Laura Lemay
Rafe Coburn
Jennifer Kyrnin

Sams **Teach Yourself**

HTML, CSS & JavaScript

Web Publishing

in **One Hour a Day**

Seventh Edition

800 East 96th Street, Indianapolis, Indiana 46240

Sams Teach Yourself HTML, CSS & JavaScript Web Publishing in One Hour a Day, Seventh Edition

ISBN-13: 978-0-672-33623-2
ISBN-10: 0-672-33623-5

Library of Congress Control Number: 2015918052

Printed in the United States of America

3   16

Trademarks

Warning and Disclaimer

Special Sales

For information about buying this title in bulk quantities, or for special sales opportunities (which may include electronic versions; custom cover designs; and content particular to your business, training goals, marketing focus, or branding interests), please contact our corporate sales department at corpsales@pearsoned.com or (800) 382-3419.

For government sales inquiries, please contact governmentsales@pearsoned.com.

For questions about sales outside the U.S., please contact international@pearsoned.com.

Contents at a Glance

Table of Contents

PART III: Doing More with HTML and CSS

LESSON 7: Formatting Text with HTML and CSS   121

PART VI: Going Live on the Web

About the Authors

Rafe Colburn is an author and web developer with more than 15 years of experience building websites. His other books include *Special Edition Using SQL* and *Sams Teach Yourself CGI in 24 Hours*. You can read his blog at http://rc3.org or find him on Twitter as @rafeco.

Jennifer Kyrnin is an author and web designer who has been working on the Internet since 1995. Her other books include *Sams Teach Yourself Bootstrap in 24 Hours*, *Sams Teach Yourself Responsive Web Design in 24 Hours*, and *Sams Teach Yourself HTML5 Mobile Application Development in 24 Hours*. She can be found at http://htmljenn.com/ or on Twitter as @htmljenn.

Laura Lemay is one of the world's most popular authors on web development topics. She is the original author of *Sams Teach Yourself Web Publishing with HTML*, *Sams Teach Yourself Java in 21 Days*, and *Sams Teach Yourself Perl in 21 Days*.

We Want to Hear from You!

As the reader of this book, *you* are our most important critic and commentator. We value your opinion and want to know what we're doing right, what we could do better, what areas you'd like to see us publish in, and any other words of wisdom you're willing to pass our way.

We welcome your comments. You can email or write to let us know what you did or didn't like about this book—as well as what we can do to make our books better.

Please note that we cannot help you with technical problems related to the topic of this book.

When you write, please be sure to include this book's title and author as well as your name and email address. We will carefully review your comments and share them with the author and editors who worked on the book.

Email: feedback@samspublishing.com

Mail: Sams Publishing
         ATTN: Reader Feedback
         800 East 96th Street
         Indianapolis, IN 46240 USA

Reader Services

Register your copy of *Sams Teach Yourself HTML, CSS & JavaScript Web Publishing in One Hour a Day* (ISBN 978-0-672-33623-2) at **informit.com/register** for convenient access to downloads, updates, and corrections as they become available.

Introduction

Over the past decade, the Web has become completely integrated into the fabric of society. Most businesses have websites, and it's unusual to see a commercial on television that doesn't display a URL. The simple fact that most people know what a URL *is* speaks volumes. People who didn't know what the Internet was several years ago are now reconnecting with their high school friends on Facebook.

Perhaps the greatest thing about the Web is that you don't have to be a big company to publish things on it. The only things you need to create your own website are a computer with access to the Internet and the willingness to learn. Obviously, the reason you're reading this is that you have an interest in web publishing. Perhaps you need to learn about it for work, or you're looking for a new means of self-expression, or you want to post baby pictures on the Web so that your relatives all over the country can stay up-to-date. The question is, how do you get started?

There's more than enough information on the Web about how to publish websites like a seasoned professional. There are tutorials, reference sites, tons of examples, and free tools to make it easier to publish on the Web. However, the advantage of reading this book instead is that all the information you need to build websites is organized in one place and presented in an orderly fashion. It has everything you need to master HTML, publish sites to a server on the Web, create graphics for use on the Web, and keep your sites running smoothly.

But wait, there's more. Other books on how to create web pages just teach you the basic technical details, such as how to produce a boldface word. In this book, you'll also learn why you should be producing a particular effect and when you should use it. In addition, this book provides hints, suggestions, and examples of how to structure your overall website, not just the words on each page. This book won't just teach you how to create a website—it'll teach you how to create a great website and how to get people to come visit it.

In this book, examples are written in valid HTML5 and CSS3 using tags that work in all current browsers wherever possible. Exceptions and caveats are noted whenever I use tags that are obsolete or not included in HTML5.

NOTE   Visit our website and register this book at www.informit.com/
register for convenient access to any updates, downloads, or
errata that might be available for this book.

Who Should Read This Book

Is this book for you? That depends:

- If you've seen what's out on the Web and you want to contribute your own content, this book is for you.

- If you work for a company that wants to create a website and you're not sure where to start, this book is for you.

- If you're an information developer, such as a technical writer, and you want to learn how the Web can help you present your information online, this book is for you.

- If you're just curious about how the Web works, some parts of this book are for you, although you might be able to find what you need on the Web itself.

- If you've created web pages before with text, images, and links, and you've played with a table or two and set up a few simple forms, you may be able to skim the first half of the book. The second half should still offer you a lot of helpful information.

What This Book Contains

The lessons are arranged in a logical order, taking you from the simplest tasks to more advanced techniques:

- Part I: Getting Started

  In Part I, you'll get a general overview of the World Wide Web and what you can do with it. You'll also write your first (basic) web page with HTML and CSS.

- Part II: Creating Web Pages

  In Part II, you'll learn how to write simple documents in the HTML language and style them with CSS. You'll learn how to create lists on your pages as well as paragraphs of text, and you'll learn how to link your pages with hypertext links.

- Part III: Doing More with HTML and CSS

  In Part III, you'll learn the meat of building web pages. You'll learn how to format text and style a page using CSS. You'll learn how to add images and create tables and forms and place them on your pages. You'll also learn how to lay out your web pages with CSS and make them responsive to the devices that are viewing them.

- Part IV: Using JavaScript and jQuery

  In Part IV, you'll learn how you can extend the functionality of your web pages by adding JavaScript to them. First, we provide an overview of JavaScript and of jQuery. We provide some specific JavaScript examples you can use on your own pages. And you learn how to make inline frames and linked windows.

- Part V: Designing for Everyone

  Part V gives you hints for creating a well-constructed website, and you'll learn how to design for mobile devices as well as make your site accessible so that it is usable by people with disabilities.

- Part VI: Going Live on the Web

  In Part VI, you'll learn how to put your site up on the Web, including how to advertise the work you've done. You'll also learn how to use some of the features of your web server to make your life easier. And you'll get some tips for making your site searchable in the most popular search engines with search engine optimization (SEO).

What You Need Before You Start

There are lots of books about how to use the Web. This book isn't one of them. We're assuming that if you're reading this book, you already have a working connection to the Internet, you have a modern web browser such as Chrome, Safari, Firefox, Opera, Internet Explorer version 10, or Microsoft Edge, and that you're familiar with the basics of how the Web and the Internet work. You should also have at least a passing acquaintance with some other elements of the Internet, such as email and FTP, because we refer to them in general terms in this book.

In other words, you need to have used the Web to provide content for the Web. If you meet this one simple qualification, read on!

Many of the screenshots in this book are made on a Macintosh computer, but you can do all the work on Windows or a Linux machine if that's what you use. You should just be familiar with how your operating system works and where common programs are located.

Conventions Used in This Book

This book uses special typefaces and other graphical elements to highlight different types of information.

Special Elements

Three types of "boxed" elements present pertinent information that relates to the topic being discussed: Note, Tip, and Caution as follows:

NOTE — Notes highlight special details about the current topic.

TIP — It's a good idea to read the tips because they present shortcuts or trouble-saving ideas for performing specific tasks.

CAUTION — Don't skip the cautions. They help you avoid making bad decisions or performing actions that can cause you trouble.

▼ Task

Tasks demonstrate how you can put the information in a lesson into practice by giving you a real working example.

▲

HTML Input and Output Examples

Throughout the book, we present exercises and examples of HTML input and output.

Input ▼

An input icon identifies HTML code that you can type in yourself.

Output ▼

An output icon indicates the results of the HTML input in a web browser such as Microsoft Internet Explorer.

Special Fonts

Several items are presented in a monospace font, which can be plain or italic. Here's what each one means:

- `plain mono`—Applied to commands, filenames, file extensions, directory names, and HTML input. For example, HTML tags such as `<table>` and `<p>` appear in this font.

- `mono italic`—Applied to placeholders. A placeholder is a generic item that replaces something specific as part of a command or computer output. For instance, the term represented by `filename` would be the real name of the file, such as `myfile.txt`.

Workshop

In the "Workshop" section, you can reinforce your knowledge of the concepts in the lesson by answering quiz questions or working on exercises. The Q&A provides additional information that didn't fit in neatly elsewhere in the lesson.

LESSON 1
What Is Web Publishing?

A journey of a thousand miles begins with a single step, and here you are in Lesson 1 of a journey that will show you how to write, design, and publish pages on the World Wide Web. But before beginning the actual journey, you should start simple, with the basics. You'll learn the following:

- How the World Wide Web really works

- What web browsers do, and which browsers your audience will be using

- What a web server is, and why you need one

- Some information about *uniform resource locators* (URLs)

These days, the Web is pervasive, and today's lesson might seem like old news. If so, feel free to skim it and skip ahead to Lesson 2, "Getting Your Tools in Order," where you'll discover the first steps you need to take to learn to create web pages.

Thinking Like a Web Publisher

You're almost certainly already familiar with the Web as a user. You open your favorite web browser and visit websites where you look up information, shop, or keep up with what your friends are doing. You may also use your web browser to read your email, check your calendar, and do your work.

Being a web publisher means understanding what happens when you enter an address in your web browser or click a link and visit a website. But first, before I get into explaining the Web at a technical level, I want to define it at a conceptual level.

The Web is

- A hypertext information system
- Cross-platform
- Distributed
- Dynamic
- Interactive

So, let's look at all these words and see what they mean in the context of how you use the Web as a publishing medium.

The Web Is a Hypertext Information System

The idea behind hypertext is that instead of reading text in a rigid, linear structure (such as a book), you can skip easily from one point to another. You can get more information, go back, jump to other topics, and navigate through the text based on what interests you at the time.

Hypertext enables you to read and navigate text and visual information in a nonlinear way, based on what you want to know next.

When you hear the term *hypertext*, think *links*. (In fact, some people still refer to links as hyperlinks.) Whenever you visit a web page, you're almost certain to see links throughout the page. Some of the links might point to locations within that same page, others to pages on the same site, and still others might point to pages on other sites. Hypertext was an old concept when the Web was invented—it was found in applications such as HyperCard and various help systems. However, the World Wide Web redefined how large a hypertext system could be. Even large websites were hypertext systems of a scale not before seen, and when you take into account that it's no more difficult to link to a document on a server in Australia from a server in the United States than it is to link to a document stored in the same directory, the scope of the Web becomes truly staggering.

NOTE

> Nearly all large corporations and medium-sized businesses and organizations are using web technology to manage projects, order materials, and distribute company information in a paperless environment. By locating their documents on a private, secure web server called an *intranet*, they take advantage of the technologies the World Wide Web has to offer while keeping the information contained within the company.

The Web Is Cross-Platform

If you can access the Internet, you can access the World Wide Web, regardless of whether you're working on a smartphone, a tablet, a brand new laptop, or a desktop computer you bought at the flea market. If you think Windows menus and buttons look better than Macintosh menus and buttons or vice versa (or if you think both Macintosh and Windows people are weenies), it doesn't matter. The World Wide Web isn't limited to any one kind of machine or developed by any one company. The Web is entirely cross-platform.

Cross-platform means that you can access web information equally well from any computer hardware running any operating system using any display.

The Cross-Platform Ideal

The whole idea that the Web is—and should be—cross-platform is strongly held to by purists. The reality, however, is somewhat different. With the introduction over the years of numerous special features, technologies, and media types, the cross-platform nature of the Web has been compromised. Web authors can choose to use nonstandard features, like Flash, but in doing so they limit the potential audience for their site, especially as more and more people switch to smartphones and mobile devices to view the Web. Web publishers also must choose between creating native applications for mobile devices or using modern web standards to build web applications that are more cross-platform compatible. It's up to individual creators to decide whether to compromise cross-platform flexibility for the greater capabilities of a proprietary platform.

The Web Is Distributed

Web content can take up a great deal of storage, particularly when you include images, audio, and video. To store all the information published on the Web, you would need an untold amount of disk space, and managing it would be almost impossible. (Not that there aren't people who try.)

The Web succeeds at providing so much information because that information is distributed globally across millions of websites, each of which contributes the space for the information it publishes. These sites reside on one or more computers, referred to as web servers. A *web server* is just a computer that listens for requests from web browsers and responds to that request. You, as a consumer of that information, request a resource from the server to view it. You don't have to install it or do anything other than point your browser at that site.

A *website* is a location on the Web that publishes some kind of information. When you view a web page, your browser connects to that website to get that information.

Each website, and each page or bit of information on that site, has a unique address. This address is called a *uniform resource locator* or URL. When people tell you to visit a site at http://www.nytimes.com/, they've just given you a URL. Whenever you use a browser to visit a website, you get there using a URL. You'll learn more about URLs later in this lesson in the "Uniform Resource Locators" section.

The Web Is Dynamic

If you want a permanent copy of some information that's stored on the Web, you have to save it locally because the content can change any time, even while you're viewing the page.

If you're browsing that information, you don't have to install a new version of the help system, buy another book, or call technical support to get updated information. Just launch your browser and check out what's there.

If you're publishing on the Web, you can make sure that your information is up-to-date all the time. You don't have to spend a lot of time re-releasing updated documents. There's no cost of materials. You don't have to get bids on numbers of copies or quality of output. Color is free. And you won't get calls from hapless customers who have a version of the book that was obsolete four years ago.

Consider a book published and distributed entirely online, such as *Little Brother* by Cory Doctorow (which you can find at http://craphound.com/littlebrother/). He can correct any mistakes in the book and simply upload the revised text to his website, making it instantly available to his readers. He can post pointers to foreign language translations of the book as they arrive. The website for the book appears in Figure 1.1.

FIGURE 1.1
The website for
Little Brother.

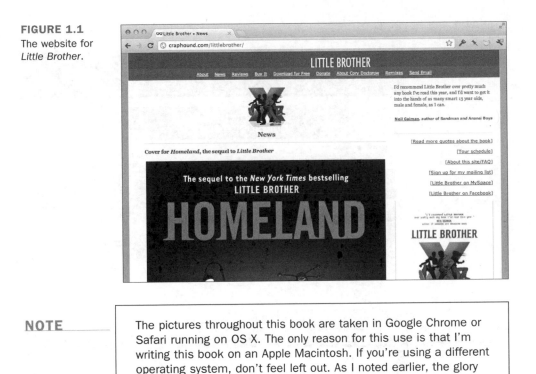

1

<table>
<tr><td>NOTE</td><td>The pictures throughout this book are taken in Google Chrome or Safari running on OS X. The only reason for this use is that I'm writing this book on an Apple Macintosh. If you're using a different operating system, don't feel left out. As I noted earlier, the glory of the Web is that you see the same information regardless of the platform you're using.</td></tr>
</table>

For some sites, the capability to update the site on-the-fly, at any moment, is precisely why the site exists. Figure 1.2 shows the home page for the BBC News, a site that's updated 24 hours a day to reflect up-to-the-minute news as it happens. Because the site is up and available all the time, it has an immediacy that newspapers cannot match. Visit the BBC News at http://www.bbc.co.uk/news/world/.

These days, you don't even need to reload a web page to receive updated information. Through the use of JavaScript, which I discuss starting in Lesson 17, "Introducing JavaScript," you can update the contents of a page in real time. The scores and statistics on the NBA game page in Figure 1.3 are updated in place as the game progresses.

FIGURE 1.2
The BBC News.

FIGURE 1.3
Live game updates
on the CBS Sports
website.

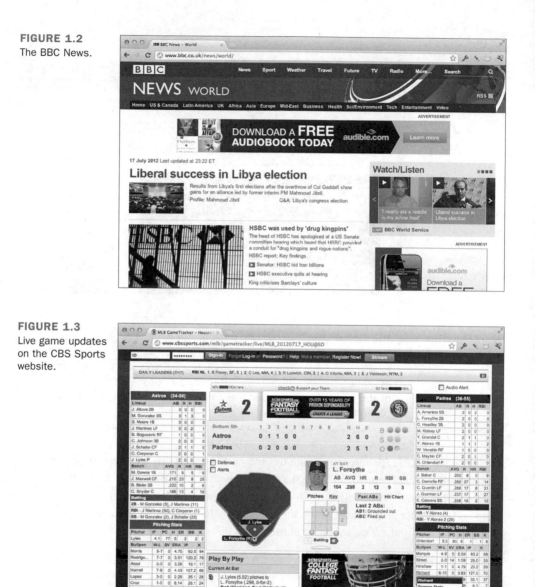

The Web Is Interactive

Interactivity is the capability to "talk back" to the web server. More traditional media, such as television, isn't interactive in the slightest; all you do is sit and watch as shows are played at you. Other than changing the channel, you don't have much control over

1

what you see. The Web is inherently interactive; the act of selecting a link and jumping to another web page to go somewhere else on the Web is a form of interactivity. In addition to this simple interactivity, however, the Web enables you to communicate with the publisher of the pages you're reading and with other readers of those pages.

Indeed, the most popular sites on the Web these days are about interacting with other users of the site rather than with the site's publisher. That's what people mean when they say "social media." Rather than spending money to hire writers and cameramen, now sites are spending money to hire programmers to create spaces for people to share content they create with one another. These days, it's not uncommon to see people on TV reading viewer posts from Twitter or Facebook out loud on the air. Such is the degree to which this form of media has taken hold.

As a web publisher, you'll need to decide the type of interaction you want your site to provide. You can publish web pages without any outlet for users to interact. You can enable users to submit feedback privately. You can enable them to publish public comments and converse with you and with each other. You can provide forums that enable users to interact with one another directly. You can provide games or other interactive features. You can even incorporate interactive features from other websites into your own so that you can integrate your site with the sites to which your users already belong. For example, Figure 1.4 shows a Facebook widget incorporated into a third-party website.

FIGURE 1.4
A Facebook widget.

Web Browsers

A web browser, as mentioned earlier, is the application you use to view pages and navigate the World Wide Web. A wide array of web browsers is available for just about every platform you can imagine. Microsoft Internet Explorer, for example, is included with Windows, and Safari is included with OS X. Mozilla Firefox, Google Chrome, and Opera are all available as free downloads. Likewise, more and more people are using browsers on mobile devices and tablets. iPhone and iPad use Mobile Safari. The Android mobile platform has its own browser. There are also other mobile platforms, like BlackBerry and Windows Phone, and third-party browsers for both Android and iPhone. Not too many years ago, Internet Explorer was the dominant browser for Windows, the OS X market share was less than 5%, and mobile browsers were so limited that they wouldn't work with regular web pages at all. Back then, developers sometimes chose to support Internet Explorer and ignore other browsers. That is no longer a viable strategy.

NOTE

> Choosing to develop for a specific browser, such as Internet Explorer, is only suitable when you know a limited audience using the targeted browser software will view your website. Developing this way is a common practice in corporations implementing intranets. In these situations, it's a fair assumption that all users in the organization will use the browser supplied to them and, accordingly, it's possible to design the web pages on an intranet to use the specific capabilities of the browser in question.

What the Browser Does

The core purpose of a web browser is to connect to web servers, request documents, and then properly format and display those documents. Web browsers can also display files on your local computer, download files that are not meant to be displayed, and in some cases even allow you to send and retrieve email. What the browser is best at, however, is retrieving and displaying web documents. Each web page is written in a language called the *Hypertext Markup Language* (HTML) that includes the text of the page, a description of its structure, and links to other documents, images, or other media. The browser takes the information it gets from the web server and formats it for your display. Different browsers might format and display the same file in diverse ways, depending on the capabilities of that system and how the browser is configured.

An Overview of Some Popular Browsers

There's a good chance you use only one browser, or two, if you use a browser on a computer and one on a mobile device. However, your website will probably be visited by a variety of browsers, and to publish on the Web successfully, you'll need to be aware of them. This section describes some of the most popular browsers on the Web. They're in no way the only browsers available, and if the browser you're using isn't listed here, don't feel that you have to use one of these. Whichever browser you have is fine as long as it works for you.

Google Chrome

Google Chrome is currently the most popular web browser. Its market share has shown incredible growth because the browser offers great performance and stability and is updated often, plus it is used on both desktop and mobile devices. It uses the same HTML engine as Apple's Safari browser, an open source engine called WebKit. It's available as a free download at http://www.google.com/chrome/. You'll see Google Chrome used for the screenshots in this book, and I'll be talking about its special features for people creating websites, starting in Lesson 2.

Microsoft Internet Explorer

Microsoft's browser, Microsoft Internet Explorer, is included with Microsoft Windows and is still the second most popular web browser. It has lost market share to other browsers because new versions are not released as often as Google Chrome and Mozilla Firefox. However, a huge number of people still use Internet Explorer, and it is the most unlike other browsers like Chrome, Firefox, and Safari. According to the website CanIUse.com, Internet Explorer 10 offers 49% support of HTML5 features, and Internet Explorer 11 offers 58% support.

NOTE

If you're serious about web design, you should install all the popular browsers on your system and use them to view your pages after you've published them. That way, you can make sure that everything is working properly. Even if you don't use a particular browser on a day-to-day basis, your site will be visited by people who do. If you are interested in checking cross-browser compatibility issues, start with Microsoft Internet Explorer and Mozilla Firefox, and include Google Chrome, too.

Figure 1.5 shows Microsoft Edge—the successor to Internet Explorer—running under Windows 10.

FIGURE 1.5
Microsoft Edge
(Windows 10).

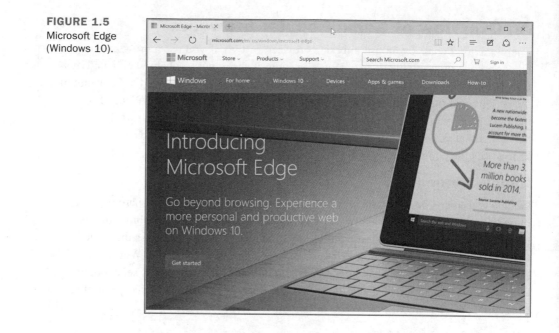

One other important point to make about Internet Explorer is that the different versions differ greatly. Version 10 of Internet Explorer was released in 2012, but many users haven't upgraded from version 9, version 8, or even version 7. Internet Explorer differs widely between versions, so to get a site to work properly you need to test in each version. Web publishers have dropped support for version 6, and most have also dropped version 7, and Microsoft recommends that all users upgrade to a newer version. And in 2015 Microsoft released a new browser Microsoft Edge—the default browser for Windows 10.

Mozilla Firefox

Mozilla Firefox is a free, open source web browser that makes up roughly 15% of the browser market as of July 2015. Netscape Navigator was the first popular commercial web browser. Version 1.0 was released in 1994. In 1998, Netscape Communications opened the source code to their web browser and assigned some staff members to work on making it better. Seven years and many releases later, the result of that effort was Mozilla Firefox. Netscape Communications, since acquired by America Online, no longer has any official ties to the Mozilla Foundation, which is now an independent nonprofit organization.

Firefox became popular in large part because it was free from the security issues that plagued Internet Explorer. In addition, a large number of Firefox extensions improve the browser experience, and Firefox has done a good job of keeping up with web standards as they have evolved. Firefox is available for Windows, Mac OS X, and Linux and is a free download at http://www.mozilla.com/.

1

Apple Safari

Safari is the default browser for OS X. There is also a mobile version of this browser installed on the Apple iPhone and iPad. It is based on open source technology, and its support for web standards is at a similar level to Firefox. Right now, Safari has around 9% of the browser market share.

Mobile Browsers

No discussion of browsers would be complete without talking about mobile browsers. The big three are Chrome, Safari, and Android. As of July 2015, Chrome has 31% of the market share for mobile browsers, with Safari and Android at 24% and 15%, respectively.

Google Chrome came on the market for mobile devices before 2014 and became the most popular browser on mobile devices in early 2015. It uses the same engine as the desktop version of the browser and offers the performance and reliability people have come to expect of Chrome. Safari is the browser Apple includes with iOS devices like the iPhone and iPad. It offers very strong HTML5 support and, apart from screen size, provides an experience very similar to a desktop browser. Similarly, Android provides a browser that also provides a high-quality web experience. All three of them are based on the WebKit rendering engine, just like Safari and Chrome for the desktop. I'll discuss the considerations that go into building sites that are friendly to mobile devices in Lesson 21, "Designing for the Mobile Web."

Other Browsers

As of July 2015, Google Chrome has the lion's share of the market for web browsers on both desktop and mobile devices. The remaining browsers all share a relatively small slice of the pie—13% or less. For example, Opera (http://www.operasoftware.com/) has a niche market with only 5% share. It's small, fast, free, and available for a number of platforms, including Windows, Mac OS X, and Linux. It's also standards compliant. For UNIX users who use KDE, there's Konqueror. There are various Mozilla offshoots, such as Camino for Mac OS X. Likewise, command-line browsers such as Lynx and Links are available to provide an all-text view of web pages. There are also a number of browsers that provide access to the Web for people with various special needs. It makes sense to code to common standards to accommodate all these types of browsers.

Web Servers

To view and browse pages on the Web, all you need is a web browser. To publish pages on the Web, you need a web server.

A *web server* is the program that runs on a computer and is responsible for replying to web browser requests for whatever content is associated with a particular URL. You need a web server to publish documents on the Web. One point of confusion is that the computer on which a server program runs is also referred to as a server. So, when someone uses the term *web server*, she could be referring to a program used to respond to requests for web pages or the computer on which that program runs.

When you use a browser to request a page on a website, that browser makes a web connection to a server using HTTP. The server accepts the connection, sends the contents of the requested files, and then closes the connection. The browser then formats the information it got from the server.

On the server side, many different browsers can connect to the same server to get the same information. The web server is responsible for handling all these requests.

Web servers do more than just serve files. They're also responsible for managing form input and for linking forms and browsers with programs such as databases running on the server.

As with browsers, many different servers are available for many different platforms, each with many different features. For now, all you need to know is what the server is there for; you'll learn more about web servers in Lesson 23, "How to Publish Your Site."

Uniform Resource Locators

As you learned earlier, a URL is a pointer to some bit of data on the Web, be it a web document, an image, a style sheet, or a JavaScript script. You'll learn about all of these later. The URL provides a universal, consistent method for finding and accessing information.

In addition to typing URLs directly into your browser to go to a particular page, you also use URLs when you create a hypertext link within a document to another document. So, any way you look at it, URLs are important to how you and your browser get around on the Web.

URLs contain information about the following:

- How to get to the information (which protocol to use: FTP, HTTP, or file)
- The Internet hostname of the computer where the content is stored (www.ncsa.uiuc.edu, ftp.apple.com, netcom16.netcom.com, and so on)
- The directory or other location on that site where the content is located

You also can use special URLs for tasks such as sending mail to people (called *Mailto URLs*) and running JavaScript code. You'll learn all about URLs and what each part means in Lesson 6, "Working with Links."

Defining Web Publishing Broadly

When the Web was invented, web publishing meant one thing: creating web pages as individual files and uploading them to a server so that people could view them in their browsers. Since then, pretty much everything has changed.

A few websites still include hand-coded web pages that the creator uploads, but most websites are created using software that runs on the server. Web pages have gotten more complex, as have websites. These days, most content on web pages is written using applications that live on the Web as well. For example, you can create a blog at WordPress.com and immediately begin posting content through the WordPress web interface.

Whether you're posting status updates on Twitter, writing comments on a news site, publishing a blog through a tool, or editing articles on Wikipedia, you're publishing on the Web. In most cases, you are not required to directly write HTML on your own. Generally, the pages live in templates that someone else created, and often you can format the content you create using a graphical editor or with simplified markup that enables you to avoid the use of HTML.

Ultimately the content, however you enter it, will be converted to HTML before it is displayed to users. So if you publish something and it doesn't look right, you'll need to know HTML if you want to fix it. You'll need to be able to differentiate between the parts of the page you control and the parts that are built in to the publishing application that you're using. And if you want to take greater control of the appearance of your site, you will probably need to know HTML to update the templates that are used to give your pages their own look and feel.

So no matter what approach you take to web publishing, you will likely benefit by starting with the basics and learning how web publishing works from end to end. You may never write individual web pages by hand, but understanding how to do so will prepare you to build websites using whichever tool you ultimately choose.

Summary

To publish on the Web, you have to understand the basic concepts that make up the parts of the Web. In this lesson, you learned three major concepts. First, you learned about a few of the more useful features of the Web for publishing information. Second, you learned about web browsers and servers and how they interact to deliver web pages. Third, you learned about what a URL is and why it's important to web browsing and publishing.

Workshop

Each lesson in this book contains a workshop to help you review the topics you learned. The first section of this workshop lists some common questions about the Web. Next, you'll answer some questions that I'll ask you about the Web. The answers to the quiz appear in the next section. At the end of each lesson, you'll find some exercises that will help you retain the information you learned about the Web.

Q&A

Q Who runs the Web? Who controls all these protocols? Who's in charge of all this?

A No single entity owns or controls the World Wide Web. Given the enormous number of independent sites that supply information to the Web, for any single organization to set rules or guidelines would be impossible. Two groups of organizations, however, have a great influence over the look and feel and direction of the Web itself.

The first is the *World Wide Web Consortium* (W3C), based at Massachusetts Institute of Technology in the United States and INRIA in Europe. The W3C is made up of individuals and organizations interested in supporting and defining the languages and protocols that make up the Web (HTTP, HTML, XHTML, and so on). It also provides products (browsers, servers, and so on) that are freely available to anyone who wants to use them. The W3 Consortium is the closest anyone gets to setting the standards for and enforcing rules about the World Wide Web. You can visit the Consortium's home page at http://www.w3.org/.

The second group of organizations that influences the Web is the browser developers themselves, most notably Google, Apple, Microsoft, and the Mozilla Foundation. The competition to be the most popular and technically advanced browser on the Web can be fierce. A group of people and companies interested in the future of the Web have created an organization called the Web Hypertext Application Technology Working Group (or WHATWG). The WHATWG, along with the W3C, wrote the HTML5 specification.

Going forward, the WHATWG has abandoned version numbers for the HTML specification entirely. Instead, HTML will be a "living standard" and incorporate both experimental and widely supported features. The goal is to make sure that the specification evolves to match the features that browser makers have agreed to add to their browsers. If a proposed feature does not reach consensus, it is removed from the specification. This is an attempt to prevent the problems of the past where the process of creating the HTML specification diverged from the work the browser makers were doing.

Q I've heard that the Web changes so fast that it's almost impossible to stay current. Is this book doomed to be out-of-date the day it's published?

A Although it's true that things do change on the Web, the vast majority of the information in this book will serve you well far into the future. HTML is as stable now as it has ever been, and once you learn the core technologies of *Hypertext Markup Language* (HTML), *Cascading Style Sheets* (CSS), and JavaScript, you can add on other things at your leisure.

Quiz

1. What's a URL?
2. What's required to publish documents on the Web?

Quiz Answers

1. A URL, or uniform resource locator, is an address that points to a specific document or bit of information on the Internet.
2. You need access to a web server. Web servers, which are programs that serve up documents over the Web, reply to web browser requests for files and send the requested pages to many different types of browsers. They also manage form input and handle database integration.

Exercises

1. Start thinking more about web publishing as you surf the Web. Look at how URLs are constructed. Pay attention to how the pages are constructed. Soon you'll understand how these pages are built from the inside out.
2. Download a different browser than the one you ordinarily use and try it out for a while. If you're using Internet Explorer, try out Firefox, Chrome, Safari, or even a command-line browser such as Lynx or Links. To really see how things have changed and how some users who don't upgrade their browser experience the Web, download an old browser from http://browsers.evolt.org/ and try it out.

LESSON 2
Getting Your Tools in Order

When you start on a project, whether it's writing a book or painting a room, you don't just jump in and grab a brush or start typing. You come up with a plan to complete the project and gather the materials you need to get the work done. Your plan may be as simple as deciding to paint the walls before you paint the ceiling, or it may be as complex as a detailed outline of everything you plan to write in your book.

The same goes for materials. If you're painting a room, you need brushes, paint, and maybe something to prevent getting paint where you don't want it. Likewise, if you're writing a book, you'll want to install a word processor and perhaps gather the research materials you need to support your writing. Just as with most other projects, the process of writing and designing web pages takes some planning and thought before you start flinging text and graphics around and linking them wildly to each other. Likewise, you'll want to make sure you have everything you need on your computer to build web pages, as well as a place on the Web to host your website when you're finished.

To prepare to publish on the Web, you must

- Learn the differences between a web server, a website, a web page, and a home page.
- Set up your computer so that you can start creating web pages.

Anatomy of a Website

First, here's a look at some simple terminology I use throughout this book. You need to know what the following terms mean and how they apply to the body of work you're developing for the Web:

- **Website**—A collection of one or more web pages linked together in a meaningful way that, as a whole, describes a body of information or creates an overall effect (see Figure 2.1).

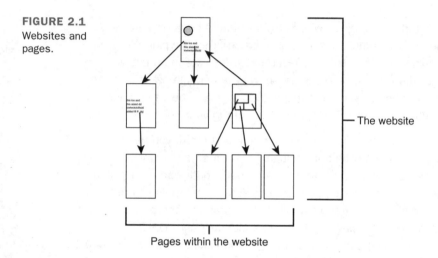

FIGURE 2.1
Websites and pages.

The website

Pages within the website

- **Web server**—A computer on the Internet or an intranet that delivers web pages and other files in response to browser requests. (An intranet is a network that uses Internet protocols but is not publicly accessible.)

- **Web page**—A single document on a website, usually consisting of a *Hypertext Markup Language* (HTML) document and any items that are displayed within that document, such as inline images or style sheets.

- **Home page**—The entry page for a website, which can link to additional pages on the same website or pages on other sites.

Each website is hosted on a web server. Throughout the first few lessons in this book, you'll learn how to develop well thought-out and well-designed websites. Later, you'll learn how to publish your site on an actual web server.

A *web page* is an individual element of a website in the same way that a page is a single element of a book or a newspaper (although, unlike paper pages, web pages can be of any length). Web pages sometimes are called *web documents*. Both terms refer to the same thing. A web page consists of an HTML document and all the other components that are included on the page, such as images or other media.

NOTE

> Most websites aren't built out of individual pages these days. Rather, they are created using applications that publish web content stored in a database of some kind through a common set of templates. The URLs on the site act as input for the publishing application. In this book, you'll still be creating web pages in the traditional sense, because it's the easiest way to learn.

If you're publishing a website, the home page is the first or topmost page on your website. It's the intended entry point that provides access to the rest of the pages on the site (see Figure 2.2).

CAUTION

> Most of your customers will access your site through your home page, but some will enter your site through other pages. The nature of the Web is that people can link to any page on your site. If you have interesting information on a page other than your home page, people will link directly to that page. On the other pages of your site, you shouldn't assume that the visitor has seen your home page.

FIGURE 2.2
A home page.

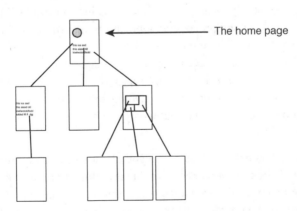

The home page

A home page often contains an overview of the content of the website, available from that starting point—for example, in the form of a table of contents or a set of icons. If you don't have too much content, you might include everything on that single page—making your home page and your website the same thing. A personal home page might include a link to a person's resumé and a link to his Twitter account and his photos on Flickr. A restaurant's home page will likely include the restaurant's hours and location, and links to the menu and directions to the restaurant. A corporate home page usually describes what the company does and contains links like "About the Company," "Products and Services," and "Customer Support."

Setting Up Your Computer for Web Publishing

First of all, if you just want to post some words or pictures on a web page, you don't really need to do anything to set up your computer. You can just open a browser, find a site that enables you to publish your content like Tumblr or Wix, and then publish from within the browser.

If you want to learn how to create websites from scratch, set up your own computer so that you can create web pages and view them locally. The only two tools you absolutely must have to experiment with web publishing are a text editor and a web browser. You learned a bit about web browsers in the previous lesson, so let's talk about text editors first.

Text Editors

HTML files are plain-text files and should be edited using a tool that works with plain-text files. What this essentially means is that you are going to learn HTML, you shouldn't be editing your files with a word processing application like Microsoft Word or an online application like Google Docs. Those types of programs allow you to edit files in what will be their final format and then save the results in a document format like Microsoft Word's proprietary format. Confusingly, these types of applications will also enable you to save your documents as HTML documents. Doing so may be sufficient to meet your needs in terms of producing a document but won't teach you the first thing about HTML, which is your goal.

If you've used text editors before, chances are you already have a favorite. People tend to be highly opinionated about what makes a good text editor. If you haven't used one at all or haven't used one much, you'll need a recommendation. To get started, you can use the text editor that's provided with your computer's operating system; they all have one.

If you're a Windows user, you can use the Notepad application. If you are using OS X, you can start with TextEdit. If you are a Linux user, you can start with vi or Emacs.

Notepad, TextEdit, and vi offer very limited functionality, and if you do a lot of text editing, you'll want to track down another more powerful application to do your text editing. Here's a list of a few editors often used by people who create websites:

- Komodo Edit is a free, open source version of the popular Komodo IDE. It runs on Windows, Macintosh, and Linux and offers a lot of features of an IDE. You can download it at http://komodoide.com/komodo-edit/.

- HTML-Kit is a popular text editor specifically for web pages for Windows. You can download it at http://www.htmlkit.com/. You can use an older version for free or you can pay for the latest and greatest.

- Notepad++ is a free, open source text editor for Windows that is very popular. You can download it at http://notepad-plus-plus.org/.

- TextWrangler is a popular, free text editor for OS X. It was created by Bare Bones Software, and you can download it at their website at http://www.barebones.com/products/textwrangler/. You may also be interested in BBEdit, a more powerful text editor with a licensing fee.

- Coda is a text editor specifically for people creating web pages by Panic. It includes a lot of development features like source control and database connectivity. You can find it at http://panic.com/coda/. It also has a licensing fee.

You'll want to find your text editor and open the application. If you're using TextEdit on OS X, make sure that it's in plain-text mode. If the document window has controls that let you choose a font or apply other formatting, go to the Format menu and select Make Plain Text. Once you have your editor open, you can type in some stuff and, if you like, save the file you're editing. The main thing to make note of is that simply typing in characters with your keyboard is the only thing you're able to do. You have no formatting options whatsoever—that's what's meant by *plain text*.

NOTE

You can work through every lesson in this book using Notepad or TextEdit, but most web developers find that using a more powerful tool improves their productivity significantly. Many provide highlighting that makes your documents easier to read. All of them also enable you to have multiple documents open at once and enable you to treat a group of files as a project. It would be tough to find a new tool that suits you before you have even started, but I would encourage you to look into different editors as you make your way through the book. And many of the commercial editors have free trials, so you can try them out before you buy.

Figure 2.3 is a screenshot of the OS X text editor TextEdit. It is notable mainly due to the fact that it has no text formatting menu or toolbar at all. This is what you're looking for in a text editor; it should enable you to edit the contents of the file without applying formatting of any kind.

FIGURE 2.3
TextEdit on OS X.

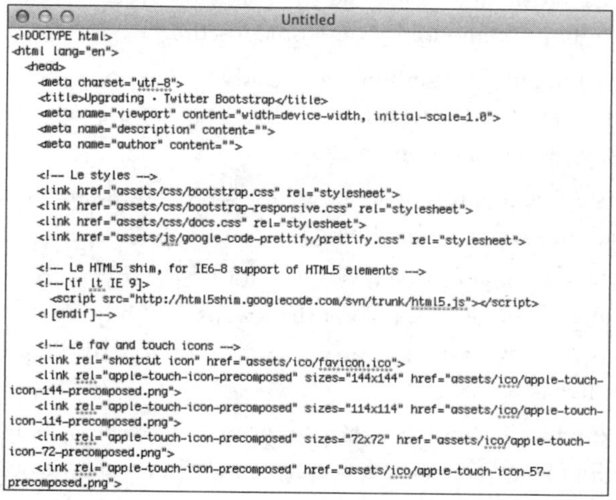


```
<!DOCTYPE html>
<html lang="en">
  <head>
    <meta charset="utf-8">
    <title>Upgrading · Twitter Bootstrap</title>
    <meta name="viewport" content="width=device-width, initial-scale=1.0">
    <meta name="description" content="">
    <meta name="author" content="">

    <!-- Le styles -->
    <link href="assets/css/bootstrap.css" rel="stylesheet">
    <link href="assets/css/bootstrap-responsive.css" rel="stylesheet">
    <link href="assets/css/docs.css" rel="stylesheet">
    <link href="assets/js/google-code-prettify/prettify.css" rel="stylesheet">

    <!-- Le HTML5 shim, for IE6-8 support of HTML5 elements -->
    <!--[if lt IE 9]>
      <script src="http://html5shim.googlecode.com/svn/trunk/html5.js"></script>
    <![endif]-->

    <!-- Le fav and touch icons -->
    <link rel="shortcut icon" href="assets/ico/favicon.ico">
    <link rel="apple-touch-icon-precomposed" sizes="144x144" href="assets/ico/apple-touch-
icon-144-precomposed.png">
    <link rel="apple-touch-icon-precomposed" sizes="114x114" href="assets/ico/apple-touch-
icon-114-precomposed.png">
    <link rel="apple-touch-icon-precomposed" sizes="72x72" href="assets/ico/apple-touch-
icon-72-precomposed.png">
    <link rel="apple-touch-icon-precomposed" href="assets/ico/apple-touch-icon-57-
precomposed.png">
```

A Web Browser

As mentioned in the previous lesson, a number of popular web browsers are available, and you can use any that you like to surf the Web on a day-to-day basis. However, as you're working through the lessons in this book, I'm going to recommend one browser in particular: Google Chrome. The main reason is that Google Chrome offers a number of powerful tools aimed at helping people create websites. Other browsers have similar tools, but I'm going to make reference to the Google Chrome Developer Tools specifically in the text, and you'll find it easier to follow along if you're using Google Chrome as well. If you feel confident, you can choose another browser if you prefer. (You'll need to translate the parts where I mention Google Chrome to your own browser, but I'd encourage you to download Google Chrome and work through the next section regardless of which browser you plan to ultimately use, especially if you're completely unfamiliar with these kinds of tools). You can download Google Chrome at http://google.com/chrome.

Using the Google Chrome Developer Tools

After you've downloaded and installed Google Chrome, open the application, and navigate to http://getbootstrap.com/. Bootstrap is a generic framework for web pages and is discussed later. For now, it's useful because the source code for the web pages was written to be easily readable. In Chrome's View menu, open the Developer submenu, and then click Developer Tools. At this point, the Developer Tools will open, as shown in Figure 2.4.

FIGURE 2.4
The Google Chrome Developer Tools.

> **TIP**
>
> There is also a keyboard shortcut to open the Developer Tools. On Windows, you can open them by pressing Control+Shift+I. On OS X, you can open them with Command+Option+I. You'll find yourself using the Developer Tools a lot, so it's definitely worth memorizing the keyboard shortcut.

The Developer Tools opens as a panel in the browser, covering the bottom of the web page. If you prefer, you can click the button on the upper right to detach the Developer Tools from the browser window. This allows you to see more in both windows, but you'll have to switch between them. You can also move the tools to the side of your browser window rather than the bottom if you prefer. Position the Developer Tools however you feel the most comfortable.

From the earliest days of the Web, browsers have supported a feature called "View Source" that displays the actual HTML source code for the web page that you're viewing. In Google Chrome, you can view the source for the current page by selecting View Source from the Developer submenu of the browser's View menu. The source for http://getbootstrap.com/ appears in Figure 2.5.

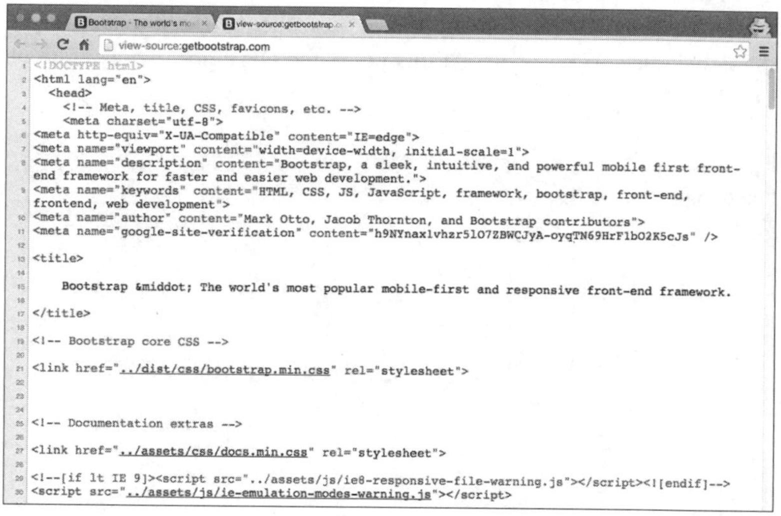

FIGURE 2.5

The source code for http:// getbootstrap.com/.

The Developer Tools are a much more powerful extension of this concept. The Developer Tools have a number of tabs. When you open them, the Elements tab is displayed. This tab contains the source of the page, sort of. When a browser downloads a web page, it transforms it so that the engine that formats the HTML and presents it can understand it. Depending on the validity of the web page, this transformation is pretty minor. The Elements tab presents the HTML as the browser sees it. View Source shows the actual HTML that the browser downloaded, so if you compare the contents of the View Source window with the contents of the Elements tab, you'll see a few differences that illustrate what I'm talking about.

Don't worry about what any of the actual HTML does right now, I'll dig into that soon enough. For now, just focus on the tool. When you move your mouse over the elements in the Elements tab, the part of the web page associated with the element under the mouse will be highlighted so that you can see how the HTML corresponds to the HTML source. When you click one of the elements, the panes to the right of the window are updated with the style information for that element. Later, when you start working with Cascading Style Sheets, this feature will be really helpful because it shows exactly how the browser interprets your styles.

Finally, on the bottom row, you'll find a number of buttons. The first is the button that detaches or reattaches the tools window. The next opens the JavaScript console, which is discussed starting in Lesson 17, "Introducing JavaScript." The next button looks like a magnifying glass. If you click it, you can then click content on the web page, and the HTML element corresponding to it will be selected in the Elements tab. This is useful when you want to inspect a particular element on the page.

Finally, the next buttons show the nesting order of the tags for the selected elements. These are useful for moving through the structure of the web page. You'll learn more about how pages are structured in lessons to come.

Exercise 2.1: Using the Inspector ▼

Before moving on, it's worth seeing exactly how the Inspector works to see how to use the Developer Tools to find specific elements on the page in the Elements view. If you're not viewing http://getbootstrap.com/ in your browser, go ahead and open it, and then open the Chrome Developer Tools. You may want to go ahead and try the keyboard shortcut mentioned earlier in a tip. As I said, as you progress you'll find yourself doing this a lot.

Once the browser tools are open, click the "inspect" button in the Developer Tools. It's the first button on the left in the bottom row—a magnifying glass. The button will turn blue, indicating that the Developer Tools are ready to inspect the element that you click. At this point, move the mouse over the browser window until you locate the large heading near the top of the page. The browser window should look something like the one in Figure 2.6.

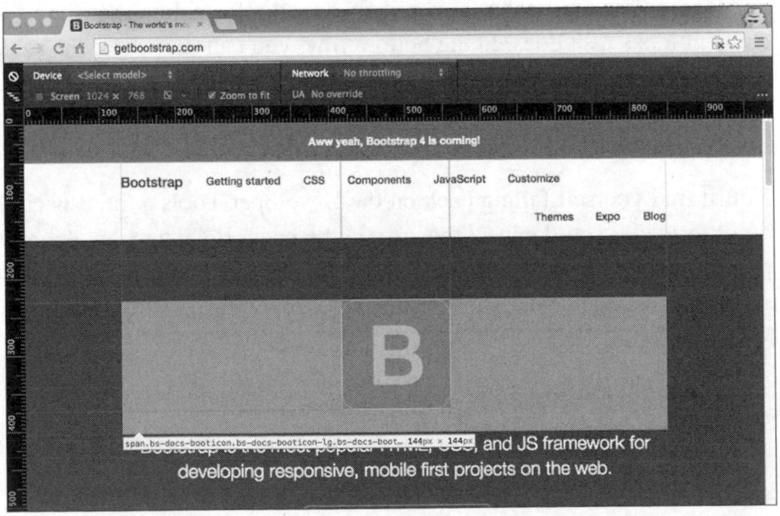

FIGURE 2.6
Inspecting the
Bootstrap page.

▼ As you can see, the heading is highlighted, and some information about the size of the element is provided in a tool tip. This is the element I want you to inspect, so you should locate it in your browser and click it. As you saw in Figure 2.4, the source of the page shown in the Elements is mostly collapsed when you initially open the Developer Tools. When you inspect an element, the source is expanded enough to show you the HTML source corresponding to whatever it was on the page that you clicked. The Developer Tools window should now be displaying the HTML tags used to create the heading you clicked. It will look like Figure 2.7.

FIGURE 2.7
Inspecting the
B icon in the
Developer Tools.

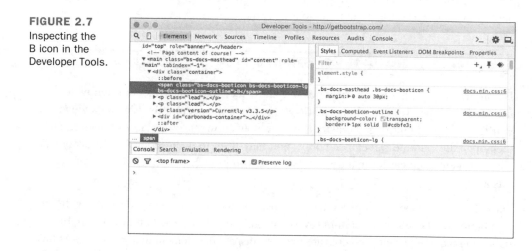

I don't expect to understand much of what you see in the Developer Tools window yet, but let me go over the highlights. In the left panel, you'll see the actual HTML source for the page. In the right column, you'll find style information that shows why the selected element looks as it does. In the bottom row, you can see where the selected element falls within the structure of the page. The selected element is the "span" around the Bootstrap B at the right end of the bottom bar. It is four levels deep in the page and has three CSS classes applied to it.

You'll find yourself falling back on the Developer Tools a lot, especially when things don't look like you'd expect them to on the page. It shows how the browser sees your page and makes it easy to drill down to exactly the element you want to find, which is

▲ especially useful as your pages grow larger and more complex.

What Do You Want to Do on the Web?

This question might seem silly. You wouldn't have bought this book if you didn't already have some idea of what you want to publish. But maybe you don't really know what you want to put on the Web, or you have a vague idea but nothing concrete. Maybe it has suddenly become your job to work on the company website, and someone handed you this book and said, "Here, this will help." Maybe you're a software developer who's suddenly in charge of building a web interface for a product or building a web application. Maybe you just want to do something similar to some other web page you've seen and thought was particularly cool.

What you want to put on the Web is what I refer to throughout this book as your content. *Content* is a general term that can refer to text, graphics, media, forms, and so on. If you tell someone what your web pages are about, you're describing your content.

The only thing that limits what you can publish on the Web is your own imagination. In fact, if what you want to do seems especially wild or half-baked, that's an excellent reason to try it. The most interesting websites are the ones that stretch the boundaries of what the Web is supposed to be capable of.

You might also find inspiration in looking at other websites similar to the one you have in mind. If you're building a corporate site, look at the sites belonging to your competitors and see what they have to offer. If you're working on a personal site, visit sites that you admire and see whether you can find inspiration for building your own site. Decide what you like about those sites and you want to emulate and where you can improve on those sites when you build your own.

These days, the barriers to building many kinds of websites are extremely low. If you want to publish text and photos, you can use one of any number of free blogging sites to set up a site in minutes, as long as blogging software suits your needs. Experimenting is easier than ever. Try something, see whether it takes off, and then build from there.

If you really have no idea of what to put up on the Web, don't feel that you have to stop here, put this book away, and come up with something before continuing. Maybe by reading through this book, you'll get some ideas (and this book will be useful even if you don't have ideas). I've personally found that the best way to come up with ideas is to spend an afternoon browsing on the Web and exploring what other people have done.

Wireframing Your Website

The next step in planning your website is to figure out what content goes on which pages and to come up with a scheme for navigating between those pages. If you have a lot of content that needs to be linked together in sophisticated ways, sitting down and making a specific plan of what goes where will be incredibly useful later as you develop and link each individual page.

What's Wireframing, and Why Do I Need It?

Wireframes provides a rough outline of what the website will look like when it's done, showing which content will appear on which pages and how they will be connected together. With that representation in hand, you can develop each page without trying to remember exactly where that page fits into the overall website and its often complex relationships to other pages.

In the case of really large sites, wireframes enable different people to develop various portions of the same website. With clear wireframes, you can minimize duplication of work and reduce the amount of contextual information each person needs to remember.

For smaller websites, or websites built using content management applications that provide a specific structure, wireframes might be unnecessary. For larger and more complex projects, however, the existence of wireframes can save enormous amounts of time and frustration. If you can't keep all the parts of your content and their relationships in your head, consider creating a wireframe.

So, what do wireframes look like? Generally speaking, they are collections of documents or images, each of which represents a certain type of page on a website. The documents contain a rough diagram of the page, illustrating how the various components of the page will be positioned, how much space they should take up, and what function they will serve. For example, the wireframes for a newspaper website would include a diagram of the home page, the home page for sections of the paper, and a wireframe for article pages. The wireframes might also include the registration form for the site and a page that can be used to purchase advertisements. An example wireframe created using a tool called Balsamiq is included in Figure 2.8.

Don't feel that your wireframes have to be pretty or built in specific wireframing software. The point of wireframing is that it organizes your web pages in a way that works for you. If you like index cards and string, work with these tools. If a simple outline on paper or on the computer works better, use that instead.

FIGURE 2.8
A wireframe for a newspaper home page.

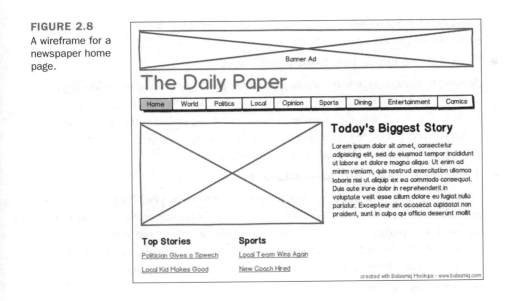

2

Hints for Wireframing

Some things to think about when developing your wireframes are as follows:

- **Which topics will go on each page?**

   Trying to figure out how much information to put on one page can be tricky. Some websites put all of their content on one long, cleverly designed page. Others split it up between a great many pages. Still others use modern techniques to dynamically load parts of the page on demand without ever really moving from one page to another. Without getting too fancy, your best bet is to organize your content so that each page consists of information on a single topic. If your pages become more than a few screens long, it might be time to split them into logical subtopics.

- **What are the primary forms of navigation between pages?**

   What links will you need for your visitors to navigate from page to page? They are the main links in your document that enable your visitors to accomplish the goals you defined in the first section. Links for forward, back, up, down, and home all fall under the category of primary navigation.

- **What alternative forms of navigation are you going to provide?**

   In addition to the simple navigation links, some websites contain extra information that's parallel to the main web content, such as a glossary of terms, an alphabetic index of concepts, copyright information, or a credits page. Consider these extra forms of information when designing your plan, and think about how you're going to link them into the main content.

- **What will you put on your home page?**

Because the home page is the starting point for the rest of the information in your website, consider what sort of information you're going to put on the home page. A blog? A general summary of what's to come? A list of links to other topics? Whatever you put on the home page, make sure that it's compelling enough so that members of your intended audience want to stick around.

- **How will visitors to inner pages establish context?**

Unless your website requires customers to register to view your content, there's a good chance that users could arrive on any page on your site by way of a search engine. It's important to make sure that customers can figure out which site they're on and that there's more information that they may also be interested in. You can generally establish this context through your design and navigation.

- **What are your goals?**

As you design the framework for your website, keep your goals in mind, and make sure that you aren't obscuring your goals with extra information or content.

TIP

> Several utilities and packages can assist you in creating wireframes. Some free tools include Mockingbird (http://gomockingbird.com/), Denim (http://dub.washington.edu:2007/denim/), and Gliffy (https://www.gliffy.com/uses/wireframe-software/). In addition, several mobile apps for iOS and Android devices help you create website mockups.

Web Hosting

At some point, you'll want to move the websites you create from your local computer to a server on the Internet. Before doing so, you must decide exactly what kind of hosting arrangement you want. The simplest approach is to get a web hosting account that enables you to upload your HTML files, images, style sheets, and other web content to a server that's visible on the Web. This approach enables you to easily create web pages (and websites) locally and publish them on the server without making changes to them.

Using a Content-Management Application

The other option is to use an application to publish content on the Web. This can make more sense if your idea for a website falls into an existing category with publishing tools available for it. For example, if you want to publish a blog, you can use sites like TypePad (http://typepad.com/), Blogger (http://blogger.com), WordPress (http://wordpress.com/), or Tumblr (http://tumblr.com), among many others. The advantage of these applications is that it's easy to set up a site, pick a theme, and start publishing content on the Web through a web interface. There's no need to build the web pages by hand, set up a hosting account, or even deal with editing files by hand.

There are also online tools like Wix (http://www.wix.com/), Squarespace (http://squarespace.com/), and Weebly (http://www.weebly.com/) that let you build a more open format website than a blog. These applications make it easy to create a website using their many templates, and they include other features like domain names, ecommerce, image and multimedia collections, and more. The advantage of using these applications is that they are easy to set up and create more professional-looking sites than blogging platforms.

2

Generally with either of these types of applications, all you need to do to get started is fill out a form, choose a URL, and pick a theme for your website. Then you can enter your content by way of forms, enabling you to avoid writing the HTML for the pages yourself. Some of them even include WYSIWYG editors so that you can format the content you enter without using HTML.

However, that doesn't mean that you don't need to learn anything about HTML or *Cascading Style Sheets* (CSS). Even if you're not creating the pages by hand, you'll still need to understand how pages are structured when you start entering content or modifying themes yourself. If you don't understand how web pages are built, you won't know how to track down and fix problems with the markup on your website, whether you're responsible for writing it or not.

For most people taking their first steps into web publishing, using an application to get started is the best approach, because it enables you to start putting the content you're interested in on the Web immediately without figuring out too many things for yourself. However, people run into limitations in these applications that leave them wanting to take more control of their websites and go further on their own. This book will help you do so.

Setting Up Your Own Web Hosting

If you do want to create and upload your own web pages, you'll need to choose a company that will provide you with the space you need. There are a huge number of hosting companies that provide web space to people who want to launch their own websites. Companies like DreamHost (http://dreamhost.com/) and Pair.com (http://pair.com/) have been in the hosting business for many years and offer a variety of affordable hosting plans, but there are plenty of other options, too. Many people subscribe to hosting plans from the company that they use to register the domain name for their website or go with hosting companies that are in their local area.

If you choose to go this route, the steps for going from setting up a hosting account to making your pages available on the Web are as follows:

1. Optionally, register a domain name. If you want your website to appear at a URL like mycoolsite.com or mycompany.com, you'll need to register that domain name if you haven't already. There are a number of domain registrars; just enter "domain registration" in your favorite search engine to see a large number of ads and search results for companies that offer domain registration.

2. Pick out a web hosting company and sign up for an account. If you're going to be putting your pages on an internal or external server belonging to your employer or your school, you won't need your own hosting. But if you're creating a new website that will be available on the Internet, you'll need some sort of hosting arrangement.

3. Associate your domain name with your new website, if you have registered one. Your domain registrar and hosting company should provide instructions for setting it up so that your domain name points to your hosting account. That way when users enter your domain name in a URL, they'll get the content that you upload to your server.

4. Start uploading your content. Once your web hosting is set up, you can use whatever tool you prefer to start uploading web content to the server. Many hosts provide a web interface that will allow you to upload content, but most hosts will also let you use a file transfer tool that supports *File Transfer Protocol* (FTP), *Secure Copy* (SCP), or *Secure FTP* (SFTP) to get your files to the server.

There will be a much more extensive discussion of web hosting and how to publish your site in Lesson 23, "How to Publish Your Site," but I wanted to give you a head start if you're eager to start publishing on the Web.

Summary

In this lesson, I explained how to get set up to productively work on web pages. You learned about how to use the Developer Tools built in to Google Chrome to assist in working on web pages and how to find a text editor that you can use to create web pages. You also learned about setting goals for your website and about finding hosting for your site. I also explained how wireframes are used to create a map of your website before you start creating it in HTML.

Workshop

The first section of the workshop lists some of the common questions people ask while planning a website, along with an answer to each. Following that, you have an opportunity to answer some quiz questions yourself. If you have problems answering any of the questions in the quiz, go to the next section, where you'll find the answers. The exercises help you formulate some ideas for your own website.

Q&A

Q Getting organized seems like an awful lot of work. All I want to do is make something simple, and you're telling me I have to have plans and wireframes. Are all the steps listed here really necessary?

A If you're doing something simple, you won't need to do much, if any, of the stuff I recommended in this lesson. However, if you're talking about developing two or three interlinked pages or more, having a plan before you start will really help. If you just dive in, you might discover that keeping everything straight in your head is too difficult. And the result might not be what you expected, making it hard for people to get the information they need out of your website as well as making it difficult for you to reorganize it so that it makes sense. Having a plan before you start can't hurt, and it might save you time in the long run.

Q You talked a lot in this lesson about organizing topics and pages, but you said nothing about the design and layout of individual pages. Why?

A I discuss design and layout later in this book, after you've learned more about the sorts of layout that HTML (the language used for web pages) can do and the stuff that it just can't do.

Q What if I don't like any of the basic structures you talked about in this lesson?

A Then design your own. As long as your visitors can find what they want or do what you want them to do, no rules say you *must* use a hierarchy or a linear structure. I presented these structures only as potential ideas for organizing your web pages.

Quiz

1. How would you briefly define the meaning of the terms *website*, *web server*, and *web pages*?
2. In terms of web publishing, what's the meaning of the term *home page*?
3. Regardless of the navigation structure you use in your website, there's one link that should typically appear on each of your web pages. What is it?
4. What's the purpose of a wireframe?

Quiz Answers

1. A *website* is one or more web pages linked together in a meaningful way. A *web server* is the actual computer that stores the website (or, confusingly enough, the piece of software that responds to requests for pages from the browser). *Web pages* are the individual elements of the website, like a page is to a book.

2. A *home page*, in terms of web publishing, is the entry point to the rest of the pages in your website (the first or topmost page).

3. You should try to include a link to your home page on each of the pages in your website. That way, users can always find their way back home if they get lost.

4. A wireframe provides an overall outline of what the website will look like when it's done. It helps organize your web pages in a way that works for you. It is most beneficial for a larger website.

Exercises

1. Come up with a list of several goals that your visitors might have for your web pages. The clearer your goals are, the better.

2. After you set your goals, visit sites on the Web that cover topics similar to those you want to cover in your own website. As you examine the sites, ask yourself whether they're easy to navigate and have good content. Then make a list of what you like about the sites. How would you make your website better?

LESSON 3
Introducing HTML and CSS

Now that you've learned all about the Web at a high level and you've gotten your computer set up, you're probably ready to write a web page. That is, after all, why you bought this book. Wait no longer! In this lesson, you get to create your very first (albeit brief) web page, learn about HTML (the language for writing web pages), and learn about the following:

- What HTML is and why you have to use it

- What you can and cannot do when you design HTML pages

- What HTML tags are and how to use them

- How to write pages that conform to the HTML standard

- How you can use Cascading Style Sheets to control the look and feel of your pages

What HTML Is (And What It Isn't)

Take note of just one more thing before you start writing web pages. You should know what HTML is, what it can do, and most important, what it can't do.

HTML stands for *Hypertext Markup Language*. HTML was originally based on the *Standard Generalized Markup Language* (SGML), a much larger, more complicated document-processing system. To write HTML pages, you won't need to know much about SGML. However, knowing that one of the main features of SGML is that it describes the general structure of the content inside documents—rather than its actual appearance on the page or onscreen—does help. This concept might be a bit foreign to you if you're used to working with WYSIWYG (What You See Is What You Get) editors, so let's go over the information carefully.

HTML Describes the Structure of a Page

HTML, by virtue of its SGML heritage, is a language for describing the structure of a document, not its actual presentation. The idea here is that most documents have common elements—for example, titles, paragraphs, and lists. Before you start writing, therefore, you can identify and define the set of elements in that document and name them appropriately (see Figure 3.1).

FIGURE 3.1
Document elements.

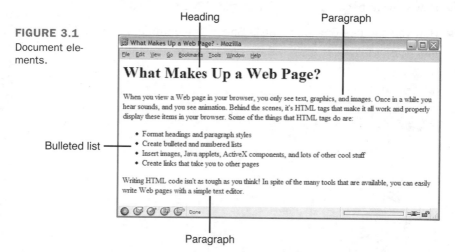

If you've worked with word processing programs that use style sheets (such as Microsoft Word) or paragraph catalogs (such as FrameMaker), you've done something similar; each section of text conforms to one of a set of styles that are predefined before you start working.

HTML defines a set of common elements for web pages: headings, paragraphs, lists, and tables. It also defines character formats such as boldface and code examples. These elements and formats are indicated inside HTML documents using *tags*. Each tag has a specific name and is set off from the content of the document using a notation that I discuss a bit later.

HTML Does Not Describe Page Layout

When you're working with a word processor or page layout program, styles are not just named elements of a page; they also include formatting information such as the font size and style, indentation, underlining, and so on. So, when you write some text that's supposed to be a heading, you can apply the Heading style to it, and the program automatically formats that paragraph for you in the correct style.

HTML doesn't go this far. For the most part, the HTML specification doesn't say anything about how a page looks when it's viewed. HTML tags just indicate that an element is a heading or a list; they say nothing about how that heading or list is to be formatted. The only thing you have to worry about is marking which section is supposed to be a heading, not how that heading should look.

3

NOTE

> Although HTML doesn't say much about how a page looks when it's viewed, *Cascading Style Sheets* (CSS) enable you to apply advanced formatting to HTML tags. HTML has evolved to the point where web publishers are intended to use CSS for formatting instructions. You'll learn about CSS later in the book.

Web browsers, in addition to providing the networking functions to retrieve pages from the Web, double as HTML formatters. When you read an HTML page into a browser such as Firefox, Chrome, or Internet Explorer, the browser interprets, or *parses*, the HTML tags and formats the text and images on the screen. The browser has mappings between the names of page elements and actual styles on the screen; for example, headings might appear in a larger font than the text on the rest of the page. The browser also wraps all the text so that it fits into the current width of the window.

Different browsers running on diverse platforms style elements differently. For the most part, browsers have standardized on the styles associated with the various HTML tags, but there are some cases where they differ. Some non-smartphones display web pages very differently than desktop and smartphone browsers; for example, they might not provide support for multiple fonts or even italics on a web page. More importantly, browsers intended to be accessible to the disabled, like screen readers for the visually impaired, use a radically different set of "styles" to enable users to access web pages. In these cases, the idea that HTML describes the structure of a document rather than its appearance is crucially important.

How the Visual Styles for Tags Evolved

In practice, most HTML tags are rendered in a fairly standard manner, on desktop computers at least. When the earliest browsers were written, somebody decided that links would be underlined and blue, visited links would be purple, and emphasized text would appear in italic. Similar decisions were made about every other tag. Since then, pretty much every browser maker has followed that convention. These conventions blurred the line separating structure from presentation, but in truth the line still exists, even if it's not obvious.

Why It Works This Way

If you're used to writing and designing documents that will wind up printed on paper, this concept might seem almost perverse. No control over the layout of a page? The whole design can vary depending on where the page is viewed? This is awful! Why on earth would a system work like this?

Remember in Lesson 1, "What Is Web Publishing?" when I mentioned that one of the cool things about the Web is that it's cross-platform and that web pages can be viewed on any computer system, on any size screen, with any graphics display? If the final goal of web publishing is for your pages to be readable by anyone in the world, you can't count on your readers having the same computer systems, the same screen size, the same number of colors, or the same fonts that you have. The Web takes into account all these differences and enables all browsers and all computer systems to be on equal ground.

The Web, as a design medium, is not a new form of paper. The Web is an entirely different medium, with its own constraints and goals that are very different from working with paper. The most important rules of web page design, as I'll keep harping on throughout this book, are the following:

DO	DON'T
DO design your pages so that they work in most browsers.	**DON'T** design your pages based on what they look like on your computer system and on your browser.
DO focus on clear, well-structured content that's easy to read and understand.	

Throughout this book, you'll see examples of HTML code and what they look like when displayed.

How Markup Works

HTML is a *markup language*. Writing in a markup language means that you start with the text of your page and add special tags around words and paragraphs. The tags indicate the different parts of the page and produce different effects in the browser. You'll learn more about tags and how they're used in the next section.

HTML has a defined set of tags you can use. You can't make up your own tags to create new styles or features. And just to make sure that things are really confusing, various browsers support different sets of tags.

What HTML Files Look Like

Enough theory. It's time to get into writing HTML. HTML documents are plain-text files (ASCII), which means that they contain no platform- or program-specific information. Any editor that supports text (which should be just about any editor; read more about this subject in Lesson 2, "Getting Your Tools in Order") can be used to create them.

HTML files contain the following:

- The text of the page itself
- HTML tags that identify page elements, structure, formatting, and hypertext links to other pages or to included media

Most HTML tags look something like the following:

```
<thetagname>affected text</thetagname>
```

The tag name itself (here, `thetagname`) is enclosed in angle brackets (`< >`). HTML tags generally have a beginning and an ending tag surrounding the text they affect. The beginning tag "turns on" a feature (such as headings, bold, and so on), and the ending tag turns it off. Closing tags contain the tag name preceded by a slash (`/`). The opening tag (for example, `<p>` for paragraphs) and closing tag (for example, `</p>` for paragraphs) compose what is officially called an *HTML element*.

CAUTION

Be aware of the difference between the forward slash (/) mentioned with relation to tags, and backslashes (\), which are used by Windows in directory references on hard drives (as in C:\window or other directory paths). If you accidentally use the backslash in place of a forward slash in HTML, the browser won't recognize the ending tags.

3

Not all HTML tags have both an opening and a closing tag. Some tags are only one-sided, and still other tags are containers that hold extra information and text inside the brackets. You'll learn the proper way to open and close the tags as the book progresses.

Some HTML tags have additional text inside them that provides additional information about the tags. These are called *attributes*, and they are usually defined as name=value pairs that follow the tag name separated by a space. An HTML tag with an attribute looks something like this:

```
<thetagname theattribute="theattributevalue">affected text</thetagname>
```

HTML tags are not case sensitive; that is, you can specify them in uppercase, in lower-case, or in any mixture. So, `<HTML>` is the same as `<html>`, which is the same as `<HtMl>`. This is true for attributes as well.

▼ Exercise 3.1: Creating Your First HTML Page

Now that you've seen what an HTML tag looks like, it's your turn to create a web page that uses a few. Start with a simple example so that you can get a basic feel for HTML.

To get started writing HTML, you don't need a web server, web hosting, or even a con-nection to the Internet. All you really need is an application in which you can create your HTML files and a browser to view them. You can write, link, and test whole suites of web pages without even touching a network. In fact, that's what you're going to do for the majority of this book. Later, I discuss publishing everything on the Web so that other people can see your work.

CAUTION	Many word processors are including HTML modes or mechanisms for creating HTML or XML code. This feature can produce unusual results or files that simply don't behave as you expect. Using a word processor to generate HTML is not a good idea if you plan on editing the web pages later. They also don't provide the opportunity to learn HTML, so they make a poor companion for this book. When you work on the examples in this book, you should use a regular text editor.

Open your text editor and type the following code. You don't have to understand what any of it means at this point. You'll learn more about much of this in this lesson and the following lesson. This simple example is just to get you started:

```
<!DOCTYPE html>
<html>
<head>
```

```
<title>My Sample HTML Page</title>
</head>
<body>
<h1>This is an HTML Page</h1>
</body>
</html>
```

NOTE

Note that the `<!DOCTYPE>` tag in the previous example looks a little different from the others, starting with the fact that it begins with an exclamation point. The purpose of the `DOCTYPE` is to tell validators and browsers which specification your page was written to—in this case, HTML5.

After you create your HTML file, save it. When you choose a name for the file, follow these two rules:

- The filename should have an extension of `.html` (`.htm` is OK, but not preferred)—for example, `myfile.html`, `text.html`, or `index.htm`. Most web software requires your files to have these extensions, so get into the habit of doing it now. (If you are using Windows, make sure that your computer is configured to show file extensions. If it isn't, you'll find yourself creating files named things like `myfile.html.txt`, which your browser will not think are HTML files.)

- Use short, simple names. Don't include spaces or special characters (bullets, accented characters)—just letters and numbers are fine. Be sure to choose descriptive, readable names for your files. They'll help you keep track of what they're used for, and they can help make your site friendlier to search engines.

Exercise 3.2: Viewing the Result

Now that you have an HTML file, start your web browser. After your browser is running, look for a menu item or button labeled Open, Open File. Choosing it enables you to browse your local disk. The Open command (or its equivalent) opens a document from your local disk, parses it, and displays it. By using your browser and the Open command, you can write and test your HTML files on your computer in the privacy of your own home. (On most computers, you can just drag the icon from your HTML file into an open browser window if you prefer.)

If you don't see something similar to what's shown in Figure 3.2 (for example, if parts are missing or if everything looks like a heading), go back into your text editor and

▼ compare your file to the example. Make sure that all your tags have closing tags and that all your < characters are matched by > characters. You don't have to quit your browser to do so; just fix the file and save it again under the same name.

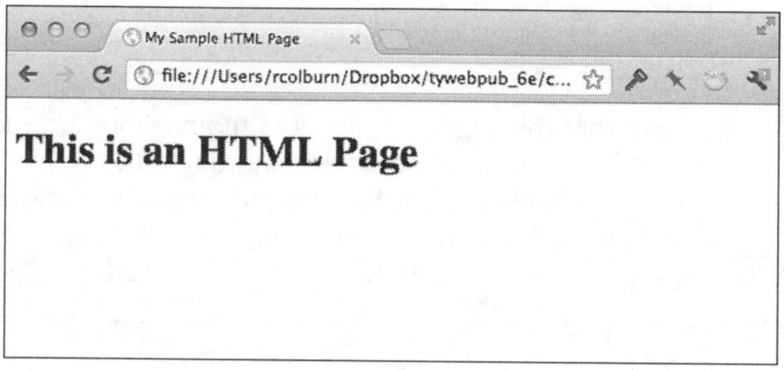

FIGURE 3.2
The sample HTML file.

Next, go back to your browser. Locate and choose a menu item or button called Refresh or Reload. The browser will read the new version of your file, and voilà! You can edit and preview and edit and preview until you get the file right.

If you're getting the actual HTML text repeated in your browser rather than what's shown in Figure 3.2, make sure that your HTML file has an .html or .htm extension. This file extension tells your browser that it's an HTML file. The extension is important.

If things are going really wrong—if you're getting a blank screen or you're getting some really strange characters—something is wrong with your original file. If the text editor can't read the file or if the result is garbled, you haven't saved the original file in the right format. Go back into your original editor and try saving the file as text only again. Then try viewing the file again in your browser until you get it right.

Once you've opened the file in the browser, go ahead and take a look at it using the Chrome Developer Tools. Once you've opened the Developer Tools, you can view the source of the page in the Elements tab. Go ahead and mouse over the elements in the source window to see the corresponding markup highlighted on the page. The Elements
▼ view of the page is shown in Figure 3.3.

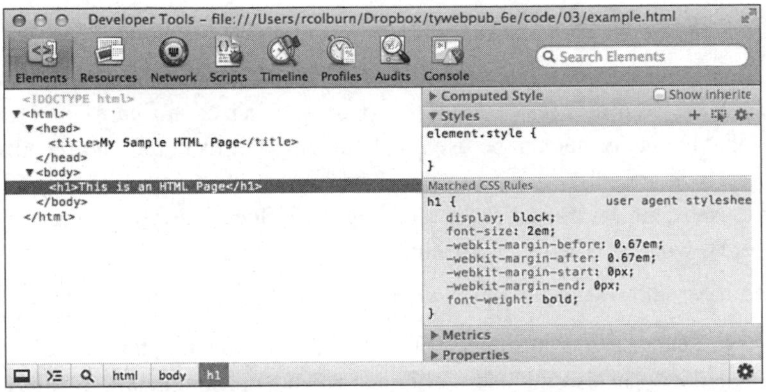

FIGURE 3.3
The Developer
Tools view of the
sample HTML file.

Text Formatting and HTML

When an HTML page is parsed by a browser, any formatting you might have done with whitespace characters—that is, any extra spaces, tabs, returns, and so on—is ignored. The only thing that specifies formatting in an HTML page is an HTML tag. If you spend hours carefully editing a plain text file to have nicely formatted paragraphs and columns of numbers but don't include any tags, when a web browser loads the page, all the text will flow into one paragraph. All your work will have been in vain.

NOTE

> There are two exceptions to this rule: the `<pre>` tag and the CSS `pre` property. You'll learn about both of them in Lesson 7, "Formatting Text with HTML and CSS."

The advantage of having all whitespace (spaces, tabs, returns) ignored is that you can put your tags wherever you want. The following examples all produce the same output. Try them!

```
<h1>Everything You Need to Know About HTML </h1>

<h1>
Everything You Need to Know About HTML</h1>


<h1>
Everything You Need to Know About HTML          </h1>


<h1>     Everything You Need to Know
About HTML </h1>
```

HTML Attributes

HTML elements can be modified by attributes. Attributes are placed within the opening tag in an element. Many elements support specialized attributes, and there are also a few global elements that can be used with any tag. For example, the ID attribute is used to specify an identifier that uniquely identifies that element on the page. These identifiers are used with JavaScript and Cascading Style Sheets, as you'll learn in later lessons. Here's what a tag with an attribute looks like:

```
<h1 id="theTopHeading">Everything You Need to Know About HTML</h1>
```

As you can see, the attribute is placed within the opening tag, to the right of the tag name. You can also include multiple attributes in a single tag, as follows:

```
<h1 id="theTopHeading" class="first">Everything You Need to Know About HTML</h1>
```

The `class` attribute is another global attribute that can be used to establish arbitrary groups of elements. You can assign the same class to multiple elements so that they can be referenced as a group via CSS or JavaScript.

The third global attribute you'll use a lot is `style`, which I talk about in the following section. There are also a number of attributes that are associated with specific elements or families of elements. I'll talk about those attributes along with the associated elements.

Using the `style` Attribute

Earlier in this lesson, I mentioned Cascading Style Sheets as a way you could control the look and feel of your pages. As I mentioned, although there are default styles associated with tags, their main purpose is to describe the structure of a document. Cascading Style Sheets are a way to control how the browser renders HTML elements.

For example, in this lesson, I've used the `<h1>` tag a couple of times. Browsers print text enclosed inside an `<h1>` tag in a large, boldface font and leave some whitespace after the heading before printing something else. Using CSS, you can tell the browser to render the `<h1>` tag differently than it normally would. CSS provides a lot of flexibility in how you can alter the appearance of any type of element, and the styles can be applied in a number of different ways.

The advantage of CSS is that it can be used in various ways. For example, you can put all your styles into a separate file and link to that file from your web page. That way, if you want to change the appearance an entire site, you can simply edit your CSS file and make changes that span every page that links to your style sheet. Or, if you prefer, you can include styles at the top of your page so that they apply only to that page. Style sheets affect the entire page; there's also a way to apply styles one tag at a time, using the `style` attribute. You can also include styles inside the tags themselves using the `style` attribute.

You can also control the specificity of the styles you create based on how you define them. For example, you can write rules that apply to all tags of a specific type, such as all `<h1>` elements. Or you can specify classes for your elements and then write rules that apply only to members of that class. Classes are categories or labels that are assigned to tags using the `class` attribute. For example, you could create a class called `headline` and then make all `<h1>` elements in the `headline` class red. You can also write rules that apply to single elements by assigning them a unique identifier using the `id` attribute and writing rules that apply to that identifier. Here's an example of an `<h1>` tag that includes both a class and an ID:

```
<h1 class="headline" id="leadstoryheadline">Lead Story Headline</h1>
```

One thing you'll find as you progress through the book is that CSS can serve as a replacement for some tags. As I describe various tags, I explain how you can achieve the same effects using CSS instead. Best practices suggest you should use HTML to describe the structure of pages and CSS to define their appearance. The coverage of CSS in this book culminates with Lesson 15, "Advanced CSS: Page Layout in CSS," which explains how to use CSS to manage the entire layout of the page or even the entire layout of a site.

3

Including Styles in Tags

As mentioned previously, the `style` attribute can be used with any tag. By including the `style` attribute in a tag, you can specify one or more style rules within a tag itself. Here's an example using the `<h1>` tag, which I introduced earlier:

```
<h1 style="font-family: Verdana, sans-serif;">Heading</h1>
```

The `style` attribute of the `<h1>` tag contains a style declaration. All style declarations follow this same basic pattern, with the property on the left and the value associated with that property on the right. The rule ends with a semicolon, and you can include more than one in a `style` attribute by placing semicolons between them. If you're only including one rule in the `style` attribute, the semicolon is optional, but it's a good idea to include it. In the preceding example, the property is `font-family`, and the value is `Verdana, sans-serif`. This attribute modifies the standard `<h1>` tag by changing the font to Verdana, and if the user doesn't have that font installed on his system, whichever sans-serif font the browser selects. (Sans-serif fonts are those that do not include *serifs*, the small lines at the ends of characters.)

Many, many properties can be used in style declarations. As previously mentioned, putting a declaration into a `style` attribute is just one of several ways that you can apply styles to your document.

A Short History of HTML Standards

HTML 2.0 was the original standard for HTML and the set of tags that all browsers should support. Most of the tags in that original specification are still supported and still make up the core of HTML. You can create perfectly good web pages using only tags that were included in HTML 2.0.

The HTML 3.2 specification was developed in early 1996. Several software vendors, including IBM, Microsoft, Netscape Communications Corporation, Novell, SoftQuad, Spyglass, and Sun Microsystems, joined with the W3C to develop this specification. Some of the primary additions to HTML 3.2 included features such as tables, applets, and text flow around images.

HTML 4.0, first introduced in 1997, incorporated many new features that gave designers greater control over page layout than HTML 2.0 and 3.2. Like HTML 2.0 and 3.2, the W3C created the HTML 4.0 standard.

Frames (originally introduced in Netscape 2.0) and floating frames (originally introduced in Internet Explorer 3.0) were introduced with the HTML 4.0 specification. Frames are discussed in more detail in Lesson 20, "Working with Frames and Linked Windows." By far, however, the most important change in HTML 4.0 was its increased integration with Cascading Style Sheets.

XHTML

The specification that followed HTML 4.0 was XHTML 1.0, which was followed by XHTML 1.1. The most significant new change introduced with XHTML was that it required that HTML documents to also be valid *Extensible Markup Language* (XML) documents. The *X* in XHTML stands for XML. XML is another markup standard derived from SGML. XML is a language used to create other markup languages, and XHTML is one such language. The main difference from HTML is that XHTML requires documents to conform to XML's strict rules for document structure. Whereas HTML 4 was forgiving of unclosed elements, XML requires that every tag be closed, every attribute have a value, and more.

Technically, XHTML and HTML 4 were *very* similar. The actual tags and attributes are almost the same, but the XML rules required large changes to many websites.

While XHTML has been superseded by HTML5, most websites that currently exist were built using XHTML. If you're working on a site that was built with XHTML, you must adhere to a few rules if you want your HTML markup to be valid XHTML. All of these rules are a direct result of the fact that to be valid, an XHTML document must be valid XML as well. Here's a list:

- All the tags in your document must be lowercase.
- Any tags that do not have closing tags must be closed using a slash after the tag name. So the `<br>` tag would be written as `<br />`.
- All attributes must have a value. You'll see later that some attributes don't have any values associated with them. XHTML requires that you use the attribute name as the value in these cases. So they follow the form `attribute="attribute"`.

The Current and Evolving Standard: HTML5

While the W3C is still involved in web standards, a new group, the WHATWG, is busy creating a new standard for HTML: HTML5. The goal of HTML5 is to make sure that the HTML standard accurately reflects the state of the Web as it exists now. The WHATWG, or Web Hypertext Application Technology Working Group, includes representatives from all the major browser makers and is writing an HTML specification that includes only features that all the browser vendors have reached a consensus on supporting.

HTML5 does not demand that web pages be valid XML, relaxing some of the rules that XHTML 1.0 imposed. However, today's valid HTML or XHTML will still be valid in HTML5 when it's fully adopted.

While no current browsers offer 100% support for HTML5, most popular browsers support over 80%. To find out whether a particular browser offers support for an HTML5 feature, go to http://caniuse.com/, which maintains a list of all the features in HTML5 and which version of each browser supports them, along with the percentage of users whose browsers support that feature. For example, at the time of the writing, 87% of users currently have browsers that fully support the HTML5 form features. However, only 9% of users have browsers that support SVG favicons.

Another important note about HTML5 is that the WHATWG has decided to do away with the concept of versions for HTML period. The HTML specification is being written to reflect the current and future state of the industry and will evolve over time with browsers. This is a new experiment designed to make sure that the specification process more accurately reflects the evolution of the Web.

3

Summary

In this lesson, you learned some basic points about what HTML is and how you create HTML files. You learned a bit about the history of HTML and the reasons why the HTML specification has changed several times since the beginning. You also learned how CSS can be used to augment your HTML. You created your first web page with some basic tags. It wasn't so bad, was it? You also learned a bit about the current standard version of HTML, XHTML, and how to apply styles using CSS. In the following lesson, you'll expand on this and learn more about adding headings, text, and lists to your pages.

Workshop

Now that you've had an introduction to HTML and a taste of creating your first (very simple) web page, here's a workshop that will guide you toward more of what you'll learn. A couple of questions and answers that relate to HTML formatting are followed by a brief quiz and answers about HTML. The exercises prompt you to examine the code of a more advanced page in your browser.

Q&A

Q Can I do *any* formatting of text in HTML?

A You can apply some formatting to strings of characters. CSS has superseded most of the tags for formatting text. However, browsers still support the older text formatting elements. You'll learn some formatting tricks in Lesson 7.

Q I have some existing XHTML pages that I work on. Should I convert them to HTML5?

A To have correct HTML5, you just need the simplified DOCTYPE at the top of your document. By just changing that, you have converted to HTML5. Then you will not be limited by the constraints of XHTML and can use all the new features of HTML5. HTML5 is well supported by browsers, especially if all you do is change the DOCTYPE, so there really is no reason not to convert any old pages you edit.

Quiz

1. What does HTML stand for? How about XHTML?
2. What's the primary function of HTML?
3. Why doesn't HTML control the layout of a page?
4. What's the basic structure of an HTML tag?

Quiz Answers

1. HTML stands for Hypertext Markup Language. XHTML stands for Extensible Hypertext Markup Language.

2. HTML enables you to describe the structure of a document so that it can be styled, either using HTML tags or using CSS.

3. HTML doesn't control the layout of a page because it's designed to be cross-platform. It takes the differences of many platforms into account and allows all browsers and all computer systems to be on equal ground.

4. Most HTML elements consist of opening and closing tags, and they surround the text that they affect. The tags are enclosed in brackets (<>). The beginning tag turns on a feature, and the ending tag, which is preceded by a forward slash (/), turns it off.

Exercises

1. Before you actually start writing a meatier HTML page, getting a feel for what an HTML page looks like certainly helps. Luckily, you can find plenty of source material to look at. Every page that comes over the wire to your browser is in HTML (or perhaps XHTML) format.

   One feature of Chrome's Developer Tools (and developer tools provided by other browsers) is the ability to edit the content and style of pages while they are being displayed. Use the Chrome Developer Tools to make some changes to a web page as you watch.

   For example, go to the HTML5 article in Wikipedia (http://en.wikipedia.org/wiki/HTML5) and open the Chrome Developer Tools. Use the inspector tool to go to the article title. Double-click the title and change it to something else. You'll see the change reflected on the page. If you're feeling adventurous, you can also change the styles associated with the page to alter its appearance. None of these changes will be preserved, so feel free to experiment.

   When you're working on your own web pages, you can use the Developer Tools to experiment rather than editing your files, saving your changes, and reloading the web page. Just edit your pages in the Developer Tools and then transfer the changes back to your files once you're happy with the results you see.

2. Try viewing the source of your own favorite web pages, either using View Source or with the Developer Tools. You should start seeing some similarities in the way pages are organized and get a feel for the kinds of tags that HTML uses. You can learn a lot about HTML by comparing the text onscreen with the source for that text.

3

LESSON 4
Learning the Basics of HTML

Over the first three lessons, you learned about the World Wide Web, how to prepare to build websites, and why you need to use HTML to create a web page. In Lesson 3, "Introducing HTML and CSS," you even created your first very simple web page. In this lesson, you learn about each of the basic HTML tags in more depth, and begin writing web pages with headings, paragraphs, and several different types of lists. We focus on the following topics and HTML tags:

- Tags for overall page structure: `<html>`, `<head>`, and `<body>`

- Tags for titles, headings, and paragraphs: `<title>`, `<h1>` through `<h6>`, and `<p>`

- Tags for comments: `<!-- ... -->`

Structuring Your HTML

HTML defines three tags that are used to define the page's overall structure and provide some simple header information. These three tags—`<html>`, `<head>`, and `<body>`—make up the basic skeleton of every web page. They also provide simple information about the page (such as its title or its author) before loading the entire thing. The page structure tags don't affect what the page looks like when it's displayed; they're only there to help browsers.

The DOCTYPE **Identifier**

Although it's not a page structure tag, the XHTML 1.0 and HTML5 standards impose an additional requirement on your web pages. The first line of each page must include a DOCTYPE identifier that defines the HTML version to which your page conforms, and in some cases, the Document Type Definition (DTD) that defines the specification. This is followed by the `<html>`, `<head>`, and `<body>` tags. In the following example, the HTML5 document type appears before the page structure tags:

```
<!DOCTYPE html>
<html>
<head>
<title>Page Title</title>
</head>
<body>
...your page content...
</body>
</html>
```

The `<html>` Tag

The first page structure tag in every HTML page is the `<html>` tag. It indicates that the content of this file is in the HTML language. The `<html>` tag should immediately follow the DOCTYPE identifier (as mentioned in the previous note), as shown in the following example.

All the text and HTML elements in your web page should be placed within the beginning and ending HTML tags, like this:

```
<!DOCTYPE html>
<html>
...your page...
</html>
```

The `<html>` tag serves as a container for all of the tags that make up the page. It is required because both XML and SGML specify that every document have a root element. Were you to leave it out, which you shouldn't do because it would make your page invalid, the browser would make up an `<html>` tag for you so that the page would make sense to its HTML processor.

The `<head>` Tag

The `<head>` tag is a container for the tags that contain information about the page, rather than information that will be displayed on the page. Generally, only a few tags are used in the `<head>` portion of the page (most notably, the page title, described later). You should never put any of the text of your page into the header (between `<head>` tags).

Here's a typical example of how you properly use the `<head>` tag. (You'll learn about `<title>` later.)

```
<!DOCTYPE html>
<html>
<head>
<title>This is the Title. It will be explained later on</title>
</head>
...your page...
</html>
```

4

The `<body>` Tag

The content of your HTML page (represented in the following example as ...*your page*...) resides within the `<body>` tag. This includes all the text and other content (links, pictures, and so on). In combination with the `<html>` and `<head>` tags, your page will look something like this:

```
<!DOCTYPE html><html>
<head>
<title>This is the Title. It will be explained later on</title>
</head>
<body>
...your page...
</body>
</html>
```

You might notice here that the tags are nested. That is, both `<body>` and `</body>` tags go inside the `<html>` tags; the same with both `<head>` tags. All HTML tags work this way, forming individual nested sections of text. You should be careful never to overlap tags. That is, never do something like the following:

```
<!DOCTYPE html><html>
<head>
<body>
</head>
</body>
</html>
```

Whenever you close an HTML tag, make sure that you're closing the most recent unclosed tag. (You'll learn more about closing tags as you go on.)

NOTE

In HTML, closing some tags is optional. In fact, in HTML 4.0 and earlier, closing tags were forbidden in some cases. The XHTML standard requires your markup to be well-formed XML, which leads to the requirement that all tags be closed. Because the examples shown in this book use HTML5, closing tags will be used only when they are required, but if you are working with XHTML you must close them.

The Title

Each HTML page needs a title to indicate what the page describes. It appears in the title bar of the browser when people view the web page. The title is stored in your browser's bookmarks and in search engines when they index your pages. Use the `<title>` tag to give a page a title.

`<title>` tags are placed within the `<head>` tag and are normally used to describe the contents of the page, as follows:

```
<!DOCTYPE html><html>
<head>
<title>The Lion, The Witch, and the Wardrobe</title>
</head>
<body>
...your page...
</body>
</html>
```

Each page can have only one title, and that title can contain only plain text; that is, no other tags should appear inside the title.

Try to choose a title that's both short and descriptive of the content. Your title should be relevant even out of context. If someone browsing on the Web follows a random link and ends up on this page, or if a person finds your title in a friend's browser history list, would he have any idea what this page is about? You might not intend the page to be used independently of the pages you specifically linked to it, but because anyone can link to any page at any time, be prepared for that consequence and pick a helpful title.

NOTE

> When search engines index your pages, each page title is captured and listed in the search results. The more descriptive your page title, the more likely it is that someone will choose your page from all the search results.

Also, because browsers put the title in the title bar of the window, you might have a limited amount of space. (Although the text within the `<title>` tag can be of any length, it might be cut off by the browser when it's displayed.) Here are some examples of good titles:

```
<title>Poisonous Plants of North America</title>
<title>Image Editing: A Tutorial</title>
<title>Upcoming Cemetery Tours, Summer 1999</title>
<title>Installing the Software: Opening the CD Case</title>
<title>Laura Lemay's Awesome Home Page</title>
```

Here are some not-so-good titles:

```
<title>Part Two</title>
<title>An Example</title>
<title>Nigel Franklin Hobbes</title>
<title>Minutes of the Second Meeting of the Fourth Conference of the
Committee for the Preservation of English Roses, Day Four, After Lunch</title>
```

Figure 4.1 shows how the following title looks in a browser:

```
<title>The Lion, the Witch, and the Wardrobe</title>
```

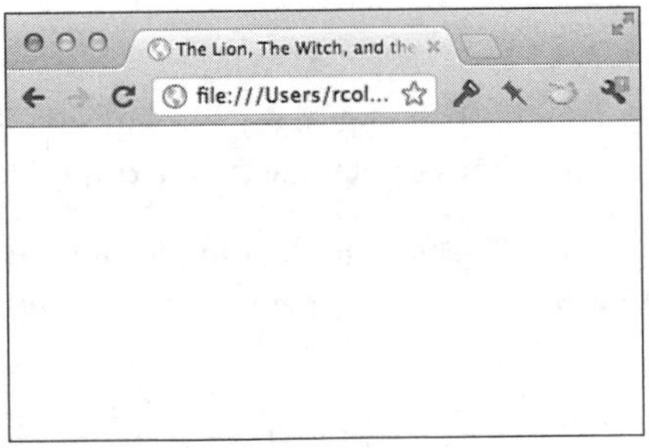

FIGURE 4.1
The title appears in the tab bar, not on the page.

4

Headings

Headings are used to add titles to sections of a page. HTML defines six levels of headings. Heading tags look like the following:

```
<h1>Installing Your Safetee Lock</h1>
```

The numbers indicate heading levels (h1 through h6). The headings, when they're displayed, aren't numbered. They're displayed in larger and bolder text so that they stand out from regular text.

Think of the headings as items in an outline. If the text you're writing is structured, use the headings to express that structure, as shown in the following code:

```
<h1>Movies</h1>
  <h2>Action/Adventure</h2>
    <h3>Caper</h3>
    <h3>Sports</h3>
    <h3>Thriller</h3>
    <h3>War</h3>
  <h2>Comedy</h2>
    <h3>Romantic Comedy</h3>
    <h3>Slapstick</h3>
  <h2>Drama</h2>
    <h3>Buddy Movies</h3>
    <h3>Mystery</h3>
    <h3>Romance</h3>
  <h2>Horror</h2>
```

Notice that I've indented the headings in this example to better show the hierarchy. They don't have to be indented in your page; in fact, the browser ignores the indenting.

TIP

Even though the browser ignores any indenting you include in your code, you will probably find it useful to indent your code so that it's easier to read. You'll find that any lengthy examples in this book are indented for that reason, and you'll probably want to carry that convention over to your own HTML code.

Unlike titles, headings can be any length, spanning many lines of text. Because headings are emphasized, however, having many lines of emphasized text might be tiring to read.

A common practice is to use a first-level heading at the top of your page to either duplicate the title or to provide a shorter or less context-specific form of the title. If you have a page that shows several examples of folding bed sheets—for example, part of a long presentation on how to fold bed sheets—the title might look something like the following:

```
<title>How to Fold Sheets: Some Examples</title>
```

The topmost heading, however, might just be as follows:

```
<h1>Examples</h1>
```

<table>
<tr><td>CAUTION</td><td>Don't use headings to display text in boldface type or to make certain parts of your page stand out more. Although the result might look as you intend, the markup will not represent the structure of your page. This comes into play for search engines, accessibility, and some browsers.</td></tr>
</table>

Figure 4.2 shows the following headings as they appear in a browser:

Input ▼

```
<h1>Mythology Through the Ages</h1>
  <h2>Common Mythological Themes</h2>
  <h2>Earliest Known Myths</h2>
  <h2>Origins of Mythology</h2>
   <h3>Mesopotamian Mythology</h3>
   <h3>Egyptian Mythology</h3>
    <h4>The Story of Isis and Osiris</h4>
    <h4>Horus and Set: The Battle of Good vs. Evil</h4>
    <h4>The Twelve Hours of the Underworld</h4>
    <h4>The River Styx</h4>
  <h2>History in Myth</h2>
```

4

Output ▼

FIGURE 4.2
HTML heading elements.

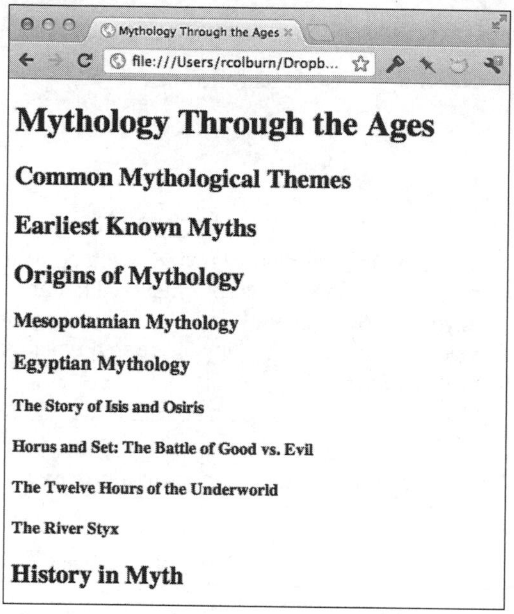

TIP

From a visual perspective, headings 4 through 6 aren't visually interesting, but they do have meaning in terms of the document's structure. If using more than three levels of headings makes sense for the document you're creating, you can use those tags and then use styles to make them appear as you intend.

Paragraphs

Now that you have a page title and several headings, you can add some ordinary paragraphs to the page.

Paragraphs are created using the `<p>` tag. The Enigern story should look like this:

```
<p>Slowly and deliberately, Enigern approached the mighty dragon.
A rustle in the trees of the nearby forest distracted his attention
for a brief moment, a near fatal mistake for the brave knight.</p>
<p>The dragon lunged at him, searing Enigern's armor with a rapid
blast of fiery breath. Enigern fell to the ground as the dragon
hovered over him. He quickly drew his sword and thrust it into the
dragon's chest.</p>
```

What if you want more (or less) space between your paragraphs than the browser provides by default? The answer is to use CSS. As you'll see, it provides fine control over the spacing of elements on the page, among other things. Figure 4.3 shows what happens when I add another paragraph about Enigern and the dragon to the page. The paragraph breaks are added between the closing and opening `<p>` tags in the text.

Input ▼

```
<p>The dragon fell to the ground, releasing an anguished cry and
seething in pain. The thrust of Enigern's sword proved fatal as
the dragon breathed its last breath. Now Enigern was free to
release Lady Aelfleada from her imprisonment in the dragon's lair. </p>
```

Output ▼

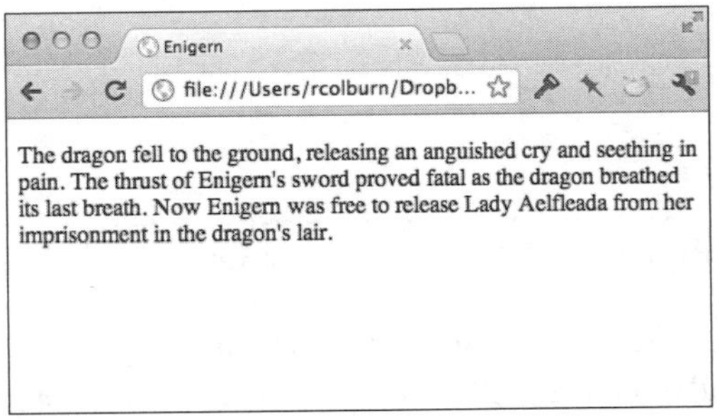

FIGURE 4.3
An HTML paragraph.

The dragon fell to the ground, releasing an anguished cry and seething in pain. The thrust of Enigern's sword proved fatal as the dragon breathed its last breath. Now Enigern was free to release Lady Aelfleada from her imprisonment in the dragon's lair.

4

The closing `</p>` tag, while not required, is important for defining the exact contents of a paragraph for CSS. Most web designers use it automatically, but if you don't need it, you can leave it out of your HTML.

Comments

You can put comments into HTML pages to describe the page itself or to provide some kind of indication of the status of the page. Some source code control programs store the page status in comments, for example. Text in comments is ignored when the HTML file is parsed; comments never show up onscreen—that's why they're comments. Comments look like the following:

```
<!-- This is a comment -->
```

Here are some examples:

```
<!-- Rewrite this section with less humor -->
<!-- Neil helped with this section -->
<!-- Go Tigers! -->
```

As you can see from Figure 4.4, users can view your comments using the View Source functionality in their browsers, so don't put anything in comments that you don't want them to see.

FIGURE 4.4
HTML comments displayed within the source for a page.

▼ **Exercise 4.1: Creating a Real HTML Page**

At this point, you know enough to get started creating simple HTML pages. You understand what HTML is, you've been introduced to a handful of tags, and you've even opened an HTML file in your browser. You haven't created any links yet, but you'll get to that soon enough, in Lesson 6, "Working with Links."

This exercise shows you how to create an HTML file that uses the tags you've learned about up to this point. It'll give you a feel for what the tags look like when they're displayed onscreen and for the sorts of typical mistakes you're going to make. (Everyone makes them, and that's why using an HTML editor that does the typing for you is often helpful. The editor doesn't forget the closing tags, leave off the slash, or misspell the tag itself.)

So, create a simple example in your text editor. Your example doesn't have to say much of anything; in fact, all it needs to include are the structure tags, a title, a couple of head-
▼ ings, and a paragraph or two. Here's an example:

Input ▼

```
<!DOCTYPE html><html>
<head>
<title>Camembert Incorporated</title>
</head>
<body>
<h1>Camembert Incorporated</h1>
<p>"Many's the long night I dreamed of cheese -- toasted, mostly."
-- Robert Louis Stevenson</p>
<h2>What We Do</h2>
<p>We make cheese. Lots of cheese; more than eight tons of cheese
a year.</p>
<h2>Why We Do It</h2>
<p>We are paid an awful lot of money by people who like cheese.
So we make more.</p>
</body>
</html>
```

Save the example to an HTML file, open it in your browser, and see how it came out. Figure 4.5 shows what the cheese factory example looks like.

Output ▼

4

FIGURE 4.5
The cheese factory example.

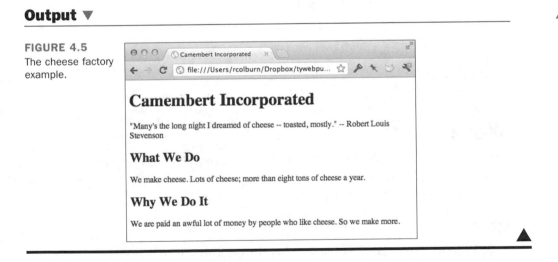

Summary

HTML, a text-only markup language used to describe hypertext pages on the World Wide Web, describes the structure of a page, not its appearance.

In this lesson, you learned what HTML is and how to write and preview simple HTML files. You also learned about the HTML tags shown in Table 4.1.

TABLE 4.1 HTML Tags from Lesson 4

Tag	Use
`<html> .. </html>`	The entire HTML page
`<head> .. </head>`	The head, or prologue, of the HTML page
`<body> .. </body>`	All the other content in the HTML page
`<title> .. </title>`	The title of the page
`<h1> .. </h1>`	First-level heading
`<h2> .. </h2>`	Second-level heading
`<h3> .. </h3>`	Third-level heading
`<h4> .. </h4>`	Fourth-level heading
`<h5> .. </h5>`	Fifth-level heading
`<h6> .. </h6>`	Sixth-level heading
`<p> .. </p>`	A paragraph

Workshop

You've learned a lot in this lesson, and the following workshop will help you remember some of the most important points. I've anticipated some of the questions you might have in the first section of the workshop.

Q&A

Q In some web pages, I've noticed that the page structure tags (`<html>`, `<head>`, `<body>`) aren't used. Do I really need to include them if pages work just fine without them?

A Most browsers handle plain HTML without the page structure tags. The only tag that is required in HTML5 is the `<title>` tag. But it's a good idea to get into the habit of using the structure tags now. Including these tags ensures that browsers handle your markup properly. And, using these tags is the correct thing to do if you want your pages to conform to true HTML format.

Q Is the `<p>` tag the general-purpose tag for use when styling a page?

A No. The `<div>` tag is the general-purpose tag for containing content on a page. The `<p>` tag is intended specifically to hold paragraphs of text. There are many tags that are not valid when placed within a `<p>` tag, including `<div>`. You'll learn more about `<div>` in Lesson 7, "Formatting Text with HTML and CSS."

Q Is it possible to put HTML tags inside comments?

A Yes, you can enclose HTML tags within comments, and the browser will not display them. In fact, it's common to use comments to temporarily hide sections of a page, especially when testing things. Programmers (and web developers) generally refer to this as "commenting it out."

Quiz

1. What three HTML tags are used to describe the overall structure of a web page, and what do each of them define?

2. Where does the `<title>` tag go, and what is it used for?

3. How many different levels of headings does HTML support? What are their tags?

4. Why is it a good idea to use two-sided paragraph tags, even though the closing tag `</p>` is optional in HTML?

4

Quiz Answers

1. The `<html>` tag indicates that the file is in the HTML language. The `<head>` tag specifies that the lines within the beginning and ending points of the tag are the prologue to the rest of the file. The `<body>` tag encloses the remainder of your HTML page (text, links, pictures, and so on).

2. The `<title>` tag is used to indicate the title of a web page in a browser's title bar and bookmarks. It is also used by search engines. This tag always goes inside the `<head>` tags.

3. HTML supports six levels of headings. Their tags are `<h1 .. /h1>` through `<h6 .. /h6>`.

4. The closing `</p>` tag becomes important when using CSS to style your text. Closing tags also are required for XHTML 1.0.

Exercises

1. Using the Camembert Incorporated page as an example, create a page that briefly describes topics that you would like to cover on your own website.

2. Create a second page that provides further information about one of the topics you listed in the first exercise. Include a couple of subheadings (such as those shown in Figure 4.2). If you feel really adventurous, complete the page's content and include lists where you think they enhance the page. This exercise will help prepare you for Lesson 5, "Organizing Information with Lists."

LESSON 5
Organizing Information with Lists

In the previous lesson, you learned about the basic elements that make up a web page. In this lesson, I introduce lists, which, unlike the other tags that have been discussed thus far, are composed of multiple tags that work together. As you'll see, lists come in a variety of types and can be used not only for traditional purposes, like shopping lists or bulleted lists, but also for creating outlines or even navigation for websites. In this lesson, you'll learn the following:

- How to create numbered lists

- How to create bulleted lists

- How to create definition lists

- The *Cascading Style Sheets* (CSS) properties associated with lists

Lists: An Overview

Lists are a general-purpose container for collections of things. They come in three varieties. Ordered lists are numbered and are useful for presenting things like your top 10 favorite songs from 2015 or the steps to bake a cake. Unordered lists are not numbered and by default are presented with bullets for each list item. However, these days unordered lists are often used as a general-purpose container for any list-like collection of items. Yes, they're frequently used for bulleted lists of the kind you might see on a PowerPoint slide, but they're also used for things like collections of navigation links and even pull-down menus. Finally, definition lists are used for glossaries and other items that pair a label with some kind of description.

> **NOTE**
>
> Older HTML standards also supported two additional list types: menu lists (`<menu>`) and directory lists (`<dir>`). Menu lists were deprecated until HTML5, but they have been reinstated for use as lists of commands.

All the list tags have the following common elements:

- Each list has an outer element specific to that type of list. For example, `<ul>` and `</ul>` for unordered lists, `<ol>` and `</ol>` for ordered lists, or `<dl>` and `</dl>` for definition lists.

- Each list item has its own tag: `<dt>` and `<dd>` for the glossary lists, and `<li>` for the other lists.

> **NOTE**
>
> The closing tags for `<dd>`, `<dt>`, and `<li>` were optional in HTML. To comply with HTML5, use closing tags of `</dd>`, `</dt>`, `</li>`.

Although the tags and the list items can be formatted any way you like in your HTML code, I prefer to arrange the tags so that the list tags are on their own lines and each new item starts on a new line. This way, you can easily select the whole list as well as the individual elements. In other words, I find the following HTML

```
<p>Dante's Divine Comedy consists of three books:</p>
<ul>
  <li>The Inferno</li>
  <li>The Purgatorio</li>
  <li>The Paradiso</li>
</ul>
```

easier to read than

```
<p>Dante's Divine Comedy consists of three books:</p>
<ul><li>The Inferno</li><li>The Purgatorio</li><li>The Paradiso</li></ul>
```

although both result in the same output in the browser.

Numbered Lists

Numbered lists are surrounded by the `<ol>`...`</ol>` tags (`ol` stands for *ordered list*), and each item within the list is included in the `<li>`...`</li>` (list item) tag.

When the browser displays an ordered list, it numbers and indents each of the elements sequentially. You don't have to perform the numbering yourself and, if you add or delete items, the browser renumbers them the next time the page is loaded.

Ordered lists are lists in which each item is numbered or labeled with a counter of some kind (like letters or roman numerals).

Use numbered lists only when the sequence of items on the list is relevant. Ordered lists are good for steps to follow or instructions to the readers, or when you want to rank the items in a list. If you just want to indicate that something has a number of elements that can appear in any order, use an unordered list instead.

For example, the following is an ordered list of steps that explain how to boil an egg. You can see how the list is displayed in a browser in Figure 5.1.

Input ▼

```
<h1>How to Boil an Egg</h1>
<ol>
    <li>Put eggs in a pot filled with cold water</li>
    <li>Bring the water to a boil</li>
    <li>Take the pot off the heat, cover it, and let it sit for
        12 minutes</li>
    <li>Remove the eggs from the hot water and cool them by
        running water over them or placing them in a bowl of
        ice water to cool off</li>
    <li>Peel and eat</li>
</ol>
```

5

Output ▼

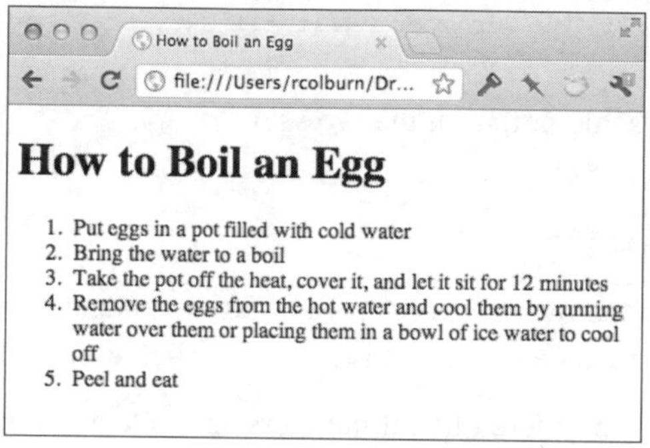

FIGURE 5.1
An ordered list in
HTML.

Customizing Ordered Lists

There are two customizations that are specific to ordered lists. The first enables you to change the numbering style for the list, and the second enables you to change the numbering itself. There are two ways to change the numbering style: the CSS property list-style-type, and the type attribute, which is obsolete in HTML5. If you're creating a new ordered list, you should always use the CSS property, however, you may see existing Web pages in which the type attribute is used instead.

Table 5.1 lists the numbering styles.

TABLE 5.1 Ordered List Numbering Styles

CSS Value	Attribute Value	Description
decimal	1	Standard Arabic numerals (1, 2, 3, 4, and so on)
lower-alpha	a	Lowercase letters (a, b, c, d, and so on)
upper-alpha	A	Uppercase letters (A, B, C, D, and so on)
lower-roman	i	Lowercase Roman numerals (i, ii, iii, iv, and so on)
upper-roman	I	Uppercase Roman numerals (that is, I, II, III, IV, and so on)

You can specify types of numbering in the <ol> tag using the style attribute, like this:

```
<ol style="list-style-type: lower-alpha;">
```

By default, the decimal type is assumed.

As an example, consider the following list:

```
<p>The Days of the Week in French:</p>
<ol>
    <li>Lundi</li>
    <li>Mardi</li>
    <li>Mercredi</li>
    <li>Jeudi</li>
    <li>Vendredi</li>
    <li>Samedi</li>
    <li>Dimanche</li>
</ol>
```

If you were to set the list style type upper-roman to the to the <ol> tag, as follows, it would appear in a browser as shown in Figure 5.2:

Input ▼

```
<h1>The days of the week in French</h1>
<ol style="list-style-type: upper-roman;">
    <li>Lundi</li>
    <li>Mardi</li>
    <li>Mercredi</li>
    <li>Jeudi</li>
    <li>Vendredi</li>
    <li>Samedi</li>
    <li>Dimanche</li>
</ol>
```

5

Output ▼

FIGURE 5.2
An ordered list
displayed using an
alternative number-
ing style.

Let me digress briefly to talk about how you can use Chrome's Developer Tools to edit styles on the fly. If you want to see what the list in Figure 5.2 looks like with the `lower-roman` list style, you can change the `style` attribute directly and see the results. Just open the developer tools, make sure the elements tab is open, and then click on the `style` attribute of the `<ol>` tag. You can then edit the attribute and see the page change instantly. The updated developer tools window is shown in Figure 5.3.

FIGURE 5.3
The Chrome developer tools with the updated `<ol>` tag.

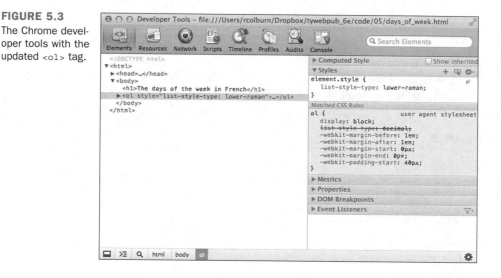

You can also use the `list-style-type` property with the `<li>` tag, changing the numbering type in the middle of the list, but you need to change every list item following it if you want them all to have the same new type. Using the `start` attribute, you can specify the number or letter with which to start your list. The default starting point is 1, of course. You can change this number by using `start`. `<ol start="4">`, for example, would start the list at number 4, whereas `<ol style="list-style-type: lower-alpha" start="3">` would start the numbering with `c` and move through the alphabet from there. The value for the `start` attribute should always be a decimal number, regardless of the numbering style being used.

For example, you can list the last six months of the year and start numbering with the Roman numeral VII as follows. The results appear in Figure 5.4.

Input ▼

```
<p>The Last Six Months of the Year (and the Beginning of the Next Year):</p>
<ol style="list-style-type: upper-roman;" start="7">
    <li>July</li>
    <li>August</li>
    <li>September</li>
    <li>October</li>
    <li>November</li>
    <li>December</li>
    <li style="list-style-type: lower-roman;">January</li>
</ol>
```

Output ▼

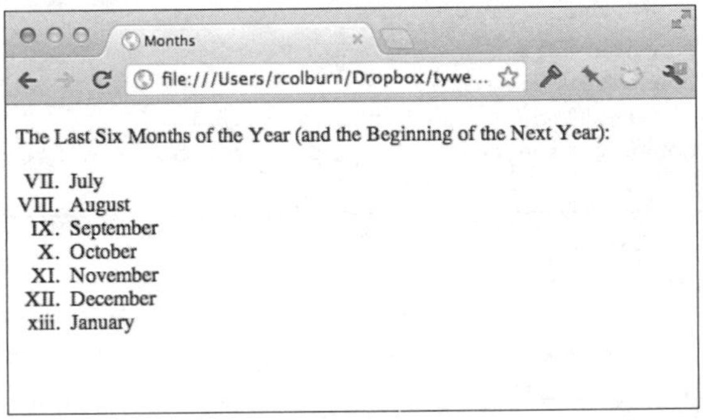

FIGURE 5.4
An ordered list with an alternative numbering style and starting number.

As with the `type` attribute, you can change the value of an entry's number at any point in a list. You do so by using the `value` attribute in the `<li>` tag. Assigning a `value` in an `<li>` tag restarts numbering in the list starting with the affected entry.

Suppose that you wanted the last three items in a list of ingredients to be `10`, `11`, and `12` rather than `6`, `7`, and `8`. You can reset the numbering at `Eggs` using the `value` attribute, as follows:

```
<h1>Cheesecake Ingredients</h1>
<ol>
    <li>Quark Cheese</li>
    <li>Honey</li>
    <li>Cocoa</li>
    <li>Vanilla Extract</li>
    <li>Flour</li>
    <li value="10">Eggs</li>
    <li>Walnuts</li>
    <li>Margarine</li>
</ol>
```

5

Unordered Lists

Unordered lists are often referred to as bulleted lists. Instead of being numbered, each element in the list has the same marker. The markup to create an unordered list looks just like an ordered list except that the list is created by using `<ul>...</ul>` tags rather than `ol`. The elements of the list are placed within `<li>` tags, just as with ordered lists.

Browsers have standardized on using a solid bullet to mark each item in an unordered list by default. Text browsers usually use an asterisk for these lists. The following input and output example shows an unordered list. Figure 5.5 shows the results in a browser.

Input ▼

```
<p>Things I like to do in the morning:</p>
<ul>
    <li>Drink a cup of coffee</li>
    <li>Watch the sunrise</li>
    <li>Listen to the birds sing</li>
    <li>Hear the wind rustling through the trees</li>
    <li>Curse the construction noises for spoiling the peaceful mood</li>
</ul>
```

Output ▼

FIGURE 5.5
An unordered list.

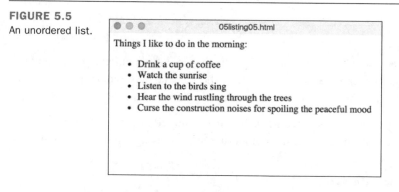

Customizing Unordered Lists

As with ordered lists, unordered lists can be customized using the `type` attribute or the `list-style-type` property. As mentioned in the section on ordered lists, the `type` attribute is no longer valid for HTML5. The bullet styles are as follows:

- ■ **"disc"**—A disc or bullet; this style is the default.
- ■ **"square"**—Obviously, a square rather than a disc.
- ■ **"circle"**—As compared with the disc, which most browsers render as a filled circle, this value should generate an unfilled circle.

In this case, the values for list-style-type and for the type attribute are the same. In the following input and output example, you see a comparison of these three types as rendered in a browser (see Figure 5.6):

Input ▼

```
<ul style="list-style-type: disc">
  <li>DAT - Digital Audio Tapes</li>
  <li>CD - Compact Discs</li>
  <li>Cassettes</li>
</ul>
<ul style="list-style-type: square">
  <li>DAT - Digital Audio Tapes</li>
  <li>CD - Compact Discs</li>
  <li>Cassettes</li>
</ul>
<ul style="list-style-type: circle">
  <li>DAT - Digital Audio Tapes</li>
  <li>CD - Compact Discs</li>
  <li>Cassettes</li>
</ul>
```

5

Output ▼

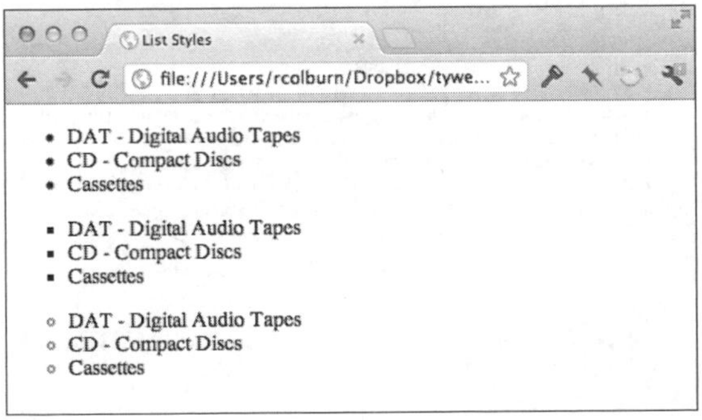

FIGURE 5.6
Unordered lists
with different bullet
types.

If you don't like any of the bullet styles used in unordered lists, you can substitute an image of your own choosing in place of them. To do so, use the `list-style-image` property. By setting this property, you can use an image of your choosing for the bullets in your list. Here's an example:

```
<ul style="list-style-image: url(/bullet.gif);">
    <li>Example</li>
</ul>
```

Don't worry much about what this all means right now. I discuss images later in Lesson 9, "Using Images on Your Web Pages." Right now, all you need to know is that the URL in parentheses should point to the image you want to use.

As you've seen in the screenshots so far, when items are formatted in a list and the list item spans more than one line, the lines of text that follow the first are aligned with the beginning of the text on the first line. If you prefer that they begin at the position of the bullet or list number, as shown in Figure 5.7, use the `list-style-position` property:

```
<ul style="list-style-position: inside;">
    <li>Always use Pillsbury's Best Flour.</li>
    <li>Sift flour twice before adding to cakes or breakfast cakes.</li>
    <li>Make all measurements level by using edge of knife to lightly
        scrape off from top of cup or spoon until material is even with
        the edges.</li>
    <li>Use same sized cups or spoons in measuring for the same recipe.</li>
    <li>Before starting to make recipe, read through carefully, then put
        on table all the materials and tools needed in making that particular
        recipe.</li>
</ul>
```

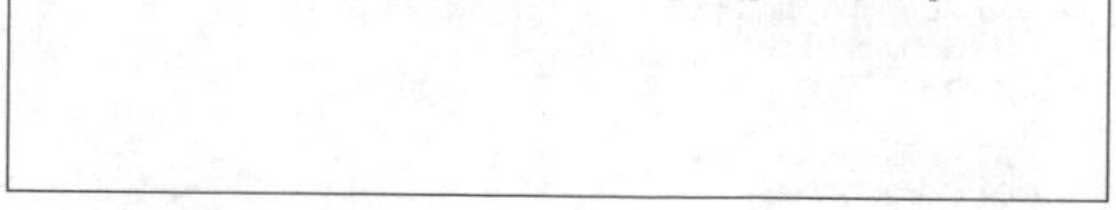

FIGURE 5.7
How the `list-style-position` property affects the layout of lists.

The default value is `outside`, and the only alternative is `inside`. Finally, if you want to modify several list-related properties at once, you can simply use the `list-style` property. You can specify three values for `list-style`: the list style type, the list style position, and the URL of the image to be used as the bullet style. This property is just a shortcut for use if you want to manipulate several of the list-related properties simultaneously. Here's an example:

```
<ul style="list-style: circle inside URL(/bullet.gif)">
    <li>Example</li>
</ul>
```

Definition Lists

Definition lists differ slightly from other lists. Each list item in a definition list has two parts:

- A term
- The term's definition

Each part of the glossary list has its own tag: `<dt>` for the term (*definition term*), and `<dd>` for its definition (*definition description*). `<dt>` and `<dd>` usually occur in pairs, although most browsers can handle single terms or definitions. The entire glossary list is indicated by the tags `<dl>...</dl>` (*definition list*).

The following is a glossary list example with a set of herbs and descriptions of how they grow (see Figure 5.8):

Input ▼

5

```
<dl>
    <dt>Basil</dt>
    <dd>Annual. Can grow four feet high; the scent of its tiny white
        flowers is heavenly</dd>
    <dt>Oregano</dt>
        <dd>Perennial. Sends out underground runners and is difficult
            to get rid of once established.</dd>
    <dt>Coriander</dt>
        <dd>Annual. Also called cilantro, coriander likes cooler
            weather of spring and fall.</dd>
</dl>
```

Output ▼

FIGURE 5.8
A definition list.

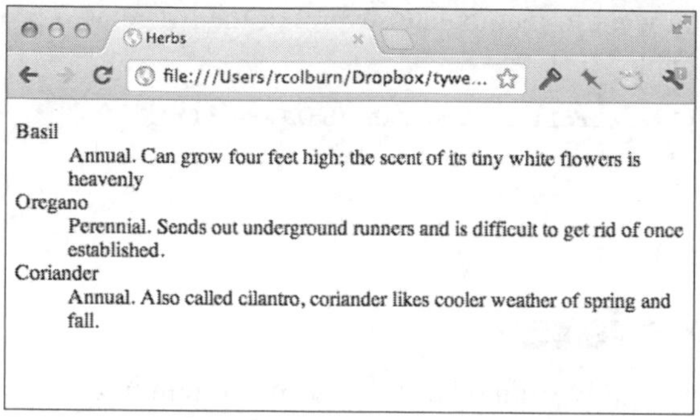

Definition lists usually are formatted in browsers with the terms and definitions on separate lines, and the left margins of the definitions are indented.

You don't have to use definition lists for terms and definitions, of course. You can use them anywhere that the same sort of list is needed. Here's an example involving a list of frequently asked questions:

```
<dl>
<dt>What is the WHATWG?</dt>
<dd>The Web Hypertext Application Technology Working Group (WHATWG) is a growing
community of people interested in evolving the Web. It focuses primarily on the
development of HTML and APIs needed for Web applications.</dd>
<dt>What is the WHATWG working on?</dt>
<dd>The WHATWG's main focus is HTML5. The WHATWG also works on Web Workers and
occasionally specifications outside WHATWG space are discussed on the WHATWG
mailing list and forwarded when appropriate.</dd>
<dt>How can I get involved?</dt>
<dd>There are lots of ways you can get involved, take a look and see What you can
do!</dd>
<dt>Is participation free?</dt>
<dd>Yes, everyone can contribute. There are no memberships fees involved, it's an
open process. You may easily subscribe to the WHATWG mailing lists. You may also
join the the W3C's new HTMLWG by going through the slightly longer application
process.</dd>
</dl>
```

Nesting Lists

What happens if you put a list inside another list? Nesting lists is fine as far as HTML is concerned; just put the entire list structure inside another list as one of its elements. The nested list just becomes another element of the first list, and it's indented from the rest of the list. Lists like this work especially well for menu-like entities in which you want to show hierarchy (for example, in tables of contents) or as outlines.

Indenting nested lists in HTML code itself helps show their relationship to the final layout:

```
<ol>
      <li>WWW</li>
      <li>Organization</li>
      <li>Beginning HTML</li>
    <li>
          <ul>
              <li>What HTML is</li>
            <li>How to Write HTML</li>
            <li>Doc structure</li>
            <li>Headings</li>
            <li>Paragraphs</li>
            <li>Comments</li>
          </ul>
    </li>
      <li>Links</li>
      <li>More HTML</li>
</ol>
```

Many browsers format nested ordered lists and nested unordered lists differently from their enclosing lists. They might, for example, use a symbol other than a bullet for a nested list, or they might number the inner list with letters (a, b, c) rather than numbers. Don't assume that this will be the case, however, and refer back to "section 8, subsection b" in your text because you can't determine what the exact formatting will be in the final output. If you do need to be sure which symbols or numbering scheme will be used for a list, specify a style using CSS.

The following input and output example shows a nested list and how it appears in a browser (see Figure 5.9):

5

Input ▼

```
<h1>Peppers</h1>
<ul>
  <li>Bell</li>
  <li>Chile</li>
  <li>
    <ul>
      <li>Serrano</li>
      <li>Jalapeno</li>
      <li>Habanero</li>
      <li>Anaheim</li>
    </ul>
  </li>
  <li>Szechuan</li>
  <li>Cayenne</li>
</ul>
```

Output ▼

FIGURE 5.9
Nested lists.

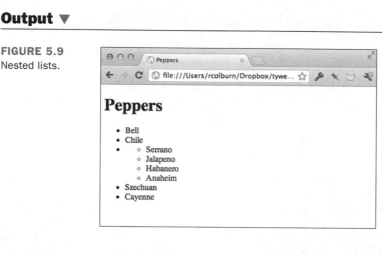

DO	DON'T
DO remember that you can change the numbering and bullet styles for lists to suit your preference.	**DON'T** use the deprecated list types; use one of the other lists instead.
DO feel free to nest lists to any extent that you like.	**DON'T** number or format lists yourself; use the list tags.
	DON'T use list tags to indent text on a page; use Cascading Style Sheets.

Other Uses for Lists

Lists have moved a long way past simple bullets. As it turns out, lists are very useful when designing web pages because of the structure they provide. Semantically speaking, there are many common elements of web design that naturally lend themselves to list-like structures. Here are some advanced examples of how lists are used that combine a number of concepts that will be introduced throughout the book.

Many websites have lots of navigation links to present, and to keep from cluttering up the page, they use nested pull-down menus similar to those used in desktop applications. In this lesson, you've already seen that you can create nested lists in HTML. You can put your navigation links in such lists and then use CSS to radically change their appearance so that rather than looking like other lists, they instead look and behave like menus. There's an example of such menus in Figure 5.10.

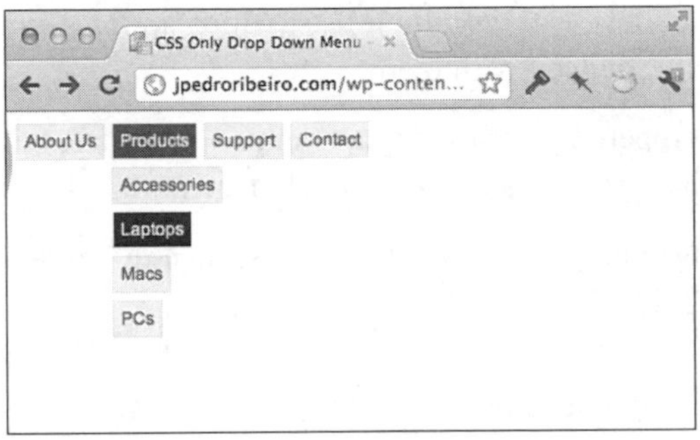

FIGURE 5.10
Pull-down navigation menus implemented using lists.

Using a combination of JavaScript and CSS, you can turn a standard HTML list into a sortable user interface element for a web application. You can see an example in Figure 5.11.

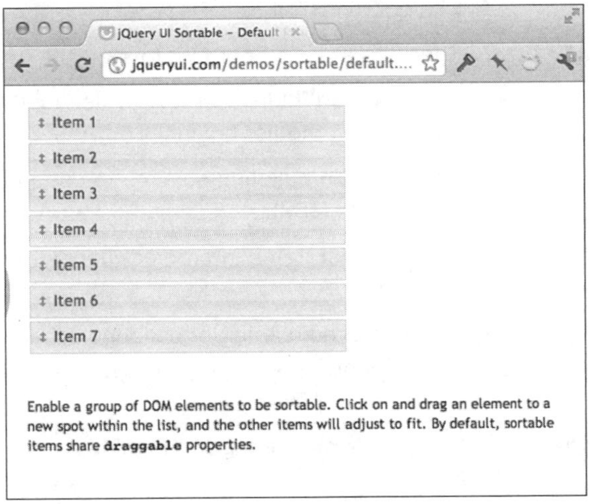

FIGURE 5.11
A sortable list.

5

You'll see other uses of lists in later lessons. With the introduction of Cascading Style Sheets, lists became one of the fundamental building blocks of web pages.

Summary

In this relatively brief lesson, you got a look at HTML lists. Lists are a core structural element for presenting content on web pages and can be used for everything from the list of steps in a process to a table of contents to a structured navigation system for a website. They come in three varieties: ordered lists, which are numbered; unordered lists, which by default are presented bullets; and definition lists, which are presented as a series of terms and the definitions associated with them.

Not only are there CSS properties specifically associated with lists, but lists can also be styled using properties that apply to any block-level element, like lists and list items.

The full list of HTML tags discussed in this lesson is shown in Table 5.2, and the CSS properties are shown in Table 5.3.

TABLE 5.2   HTML Tags from Lesson 5

Tag	Attribute	Use
`<ol>...</ol>`		An ordered (numbered) list. Each of the items in the list begins with `<li>`.
	`type`	Specifies the numbering scheme to use in the list. Replaced with CSS in HTML5.
	`start`	Specifies at which number to start the list.
`<ul>...</ul>`		An unordered (bulleted or otherwise marked) list. Each of the items in the list begins with `<li>`.
	`type`	Specifies the bulleting scheme to use in the list. Replaced with CSS in HTML5.
`<li>...</li>`		Individual list items in ordered, unordered, menu, or directory lists.
	`type`	Resets the numbering or bulleting scheme from the current list element. Applies only to `<ul>` and `<ol>` lists. Replaced with CSS in HTML5.
	`value`	Resets the numbering in the middle of an ordered (`<ol>`) list.
`<dl>...</dl>`		A glossary or definition list. Items in the list consist of pairs of elements: a term and its definition.
`<dt>...</dt>`		The term part of an item in a glossary list.
`<dd>...</dd>`		The definition part of an item in a glossary list.

TABLE 5.3   CSS Properties from Lesson 5

Property	Use/Values
list-style-type	Used to specify the bullet style or numbering style for the list. Valid values are disc, circle, square, decimal, lower-roman, upper-roman, lower-alpha, upper-alpha, and none.
list-style-image	The image to use in place of the bullets for a list. The value should be the URL of the image.
list-style-position	Defines the alignment of lines of text in list items after the first. Values are inside and outside.
list-style	Enables you to set multiple list properties at once: list style type, list style position, and the URL of the bullet style.

Workshop

You've learned how to create and customize lists in HTML. In this section, you'll see the answers to some common questions about lists, as well as some exercises that should help you remember the things you've learned.

Q&A

Q My glossaries came out formatted really strangely! The terms are indented farther in than the definitions!

A Did you mix up the `<dd>` and `<dt>` tags? The `<dt>` tag is always used first (the definition term), and the `<dd>` follows (the definition description). I mix them up all the time. There are too many d tags in definition lists.

Q Is it possible to change the amount that list items are indented, or remove the indentation entirely?

A Yes, the properties used to control list indentation are `margin-left` and `padding-left`. Some browsers use one and some use the other, so you need to set both of them to change the indentation for your lists. You might need to use negative margins to get the text to line up the way you want.

5

Quiz

1. Ordered and unordered lists use the `<li>` tag for list items. What tags are used by definition lists?

2. Is it possible to nest an ordered list within an unordered list or vice versa?

3. Which attribute is used to set the starting number for an ordered list? What about to change the value of an element within a list?

4. What are the three types of bullets that can be specified for unordered lists using the `list-style-type` CSS property?

Quiz Answers

1. Definition lists use the `<dt>` and `<dd>` tags for list items.

2. Yes, you can nest ordered lists within unordered lists or vice versa. You can also nest lists of the same type, too.

3. With the `<ol>` tag, the `start` attribute is used to specify the starting value for the list. To change the numbering within a list, the `value` attribute is used.

4. The bullet types supported by the `list-style-type` property are `disc`, `circle`, and `square`. The default is `disc`.

Exercises

1. Use nested lists to create an outline of the topics covered in this book so far.

2. Use nested lists and the `list-style-type` CSS property to create a traditional outline of the topics you plan to cover on your own website.

LESSON 6
Working with Links

After finishing the preceding lesson, you now have a couple of pages that have some headings, text, and lists in them. These pages are all well and good, but rather boring. The real fun starts when you learn how to create hypertext links and link your pages to the Web. In this lesson, you'll learn just that. Specifically, you'll learn about the following:

- The HTML link tag (<a>) and its various parts

- How to link to other pages using relative and absolute paths

- How to link to other pages on the Web using URLs

- How to use links and anchors to link to specific locations inside pages

- URLs: the various parts of the URL and the kinds of URLs you can use

Creating Links

To create a link in HTML, you need two things:

- The name of the file (or the URL) to which you want to link
- The text that will serve as the clickable link

Only the text included within the link tag is actually visible on your page. When your readers click the link, the browser loads the URL associated with the link.

The Link Tag: `<a>`

To create a link in an HTML page, you use the HTML link tag `<a>...</a>`. The `<a>` tag is also called an *anchor* tag because it also can be used to create anchors for links. (You'll learn more about creating anchors later in this lesson.) The most common use of the link tag, however, is to create links to other pages.

Unlike the tags you learned about in the preceding lesson, the `<a>` tag requires attributes in order to be useful. You've seen optional attributes for tags, and attributes like `style` that can be used with basically any tag. The `<a>` tag uses attributes to define the link. So, rather than the opening `<a>` tag having just the tag name inside brackets, it looks something like the following:

```
<a href="menu.html" title="The Twelve Caesars">
```

The additional attributes (in this example, `href`, and `title`) describe the link itself. The attribute you'll probably use most often is the `href` attribute, which is short for *hypertext reference*. You use the `href` attribute to specify the name or URL to which this link points.

NOTE

> HTML5 made `<a>` tags with no attributes valid as placeholder links for use with CSS and scripts.

Like most HTML tags, the link tag also has a closing tag, `</a>`. All the text between the opening and closing tags will become the actual link on the screen and be highlighted, underlined, or otherwise marked as specified in the page's style sheet when the web page is displayed. That's the text you or your readers will click to follow the link to the URL in the `href` attribute.

Figure 6.1 shows the parts of a typical link using the `<a>` tag, including the `href`, the text of the link, and the closing tag.

FIGURE 6.1
A link on a web page.

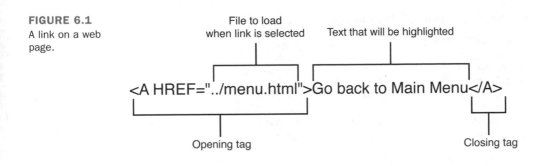

The following example shows a simple link and what it looks like (see Figure 6.2):

Input ▼

```
Go back to <a href="menu.html">Main Menu</a>
```

Output ▼

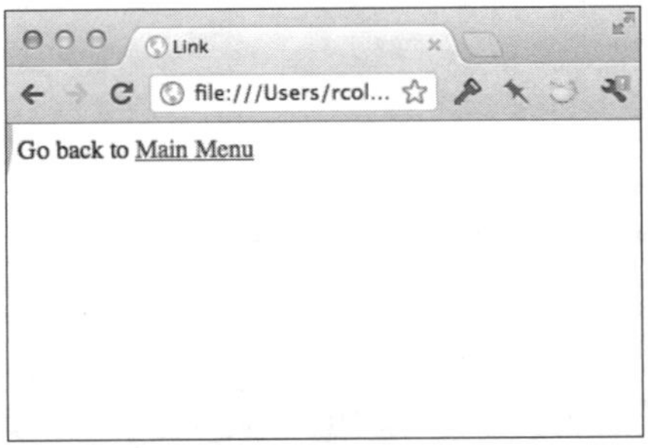

FIGURE 6.2
How a browser displays a link.

Go back to Main Menu

Exercise 6.1: Linking Two Pages   ▼   6

Now you can try a simple example with two HTML pages on your local disk. You'll need your text editor and your web browser for this exercise. Because both the pages you'll work with are on your local disk, you don't need to be connected to the Internet. (Be patient; you'll get to do network stuff in the next section.)

Create two HTML pages and save them in separate files. Here's the code for the two HTML files I created for this section, which I called menu.html and claudius.html. What your two pages look like or what they're called really doesn't matter. However, make sure that you insert your own filenames if you're following along with this example.   ▼

▼ The following is the first file, called `menu.html`:

```
<!DOCTYPE html>
<html>
<head>
<title>The Twelve Caesars</title>
</head>
<body>
<h1>"The Twelve Caesars" by Suetonius</h1>
<p>Seutonius (or Gaius Suetonius Tranquillus) was born circa A.D. 70
and died sometime after A.D. 130. He composed a history of the twelve
Caesars from Julius to Domitian (died A.D. 96). His work was a
significant contribution to the best-selling novel and television
series "I, Claudius." Suetonius' work includes biographies of the
following Roman emperors:</p>
<ul>
 <li>Julius Caesar</li>
 <li>Augustus</li>
 <li>Tiberius</li>
 <li>Gaius (Caligula)</li>
 <li>Claudius</li>
 <li>Nero</li>
 <li>Galba</li>
 <li>Otho</li>
 <li>Vitellius</li>
 <li>Vespasian</li>
 <li>Titus</li>
 <li>Domitian</li>
</ul>
</body>
</html>
```

The list of menu items (Julius Caesar, Augustus, and so on) will be links to other pages. For now, just type them as regular text; you'll turn them into links later.

The following is the second file, `claudius.html`:

```
<!DOCTYPE html>
<html>
<head>
<title>The Twelve Caesars: Claudius</title>
</head>
<body>
<h2>Claudius Becomes Emperor</h2>
<p>Claudius became Emperor at the age of 50. Fearing the attack of
Caligula's assassins, Claudius hid behind some curtains. After a guardsman
discovered him, Claudius dropped to the floor, and then found himself
declared Emperor.</p>
<h2>Claudius is Poisoned</h2>
<p>Most people think that Claudius was poisoned. Some think his wife
```
▼ Agrippina poisoned a dish of mushrooms (his favorite food). His death

```
was revealed after arrangements had been made for her son, Nero, to
succeed as Emperor.</p>
<p>Go back to Main Menu</p>
</body>
</html>
```

CAUTION

Make sure that both of your files are in the same directory or folder. If you haven't called them `menu.html` and `claudius.html`, make sure that you take note of the filenames because you'll need them later.

Create a link from the menu file to the claudius file. Edit the `menu.html` file, and put the cursor at the following line:

```
<li>Claudius</li>
```

You'll want to nest the `<a>` tag inside the existing `<li>` tag. First, put in the link tags themselves (the `<a>` and `</a>` tags) around the text that you want to use as the link:

```
<li><a>Claudius</a></li>
```

Now add the URL that you want to link to as the `href` part of the opening link tag. In this case the URL is simply a pointer to the other file you've created. Enclose the name of the file in quotation marks (straight quotes ["], not curly or typesetter's quotes ["]), with an equal sign between `href` and the name. Filenames in links are case sensitive, so make sure that the filename in the link is identical to the name of the file you created. (`Claudius.html` is not the same file as `claudius.html`; it has to be exactly the same case.) Here I've used `claudius.html`; if you used different files, use those filenames.

```
<li><a href="claudius.html">Claudius</a></li>
```

Now start your browser, select Open File (or its equivalent in your browser), and open the `menu.html` file. The paragraph you used as your link should now show up as a link that is in a different color, underlined, or otherwise highlighted. Figure 6.3 shows how it looked when I opened it.

Now when you click the link, your browser should load and display the `claudius.html` page, as shown in Figure 6.4.

6

▼ **FIGURE 6.3**
The `menu.html` file
with link.

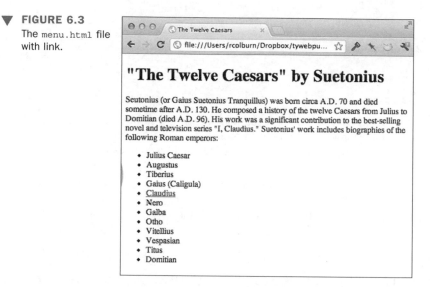

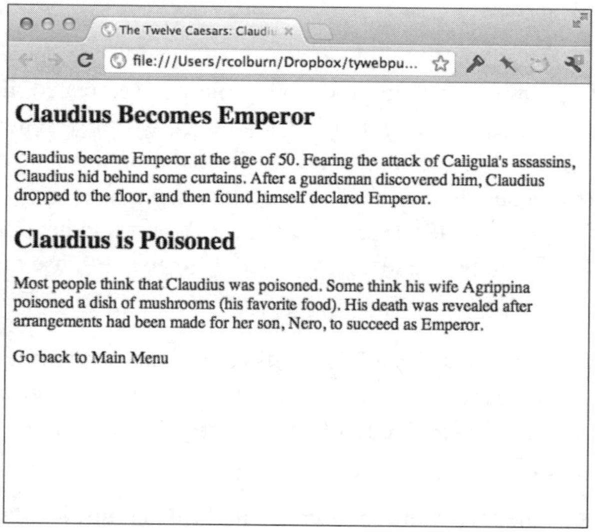

FIGURE 6.4
The
`claudius.html`
page.

If your browser can't find the file when you click on the link, make sure that the name
of the file in the `href` part of the link tag is the same as the name of the file on the disk,
uppercase and lowercase match, and both files are in the same directory. Remember to
▼ close your link, using the `</a>` tag, at the end of the text that serves as the link. Also,

make sure that you have quotation marks at the beginning and end of the filename (some- ▼ times you can easily forget) and that both quotation marks are ordinary straight quotes. All these things can confuse the browser and prevent it from finding the file or displaying the link properly.

Now you can create a link from the caesar page back to the menu page. A paragraph at the end of the `claudius.html` page is intended for just this purpose:

```
<p>Go back to Main Menu</p>
```

Add the link tag with the appropriate `href` to that line, such as the following in which `menu.html` is the original menu file:

```
<p><a href="menu.html">Go back to Main Menu</a></p>
```

Nesting Tags Properly

When you include tags inside other tags, make sure that the closing tag closes the tag that you most recently opened. That is, enter

```
<p> <a> .. </a> </p>
```

rather than

```
<p> <a> .. </p> </a>
```

Improper nesting of tags is invalid and could prevent your page from being displayed properly, so always make sure that you close the most recently opened tag first.

Now when you reload the Claudius file, the link will be active, and you can jump between the menu and the detail page by clicking on those links. ▲

Linking Local Pages Using Relative and Absolute Pathnames

6

The example in the preceding section shows how to link together pages that are contained in the same folder or directory on your local disk. This section continues that thread, linking pages that are still on the local disk but might be contained in different directories or folders on that disk.

NOTE ———— Folders and directories are the same thing, but they're called different names depending on whether you're on Macintosh, Windows, or UNIX. I'll simply call them *directories* from now on to make your life easier.

When you specify just the filename of a linked file within quotation marks, as you did earlier, the browser looks for that file in the same directory as the current file. This is true even if both the current file and the file being linked to are on a server somewhere else on the Internet; both files are contained in the same directory on that server. It is the simplest form of a relative pathname.

Relative pathnames point to files based on their locations relative to the current file. They can include directory names, or they can point to the path you would take to navigate to that file if you started at the current directory or folder. A pathname might, for example, include directions to go up two directory levels and then go down two other directories to get to the file.

To specify relative pathnames in links, you must use UNIX-style paths regardless of the system you actually have. You therefore separate directory or folder names with forward slashes (/), and you use two dots to refer generically to the directory above the current one (..).

Table 6.1 shows some examples of relative pathnames and where they lead.

TABLE 6.1   Relative Pathnames

Pathname	Means
href="file.html"	file.html is located in the current directory.
href="files/file.html"	file.html is located in the directory called files (and the files directory is located in the current directory).
href="files/morefiles/file.html"	file.html is located in the morefiles directory, which is located in the files directory, which is located in the current directory.
href="../file.html"	file.html is located in the directory one level up from the current directory (the parent directory).
href="../../files/file.html"	file.html is located two directory levels up, in the directory files.

Absolute Pathnames

You can also specify the link to another page on your local system by using an absolute pathname.

Absolute pathnames point to files based on their absolute locations on the file system. Whereas relative pathnames point to the page to which you want to link by describing its location relative to the current page, absolute pathnames point to the page by starting at the top level of your directory hierarchy and working downward through all the intervening directories to reach the file.

Absolute pathnames always begin with a slash, which is the way they're differentiated from relative pathnames. Following the slash are all directories in the path from the top level to the file you are linking.

NOTE

> *Top* has different meanings, depending on how you're publishing your HTML files. If you're just linking to files on your local disk, the top is the top of your file system (/ on UNIX, or the disk name on a Macintosh or PC). When you're publishing files using a web server, the top is the directory where the files served by the web server are stored, commonly referred to as the *document root*.

Table 6.2 shows some examples of absolute pathnames on a local computer and what they mean.

TABLE 6.2 Absolute Pathnames Examples

Pathname	Means
href="/home/lemay/file.html"	`file.html` is located in the directory `/home/lemay` (typically on UNIX systems).
href="/d|/files/html/file.htm"	`file.htm` is located on the `D:` disk in the directory `files/html` (on Windows systems).
href="/Macintosh%20HD/HTML%20Files/file.html"	`file.html` is located on the disk `Macintosh HD`, in the folder `HTML Files` (typically on OS X systems).

In the last example, the series of characters "%20" represents a space. It has been encoded so that the space character does not cause issues. You'll learn more about this encoding later on.

6

Should You Use Relative or Absolute Pathnames?

The answer to that question is, "It depends." If you have a set of files that link only to other files within that set, using relative pathnames makes sense. On the other hand, if the links in your files point to files that aren't within the same hierarchy, you probably want to use absolute links. Generally, a mix of the two types of links makes the most sense for complex sites.

I can explain this better with an example. Let's say that your site consists of two sections, /stuff and /things. If you want to link from the file index.html in /stuff to history.html in /stuff (or any other file in /stuff), you use a relative link. That way, you can move the /stuff directory around without breaking any of the internal links. On the other hand, if you want to create a link in /stuff/index.html to /things/index.html, an absolute link is probably called for. That way, if you move /stuff to /more/stuff, your link will still work.

The rule of thumb I generally use is that if pages are part of the same collection, I use relative links, and if they're part of different collections, I use absolute links.

Links to Other Documents on the Web

So, now you have a whole set of pages on your local disk, all linked to each other. In some places in your pages, however, you want to refer to a page somewhere else on the Internet—for example, to The First Caesars page by Dr. Ellis Knox at Boise State University for more information on the early Roman emperors. You also can use the link tag to link those other pages on the Internet, which I'll call *remote* pages. *Remote pages* are contained somewhere on the Web other than the system on which you're currently working.

The HTML code you use to link pages on the Web looks exactly the same as the code you use for links between local pages. You still use the <a> tag with an href attribute, and you include some text to serve as the link on your web page. Rather than a filename or a path in the href, however, you use the URL of that page on the Web, as Figure 6.5 shows.

FIGURE 6.5
Link to remote files.

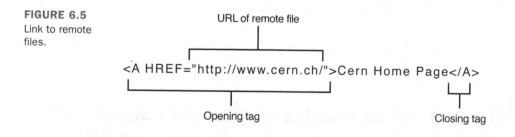

Exercise 6.2: Linking Your Caesar Pages to the Web ▼

Go back to those two pages you linked earlier today—the ones about the Caesars. The `menu.html` file contains several links to other local pages that provide information about 12 Roman emperors.

Now suppose that you want to add a link to the bottom of the menu file to point to The Twelve Caesars page on Wikipedia, whose URL is http://en.wikipedia.org/wiki/ The_Twelve_Caesars.

First, add the appropriate text for the link to your menu page, as follows:

```
<p><i>The Twelve Caesars</i> article in Wikipedia has more information on
these Emperors.</p>
```

What if you don't know the URL of the home page for The Twelve Caesars page (or the page to which you want to link), but you do know how to get to it by following several links on several different people's home pages? Not a problem. Use your browser to find the home page for the page to which you want to link. Figure 6.6 shows what The Twelve Caesars page looks like in a browser.

FIGURE 6.6
The Twelve
Caesars page.

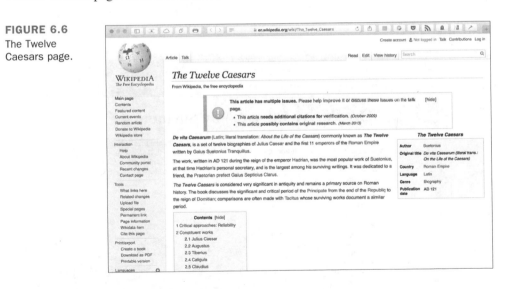

You can find the URL of the page you're currently viewing in your browser in the address box at the top of the browser window. To find the URL for a page you want to link to, use your browser to go to the page, copy the URL from the address field, and paste it into the `href` attribute of the link tag. No typing!

▼

▼ After you have the URL of the page, you can construct a link tag in your menu file and paste the appropriate URL into the link, like this:

Input ▼

```
<p>"<em><a href="http://en.wikipedia.org/wiki/The_Twelve_Caesars">
The Twelve Caesars</a></em>" article in Wikipedia has more information on these
Emperors.</p>
```

In that code I also italicized the title of the page using the `<em>` tag. You'll learn more about that tag and other text formatting tags in Lesson 7, "Formatting Text with HTML and CSS."

Of course, if you already know the URL of the page to which you want to link, you can just type it into the `href` part of the link. Keep in mind, however, that if you make a mistake, your browser won't be able to find the file on the other end. Many URLs are too complex for humans to be able to remember them; I prefer to copy and paste whenever I can to cut down on the chances of typing URLs incorrectly.

Figure 6.7 shows how the `menu.html` file, with the new link in it, looks when it is displayed.

Output ▼

FIGURE 6.7
The Twelve
Caesars link.

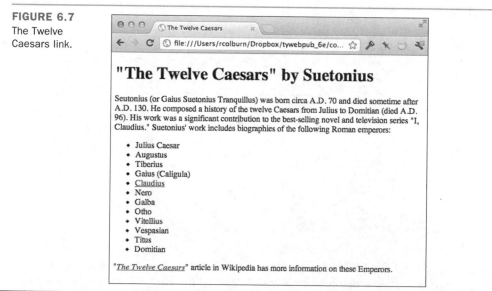

Exercise 6.3: Creating a Link Menu ▼

Now that you've learned how to create lists and links, you can create a *link menu*. Link menus are links on your web page that are arranged in list form or in some other short, easy-to-read, and easy-to-understand format. Link menus are terrific for pages that are organized in a hierarchy, for tables of contents, or for navigation among several pages. Web pages that consist of nothing but links often organize the links in menu form.

The idea of a link menu is that you use short, descriptive terms as the links, with either no text following the link or with a further description following the link itself. Link menus look best in a bulleted or unordered list format, but you also can use glossary lists or just plain paragraphs. Link menus enable your readers to scan the list of links quickly and easily, a task that might be difficult if you bury your links in body text.

In this exercise, you'll create a web page for a set of book reviews. This page will serve as the index to the reviews, so the link menu you'll create is essentially a menu of book names.

Start with a simple page framework: a first-level heading and some basic explanatory text:

```
<!DOCTYPE html>
<html>
<head>
<title>Really Honest Book Reviews</title>
</head>
<body>
<h1>Really Honest Book Reviews</h1>
<p>I read a lot of books about many different subjects. Though I'm not a
book critic, and I don't do this for a living, I enjoy a really good read
every now and then. Here's a list of books that I've read recently:</p>
```

Now add the list that will become the links, without the link tags themselves. It's always easier to start with link text and then attach actual links afterward. For this list, you'll use a tag to create a bulleted list of individual books. The `<ol>` tag wouldn't be appropriate because the numbers would imply that you were ranking the books in some way. Here's the HTML list of books, and Figure 6.8 shows the page as it currently looks with the introduction and the list:

6

Input ▼

```
<ul>
  <li><em>The Rainbow Returns</em> by E. Smith</li>
  <li><em>Seven Steps to Immeasurable Wealth</em> by R. U. Needy</li>
  <li><em>The Food-Lovers Guide to Weight Loss</em> by L. Goode</li>
```
▼

```
▼   <li><em>The Silly Person's Guide to Seriousness</em> by M. Nott</li>
    </ul>
    </body>
    </html>
```

Output ▼

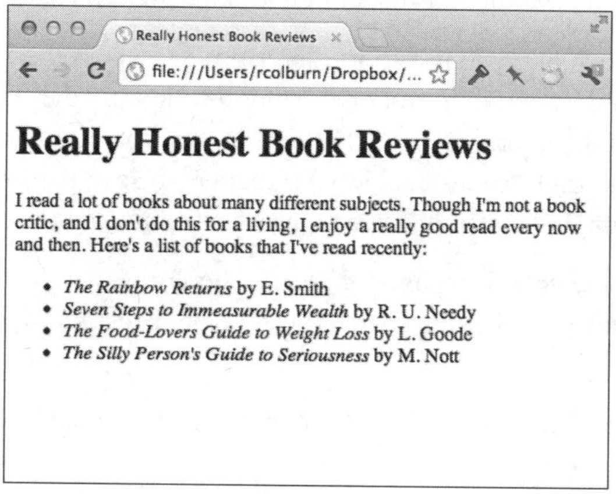

FIGURE 6.8
A list of books.

> In the previous example, you'll see the use of the `<em>` tag. This tag is used to indicate that the text within it should be emphasized. By convention, browsers emphasize the text using italics.

NOTE

Now, modify each of the list items so that they include links. You need to keep the `<li>` tag in there because it indicates where the list items begin. Just add the `<a>` tags around the text itself. Here you'll link to filenames on the local disk in the same directory as this file, with each file containing the review for the particular book:

```
<ul>
 <li><a href="rainbow.html"><em>The Rainbow Returns</em> by E. Smith</a></li>
 <li><a href="wealth.html"><em>Seven Steps to Immeasurable Wealth</em> by R. U.
 Needy</a></li>
 <li><a href="food.html"><em>The Food-Lovers Guide to Weight Loss</em> by L.
 Goode</a></li>
 <li><a href="silly.html"><em>The Silly Person's Guide to Seriousness</em> by M.
 Nott</a></li>
▼ </ul>
```

The menu of books looks fine, although it's a little sparse. Your readers don't know anything about each book (although some of the book names indicate the subject matter) or whether the review is good or bad. An improvement would be to add some short explanatory text after the links to provide hints of what is on the other side of the link:

Input ▼

```
<ul>
 <li><a href=rainbow.html"><em>The Rainbow Returns</em> by E. Smith</a>. A
 fantasy story set in biblical times. Slow at times, but interesting.</li>
 <li><a href="wealth.html"><em>Seven Steps to Immeasurable Wealth</em> by R. U.
 Needy</a>. I'm still poor, but I'm happy! And that's the whole point.</li>
 <li><a href="food.html"><em>The Food-Lovers Guide to Weight Loss</em> by L.
Goode
 </a>. At last! A diet book with recipes that taste good!</li>
 <li><a href="silly.html"><em>The Silly Person's Guide to Seriousness</em> by M.
 Nott</a>. Come on ... who wants to be serious?</li>
 </ul>
```

The final list looks like Figure 6.9.

Output ▼

FIGURE 6.9
The final menu listing.

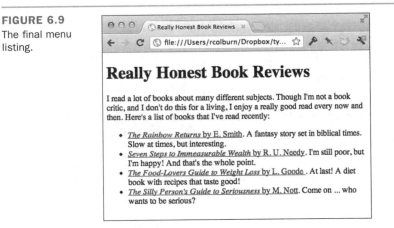

You'll use link menus similar to this one throughout this book.

6

Linking to Specific Places Within Documents

The links you've created so far in this lesson have been from one point in a page to another page. But what if, rather than linking to that second page in general, you want to link to a specific place within that page—for example, to the fourth major section down?

You can do so by referring to the ID of the element you want to link to specifically in the URL in your link. When you follow the link with your browser, the browser will load the second page and then scroll down to the element you specify. (Figure 6.10 shows an example.)

FIGURE 6.10
Links and anchors.

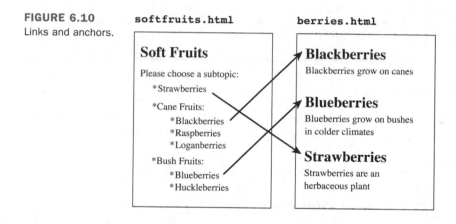

You can use links to jump to a specific element within the same page. For example, you can assign IDs to the headings at the beginning of each section and include a table of contents at the top of the page that has links to the sections.

The `id` attribute can be used with any element on a page. The only requirement is that each ID is unique within that page. For example, here's a heading with an ID:

```
<h2 id="contents">Table of Contents</a>
```

IDs are also often used when styling pages. I'll discuss that more in Lesson 8, "Using CSS to Style a Site."

Creating Links and Anchors

When you create links using `<a>`, the link has two parts: the `href` attribute in the opening `<a>` tag, and the text between the opening and closing tags that serves as a hot spot for the link.

For example, to create an anchor at the section of a page labeled Part 4, you might add an ID `part4` to the heading, similar to the following:

```
<h1 id="part4">Part Four: Grapefruit from Heaven</h1>
```

To point to an anchor in a link, use the same form of link that you would when linking to the whole page, with the filename or URL of the page in the `href` attribute. After the name of the page, however, include a hash sign (#) and the ID of the element exactly as it appears in the `id` attribute of that element (including the same uppercase and lowercase characters!), as follows:

```
<a href="mybigdoc.html#part4">Go to Part 4</a>
```

This link tells the browser to load the page `mybigdoc.html` and then to scroll down to the anchor named `part4`. The text inside the anchor definition will appear at the top of the screen.

The `name` Attribute of the `<a>` Tag

Before browsers supported linking to elements directly using their IDs, you had to use the `name` attribute of the `<a>` tag to create anchors on the page to which you could link. Rather than including the `href` attribute in your `<a>` tag to link to a location, you included the `name` attribute to indicate that the `<a>` was an anchor to which someone could link. For example, you would write the previous example as follows:

```
<h1><a name="part4"></a>Part Four: Grapefruit from Heaven</h1>
```

The tag wouldn't produce a visible change on the page, but it would provide an anchor to which you could link. Best practices recommend that you avoid using the `name` attribute and use the ID attribute instead. You can use the ID attribute on any HTML element, not just the `<a>` tag. However, you may still encounter old markup that uses the `<a>` tag in this way.

Exercise 6.4: Linking Sections Between Two Pages   ▼   6

Now let's create an example with two pages. These two pages are part of an online reference to classical music, in which each web page contains all the references for a particular letter of the alphabet (`a.html`, `b.html`, and so on). The reference could have been organized such that each section is its own page. Organizing it that way, however, would have involved several pages to manage, as well as many pages the readers would have to load if they were exploring the reference. Bunching the related sections together under lettered groupings is more efficient in this case.

The first page you'll look at is for M; the first section looks like the following in HTML:

Input ▼

```
<!DOCTYPE html>
<html>
<head>
<title>Classical Music: M</title>
</head>
<body>
<h1>M</h1>
<h2>Madrigals</h2>
<ul>
 <li>William Byrd, <em>This Sweet and Merry Month of May</em></li>
 <li>William Byrd, <em>Though Amaryllis Dance</em></li>
 <li>Orlando Gibbons, <em>The Silver Swan</em></li>
 <li>Claudio Monteverdi, <em>Lamento d'Arianna</em></li>
 <li>Thomas Morley, <em>My Bonny Lass She Smileth</em></li>
 <li>Thomas Weelkes, <em>Thule, the Period of Cosmography</em></li>
 <li>John Wilbye, <em>Sweet Honey-Sucking Bees</em></li>
</ul>
<p>Secular vocal music in four, five and six parts, usually a capella.
15th-16th centuries.</p>
<p><em>See Also</em>
Byrd, Gibbons, Lassus, Monteverdi, Morley, Weelkes, Wilbye </p>
</body>
</html>
```

Figure 6.11 shows how this section looks when it's displayed.

Output ▼

FIGURE 6.11
Part M of the
Online Music
Reference.

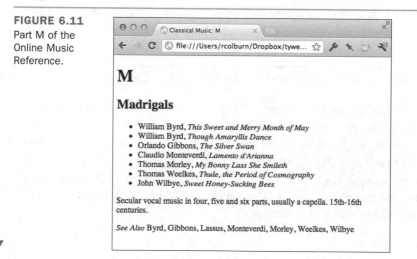

In the last line (the See Also), linking the composer names to their respective sections elsewhere in the reference would be useful. If you use the procedure you learned earlier today, you can create a link here around the word Byrd to the page b.html. When your readers select the link to b.html, the browser drops them at the top of the Bs. Those hapless readers then have to scroll down through all the composers whose names start with *B* (and there are many of them: Bach, Beethoven, Brahms, Bruckner) to get to Byrd—a lot of work for a system that claims to link information so that you can find what you want quickly and easily.

What you want is to be able to link the word Byrd in m.html directly to the section for Byrd in b.html. Here's the relevant part of b.html you want to link. (I've deleted all the Bs before Byrd to make the file shorter for this example. Pretend they're still there.)

```
<!DOCTYPE html><html>
<head>
<title>Classical Music: B</title>
</head>
<body>
<h1>B</h1>
<!-- I've deleted all the Bs before Byrd to make things shorter -->
<h2>Byrd, William, 1543-1623</h2>
<ul>
 <li>Madrigals
  <ul>
    <li><em>This Sweet and Merry Month of May</em></li>
    <li><em>Though Amaryllis Dance</em></li>
    <li><em>Lullabye, My Sweet Little Baby</em></li>
  </ul>
 </li>
 <li>Masses
  <ul>
    <li><em>Mass for Five Voices</em></li>
    <li><em>Mass for Four Voices</em></li>
    <li><em>Mass for Three Voices</em></li>
  </ul>
 </li>
 <li>Motets
  <ul>
    <li><em>Ave verum corpus a 4</em></li>
  </ul>
 </li>
</ul>
<p><em>See Also</em>
 Byrd, Gibbons, Lassus, Monteverdi, Morley, Weelkes, Wilbye</p>
</body>
</html>
```

6

▼ You'll need to add an ID to the section heading for Byrd. You then can link to that ID from the See Also instances in the file for *M*.

You can choose any ID you want for the element, but each ID in the page must be unique. (If you have two elements with the ID `fred` in the same page, how would the browser know which one to choose when a link to that ID is selected?) A good, unique ID for this example is simply `byrd` because `byrd` can appear only one place in the file, and this is it. Adding the ID is as simple as adding the `id` attribute to your `<h2>` element:

```
<h2 id="byrd">Byrd, William, 1543-1623</h2>
```

So, you've added your ID to the heading and its name is `"byrd"`. Now go back to the See Also line in your `m.html` file:

```
<p><em>See Also</em>
 Byrd, Gibbons, Lassus, Monteverdi, Morley, Weelkes, Wilbye</p>
```

You're going to create your link here around the word `Byrd`, just as you would for any other link. But what's the URL? As you learned previously, pathnames to anchors look similar to the following:

```
page_name#anchor_name
```

If you're creating a link to the `b.html` page itself, the `href` is as follows:

```
<a href="b.html">
```

Because you're linking to a section inside that page, add the anchor name to link that section so that it looks like this:

```
<a href="b.html#byrd">
```

Note the small `b` in `byrd`. Anchor names and links are case sensitive; if you put `#Byrd` in your `href`, the link might not work properly. Make sure that the anchor name you use in the `name` attribute and the anchor name in the link after the `#` are identical.

CAUTION

> A common mistake is to put a hash sign in both the anchor name and the link to that anchor. You use the hash sign only to separate the page and the anchor in the link. Anchor names should never have hash signs in them.

So, with the new link to the new section, the See Also line looks like this:

```
<p><em>See Also</em>
 <a href="b.html#byrd">Byrd</a>,
 Gibbons, Lassus, Monteverdi, Morley, Weelkes, Wilbye</p>
```
▼

Of course, you can go ahead and add anchors and links to the other parts of the reference ▼ for the remaining composers.

With all your links and anchors in place, test everything. Figure 6.12 shows the Madrigals section with the link to Byrd ready to be selected.

FIGURE 6.12
The Madrigals section with a link to Byrd.

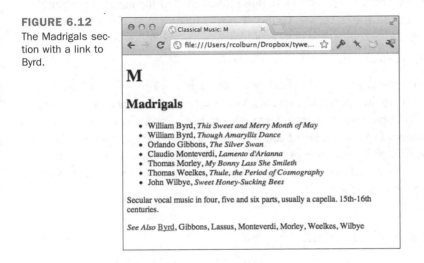

Figure 6.13 shows the screen that pops up when you select the Byrd link. If the page fits entirely within the window, the browser will not be able to move down to the anchor, so you may need to reduce the size of your browser window to see how the link to the anchor takes you to the correct spot on the page.

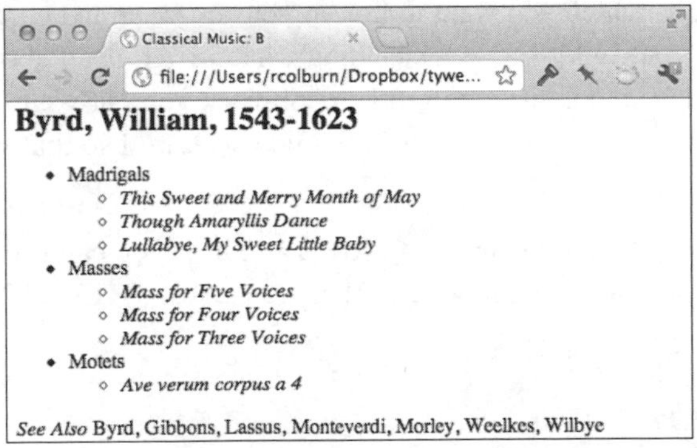

FIGURE 6.13
The Byrd section.

Linking to Elements in the Same Document

What if you have only one large page, and you want to link to sections within that page? You can link to them as well. For longer pages, using IDs can be an easy way to jump around within sections. To link to sections, you just need to add IDs to each section the way you usually do. Then, when you link to those IDs, leave off the name of the page itself, but include the hash sign and the ID. So, if you're linking to an element with the ID `section5` in the same page as the link, the link looks like the following:

```
Go to <a href="#section5">The Fifth Section</a>
```

When you leave off the page name, the browser assumes that you're linking to the current page and scrolls to the appropriate section. You'll get a chance to see this feature in action in Lesson 7. There, you'll create a complete web page that includes a table of contents at the beginning. From this table of contents, the reader can jump to different sections in the same web page. The table of contents includes links to each section heading. In turn, other links at the end of each section enable the user to jump back to the table of contents or to the top of the page.

Anatomy of a URL

So far in this book, you've encountered URLs twice: in Lesson 1, "What Is Web Publishing?," as part of the introduction to the Web; and in this lesson, when you created links to remote pages. If you've ever done much exploring on the Web, you've encountered URLs as a matter of course. You couldn't start exploring without a URL.

As I mentioned in Lesson 1, URLs are *uniform resource locators*. In effect, URLs are street addresses for bits of information on the Internet. Most of the time, you can just navigate to the page to which you want to link in your browser and copy the URL from the address bar into your link. But understanding what a URL is all about and why it can sometimes be so long and complex is useful. Also, when you put your own information up on the Web, knowing something about URLs will be useful so that you can tell people where your web page is.

In this section, you learn what the parts of a URL are, how you can use them to get to information on the Web, and the kinds of URLs you can use (HTTP, FTP, mailto, and so on).

Parts of URLs

Most URLs contain (roughly) three parts: the protocol, the hostname, and the directory or filename (see Figure 6.14).

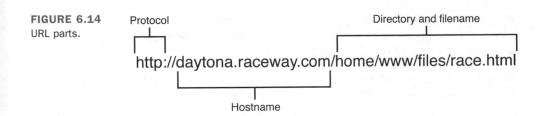

FIGURE 6.14
URL parts.

The *protocol* is the way in which the page is accessed; that is, it's the means of communication your browser uses to get the file. If the protocol in the URL is http, the browser will attempt to use the *Hypertext Transfer Protocol* (HTTP) to talk to the server. For a link to work, the host named in the link must be running a server that supports the protocol that's specified. So if you use an ftp URL to connect to www.example.com, the link won't work if that server isn't running *File Transfer Protocol* (FTP) server software.

The *hostname* is the address of the computer on which the information is stored, like www.google.com, ftp.apple.com, or www.aol.com. The same hostname can support more than one protocol, as follows:

http://example.com
ftp://example.com

It's one machine that offers two different information services, and the browser will use different methods of connecting to each. So long as both servers are installed and available on that system, you won't have a problem.

The hostname part of the URL might include a port number. The port number tells your browser to open a connection using the appropriate protocol on a specific network port. The only time you'll need a port number in a URL is if the server responding to the request has been explicitly installed on that port. If the server is listening on the default port, you can leave the port number out.

If a port number is necessary, it's placed after the hostname but before the directory, as follows:

http://my-public-access-unix.com:1550/pub/file

If the port is not included, the browser tries to connect to the default port number associated with the protocol in the URL. The default port for HTTP is 80, so links to http://www.example.com:80/ and http://www.example.com/ are equivalent.

The *path* is the location of the file or other form of information on the host. The path does not necessarily point to a physical directory and file on the server. Some web applications generate content dynamically and just use the directory information as

6

an identifier. For the files you'll be working with while learning HTML, the directory information will point to files that exist on your computer. The path of the root URL on a server is just /, as in http://www.example.com/.

After the path, some URLs include a *query*. The query is separated from the rest of the URL by a question mark. The query is made up of name and value pairs, separated by ampersands (&). An equals sign (=) separates the names and values. Here's an example:

http://www.example.com/search?q=urls

The query portion of a URL isn't typically used with regular HTML files, but it can be accessed by web applications and can be used with JavaScript. These query parameters will not be discussed much in this book, but you'll see an awful lot of them when you're visiting websites.

The final part of a URL is the anchor, which was described in the previous section.

Special Characters in URLs

A *special character* in a URL is anything that is not an upper- or lowercase letter, a number (0–9), or one of the following symbols: dollar sign ($), dash (-), underscore (_), or period (.). You might need to specify any other characters by using special URL escape codes to keep them from being interpreted as parts of the URL itself.

These special characters are replaced by codes that consist of a percent sign followed by two hexadecimal digits, which consist of digits (0–9) and letters (A–F). For example, once a URL has been encoded, %20 replaces a space, %3f replaces a question mark, and %2f replaces a slash. (Spaces are also sometimes encoded as + signs, and + signs are encoded as %2b.) The need for encoding these characters makes sense because such characters can have a specific meaning when seen within a URL. The slash is the path separator in a URL, and a question mark separates the path in a URL from the query. Spaces that aren't encoded are hard to interpret in many contexts.

Suppose that you have a directory named `All My Files`. Your first pass at a URL with this name in it might look like the following:

http://myhost.com/harddrive/All My Files/www/file.html

If you put this URL in quotation marks in a link tag, it might work (but only if you put it in quotation marks). Because the spaces are considered special characters to the URL, however, some browsers might have problems with them and not recognize the pathname correctly. For full compatibility with all browsers, use %20, as follows:

http://myhost.com/harddrive/All%20My%20Files/www/file.html

CAUTION

> If you make sure that your file and directory names are short and use only alphanumeric characters, you won't need to include special characters in URLs. Special characters can be problematic in a variety of ways. When you're creating your own pages, you should avoid using spaces in filenames as well as other non-alphanumeric characters whenever possible. The two exceptions are _ and -, which are the preferred separators between words in URLs.

The `rel` Attribute

One additional attribute that's supported by the `<a>` tag is the `rel` attribute, which is used to describe the relationship between the linking document and the document that the user is linking to. There's a set of specific values that should be used with this attribute. The most well known is the `nofollow` attribute, which indicates that search engines should not factor that link into their ranking of the document that is linked. `nofollow` is intended as a measure to fight search engine spam. You would use it like this:

```
<a href="http://www.example.com/" rel="nofollow">Link to example site</a>
```

There are a number of other values that can be used with `rel` as well. You can see a full list of the accepted values at the Microformats website at the following URL: http://microformats.org/wiki/existing-rel-values.

Kinds of URLs

Many kinds of URLs are defined by the Uniform Resource Locator specification. This section describes some of the more popular URLs and some situations to look out for when using them.

HTTP

HTTP URLs are by far the most common type of URLs because they point to other documents on the Web. HTTP is the protocol that World Wide Web servers use to communicate with web browsers.

HTTP URLs follow this basic URL form:

http://www.example.com/home/foo/

If the URL ends in a slash, the last part of the URL is considered a directory name. The file that you get using a URL of this type is the default file for that directory as defined by the HTTP server, usually a file called `index.html`. If the web page you're designing

6

is the top-level file for all a directory's files, calling it `index.html` is a good idea. Putting such a file in place will also keep users from browsing the directory where the file is located.

You also can specify the filename directly in the URL. In this case, the file at the end of the URL is the one that is loaded, as in the following examples:

http://www.foo.com/home/foo/index.html

http://www.foo.com/home/foo/homepage.html

Using HTTP URLs such as the following, where `foo` is a directory, is also usually acceptable:

http://www.foo.com/home/foo

In this case, because `foo` is a directory, this URL should have a slash at the end. Most web servers can figure out that this is a link to a directory and redirect to the appropriate file. Including the trailing slash helps the pages load more quickly.

Anonymous FTP

FTP URLs are used to point to files located on FTP servers—usually anonymous FTP servers; that is, the ones that allow you to log in using `anonymous` as the login ID and your email address as the password. FTP URLs also follow the standard URL form, as shown in the following examples:

ftp://ftp.foo.com/home/foo
ftp://ftp.foo.com/home/foo/homepage.html

Because you can retrieve either a file or a directory list with FTP, the restrictions on whether you need a trailing slash at the end of the URL aren't the same as with HTTP. The first URL here retrieves a listing of all the files in the `foo` directory. The second URL retrieves and parses the file `homepage.html` in the `foo` directory.

NOTE

Navigating FTP servers using a web browser can often be much slower than navigating them using FTP itself because the browser doesn't hold the connection open. Instead, it opens the connection, finds the file or directory listing, displays the listing, and then closes down the FTP connection. If you select a link to open a file or another directory in that listing, the browser constructs a new FTP URL from the items you selected, reopens the FTP connection by using the new URL, gets the next directory or file, and closes it again. For this reason, FTP URLs are best for when you know exactly which file you want to retrieve rather than for when you want to browse an archive.

Although your browser uses FTP to fetch the file, if it's an HTML file, your browser will display it just as it would if it were fetched using HTTP. Web browsers don't care how they get files. As long as they can recognize the file as HTML, either because the server explicitly says that the file is HTML or by the file's extension, browsers will parse and display that file as an HTML file. If they don't recognize it as an HTML file, no big deal. Browsers can either display the file if they know what kind of file it is or just save the file to disk.

Non-Anonymous FTP

All the FTP URLs in the preceding section are used for anonymous FTP servers. You also can specify an FTP URL for named accounts on an FTP server, like the following:

ftp://*username:password*@ftp.foo.com/home/foo/homepage.html

In this form of the URL, the *username* part is your login ID on the server, and *password* is that account's password. Note that no attempt is made to hide the password in the URL. Be very careful that no one is watching you when you're using URLs of this form—and don't put them into links that someone else can find!

Furthermore, the URLs that you request might be cached or logged somewhere, either on your local machine or on a proxy server between you and the site you're connecting to. For that reason, it's probably wise to avoid using this type of non-anonymous FTP URL altogether. You may find yourself using non-anonymous FTP to upload your HTML files (or other files related to websites) to a web server in order to publish them. Normally, it's best to connect to the FTP server using a dedicated FTP client rather than the browser. Using FTP to publish web content will be covered in Lesson 23, "How to Publish Your Site."

Mailto

Mailto URLs are used to send electronic mail. If the browser supports mailto URLs, when a link that contains one is selected, the browser will open a new outgoing email in your default email application and send that message to the address in the link when you're done. Depending on how the user's browser and email client are configured, mailto links might not work at all for them.

The mailto URL is different from the standard URL form. It looks like the following:

mailto:*internet_email_address*

Here's an example:

mailto:lemay@lne.com

6

NOTE   If your email address includes a percent sign (%), you have to use the escape character %25 instead. Percent signs are special characters to URLs and thus to mailto URLs.

Unlike the other URLs described here, the mailto URL works strictly on the client side. The mailto link just tells the browser to compose an email message to the specified address. It's up to the browser to figure out how that should happen. Most browsers will also let you add a default subject to the email by including it in the URL like this:

mailto:lemay@lne.com?subject=Hi there!

When the user clicks the link, most browsers will automatically stick Hi there! in the subject of the message. You can also define Cc and Bcc addresses like this:

mailto:lemay@lne.com?cc=htmljenn@gmail.com

Some even support putting body text for the email message in the link with the body= query. Then you can combine them all together, like this:

mailto:lemay@lne.com?subject=Hi there!&cc=htmljenn@gmail.com&body=Body text.

File

File URLs are intended to reference files contained on the local disk. In other words, they refer to files located on the same system as the browser. For local files, URLs have an empty hostname (three slashes rather than two):

file:///dir1/dir2/file

You'll use file URLs a lot when you're testing pages you've created locally, although it's easier to use the browser's "Open File" functionality or drag and drop to open local files in your browser than it is to type in a file URL. Another use of file URLs is to create a local startup page for your browser with links to sites you use frequently. In this instance, because you'll be referring to a local file, using a file URL makes sense.

The problem with file URLs is that they reference local files, where *local* means on the same system as the browser pointing to the file—not the same system from which the page was retrieved! If you use file URLs as links in your page, and someone from elsewhere on the Internet encounters your page and tries to follow those links, that person's browser will attempt to find the file on her local disk (and generally will fail). Also, because file URLs use the absolute pathname to the file, if you use file URLs in your page, you can't move that page elsewhere on the system or to any other system.

If your intention is to refer to files that are on the same file system or directory as the current page, use relative pathnames rather than file URLs. With relative pathnames for local files and other URLs for remote files, you shouldn't need to use a file URL at all.

Summary

In this lesson, you learned about links. Links turn the Web from a collection of unrelated pages into an enormous, interrelated information system.

To create links, you use the `<a>...</a>` tag pair, called the *link* or *anchor* tag. The anchor tag has attributes for creating links (the `href` attribute) and anchor names (the `name` attribute).

When linking pages that are stored on the local disk, you can specify their pathnames in the `href` attribute as relative or absolute paths. For local links, relative pathnames are preferred because they enable you to move local pages more easily to another directory or to another system. If you use absolute pathnames, your links will break if you change anything in the hard-coded path.

If you want to link to a page on the Web (a remote page), the value of the `href` attribute is the URL of that page. You can easily copy the URL of the page you want to link. Just go to that page by using your favorite web browser, and then copy and paste the URL from your browser into the appropriate place in your link tag.

To create links to specific parts of a page, set an anchor at the point you want to link to with the `id` attribute on an element at that part of the page. You then can link directly to that ID by using the name of the page, a hash sign (#), and the ID.

Finally, URLs (*uniform resource locators*) are used to point to pages, files, and other information on the Internet. Depending on the type of information, URLs can contain several parts, but most contain a protocol type and location or address. URLs can be used to point to many kinds of information but are most commonly used to point to web pages (http), FTP directories or files (ftp), or electronic mail addresses (mailto).

6

Workshop

Congratulations, you learned a lot in this lesson! Now it's time for the workshop. Many questions about links appear here. The quiz focuses on other items that are important for you to remember, followed by the quiz answers. In the following exercises, you'll take the list of items you created in Lesson 5, "Organizing Information with Lists," and link them to other pages.

Q&A

Q **My links aren't being highlighted in blue or purple at all. They're still just plain text.**

A Is the filename in a `name` attribute rather than in an `href`? Did you remember to close the quotation marks around the filename to which you're linking? Both of these errors can prevent links from showing up as links.

Q **I put a URL into a link, and it shows up as highlighted in my browser, but when I click it, the browser says "unable to access page." If it can't find the page, why did it highlight the text?**

A The browser highlights text within a link tag whether or not the link is valid. In fact, you don't even need to be online for links to show up as highlighted links, although you can't get to them. The only way you can tell whether a link is valid is to select it and try to view the page to which the link points.

As to why the browser couldn't find the page you linked to—make sure that you're connected to the network and that you entered the URL into the link correctly. Also verify that you have both opening and closing quotation marks around the filename and that those quotation marks are straight quotes. If your browser prints link destinations in the status bar when you move the mouse cursor over a link, watch that status bar and see whether the URL that appears is actually the URL you want.

Finally, try opening the URL directly in your browser and see whether that solution works. If directly opening the link doesn't work either, there might be several reasons why. The following are two common possibilities:

- The server is overloaded or is not on the Internet.

  Machines go down, as do network connections. If a particular URL doesn't work for you, perhaps something is wrong with the machine or the network. Or maybe the site is popular, and too many people are trying to access it simultaneously. Try again later. If you know the people who run the server, you can try sending them electronic mail or calling them.

- The URL itself is bad.

  Sometimes URLs become invalid. Because a URL is a form of absolute pathname, if the file to which it refers moves around, or if a machine or directory name gets changed, the URL won't be valid anymore. Try contacting the person or site you got the URL from in the first place. See whether that person has a more recent link.

Be sure to read the error message provided by the browser carefully. Often it will describe the reason why the link can't be opened, indicating whether it is a network problem or a problem with the URL.

Q Can I put any URL in a link?

A You bet. If you can get to a URL using your browser, you can put that URL in a link. Note, however, that some browsers support URLs that others don't. For example, Lynx is really good with mailto URLs (URLs that enable you to send electronic mail to a person's email address). When you select a mailto URL in Lynx, it prompts you for a subject and the body of the message. When you're done, it sends the mail.

Q Can I use images as links?

A Yup, in more ways than one, actually. You'll learn how to use images as links and define multiple links within one image using image maps in Lesson 9, "Using Images on Your Web Pages."

Q My links aren't pointing to my anchors. When I follow a link, I'm always dropped at the top of the page rather than at the anchor. What's going on here?

A Are you specifying the anchor name in the link after the hash sign the same way that it appears in the anchor itself, with all the uppercase and lowercase letters identical? Anchors are case sensitive, so if your browser can't find an anchor name with an exact match, the browser might try to select something else in the page that's closer. This is dependent on browser behavior, of course, but if your links and anchors aren't working, the problem usually is that your anchor names and your anchors don't match. Also, remember that anchor names don't contain hash signs—only the links to them do.

Q Is there any way to indicate a subject in a mailto URL?

A If you include `?subject=Your%20subject` in the mailto URL, it will work with most email clients. Here's what the whole link looks like:

```
<a href="mailto:someone@example.com?subject=Your%20subject">Send email</a>
```

Quiz

1. What two things do you need to create a link in HTML?
2. What's a relative pathname? Why is it advantageous to use one?
3. What's an absolute pathname?
4. What's an anchor, and what is it used for?
5. Besides HTTP (web page) URLs, what other kinds are there?

6

Quiz Answers

1. To create a link in HTML, you need the name or URL of the file or page to which you want to link and the text that your readers can select to follow the link.

2. A relative pathname points to a file, based on the location that's relative to the current file. Relative pathnames are portable, meaning that if you move your files elsewhere on a disk or rename a directory, the links require little or no modification.

3. An absolute pathname points to a page by starting at the top level of a directory hierarchy and working downward through all intervening directories to reach the file.

4. An anchor marks a place that you can link to inside a web document. A link on the same page or on another page can then jump to that specific location instead of the top of the page.

5. Other types of URLs are FTP URLs (which point to files on FTP servers); file URLs (which point to a file contained on a local disk); and mailto URLs (which are used to send electronic mail).

Exercises

1. Remember the list of topics that you created in Lesson 5 in the first exercise? Create a link to the page you created in Lesson 5's second exercise (the page that described one of the topics in more detail).

2. Now open the page that you created in Lesson 5's second exercise, and create a link back to the first page. Also, find some pages on the World Wide Web that discuss the same topic and create links to those pages, too. Good luck!

LESSON 7
Formatting Text with HTML and CSS

Over the previous lessons, you learned the basics of HTML, including tags used to create page structure and add links. With that background, you're now ready to learn more about what HTML and CSS can do in terms of text formatting and layout. In this lesson, you'll learn about many of the remaining tags in HTML that you'll need to know to construct pages, including how to use HTML and CSS to do the following:

- Specify the appearance of individual characters (bold, italic, underlined)
- Include special characters (characters with accents, copyright marks, and so on)
- Create preformatted text (text with spaces and tabs retained)
- Align text left, right, and centered
- Change the font and font size
- Create other miscellaneous HTML text elements, including line breaks, rule lines, addresses, and quotations

Character-Level Elements

When you use HTML tags to create paragraphs, headings, or lists, those tags affect that block of text as a whole—changing the font, changing the spacing above and below the line, or adding characters (in the case of bulleted lists). They're referred to as *block-level elements*.

Character-level elements are tags that affect words or characters within other HTML tags and change the appearance of that text so that it's somehow different from the surrounding text—making it bold or underlined, for example. Tags like `<p>`, `<ul>`, and `<h1>` are block-level elements. The only character-level element you've seen so far is the `<a>` tag.

NOTE

> In HTML4 it was not valid to nest a block-level element within a character-level element. For example, if you create a heading that is also a link, the `<a>` tag was required to always appear within the heading tag. But HTML5 changed that rule, making it possible to link entire paragraphs or other blocks of content by wrapping them with an `<a>` tag.

To change the appearance of a set of characters within text, you can use one of two methods: semantic HTML tags or *Cascading Style Sheets* (CSS).

Semantic HTML Tags

Semantic tags describe the meaning of the text within the tag, not how it should look in the browser. For example, semantic HTML tags might indicate a definition, a snippet of code, or an emphasized word. This can be a bit confusing because there are de facto standards that correlate each of these tags with a certain visual style. In other words, even though a tag like `<strong>` would mean different things to different people, most browsers display it in boldface, but it has the semantic meaning of strong emphasis.

Each character style tag has both opening and closing sides and affects the text within those two tags. The following are semantic HTML tags:

`<em>` This tag indicates that the characters are emphasized in some way. Most browsers display `<em>` in italics. For example:

```
<p>The anteater is the <em>strangest</em> looking animal,
isn't it?</p>
```

`<strong>` With this tag, the characters are more strongly emphasized than with `<em>`—usually in boldface. Consider the following:

```
<p>Take a <strong>left turn</strong> at <strong>Dee's Hop
Stop</strong></p>
```

`<code>` This tag indicates that the text inside is a code sample and displays it in a fixed-width font such as Courier. For example:

```
<p><code>#include "trans.h"</code></p>
```

`<samp>` This tag indicates sample text and is generally presented in a fixed-width font, like `<code>`. An example of its usage follows:

```
<p>The URL for that page is <samp>http://www.cern.ch/
</samp></p>
```

`<kbd>` This tag indicates text that's intended to be typed by a user. It's also presented in a fixed-width font. Consider the following:

```
<p>Type the following command: <kbd>find . -name "prune"
-print</kbd></p>
```

`<var>` This tag indicates the name of a variable, or some entity to be replaced with an actual value. Often it's displayed as italic or underline and is used as follows:

```
<p><code>chown</code> <var>your_name for the_file
</var></p>
```

`<dfn>` This tag indicates a definition. `<dfn>` is used to highlight a word (usually in italics) that will be defined or has just been defined, as in the following example:

```
<p>Styles that are named after how they are actually
used are called
<dfn>logical styles</dfn></p>
```

`<cite>` This tag indicates the cited title of a work—usually displayed in italics. It is written as in the following:

```
<p>"use the Force, Luke" <cite>"Star Wars"</cite> (1976)</p>
```

`<abbr>` This tag indicates the abbreviation of a word, as in the following:

```
<p>Use the standard two-letter state abbreviation
(such as <abbr>CA</abbr> for California)</p>
```

NOTE

> Only the `<abbr>` tag made it into HTML5, `<acronym>` has been removed due to redundancy. You may still see it used, but you should use the `<abbr>` tag instead.

The following code snippets demonstrate each of the semantic HTML tags mentioned, and Figure 7.1 illustrates how all the tags are displayed.

Input ▼

```
<p>The anteater is the <em>strangest</em> looking animal, isn't it?</p>
<p>Take a <strong>left turn</strong> at <strong>Dee's Hop Stop
</strong></p>
<p><code>#include "trans.h"</code></p>
<p>The URL for that page is <samp>http://www.cern.ch/</samp></p>
<p>Type the following command: <kbd>find . -name "prune" -print</kbd></p>
<p><code>chown </code><var>your_name the_file</var></p>
<p>Styles that are named after how they are used are called <dfn>logical
styles</dfn></p>
<p>Eggplant has been known to cause nausea in some
people<cite> (Lemay, 1994)</cite></p>
<p>Use the standard two-letter state abbreviation (such as
<abbr>CA</abbr> for California)</p>
```

Output ▼

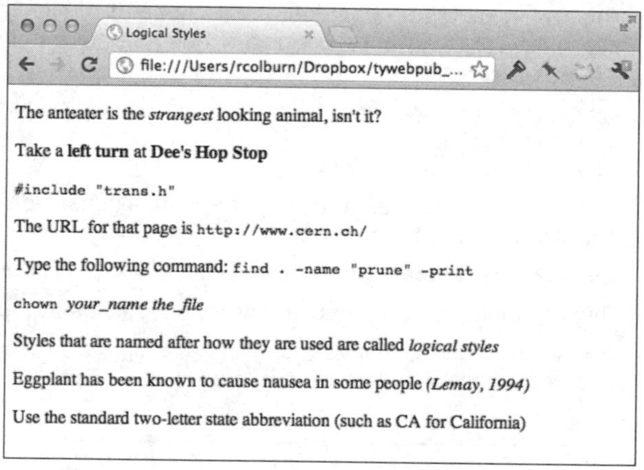

FIGURE 7.1
Various semantic tags displayed in a browser.

> The anteater is the *strangest* looking animal, isn't it?
>
> Take a **left turn** at **Dee's Hop Stop**
>
> `#include "trans.h"`
>
> The URL for that page is `http://www.cern.ch/`
>
> Type the following command: `find . -name "prune" -print`
>
> `chown` *your_name the_file*
>
> Styles that are named after how they are used are called *logical styles*
>
> Eggplant has been known to cause nausea in some people *(Lemay, 1994)*
>
> Use the standard two-letter state abbreviation (such as CA for California)

Changes to Physical Style Tags in HTML5

Over time, a number of physical style tags were added to HTML as well. You should avoid using them and use CSS or the semantic equivalents instead, but if you decide to use them, HTML5 has given them semantic meanings:

`<b>`	Text that is usually bold
`<i>`	Text that is usually displayed as italic
`<u>`	Text that is usually displayed as underlined
`<small>`	Text that displays as small print

`<sub>`	Subscript
`<sup>`	Superscript

Character Formatting Using CSS

You've already seen how styles can be used to modify the appearance of various elements. Any of the effects associated with the tags introduced in this lesson can also be created using CSS. Before I go into these properties, however, I want to talk a bit about how to use them. As I've said before, the `style` attribute can be used with most tags. However, most tags somehow affect the appearance of the text that they enclose. There's a tag that doesn't have any inherent effect on the text that it's wrapped around: the `<span>` tag. It exists solely to be associated with style sheets. It's used exactly like any of the other tags you've seen in this lesson. Simply wrap it around some text, like this:

```
<p>This is an example of the <span>usage of the span tag</span>.</p>
```

Used by itself, the `<span>` tag has absolutely no effect. Paired with the `style` attribute, it can take the place of any of the tags you've seen in this lesson and can do a lot more than that, as well.

The Text Decoration Property

The `text-decoration` property is used to specify which, if any, decoration will be applied to the text within the affected tag. The valid values for this property are `underline`, `overline`, `line-through`, and `blink`. The application of each of them is self-explanatory. However, here's an example that demonstrates how to use each of them:

```
<p>Here is some <span style="text-decoration: underline;">underlined text
</span>.</p>
<p>Here is some <span style="text-decoration: overline;">overlined text</span>.
</p>
<p>Here is some <span style="text-decoration: line-through;">line-through text
</span>.</p>
<p>Here is some <span style="text-decoration: blink;">blinking text</span>.</p>
```

The cool thing is that you can use these styles along with all the other properties you'll see in this lesson with any tag that contains text. Take a look at this example:

```
<h1 style="text-decoration: underline;">An Underlined Heading</h1>
```

Using the `style` attribute, you can specify how the text of the heading appears. As you can see, using the `style` attribute involves a lot more typing than using the `<u>` tag. The tradeoff is that there are many other ways to specify styles that are much more efficient

7

than using the `style` attribute. Later, you'll see how to use style sheets to control the appearance of many elements simultaneously.

Font Properties

When you want to modify the appearance of text, the other major family of properties you can use is font properties. You can use font properties to modify pretty much any aspect of the type used to render text in a browser. One of the particularly nice things about font properties is that they're much more specific than the tags that you've seen so far.

First, let's look at some of the direct replacements for tags you've already seen. The `font-style` property can be used to italicize text. It has three possible values: `normal`, which is the default; `italic`, which renders the text in the same way as the `<i>` tag; and `oblique`, which is a slanted version of the standard typeface. Most fonts provide an italic version, which has letterforms separate from the normal version or an oblique version, but not both. When you specify that text should be `oblique` or `italic`, the browser will choose whichever of the two is available. If neither variant is installed, the browser will usually generate its own oblique version of the font. Here are some examples:

```
<p>Here's some <span style="font-style: italic;">italicized text</span>.</p>
<p>Here's some <span style="font-style: oblique;">oblique text</span>
(which may look like regular italics in your browser).</p>
```

Now let's look at how you use CSS to create boldfaced text. In the world of HTML, you have two options: bold and not bold. With CSS, you have many more options. In practice, text is either bold or normal. To specify that text should be boldface, the `font-weight` property is used. Valid values are `normal` (the default), `bold`, `bolder`, `lighter`, and 100 through 900, in units of 100. Here are some examples:

```
<p>Here's some <span style="font-weight: bold;">bold text</span>.</p>
<p>Here's some <span style="font-weight: bolder;">bolder text</span>.</p>
<p>Here's some <span style="font-weight: lighter;">lighter text</span>.</p>
<p>Here's some <span style="font-weight: 700;">bolder text</span>.</p>
```

TIP

In some cases, computers will have a bold variation of a font, an italic variation, and a normal variation but not a bold, italic variation. If you specify that text has a `font-weight` of `bold` and a `font-style` of `italic` or `oblique`, the browser will substitute an oblique version of the bold font that it creates on the fly, and the result will often be ugly text. If you are concerned with nice typography, make sure to only specify font variations that are normally installed.

You can also set the typeface for text using the `font-family` property. In addition, you can set the specific font for text, but I'm not going to discuss that until later in the lesson. In the meantime, let's look at how you can set the font to a member of a particular font family. The specific font will be taken from the user's preferences. The property to modify is `font-family`. The possible values are `serif`, `sans-serif`, `cursive`, `fantasy`, and `monospace`. So, if you want to specify that a monospace font should be used with CSS rather than the now obsolete `<tt>` tag, use the following code:

```
<p><span style="font-family: monospace;">This is monospaced text.</span></p>
```

Now let's look at one capability not available using regular HTML tags. Using the `font-variant` property, you can have your text rendered so that lowercase letters are replaced with small capital letters. The two values available are `normal` and `small-caps`. Here's an example:

```
<p><span style='font-variant: small-caps;'>This Text Uses Small Caps.</span></p>
```

The web page in Figure 7.2 contains some text that uses the `font-variant` property as well as all the other properties described in this section.

Output ▼

FIGURE 7.2
Text styled using CSS.

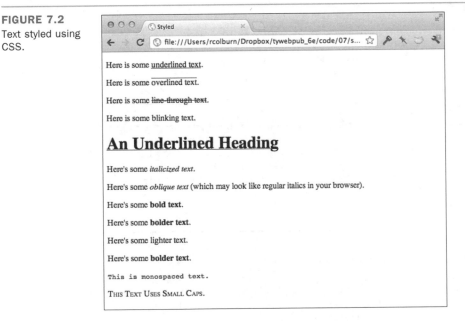

7

Preformatted Text

Most of the time, text in an HTML file is formatted based on the HTML tags used to mark up that text. In Lesson 3, "Introducing HTML and CSS," I mentioned that any extra whitespace (spaces, tabs, returns) that you include in your HTML source is stripped out by the browser.

The one exception to this rule is the preformatted text tag `<pre>`. Any whitespace that you put into text surrounded by the `<pre>` and `</pre>` tags is retained in the final output. With these tags, the spacing in the text in the HTML source is preserved when it's displayed on the page.

The catch is that preformatted text usually is displayed (in graphical displays, at least) in a monospaced font such as Courier. Preformatted text is excellent for displaying code examples in which you want the text formatted with exactly the indentation the author used. Because you can use the `<pre>` tag to align text by padding it with spaces, you can use it for simple tables. However, the fact that the tables are presented in a monospaced font might make them less than ideal. (You'll learn how to create real tables in Lesson 10, "Building Tables.") The following is an example of a table created with `<pre>`:

Input ▼

```
<pre>
          Diameter    Distance    Time to      Time to
          (miles)     from Sun    Orbit        Rotate
                      (millions
                      of miles)

          -----------------------------------------------------------
Mercury   3100            36       88 days      59 days
Venus     7700            67      225 days     244 days
Earth     7920            93      365 days      24 hrs
Mars      4200           141      687 days      24 hrs 24 mins
Jupiter   88640          483       11.9 years    9 hrs 50 mins
Saturn    74500          886       29.5 years   10 hrs 39 mins
Uranus    32000         1782       84 years     23 hrs
Neptune   31000         2793      165 days      15 hrs 48 mins
Pluto     1500          3670      248 years      6 days 7 hrs</pre>
```

Figure 7.3 shows how it looks in a browser.

Output ▼

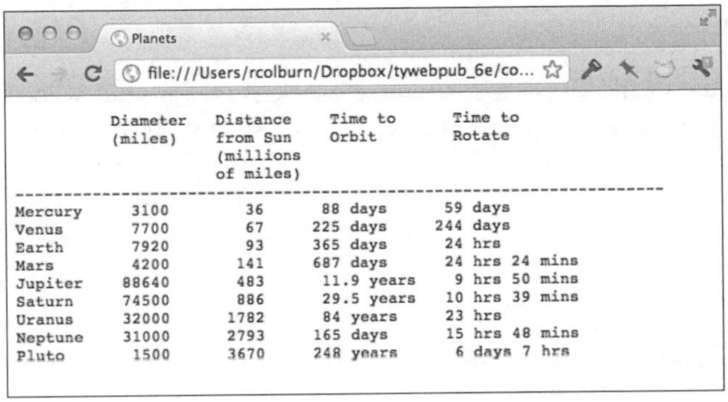

FIGURE 7.3
A table created
using `<pre>`,
shown in a
browser.

When you're creating text for the `<pre>` tag, you can use link tags and character styles but not element tags such as headings or paragraphs. You should break your lines with hard returns and try to keep your lines to 60 characters or fewer. Some browsers might have limited horizontal space in which to display text. Because browsers usually won't reformat preformatted text to fit that space, you should make sure that you keep your text within the boundaries to prevent your readers from having to scroll from side to side.

Be careful with tabs in preformatted text. The actual number of characters for each tab stop varies from browser to browser. One browser might have tab stops at every fourth character, whereas another may have them at every eighth character. You should convert any tabs in your preformatted text to spaces so that your formatting isn't messed up if it's viewed with different tab settings than in the program you used to enter the text.

The `<pre>` tag is also excellent for converting files that were originally in some sort of text-only form, such as email messages, into HTML quickly and easily. Just surround the entire content of the message within `<pre>` tags and you have instant HTML, as in the following example:

```
<pre>
To: lemay@lne.com
From: jokes@lne.com
Subject: Tales of the Move From Hell, pt. 1

I spent the day on the phone today with the entire household
services division of northern California, turning off services,
turning on services, transferring services and other such fun
things you have to do when you move.

It used to be you just called these people and got put on hold for
an interminable amount of time, maybe with some nice music, and
then you got a customer representative who was surly and hard of
```

7

```
hearing, but with some work you could actually get your phone
turned off.
</pre>
```

One creative use of the `<pre>` tag is to create ASCII art for your web pages. The following HTML input and output example shows a simple ASCII-art cow:

Input ▼

```
<pre>
       (  )
Moo (oo)
     \/------\
      ||    | \
      ||---W|| *
      ||    ||
</pre>
```

Figure 7.4 displays the result.

Output ▼

FIGURE 7.4
A bit of ASCII art that illustrates how preformatted text works.

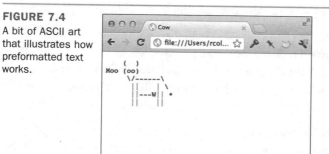

Horizontal Rules (or Thematic Breaks)

The `<hr>` tag, which has no closing tag in HTML and no text associated with it, creates a horizontal line on the page. As of HTML5, the tag has also been given a semantic meaning—thematic break. It's represented by a horizontal line as it always has been, but it has now been ascribed a semantic meaning as well. It represents a change of topic within a section or, for example, a change in scene in a story.

Closing Empty Elements

The `<hr>` tag has no closing tag in HTML. To convert this tag to XHTML, add a space and a forward slash to the end of the tag:

```
<hr />
```

If the horizontal line has attributes associated with it, the forward slash still appears at the end of the tag.

The following input shows a horizontal rule used to separate two sections in Emily Bronte's novel *Wuthering Heights*:

Input ▼

```
<p>At first, on hearing this account from Zillah, I determined
to leave my situation, take a cottage, and get Catherine to
come and live with me: but Mr. Heathcliff would as soon permit
that as he would set up Hareton in an independent house; and
I can see no remedy, at present, unless she could marry again;
and that scheme it does not come within my province to arrange.</p>
<hr>
<p>Thus ended Mrs. Dean's story.  Notwithstanding the doctor's
prophecy, I am rapidly recovering strength; and though it be
only the second week in January, I propose getting out on
horseback in a day or two, and riding over to Wuthering Heights,
to inform my landlord that I shall spend the next six months
in London; and, if he likes, he may look out for another
tenant to take the place after October.  I would not pass
another winter here for much.</p>
```

Figure 7.5 shows how it appears in a browser.

Output ▼

FIGURE 7.5
An example of how horizontal rules are used to separate sections.

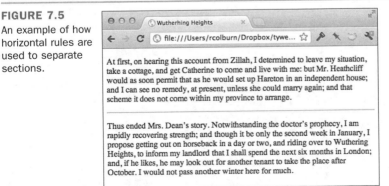

7

Attributes of the `<hr>` Tag

If you're working in HTML5, this one is easy. HTML5 does not support any attributes of the `<hr>` element other than those supported by all elements. However, past versions of HTML supported a number of attributes that could be used to modify the appearance of a horizontal rule. If you are creating new web pages, you should use CSS to style your horizontal rules. However, you may encounter these attributes in existing HTML.

The `size` attribute indicates the thickness, in pixels, of the rule line. The default is 2, and this also is the smallest that you can make the rule line.

To change the thickness of an `<hr>` with CSS, use the `height` property, which I'll discuss in Lesson 8, "Using CSS to Style a Site."

The `width` attribute specifies the horizontal width of the rule line. You can specify the exact width of the rule in pixels. You can also specify the value as a percentage of the browser width (for example, 30% or 50%). If you set the width of a horizontal rule to a percentage, the width of the rule will change to conform to the window size if the user resizes the browser window. You should use the `width` CSS property instead. I'll also talk about width in the following lesson. Most browsers automatically center `<hr>` tags. Figure 7.6 shows the result of the following code, which displays some sample rule line widths:

Input ▼

```
<h2>100%, Default Size</h2>
<hr>
<h2>75%, Size 2</h2>
<hr width="75%" size="2">
<h2>50%, Size 4</h2>
<hr width="50%" size="4">
<h2>25%, Size 6</h2>
<hr width="25%" size="6">
<h2>10%, Size 8</h2>
<hr width="10%" size="8">
```

Output ▼

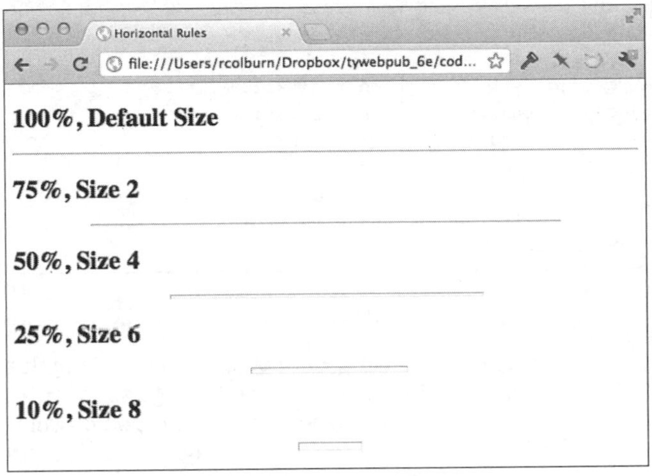

FIGURE 7.6
Examples of rule
line widths and
heights.

If you specify a `width` smaller than the actual width of the browser window, you can also specify the alignment of that rule with the `align` attribute, making it flush left (`align="left"`), flush right (`align="right"`), or centered (`align="center"`). By default, rule lines are centered. Like all of the other `<hr>` attributes, the `align` attribute has been replaced with CSS in HTML5 for all elements that once used it. Alignment will be covered in the following lesson.

Finally, the obsolete `noshade` attribute causes the browser to draw the rule line as a plain line without the three-dimensional shading.

Line Break

The `<br>` tag breaks a line of text at the point where it appears. When a web browser encounters a `<br>` tag, it restarts the text after the tag at the left margin (whatever the current left margin happens to be for the current element). You can use `<br>` within other elements, such as paragraphs or list items; `<br>` won't add extra space above or below the new line or change the font or style of the current entity. All it does is restart the text at the next line.

The following example shows a simple paragraph in which each line (except for the last, which ends with a closing `<p>` tag) ends with a `<br>`:

7

Input ▼

```
<p>Tomorrow, and tomorrow, and tomorrow,<br>
Creeps in this petty pace from day to day,<br>
To the last syllable of recorded time;<br>
And all our yesterdays have lighted fools<br>
The way to dusty death. Out, out, brief candle!<br>
Life's but a walking shadow; a poor player,<br>
That struts and frets his hour upon the stage,<br>
And then is heard no more: it is a tale <br>
Told by an idiot, full of sound and fury, <br>
Signifying nothing.</p>
```

NOTE

clear is an obsolete attribute of the <br> tag. It's used with images that have text wrapped alongside them. You'll learn about this attribute in Lesson 9, "Using Images on Your Web Pages." Like similar attributes of other tags, the clear attribute has been replaced with CSS.

Figure 7.7 shows how it appears in a browser.

Output ▼

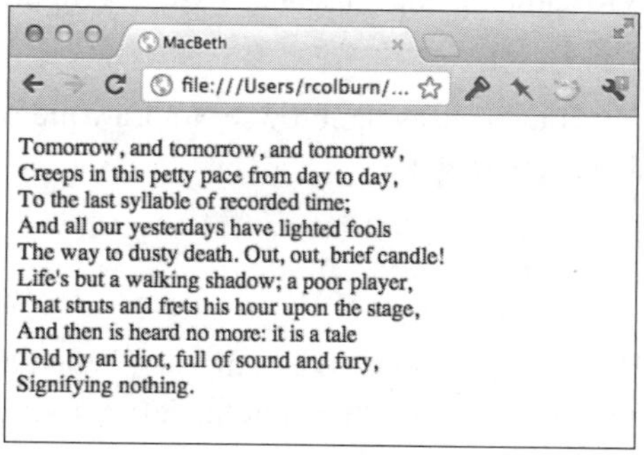

FIGURE 7.7
Line breaks.

Tomorrow, and tomorrow, and tomorrow,
Creeps in this petty pace from day to day,
To the last syllable of recorded time;
And all our yesterdays have lighted fools
The way to dusty death. Out, out, brief candle!
Life's but a walking shadow; a poor player,
That struts and frets his hour upon the stage,
And then is heard no more: it is a tale
Told by an idiot, full of sound and fury,
Signifying nothing.

Addresses

The address tag <address> is used to supply contact information on web pages. Address tags usually go at the bottom of the web page and are used to indicate who wrote the web page, whom to contact for more information, the date, any copyright notices or other warnings, and anything else that seems appropriate.

Signing each of your web pages using the `<address>` tag is an excellent way to make sure that people can get in touch with you and that visitors who arrive on your web page by way of an external link can see who created it. `<address>` is a block-level tag, and some browsers italicize the text inside it.

The following input shows an address:

Input ▼

```
<address>
Laura Lemay <a href="mailto:lemay@lne.com">lemay@lne.com</a><br />
A service of Laura Lemay, Incorporated <br />
last revised July 10, 2012 <br />
Copyright Laura Lemay 2012 all rights reserved <br />
Void where prohibited. Keep hands and feet inside the vehicle at all times.
</address>
```

Figure 7.8 shows it in a browser.

Output ▼

FIGURE 7.8
An address block.

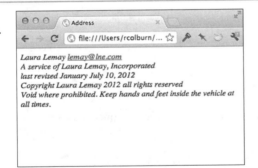

As you can see, by default many browsers italicize the contents of address blocks. To render them in normal text, you can use styles to set the `font-style` property to `normal`.

Quotations

The `<blockquote>` tag is used to indicate that a block of text represents an extended quotation. The `<blockquote>` tag is a block-level element. By default, `<blockquote>` elements are indented, although that can be changed with CSS. For example, the

7

Macbeth soliloquy I used in the example for line breaks would have worked better as a `<blockquote>` than as a simple paragraph. Here's an example:

```
<p>From Shakespeare's <cite>MacBeth</cite>:

<blockquote>Tomorrow, and tomorrow, and tomorrow,<br>
Creeps in this petty pace from day to day,<br>
To the last syllable of recorded time;<br>
And all our yesterdays have lighted fools<br>
The way to dusty death. Out, out, brief candle!<br>
Life's but a walking shadow; a poor player,<br>
That struts and frets his hour upon the stage,<br>
And then is heard no more: it is a tale <br>
Told by an idiot, full of sound and fury, <br>
Signifying nothing.</blockquote>
```

As with paragraphs, you can split lines in a `<blockquote>` using the line break tag, `<br>`. The following input example shows an example of this use:

Input ▼

```
<blockquote>
Guns aren't lawful, <br />
nooses give.<br />
gas smells awful.<br />
You might as well live.
</blockquote>
<p>-- Dorothy Parker</p>
```

Figure 7.9 shows how the preceding input example appears in a browser.

Output ▼

FIGURE 7.9
A block quotation.

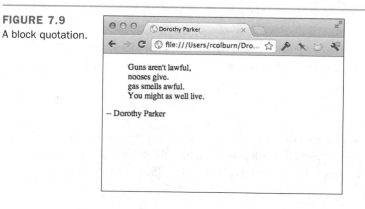

The `<blockquote>` tag supports one attribute, `cite`. The value of the `cite` attribute is the URL that is the source of the quotation inside the `<blockquote>` tag. For example, the `<blockquote>` tag for the preceding Dorothy Parker quotation could point back to the original source using the `cite` attribute:

```
<blockquote cite="http://www.poetryfoundation.org/poem/174101">
Guns aren't lawful, <br />
nooses give.<br />
gas smells awful.<br />
You might as well live.
</blockquote>
<p>-- Dorothy Parker</p>
```

The cite attribute does not produce visible changes on the page, and for that reason best practices recommend that you not use it. Instead, you should use the `<cite>` tag directly on the page to indicate the author, title, or URL of the work referenced.

For inline quotations, you should use the `<q>` tag, and, optionally, the `cite` attribute to indicate them and provide the source URL. The `<q>` tag does not affect the visual display of the page. Here's an example of how it's used:

```
<p>As Albert Einstein said,
"<q cite="https://en.wikiquote.org/wiki/Albert_Einstein">
I never think of the future. It comes soon enough.</q>"</p>
```

Finally, the `<cite>` element is used to cite the author, title, or URL of the work quoted. Like the `<q>` tag, it does not affect the visual display of the page in any way, although both can be styled using CSS. And, as previously mentioned, the `<cite>` tag contents are visible on the page and are the recommended method to cite quotations. Here's how the `<cite>` tag is used:

```
<p>In Roger Ebert's book <cite>The Great Movies</cite>, he lists
<cite>The Wizard of Oz</cite> as one of the great films.</p>
```

Figure 7.10 shows how all three tags are used.

FIGURE 7.10
Use of the `<blockquote>`, `<q>` and `<cite>` tags.

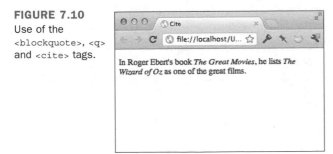

7

Special Characters

As you've already learned, HTML files are ASCII text and should contain no formatting or fancy characters. In fact, the only characters you should put in your HTML files are the characters that are actually printed on your keyboard. If you have to hold down any key other than Shift or type an arcane combination of keys to produce a single character, you can't use that character in your HTML file. This includes characters you might use every day, such as em dashes and curly quotes. (If you are using a word processor that does automatic curly quotes, you should find another HTML editor that writes text files instead.)

"But wait a minute," you say. "If I can type a character like a bullet or an accented *a* on my keyboard using a special key sequence, and I can include it in an HTML file, and my browser can display it just fine when I look at that file, what's the problem?"

The problem is that the internal encoding your computer does to produce that character (which enables it to show up properly in your HTML file and in your browser's display) probably won't translate to other computers. Someone on the Internet who's reading your HTML file with that funny character in it might end up with some other character or just plain garbage.

So, what can you do? HTML provides a reasonable solution. It defines a special set of codes, called *character entities*, that you can include in your HTML files to represent the characters you want to use. When interpreted by a browser, these character entities display as the appropriate special characters for the given platform and font.

Some special characters don't come from the set of extended ASCII characters. For example, quotation marks and ampersands can be presented on a page using character entities even though they're found within the standard ASCII character set. These characters have a special meaning in HTML documents within certain contexts, so they can be represented with character entities to avoid confusing web browsers. Modern browsers generally don't have a problem with these characters, but it's not a bad idea to use the entities anyway.

CAUTION

> HTML validators will complain when they encounter ampersands that are not part of entities, so you always want to encode them using entities on your pages.

Character Encoding

Before I can talk about how to add special characters to your web page, I first have to talk a little bit about character encoding. When we think of text, we think of characters like "a" or "6" or "&" or a space. Computers, however, think of them as numbered entries in a list. Each of these lists of characters is referred to as a character set.

One character set you may have heard of is ASCII, which contains 128 characters, including the upper and lowercase letters, numbers, punctuation, and a number of other special characters like space, carriage return, and tab. The space character is in the 32nd position of the list of ASCII characters. When you convert that to hexadecimal (base 16) notation, it's in position 20. That may ring a bell—back in Lesson 6, you learned that when URL encoding is used, spaces are encoded as %20. That's because encoded characters in URL encoded are numbered by their position in the list of ASCII characters.

When a web page is displayed, the browser looks up all of the characters on the page in the character set that is being used to display the page. There are a number of ways to specify which character set is used for a page. If none of them are used, the browser displays the page using its default encoding. There are a whole lot of character sets available; you can see a list of them from Chrome's View Encoding menu in Figure 7.11.

FIGURE 7.11
A list of some of the character encodings supported by Google Chrome.

```
✓ Auto Detect

✓ Unicode (UTF-8)
  Western (ISO-8859-1)
  Western (Windows-1252)
  Hebrew (Windows-1255)
  South European (ISO-8859-3)
  Korean

  Unicode (UTF-16LE)
  Arabic (Windows-1256)
  Arabic (ISO-8859-6)
  Baltic (ISO-8859-4)
  Baltic (ISO-8859-13)
  Baltic (Windows-1257)
  Celtic (ISO-8859-14)
  Central European (ISO-8859-2)
  Central European (Windows-1250)
  Chinese Simplified (GBK)
```

For the most part, as long as you stick with using characters from the list of 128 characters in the ASCII character set, your page will look fine regardless of which encoding is selected because all the characters are based on ASCII. You run into problems when you get past those 128 initial characters. This becomes important if you want to use special characters like em dashes, smart quotation marks, or letters with accents.

There is a lot more that can be said about character encoding; in fact, large books have been written on the topic. At this point, I'm just going to give you a shortcut. To ensure that your special characters always look the way they're supposed to, you just have to

7

make sure that your pages specify that they are encoded in UTF-8 and that you use the entities that I'll describe shortly for any characters that are not in the 128 characters in the ASCII set. If you do both of those things, you'll never run into problems with browsers not displaying the characters that you intend.

> **NOTE**
>
> UTF-8 is a character set that's backward compatible with ASCII and that supports every character in the Unicode character set. This is important because Unicode supports a huge number of characters in a large number of alphabets. It's extremely unlikely that you would ever want to use a character that is not supported by Unicode.

The question is, how do you specify that your web pages use the UTF-8 character set? The character set can be configured at the web server level, and I'll discuss that in Lesson 23, "How to Publish Your Site." You can specify the encoding at the page level. If you are using HTML5, you should begin your page like this:

```
<!DOCTYPE HTML>
<html>
<head>
<meta charset="UTF-8">
```

The character set is specified using the `<meta>` tag. For HTML5, the character set is specified using the following `<meta>` tag:

```
<meta charset="utf-8">
```

UTF-8 was created to provide a single character set that would encompass the huge number of characters used in various languages around the world, and it should be used for all web pages unless there is a very good reason not to.

Character Entities for Special Characters

Character entities take one of two forms: named entities and numbered entities.

Named entities begin with an ampersand (&) and end with a semicolon (;). In between is the name of the character (or, more likely, a shorthand version of that name, such as `agrave` for an *a* with a grave accent, or `reg` for a registered trademark sign). Unlike other HTML tags, the names are case sensitive, so you should make sure to type them in exactly. Named entities look something like the following:

```
&agrave;
&quot;
```

```
&laquo;
&copy;
```

The numbered entities also begin with an ampersand and end with a semicolon, but rather than a name, they have a pound sign (#) and a number. The numbers correspond to character positions in the character set for the web page. In this lesson, I'll assume you're using UTF-8. Every character you can type or for which you can use a named entity also has a numbered entity. Numbered entities look like the following:

```
&#224;
&#34;
&#171;
&#169;
```

You can use either numbers or named entities in your HTML file by including them in the same place that the character they represent would go. So, to place the word *résumé* in your HTML file, you would use either

```
r&eacute;sum&eacute;
```

or

```
r&#233;sum&#233;
```

If you use named entities, the character set is not important because the browser will translate the named entity into the appropriate character in the character set specified for the page. You can find a full list of the named entities at

http://www.w3.org/TR/2011/WD-html5-20110113/named-character-references.html

Given that UTF-8 supports more than 100,000 characters, it's tough to print a table of all of them. However, one resource you can use to look up UTF-8 characters is the resource at http://www.utf8-chartable.de/. Remember that you'll need to use the decimal representations in your entities.

Character Entities for Reserved Characters

For the most part, character entities exist so that you can include special characters that aren't part of the standard ASCII character set. However, there are several exceptions for the few characters that have special meaning in HTML itself. You must use entities for these characters, too.

Suppose that you want to include a line of code that looks something like the following in an HTML file:

```
<p><code>if x < 0 do print i</code></p>
```

7

Doesn't look unusual, does it? Unfortunately, this is not valid HTML as written. Why? The problem is with the < (less-than) character. To an HTML browser, the less-than character means "this is the start of a tag." Because the less-than character isn't actually the start of a tag in this context, your browser might get confused. You'll have the same problem with the greater-than character (>) because it means the end of a tag in HTML, and with the ampersand (&) because it signals the beginning of an entity. Written correctly for HTML, the preceding line of code would look like the following instead:

```
<p><code>if x &lt; 0 do print i</code></p>
```

Use of these entities is also important if you want to print HTML tags in your web pages, like this:

```
<p>The <code>&lt;p&gt;</code> element represents a paragraph.</p>
```

HTML provides named entities for each of these characters, and one for the double quotation mark, too, as shown in Table 7.1.

TABLE 7.1 Escape Codes for Characters Used by Tags

Entity	Result
<	<
>	>
&	&

Fonts and Font Sizes

Earlier in this lesson, I described a few font-related properties that you can manipulate using CSS. In fact, you can use CSS to control all font usage on the page. I also described how the `font-family` property can be used to specify that text should be rendered in a font belonging to a particular general category, such as monospace or serif. You can also use the `font-family` property to specify a specific font.

You can provide a single font or a list of fonts, and the browser will search for each of the fonts until it finds one on your system that appears in the list. You can also include a generic font family in the list of fonts if you like. Here are some examples:

```
<p style="font-family: Verdana, Trebuchet, Arial, sans-serif;">
This is sans-serif text.</p>
<p style="font-family: 'Courier New', monospace;">This is
monospace text.</p>
<p style="font-family: Georgia;">This text will appear in the
Georgia font, or, if that font is not installed, the browser's
default font.</p>
```

You can also use CSS to specify font size. CSS provides a lot of flexibility and power when it comes to specifying how large things are. You can specify sizes in a variety of units. I'll dig deep into how sizes work in CSS in Lesson 8, "Using CSS to Style a Site," but I'll provide a preview here. Let's start with the basics. To change the font size for some text, the `font-size` property is used. The value is a size (relative or absolute) in any of the units of measure supported by CSS.

The simplest is the percentage size, relative to the current font size. So, to make the font twice as large as the size inherited from the enclosing element, just use the following:

```
<p>This text is normal sized, and this text is
<span style="font-size: 200%;">twice that size</span>.</p>
```

You can also specify the size in any of a number of units. For example, the `px` unit specifies the height in pixels. To set your text to be 12 pixels high, the following style declaration is used:

```
<p style="font-size: 12px;">This text is 12 pixels tall.</p>
```

CAUTION

One thing to watch out for: When you specify units in CSS, you must leave no spaces between the number of units and unit specification. In other words, `12px` and `100%` are valid, and `12 px` and `100 %` aren't.

DO	DON'T
DO list backup fonts when specifying a font family in order to make it more likely that your users will have one of the fonts you specify.	**DON'T** use too many different fonts on the same page. **DON'T** use absolute font sizes with CSS if you can help it, because some browsers won't let users alter the text size if you do so.

Exercise 7.1: Creating a Real HTML Page ▼

Here's your chance to apply what you've learned and create a real web page. No more disjointed or overly silly examples. The web page you'll create in this section is a real one, suitable for use in the real world (or the real world of the web, at least).

7

▼

▼ Your task for this example is to design and create a home page for a bookstore called The Bookworm, which specializes in old and rare books.

Planning the Page   First, consider the content you want to include on this page. The following are some ideas for topics for this page:

- The address and phone number of the bookstore
- A short description of the bookstore and why it's unique
- Recent titles and authors
- Upcoming events

Now come up with some ideas for the content you're going to link to from this page. Each title in a list of recently acquired books seems like a logical candidate. You also can create links to more information about each book, its author and publisher, its price, and maybe even its availability.

The Upcoming Events section might suggest a potential series of links, depending on how much you want to say about each event. If you have only a sentence or two about each one, describing them on this page might make more sense than linking them to another page. Why make your readers wait for each new page to load for just a couple of lines of text?

Other interesting links might arise in the text itself, but for now, starting with the basic link plan is enough.

Beginning with a Framework   Next, create the framework that all HTML files must include: the document structure, a title, and some initial headings. Note that the title is descriptive but short; you can save the longer title for the `<h1>` element in the body of the text. The four `<h2>` subheadings help you define the four main sections you'll have on your web page:

```
<!DOCTYPE html>
<html>
<head>
<meta charset="UTF-8">
<title>The Bookworm Bookshop</title>
</head>
<body>
<h1>The Bookworm: A Better Book Store</h1>
<h2>Contents</h2>
<h2>About the Bookworm Bookshop</h2>
<h2>Recent Titles (as of July 11, 2012)</h2>
<h2>Upcoming Events</h2>
</body>
▼ </html>
```

Each heading you've placed on your page marks the beginning of a particular section. You'll add IDs to each of the topic headings so that you can jump from section to section with ease. The IDs are simple: top for the main heading; contents for the table of contents; and about, recent, and upcoming for the three subsections on the page. With the IDs in place, the revised code looks like the following:

Input ▼

```
<!DOCTYPE html>
<html>
<head>
<meta charset="UTF-8">
<title>The Bookworm Bookshop</title>
</head>
<body>
<h1 id="top">The Bookworm: A Better Book Store</h1>
<h2 id="contents">Contents</h2>
<h2 id="about">About the Bookworm Bookshop</h2>
<h2 id="recent">Recent Titles (as of July 11, 2012)</h2>
<h2 id="upcoming">Upcoming Events</h2>
</body>
</html>
```

Adding Content   Now begin adding the content. You're undertaking a literary endeavor, so starting the page with a nice quote about old books would be a nice touch. Because you're adding a quote, you can use the <blockquote> tag to make it stand out as such. Also, the name of the poem is a citation, so use <cite> there, too.

Insert the following code on the line after the level 1 heading:

Input ▼

```
<blockquote>
"Old books are best---how tale and rhyme<br>
Float with us down the stream of time!"<br>
-- Clarence Urmy, <cite>Old Songs are Best</cite>
</blockquote>
```

Immediately following the quote, add the address for the bookstore. Since it contains contact information, it's appropriate to use the <address> tag, as follows:

Input ▼

```
<address style="font-style: normal;">The Bookworm Bookshop<br />
1345 Applewood Dr<br />
Springfield, CA 94325<br />
(415) 555-0034
</address>
```

▼ **Adding the Table of Contents**   The page you're creating will require a lot of scrolling to get from the top to the bottom. One nice enhancement is to add a small table of contents at the beginning of the page, listing the sections in a bulleted list. If a reader clicks one of the links in the table of contents, he'll automatically jump to the section that's of most interest to him. Because you've added the IDs already, it's easy to see where the links will take you.

You already have the heading for the table of contents. You just need to add the bulleted list and then create the links to the other sections on the page. The code looks like the following:

Input ▼

```
<h2 id="contents">Contents</h2>
<ul>
 <li><a href="#about">About the Bookworm Bookshop</a></li>
 <li><a href="#recent">Recent Titles</a></li>
 <li><a href="#upcoming">Upcoming Events</a></li>
</ul>
```

Figure 7.12 shows an example of the introductory portion of the Bookworm Bookshop page as it appears in a browser.

Output ▼

FIGURE 7.12
The top section of the Bookworm Bookshop page.

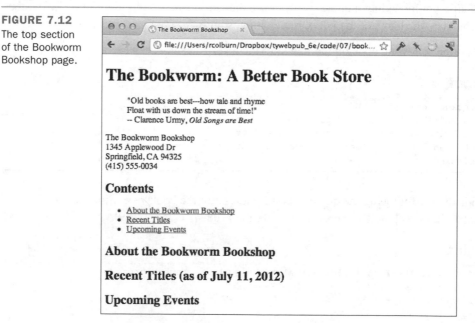

▼

Creating the Description of the Bookstore Now you come to the first descriptive subheading on the page, which you've added already. This section gives a description of the bookstore. After the heading (shown in the first line of the following example), I've arranged the description to include a list of features to make them stand out from the text better:

Input ▼

```
<h2 id="about">About the Bookworm Bookshop</h2>
<p>Since 1933, The Bookworm Bookshop has offered
rare and hard-to-find titles for the discerning reader.
The Bookworm offers:</p>
<ul>
<li>Friendly, knowledgeable, and courteous help</li>
<li>Free coffee and juice for our customers</li>
<li>A well-lit reading room so you can "try before you buy"</li>
<li>Four friendly cats: Esmerelda, Catherine, Dulcinea and Beatrice</li>
</ul>
```

Add a note about the hours the store is open and emphasize the actual numbers:

Input ▼

```
<p>Our hours are <strong>10am to 9pm</strong> weekdays,
<strong>noon to 7</strong> on weekends.</p>
```

Then, end the section with links to the table of contents and the top of the page, using the implicit `top` anchor:

Input ▼

```
<p><a href="#contents">Back to Contents</a> | <a href="#top">Back to Top</a></p>
```

Figure 7.13 shows you what the About the Bookworm Bookshop section looks like in a browser.

▼ **Output** ▼

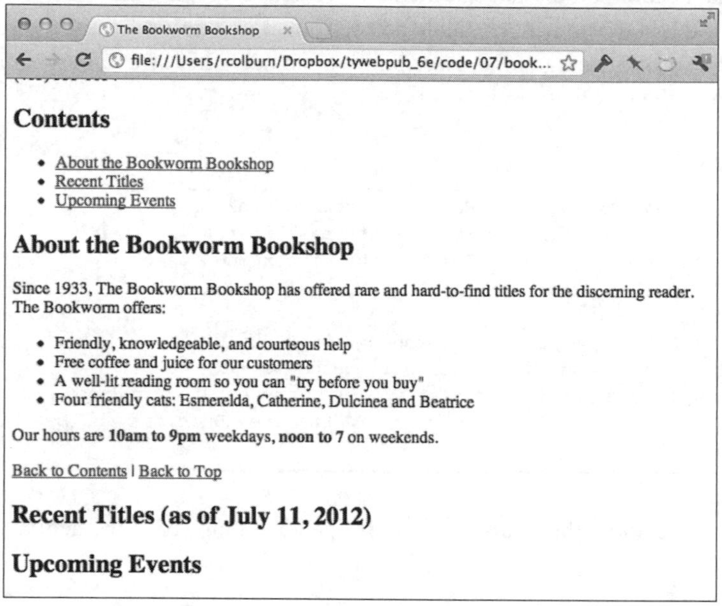

FIGURE 7.13
The About the
Bookworm
Bookshop section.

Creating the Recent Titles Section   The Recent Titles section itself is a classic link menu, as I described earlier in this section. Here you can put the list of titles in an unordered list, with the titles themselves as citations, by using the `<cite>` tag. End the section with another horizontal rule.

After the Recent Titles heading (shown in the first line in the following example), enter the following code:

```
<h2 id="recent">Recent Titles (as of July 11, 2012)</h2>
<ul>
<li>Sandra Bellweather, <cite>Belladonna</cite></li>
<li>Jonathan Tin, <cite>20-Minute Meals for One</cite></li>
<li>Maxwell Burgess, <cite>Legion of Thunder</cite></li>
<li>Alison Caine, <cite>Banquo's Ghost</cite></li>
</ul>
```

Now add the anchor tags to create the links. How far should the link extend? Should it include the whole line (author and title) or just the title of the book? This decision is a matter of preference, but remember that people viewing your page on mobile devices need longer links to be able to tap them with their fingers. Here, I linked only the titles of the books. At the same time, I also added links to the table of contents and the top of the ▼ page:

Input ▼

```
<h2 id="recent">Recent Titles (as of July 11, 2012)</h2>
  <ul>
    <li>Sandra Bellweather, <a href="belladonna.html">
      <cite>Belladonna</cite></a></li>
    <li>Johnathan Tin, <a href="20minmeals.html">
      <cite>20-Minute Meals for One</cite></a></li>
    <li>Maxwell Burgess, <a href="legion.html">
      <cite>Legion of Thunder</cite></a></li>
    <li>Alison Caine, <a href="banquo.html">
      <cite>Banquo's Ghost</cite></a></li>
  </ul>
  <p><a href="#contents">Back to Contents</a> | <a href="#top">Back to Top</a></p>
```

Note that I put the `<cite>` tag inside the link tag `<a>`. I could have just as easily put it outside the anchor tag; character style tags can go just about anywhere. But as I mentioned once before, be careful not to overlap tags. Your browser might not be able to understand what's going on, and it's invalid. In other words, don't do the following:

```
<a href="banquo.html"><cite>Banquo's Ghost</a></cite>
```

Take a look at how the Recent Titles section appears in Figure 7.14.

Output ▼

FIGURE 7.14
The Recent Titles
section.

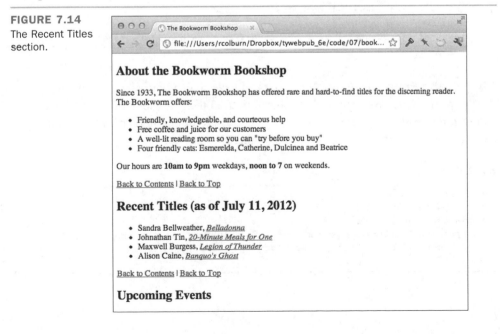

7

▼ **Completing the Upcoming Events Section** Next, move on to the Upcoming Events section. In the planning stages, you weren't sure whether this would be another link menu or whether the content would work better solely on this page. Again, this decision is a matter of preference. Here, because the amount of extra information is minimal, creating links for just a couple of sentences doesn't make much sense. So, for this section, create an unordered list using the `<ul>` tag. I've boldfaced a few phrases near the beginning of each paragraph. These phrases emphasize a summary of the event itself so that the text can be scanned quickly and ignored if the readers aren't interested.

As in the previous sections, you end the section with links to the top and to the table of contents:

```
<h2 id="upcoming">Upcoming Events</h2>
  <ul>
    <li><strong>The Wednesday Evening Book Review</strong> meets, appropriately,
    on Wednesday evenings at 7 pm for coffee and a round-table discussion.
    Call the Bookworm for information on joining the group.</li>
    <li><strong>The Children's Hour</strong> happens every Saturday at 1 pm and
    includes reading, games, and other activities. Cookies and milk are
    served.</li>
    <li><strong>Carole Fenney</strong> will be at the Bookworm on Sunday,
    January 19, to read from her book of poems <cite>Spiders in the Web.</
    cite></li>
    <li><strong>The Bookworm will be closed</strong> March 1st to remove a family
    of bats that has nested in the tower. We like the company, but not
    the mess they leave behind!</li>
  </ul>
  <p><a href="#contents">Back to Contents</a> | <a href="#top">Back to
  Top</a></p>
```

Signing the Page To finish, sign what you have so that your readers know who did the work. Here, I've separated the signature from the text with a rule line. I've also included the most recent revision date, my name as the webmaster, and a basic copyright (with a copyright symbol indicated by the numeric escape `&#169;`):

Input ▼

```
<address>
  Last Updated: July 11, 2012<br>
  Webmaster: Laura Lemay
  <a href="mailto:lemay@bookworm.com">lemay@bookworm.com</a><br>
  &copy; copyright 2012 the Bookworm<br>
</address>
```
▼

Figure 7.15 shows the signature at the bottom portion of the page as well as the Upcoming Events section.

Output ▼

FIGURE 7.15
The Upcoming Events section and the page signature.

Reviewing What You've Got   Here's the HTML code for the page so far:

```
<!DOCTYPE html>
<html>
  <head>
    <meta charset="UTF-8">
    <title>The Bookworm Bookshop</title>
  </head>
  <body>
    <h1>The Bookworm: A Better Book Store</h1>
    <blockquote>
      "Old books are best---how tale and rhyme<br>
      Float with us down the stream of time!"<br>
      -- Clarence Urmy, <cite>Old Songs are Best</cite>
    </blockquote>
    <address style="font-style: normal">The Bookworm Bookshop<br>
      1345 Applewood Dr<br>
      Springfield, CA 94325<br>
      (415) 555-0034
    </address>
```

7

```
<h2 id="contents">Contents</h2>
<ul>
  <li><a href="#about">About the Bookworm Bookshop</a></li>
  <li><a href ="#recent">Recent Titles</a></li>
  <li><a href ="#upcoming">Upcoming Events</a></li>
</ul>

<h2 id="about">About the Bookworm Bookshop</h2>
  <p>Since 1933, The Bookworm Bookshop has offered
  rare and hard-to-find titles for the discerning reader.
  The Bookworm offers:</p>
  <ul>
    <li>Friendly, knowledgeable, and courteous help</li>
    <li>Free coffee and juice for our customers</li>
    <li>A well-lit reading room so you can "try before you buy"</li>
    <li>Four friendly cats: Esmerelda, Catherine, Dulcinea and Beatrice</li>
  </ul>
  <p>Our hours are <strong>10am to 9pm</strong> weekdays,
  <strong>noon to 7</strong> on weekends.</p>
  <p><a href="#contents">Back to Contents</a> | <a href="#top">Back to Top
  </a></p>
<h2 id="recent">Recent Titles (as of July 11, 2012)</h2>
  <ul>
    <li>Sandra Bellweather, <a href="belladonna.html">
      <cite>Belladonna</cite></a></li>
    <li>Johnathan Tin, <a href="20minmeals.html">
      <cite>20-Minute Meals for One</cite></a></li>
    <li>Maxwell Burgess, <a href="legion.html">
      <cite>Legion of Thunder</cite></a></li>
    <li>Alison Caine, <a href="banquo.html">
      <cite>Banquo's Ghost</cite></a></li>
  </ul>
  <p><a href="#contents">Back to Contents</a> | <a href="#top">Back to Top</
a></p>

<h2 id="upcoming">Upcoming Events</h2>
  <ul>
    <li><strong>The Wednesday Evening Book Review</strong> meets,
    appropriately, on Wednesday evenings at 7 pm for coffee and a round-table.
    discussion Call the Bookworm for information on joining the group.</li>
    <li><strong>The Children's Hour</strong> happens every Saturday at 1 pm
    and includes reading, games, and other activities. Cookies and milk are
    served.</li>
    <li><strong>Carole Fenney</strong> will be at the Bookworm on Sunday,
    January 19, to read from her book of poems <cite>Spiders in the Web.
    </cite></li>
    <li><strong>The Bookworm will be closed</strong> March 1st to remove a
    family of bats that has nested in the tower. We like the company, but not
    the mess they leave behind!</li>
```

```
  </ul>
  <p><a href="#contents">Back to Contents</a> | <a href="#top">Back to
    Top</a></p>

  <address>
    Last Updated: July 11, 2012<br>
    Webmaster: Laura Lemay
    <a href="mailto:lemay@bookworm.com">lemay@bookworm.com</a><br>
    &copy; copyright 2012 the Bookworm<br>
  </address>

  </body>
</html>
```

Now you have some headings, some text, some topics, and some links, which form the basis for an excellent web page. With most of the content in place, now you need to consider what other links you might want to create or what other features you might want to add to this page.

For example, the introductory section has a note about the four cats owned by the bookstore. Although you didn't plan for them in the original organization, you could easily create web pages describing each cat (and showing pictures) and then link them back to this page, one link (and one page) per cat.

Is describing the cats important? As the designer of the page, that's up to you to decide. You could link all kinds of things from this page if you have interesting reasons to link them (and something to link to). Link the bookstore's address to an online mapping service so that people can get driving directions. Link the quote to an online encyclopedia of quotes. Link the note about free coffee to the Coffee home page.

My reason for bringing up this point here is that after you have some content in place on your web pages, there might be opportunities for extending the pages and linking to other places that you didn't think of when you created your original plan. So, when you're just about finished with a page, stop and review what you have, both in the plan and on your web page.

For the purposes of this example, stop here and stick with the links you have. You're close enough to being done, and I don't want to make this lesson any longer than it already is!

Testing the Result Now that all the code is in place, you can preview the results in a browser. Figures 7.12 through 7.15 show how it looks in a browser. Actually, these figures show what the page looks like after you fix the spelling errors, the forgotten closing tags, and all the other strange bugs that always seem to creep into an HTML file the first time you create it. These problems always seem to happen no matter how good you are

▼ at creating web pages. If you use an HTML editor or some other help tool, your job will be easier, but you'll always seem to find mistakes. That's what previewing is for—so you can catch the problems before you actually make the document available to other people. Plus, the more browsers that you view your pages in, the fewer problems your customers ▲ will see.

Summary

Tags, tags, and more tags! In this lesson, you learned about most of the remaining tags in the HTML language for presenting text, and quite a few of the tags for additional text formatting and presentation. You also put together a real-life HTML home page. You could stop now and create quite presentable web pages, but more cool stuff is to come. So, don't put down the book yet.

Table 7.2 presents a quick summary of all the tags and attributes you've learned about in this lesson. Table 7.3 summarizes the CSS properties that have been described in this lesson.

TABLE 7.2 HTML Tags from Lesson 7

Tag	Attribute	Use
`<address>...</address>`		A signature for each web page; typically occurs near the bottom of each document and contains contact or copyright information.
`<b>...</b>`		Bold text.
`<blockquote>...</blockquote>`		A quotation longer than a few words.
	cite	The URL that was the source for the quotation.
`<cite>...</cite>`		A citation.
`<code>...</code>`		A code sample.
`<dfn>...</dfn>`		A definition, or a term about to be defined.
`<em>...</em>`		Emphasized text.
`<i>...</i>`		Italic text.
`<kbd>...</kbd>`		Text to be typed in by the user.
`<pre>...</pre>`		Preformatted text; all spaces, tabs, and returns are retained. Text is printed in a monospaced font.

Tag	Attribute	Use
`<q>...</q>`		An inline quotation.
	`cite`	The URL that was the source for the quotation.
`<samp>...</samp>`		Sample text.
`<small>...</small>`		Text in a smaller font than the text around it.
`<strong>...</strong>`		Strongly emphasized text.
`<sub>...</sub>`		Subscript text.
`<sup>...</sup>`		Superscript text.
`<u>...</u>`		Underlined text.
`<var>...</var>`		A variable name.
`<span>...</span>`		A generic tag used to apply styles to a particular bit of text.
`<hr>`		A horizontal rule line at the given position in the text. There's no closing tag in HTML for `<hr>`; for XHTML, add a space and forward slash (/) at the end of the tag and its attributes (for example, `<hr size="2" width="75%" />`).
	`size`	The thickness of the rule, in pixels. (Obsolete in HTML5.)
	`width`	The width of the rule, either in exact pixels or as a percentage of page width (for example, 50%). (Obsolete in HTML5.)
	`align`	The alignment of the rule on the page. Possible values are `left`, `right`, and `center`. (Obsolete in HTML5.)
	`noshade`	Displays the rule without three-dimensional shading. (Obsolete in HTML5.)
` `		A line break; starts the next character on the next line but doesn't create a new paragraph or list item. There's no closing tag in HTML for ` `; for XHTML, add a space and forward slash (/) at the end of the tag and its attributes (for example, `<br clear="left" />`).

7

TABLE 7.3 CSS Properties from Lesson 7

Property	Use/Values
text-decoration	Specifies which sort of decoration should be applied to the text. The values are underline, overline, line-through, blink, and none.
font-style	Specifies whether text should be italicized. The three values are normal, italic, and oblique.
font-weight	Specifies the degree to which text should be emboldened. Options are normal, bold, bolder, lighter, and 100 to 900.
font-family	Enables you to specify the font used for text. You can choose families such as serif, sans serif, and monospace, or specific font names. You can also specify more than one font or font family.
font-variant	Sets the font variant to normal or small-caps.
font-size	Enables you to specify the font size in any unit supported by CSS.

Workshop

Here you are at the close of this lesson (a long one!) and facing yet another workshop. This lesson covered a lot of ground, so I'll try to keep the questions easy. There are a couple of exercises that focus on building some additional pages for your website. Ready?

Q&A

Q If line breaks appear in HTML, can I also do page breaks?

A HTML doesn't have a page break tag. Consider what the term *page* means in a web document. If each document on the web is a single page, the only way to produce a page break is to split your HTML document into separate files and link them.

Even within a single document, browsers have no concept of a page; each HTML document simply scrolls by continuously. If you consider a single screen a page, you still can't have what results in a page break in HTML. The screen size in each browser is different. It's based on not only the browser itself, but also the size of the monitor on which it runs, the number of lines defined, the font currently being used, and other factors that you cannot control from HTML.

When you're designing your web pages, don't get too hung up on the concept of a page the way it exists in paper documents. Remember, HTML's strength is its flexibility for multiple kinds of systems and formats. Instead, think in terms of creating small chunks of information and how they link together to form a complete presentation.

If page breaks are essential to your document, you might consider saving it in the PDF format and making it available for download.

Q How can I include em dashes or curly quotes (typesetter's quotes) in my HTML files?

A There are entities for all of these characters, but they might not be supported by all browsers or on all platforms. Most people still don't use them. To add an em dash, use `&mdash;`. The curly quote entities are `&ldquo;` for the left quote and `&rdquo;` for the right quote. Similarly, you can create curly single quotes using `&lsquo;` and `&rsquo;`.

Quiz

1. What makes an HTML tag semantic?
2. What are some things that the `<pre>` (preformatted text) tag can be used for?
3. What's the most common use of the `<address>` tag?
4. Without looking at Table 7.2, list eight semantic tags and what they're used for.

Quiz Answers

1. Semantic HTML tags are tags that provide meaning to the enclosed content, beyond just the framework of the document.
2. Preformatted text can be used for text-based tables, code examples, ASCII art, and any other web page content that requires extra spaces to align characters.
3. The `<address>` tag is most commonly used for signature-like entities on a web page. These include the name of the author of the web page, contact information, dates, copyright notices, or warnings. Address information usually appears at the bottom of a web page.
4. The semantic tags are `<em>` (for emphasized text), `<strong>` (for strongly emphasized text), `<code>` (for programming code), `<samp>` (similar to `<code>`), `<kbd>` (to indicate user keyboard input), `<var>` (for variable names), `<dfn>` (for definitions), and `<cite>` (for short quotes or citations).

7

Exercises

1. Now that you've had a taste of building your first really thorough web page, take a stab at your own home page. What can you include that would entice people to dig deeper into your pages? Don't forget to include links to other pages on your site.

2. Try out your home page in several browsers. Web developers have to get used to the fact that their designs are at the mercy of their users, and it's best to see right away how different browsers and platforms treat pages.

LESSON 8
Using CSS to Style a Site

In the past few lessons, I've discussed how to lay out web pages using *Hypertext Markup Language* (HTML) tags. In this lesson, I describe how you can create complex pages using Cascading Style Sheets (CSS). You've already learned about the advantages CSS can provide for formatting smaller snippets of text. In this lesson, you'll learn how to use CSS to control the appearance of an entire page.

The following topics are covered:

- Creating style sheets and including them in a page
- Linking to external style sheets
- Using selectors to apply styles to elements on a page
- Examining units of measure supported by CSS
- Considering the CSS box model
- Positioning elements using CSS
- Applying styles to tables and the `<body>` tag
- Using CSS to create multicolumn layouts

Including Style Sheets in a Page

Thus far, when I've discussed style sheets, I've applied them using the `style` attribute. For example, I've shown how you can modify the font for some text using tags such as `<span>` or how you can modify the appearance of a list item by applying a style within an `<li>` tag. If you rely on the `style` attribute of tags to apply CSS, if you want to embolden every paragraph on a page, you need to put `style="font-weight: bold"` in every `<p>` tag. This is no improvement over just using `<p><b>` and `</b></p>` instead. The good news is that the style attribute is the least efficient method of applying styles to a page or a site. In this section, I'll explain more powerful approaches.

Creating Page-Level Styles

First, let's look at how we can apply styles to our page at the page level. Thus far, you've seen how styles are applied, but you haven't seen any style sheets. Here's what one looks like:

```
<style type="text/css">
h1 { font-size: x-large; font-weight: bold; }
h2 { font-size: large; font-weight: bold; }
</style>
```

The `<style>` tag should be included within the `<head>` tag on your page. The `type` attribute indicates the MIME type of the style sheet. `text/css` is the only value you'll use. It's not required in HTML5, and most designers leave it out. The body of the style sheet consists of a series of rules. All rules have the same structure:

```
selector { property1: value1; property2: value2; .. }
```

Each rule consists of a selector followed by a list of properties and values associated with those properties. All the properties being set for a selector are enclosed in curly braces, as shown in the example. You can include any number of properties for each selector, and they must be separated from one another using semicolons. You can also include a semicolon following the last property/value pair in the rule, or not, but best practices recommend that you do.

You should already be familiar with CSS properties and values because that's what you use in the `style` attribute of tags. Selectors are something new. I discuss them in detail in a bit. The ones I've used thus far have the same names as tags. If you use `h1` as a selector, the rule will apply to any `<h1>` tags on the page. By the same token, if you use `p` as your selector, it will apply to `<p>` tags.

Creating Sitewide Style Sheets

You can't capture the real efficiency of style sheets until you start creating sitewide style sheets. You can store all of your style information in a file and include it in your Web pages using an HTML tag. A CSS file contains the body of a `<style>` tag. To turn the style sheet from the previous section into a separate file, you could just save the following to a file called `styles.css`:

```
h1 { font-size: x-large; font-weight: bold; }
h2 { font-size: large; font-weight: bold; }
```

In truth, the extension of the file is irrelevant, but the extension `.css` is the de facto standard for style sheets, so you should probably use it. After you've created the style sheet file, you can include it in your page using the `<link>` tag, like this:

```
<link rel="stylesheet" href="styles.css" type="text/css" >
```

The `type` attribute is the same as that of the `<style>` tag and is not required in HTML5. The `href` attribute is the same as that of the `<a>` tag. It can be a relative URL, an absolute URL, or even a fully qualified URL that points to a different server. As long as the browser can fetch the file, any URL will work. This means that you can just as easily use other people's style sheets as your own.

There's another attribute of the link tag, too: `media`. This enables you to specify different style sheets for different display mediums. For example, you can specify one for print, another for screen display, and others for things like aural browsers for use with screen readers. Not all browsers support the different media types, but if your style sheet is specific to a particular medium, you should include it. The options are `screen`, `print`, `projection`, `aural`, `braille`, `tty`, `tv`, `embossed`, `handheld` and `all`. I go into more uses for this attribute in Lesson 16, "Using Responsive Web Design."

You can also specify titles for your style sheets using the `title` attribute, as well as alternative style sheets by setting the `rel` attribute to `alternative style sheet`. Theoretically, this means that you could specify multiple style sheets for your page (with the one set to `rel="stylesheet"` as the preferred style sheet). The browser would then enable the user to select from among them based on the title you provide. You can use JavaScript to select from the different style sheets.

As it is, you can include links to multiple style sheets in your pages, and all the rules will be applied. This means that you can create one general style sheet for your entire site, and then another specific to a page or to a section of the site, too.

As you can see, the capability to link to external style sheets provides you with a powerful means for managing the look and feel of your site. After you've set up a sitewide

8

style sheet that defines the styles for your pages, changing things such as the headline font and background color for your pages all at once is trivial. Before CSS, making these kinds of changes required a lot of manual labor or a facility with tools that had search and replace functionality for multiple files. Now it requires quick edits to a single linked style sheet.

Selectors

You've already seen one type of selector for CSS: element names. Any tag can serve as a CSS selector, and the rules associated with that selector will be applied to all instances of that tag on the page. You can add a rule to the `<b>` tag that sets the font weight to normal if you choose to do so, or you can italicize every paragraph on your page by applying a style to the `<p>` tag. Applying styles to the `<body>` tag using the body selector enables you to apply pagewide settings. However, you can apply styles on a more granular basis in a number of ways and apply them across multiple types of elements using a single selector.

First, there's a way to apply styles to more than one selector at the same time. Suppose, for instance, that you want all unordered lists, ordered lists, and paragraphs on a page to be displayed using blue text. Instead of writing individual rules for each of these elements, you can write a single rule that applies to all of them. Here's the syntax:

```
p, ol, ul { color: blue; }
```

A comma-separated list indicates that the style rule should apply to all the tags listed. The preceding rule is just an easier way to write the following:

```
p { color: blue; }
ol { color: blue; }
ul { color: blue; }
```

Contextual Selectors

Contextual selectors are also available. These are used to apply styles to elements only when they're nested within other specified elements. Take a look at this rule:

```
ol em { color: blue; }
```

The fact that I left out the comma indicates that this rule applies only to `em` elements that are nested within ordered lists. Let's look at two slightly different rules:

```
p cite { font-style: italic; font-weight: normal; }
li cite { font-style: normal; font-weight: bold; }
```

In this case, `<cite>` tags that appear within `<p>` tags will be italicized. If a `<cite>` tag appears inside a list item, the contents will be rendered in boldface. Let's add in one more rule:

```
cite { color: green; }
p cite { font-style: italic; font-weight: normal; }
li cite { font-style: normal; font-weight: bold; }
```

In this case, we have one rule that applies to all `<cite>` tags, and the two others that you've already seen. In this case, the contents of all `<cite>` tags will be green, and the appropriately nested `<cite>` tags will take on those styles, too. Here's one final example:

```
cite { color: green; }
p cite { font-style: italic; font-weight: normal; color: red; }
li cite { font-style: normal; font-weight: bold; color: blue; }
```

In this case, the nested styles override the default style for the `<cite>` tag because they are a more *specific* style definition. The contents of `<cite>` tags that don't meet the criteria of the nested rules will appear in green. The nested rules will override the color specified in the less-specific rule, so for `<cite>` tags that are inside `<p>` tags, the contents will be red. Inside list items, the contents will be blue.

The ability to override property settings by using more specific selectors is what provides the ability to set styles with the precision of the `style` attribute from a style sheet. This is called CSS *specificity*.

Classes and IDs

Sometimes selecting by tag (even using contextual selectors) isn't specific enough for your needs, and you must create your own classifications for use with CSS. There are two attributes supported by all HTML tags: `class` and `id`. The `class` attribute is used to classify elements, and the `id` attribute is for assigning identifiers to unique elements.

To apply a selector to a class, use a leading . in the class name in your style sheet. So, if you have a tag like this

```
<div class="imprtnt">Some text.</div>
```

then you write the rule like this

```
.imprtnt { color: red; font-weight: bold; }
```

Any element with the class `imprtnt` will appear in bold red text. If you want to give this treatment to only important `<div>`s, you can include the element name along with the class name in your rule.

```
div.imprtnt { color: red; font-weight: bold; }
p.imprtnt { color: blue; font-weight: bold; }
```

In this case, if a `<p>` tag is has the class `imprtnt`, the text inside will be blue. If a `<div>` has the `imprtnt` class, its text will be red. You could also rewrite the preceding two rules as follows:

```
.imprtnt { font-weight: bold; }
div.imprtnt { color: red; }
p.imprtnt { color: blue; }
```

All members of the `imprtnt` class will be bold and `<div>` tags with the class `imprtnt` will be red, whereas paragraphs with the class will be blue. If you assigned the `imprtnt` class to another tag, like `<li>`, the default color would be applied to it.

Whenever you want to specify styles for a single element, assign it an ID. The element must be unique on the page—the only element with that identifier. As you'll learn later in the book, assigning IDs to elements is also very useful when using JavaScript because doing so lets you write scripts that reference individual items specifically. For now, however, let's look at how IDs are used with CSS. Generally, a page will have only one footer. To identify it, use the `id` attribute:

```
<div id="footer">
Copyright 2010, Example Industries.
</div>
```

You can then write CSS rules that apply to that element by referencing the ID. Here's an example:

```
#footer { font-size: small; }
```

As you can see, when you refer to IDs in your style sheets, you need to prepend a # on the front to distinguish them from class names and element names. Note that there's no additional facility for referring to IDs that are associated with particular elements. IDs are required to be unique, so there's no need to qualify them further. Finally, there's nothing to say that you can't mix up all these selectors in one rule, like so:

```
h1, #headline, .heading, div.imprtnt { font-size: large; color: green; }
```

As you can see, I've included several types of selectors in one rule. This is perfectly valid if you want to set the same properties for a number of different selectors. Classes also work with contextual selectors:

```
ul li.important { color: red; }
```

In this case, list items in the `imprtnt` class will be red if they occur in an unordered list. If they're in an ordered list, the rule will not be applied.

8

CAUTION

> One common mistake is to include the . when assigning classes
> or the # when assigning IDs. The punctuation should only be
> used in the style sheet. In the attributes, leave them off. So
> `id="primary"` is correct; `id="#primary"` is not.

You can also use selectors that are applied only to elements that have all of the classes specified for a rule. For example, you can set up three selectors like this:

```
.yellow { color: yellow; }
.blue { color: blue; }
.yellow.blue { color: green; }
```

The paragraph that follows would be green because it has the class `blue` and the class `yellow`:

```
<p class="blue yellow">My green paragraph.</p>
```

What Cascading Means

You may be wondering where the *cascading* in Cascading Style Sheets comes from. They are so named because styles cascade from parent elements to their children. To override a style that has been applied via cascading, you just need to set the same property using a more specific selector.

Here's an example style sheet that will illustrate how cascading works:

```
body { font-size: 200%; }
div { font-size: 80%; }
p { font-size: 80%; }
span.smaller { font-size: 80%; font-weight: bold; }
#smallest { font-size: 80%; font-weight: normal; }
```

Figure 8.1 shows what the page looks like when that style sheet is applied to the following HTML:

Input ▼

```
<div>
  This text is in a div but not in a paragraph.

  <p>This test is in a paragraph.</p>

  <p><span class="smaller">This is in a span with the class "smaller"
inside a paragraph.</span></p>
```

```
<p><span class="smaller"><span id="smallest">This text is in a
span with the ID "smallest".</span></span></p>
</div>
```

Output ▼

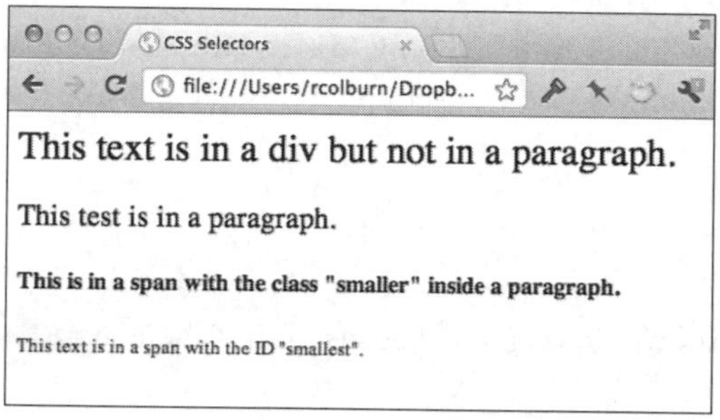

FIGURE 8.1
How cascading
styles work.

When percentage units are used in style sheets, the percentage is applied to the value that's inherited as the styles cascade down. To start, all the text on the page is set to a font size of 200% using the selector for the `<body>` tag. Then I use a variety of selectors to make the text progressively smaller as the styles cascade down through the style sheet. With CSS, the styles that are applied to a given element are calculated from all the selectors that match that style in the style sheet.

It's also possible to override styles. This style sheet sets the font weight for spans with the class `smaller` to `bold`. The element with the ID `smallest` has its font weight set to normal. In Figure 8.1, you'll see that the last line is not bold. It inherits the font weight from the `span.smaller` selector, but the `#smallest` selector overrides it.

Units of Measure

One of the most confusing aspects of CSS is the units of measure it provides. Four types of units can be specified in CSS: length units, percentage units, color units, and URLs.

There are two kinds of length units: absolute and relative. *Absolute* units theoretically correspond to a unit of measure in the real world, such as an inch, a centimeter, or a point. *Relative* units are based on some more arbitrary unit of measure. Table 8.1 contains a full list of length units.

TABLE 8.1 Length Units in CSS

Unit	Measurement
em	Relative; height of the element's font
ex	Relative; height of x character in the element's font
px	Relative; pixels, which are relative to the viewing device
in	Absolute; inches
cm	Absolute; centimeters
mm	Absolute; millimeters
pt	Absolute; points
pc	Absolute; picas
rem	Relative; height of the root element's font (new in CSS3)
vh	Relative; percent of the viewport height (new in CSS3)
vw	Relative; percent of the viewport width (new in CSS3)

8

The absolute measurements seem great, except that an inch isn't really an inch when it comes to measuring things on a screen. Given the variety of browser sizes and resolutions supported, the browser doesn't really know how to figure out what an inch is. For example, you might have a laptop with a 15-inch display running at 1440 by 900 pixels. I might have a 23-inch CRT running at roughly the same resolution. If the browser thinks that one inch is 96 pixels, a headline set to 1in may appear as less than an inch on your monitor or more than an inch on mine. Using relative units is safer.

In this lesson, I use one length unit: px. It's my favorite for sizing most things. However, other relative units can also be useful. For example, if you want paragraphs on your page to appear as double spaced, you can specify them like this:

```
p { line-height: 2em; }
```

CSS3 also brings in three new relative units that are very useful: rem, vh, and vw. The rem unit acts like the em unit; it is relative to the font size. But rather than being relative to the current element's font size, it's relative to the base font size for the whole page. This means that you can set values that don't combine with each other. Many designers did not like the em unit because it would combine and result in font sizes that were much larger or smaller than they expected. rem acts the way most designers expect.

The other two new units are vh and vw. These are relative to the viewport window. This is particularly useful if you are designing pages to look good on mobile and smaller screen devices. By setting the text size to be relative to the viewport, you can ensure that it will be legible even on small screens.

Percentage units are also extremely common. They're written as you'd expect: `200%` (with no spaces). The thing to remember with percentages is that they're always relative to something. If you set a font size to 200%, it will be double the size of the font it inherited through CSS, or 200% of the browser's default font size if no font size has been applied to that element. If you set a `<div>`'s width to 50%, it will be half as wide as the enclosing element (or the browser window, if there's no enclosing element). When you use percentages, always keep in mind what you're talking about a percent of.

Using Percentage Units

When you use percentages as units, bear in mind that the percentage applies not to the size of the page, but rather to the size of the box that encloses the box to which the style applies. For example, if you have a `<div>` with its width set to 50% inside a `<div>` with its width set to `500px`, the inner `<div>` will be 250 pixels wide. However, if the outer `<div>` were also set to 50%, it would be half as wide as the browser window, and the inner `<div>` would be 25% of the width of the browser window.

Color units can be specified in a variety of ways. Some colors can be specified by name, or you can use color codes. I'll talk about how colors are specified shortly.

Most of the time, when you use URL units, they're used in the `<a>` tag or `<img>` tag. In CSS, they're usually included to specify the location of a background image or a bullet image for a list. Generally, URLs are specified like this:

```
url('http://www.example.com/')
```

Specifying Colors

As you've already seen, browsers understand some color names. Unfortunately, once you get past a few common names like `black` and `white`, things become more uncertain. It's better to define colors by the specific shade. For reasons related to the way computer displays work, in CSS and HTML, colors are created by mixing red, green, and blue. When you specify a color, you specify the intensity of those three colors and a distinct color results.

Aside from color names, there are several ways to specify colors using CSS:

- **Hexadecimal**—A six-character string that comprises three two-digit hexadecimal numbers that represent the intensity of red, green, and blue on a scale of 00 to FF (255 in decimal)

- **Hexadecimal shorthand**—A three-character string that comprises three single-digit hexadecimal numbers that are duplicated to represent the intensity of red, green, and blue on a scale of 00 to FF (255 in decimal)
- **RGB**—Three percentages representing the intensity of red, green, and blue
- **RGB**—Three decimal numbers representing the intensity of red, green, and blue on a scale of 0 to 255
- **HSL**—Three numbers representing the hue (from 0 to 360 degrees), saturation percentage, and lightness percentage
- **Transparency or alpha channel**—Add a fourth number to the RGB and HSL colors that ranges from 0 to 1 to specify the opacity

8

The approaches differ in terms of notation and precision. The methods that scale from 0 to 255 are more precise than the percentages, which run from 0 to 100, and the single hexadecimal digits, which are meant as a shorthand for writing common colors.

In practical terms, nearly everyone uses the six digit hexadecimal strings because that form of notation was supported in HTML for defining colors as well. The other approaches were not. Let's examine a few shades to look a little deeper at how CSS colors work:

black rgb(0,0,0) 000000 hsl(0,0,0)

white rgb(255,255,255) FFFFFF hsl(0,0,100)

red rgb(255,0,0) FF0000 hsl(0,100,50)

yellow rgb(255,255,0) FFFF00 hsl(60,100,50)

coral rgb(255,127,80) FF7F50 hsl(16,100,66)

As you can see, black is created by setting all three colors to zero intensity. White is created by setting all three colors to maximum intensity. The brightest shade of red has the hue red (0) at 100% saturation and 50% lightness. Yellow is maximum red and green and no blue. Coral is a mixture of all three shades, with an emphasis on red. The RGB units and hexadecimal units are identical—the only difference is in notation.

CSS added the ability to make colors transparent with the alpha channel on RGB and HSL colors. Colors are assumed to be 100% opaque. However, if you convert to RGBa or HSLa by adding a number from 0 to 1, you can make your colors see through. For example, red (`rgb(255,0,0)`) becomes pink when displayed at 50% transparent on a white background.

```
rgba(255,0,0,0.5)
```

Web designers tend to prefer RGB or HSL notation because it is very easy to add opacity information by switching to RGBa or HSLa.

Given that there are millions of possible colors, how do you find the colors you want to use? Generally speaking, you'll either use a color picker to choose a color from a palette, or you'll use a sampling tool to grab a color from a source on your screen—a picture, a Web page, whatever.

Color Schemer, available at http://www.colorschemer.com/online.html, is one of the better color pickers on the Web. It enables you to view several colors next to each other to see how they match and will even suggest colors that match the ones you choose. The current Color Schemer interface appears in Figure 8.2.

FIGURE 8.2
Color Schemer.

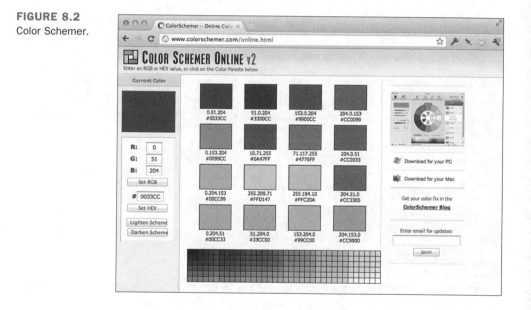

Another is Adobe Color CC at https://color.adobe.com/. It makes it easy to create your own color schemes and to browse and rate color schemes created by others. It's a great place to find inspiration if you're thinking about adding color to a site.

If you want to sample colors from Web pages, there are browser add-ons like ColorZilla for Firefox or Eye Dropper for Google Chrome. Most graphics programs also provide color sampling tools that you can use.

Editing Styles with Developer Tools

When you start working with full-fledged style sheets, it becomes easier to manipulate those style sheets using the Chrome Developer Tools (or the tools for other browsers). Figure 8.3 shows the Chrome Developer Tools for the page in Figure 8.1.

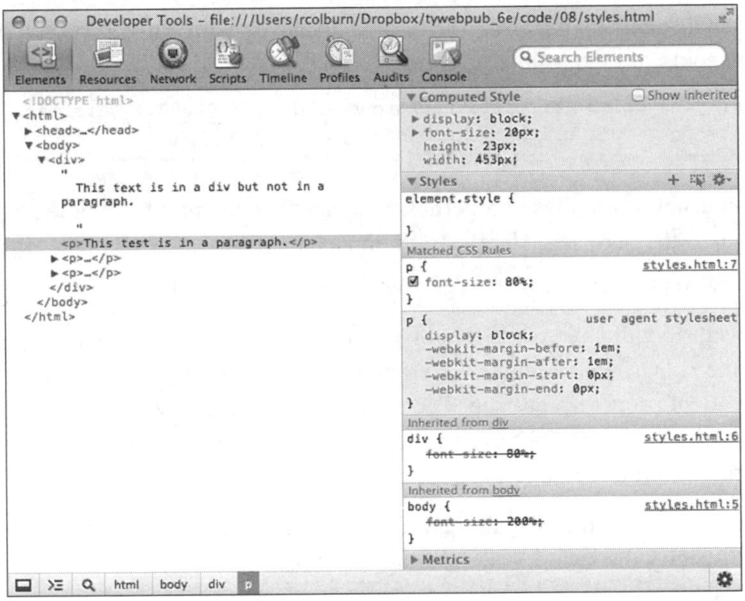

8

FIGURE 8.3
Viewing and modi-
fying CSS in the
Chrome Developer
Tools.

As you can see, the styles that apply to the current element are displayed on the right. In this case, the style sheet on the page supplies one style that sets the `font-size` to `80%` for `<p>` tags, and the user agent style sheet provides others. The user agent style sheet represents the browser defaults. There are also inherited styles listed, with the rules marked out. That's because the style for the `<p>` tag overrides them.

You can click on the styles in the panel to the right to modify the values, disable and re-enable the styles, and even add new style rules. This enables you to experiment with the styles on the page easily.

As your style sheets become more complex, a large number of styles can be applied to a specific element. The Computed Styles provide a view of the actual styles applied to the element from all sources.

Using Color

Using CSS, you can easily set up a color scheme for your entire website or just tweak the colors of specific elements on a page. There are two key properties when it comes to assigning colors to elements using CSS—color and background-color. For elements with borders, you can also set the border color using the border-color property.

To indicate that a paragraph should be displayed with white text on a black background, you could use the following code:

```
<p style="color: #ffffff; background-color: #000000;">This paragraph has
white text on a black background.</p>
```

You can also use these properties to adjust the colors on the whole page by applying them to the body tag. Here's an example:

```
<body style="color: #ffffff; background-color: #0000ff;">
```

This page will have white text on a blue background. You can also specify colors as part of the background and border properties, which allow you to set the values for a whole family of properties at once. The background property will be discussed in Lesson 9, "Using Images on Your Web Pages," because most of its subproperties are associated with background images.

To set the link color for all the links on a page, you need to use a style sheet for the page and specify the style for the <a> tag, like this:

```
<style>
    a { color: #ff9933; }
</style>
```

What about active links and visited links? CSS provides pseudo-classes that apply to links in particular states, as follows:

a:link	Applies to unvisited links.
a:visited	Applies to links that the user has visited.
a:hover	Applies to links when the user has her mouse pointer over the link.
a:active	Like the alink attribute, this selector is used when the user is clicking on the link.

As you can see, these selectors provide access to an additional state that the old attributes did not: the hover state. Here's an example that specifies the colors for links in each of their states:

```
<style type="text/css">
    a { color: #ff9933; }
    a:visited { color: #bbbbbb; }
    a:hover { color: #E58A2E; }
    a:active { color: #FFA64D; }
</style>
```

Pseudo-classes are most commonly used with links, but there are a number of other pseudo-classes that can also be used that I'll talk about later in this lesson.

Links

You already know how to adjust the colors of elements on a page, but links are a bit different. They're more complicated than other types of elements because they can exist in multiple states: an unvisited link, a visited link, an active link, and a link that the user currently has the pointer over. Using CSS, you can change the color of a link when the user mouses over it (referred to as the *hover* state) as opposed to when he's currently clicking it (the *active* state).

Another advantage of CSS is that you can change the color schemes for links on the same page rather than being forced to use one scheme throughout. Finally, you can turn off link underlining if you want. For example, here's a style sheet that turns off link underlining for navigation links, renders them in boldface, and keeps the same color for visited and unvisited links:

```
a:link   { color: blue; }
a:active { color: red; }
a:visited { color: purple; }
a:hover  { color: red; }
a.nav    { font-weight: bold;
        text-decoration: none; }
a.nav:hover, a.nav: active { background-color: yellow;
              color: red; }
a.nav:link, a.nav:visited { color: green; }
```

From the style sheet, you can see that for all `<a>` tags in the class `nav`, the `text-decoration` property is set to `none`, which turns off underlining, and `font-weight` is set to `bold`. For `<a>` tags on the rest of the page, the underlining remains on, but I've set it up so that when the mouse is over the links, they turn red. For navigation links, when the mouse is over the links, the background of the element turns yellow and the text turns red.

CAUTION

> You can use pretty much any property you like with the pseudo-selectors for links, and browsers that support them will dynamically reflow the page to accommodate the change. However, changes that affect the size of the element (such as boldfacing the text dynamically or increasing the font size) can be very jarring to users, so use them cautiously.

The Box Model

When working with CSS, it helps to think of every element on a page as being contained within a box. This is true of inline elements like `<a>` or block-level elements like `<p>`. Each of these boxes is contained within three larger boxes, and the entire set of four is referred to as the CSS box model. Figure 8.4 shows a diagram of the box model.

FIGURE 8.4
The CSS box model.

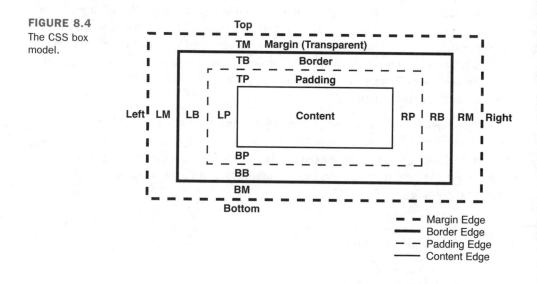

The innermost box contains the content of the element. Surrounding that is the padding, then the border, and finally, the outermost layer (the margin). In addition to properties that you can use to change how the content is displayed, CSS provides properties that can be used to change the padding, border, and margins around each box. In this section, you'll learn how to modify all the layers in the box model. If you get confused about how the layers are ordered, just refer to Figure 8.4.

The Chrome Developer Tools will display the box properties for an element so that you can see its current size along with its border, margin, and padding. You can use the Inspect tool to choose an element on the page, or you can locate an element in the source by way of the Elements tab. Then choose Metrics in the right column, and you'll see a box representing the element along with its properties. You can see the Metrics view in Figure 8.5.

FIGURE 8.5
The Metrics view in the Chrome Developer Tools.

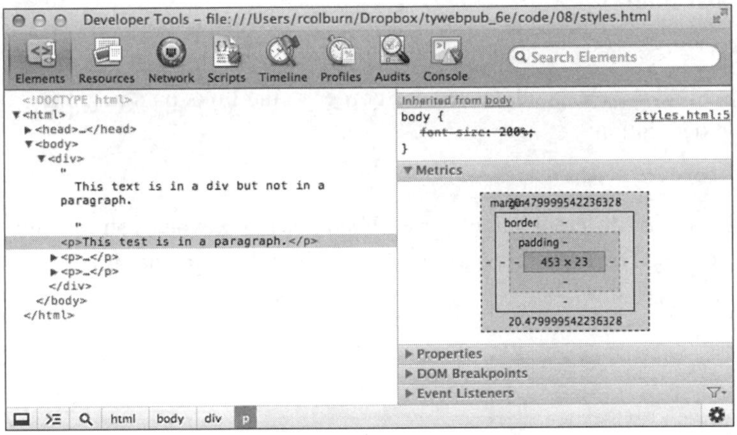

Borders

Before I talk about padding or margins, I want to talk about borders. CSS provides several properties for adding borders around elements and changing how they are displayed. Using CSS, you can apply a border to any box.

The `border-style` property specifies the type of border that will be displayed. Valid options for the `border-style` are `none`, `dotted`, `dashed`, `solid`, `double`, `groove`, `ridge`, `inset`, `outset`, and `inherit`. Most of the styles alter the border appearance, but `none` and `inherit` are special. Setting the `border-style` to `none` disables borders, and `inherit` uses the `border-style` inherited from a less-specific selector.

The `border-width` property specifies how wide the border around a box should be. Borders are usually specified in pixels, but any CSS unit of measurement can be used. To create a 1-pixel, dashed border around all the anchors on a page, you use the following CSS:

```
a { border-width: 1px; border-style: solid; }
```

The final border style, `border-color`, is used to set the color for a border. To set the border color for links to red, you use the following style declaration:

```
a { border-color: red; }
```

You can also set border properties for an element using what's called a *shorthand property*. Instead of using the three separate border properties, you can apply them all simultaneously as long as you put the values in the right order, using the `border` property. It's used as follows:

```
selector { border: style width color; }
```

So, to add a three-pixel dashed red border to the links on a page, you use the following style decoration:

```
a { border: dashed 3px red; }
```

You can use different values for each side of a box when you're using any of the box properties. There are two ways to do so. The first is to add directions to the property names, as follows:

```
a {
  border-left-width: 3px;
  border-left-style: dotted;
  border-left-color: green;
}
```

The directions are `top`, `bottom`, `left`, and `right`. Alternatively, you can set the values for each side. If you specify four values, they will be applied to the top, right, bottom, and left, in that order. If you specify two values, they will be applied to the top and bottom and left and right. And if you set three values, they will be set to the top, right, and left the same, and bottom. To set different border widths for all four sides of a box, you use the following style:

```
p.box { border-width: 1px 2px 3px 4px; }
```

That's equivalent to the following:

```
p.box {
  border-top-width: 1px;
  border-right-width: 2px;
  border-bottom-width: 3px;
  border-left-width: 4px;
}
```

To apply different values for the `border` shortcut property to different sides of a box, it's necessary to use the directional property names. You can't supply multiple values for the components of the shortcut property. However, CSS will apply the styles in the order they appear in the CSS document, so you can use styles like this to change the properties of just one side:

Input ▼

```
p {
  border: solid  2px red ;
  border-bottom: dashed 4px green;
}
```

The results are shown in Figure 8.6.

Output ▼

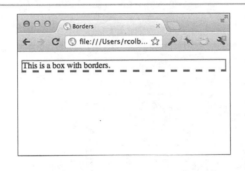

FIGURE 8.6
Border styles.

If you want to experiment with border styles, colors, and widths, you can open the example page in the Developer Tools and modify the styles directly.

Margins and Padding

In the box model, there are two ways to control whitespace around a box. Padding is the whitespace inside the border, and the margin is the whitespace outside the border, separating the box from surrounding elements. Let's look at an example that illustrates how padding and margins work. The web page that follows has one `<div>` nested within another. The outer `<div>` has a solid black border; the inner `<div>` has a dotted black border. The page appears in Figure 8.7.

Input ▼

```
<html>
<head>
  <title>Nested Elements</title>
  <style type="text/css">
    .outer { border: 2px solid black; }
    .inner { border: 2px dotted black;
```

```
            padding: 0;
            margin: 0; }
     </style>
  </head>
  <body>
  <div class="outer">
  Outer.
  <div class="inner">
  Friends, Romans, countrymen, lend me your ears;<br />
  I come to bury Caesar, not to praise him.<br />
  The evil that men do lives after them;<br />
  The good is oft interred with their bones;<br />
  So let it be with Caesar. The noble Brutus<br />
  </div>
  </div>

  </body>
  </html>
```

Output ▼

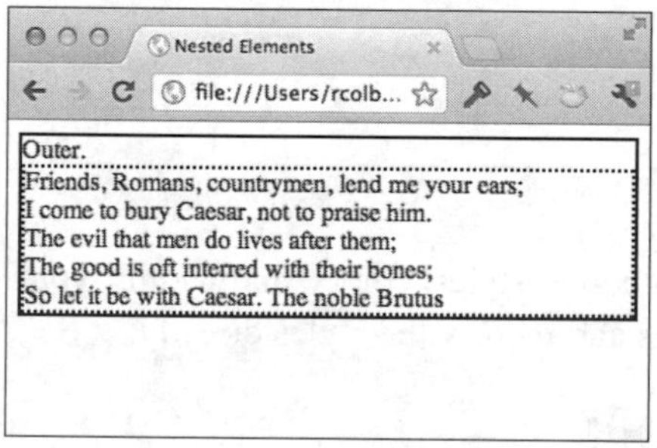

FIGURE 8.7
Nested <div>s
with no margins or
padding.

As you can see, the text in the inner <div> is jammed right up against the border, and the inner border and outer border are flush against each other. That's because I've set both the padding and the margin of the inner <div> to 0. (When you're setting a property to 0 there's no need to specify a unit.) The results in Figure 8.8 show what happens if I change the style sheet to this:

Input ▼

```
.outer { border: 2px solid black; }
.inner { border: 2px dotted black;
     padding: 15px;
     margin: 15px; }
```

Output ▼

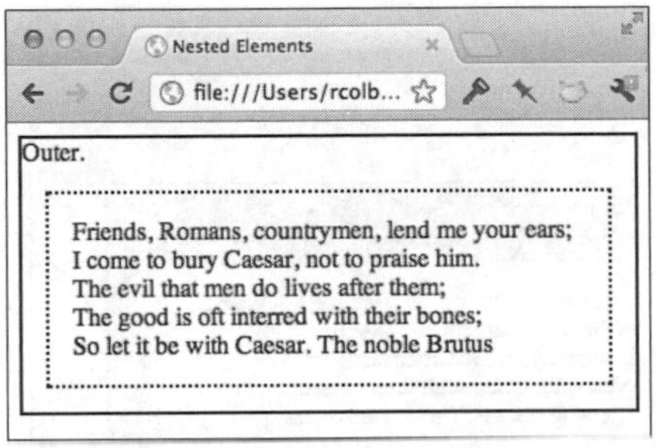

FIGURE 8.8
The inner `<div>` has 15 pixels of padding and margin here.

As you can see, I've created some space between the border of the inner `<div>` and the text inside the inner `<div>` using `padding`, and some space between the border of the inner `<div>` and the border of the outer `<div>` using `margin`. Now let's look at what happens when I add some margin and padding to the outer `<div>`, too. I'm also going to give both the inner and outer `<div>`s background colors so that you can see how colors are assigned to whitespace. (I discuss backgrounds and background colors in a later lesson.) The results are in Figure 8.9. Here's the new style sheet:

Input ▼

```
.outer { border: 2px solid black;
    background-color: gray;
    padding: 15px;
    margin: 40px; }
.inner { border: 2px dotted black;
    background-color: white;
    padding: 15px;
    margin: 15px; }
```

Output ▼

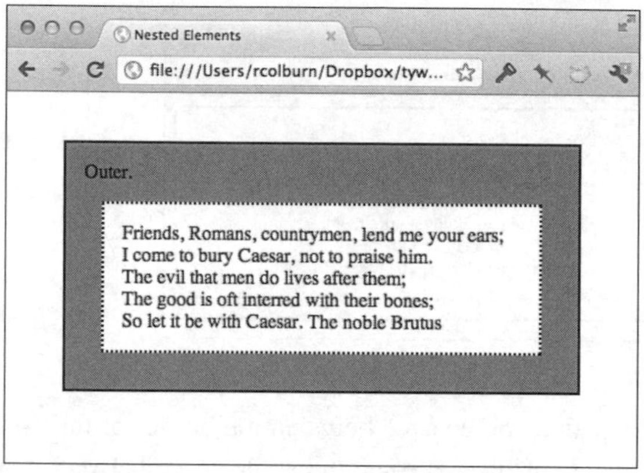

FIGURE 8.9
Both the inner
`<div>` and the
outer `<div>` have
margin and
padding.

I gave the outer `<div>` a large 40-pixel margin so that you could see how it moves the borders away from the edges of the browser window. Note also that there's now space between the text in the outer `<div>` and the border. You can also see that the padding of the outer `<div>` and the margin of the inner `<div>` are combined to provide 30 pixels of whitespace between the border of the outer `<div>` and the border of the inner `<div>`. Finally, it's important to understand the behavior of the background color. The background color is applied to the padding, but not to the margin. So, the 15-pixel margin outside the inner `<div>` takes on the background color of the outer `<div>`, and the margin of the outer `<div>` takes on the background color of the page.

Collapsing Margins

In the CSS box model, horizontal margins are never collapsed. (If you put two items with horizontal margins next to each other, both margins will appear on the page.) Vertical margins, however, are collapsed. Only the larger of the two vertical margins is used when two elements with margins are next to each other. For example, if a `<div>` with a 40-pixel bottom margin is above a `<div>` with a 20-pixel top margin, the margin between the two will be 40 pixels, not 60 pixels.

To center text within a box, the `text-align: center;` style property is used. The question now is this: How do you center a box on the page? In addition to passing units of measure or a percentage to the margin property, you can set the margin to `auto`. In theory, this means to set this margin to the same value as the opposite margin. However, if you set both the left and the right margins to `auto`, your element will be centered. To do so, you can use the `margin-left` and `margin-right` properties or provide multiple values for the `margin` property. So, to center a `<div>` horizontally, the following style sheet is used. (The newly centered `<div>` is in Figure 8.10.)

Input ▼

```
.inner { border: 2px dotted black;
    background-color: white;
    padding: 15px;
    width: 50%;
    margin-left: auto;
    margin-right: auto;
    }
```

Output ▼

FIGURE 8.10
A centered `<div>`.

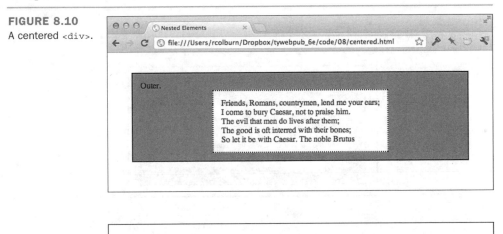

TIP

If you want elements to overlap each other, you can apply negative margins to them rather than positive margins.

I used the `width` property in that style sheet to shrink the `<div>` so that it could be centered. I explain how to resize elements using CSS later in the lesson.

Another thing to remember is that the `<body>` of the page is a box, too. Here's a style sheet that includes new values for the `border`, `margin`, and `padding` properties of the `<body>` tag. It also includes some changes to the outer `<div>` to illustrate how the changes to the `<body>` tag work. You can see the updated page in Figure 8.11.

Input ▼

```
.outer { border: 2px solid black;
    background-color: gray;
    padding: 15px; }
.inner { border: 2px dotted black;
    background-color: white;
    padding: 15px;
    margin: 15px; }
body { margin: 20px;
    border: 3px solid blue;
    padding: 20px;
    background-color: yellow;
    }
```

Output ▼

FIGURE 8.11
Treating the body of a document as a box.

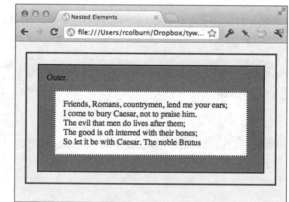

In this example, you can see that you can adjust the margin, padding, and border of a document's body. However, unlike other boxes, the background color is applied to the margin as well as the padding.

Controlling Size and Element Display

The one box in the box model I haven't discussed is the content box. For starters, there are two types of content boxes: block and inline. In previous lessons, I've discussed block-level elements versus inline elements; this distinction is important in CSS. Block elements are, by default, as wide as the container you place them within, and you can modify their height and width using CSS. Block elements are also preceded and followed by line breaks. Inline elements are only as wide as they need to be to display their contents, as well as the margins, borders, and padding that you apply to them.

Each element is, by default, either a block element or an inline element, but CSS provides the `display` property to allow you to change this behavior. The block property supports three values: `block`, `inline`, and `none`. For example, if you want the elements in a list to appear inline rather than each appearing on its own line, as shown in Figure 8.12, you use the following style:

```
ul.inline li { display: inline; }
```

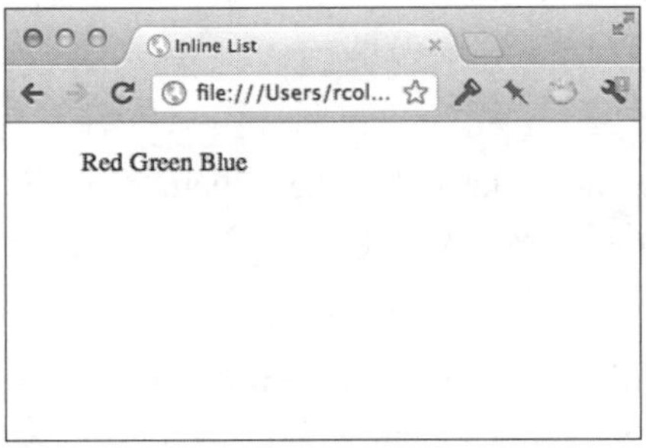

FIGURE 8.12
Inline list items.

Setting the `display` property to `none` removes the selected elements from the page entirely. Hiding elements with this property is useful if you want to use JavaScript to dynamically hide and show items on the page. Using JavaScript to modify page styles is discussed starting in Lesson 17, "Introducing JavaScript."

There are two properties for controlling the size of a block: `width` and `height`. They enable you to set the size of the box using any of the units of measurement mentioned previously. If you use a percentage for the height or width, that percentage is applied to the size of the containing element.

To make the header of your page 100 pixels high and half the width of the browser, you could use the following rule:

```
#header { width: 50%; height: 100px; }
```

The following paragraph will appear to be very narrow, but the box in which it resides will be as wide as the browser window unless you specify a width.

```
<p>one.<br>two.<br>three.<br></p>
```

It's possible to set maximum and minimum heights and widths for elements to account for differences in the size of users' browser windows. The properties that enable you to do so are `max-width`, `min-width`, `max-height`, and `min-height`. Let's say you've created a page design that only looks right if it's at least 600 pixels wide. You could use the following style:

```
#container { min-width: 600px; }
```

The element with the ID `container` will expand to fit the size of the browser window as long as it's at least 600 pixels wide. If the browser is smaller than 600 pixels wide, the contents of the element will scroll off the screen. Likewise, you may want to constrain the maximum size of an element so that lines of text do not become so long that they're difficult to read. To do so, use the following style:

```
#container { max-width: 800px; }
```

You can also use both styles together to keep the size of your page within a certain range, regardless of the size of the user's browser window:

```
#container { min-width: 600px; max-width: 800px; }
```

Normally elements in HTML are sized to fit the content that is placed within them. However, if you constrain the size of an element with a size or a maximum size and then place content inside the element that won't fit, the browser has to decide what to do with it. By default, when content won't fit inside its box, the browser just displays the overflow as best it can. As you can see from Figure 8.13, the results are not always pretty.

FIGURE 8.13
Content that is too large for its container.

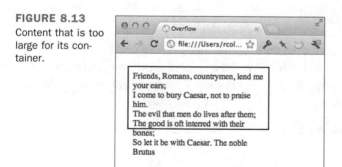

The border shows the dimensions of the box specified in the style sheet. Because there's too much text to fit inside the box, it runs over the border and down the page. Using the CSS `overflow` property, you can tell the browser what to do when these situations arise. The values are `visible` (this is the default), `hidden`, `scroll`, `auto`, and `inherit`. You can see how the different overflow settings look in Figure 8.14.

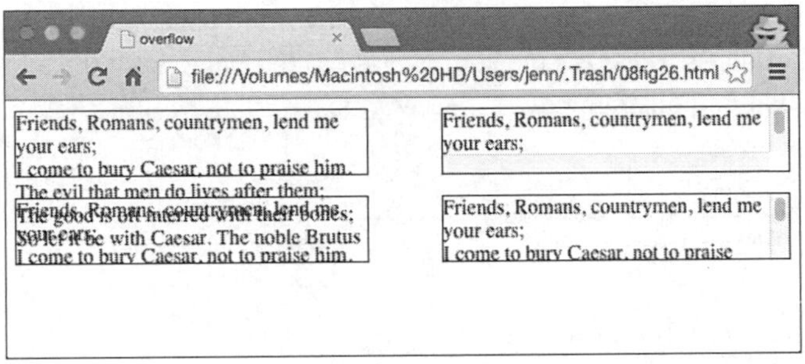

FIGURE 8.14
Different ways of dealing with overflow.

When overflow is `hidden`, the content that does not fit in the box is not displayed at all. Both `scroll` and `auto` add scrollbars to enable users to view the entire contents of the box. When the setting is `scroll`, the scrollbars are always displayed, whereas when the setting is `auto`, the scrollbars display only if needed. When overflow is visible, content that overflows the box is not taken into account when laying out other items on the page, and the overflow content bleeds onto other content on the page. When you are sizing elements on the page manually, you should always account for potential overflow so that it doesn't break the layout of your page.

Float

Normally, block-level elements flow down the page from top to bottom. If you want to alter the normal flow of the page, you can use absolute positioning, which I discuss in a bit, or you can use the `float` property. The `float` property is used to indicate that an element should be placed as far as possible to the left or right on the page and that any other content should wrap around it. This is best illustrated with an example. First, take a look at the page in Figure 8.15.

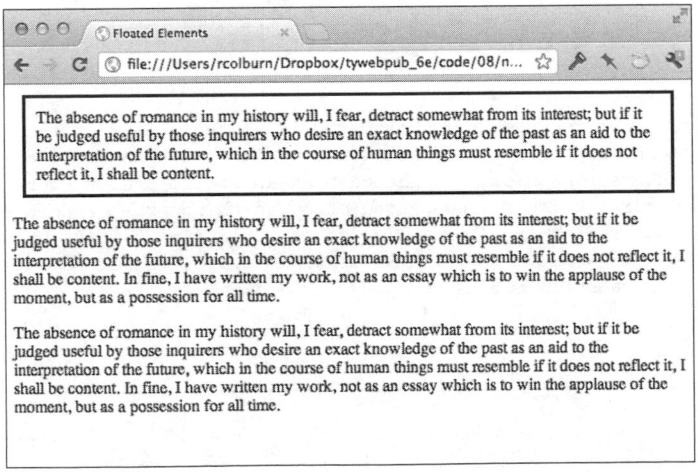

FIGURE 8.15
A page with no floating elements.

As you can see, the three boxes run straight down the page. I've added a border to the first box, but that's it. Here's the source code to the page, with the addition of a few other properties that demonstrate how `float` works:

Input ▼

```html
<!DOCTYPE html>
<html>
<head>
  <title>Floated Elements</title>
  <style type="text/css" media="screen">
    .right {
      border: 3px solid black;
      padding: 10px;
      margin: 10px;
      float: right;
      width: 33%; }

    .bottom { clear: both; }
  </style>
</head>
<body>
<p class="right">
The absence of romance in my history will, I fear, detract somewhat
from its interest; but if it be judged useful by those inquirers who
desire an exact knowledge of the past as an aid to the interpretation
of the future, which in the course of human things must resemble if
it does not reflect it, I shall be content.
</p>
<p class="main">
The absence of romance in my history will, I fear, detract somewhat
from its interest; but if it be judged useful by those inquirers who
desire an exact knowledge of the past as an aid to the interpretation
of the future, which in the course of human things must resemble if
it does not reflect it, I shall be content. In fine, I have written
my work, not as an essay which is to win the applause of the moment,
but as a possession for all time.
</p>
<p class="bottom">
The absence of romance in my history will, I fear, detract somewhat
from its interest; but if it be judged useful by those inquirers who
desire an exact knowledge of the past as an aid to the interpretation
of the future, which in the course of human things must resemble if
it does not reflect it, I shall be content. In fine, I have written
my work, not as an essay which is to win the applause of the moment,
but as a possession for all time.
</p>
</body>
</html>
```

As you can see from the style sheet, I've set the `float` property for elements with the class "right" to `right`. I've also added some padding, a margin, and a border to that class for aesthetic purposes and set the width for that class to 33% so that it isn't as wide as the browser window. I've also put the second paragraph on the page in the class `bottom`, and I've added the `clear: both` property to it. Figure 8.16 shows the results.

8

Output ▼

FIGURE 8.16
A page with a
`<div>` floated to
the right.

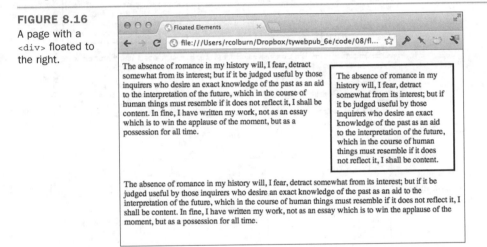

The `<div>` is moved over to the right side of the page, and the first paragraph appears next to it. The `float: right` property indicates that the rest of the page's content should flow around it. The bottom paragraph does not flow around the `<div>` because I've applied the `clear: both` property to it, which cancels any float that has been set. The options for `float` are easy to remember: `left`, `right`, and `none`. The options for clear are `none`, `left`, `right`, and `both`.

Using the `clear` property, you have the option of clearing either the left or the right float without canceling both at the same time. This proves useful if you have a long column on the right and a short one on the left and you want to maintain the float on the right even though you're canceling it on the left (or vice versa).

Now let's look at how floated elements work together. Figure 8.17 shows what happens when you have two right-floating elements together, and Figure 8.18 shows the effect with a left-floating element and a right-floating element.

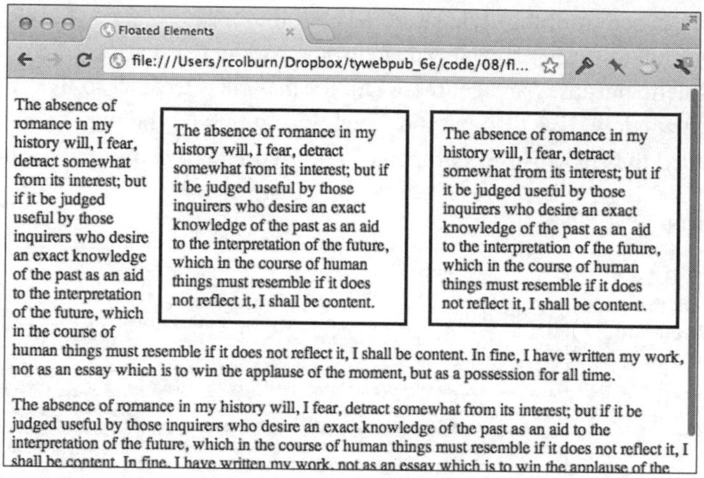

FIGURE 8.17
Two right-floating elements together.

FIGURE 8.18
A left-floating and a right-floating element together.

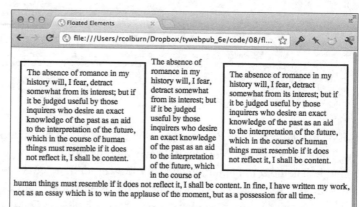

As you can see, when you put two floating elements together, they appear next to each other. If you want the second one to appear below the first, you need to use the `clear` property as well as the `float` property in the rule, as shown in this style sheet:

Input ▼

```
.right {
  border: 3px solid black;
  padding: 10px;
  margin: 10px;
  float: right;
```

8

```
    width: 33%; }

#second { clear: right; }

.bottom { clear: both; }
```

The additional `<div>` I've added has been given the ID second so that it inherits all the styles of the class `right` and the style rule associated with the ID `second`. The result is in Figure 8.19.

Output ▼

FIGURE 8.19
Two floating ele-
ments that are
aligned vertically.

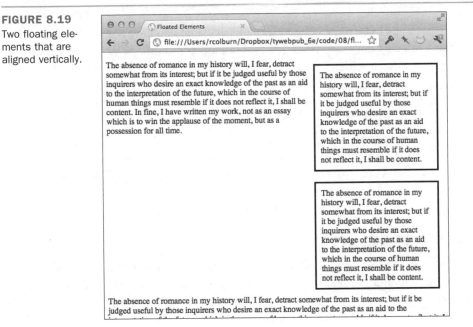

More Selectors

A number of other CSS selectors provide even more fine-grained control over which elements on the page have styles applied to them. You can always group elements in an arbitrary fashion using classes, identify single elements using IDs, and add `<span>` and `<div>` elements to the page to provide structure to which styles can be applied. These additional selectors make it easier to apply styles to very specific items on a page without altering the structure of the page itself. The only catch is that some of these selectors are incompatible with old browsers, especially versions of Internet Explorer prior to version 8.

You've already seen the basic descendant selector, which looks like this:

```
p span.important { font-weight: bold }
```

That selector matches any `<span>` tag with the class important that's nested inside a `<p>` tag. The child selector is slightly stricter; it looks like this:

```
p > span.important { font-weight: bold }
```

That selector only matches if the `<span>` tag is a child of the `<p>` tag. It would not match the `<span>` tag in the following paragraph, whereas the descendant selector would:

```
<p>This is a paragraph. <em>This is an
<span class="imprtnt">important</span> sentence.</em></p>
```

Let's say that you have some nested lists on a page, and you have a style that should only apply to items in the top-level list. This is another example in which the descendant selector would make sense:

```
ul.topmost > li { color: green; }
```

The items in the topmost list would be green. The items in the other lists would not.

Finally, there's the next sibling selector, which uses the + operator. The selector `h1 + p` matches the first paragraph that follows a first level heading, assuming they both have the same parent. You could use this rule if you wanted to add special styling to the lead paragraphs for stories on your site. The ~ selector matches any siblings, not just the first. So `h1 ~ p` would match any paragraph that follows an `<h1>` tag.

Pseudo-Classes

A couple of pseudo-classes can also be used to apply styles to content based on its position on the page. For example, the `:first-letter` pseudo-class selects only the first letter in each of the elements selected by the selector. Likewise, the `:first-line` pseudo-class selects the first line of text in the element.

Let's say you want to create what's known as a drop-cap, a large capital letter at the beginning of a block of text. You could do it by wrapping the character in a `<span>` tag, but using the `:first-letter` pseudo-class, you can avoid adding an element to the page. To create the drop-cap, you'll need to increase the font size, float the character to the left, and manipulate the padding to be sure that the appearance is correct. Figure 8.20 shows the result.

```
p:first-letter {
  font-size: 300%;
  float: left;
  font-family: sans-serif;
  padding: 0 5px;
}
```

8

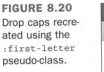

FIGURE 8.20
Drop caps recre-
ated using the
`:first-letter`
pseudo-class.

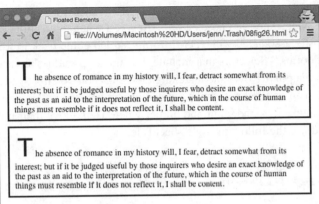

As you can see, both paragraphs have the drop cap. This is where the next sibling selector comes in handy. I can use the selector I introduced earlier to ensure that only the first
paragraph on the page has the drop cap, as shown in Figure 8.21.

Input ▼

```
h1 + p:first-letter {
  font-size: 300%;
  float: left;
  font-family: sans-serif;
  padding: 0 5px;
}
```

Output ▼

FIGURE 8.21
Using the sibling
selector limits the
drop cap to the
first paragraph.

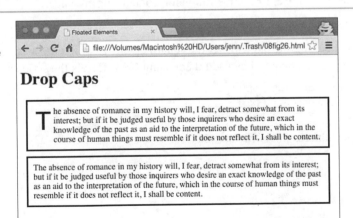

The `:hover` and `:focus` pseudo-classes are applied based on how the user is interacting with the page. The `:focus` selector is triggered when a matching element has focus. Focus is mostly associated with HTML forms, so I'll come back to it in Lesson 12, "Designing Forms." Selectors that include the `:hover` pseudo-class are activated when the user has his pointer over the matching element. You've already see how the `:hover` pseudo-class can be used with links—it can in fact be used with any element on a page. To change the background color and border when users move their pointer over a paragraph, you'd use the following style sheet rule:

```
p:hover {
  background-color: yellow;
  border: 1px solid green;
}
```

Over time, CSS has evolved to enable you to make your pages more dynamic only through the use of style sheets. At one time, if you wanted to change styles on your page after it loaded, you had to write a script using JavaScript, which I'll discuss later in the book. Now, a number of CSS selectors enable you to add dynamic content to your pages without scripting.

You can even use CSS to modify the contents of the page directly using the `:before` and `:after` selectors. The newer notation is `::before` and `::after`, but `:before` and `:after` are more widely supported. These selectors create a pseudo-element that's the first child of the matched element. You can use a style property called `content` to insert any content you like into that pseudo-element, and it will be displayed on the screen. Using `:before`, `:after`, and `content`, you can make changes to the actual content of your page.

Let's say I have a style guide for my site that requires me to place square brackets around any abbreviation I use. I have the following content for my page:

```
<p><abbr>NASA</abbr> is responsible for the US space program.</p>
```

Rather than editing the page to add the square brackets, which are a stylistic element more than proper content, I can add them using CSS. Here's the style sheet:

```
abbr:before { content: "[" }
abbr:after { content: "]" }
```

You can see the results in Figure 8.22.

Output ▼

FIGURE 8.22
Content added to a page using the `:before` and `:after` pseudo-elements.

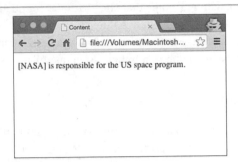

[NASA] is responsible for the US space program.

8

A number of other pseudo-classes can be used, but they are not as widely supported in browsers as the other pseudo-classes I've discussed. Specifically, Internet Explorer did not add support for them until version 9. You can read about the additional pseudo-classes, as well as the ones that have been discussed in the Mozilla developer documentation: https://developer.mozilla.org/en-US/docs/CSS/Pseudo-classes.

Attribute Selectors

CSS also provides selectors that match the attributes associated with elements. For example, here's a simple selector that matches paragraphs with the class `highlight`:

```
p[class="highlight"] { font-weight: bold; }
```

That's not really any more useful than simply using the selector `p.highlight`. The important point is that the selector works with any attribute name and value. You can also use the `=~` operator with attributes. In that case, it will match any value in a list of values, separated by spaces. Here's an example:

```
p[class=~"highlight"] { font-weight: bold; }
```

In that case, the selector would match a paragraph like the following:

```
<p class="major highlight">This is a major highlight.</p>
```

The class "highlight" is one member of the list of classes, so it matches the selector thanks to the presence of the `=~` operator.

You can also leave out the attribute value entirely and match any element that has the listed attribute. The rule that follows will match paragraphs that have any class at all:

```
p[class] { font-weight: bold; }
```

There are several other attribute selectors that you may find useful as well. The `^=` attribute selector matches elements with attributes that start with the supplied value. The `*=` attribute selector matches elements with attribute values that contain the value passed to the operator. You can match attribute values that end with a certain string using `$=`. Finally, the `|=` operator matches any value in a hyphen-separated list of values.

The `<body>` Tag

I've already mentioned that you can adjust the margin, padding, and border of a page by applying styles to the `<body>` tag. More important, any styles that you want to apply on a page-wide basis can be assigned to the page's body. You already know about setting the background color for the page by using `style="background-color: black"` in your `<body>` tag. That's really just the beginning. If you want the default font for all the text on your page to appear in the Georgia font, you can use the following style:

```
body { font-family: Georgia; }
```

That's a lot easier than changing the `font-family` property for every tag that contains text on your page. You can modify the background and text colors of your page like this:

```
body { color: white;
    background-color: black; }
```

One of the main advantages of taking this approach, aside from the fact that it's how the standard says you should do things, is that then you can put the style into a linked style sheet and set the background color for your whole site on one page.

Many layouts require that elements be flush with the edge of the browser. In these cases, you need to set the margin to `0` for your `<body>` tag. To turn off margins, just use this rule:

```
body { margin: 0px; }
```

Summary

In the preceding lessons, I've given you a taste of how to use CSS. You didn't get the full flavor because I used them only within the context of the `style` attribute of tags. In this lesson, I discussed how you can create style sheets either as part of a page or as a standalone file that can be included by any page. I also moved beyond properties that discuss text formatting to explain how to use CSS to lay out an entire page.

By understanding how browsers render pages and how you can affect that process using CSS, you can achieve the effects you want without writing loads of markup that's difficult to understand and maintain.

You'll continue to be introduced to new CSS properties in the lessons that follow. In Lesson 9, I explain how to use CSS to create pages that respond to the devices viewing them, in Lesson 10 I show you how to change colors on the page and provide all the details on using CSS to define the backgrounds of pages and specific elements. Lesson 16 takes a deeper look at CSS selectors and explains how to create entire page layouts using CSS.

Workshop

In this lesson, you learned about Cascading Style Sheets, the wonderful supplement to HTML that makes formatting your pages less painful. Throughout the rest of this book, I use CSS where appropriate, so please review this workshop material before continuing.

Q&A

Q My CSS isn't working like I'd expect. What should I do?

A CSS probably doesn't seem that clear in the first place, and things can only get messier when you actually start applying styles to your pages. You should be sure to test your pages in every browser you can find, and don't be afraid to experiment. Just because something seems like it should work doesn't mean it will. The W3C also provides a CSS Validator (http://jigsaw.w3.org/css-validator/) that you can use to make sure that your CSS syntax is correct. You should probably use it all the time, but even if you don't, it can still help out if you get stuck.

Q Are there naming rules for classes and IDs?

A Yes, there are. A name must start with a letter and can contain only letters, numbers, or dashes (-). Some browsers may not enforce these rules, but to be safe, you should adhere to them.

Q What are the relevant CSS standards?

A There are three CSS recommendations from the W3C: CSS1, CSS2, and CSS3. Most modern browsers support a large part of CSS1 and CSS2, as well as parts of CSS3. You can find out more at http://www.w3.org/Style/CSS/. If you're curious about how well your browser supports CSS or the effect that properties have in real browsers, you can check out the CSS test suites at http://www.w3.org/Style/CSS/Test/. CSS2 and CSS3 include a number of additional selectors.

Quiz

1. Why can't absolute units be used reliably in CSS?
2. True or false: Including style sheets on your page requires features provided by a web server.
3. Is the margin or padding of an element inside the border?

Quiz Answers

1. Absolute units have problems in CSS because there's no way to know exactly what sort of display medium the user has. An inch on one monitor might be completely different than an inch on another.
2. The answer is false; you can use the `<link>` tag to load external style sheets.
3. The padding of an element is inside the border of an element, and the margin is outside.

Exercises

1. If you've already created some web pages, go back and try to figure out how you could apply CSS to them.
2. Examine the style sheets used by some websites that you admire. Take a look at how they use classes and IDs in their markup.
3. Create a web page that includes a sidebar on the left, with text wrapped around it. Create a navigation menu at the bottom that is positioned below the sidebar.

LESSON 9
Using Images on Your Web Pages

Few things can do more to make a web page more interesting than a strategically placed image or an attractive color scheme. Effective use of images and color is one of the key things that separates professionally designed sites from those designed by novices. The process of selecting images, resizing them and saving them in the proper format, and integrating them into a page can be intimidating, but this lesson will explain how it's done.

This lesson covers the following topics:

- The kinds of images you can use in web pages

- How to include images on your web page, either alone or alongside text

- How to use images in links

- How to set up and assign links to regions of images using client-side imagemaps

- How to provide alternatives for browsers that can't view images

- How to use images as backgrounds for page elements

- How and when to use images on your web pages

- A few tips on image etiquette

Images on the Web

Images displayed on the Web should be converted to one of the formats supported by most browsers: GIF, JPEG, or PNG. Every popular browser supports all three. HTML5 introduces support for SVG images. Many other image formats are supported by some browsers and not others. You should avoid them.

Let's assume that you already have an image you want to put on your web page. How do you get it into PNG, GIF, or JPEG format so it can be viewed on your page? Most image editing programs, such as Adobe Photoshop (http://www.adobe.com/), iPhoto (http://apple.com/), Picasa (http://picasa.google.com/), and GIMP (http://gimp.org/), will convert images to the popular formats. You might have to look under the option for Save As or Export to find the conversion option. There are also freeware and shareware programs for most platforms that do nothing but convert between image formats as well as online photo editors available at http://pixlr.com/ and http://www.picmonkey.com.

TIP

> If you're a Windows user, you can download IrfanView, which enables you to view images, and convert them to various formats, at http://www.irfanview.com/. It also provides a number of other image-manipulation features that are useful for working with images for the Web. Best of all, it's free for noncommercial use.

Remember how your HTML files have to have an `.html` or `.htm` extension to work properly? Image files have specific extensions, too. For PNG files, the extension is `.png`. For GIF files, the extension is `.gif`. For JPEG files, the extensions are `.jpg` and `.jpeg`.

Image Formats

As I just mentioned, several image formats are supported by every major web browser: GIF, JPEG, PNG, and SVG. JPEG and GIF are the old standbys, each useful for different purposes. PNG was designed as a replacement for the GIF format. SVG or scalable vector graphics are an *Extensible Markup Language* (XML) format to add vector drawings to web pages. To design web pages, you must understand and be able to apply all the image formats and to decide which is appropriate to use in each case.

GIF

Graphics Interchange Format, also known as GIF, was once the most widely used image format. It was developed by CompuServe to fill the need for a cross-platform image format.

9

NOTE | GIF is pronounced *jiff*, like the peanut butter, not with a hard *G* as in *gift*. Really—the early documentation of GIF tools says so.

The GIF format is okay for logos, icons, line art, and other simple images. It doesn't work as well for highly detailed images because each image can only use a maximum of 256 colors. Photographs in GIF format tend to look grainy and blotchy because the color palette limits smooth color transitions. The GIF format supports transparency, which makes it easy to incorporate an image into a larger design, but not alpha transparency. Alpha transparency, which is supported by PNG, actually blends an image with what's behind it and works much better than GIF's simple transparency (which simply disables some pixels).

One feature that is unique to the GIF format among web image formats is support for simple animations. Animated GIFs don't support sound or playback control, but they can be embedded on a page without a browser plug-in, so they are assured of working on mobile devices.

JPEG

JPEG, which stands for *Joint Photographic Experts Group* (the group that developed it), is the most popular format for images on the Web. JPEG (pronounced *jay-peg*) is actually a method of compressing images that other file formats can use. The file format for which it's known is also commonly called JPG.

JPEG was designed for the storage of photographic images. Unlike GIF images, JPEG images can include any number of colors. The style of compression that JPEG uses (the compression algorithm) works especially well for photographs, so photographs compressed using the JPEG algorithm are considerably smaller than those compressed using GIF or PNG. JPEG uses a *lossy* compression algorithm, which means that some of the data used in the image is discarded to make the file smaller. Lossy compression works extremely well for photographic data, but it makes JPEG unsuitable for images that contain elements with sharp edges, such as logos, line art, and type. If you're working with photos to display on the Web, you should save them in the JPEG format.

PNG

PNG, pronounced *ping*, was originally designed as a replacement for GIFs. It stands for *Portable Network Graphics*. All current browsers support PNG, and it has some important advantages over GIF and JPEG. Like GIF, no data is lost when images are converted to PNG.

As mentioned, PNG's alpha transparency works better than GIF's more rudimentary approach and supports palette-based images (like GIF) as well as true-color and grayscale images (like JPEG). In other words, you don't have to worry about color usage with PNG, although the number of colors used will result in smaller files.

If you're creating new images that aren't photographs, PNG is the format to use. JPEG still makes more sense for photographs because of its superior compression. If you are creating new images, GIFs only really make sense if you are using GIF animation.

SVG

Scalable Vector Graphics (SVG) is a graphics format that was developed for the Web. It became a standard at the W3C in 2001, and all current web browsers support basic SVG features.

One advantage of using SVG is that they are scalable vectors. This means that they can be resized up or down without any loss of quality. This makes them well suited to responsive web design and web applications.

SVG images are written in XML and can be written directly in HTML5 documents. This makes SVG images faster to load and easy to manipulate with scripts or programs. They can also be used to create moving images and complex animations. If you look at an SVG image that has been included in HTML, it will look a lot like other HTML code. SVG uses XML to create the images, so it uses tags and attributes just like you've learned to use in HTML documents. But you don't need to go out and learn the SVG markup. Instead, a lot of tools are available to create the images for you. Most vector graphics programs like Adobe Illustrator (http://www.adobe.com/products/illustrator.html) and Inkscape (https://inkscape.org/en/) will save the images as SVG. You can then open the SVG files in a text editor and see that they are just complex XML files.

SVG is a good choice for images that need to be available at many different sizes, such as on responsive websites. It is also good for scripted images like graphs. But while all current browsers support SVG, if your site must support Internet Explorer 8 (or lower), you will need to have fallback options for SVG images.

Inline Images in HTML: The `<img>` Tag

After you have an image ready to go, you can include it on your web page. Inline images are placed in HTML documents using the `<img>` tag. This tag, like the `<hr>` and `<br>` tags, has no closing tag in HTML.

The `<img>` tag has many attributes that enable you to control how the image is presented on the page. Some attributes have been deprecated in favor of *Cascading Style Sheets* (CSS). There are only two required attributes of the image tag in HTML5: `src` and `alt`.

The most important attribute of the `<img>` tag is `src`, which is the URL of the image. There's nothing special about image URLs, so everything you learned about absolute and relative paths in Lesson 6, "Working with Links," applies. To point to a file named `image.gif` in the same directory as the HTML document, you can use the following tag:

```
<img src="image.gif">
```

For an image file one directory up from the current directory, use this tag:

```
<img src="../image.gif">
```

Apply the same rules as for URLs in the `href` part of the `<a>` tag.

You can also point to images on remote servers from the `src` attribute of an `<img>` tag, just as you can from the `href` attribute of a link. If you wanted to include the image `example.gif` from www.example.com on your web page, you could use the following tag:

```
<img src="http://www.example.com/example.gif">
```

CAUTION | Just because you can use images stored on other servers for your own web pages doesn't mean that you should. A lot of legal, ethical, and technical issues are involved with using images on other sites. I discuss them later in this lesson.

Adding Alternative Text to Images

Occasionally there are cases where your images may not be displayed as intended on your page. Maybe a user with a visual impairment visits your page with a screen reader. Perhaps it's a user on a mobile device with a slow connection that's taking too long to download your images. You can use the `alt` attribute of the `<img>` tag to describe your image so that some meaning is conveyed even when the image cannot be displayed.

You should enter a text description of the image in the `alt` attribute, like this:

```
<img src="onthebeach.jpg" alt="Atlantic Beach at sunset">
```

The `alt` attribute supports a simple text description, not markup of any kind. Therefore, you can't use whole blocks of HTML code as a replacement for an image—just a few words or phrases.

▼ **Exercise 9.1: Adding Images to a Page**

Here's the web page for a local haunted house that's open every year at Halloween. Using all the advice I've given you in the preceding lessons, you should be able to create a page like this one fairly easily. Here's the HTML code for this HTML file, and Figure 9.1 shows how it looks so far:

Input ▼

```
<!DOCTYPE html>
<html>
  <head>
    <title>Welcome to the Halloween House of Terror</title>
  </head>
  <body>
    <h1>Welcome to The Halloween House of Terror</h1>
    <p>
      Voted the most frightening haunted house three years in a
      row, the <strong>Halloween House of Terror</strong>
      provides the ultimate in Halloween thrills. Over
      <strong>20 rooms of thrills and excitement</strong> to
      make your blood run cold and your hair stand on end!
    </p>
    <p>
      The Halloween House of Terror is open from <em>October 20
        to November 1st</em>, with a gala celebration on
        Halloween night. Our hours are:
    </p>
    <ul>
      <li>Mon-Fri 5PM-midnight</li>
      <li>Sat &amp; Sun 5PM-3AM</li>
      <li><strong>Halloween Night (31-Oct)</strong>: 3PM-???</li>
    </ul>
    <p>
      The Halloween House of Terror is located at:<br>
      The Old Waterfall Shopping Center<br>
      1020 Mirabella Ave<br>
      Springfield, CA 94532
    </p>
  </body>
▼ </html>
```

Output ▼

FIGURE 9.1
The Halloween
House home page.

So far, so good. Now you can add an image to the page. Suppose that you happen to have an image of a haunted house lying around on your hard drive; it would look excellent at the top of this web page. The image, called `haunted_house.png`, is in PNG format. It's located in the same directory as the `halloween.html` page, so adding it to the page will be easy.

Now, suppose that you want to place this image above the page heading. To do so, add an `<img>` tag to the file, just before the heading:

```
<div><img src="haunted_house.png" alt="House of Terror"></div>
<h1>Welcome to The Halloween House of Terror</h1>
```

Images, like links, don't define their own text elements, so the `<img>` tag has to go inside a paragraph or heading element.

When you reload the `halloween.html` page, your browser should include the haunted house image on the page, as shown in Figure 9.2.

If the image doesn't load and your browser displays a funny-looking icon in its place, make sure that you entered the filename properly in the HTML file. Image filenames are case sensitive, so all the uppercase and lowercase letters have to be correct.

If the case isn't the problem, double-check the image file to make sure that it is indeed a GIF or JPEG image and that it has the proper file extension.

▼

FIGURE 9.2
The Halloween
House home page
with the haunted
house.

If one image is good, two would be really good, right? Try adding another <img> tag next to the first one, as follows, and see what happens:

Input ▼

```
<div><img src="haunted_house.png" alt="House of Terror">
<img src="haunted_house.png" alt="House of Terror"></div>
<h1>Welcome to The Halloween House of Terror</h1>
```

Output ▼

Figure 9.3 shows how the page looks in a browser. The two images are adjacent to each other, as you would expect.

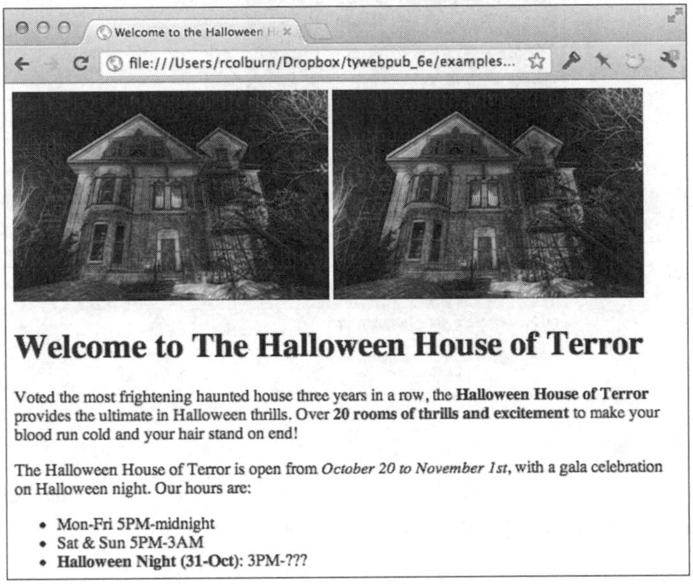
Welcome to the Halloween H
file:///Users/rcolburn/Dropbox/tywebpub_6e/examples...
Welcome to The Halloween House of Terror
Voted the most frightening haunted house three years in a row, the Halloween House of Terror provides the ultimate in Halloween thrills. Over 20 rooms of thrills and excitement to make your blood run cold and your hair stand on end!
The Halloween House of Terror is open from October 20 to November 1st, with a gala celebration on Halloween night. Our hours are:
Mon-Fri 5PM-midnight
Sat & Sun 5PM-3AM
Halloween Night (31-Oct): 3PM-???

FIGURE 9.3
Multiple images.

And that's all there is to adding images! ▲

Images and Text

In the preceding exercise, you put an inline image on a page with text below it. You also can include an image inside a line of text. In fact, this is what the phrase "inline image" actually means—it's *in* a *line* of text.

To include images inside a line of text, just add the <img> tag inside an element tag (<h1>, <p>, <address>, and so on), as in the following line:

```
<h2><img src="house.jpg" alt="House of Terror">The Halloween House of Terror!!
</h2>
```

Figure 9.4 shows the difference you can make by putting the image inline with the heading. (I've also shortened the heading itself and changed it to <h2> so that it all fits on one line.)

FIGURE 9.4
The Halloween
House page with
an image inside
the heading.

The image doesn't have to be large, and it doesn't have to be at the beginning of the text.
You can include an image anywhere in a block of text, as in the following:

Input ▼

```
<blockquote>
      Love, from whom the world <img src="world.gif"> begun,<br>
      Hath the secret of the sun. <img src="sun.gif"><br>
      Love can tell, and love alone, Whence the million stars
      <img src="star.gif"> were strewn<br>
      Why each atom <img src="atom.gif"> knows its own.<br>
      --Robert Bridges
   </blockquote>
```

Figure 9.5 shows how this block looks.

Output ▼

FIGURE 9.5
Images can go anywhere in text.

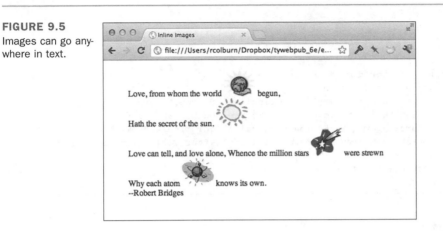

Text and Image Alignment

In these examples, the bottom of the image and the bottom of the text are aligned. You can change how inline images align with text using the `vertical-align` CSS property.

The values supported by the `vertical-align` property are as follows:

`baseline`	Aligns the bottom of the image with the baseline of its parent. This is the default.
`top`	Aligns the top of the image with the top of the line (which may be the top of the text or the top of another image).
`middle`	Aligns the center of the image with the middle of lowercase letters in the parent element.
`bottom`	Aligns the bottom of the image with the bottom of the line.
`text-top`	Aligns the top of the image with the top of the parent element's font (whereas `top` aligns the image with the topmost item in the line).
`text-bottom`	Aligns the bottom of the image with the bottom of the parent element's font.
`sub`	Aligns the element as if it were a subscript.
`sup`	Aligns the element as if it were a superscript.
`length`	Raises or lowers the element by the specified length. Negative values are allowed.
`%`	Raises or lowers the element in a percent of the `line-height` property. Negative values are allowed.

Figure 9.6 shows the Robert Bridges poem from the previous section with the world image unaligned, the sun image aligned to the top of the line, the star image aligned to the middle, and the atom aligned to the bottom of the text.

Input ▼

```
<blockquote>
      Love, from whom the world
      <img src="world.gif"> begun,<br>
      Hath the secret of the sun.
      <img src="sun.gif" style="vertical-align: top;"><br>
      Love can tell, and love alone, Whence the million stars
      <img src="star.gif" style="vertical-align: middle;"> were strewn<br>
      Why each atom <img src="atom.gif" style="vertical-align: bottom;">
      knows its own.<br>
      --Robert Bridges
</blockquote>
```

Output ▼

FIGURE 9.6
Images unaligned, aligned top, aligned middle, and aligned bottom.

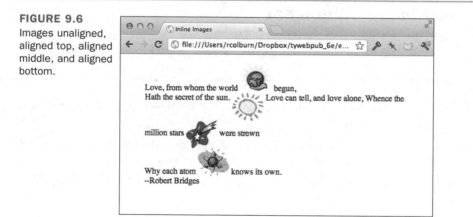

Other alignment options are shown in the following example.

Input ▼

```
<h2>vertical-align "top" versus vertical-align "text-top":</h2>
<p>
  <img src="line.gif">
  vertical-align: top <img src="uparrow.gif" style="vertical-align: top;" />
  vertical-align: text-top <img src="uparrow.gif" style="vertical-align:
  text-top;" />
</p>
```

```
<h2>align "absmiddle" versus vertical-align "middle"</h2>
<p>
  <img src="line.gif">
  align: middle <img src="forward.gif" align="middle">
  vertical-align: middle <img src="forward.gif" style="vertical-align: middle;">
</p>
<h2>vertical-align "baseline" versus vertical-align "text-bottom"</h2>
<p>
  <img src="line.gif">
  vertical-align: baseline <img src="down.gif" style="vertical-align: baseline;">
  vertical-align: text-bottom <img src="down.gif" style="vertical-align:
  text-bottom;">
</p>
```

9

Figure 9.7 shows examples of all the options as they appear in a browser. In each case, the line on the left side and the text are aligned with each other, and the position of the arrow varies.

Output ▼

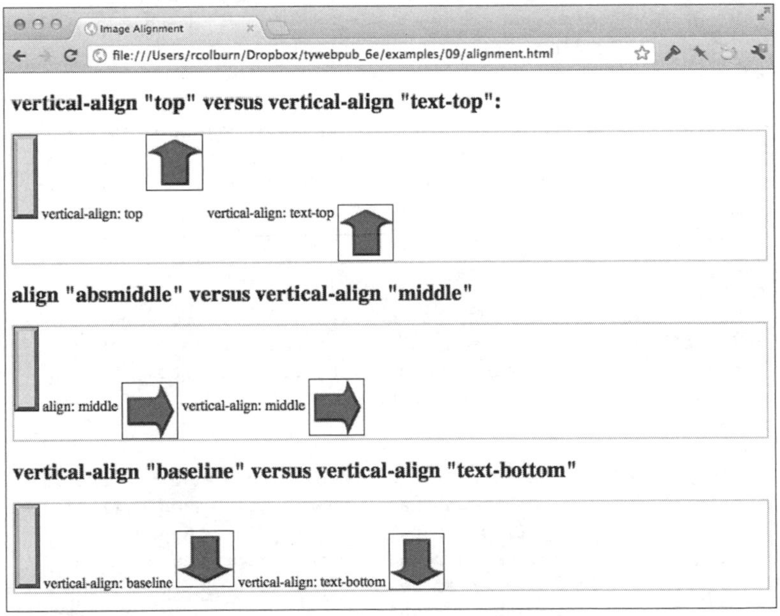

FIGURE 9.7
Image alignment
options.

Wrapping Text Next to Images

Including an image inside a line works fine if you have only one line of text. To control the flow of text around an image, you'll need to use CSS. Images are just like any other element as far as the `float` property goes, so you can use the `float` and `clear` CSS properties to control text flow around them, as discussed in the earlier lesson.

Floating Images

As you learned in Lesson 8, "Using CSS to Style a Site," the `float` property removes an element from flow of the page and aligns it with the left or right side of its container. You can float images the same way you float any other element, using the `float` property as shown in the example that follows:

Input ▼

```
<img src="tulips.gif" style="float: left;">
<h1>Mystery Tulip Murderer Strikes</h1>
<p>
  Someone, or something, is killing the tulips of New South
  Haverford, Virginia. Residents of this small town are
  shocked and dismayed by the senseless vandalism that has
  struck their tiny town.
</p>
<p>
  New South Haverford is known for its extravagant displays
  of tulips in the springtime, and a good portion of its
  tourist trade relies on the people who come from as far as
  New Hampshire to see what has been estimated as up to two
  hundred thousand tulips that bloom in April and May.
</p>
<p>
  Or at least the tourists had been flocking to New South
  Haverford until last week, when over the course of three
  days the flower of each and every tulip in the town was
  neatly clipped off while the town slept.
</p>
<p>
  "It started at the south end of town," said Augustin Frouf,
  a retired ladder-maker who has personally planted over five
  hundred pink lily-flowered tulips. "They hit the houses up
  on Elm Street, and moved down into town from there. After
  the second night, we tried keeping guard. We tried bright
  lights, dogs, everything. There was always something that
  pulled us away, and by the time we got back, they were all
  gone."
</p>
```

Figure 9.8 shows an image with some text aligned next to it. In this case, the enclosing container for the image is the body of the page, and the image is floated to the left side of that container. The rest of the content of the page flows around it.

Output ▼

FIGURE 9.8
A floated image.

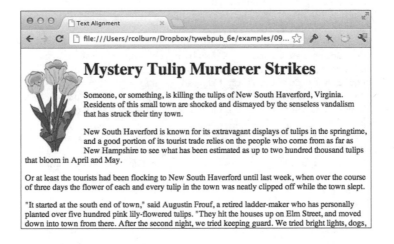

9

Stopping Text Wrapping

What if you want to stop the page content flowing around a floated image and start the next line underneath the image? A normal line break won't do it; it just breaks the line to the current margin alongside the image. A new paragraph also continues wrapping the text alongside the image. To stop wrapping text next to an image, use the `clear` CSS property. This enables you to return to the normal page flow past the floated element.

As mentioned in Lesson 8, the `clear` property can have one of three values:

`left`	Break to an empty left margin, for left-aligned images
`right`	Break to an empty right margin, for right-aligned images
`both`	Break to a line clear to both margins

For example, the following code snippet shows a picture of a tulip with some text wrapped next to it. Adding a `style` attribute to the first paragraph with `clear` set to `left` breaks the text wrapping after the heading and restarts the text after the image:

Input ▼

```
<p><img src="tulips.gif" style="float: left;"></p>
    <h1>Mystery Tulip Murderer Strikes</h1>
    <p style="clear: left;">
        Someone, or something, is killing the tulips of New South
        Haverford, Virginia. Residents of this small town are
        shocked and dismayed by the senseless vandalism that has
        struck their tiny town.
    </p>
    <p>
        New South Haverford is known for its extravagant displays
        of tulips in the springtime, and a good portion of its
        tourist trade relies on the people who come from as far as
        New Hampshire to see what has been estimated as up to two
        hundred thousand tulips that bloom in April and May.
    </p>
    <p>
        Or at least the tourists had been flocking to New South
        Haverford until last week, when over the course of three
        days the flower of each and every tulip in the town was
        neatly clipped off while the town slept.
    </p>
    <p>
        "It started at the south end of town," said Augustin Frouf,
        a retired ladder-maker who has personally planted over five
        hundred pink lily-flowered tulips. "They hit the houses up
        on Elm Street, and moved down into town from there. After
        the second night, we tried keeping guard. We tried bright
        lights, dogs, everything. There was always something that
        pulled us away, and by the time we got back, they were all
        gone."
    </p>
```

Figure 9.9 shows the result in a browser.

Output ▼

FIGURE 9.9
Line break to a
clear margin.

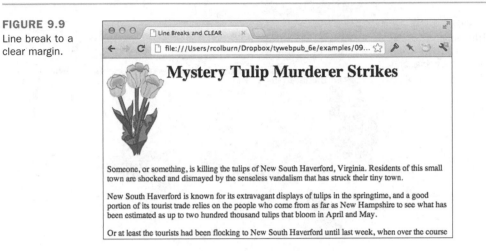

Adjusting the Space Around Images

With the capability to wrap text around an image, you also might want to add some space between the image and the text that surrounds it. In the previous lesson, you learned how to manage the whitespace around elements using CSS padding and margins. Images are like any other element when it comes to adding white space around them—you can use the `margin` and `padding` style properties with them.

The following HTML code, displayed in Figure 9.10, illustrates two examples. The upper example shows default horizontal and vertical spacing around the image, and the lower example shows how to add whitespace using padding. Both images are floated to the left. As you can see, the text next to the bottom image is aligned with the top of the padding, not the image itself.

Input ▼

```
<p><img src="eggplant.gif" style="float: left;"></p>
<p>
  This is an eggplant. We intend to stay a good ways away
  from it, because we really don't like eggplant very much.
</p>
<p style="clear: left;">
  <img src="eggplant.gif" style="float: left; padding: 50px;">
</p>
<p>
  This is an eggplant. We intend to stay a good ways away
  from it, because we really don't like eggplant very much.
</p>
```

Output ▼

FIGURE 9.10
The upper example
doesn't have
image spacing, and
the lower example
does.

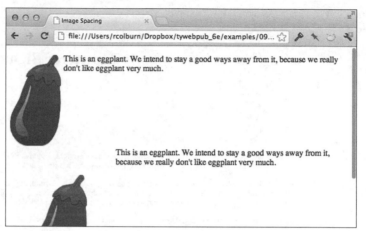

Images and Links

Can an image serve as a link? Sure it can! If you include an `<img>` tag inside a link tag (`<a>`), that image serves as a link itself:

```
<a href="index.html"><img src="uparrow.gif" alt="Up"></a>
```

If you include both an image and text in the link tag, they become links to the same URL:

```
<a href="index.html"><img src="uparrow.gif" alt="Up">Up to Index</a>
```

TIP

> One thing to look out for when you're placing images within links, with or without text, is whitespace between the `</a>` tag and the `<img>` tag or between the text and the image. Some browsers turn the whitespace into a link, and you get an odd "tail" on your images. To avoid this unsightly problem, don't leave spaces or line feeds between your `<img>` tags and `</a>` tags.

Some browsers add a border around images that appear when the image is linked. You can control the border around an image using the `border` CSS property. To remove the border, just use the `style` attribute:

```
<a href="index.html"><img src="uparrow.gif" alt="Up" style="border: none;"></a>
```

You can use any of the border-related properties that were described in the previous lesson to control the borders around an image, changing the width, color, or style. If you don't want any of the images on your page to have borders, whether they're in links or not, you can use the following style rule in your page's style sheet:

```
img { border: none; }
```

Or, if you want to disable only borders on images that are inside links, you can use this rule:

```
a img { border: none; }
```

You can always override that rule by adding a more specific rule that applies to the images that should have a border. For example, let's say you have some photos on your page that are linked to individual pages but look better with a border. First, write your image tag like this:

```
<a href="photo1detail.html"><img src="photo1.jpg" alt="Lake house"
class="photo"></a>
```

Then add the following style rule:

```
img.photo { border: 2px solid black; }
```

Even if you disabled borders for images in general using one of the previous rules, that rule will turn them back on for images with the `photo` class.

TIP

> Including borders around images that are links has really fallen out of favor with most web designers. Using them can make your design look very dated.

Exercise 9.2: Using Navigation Icons ▼

Now you can create a simple page that uses images as links. When you have a set of related web pages, it's usually helpful to create a consistent navigation scheme that is used on all the pages.

This example shows you how to create a set of icons that are used to navigate through a linear set of pages. You have three icons in GIF format: one for forward, one for back, and a third to enable the visitors to jump to the top-level contents page.

9

▼ First, you'll write the HTML structure to support the icons. Here, the page itself isn't very important, so you can just include a shell page:

Input ▼

```
<!DOCTYPE html>
<html>
  <head>
    <title>Motorcycle Maintenance: Removing Spark Plugs</title>
  </head>
  <body>
    <h1>Removing Spark Plugs</h1>
    <p>(include some info about spark plugs here)</p>
  </body>
</html>
```

Figure 9.11 shows how the page looks at the beginning.

Output ▼

FIGURE 9.11
The basic page,
with no icons.

At the bottom of the page, add your images using `<img>` tags:

Input ▼

```
<div>
  <img src="Up.png" alt="Up">
  <img src="Left.png" alt="Left">
  <img src="Right.png" alt="Right">
▼ </div>
```

Now add the anchors to the images to activate them:

Input ▼

```
<div>
  <a href="index.html"><img src="Up.png" alt="Up"></a>
  <a href="ready.html"><img src="Left.png" alt="Left"></a>
  <a href="replacing.html"><img src="Right.png" alt="Right"></a>
</div>
```

Figure 9.12 shows the result of this addition.

When you click the icons now, the browser jumps to the linked page just as it would have if you had used text links.

Output ▼

FIGURE 9.12
The basic page with navigation links.

Speaking of text, are the icons usable enough as they are? How about adding some text describing exactly what's on the other side of each link? You can add this text inside or outside the anchor, depending on whether you want the text to be a hot spot for the link, too. Here, include it outside the link so that only the image is a link. You also can position the icons so that the text is aligned with the middle of them using the `vertical-align` attribute of the `<img>` tag. Finally, because the extra text causes the icons to move onto two lines, arrange each one on its own line instead:

Input ▼

```
<!DOCTYPE html>
<html>
  <head>
    <title>Motorcycle Maintenance: Removing Spark Plugs</title>
```

```
<style type="text/css">
  img { vertical-align: middle; }
  ul { padding: 0; }
</style>
</head>
<body>
  <h1>Removing Spark Plugs</h1>
  <p>(include some info about spark plugs here)</p>
  <ul id="bottom-links">
    <li>
      <a href="index.html"><img src="Up.png" alt="Up"></a>
      Up to index
    </li>
    <li>
      <a href="ready.html"><img src="Right.png" alt="Left"></a>
      On to "Gapping the New Plugs"
    </li>
    <li>
      <a href="replacing.html"><img src="Left.png" alt="Right"></a>
      Back to "When You Should Replace your Spark Plugs"
    </li>
  </ul>
</body>
</html>
```

See Figure 9.13 for the final menu.

Output ▼

FIGURE 9.13
The basic page
with iconic links
and text.

Other Neat Tricks with Images

Now that you've learned about inline images, images as links, and how to wrap text around images, you know what *most* people do with images on web pages. But you can play with a few newer tricks, too.

Image Dimensions and Scaling

Two attributes of the `<img>` tag, `height` and `width`, specify the height and width of the image in pixels or as a percentage.

If the values for `width` and `height` are different from the actual width and height of the image, your browser will resize the image to fit those dimensions.

Here's an example `<img>` tag that uses the `height` and `width` attributes:

```
<img src="my_image.png" height="100" width="200" />
```

Although the `width` and `height` attributes are still part of HTML5, best practices recommend that you avoid using them. Instead, you should size your images with CSS. This lets your images be responsive. You will learn more about this in Lesson 16, "Using Responsive Web Design."

To specify the height and width using CSS, use the height and width properties:

```
<img src="my_image.png" style="height: 100px; width: 100px;">
```

If you leave out either the height or the width, the browser will calculate that value based on the value you provide for the other aspect. If you have an image that's 100 pixels by 100 pixels and you specify a height (using the attribute or CSS) of 200 pixels, the browser will automatically scale the width to 200 pixels, as well, preserving the original aspect ratio of the image. To change the aspect ratio of an image, you must specify both the height and the width.

As you've seen in this lesson, browsers can figure out the dimensions of images on their own. There are two reasons to specify the dimensions. The first is to alter them—to resize the image in the browser so it better fits on the page. This is how images are made responsive. You should create your images exactly as large as the largest device will be viewing them. Then use a graphics program to make the file size as small as possible. Then you can use CSS to resize the image down in smaller devices.

CAUTION

> Finding the best image size is a challenge for all web designers. You don't want images that are too large, making them slow to download on smartphones and tablets, but you don't want tiny images that look terrible on 5K displays. A good rule of thumb is to create your feature images as large or slightly larger than your page will handle. Then use CSS and responsive web design to resize it down for smaller devices. For nonfeature images, you can start with smaller initial images. You should never use CSS or the browser to make an image appear larger than it is. This will never look good. Instead, if you need a larger version of the image, go back and get a larger original.

The second reason to specify the dimensions of an image is to let the browser know ahead of time how large it is going to be. You should do this even if you aren't going to resize the image, because it enables the browser to establish the page layout before it downloads the images that will be displayed. This will help your pages display more quickly because the browser can lay out the page correctly before the images are fully downloaded. You can set the height and width of the image using the `height` and `width` attributes, the `height` and `width` style properties, or by specifying the height and width of the parent element.

Image Backgrounds

With CSS, you can specify a background image for any element and control exactly how it appears and is positioned.

To add a background image to an element, use the `background-image` style property. In the example below, I added a background image to a `<div>`, and added a few other style properties to illustrate how the background works. You can see how the example code appears in a browser in Figure 9.14.

```
<div style="background-image: url('black_rook.png');
  height: 240px; width: 240px; border: 1px solid black;
  background-color: #999;">
  An element with a background.
</div>
```

As you can see from the example, background images are tiled both horizontally and vertically. I added a grey background to the `<div>` but you can't see it at all because the background image is tiled to cover the entire background. I also added a border to show the exact size of the `<div>`.

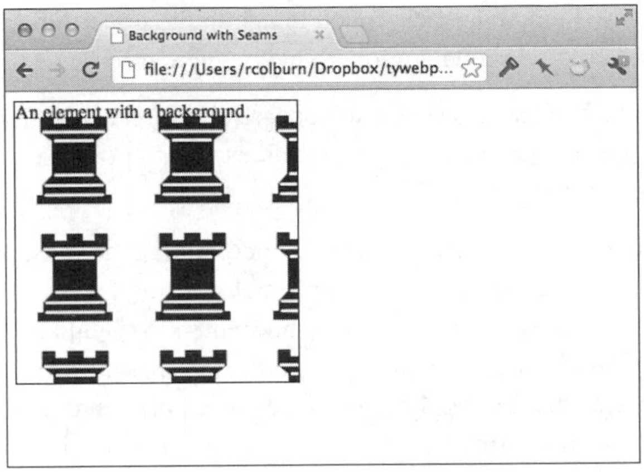

FIGURE 9.14
An element with a
tiled background.

CSS provides a number of options for controlling how backgrounds are applied. The
`background-repeat` property is used to specify how background images are tiled.
Options include `repeat` (the default, which tiles the image horizontally and vertically),
`repeat-x` (tile horizontally only), `repeat-y` (tile vertically only), and `no-repeat`. In
Figure 9.15, I've altered the `<div>` so that the background image does not repeat:

```
<div style="background-image: url('black_rook.png');
  height: 240px; width: 240px; border: 1px solid black;
  background-color: #999; background-repeat: no-repeat;">
  An element with a background.
</div>
```

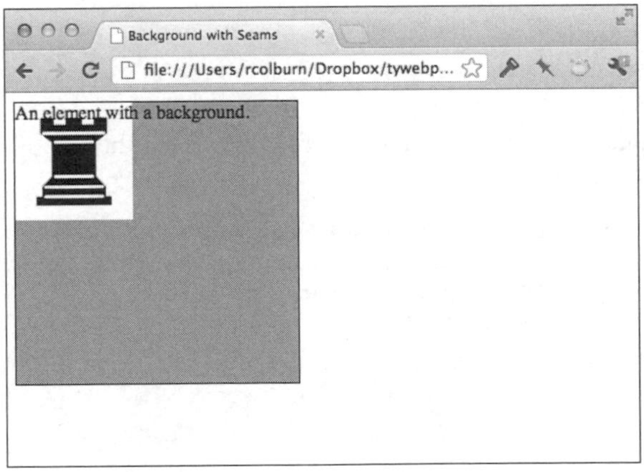

FIGURE 9.15
An element with a
nonrepeating back-
ground.

As you can see, there's only one background image in the upper-left corner of the `<div>`, and the background color is showing through everywhere else.

What if you want the background image to appear somewhere other than the upper-left corner? The `background-position` property enables you to position a background image anywhere you like within its container.

The `background-position` property is a bit more complex than most you'll see. You can either pass in two percentages, or the horizontal position (`left`, `right`, `center`), or the vertical position (`top`, `bottom`, `center`), or both the horizontal and vertical positions. If you specify only one value, the default position (`center`) will be used for the other. If you specify two values that can apply as the vertical or horizontal positions (a percentage, or `center`), the browser treats the first value as the horizontal setting and the second as vertical.

Here are some valid settings for this property:

Upper right	`100% 0%`
	`top right`
	`right top`
Center	`50% 50%`
	`center center`
	`50%`
Bottom center	`50% 100%`
	`bottom center`
	`center bottom`

Here's a tag that places the background centered 30% from the top of the `<div>`. You can see the results in Figure 9.16.

```
<div style="background-image: url('black_rook.png');
  height: 240px; width: 240px; border: 1px solid black;
  background-color: #999; background-repeat: no-repeat;
  background-position: center 30%;">
  An element with a background.
</div>
```

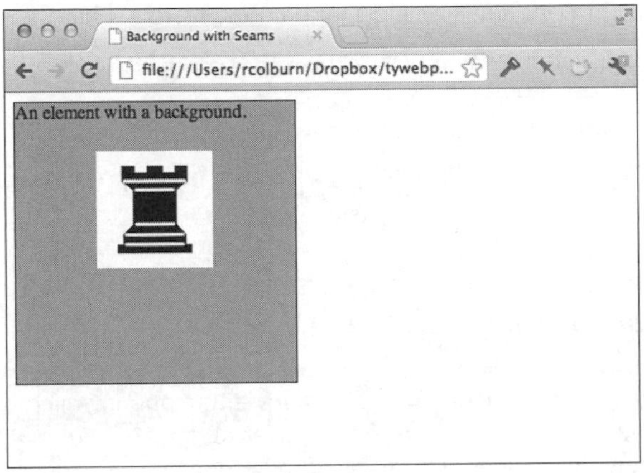

FIGURE 9.16
Using `background-position` with a background image.

You can also specify negative percentages for the background-position tag, if you want to position the background partially outside its container. This can be useful with tiled backgrounds if you don't want the upper-left corner of your background image to start in the upper-left corner of its container.

The final individual CSS property associated with backgrounds is `background-attachment`. It supports three values: `scroll`, `fixed`, and `local`. The default value is `scroll`—the background will scroll along with the element in which it is contained. `fixed` indicates that the background should not scroll at all; when the browser's viewport moves, the image maintains its position. The `local` setting means that the image will not move when its containing element moves but will scroll if the containing element itself scrolls. Usually this property is used to pin a background image to a fixed location in the browser window so that it doesn't scroll with the rest of the page.

Instead of using all these different properties to specify the background, you can use the `background` shorthand property by itself to specify all the background properties. With the `background` property, you can specify the background color, image, repeat setting, attachment, and position. All the properties are optional, but they must appear in a specific order. Here's the structure of the property:

```
background: background-color background-image background-repeat background-attachment background-position;
```

To condense the preceding specification into one property, the following tag is used:

```
<body style="background: url('backgrounds/rosemarble.gif')
no-repeat fixed center right;">
```

If you like, you can also include a background color. Here's what the new tag looks like:

```
<body style="background: #000 url('backgrounds/rosemarble.gif')
no-repeat fixed center right;">
```

Whether you use the `background` property or the individual properties for each of the background-related rules is a matter of taste.

CSS Backgrounds and the `<img>` **Tag**

Applying backgrounds to elements using CSS is an alternative to using the `<img>` tag to place images on a page. There are many situations in which both options will work. (For example, if you want to layer text over an image, you can place the text in a `<div>` and use the image as the background for that `<div>`, or you can use the `<img>` tag and then use CSS positioning to place the text over the image.)

However, there is a rule of thumb that many web designers use when choosing between the two alternatives. If an image is purely decorative, it should be included on the page as a background. If an image is part of the content of the page, you should use an `<img>` tag. So if the page is a news article, and you're including an image to illustrate the article, the `<img>` tag is appropriate. If you have a photo of a landscape that you want to use to make the heading of your page more attractive, it makes more sense to use CSS to include the image as a background in the heading.

The reason for this rule is that it makes things easier for visually challenged users who may be visiting a page using a screen reader. If you include your pretty header image using the `<img>` tag, the users' screen readers will tell them about the image on every page they visit. On the other hand, they probably would want to know about the photo accompanying a news article.

Another simple rule is to think about what you would put in the `alt` attribute for an image. If the alternate text is interesting or useful, you should use the `<img>` tag. If you can't think of anything interesting to put in the alternate text for an image, it probably should be a background for an element instead.

Using Images as Bullets

All the way back in Lesson 5, "Organizing Information with Lists," you learned about the `list-style-image` property, which enables you to use images as bullets for lists. Specifying the image URL for bullets is the same as specifying the URL for background images in CSS. The browser will substitute the default bullets with the image you specify. Here's an example, the results of which are shown in Figure 9.17.

Input ▼

```html
<!DOCTYPE html>
<html>
  <head>
    <title>Southern Summer Constellations</title>
    <style type="text/css" media="screen">
      ul {
          list-style-image: url("Bullet.png");
      }
    </style>
  </head>
  <body>
    <h1>Southern Summer Constellations</h1>

    <ul>
      <li>Canis Major</li>
      <li>Cetus</li>
      <li>Eridanus</li>
      <li>Gemini</li>
      <li>Orion</li>
      <li>Perseus</li>
      <li>Taurus</li>
    </ul>
  </body>
</html>
```

Output ▼

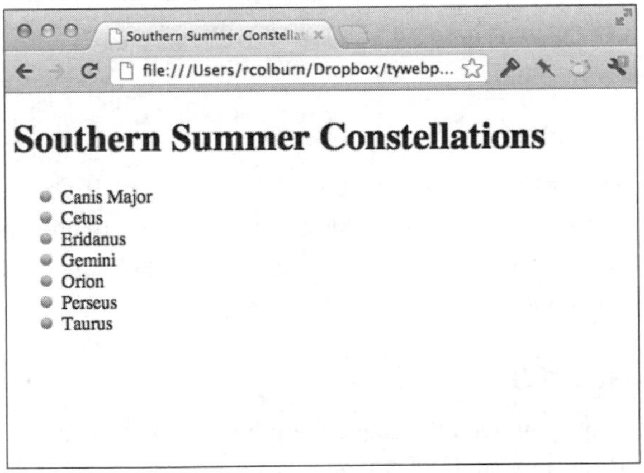

FIGURE 9.17
A list that uses
images for bullets.

You can also supply both the `list-style-image` and `list-style-type` properties so that
if the image is not found, the list will use the bullet style of your choosing.

What Is an Imagemap?

Earlier in this lesson, you learned how to create an image that doubles as a link simply by including the `<img>` tag inside a link tag (`<a>`). In this way, the entire image becomes a link.

In an imagemap, you can define regions of an image as links. You can specify that certain areas of a map link to various pages, as in Figure 9.18. Or you can create visual metaphors for the information you're presenting, such as a set of books on a shelf or a photograph with a link from each person in the picture to a page with his or her biography on it.

FIGURE 9.18
Imagemaps: different places, different links.

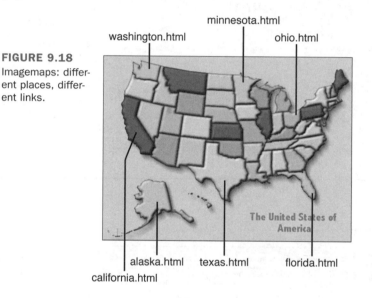

HTML5 supports the `<map>` element for creating image maps. If you don't want to use the `<map>` tag, you can also use CSS to position links over an image and hide the contents of those links, making it appear as though regions of an image are clickable. I discuss both techniques in this lesson.

Getting an Image

To create an imagemap, you need an image (of course). This image will be the most useful if it has several discrete visual areas that can be selected individually. For example, use an image that contains several symbolic elements or that can be easily broken down into polygons. Photographs generally don't make good imagemaps because their various elements tend to blend together or are of unusual shapes. Figures 9.19 and 9.20 show examples of good and poor images for imagemaps.

FIGURE 9.19
A good image for
an imagemap.

9

FIGURE 9.20
A not-so-good
image for an
imagemap.

Determining Your Coordinates

Imagemaps consist of two parts; the first is the image used for the imagemap. The second is the set of HTML tags used to define the regions of the imagemap that serve as links. To define these tags, you must determine the exact coordinates on your image that define the regions you'll use as links.

You can determine these coordinates either by sketching regions and manually noting the coordinates or by using an imagemap creation program. The latter method is easier because the program automatically generates a map file based on the regions you draw with the mouse.

The Mapedit program for Windows, Linux, and Mac OS X can help you create client-side imagemaps. You can find it online at http://www.boutell.com/mapedit/. In addition, many of the latest WYSIWYG editors for HTML pages and web graphics enable you to generate imagemaps. There's a web-based editor for imagemaps that you can try out at http://www.image-maps.com/; it creates both imagemaps and the CSS equivalents.

If you must create your imagemaps by hand, here's how. First, make a sketch of the regions that will be active on your image. Figure 9.21 shows the three types of shapes that you can specify in an imagemap: circles, rectangles, and polygons.

FIGURE 9.21
Three types of shapes are available for creating imagemaps.

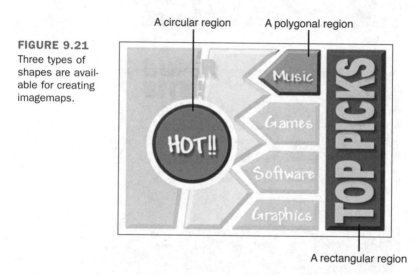

You next need to determine the coordinates for the endpoints of those regions. Most image-editing programs have an option that displays the coordinates of the current mouse position. Use this feature to note the appropriate coordinates. (All the mapping programs mentioned previously will create the <map> tag for you, but for now, following the steps manually will help you better understand the processes involved.)

Defining a Polygon

Figure 9.22 shows the x,y coordinates of a polygon region. These values are based on their positions from the upper-left corner of the image, which is coordinate 0,0. The first number in the coordinate pair indicates the x value and defines the number of pixels from the extreme left of the image. The second number in the pair indicates the y measurement and defines the number of pixels from the top of the image.

NOTE
The 0,0 origin is in the upper-left corner of the image, and positive y is down.

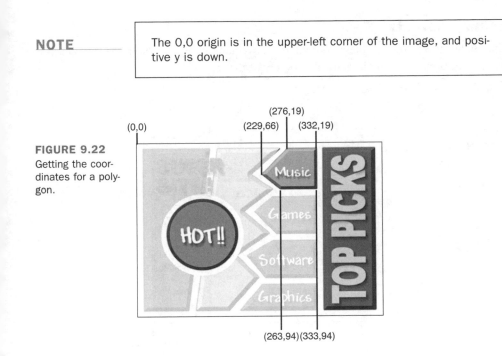

FIGURE 9.22
Getting the coordinates for a polygon.

Defining a Circle

Figure 9.23 shows how to get the coordinates for circles. Here you note the coordinates for the center point of the circle and the radius, in pixels. The center point of the circle is defined as the x,y coordinate from the upper-left corner of the image.

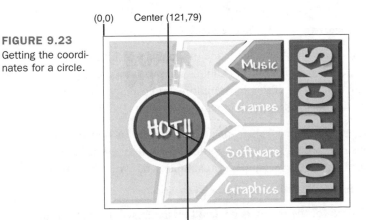

FIGURE 9.23
Getting the coordinates for a circle.

Defining a Rectangle

Figure 9.24 shows how to obtain coordinates for rectangle regions. Note the x,y coordinates for the upper-left and lower-right corners of the rectangle.

FIGURE 9.24
Getting the coordinates for a rectangle.

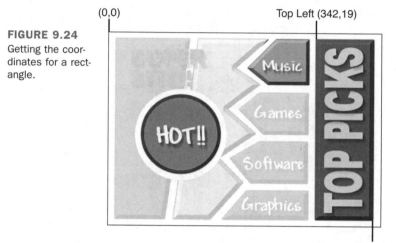

(0,0)   Top Left (342,19)

Bottom right (440,318)

The `<map>` and `<area>` Tags

If you're creating your imagemap manually and you've written down all the coordinates for your regions and the URLs they'll point to, you can include this information in the client-side imagemap tags on a web page. To include a client-side imagemap inside an HTML document, use the `<map>` tag, which looks like the following:

```
<map name="mapname"> coordinates and links </map>
```

The value assigned to the `name` attribute is the name of this map definition. This is the name that will be used later to associate the clickable image with its corresponding coordinates and hyperlink references. So, if you have multiple imagemaps on the same page, you can have multiple `<map>` tags with different names.

Between the `<map>` and the `</map>` tags, enter the coordinates for each area in the imagemap and the destinations of those regions. The coordinates are defined inside yet another new tag: the `<area>` tag. To define a rectangle, for example, you write the following:

```
<area shape="rect" coords="41,16,101,32" href="test.html">
```

The type of shape to be used for the region is declared by the `shape` attribute, which can have the values `rect`, `poly`, `circle`, and `default`. The coordinates for each shape are noted using the `coords` attribute. For example, the `coords` attribute for a `poly` shape appears as follows:

```
<area shape="poly" coords="x1,y1,x2,y2,x3,y3,...,xN,yN" href="URL">
```

Each x,y combination represents a point on the polygon. For `rect` shapes, $x1,y1$ is the upper-left corner of the rectangle, and $x2,y2$ is the lower-right corner:

```
<area shape="rect" coords="x1,y1,x2,y2" href="URL">
```

For `circle` shapes, x,y represents the center of a circular region of size *radius*:

```
<area shape="circle" coords="x,y,radius" href="URL">
```

The `default` shape is different from the others—it doesn't require coordinates to be specified. Instead, the link associated with the `default` shape is followed if the user clicks anywhere on the image that doesn't fall within another defined region.

Another attribute you need to define for each `<area>` tag is the `href` attribute. You can assign `href` any URL you usually would associate with an `<a>` link, including relative pathnames. In addition, you can assign `href` a value of `"nohref"` to define regions of the image that don't contain links to a new page.

NOTE

If you're using client-side imagemaps with frames, you can include the `target` attribute inside an `<area>` tag to open a new page in a specific window, as in this example:

```
<area shape="rect" coords="x1,y1,x2,y2" href="URL" target=
"window_name">
```

You need to include one more attribute in HTML5. Earlier in this lesson, you learned how to specify alternate text for images. In HTML5, the `alt` attribute is an additional requirement for the `<area>` tag that displays a short description of a clickable area on a client-side imagemap when you pass your cursor over it. Using the `<area>` example that I cited, the `alt` attribute appears as shown in the following example:

```
<area shape="rect" coords="41,16,101,32" href="test.html" alt="test link">
```

The `usemap` Attribute

After you've created your `<map>` tag and defined the regions of your image using `<area>` tags, the next step is to associate the map with the image. To do so, the `usemap` attribute of the `<img>` tag is used. The map name that you specified using the `name` attribute of the

9

`<map>` tag, preceded by a #, should be used as the value of the `usemap` attribute, as shown in this example:

```
<img src="image.gif" usemap="#mapname">
```

▼ Exercise 9.3: A Clickable Jukebox

Let's take a look at how to create a client-side imagemap for a real image. In this example, you'll define clickable regions on an image of a jukebox. The image you'll be using appears in Figure 9.25.

FIGURE 9.25
The jukebox image.

First, define the regions that will be clickable on this image. There are six rectangular buttons with musical categories on them, a center area that looks like a house, and a circle with a question mark inside it. Figure 9.26 shows regions on the image.

Now that you know where the various regions are, you need to find the exact coordinates of the areas as they appear in your image. You can use a mapping program like Mapedit, or you can do it manually. If you try it manually, it's helpful to keep in mind that most image-editing programs display the x and y coordinate of the image when you move the
▼ mouse over it.

FIGURE 9.26
The jukebox with areas defined.

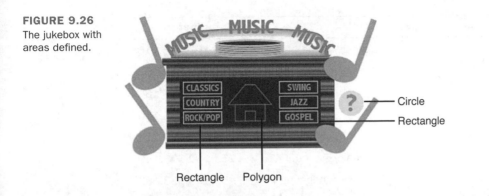

Rectangle   Polygon

9

Getting Image Coordinates from the Browser

You don't have an image-editing program? If you use Firefox as your browser, here's a trick: Create an HTML file with the image inside a link pointing to a fake file, and include the `ismap` attribute inside the `<img>` tag. You don't need a real link; anything will do. The HTML code might look something like the following:

```
<a href="nothing"><img src="myimage.gif" ismap></a>
```

When you load this into your browser, the image displays as if it were an imagemap. When you move your mouse over it, the x and y coordinates appear in the status line of the browser. Using this trick, you can find the coordinates for the map file of any point on that image.

With regions and a list of coordinates, all you need are the web pages to jump to when the appropriate area is selected. These can be documents, scripts, or anything else you can call from a browser as a jump destination. For this example, I've created several documents and stored them inside the `music` directory on my web server. These are the pages you'll define as the end points when the clickable images are selected. Figure 9.27 identifies each of the eight clickable areas in the imagemap. Table 9.1 shows the coordinates of each and the URL that's called up when it's clicked.

TABLE 9.1 Clickable Areas in the Jukebox Image

Number	Type	URL	Coordinates
1	rect	music/classics.html	101,113,165,134
2	rect	music/country.html	101,139,165,159
3	rect	music/rockpop.html	101,163,165,183

Number	Type	URL	Coordinates
4	poly	music/home.html	175,152,203,118
			220,118,247,152
			237,153,237,181
			186,181,186,153
5	rect	music/swing.html	259,113,323,134
6	rect	music/jazz.html	259,139,323,159
7	rect	music/gospel.html	259,163,323,183
8	circle	music/help.html	379,152,21

FIGURE 9.27
Eight hot spots, numbered as identified in Table 9.1.

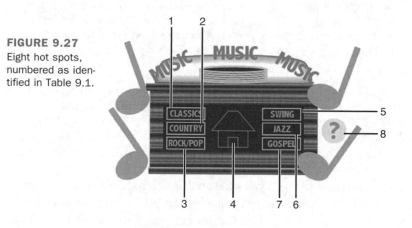

For the jukebox image, the `<map>` tag and its associated `<area>` tags and attributes look like the following:

```
<map name="jukebox">
<area shape="rect" coords="101,113, 165,134"
  href="/music/classics.html"
  alt="Classical Music and Composers">
<area shape="rect" coords="101,139, 165,159"
  href="/music/country.html"
  alt="Country and Folk Music">
<area shape="rect" coords="101,163, 165,183"
  href="/music/rockpop.html"
  alt="Rock and Pop from 50's On">
<area shape="poly" coords="175,152, 203,118, 220,118, 247,152,
  237,153, 237,181, 186,181, 186,153"
  href="code/music/home.html"
  alt="Home Page for Music Section">
```

```
<area shape="rect" coords="259,113, 323,134"
  href="/music/swing.html"
  alt="Swing and Big Band Music">
<area shape="rect" coords="259,139, 323,159"
  href="/music/jazz.html"
  alt="Jazz and Free Style">
<area shape="rect" coords="259,163, 323,183"
  href="/music/gospel.html"
  alt="Gospel and Inspirational Music">
<area shape="circle" coords="379,152, 21"
  href="/music/help.html"
  alt="Help">
</map>
```

9

The `<img>` tag that refers to the map coordinates uses `usemap`, as follows:

```
<img src="jukebox.gif" usemap="#jukebox" >
```

Finally, put the whole thing together and test it. Here's a sample HTML file for The Really Cool Music Page with a client-side imagemap, which contains both the `<map>` tag and the image that uses it:

Input ▼

```
<!DOCTYPE html>
<html>
<head>
<title>The Really Cool Music Page</title>
</head>
<body>
<div align="center">
<h1>The Really Cool Music Page</h1>
<p>Select the type of music you want to hear.<br>
 You'll go to a list of songs that you can select from.</p>
<p>
<img src="jukebox.gif" alt="Juke Box" usemap="#jukebox">
<map name="jukebox">
<area shape="rect" coords="101,113, 165,134"
  href="/music/classics.html"
  alt="Classical Music and Composers">
<area shape="rect" coords="101,139, 165,159"
  href="/music/country.html"
  alt="Country and Folk Music">
<area shape="rect" coords="101,163, 165,183"
  href="/music/rockpop.html"
  alt="Rock and Pop from 50's On">
<area shape="poly" coords="175,152, 203,118, 220,118, 247,152,
  237,153, 237,181, 186,181, 186,153"
  href="code/music/home.html"
  alt="Home Page for Music Section">
```

```
<area shape="rect" coords="259,113, 323,134"
  href="/music/swing.html"
  alt="Swing and Big Band Music">
<area shape="rect" coords="259,139, 323,159"
  href="/music/jazz.html"
  alt="Jazz and Free Style">
<area shape="rect" coords="259,163, 323,183"
  href="/music/gospel.html"
  alt="Gospel and Inspirational Music">
<area shape="circle" coords="379,152, 21"
  href="/music/help.html"
  alt="Help">
</map></p>
<p>
<a href="code/music/home.html">Home</a> |
<a href="code/music/classics.html">Classics</a> |
<a href="code/music/country.html">Country</a> |
<a href="code/music/rockpop.html">Rock/Pop</a> |
<a href="code/music/swing.html">Swing</a> |
<a href="code/music/jazz.html">Jazz</a> |
<a href="code/music/gospel.html">Gospel</a> |
<a href="code/music/help.html">Help</a>
</p>
</div>
</body>
</html>
```

Figure 9.28 shows the imagemap in a browser.

Output ▼

FIGURE 9.28
The finished Really Cool Music Page with client-side imagemap.

Image Etiquette

There are great images on sites all over the Web: cool icons, great photographs, excellent line art, and plenty of other graphics, too. You might feel the temptation to link directly to these images and include them on your own pages or save them to disk and then use them. There are a number of reasons why it's wrong to do so.

First of all, if you're linking directly to images on another site, you're stealing bandwidth from that site. Every time someone requests your page, that person is also issuing a request to the site where the image is posted and downloading the image from there. If you get a lot of traffic, you can cause problems for the remote site.

The second reason is actually a problem regardless of how you use images from other sites. If you don't have permission to use an image on your site, you're violating the rights of the image's creator. Copyright law protects creative work from use without permission, and it's granted to every creative work automatically.

The best course of action is to create your own images or look for images that are explicitly offered for free use by their creators. Even if images are made available for your use, you should download them and store them with your web pages rather than linking to them directly. Doing so prevents you from abusing the bandwidth of the person providing the images.

Summary

In this lesson you learned to place images on your web pages. Those images are normally in GIF, JPEG, PNG, or SVG format and should be small enough that they can be downloaded quickly over a slow link. You also learned that the HTML tag `<img>` enables you to put an image on a web page either inline with text or on a line by itself. The `<img>` tag has two primary attributes supported in standard HTML:

`src`	The location and filename of the image to include.
`alt`	A text string to substitute for the image in text-only browsers.

You can include images inside a link tag (`<a>`) to treat them as links. You also learned how to display images on a page using CSS, as backgrounds for elements or as list bullets.

Workshop

Now that you know how to add images and color to your pages, you can really get creative. This workshop will help you remember some of the most important points about using images on your pages.

Q&A

Q **What are the differences between GIF, PNG, and JPEG images? Is there any rule of thumb that defines when you should use one format rather than the other?**

A JPEG images are best for photographic-quality or high-resolution 3D rendered graphics because they can display true-color images to great effect. Most image-editing programs enable you to specify how much to compress a JPEG image. The size of the file decreases the more an image is compressed; however, compression can also deteriorate the quality and appearance of the image if you go overboard. You have to find just the right balance between quality and file size, and that can differ from image to image.

As a rule, you should use PNG (or GIF) for all images that are not photographs. They both offer good compression, but PNG offers a number of advantages over GIF, including support for palettes of more than 256 colors, and alpha-based transparency. There's no reason to convert existing GIFs to PNG, but if you are creating new images, PNG is almost always the better choice.

The one unique feature offered by GIFs is simple animation. Many sites are using animated GIFs rather than video for some things these days because you don't need to worry about browser support, plug-ins, or any of the overhead associated with web video if you just want to present an animated image.

Q **My client-side imagemaps aren't working. What's wrong?**

A Make sure that the pathnames or URLs in your `<area>` tags point to real files. Also, make sure the map name in the `<map>` file matches the name of the map in the `usemap` attribute in the `<img>` tag. Only the latter should have a pound sign in front of it.

Q **How can I create thumbnails of my images so that I can link them to larger external images?**

A You'll have to do that with some type of image-editing program (such as Adobe Photoshop); the Web won't do it for you. Just open up the image and scale it down to the right size.

Q **What about images that are partially transparent so that they are able to display the page background? They look like they sort of float on the page. How do I create those?**

A This is another task you can accomplish with an image-editing program. Both GIF and PNG support transparency. Most image-editing programs provide the capability to create these types of images.

Q **Can I put HTML tags in the string for the `alt` attribute?**

A That would be nice, wouldn't it? Unfortunately, you can't. All you can do is put an ordinary string in there. Keep it simple, and you should be fine.

9

Quiz

1. What's the most important attribute of the `<img>` tag? What does it do?

2. If you see a funny-looking icon rather than an image when you view your page, the image isn't loading. What are some of the reasons this could happen?

3. Why is it important to use the `alt` attribute to display a text alternative to an image? When is it most important to do so?

4. What is an imagemap?

5. Why is it a good idea to also provide text versions of links that you create on an imagemap?

6. True or false: When you use the `background` shorthand property, the order of the values is important.

Quiz Answers

1. The most important attribute of the `<img>` tag is the `src` attribute. It indicates the filename or URL of the image you want to include on your page.

2. Several things might cause an image not to load: The URL may be incorrect, the filename might not be correct (they're case sensitive), it might have the wrong file extension, it might be the wrong type of file, or you might have forgotten to load the image to the web server.

3. It's a good idea to provide text alternatives with images because some people use text-only browsers or have their graphics turned off. It's especially important to provide text alternatives for images used as links.

4. An imagemap is a special image in which different areas point to different locations on the Web.

5. It's a good idea to include text versions of imagemap links in case there are users who visit your page with text-only browsers or with images turned off. This way, they can still follow the links on the web page and visit other areas of your website.

6. True. The property will only work if you enter the values in the proper order.

Exercises

1. Create or find some images that you can use as navigation icons or buttons on one or more pages of your website. Remember that it's always advantageous to use images more than once. Create a simple navigation bar that you can use on the top or bottom of each page.

2. Create or find some images that you can use to enhance the appearance of your web pages. After you find some that you like, try to create background, text, and link colors that are compatible with them.

3. Create and test a simple client-side imagemap that links to pages that reside in different subdirectories in a website or to other sites on the World Wide Web.

4. Create and test a client-side imagemap for your own home page or for the entry page in one of the main sections of your website. Remember to include alternatives for those who are using text-only browsers or browsers designed for the disabled.

LESSON 10
Building Tables

So far in this book, you've used plain vanilla *Hypertext Markup Language* (HTML) to build and position the elements on your pages, and you've used *Cascading Style Sheets* (CSS) to fine-tune their appearance. Although you can get your point across using paragraphs and lists, some information lends itself best to being presented in tables. In this lesson, you learn how to use HTML to create them.

When tables were officially introduced in HTML 3.2, they were commonly used to lay out entire pages. More recently, that role has been taken over by CSS. With the introduction of HTML 4 and later releases, new features were added to enable tables to better perform their designated role: the presentation of tabular data.

In this lesson, you'll learn all about tables, including the following:

- Defining tables in HTML
- Creating captions, rows, and heading and data cells
- Modifying cell alignment
- Creating cells that span multiple rows or columns
- Adding color to tables
- Using tables in web pages

Creating Tables

Creating tables in HTML is a degree more complex than anything you've seen so far in this book. Think about how many different types of tables there are. A table can be a three-by-three grid with labels across the top, or two side-by-side cells, or a complex Excel spreadsheet that comprises many rows and columns of various sizes. Representing tables in HTML is heavy on tags, and the tags can be hard to keep track of when you get going.

The basic approach with table creation is that you represent tabular data in a linear fashion, specifying what data goes in which table cells using HTML tags. In HTML, tables are created from left to right and top to bottom. You start by creating the upper-left cell and finish with the bottom-right cell. This will all become clearer when you see some actual table code.

Table Parts

Before getting into the actual HTML code to create a table, here are some table-related terms you'll see throughout this lesson:

- The *caption* indicates what the table is about: for example, "Voting Statistics, 1950–1994," or "Toy Distribution Per Room at 1564 Elm St." Captions are optional.

- The *table headings* label the rows, columns, or both. Usually they're in an emphasized font that's different from the rest of the table. They're optional.

- *Table cells* are the individual squares in the table. A cell can contain normal table data or a table heading.

- *Table data* is the values in the table itself. The combination of the table headings and table data makes up the sum of the table.

Figure 10.1 shows a typical table and its parts.

FIGURE 10.1
The elements that make up a table.

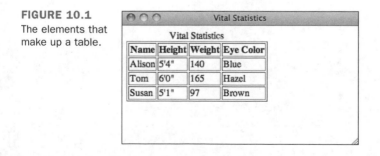

The `<table>` Element

All the components of a table are placed within a `<table>`...`</table>` element:

```
<table>
...table caption (optional) and contents...
</table>
```

Here's the code that produces the table shown in Figure 10.1. Don't be concerned if you don't know what all this means right now. For now, notice that the table starts with a `<table>` tag and its attributes and ends with a `</table>` tag:

```
<table border="1">
<caption>Vital Statistics</caption>
 <tr>
  <th>Name</th>
  <th>Height</th>
  <th>Weight</th>
  <th>Eye Color</th>
 </tr>
 <tr>
  <td>Alison</td>
  <td>5'4"</td>
  <td>140</td>
  <td>Blue</td>
 </tr>
 <tr>
  <td>Tom</td>
  <td>6'0"</td>
  <td>165</td>
  <td>Hazel</td>
 </tr>
 <tr>
  <td>Susan</td>
  <td>5'1"</td>
  <td>97</td>
  <td>Brown</td>
 </tr>
</table>
```

Summarizing the Table

Previous versions of HTML before HTML5 required that tables be summarized within the table. HTML5 removed this attribute in favor of describing tables more explicitly within the page. Specifically, tables that might be difficult to understand or where the headers are not in the first row or column should have explanatory information introducing the table. This summary should introduce the purpose of the table, explain the cell structure, and teach the reader how the table will be used.

This information can be included in several ways, including the following:

- In a prose paragraph before the table
- In the table's caption
- Inside a `<details>` element in the caption
- Next to the table in a figure or the figure's caption

This is not required if your table is used for presentation.

Rows and Cells

Now that you've been introduced to the `<table>` element, we'll move on to the rows and cells. Inside the `<table>...</table>` element, you define the actual contents of the table. Tables are specified in HTML row by row, and each row definition contains all the cells in that row. So, to create a table, you start with the top row and then each cell in turn, from left to right. Then you define a second row and its cells, and so on. The number of columns is calculated based on how many cells there are in each row.

Each table row starts with the `<tr>` tag and ends with the closing `</tr>`. Your table can have as many rows and columns as you like, but you should make sure that each row has the same number of cells so that the columns line up.

The cells within each row are created using one of two elements:

- `<th>...</th>` elements are used for heading cells. Generally, browsers center the contents of a `<th>` cell and render any text in the cell in boldface.
- `<td>...</td>` elements are used for data cells. `td` stands for *table data*.

NOTE

Closing tags are not required for `<th>`, `<td>`, and `<tr>` tags. And as long as your table data is clear without them, you can leave them out. However, if you're writing XHTML or your tables don't display correctly, you should include them. Most HTML editors include them automatically.

In this table example, the heading cells appear in the top row and are defined with the following code:

```
<tr>
 <th>Name</th>
 <th>Height</th>
 <th>Weight</th>
 <th>Eye Color</th>
</tr>
```

The top row is followed by three rows of data cells, which are coded as follows:

```
<tr>
 <td>Alison</td>
 <td>5'4"</td>
 <td>140</td>
 <td>Blue</td>
</tr>
<tr>
 <td>Tom</td>
 <td>6'0"</td>
 <td>165</td>
 <td>Blue</td>
</tr>
<tr>
 <td>Susan</td>
 <td>5'1"</td>
 <td>97</td>
 <td>Brown</td>
</tr>
```

As you've seen, you can place the headings along the top edge by defining the `<th>` elements inside the first row. Let's make a slight modification to the table. You'll put the headings along the left edge of the table instead. To accomplish this, put each `<th>` in the first cell in each row and follow it with the data that pertains to each heading. The new code looks like the following:

Input ▼

```
<tr>
 <th>Name</th>
 <td>Alison</td>
 <td>Tom</td>
 <td>Susan</td>
</tr>
<tr>
 <th>Height</th>
 <td>5'4"</td>
 <td>6'0"</td>
 <td>5'1"</td>
</tr>
<tr>
 <th>Weight</th>
 <td>140</td>
 <td>165</td>
 <td>97</td>
</tr>
<tr>
 <th>Eye Color</th>
```

10

```
<td>Blue</td>
<td>Blue</td>
<td>Brown</td>
</tr>
```

Figure 10.2 shows how this table is displayed in a browser.

Output ▼

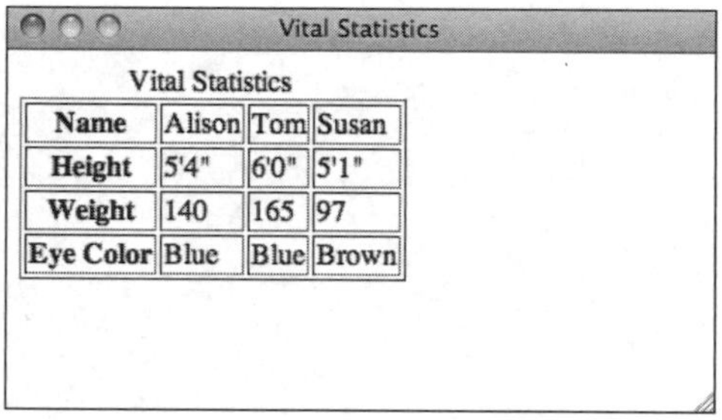

FIGURE 10.2
An example of a table that includes headings in the leftmost column.

Vital Statistics			
Name	Alison	Tom	Susan
Height	5'4"	6'0"	5'1"
Weight	140	165	97
Eye Color	Blue	Blue	Brown

Empty Cells

Both table heading cells and data cells can contain any text, HTML code, or both, including links, lists, forms, images, and other tables. But what if you want a cell with nothing in it? That's easy. Just define a cell with a `<th>` or `<td>` element with nothing inside it:

Input ▼

```
<table border="1">
<tr>
  <td></td>
  <td>10</td>
  <td>20</td>
</tr>
</table>
```

Some older browsers display empty cells of this sort as if they don't exist at all, leaving off the borders. If you want to force a *truly* empty cell, you can add a line break with no other text in that cell by itself:

Input ▼

```
<table border="1">
<tr>
  <td><br></td>
```

```
  <td>10</td>
  <td>20</td>
</tr>
</table>
```

Captions

Table captions tell your visitor what the table is for. The `<caption>` element, created just for this purpose, displays the text inside the tag as the table caption (usually centered above the table). Although you could use a regular paragraph or a heading as a caption for your table, tools that process HTML files can extract `<caption>` elements into a separate file, automatically number them, or treat them in special ways simply because they're captions.

> **NOTE**
>
> If you don't want a caption, it's optional. If your table is understandable without a caption or you have described it in some other location, you can leave it off.

The `<caption>` element goes inside the `<table>` element just before the table rows, and it contains the title of the table. It closes with the `</caption>` tag:

```
<table>
<caption>Vital Statistics</caption>
<tr>
```

You can include details inside a caption to provide additional information about the table that is hidden by default. When you include details, you need to also include a summary that acts as a title for the additional details. Chrome, Safari, and Opera all support showing and hiding content with the `<detail>` and `<summary>` tags. You can use the `<details>` and `<summary>` tags inside the `<caption>` tag:

```
<caption>
  <details>
    <summary>Vital Statistics</summary>
    <p>This table includes the name, height, and, weight of various employees.
    </p>
  </details>
</caption>
```

Figure 10.3 shows a `<detail>` element that has been clicked on to show the hidden content.

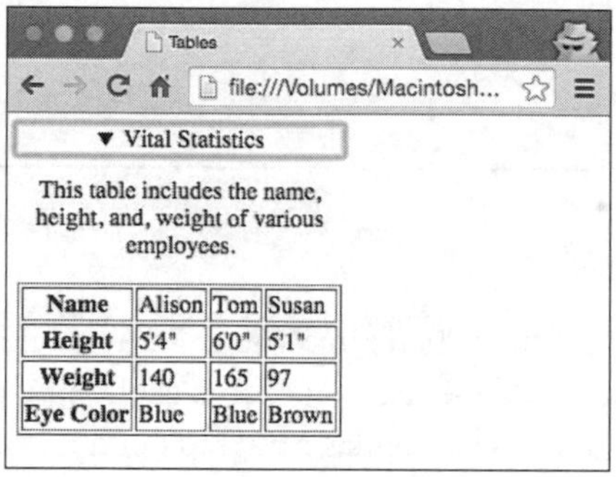

FIGURE 10.3
A visible details
area.

▼ Vital Statistics

This table includes the name,
height, and, weight of various
employees.

Name	Alison	Tom	Susan
Height	5'4"	6'0"	5'1"
Weight	140	165	97
Eye Color	Blue	Blue	Brown

▼ Exercise 10.1: Creating a Simple Table

Now that you know the basics of how to create a table, try a simple example. You'll
create a table that indicates the colors you get when you mix the three primary colors
together. Figure 10.4 shows the table you're going to re-create in this example.

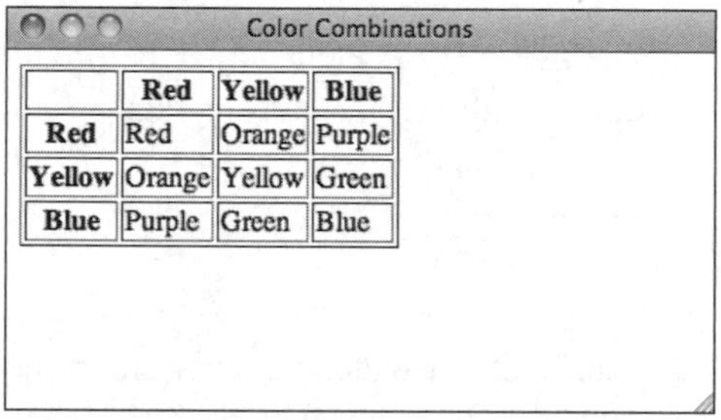

FIGURE 10.4
A simple color
table.

Color Combinations

	Red	Yellow	Blue
Red	Red	Orange	Purple
Yellow	Orange	Yellow	Green
Blue	Purple	Green	Blue

Here's a quick hint for laying out tables: Because HTML defines tables on a row-by-row
basis, sometimes it can be difficult to keep track of the columns, particularly with complex tables. Before you start actually writing HTML code, it's useful to make a sketch of
your table so that you know the heads and the values of each cell. You might even find
that it's easiest to use a word processor with a table editor (such as Microsoft Word) or
a spreadsheet to lay out your tables. Then, when you have the layout and the cell values,
you can write the HTML code for that table. Eventually, if you do this enough, you'll
▼ think of these things in terms of HTML tags, whether you want to or not.

Start with a simple HTML framework for a page that contains a table. As with all HTML ▼ files, you can create this file in any text editor:

```
<!doctype html>
<html>
  <head>
    <title>Colors</title>
  </head>
  <body>
    <table border="1">
      <!-- ...add table rows and cells here... -->
    </table>
  </body>
</html>
```

Now start adding table rows inside the opening and closing `<table>` tags (where the line `<!-- ...add table rows and cells here... -->` is). The first row is the three headings along the top of the table. The table row is indicated by `<tr>` and each cell by a `<th>` tag:

10

```
<tr>
  <th>Red</th>
  <th>Yellow</th>
  <th>Blue</th>
</tr>
```

NOTE

You can format the HTML code any way you want. As with all HTML, the browser ignores most extra spaces and returns. I like to format it like this, with the contents of the individual rows indented and the cell elements on separate lines, so that I can pick out the rows and columns more easily. But you will often see tables condensed to just one line of HTML for each row of the table to save space.

Now add the second row. The first cell in the second row is the Red heading on the left side of the table, so it will be the first cell in this row, followed by the cells for the table data:

```
<tr>
  <th>Red</th>
  <td>Red</td>
  <td>Orange</td>
  <td>Purple</td>
</tr>
```

▼

▼ Continue by adding the remaining two rows in the table, with the Yellow and Blue headings. Here's what you have so far for the entire table:

Input ▼

```
<table border="1">
<tr>
  <th>Red</th>
  <th>Yellow</th>
  <th>Blue</th>
</tr>
<tr>
  <th>Red</th>
  <td>Red</td>
  <td>Orange</td>
  <td>Purple</td>
</tr>
<tr>
  <th>Yellow</th>
  <td>Orange</td>
  <td>Yellow</td>
  <td>Green</td>
</tr>
<tr>
  <th>Blue</th>
  <td>Purple</td>
  <td>Green</td>
  <td>Blue</td>
</tr>
</tr>
</table>
```

Finally, add a simple caption. The `<caption>` element goes just after the `<table>` tag and just before the first `<tr>` tag:

```
<table border="1">
<caption>Mixing the Primary Colors</caption>
<tr>
```

▼ With a first draft of the code in place, test the HTML file in your favorite browser that supports tables. Figure 10.5 shows how it looks.

Output ▼

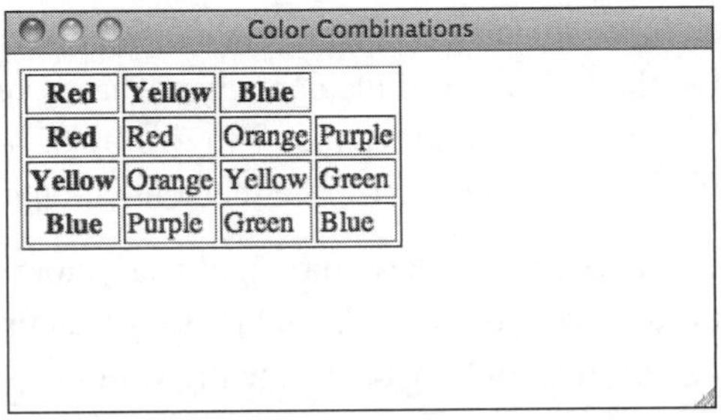

FIGURE 10.5
The not-quite-
perfect color table.

Oops! What happened with that top row? The headings are all messed up. The answer, of course, is that you need an empty cell at the beginning of that first row to space the headings out over the proper columns. HTML isn't smart enough to match it all up for you. (This is exactly the sort of error you're going to find the first time you test your tables.)

Add an empty table heading cell to that first row. (Here, it's the line `<th></th>`.)

Input ▼

```
<tr>
  <th></th>
  <th>Red</th>
  <th>Yellow</th>
  <th>Blue</th>
</tr>
```

NOTE

I used `<th>` here, but it could be `<td>` just as easily. Because there's nothing in the cell, its formatting doesn't matter.

If you try it again, you should get the right result with all the headings over the right columns, as the original example in Figure 10.4 shows.

Sizing Tables, Borders, and Cells

With the basics out of the way, now you'll look at how you can change the overall appearance of your tables. As with most other appearance features on web pages, you use CSS to design how your tables should look.

Setting Table Widths

Tables determine widths differently than other elements in HTML. Rather than each element taking up the full width of its container element, table elements only take up the width their content uses, up to the full width of the container. This is very useful when you're working with CSS designs. You can set elements to `display: table;`, and they will act more like a table cell, taking up only the space the content takes up.

But when working with actual tables, sometimes you might want more control over how wide your tables and columns are, particularly if the defaults the content provides are really strange. In this section, you'll learn how to change the width of your tables and columns.

The easiest way is to use the `width` property on the table itself. This defines how wide the table will be on the page. The `width` property can have a value that is either the exact width of the table (in pixels) or a percentage (such as 50% or 75%) of the current container width, which can therefore change if the window or container element is resized. You can also set the `width` property on your table cells, defining the width of each column.

To make a table as wide as the browser window, you add the `width` property to the table, as shown in the following line of code:

Input ▼

```
<table border="1" style="width: 100%;">
```

Figure 10.6 shows the result.

Output ▼

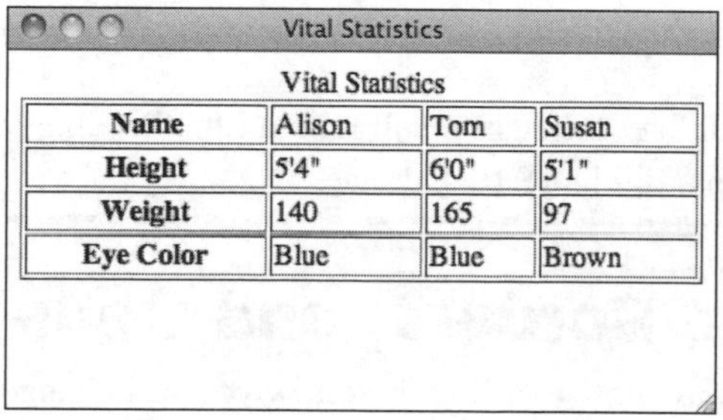

FIGURE 10.6
A table set to
100% width.

Vital Statistics			
Name	Alison	Tom	Susan
Height	5'4"	6'0"	5'1"
Weight	140	165	97
Eye Color	Blue	Blue	Brown

CAUTION

> If you make your table too narrow for whatever you put in it, the browser will ignore your settings and make the table as wide as it needs to be to display the content unless you use the CSS `overflow` property to specify otherwise. The overflow property was discussed in Lesson 8, "Using CSS to Style a Site."

It's nearly always a better idea to specify your table widths as percentages rather than as specific pixel widths. Because you don't know how wide the browser window will be, using percentages allows your table to be reformatted to whatever width the browser is. Using specific pixel widths might cause your table to run off the page. Also, if you make your tables too wide using a pixel width, your pages might not print properly.

Changing Table Borders

The `border` attribute, which appears immediately inside the opening `<table>` tag, is the most common attribute of the `<table>` element. With it, you specify whether border lines are displayed around the table. This also serves as an indicator of the type of content the table contains. But this attribute is *nonconforming* in HTML5. This means that if you use it, your HTML isn't 100% correct.

In HTML4, it was incorrect to use tables for layout, but many people continued to do so because they were easier to visualize and understand than many of the CSS methods for layout. So, HTML5 made it valid again, but with a few rules.

Tables are bad for layout because they are not accessible. They can be difficult for assistive technology to read correctly, but with a few tweaks, you can adjust your tables to use them for layout. If you use one or more of the following features, you are indicating that your table is probably a layout table and does not contain tabular data:

- Use the `role` attribute with the value `presentation`.
- Use the `border` attribute with a value of `0`.
- Use the *nonconforming* `cellspacing` or `cellpadding` attributes with the value of `0`.

By using the `caption` tag and the `border="1"` attribute, we are indicating that our table is almost certainly a nonlayout table and contains tabular data.

10

NOTE

You really should avoid using tables for layout. Even if you use the previously mentioned indicators, they are still difficult for screen readers and other assistive devices to read. This book provides information on how to use CSS for layout in Lesson 15, "Advanced CSS: Page Layout with CSS."

You can change the width of the border around the table by changing the number value in the `border` attribute. Figure 10.7 shows a table that has a border width of 10 pixels. The table and border definition looks like this:

Input ▼

```
<table border="10" style="width:100%;">
```

Output ▼

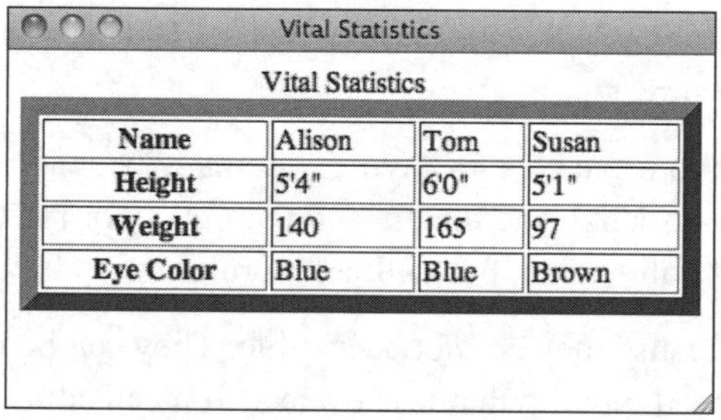

FIGURE 10.7
A table with the border width set to 10 pixels.

Vital Statistics			
Name	Alison	Tom	Susan
Height	5'4"	6'0"	5'1"
Weight	140	165	97
Eye Color	Blue	Blue	Brown

You can also adjust the borders around your tables using CSS, with much finer control than the `border` attribute provides.

You learned about borders in Lesson 8, but there's more to them when it comes to tables. For example, if you write a table like the one that follows, it will have a border around the outside, but no borders around the cells:

```
<table style="border: 1px solid red;">
    <!-- Table rows and cells go here. -->
</table>
```

To draw borders around all the cells in a table (the way the `border` attribute does), the easiest way is to use a style sheet like this:

```
<style>
table { border: 1px solid black; }
```

```
td, th { border: 1px solid black; }
</style>
```

If I applied that style sheet to the vital statistics table used in the previous example, it would appear as it does in Figure 10.8.

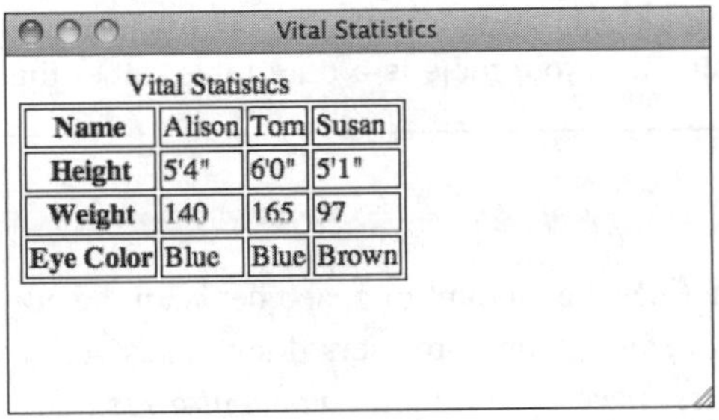

FIGURE 10.8
A table with cell borders applied using CSS.

As you can see, there are gaps between the borders on each cell for this table. To fix this, we need to use the CSS `border-collapse` property on the `table` element. It has two possible values, `separate` and `collapse`. The default is `separate`, it produces the result you see in Figure 10.8. The style sheet that follows shows how to apply it:

```
<style>
table {
    border: 1px solid black;
    border-collapse: collapse;
}
td, th {
    border: 1px solid black;
}
</style>
```

Figure 10.9 shows the results.

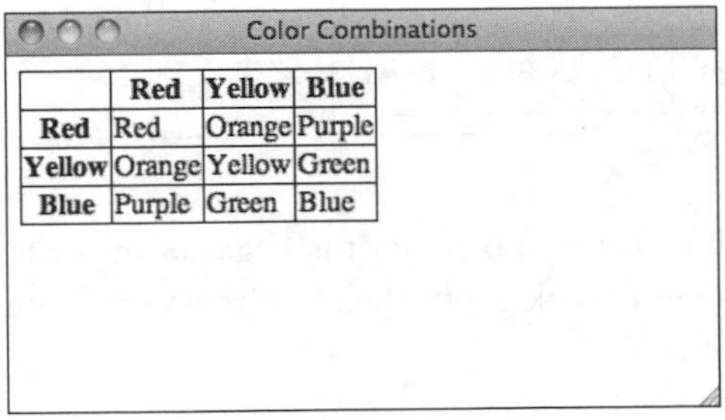

FIGURE 10.9
A table that uses the `border-collapse` property to eliminate space between cells.

10

The tables that I used for these examples included the `border` attribute to create a border. If you apply table borders using CSS, they will override the `border` attribute, so you don't need to remove it. This can be helpful because primitive browsers (including the browsers on some mobile phones) don't offer CSS support, and including the `border` attribute will ensure that borders are still displayed. It also, as mentioned previously, indicates that your table is a data table rather than a layout table.

Cell Padding

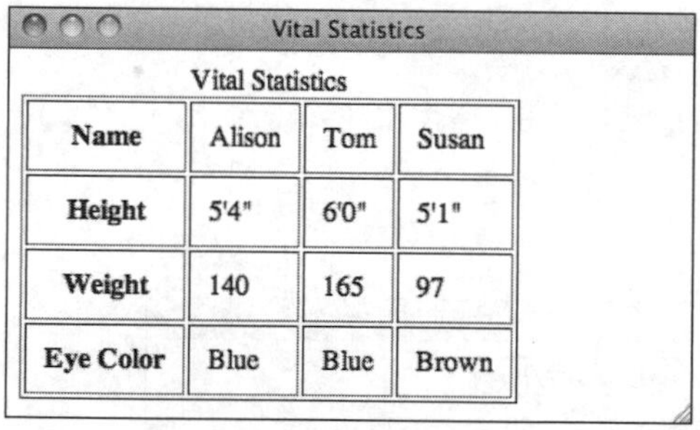

The cell padding attribute defines the amount of space between the edges of the cells and the content inside a cell. By default, many browsers draw tables with a cell padding of two pixels. You can add more space by adding the *nonconforming* `cellpadding` attribute to the `<table>` element, with a value in pixels for the amount of cell padding you want.

Here's the revised code for your `<table>` element, which increases the cell padding to 10 pixels. Figure 10.10 shows the result.

Input ▼

```
<table cellpadding="10" border="1">
```

Output ▼

FIGURE 10.10
A table with the cell padding set to 10 pixels.

A `cellpadding` attribute with a value of 0 causes the edges of the cells to touch the edges of the cell's contents. This doesn't look good when you're presenting text, but it can prove useful in other situations.

You can also specify the padding of a table cell using the `padding` property in CSS. The advantages of doing so are that you can specify the padding for the top, left, right, and bottom separately, and you can specify different padding amounts for different cells of the table if you choose to do so. For example, you can set the padding of header cells to 10 pixels on the top and 5 pixels on the sides and bottom and then set the padding to four pixels on all four sides for regular table cells. This is also the valid HTML5 method of defining padding for table cells.

To create the table in Figure 10.10 with CSS, you add the style sheet:

Input ▼

```
table {
    border: 1px solid black;
}
td, th {
    border: 1px solid black;
    padding: 10px;
}
```

10

Cell Spacing

Cell spacing is similar to cell padding except that it affects the amount of space between cells—that is, the width of the space between the inner and outer lines that make up the table border. The *nonconforming* `cellspacing` attribute of the `<table>` element affects the spacing for the table. Cell spacing is two pixels by default.

Cell spacing also includes the outline around the table, which is just inside the table's border (as set by the `border` attribute). Experiment with it, and you can see the difference. For example, Figure 10.11 shows our table with cell spacing of 8 and a border of 4, as shown in the following code:

Input ▼

```
<table border="4" cellspacing="8" cellpadding="10">
```

Output ▼

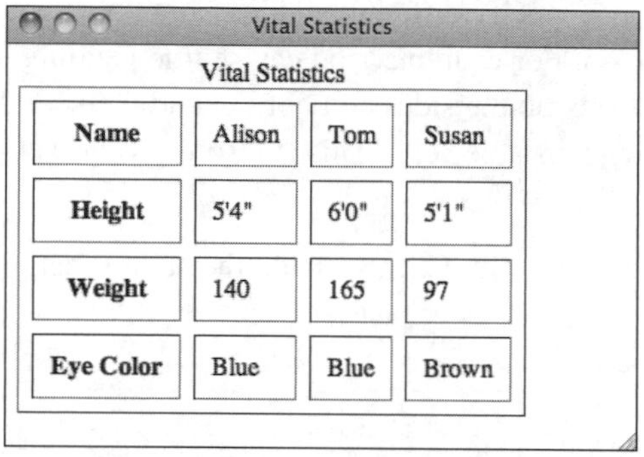

FIGURE 10.11
How increased cell
spacing looks.

The CSS equivalent of the `cellspacing` attribute is the `border-spacing` property, which must be applied to the table. To use it, the `border-collapse` property must not be set to collapse, as it eliminates cell spacing. `border-spacing` is slightly different than `padding`. With `padding`, you can specify the padding for all four sides of an element. `border-spacing` takes one or two values. If one value is specified, it is used for all four sides of each cell. If two are specified, the first sets the horizontal spacing and the second sets the vertical spacing. The table in Figure 10.12 uses the following style sheet, which sets the cell padding for each cell to 5 pixels and sets the cell spacing for the table to 10 pixels horizontally and 5 pixels vertically:

```
<style>
table {
        border-collapse: separate;
        border-spacing: 10px 5px;
}

td, th {
    border: 1px solid black;
        padding: 5px;
}
</style>
```

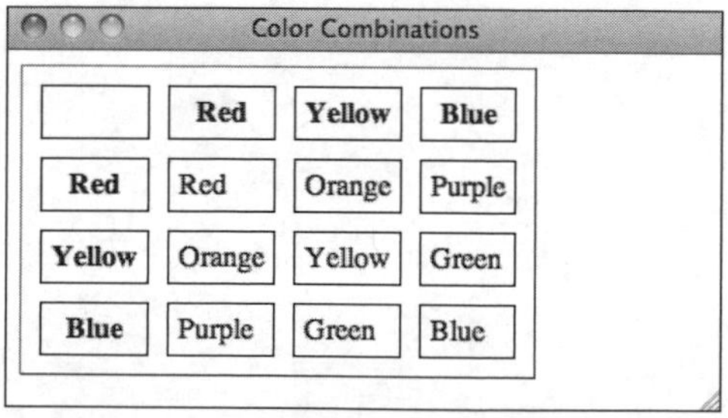

FIGURE 10.12
Using CSS to spec-
ify cell spacing and
cell padding.

Column Widths

You also can apply the `width` property to individual cells (`<th>` or `<td>`) to indicate the width of columns in a table. As with table widths, discussed earlier, you can make the `width` property in cells an exact pixel width or a percentage (which is taken as a percentage of the full table width). As with table widths, using percentages rather than specific pixel widths is a better idea because it allows your table to be displayed regardless of the window size.

Column widths are useful when you want to have multiple columns of identical widths, regardless of their contents (for example, for some forms of page layout).

Figure 10.13 shows your original table from Figure 10.1. This time, however, the table spans 100% of the screen's width. The first column is 40% of the table width, and the remaining three columns are 20% each.

To accomplish this, the column widths are applied to the heading cells as follows:

10

Input ▼

```
<table border="1" style="width:100%;">
<caption>Vital Statistics</caption>
<tr>
  <th style="width:40%;">Name</th>
  <th style="width:20%;">Height</th>
  <th style="width:20%;">Weight</th>
  <th style="width:20%;">Eye Color</th>
 </tr>
</table>
```

Output ▼

FIGURE 10.13
A table with manually set column widths.

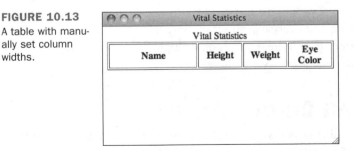

What happens if you have a table that spans 80% of the screen, and it includes the same header cells (40%, 20%, 20%, and 20%) as in the preceding example? Revise the code slightly, changing the width of the entire table to 80%, as shown in Figure 10.14. When you open the new table in your browser, you'll see that the table now spans 80% of the width of your screen. The four columns still span 40%, 20%, 20%, and 20% of the *table*. To be more specific, the columns span 32%, 16%, 16%, and 16% of the entire screen width:

Input ▼

```
<table border="1" style="width:80%;">
<caption>Vital Statistics</caption>
<tr>
  <th width="40%">Name</th>
  <th width="20%">Height</th>
  <th width="20%">Weight</th>
  <th width="20%">Eye Color</th>
 </tr>
</table>
```

Output ▼

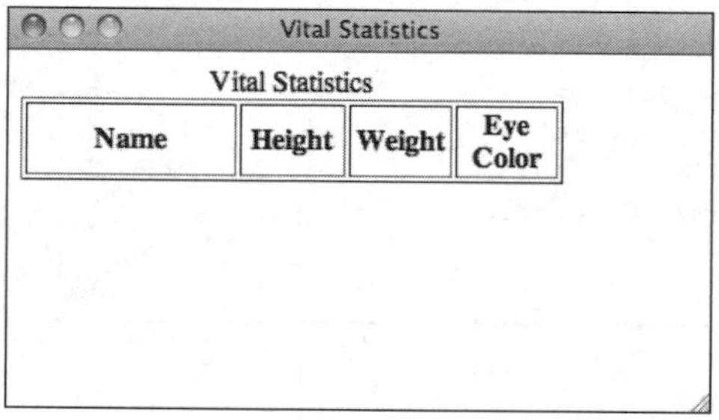

FIGURE 10.14
A modified table with manually set column widths.

If you are going to specify cell widths, make sure to specify the widths for cells only on one row or to the same values for every row. If you specify more than one value for the width of a column (by specifying different values on multiple rows of a table), there's no good way to predict which one the browser will use.

Table and Cell Color

After you have your basic table layout with rows, headings, and data, you can start refining how that table looks. You can refine tables in a couple of ways. One way is to add color to borders and cells.

This is how you change the background color of a table, a row, or a cell inside a row. You use the `background-color` property or the `background` property. You can use the `style` attribute in the `<th>` and `<td>` elements, just as you can in other elements.

Also, if you change the color of a cell, don't forget to change the color of the text inside it so that you can still read it.

Here's an example of changing the background and cell colors in a table. I've created a checkerboard using an HTML table. The table itself is white, with alternating cells in black. The checkers (here, red and black circles) are images. In the source code, I've used the `background-color` property on a `class` attribute to set background colors for some of the cells:

Input ▼

```
<!DOCTYPE html>
<html>
<head>
<title>Checkerboard</title>
<style>
  table {
    width: 50%;
    background-color:#ffffff;
  }
  tr {
    text-align: center;
  }
  td {
    width: 33%;
  }
  td.black {
    background-color: #000000;
  }
</style>
</head>
<body>
<table>
  <tr>
    <td class="black"><img src="redcircle.png"></td>
    <td><img src="redcircle.png" alt=""></td>
    <td class="black"><img src="redcircle.png"></td>
  </tr>

  <tr align="center">
    <td><img src="blackcircle.png" alt=""></td>
    <td class="black"><br></td>
    <td><img src="blackcircle.png" alt=""></td>
  </tr>
```

10

```
  <tr align="center">
    <td class="black"><br></td>
    <td><img src="blackcircle.png" alt=""></td>
    <td class="black"><br></td>
  </tr>
</table>
</body>
</html>
```

Figure 10.15 shows the result.

Output ▼

FIGURE 10.15
Table cell colors.

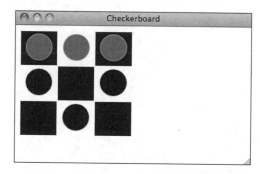

DO	**DON'T**
DO test your tables with various sizes of browser windows and mobile devices to make sure they look okay.	**DON'T** use tables just to put borders around elements on a page; use CSS.
DO increase the `padding` in your table cells to make them more readable.	**DON'T** use tables just to apply a background color to an element; use CSS instead.
	DON'T use tables for layout.

Aligning Your Table Content

Another enhancement that you can make to your tables is to adjust the alignment of their content. The `text-align` CSS property aligns content horizontally, whereas the `vertical-align` property aligns content vertically, and of course, you can use CSS properties to accomplish the same things, too. The following sections describe how to use these attributes in tables.

Table Alignment

By default, tables are displayed on a line by themselves along the left side of the page, with any text above or below the table. However, you can use the `float` style property to float tables along the left or right margins and wrap text alongside them the same way you can with images.

`float: left;` aligns the table along the left margin, and all text following that table is wrapped in the space between that table and the right side of the page. `float: right;` does the same thing, with the table aligned to the right side of the page.

In the example shown in Figure 10.16, a table that spans 70% of the width of the page is aligned to the left with the following code:

```
<table border="1" style="width: 70%; float: left;">
```

As you can see from the screenshot, one problem with wrapping text around tables is that HTML has no provision for creating margins that keep the text and the image from jamming right up next to each other. That problem can be addressed by applying a margin to the table using CSS.

10

FIGURE 10.16
A table with text alongside it. 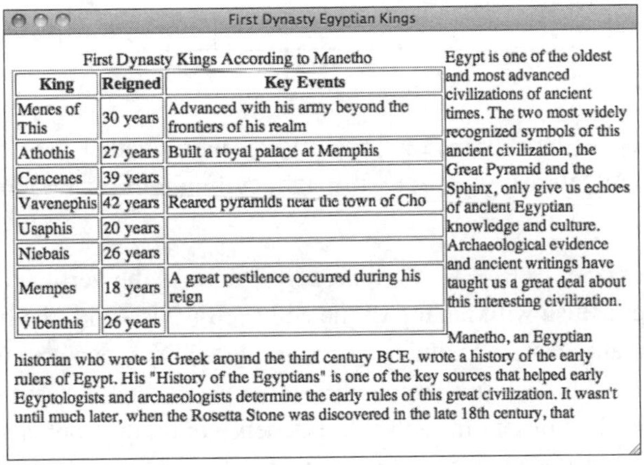

As with images, you can use the line break element with the `clear` attribute to stop wrapping text alongside a table. Centering tables is slightly more difficult. Instead of using the `float` property, you need to set the `margin-right` and `margin-left` properties to `auto`. As long as the table has an explicit width set, it will be positioned in the center of the screen horizontally:

```
<table border="1" style="width: 70%; margin-right: auto; margin-left: auto;">
```

Cell and Caption Alignment

After you have your rows and cells in place inside your table and the table is properly aligned on the page, you can align the captions and the data within each cell for the best effect, based on what your table contains. You can align the data within your cells both horizontally and vertically. Figure 10.17 shows a table of the various alignment options.

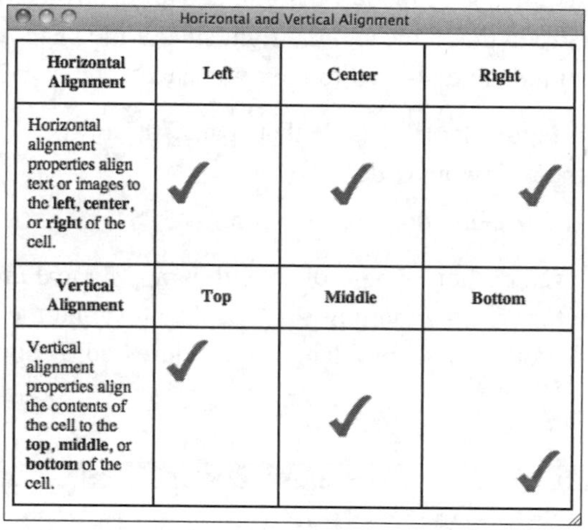

FIGURE 10.17
Aligned content within cells.

Horizontal alignment (the `text-align` property) defines whether the data within a cell is aligned with the left cell margin (`left`), the right cell margin (`right`), or centered within the two (`center`).

Vertical alignment (the `vertical-align` property) defines the vertical alignment of the data within the cell: flush with the top of the cell (`top`), flush with the bottom of the cell (`bottom`), or vertically centered within the cell (`middle`). You can also use `vertical-align: baseline;`, which is similar to `vertical-align: top;` except that it aligns the baseline of the first line of text in each cell. (Depending on the contents of the cell, this might or might not produce a different result than `vertical-align: top;`.)

By default, heading cells are centered both horizontally and vertically, and data cells are centered vertically but aligned flush left. Captions are centered horizontally, and if your caption has a height, the contents will be aligned at the top vertically.

You can override the defaults for an entire row by adding the `text-align` or `vertical-align` properties to the `<tr>` element, as in the following:

```
<tr style="text-align: right; vertical-align: middle;">
```

You can override the row alignment for individual cells by adding `align` to the `<td>` or `<th>` elements:

```
<tr style="text-align: center; vertical-align: top;">
  <td>14</td>
  <td>16</td>
  <td style="text-align:left;">No Data</td>
  <td>15</td>
</tr>
```

The following input and output example shows the various cell alignments and how they look (see Figure 10.18). I've added a style sheet that sets the cell heights to 100 pixels to make the vertical alignments easier to see:

Input ▼

```
<!DOCTYPE html>
<html>
<head>
<title>Cell Alignments</title>
    <style>
        td { height: 100px; }
    </style>
</head>
<body>
<table border="1" style="padding: 8px; width: 100%;">
  <tr>
    <th><br /></th>
    <th>Left</th>
    <th>Centered</th>
    <th>Right</th>
  </tr>

  <tr>
    <th>Top</th>
    <td style="text-align: left; vertical-align: top;"><img src="star.png" alt=""
/></td>
    <td style="text-align: center; vertical-align: top;"><img src="star.png"
alt="" /></td>
    <td style="text-align: right; vertical-align: top;"><img src="star.png"
alt="" /></td>
  </tr>

  <tr>
    <th>Centered</th>
    <td style="text-align: left; vertical-align: middle;"><img src="star.png"
alt="" /></td>
    <td style="text-align: center; vertical-align: middle;"><img src="star.png"
alt="" /></td>
```

```
    <td style="text-align: right; vertical-align: middle;"><img src="star.png"
alt="" /></td>
  </tr>

  <tr>
    <th>Bottom</th>
    <td style="text-align: left; vertical-align: bottom;"><img src="star.png"
alt="" /></td>
    <td style="text-align: center; vertical-align: bottom;"><img src="star.png"
alt="" /></td>
    <td style="text-align: right; vertical-align: bottom;"><img src="star.png"
alt="" /></td>
  </tr>
</table>
</body>
</html>
```

Output ▼

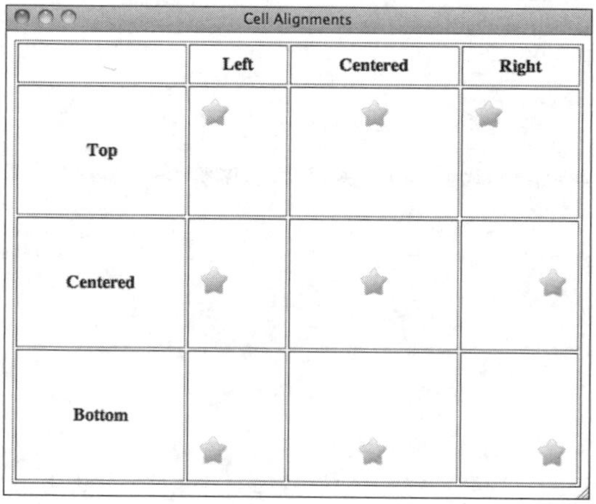

FIGURE 10.18
A matrix of cell
alignment settings.

Spanning Multiple Rows or Columns

The tables you've created up to this point all had one value per cell or the occasional empty cell. You also can create cells that span multiple rows or columns within the table. Those spanned cells then can hold headings that have subheadings in the next row or column, or you can create other special effects within the table layout. Figure 10.19 shows a table with spanned columns and rows.

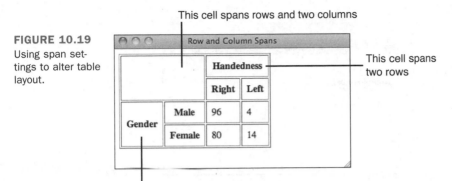

FIGURE 10.19
Using span settings to alter table layout.

This cell spans rows and two columns

This cell spans two rows

This cell spans two columns

To create a cell that spans multiple rows or columns, you add the `rowspan` or `colspan` attribute to the `<th>` or `<td>` elements, along with the number of rows or columns you want the cell to span. The data within that cell then fills the entire width or length of the combined cells, as in the following example:

10

Input ▼

```
<!DOCTYPE html>
<html>
<head>
<title>Row and Column Spans</title>
</head>
<body>
<table border="1">
  <tr>
    <th colspan="2">Gender</th>
  </tr>

  <tr>
    <th>Male</th>
    <th>Female</th>
  </tr>

  <tr>
    <td>15</td>
    <td>23</td>
  </tr>
</table>
</body>
</html>
```

Figure 10.20 shows how this table might appear when displayed.

Output ▼

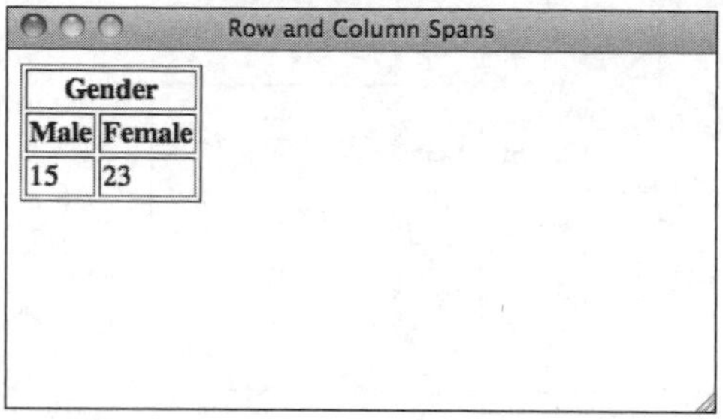

FIGURE 10.20
Using span settings to widen a column.

Note that if a cell spans multiple rows, you don't have to redefine it as empty in the next row or rows. Just ignore it and move to the next cell in the row. The span fills in the spot for you.

Cells always span downward and to the right. To create a cell that spans several columns, you add the `colspan` attribute to the leftmost cell in the span. For cells that span rows, you add `rowspan` to the topmost cell.

The following input and output example shows a cell that spans multiple rows (the cell with the word *Piston* in it). Figure 10.21 shows the result.

Input ▼

```
<!DOCTYPE html>
<html>
<head>
<title>Ring Clearance</title>
</head>
<body>
<table border="1">
  <tr>
    <th colspan="2"> </th>
    <th>Ring<br />
        Clearance</th>
  </tr>

  <tr style="text-align: center;">
    <th rowspan="2">Piston</th>
    <th>Upper</th>
    <td>3mm</td>
  </tr>

  <tr style="text-align: center;">
    <th>Lower</th>
```

```
    <td>3.2mm</td>
  </tr>
</table>
</body>
</html>
```

Output ▼

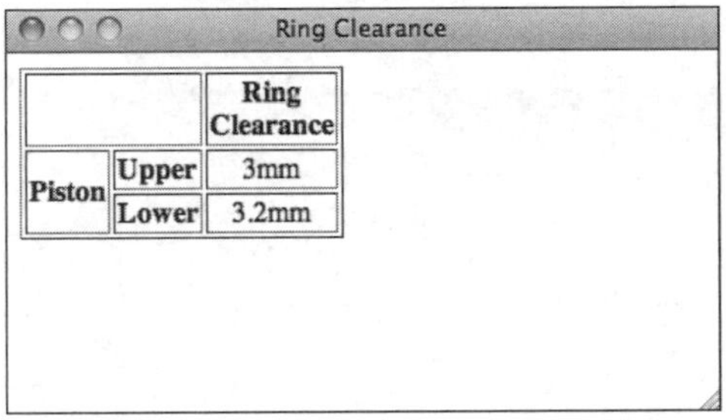

FIGURE 10.21
Cells that span
multiple rows and
columns.

Exercise 10.2: A Table of Service Specifications ▼

Had enough of tables yet? Let's do another example that takes advantage of everything you've learned here: tables that use colors, headings, normal cells, alignments, and column and row spans. This is a very complex table, so we'll go step by step, row by row, to build it.

Figure 10.22 shows the table, which indicates service and adjustment specifications from the service manual for a car.

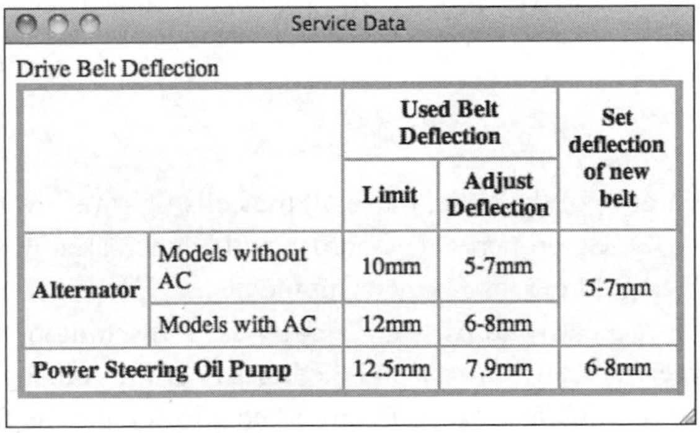

FIGURE 10.22
The really complex
service specifica-
tion table.

10

▼ There are actually five rows and columns in this table. Do you see them? Some of them span columns and rows. Figure 10.23 shows the same table with callouts drawn over it so that you can see where the rows and columns are.

With tables such as this one that use many spans, it's helpful to draw this sort of grid to figure out where the spans are and in which row they belong. Remember, spans start at the topmost row and the leftmost column.

FIGURE 10.23
Five columns, five rows.

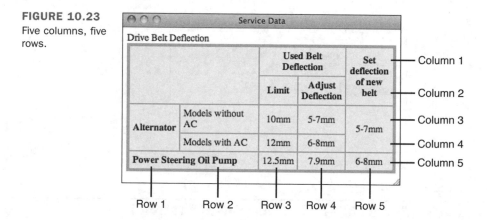

Ready? Start with the framework, just as you have for the other tables in this lesson:

```
<!DOCTYPE html>
<html>
  <head>
    <title>Service Data</title>
  </head>
  <body>
    <table border="1">
      <caption>Drive Belt Deflection</caption>
    </table>
  </body>
</html>
```

To enhance the appearance of the table, make all the cells light yellow (`#ffffcc`) by using the `background-color` property. The border will be increased in size to 5 pixels, and you'll color it deep gold (`#cc9900`) by using the `border` property. You'll make the rules between cells appear solid by using a `cellspacing` setting of `0` and increase the whitespace between the cell contents and the borders of the cells by specifying a `cellpadding` setting of `5`. The new table definition now looks like the following:

```
<table border="1" style="background-color: #ffffcc; border: 5px solid #cc9900;
```
▼ `border-collapse: collapse;">`

You should also adjust the padding on all the table cells and headers. The quickest way is ▼
with a style sheet:

```
<style>
  th, td { padding: 5px; }
</style>
```

Now create the first row. With the grid on your picture, you can see that the first cell is
empty and spans two rows and two columns (see Figure 10.24). Therefore, the HTML for
that cell would be as follows:

```
<tr>
<th rowspan="2" colspan="2"></th>
```

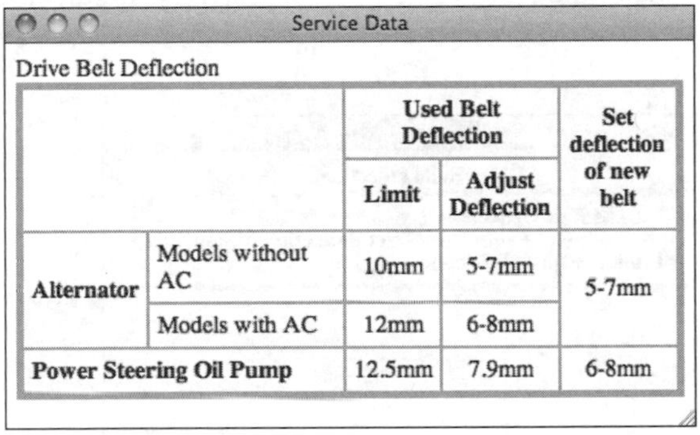

FIGURE 10.24
The first cell.

Drive Belt Deflection		Used Belt Deflection		Set deflection of new belt
		Limit	Adjust Deflection	
Alternator	Models without AC	10mm	5-7mm	5-7mm
	Models with AC	12mm	6-8mm	
Power Steering Oil Pump		12.5mm	7.9mm	6-8mm

10

The second cell in the row is the Used Belt Deflection heading cell, which spans two columns (for the two cells beneath it). The code for that cell is as follows:

```
<th colspan="2">Used Belt Deflection</th>
```

Now that you have two cells that span two columns each, there's only one left in this
row. However, this one, like the first one, spans the row beneath it:

```
<th rowspan="2">Set deflection of new belt</th>
</tr>
```

Now go on to the second row. This isn't the one that starts with the Alternator heading.
Remember that the first cell in the previous row has a `rowspan` and a `colspan` of two,
meaning that it bleeds down to this row and takes up two cells. You don't need to ▼

▼ redefine it for this row. You just move on to the next cell in the grid. The first cell in this row is the Limit heading cell, and the second cell is the Adjust Deflection heading cell:

```
<tr>
  <th>Limit</th>
  <th>Adjust Deflection</th>
</tr>
```

What about the last cell? Just like the first cell, the cell in the row above this one had a rowspan of 2, which takes up the space in this row. The only values you need for this row are the ones you already defined.

Are you with me so far? Now is a great time to try this out in your browser to make sure that everything is lining up. It'll look kind of funny because you haven't really put anything on the left side of the table yet, but it's worth a try. Figure 10.27 shows what you've got so far.

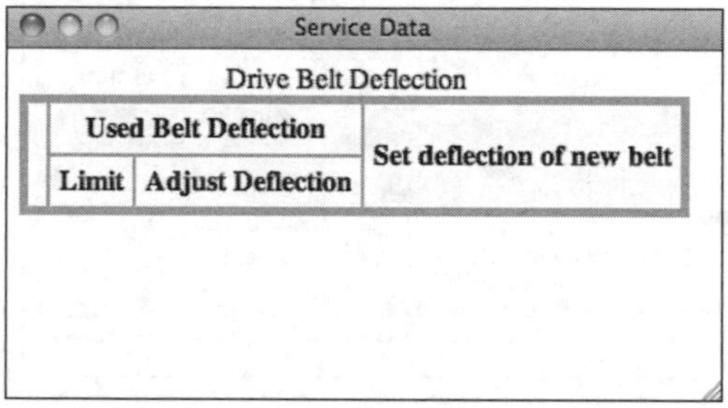

FIGURE 10.25
The table so far.

Next row! Check your grid if you need to. Here, the first cell is the heading for Alternator, and it spans this row and the one below it:

```
<tr>
  <th rowspan="2">Alternator</th>
```

Are you getting the hang of this yet?

The next three cells are pretty easy because they don't span anything. Here are their definitions:

```
<td>Models without AC</td>
<td>10mm</td>
<td>5-7mm</td>
```

The last cell in this row is just like the first one:

```
<td rowspan="2">5-7mm</td>
```
▼ `</tr>`

You're up to row number four. In this one, because of the `rowspans` from the previous row, there are only three cells to define: the cell for Models with AC, and the two cells for the numbers:

```
<tr>
  <td>Models with AC</td>
  <td>12mm</td>
  <td>6-8mm</td>
</tr>
```

NOTE

> In this table, I've made the Alternator cell a heading cell and the AC cells plain data. This is mostly an aesthetic decision on my part. I could have made all three into headings just as easily.

Now for the final row—this one should be easy. The first cell (Power Steering Oil Pump) spans two columns (the one with Alternator in it and the with/without AC column). The remaining three are just one cell each:

```
<tr>
  <th colspan="2">Power Steering Oil Pump</th>
  <td>12.5mm</td>
  <td>7.9mm</td>
  <td>6-8mm</td>
</tr>
```

That's it. You're done laying out the rows and columns. That was the hard part. The rest is just fine-tuning. Try looking at it again to make sure there are no strange errors (see Figure 10.26).

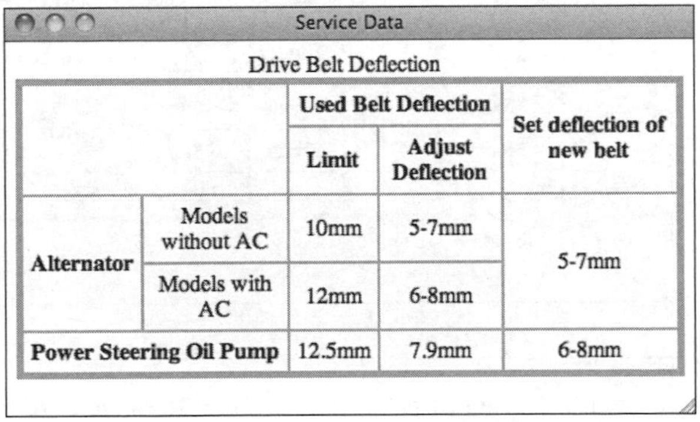

FIGURE 10.26
The table with the data rows included.

▼ Now that you have all the rows and cells laid out, adjust the alignments within the cells. The numbers should be centered, at least. Because they make up the majority of the table, center the default alignment for each row:

```
<tr style="text-align: center;">
```

The labels along the left side of the table (Alternator, Models with/without AC, and Power Steering Oil Pump) look funny if they're centered, however, so left-align them using the following code:

```
<th rowspan="2" style="text-align: left;">Alternator</th>
<td style="text-align: left;">Models without AC</td>
<td style="text-align: left;">Models with AC</td>
<th colspan="2" style="text-align: left;">Power Steering Oil Pump</th>
```

I've put some line breaks in the longer headings so that the columns are a little narrower. Because the text in the headings is pretty short to start with, I don't have to worry too much about the table looking funny if it gets too narrow. Here are the lines I modified:

```
<th rowspan="2">Set<br>deflection<br>of new belt</th>
<th>Adjust<br>Deflection</th>
```

For one final step, you'll align the caption to the left side of the table:

```
<caption style="text-align: left;">Drive Belt Deflection</caption>
```

Voilà—the final table, with everything properly laid out and aligned! Figure 10.27 shows the final result.

FIGURE 10.27
The final Drive Belt
Deflection table.

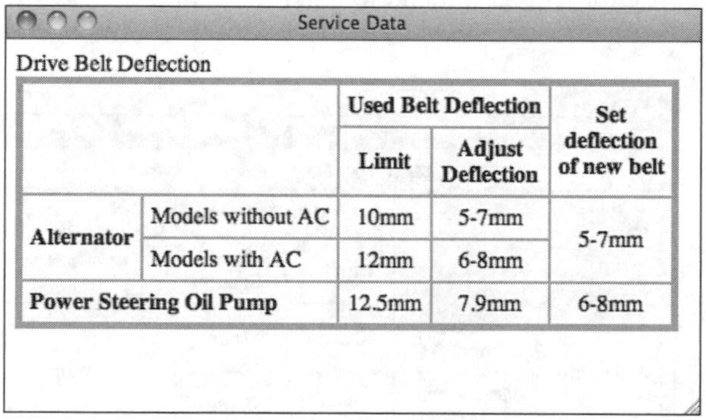

Drive Belt Deflection		Used Belt Deflection		Set deflection of new belt
		Limit	Adjust Deflection	
Alternator	Models without AC	10mm	5-7mm	5-7mm
	Models with AC	12mm	6-8mm	
Power Steering Oil Pump		12.5mm	7.9mm	6-8mm

TIP

If you got lost at any time, the best thing you can do is pull out your handy text editor and try it yourself, following along tag by tag. After you've done it a couple of times, it becomes easier.

▼

Here's the full text for the table example:

```html
<!DOCTYPE html>
<html>
  <head>
    <title>Service Data</title>
    <style>
      th, td { padding: 5px; }
    </style>
  </head>
  <body>
    <table border="1" style="background-color: #ffffcc; border: 5px solid
#cc9900;
      border-collapse: collapse;">
      <caption style="text-align: left;">Drive Belt Deflection</caption>
      <tr style="text-align: center;">
        <th rowspan="2" colspan="2"></th>
        <th colspan="2">Used Belt Deflection</th>
        <th rowspan="2">Set<br>deflection<br>of new belt</th>
      </tr>
      <tr style="text-align: center;">
        <th>Limit</th>
        <th>Adjust<br>Deflection</th>
      </tr>
      <tr style="text-align: center;">
        <th rowspan="2" style="text-align: left;">Alternator</th>
        <td style="text-align: left;">Models without AC</td>
        <td>10mm</td>
        <td>5-7mm</td>
        <td rowspan="2">5-7mm</td>
      </tr>
      <tr style="text-align: center;">
        <td style="text-align: left;">Models with AC</td>
        <td>12mm</td>
        <td>6-8mm</td>
      </tr>
      <tr style="text-align: center;">
        <th colspan="2" style="text-align: left;">Power Steering Oil Pump</th>
        <td>12.5mm</td>
        <td>7.9mm</td>
        <td>6-8mm</td>
      </tr>
    </table>
  </body>
</html>
```

10

NOTE Under normal circumstances, avoid the use of the `style` attribute and instead use a style sheet for the page and apply classes where necessary to style your table. Using the `style` attribute is the least efficient way to apply styles to a page, but it makes the example more readable.

More Advanced Table Enhancements

Tables are laid out row by row, but HTML also provides some elements that enable you to group cells into columns and modify their properties. There are also elements that enable you to group the rows in tables so that you can manage them collectively.

Grouping and Aligning Columns

Sometimes it's helpful to be able to apply styles to the columns in your tables rather than applying them to individual cells or to rows. To do so, you need to define the columns in your table with the `<colgroup>` and `<col>` elements.

The `<colgroup>`...`</colgroup>` element is used to enclose one or more columns in a group. The closing `</colgroup>` tag is optional in HTML. This element has one attribute:

- `span` defines the number of columns in the column group. Its value must be an integer greater than `0`. If `span` isn't defined, the `<colgroup>` element defaults to a column group that contains one column. If the `<colgroup>` element contains one or more `<col>` elements (described later), however, the `span` attribute is ignored.

Suppose that you have a table that measures 450 pixels in width and contains six columns. You want each of the six columns to be 75 pixels wide. The code looks something like the following:

```
<table border="1" style="width: 450px;">
  <colgroup span="6" style="width: 75px;"></colgroup>
</table>
```

Now you want to change the columns. Using the same 450-pixel-wide table, you make the first two columns 25 pixels wide and the last four columns 100 pixels wide. This requires two `<colgroup>` elements, as follows:

```
<table border="1" style="width: 450px;">
  <colgroup span="2" style="width:25px;"></colgroup>
  <colgroup span="4" style="width:100px;"></colgroup>
```

What if you don't want all the columns in a column group to be the same width or have the same appearance? That's where the `<col>` element comes into play. Whereas `<colgroup>` defines the structure of table columns, `<col>` defines their attributes. To use this element, begin the column definition with a `<col>` tag. The end tag is forbidden in this case.

Going back to your 450-pixel-wide table, you now want to make the two columns in the first column group 75 pixels wide. In the second column group, you have columns of 50,

75, 75, and 100 pixels, respectively. Here's how you format the second column group with the `<col>` tag:

```
<table border="1" style="width: 450px;">
  <colgroup span="2" style="width:75px;">
  <colgroup span="4" style="width:100px;">
    <col span="1" style="width:50px;">
    <col span="2" style="width: 75px;">
    <col span="1" style="width: 100px;">
  </colgroup>
```

You can affect more than the width of your columns. You can add any style to the `colgroup` and `col` elements, and that will be applied to the columns they span. For example, you could change the background color:

```
<colgroup span="2" style="background-color: #ffffcc;">
```

Now apply this to some *real* code. The following example shows a table that displays science and mathematics class schedules. Start by defining a table that has a 1-pixel-wide border and spans 100% of the browser window width.

Next, you define the column groups in the table. You want the first column group to display the names of the classes. The second column group consists of two columns that display the room number for the class, as well as the time that the class is held. The first column group consists of one column of cells that spans 20% of the entire width of the table. The contents of the cell are aligned vertically toward the top and centered horizontally. The second column group consists of two columns, each spanning 40% of the width of the table. Their contents are vertically aligned to the top of the cells. To further illustrate how `colgroup` works, I use the `style` attribute and `background-color` property to set each of the column groups to have different background colors.

Finally, you enter the table data the same way that you normally do. Here's what the complete code looks like for the class schedule, and the results are shown in Figure 10.28:

Input ▼

```
<!DOCTYPE html>
<html>
<head>
<title>Grouping Columns</title>
</head>
<body>
<table border="1" style="width: 100%;">
  <caption><b>Science and Mathematic Class Schedules</b></caption>
```

```
  <colgroup style="width: 20%; text-align: center; vertical-align: top;
background-color: #fcf;">
  <colgroup span="2" style="width: 40%; vertical-align: top; background-color:
#ccf;">

 <tr>
   <th>Class</th>
   <th>Room</th>
   <th>Time</th>
 </tr>

 <tr>
   <td>Biology</td>
   <td>Science Wing, Room 102</td>
   <td>8:00 AM to 9:45 AM</td>
 </tr>

 <tr>
   <td>Science</td>
   <td>Science Wing, Room 110</td>
   <td>9:50 AM to 11:30 AM</td>
 </tr>

 <tr>
   <td>Physics</td>
   <td>Science Wing, Room 107</td>
   <td>1:00 PM to 2:45 PM</td>
 </tr>

 <tr>
   <td>Geometry</td>
   <td>Mathematics Wing, Room 236</td>
   <td>8:00 AM to 9:45 AM</td>
 </tr>

 <tr>
   <td>Algebra</td>
   <td>Mathematics Wing, Room 239</td>
   <td>9:50 AM to 11:30 AM</td>
 </tr>

 <tr>
   <td>Trigonometry</td>
   <td>Mathematics Wing, Room 245</td>
   <td>1:00 PM to 2:45 PM</td>
 </tr>

 <tr>
   <th>Class</th>
   <th>Room</th>
   <th>Time</th>
```

```
    </tr>
  </table>
  </body>
</html>
```

Output ▼

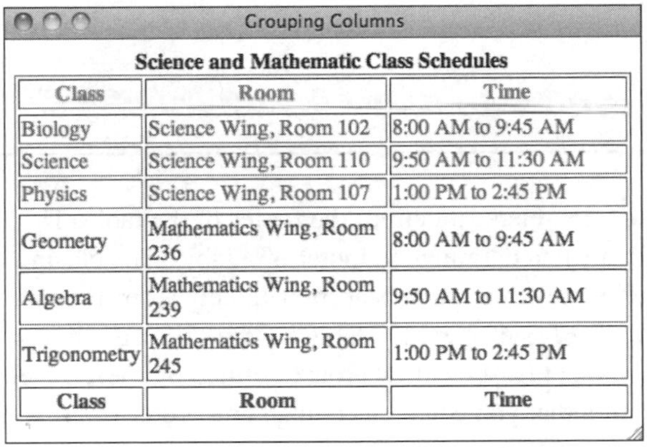

FIGURE 10.28
The class schedule with formatted column groups.

Grouping and Aligning Rows

Now that you know how to group and format columns, let's turn to the rows. You can group the rows of a table into three sections: table heading, table footer, and table body. You can modify CSS properties to emphasize the table heading and table footer and give the body of the table a different appearance.

The table header, footer, and body sections are defined by the `<thead>`, `<tfoot>`, and `<tbody>` elements, respectively. Each of these elements must contain the same number of columns.

The `<thead>...</thead>` element defines the heading of the table, which should contain information about the columns in the body of the table. Typically, this is the same type of information that you've been placing within header cells so far in the lesson.

The head of the table appears right after the `<table>` element or after `<colgroup>` elements, as the following example shows, and must include at least one row group defined by the `<tr>` element. I'm including `style` attributes in the row grouping tags to illustrate how they are used. The table is formatted as follows:

Input ▼

```
<table border="1" style="width: 100%;">
  <caption style="font-weight: bold;">Science and Mathematic Class Schedules
</caption>
  <colgroup style="width: 20%; text-align:center; vertical-align: top;">
  <colgroup span="2" style="width: 40%; vertical-align: top;">
  <thead style="background-color: red;">
  <tr>
    <th>Class</th>
    <th>Room</th>
    <th>Time</th>
  </tr>
</thead>
```

The `<tfoot>...</tfoot>` element defines the footer of the table. The starting `<tfoot>` tag is always required when defining the footer of a table. The closing `<tfoot>` tag is optional. The footer of the table can appear immediately after the table heading if one is present, or after the `<table>` element if a table heading isn't present or after the `<tbody>` element. It must contain at least one row group, defined by the `<tr>` element. A good example of information that you could place in a table footer is a row that totals columns of numbers in a table.

You usually define the footer of the table before the table body because the browser has to render the footer before it receives all the data in the table body. For the purposes of this example, we'll include the same information in the table head and the table footer. The code looks like this:

Input ▼

```
<tfoot style="background-color: blue;">
  <tr>
  <th>Class</th>
  <th>Room</th>
  <th>Time</th>
  </tr>
</tfoot>
```

After you define the heading and footer for the table, you define the rows in the table body. A table can contain more than one body element, and each body can contain one or more rows of data. This might not seem to make sense, but using multiple body sections enables you to divide up your table into logical sections. I show you one example of why this is rather cool in a little bit.

The `<tbody>...</tbody>` element defines a body section within your table. The `<tbody>` start tag is required if at least one of the following is true:

- The table contains head or foot sections.
- The table contains more than one table body.

The following example contains two table bodies, each consisting of three rows of three cells each. The body appears after the table footer, as follows:

Input ▼

```
<tbody style="background-color: yellow;">
  <tr>
    <td>Biology</td>
    <td>Science Wing, Room 102</td>
    <td>8:00 AM to 9:45 AM</td>
  </tr>
  <tr>
    <td>Science</td>
    <td>Science Wing, Room 110</td>
    <td>9:50 AM to 11:30 AM</td>
  </tr>
  <tr>
    <td>Physics</td>
    <td>Science Wing, Room 107</td>
    <td>1:00 PM to 2:45 PM</td>
  </tr>
</tbody>
<tbody style="background-color: gray;">
  <tr>
    <td>Geometry</td>
    <td>Mathematics Wing, Room 236</td>
    <td>8:00 AM to 9:45 AM</td>
  </tr>
  <tr>
    <td>Algebra</td>
    <td>Mathematics Wing, Room 239</td>
    <td>9:50 AM to 11:30 AM</td>
  </tr>
  <tr>
    <td>Trigonometry</td>
    <td>Mathematics Wing, Room 245</td>
    <td>1:00 PM to 2:45 PM</td>
  </tr>
</tbody>
</table>
```

10

Put all the preceding together, and you get a table that looks like that shown in Figure 10.29.

Output ▼

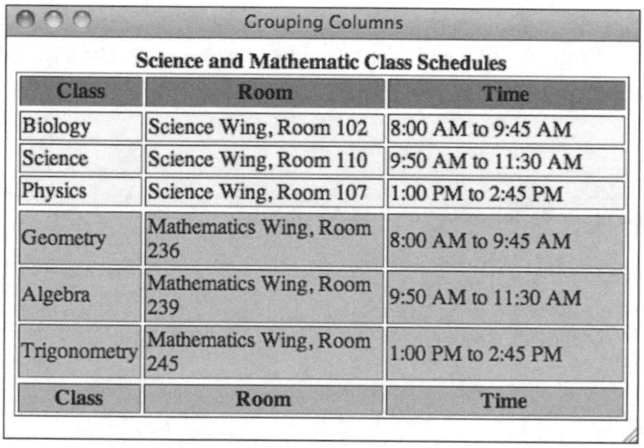

FIGURE 10.29
The class schedule with a head, two bodies, and a foot.

Grouping Columns

Science and Mathematic Class Schedules

Class	Room	Time
Biology	Science Wing, Room 102	8:00 AM to 9:45 AM
Science	Science Wing, Room 110	9:50 AM to 11:30 AM
Physics	Science Wing, Room 107	1:00 PM to 2:45 PM
Geometry	Mathematics Wing, Room 236	8:00 AM to 9:45 AM
Algebra	Mathematics Wing, Room 239	9:50 AM to 11:30 AM
Trigonometry	Mathematics Wing, Room 245	1:00 PM to 2:45 PM
Class	Room	Time

How Tables Are Used

In this lesson, I explained the usage of tables in publishing tabular data. That was the original purpose for HTML tables. In 1996, however, Netscape 2.0 introduced the option of turning off table borders, and this, along with other limitations in HTML, changed the way tables were used.

Before style sheets were invented and implemented in most browsers, there was only one way to lay out elements on a page other than straight down the middle: tables. These days, developers use CSS to lay out pages, but before CSS support in browsers became really solid, tables were the key page layout tool that most web developers used.

Even now, there are some cases in which using tables to lay out pages make sense. If you are creating a web page that will be sent out as part of an email message, tables should be used. Some email clients do not support CSS, so for more advanced layouts you're required to use tables.

Summary

In this lesson, you've learned quite a lot about tables. They enable you to arrange your information in rows and columns so that your visitors can get to the information they need quickly.

While working with tables, you learned about headings and data, captions, defining rows and cells, aligning information within cells, and creating cells that span multiple rows or columns. With these features, you can create tables for most purposes.

As you're constructing tables, it's helpful to keep the following steps in mind:

- Sketch your table, indicating where the rows and columns fall. Mark which cells span multiple rows and columns.
- Start with a basic framework and lay out the rows, headings, and data row by row and cell by cell in HTML. Include row and column spans as necessary. Test frequently in a browser to make sure that it's all working correctly.
- Modify the alignment in the rows to reflect the alignment of the majority of the cells.
- Modify the alignment for individual cells.
- Adjust line breaks, if necessary.
- Make other refinements, such as cell spacing, padding, and color.
- Test your table in multiple browsers. Different browsers might have different approaches to laying out your table or might be more accepting of errors in your HTML code.

Table 10.1 presents a quick summary of the HTML elements that you learned about in this lesson and that remain current in HTML5.

TABLE 10.1 Current HTML5 Table Elements

Tag	Use
`<table>...</table>`	Indicates a table.
`<caption>...</caption>`	Creates a caption for the table (optional).
`<colgroup>...</colgroup>`	Encloses one or more columns in a group.
`<col>`	Used to define the attributes of a column in a table.
`<thead>...</thead>`	Creates a row group that defines the heading of the table. A table can contain only one heading.
`<tfoot>...</tfoot>`	Creates a row group that defines the footer of the table. A table can contain only one footer. Must be specified before the body of the table is rendered.
`<tbody>...</tbody>`	Defines one or more row groups to include in the body of the table. Tables can contain more than one body section.

10

Tag	Use
`<tr>...</tr>`	Defines a table row, which can contain heading and data cells.
`<th>...</th>`	Defines a table cell that contains a heading. Heading cells are usually indicated by boldface and centered both horizontally and vertically within the cell.
`<td>...</td>`	Defines a table cell containing data. Table cells are in a regular font and are left-aligned and vertically centered within the cell.

Because several of the table attributes apply to more than one of the preceding elements, I'm listing them separately. Table 10.2 presents a quick summary of the HTML attributes you learned about in this lesson that remain current in HTML5.

TABLE 10.2 Current HTML5 Table Attributes

Attribute	Applied to Element	Use
border	`<table>`	Indicates whether the table will be drawn with a border. The default is no border. If border has a value, it's the width of the shaded border around the table. This attribute is nonconforming in HTML5.
span	`<colgroup>`	Defines the number of columns in a column group. Must be an integer greater than 0.
	`<col>`	Defines the number of columns that a cell spans. Must be an integer greater than 0.
colspan	`<th>` or `<td>`	Indicates the number of cells to the right of this one that this cell will span.
rowspan	`<th>` or `<td>`	Indicates the number of cells below this one that this cell will span.

Workshop

This lesson covered one of the more complex subjects in HTML: tables. Before you move on to the next lesson, work through the following questions and exercises to make sure that you've really got a good grasp of how tables work.

Q&A

Q Tables are a real hassle to lay out, especially when you get into row and column spans. That last example was awful.

A You're right. Tables are a tremendous pain to lay out by hand like this. However, if you're using writing editors and tools to generate HTML code, having the table defined like this makes more sense because you can just write out each row in turn programmatically.

Q Can you nest tables, putting a table inside a single table cell?

A Sure! As mentioned earlier, you can put any HTML code you want inside a table cell, and that includes other tables. But nesting tables can significantly slow down pages loading.

Q Is there a way to specify a beveled border like the default table borders using CSS?

A CSS actually provides three different beveled border styles: `inset`, `outset`, and `ridge`. You should experiment with them and use the one that looks the best to you.

Quiz

1. What are the basic parts of a table, and which tags identify them?
2. Which attribute is the most common attribute of the table tag, and what does it do?
3. Which attributes are used to create cells that span more than one column or row?
4. Which elements are used to define the head, body, and foot of a table?

Quiz Answers

1. The basic parts of a table (the `<table>` tag) are the caption (defined with the `<caption>` tag), header cells (`<th>`), data cells (`<td>`), and table rows (`<tr>`).
2. The `border` attribute is the most common attribute for the table tag. It specifies whether border lines are displayed around the table and how wide the borders should be. It is nonconforming in HTML5, but you will still see it on many tables to identify them as presentation or data tables.
3. The `rowspan` attribute creates a cell that spans multiple rows. The `colspan` attribute creates a cell that spans multiple columns.
4. `<thead>`, `<tbody>`, and `<tfoot>` define the head, body, and foot of a table.

Exercises

1. Here's a brainteaser for you: Create a simple nested table (a table within a table) that contains three rows and four columns. Inside the cell that appears at the second column in the second row, create a second table that contains two rows and two columns.

2. One tricky aspect of working with the HTML for tables is accounting for cells with no data. Create a table that includes empty cells and verify that once you've done so, all the rows and columns line up as you originally anticipated.

LESSON 11
Using CSS to Position Elements on the Page

When web pages display pages, the content normally flows from left to right and top to bottom. You've seen that elements can be floated to the right or left, but the basic top-to-bottom paradigm still remains. CSS enables you to position elements anywhere you like on the page, altering the default layout rules of HTML in any way that you choose. You've already seen how you can use styling to change the appearance of elements on the page. In this lesson, you'll learn how to use styles to position them as well.

These days, it's not uncommon to visit websites that look more like desktop applications than they look like traditional web pages. Such sites are created using CSS positioning, which you'll learn about in this lesson.

Positioning Schemes

To control the position of an element on the page, you first have to choose a positioning scheme. There are four positioning schemes: static, relative, absolute, and fixed. You specify which scheme to use for an element using the position CSS property.

You can put these schemes into two categories. The static and relative schemes do not alter the layout of the document, while no space is reserved in the page layout for elements positioned using the absolute and fixed schemes.

The static scheme is the default. Elements that are not floated flow down the page from left to right and top to bottom. This is referred to as the *normal flow*. The relative scheme positions the element relative to its position in the normal flow. The element's original positioned is preserved and affects the position of the subsequent elements. The absolute and fixed schemes enable you to position elements in any location you like, and elements positioned using those schemes are removed from the document layout entirely.

If you specify a position for an element other than static, you can set a position for the element. There are four positioning properties: top, left, bottom, and right. The position setting is what establishes what the values of these properties relate to. Here's an example:

```
.thing {
    position: relative;
    left: 50px;
    top: 50px;
}
```

In this case, elements in the thing class will be shifted 50 pixels down and 50 pixels to the left from the element's position in the normal flow. If I were to change position to absolute or fixed, the element would appear 50 pixels from the nearest positioned ancestor of the element, or if no such ancestor exists, the browser window itself.

Generally, when you're positioning elements, you specify a left or a right value and a top or a bottom value. If you specify conflicting values, one of the values you specify will be ignored. It's much safer to use the sizing properties to size your elements and then specify the position of one corner of your element if you want to indicate where it should be positioned.

Relative Positioning

Let's look at a page that uses relative positioning. This page illustrates both how relative positioning works and some of the problems with it. A screenshot of the page listed in the following code appears in Figure 11.1.

Input ▼

```
<!DOCTYPE html>
<html>
<head>
  <title>CSS Example</title>
  <style type="text/css">
.offset {
  border: 3px solid blue;
  padding: 10px;
  margin: 10px;
  background-color: #aaaaaa;
  position: relative;
  top: -30px;
  left: 30px;
  width: 33%; }
</style>
</head>
<body>
<p>
The absence of romance in my history will, I fear, detract somewhat
from its interest; but if it be judged useful by those inquirers who
desire an exact knowledge of the past as an aid to the interpretation
of the future, which in the course of human things must resemble if
it does not reflect it, I shall be content.
</p>
<p class="offset">
The absence of romance in my history will, I fear, detract somewhat
from its interest; but if it be judged useful by those inquirers who
desire an exact knowledge of the past as an aid to the interpretation
of the future, which in the course of human things must resemble if
it does not reflect it, I shall be content. In fine, I have written
my work, not as an essay which is to win the applause of the moment,
but as a possession for all time.
</p>
<p>
The absence of romance in my history will, I fear, detract somewhat
from its interest; but if it be judged useful by those inquirers who
desire an exact knowledge of the past as an aid to the interpretation
of the future, which in the course of human things must resemble if
it does not reflect it, I shall be content.
</p>
</body>
</html>
```

11

Output ▼

FIGURE 11.1
A page that uses
relative positioning
for an element.

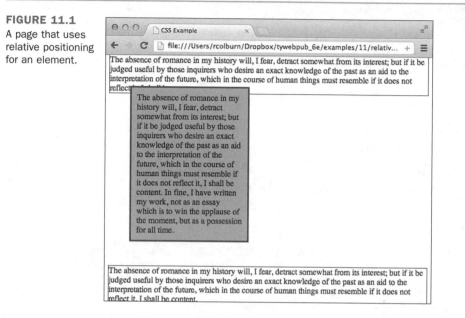

As you can see, the relatively positioned paragraph is shifted up and to the right from its natural position in the layout. You can also see that its position on the page is preserved and that the size I specified for the element is taken into account.

I used a negative value for the top property to move the element up 30 pixels, and I specified a left offset of 30 pixels, which actually moves the element 30 pixels to the right. To move the element to the left, I could have used a negative left offset or a positive right offset. The spot in the layout where the paragraph would be in the normal flow remains, creating whitespace before the third paragraph. The relative positioning of the paragraph causes it to overlap its predecessor.

By default, the element backgrounds are transparent. I added a background color to the relatively positioned box to more clearly illustrate how my page works. If I remove the background-color property from class offset, the page will look like Figure 11.2.

In this example, transparency is probably *not* the effect I'm looking for. However, taking advantage of this transparency can be useful when you create text blocks that partially overlap images or other non-text boxes.

FIGURE 11.2
Transparency of
overlapping ele-
ments.

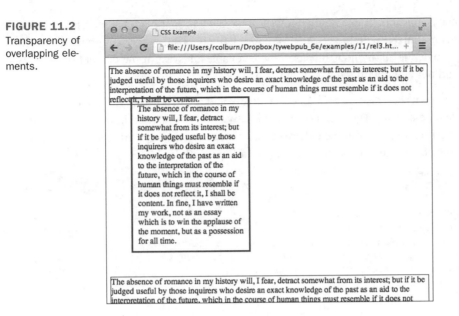

Elements are positioned relative to their containing block. A containing block is the block-level element that's the ancestor of the positioned element. In the example you just saw, the page's `<body>` element is the containing block for the paragraphs. Let's say I add a new style to the page's style sheet:

```
#positioned { position: relative; left: 50px; }
```

Then I put the three paragraphs in the preceding example in a new `<div>`:

```
<div id="positioned">
    ... the three paragraphs above ...
</div>
```

All three paragraphs will be moved 50 pixels to the right, and the offset paragraph will be positioned relative to the `<div>` that is its containing block.

In addition to containing blocks, there are also anonymous blocks. Browsers automatically create anonymous blocks when a block-level element appears within a containing block along with inline elements. Here's an example:

```
<div>
    This content is inside an anonymous block.
    <p>This is a paragraph.</p>
    This content is also inside an anonymous block.
</div>
```

11

The anonymous blocks enable the browser to create a proper page layout when inline elements are mixed with blocks. If I were to relatively position the paragraph inside the `<div>` above, the anonymous blocks are what enables the rest of the content in the `<div>` to be laid out along with the paragraph.

Inline elements can also be positioned relatively and are handled in the same fashion as block-level elements. They are positioned relative to their position in the normal flow. If you nest relatively positioned elements, the inner element is positioned relative to the location of the enclosing element, as shown in Figure 11.3:

```html
<!DOCTYPE html>
<html>
<head>
  <title>CSS Example</title>
  <style type="text/css">
    span { background-color: white; border: 1px solid black; }
    #inner { position: relative; left: 25px; top: 10px; }
    #outer { position: relative; top: 10px; }
  </style>
</head>
<body>
<p>
The absence of romance in my history will, I fear, detract somewhat <span
id="outer">from its <span id="inner">interest</span></span>; but if it be
judged useful by those inquirers who desire an exact knowledge of the past as
an aid to the interpretation of the future, which in the course of human things
must resemble if it does not reflect it, I shall be content.
</p>
</body>
</html>
```

FIGURE 11.3
Relatively positioned inline elements.

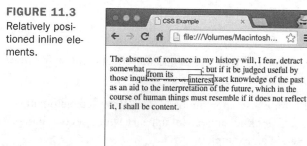

In the example, I have a `<span>` tag nested within another `<span>`. Both of the elements are relatively positioned. As you can see, the space in the layout for both is preserved, and the inner element is positioned relative to the outer element, which in turn is positioned relative to its natural location in the page layout. There is enough space left in the original layout to contain all of the relatively positioned content.

Absolute Positioning

Now let's look at absolute positioning. As mentioned previously, when an element is absolutely positioned it is removed from the normal flow entirely. However, the default coordinates of an absolutely positioned element are its position in the normal flow. So if you specify an alternate position, its position in the normal flow will not be reserved. If you do not, it will appear in the normal flow exactly as an element that is not positioned would. Before going further, I should describe the positioning properties in more detail.

Positioning Properties

As you've seen, there are four properties that can be used to specify the position of a positioned element: top, right, bottom, and left. All the positioning properties have slightly different meanings depending on the positioning scheme.

In the absolute positioning scheme, the top property specifies the distance between the top margin of the positioned element and the top inside border of its containing block. This means that while the margin and border of the containing block do affect the position of the absolutely positioned element, the block's padding does not.

In the relative positioning scheme, the top property specifies where the top margin of the positioned element should appear relative to its predecessor in the normal flow, or from the top edge of its containing block if it's the first element in that block. So if you set a top position of 100px, it will be moved 100 pixels down from its position in the normal flow. The key difference in positioning relative and absolute is that for absolutely positioned elements, the positioning is always in reference to the edges of the containing block. For relative elements, the positioning refers to adjacent elements in the normal flow if they exist.

The bottom property is exactly like the top property except that it refers to the bottom margin of the positioned element. So in the absolute scheme, it specifies the distance from the inner edge of the bottom border of the containing block. In the relative scheme, it relates to the following element in the normal flow. A positive value moves the element up the page, and a negative value moves the element down the page.

The left and right properties are similar as well. In absolute positioning schemes, positive values of the left property move elements to the right, and positive values of the right property move elements to the left. They work the same in relative schemes as well, moving elements to the left or the right relative to the adjacent blocks in the normal

11

flow. The catch is that there will only be adjacent blocks to the left or right of elements in the normal flow if they are floated.

Positioning Properties and Height and Width

You've already seen that you can specify the size of an element using the `height` and `width` properties. You can also specify the size of an element if you use more than two of the positioning properties, or only two properties if those two properties are `left` and `right` or `top` and `bottom`. When you specify the position of two parallel sides of a block, it establishes a height or width for that block. If you specify the positions of all four sizes, you specify both the height and the width of a block.

Here's a style sheet for a page with positioned `<div>` elements:

```
<style type="text/css">
  body { background-color: #aaaaaa; }
  div {
    background-color: white; border: 2px solid black; padding: 10px;
  }

  #pos {
    position: absolute;
    left: 50px;
    top: 50px;
  }

  #pos2 {
    top: 160px;
    left: 75px;
    bottom: 75px;
    right: 100px;
    position: absolute;
    overflow: hidden;
  }

  #pos3 {
    position: absolute;
    width: 50%;
    height: 50%;
    bottom: 0px;
    right: 0px;
  }
</style>
```

The resulting page is shown in Figure 11.4.

FIGURE 11.4
How size and positioning interact.

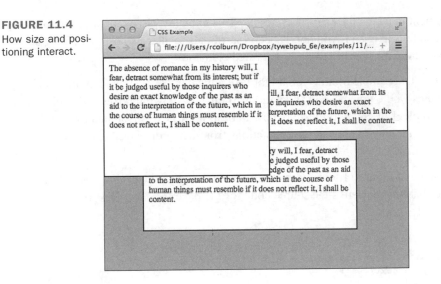

The first `<div>` is positioned using the `left` and `top` properties, and no size is specified. The left and top edges of the box are positioned as described in the style sheet, but the right side of the box runs to the edge of the page, just as it would in normal flow, and the box's height is derived from the content in it, again just as it would be in normal flow.

The second `<div>` has all four positioning properties set, which indicates exactly where all four edges of the box should appear. This establishes the exact size of the box, and if the content is larger than the box, it is treated as overflow. In this case, positioning also specifies the size of the box.

In the third example `<div>`, I use the `bottom` and `right` properties to position the box in the bottom-right corner of the page and the `height` and `width` properties to specify the size of the box. This is the preferred method of combining positioning and sizing. Rather than specifying all four positions, you should position one corner of the box (whichever makes the most sense) and then use `height` and `width` to specify a size. If you specify positions for all four sides of the box and you include a height and width, the size of the box will be taken from the size properties, and the position will be set using the `top` and `left` properties. The `bottom` and `right` properties would be ignored completely.

Nesting Absolutely Positioned Elements

As you may remember, absolutely positioned elements are positioned relative to the closest positioned ancestor. So when you nest an absolutely positioned element within another element that's positioned absolutely or relatively, the positioning will be relative

11

to the element in which the element is nested. This explains why you may want to position an element even if you don't specify attributes to alter its position. Doing so enables you to make it easier to position nested elements.

Let's look at an example of how you might take advantage of nesting. You may have seen websites where you can add annotations to images, drawing boxes and adding notes. In this example, I'm going to illustrate how to design images with annotations of that kind, along with how to prevent the annotations from being displayed except when you want to see them.

The web page in Figure 11.5 includes a `<div>` containing an image and a note I've applied to that image. Here's the source code for the page:

```
<!DOCTYPE html>
<html>
<head>
  <title>Image Notes</title>
  <style type="text/css">
    #picture {
      position: relative;
      width: 500px;
    }

    #picture img {
      width: 500px;
      margin: 0;
      padding: 0;
    }

    #note1 {
      position: absolute;
      border: 2px solid black;
      width: 340px;
      height: 300px;
      top: 40px;
      left: 40px;
      text-align: right;
    }

  </style>
</head>
<body>
  <h1>Claude Monet The Bridge at Argenteuil</h1>
  <div id="picture">
    <img src="monet.jpg">

    <div id="note1">
      This is a boat!
    </div>
```

```
</div>
</body>
</html>
```

FIGURE 11.5
A picture with a
note overlaid above
it.

I placed the picture within a relatively positioned `<div>` and then added an absolutely
positioned `<div>` within it. I chose relative positioning for the outer `<div>` because I want
to position elements within it, and yet I still want it to appear within the normal flow so
that it won't overlap elements that follow it on the page. I then nested both the image
and the `<div>` containing the note within that positioned `<div>`. The absolutely positioned `<div>` with the note is positioned relative to the positioned `<div>` within which it
is nested. That's what makes it easy to treat it as an overlay for the image, as seen in the
screenshot.

Dynamic Overlays

The previous example was a simple overlay, but there's more you can do. For example,
it's fairly common to only show the overlays over images when the user moves his
pointer over the image. You can accomplish this effect using CSS. To hide the overlay in

11

the example, I need to make two small tweaks to the CSS. I added a new rule to display the overlay, and I hid the #note1 element by default. Here are the changes:

```
#note1 {
  position: absolute;
  border: 2px solid black;
  width: 340px;
  height: 300px;
  top: 40px;
  left: 40px;
  text-align: right;
  display: none;
}

#picture:hover #note1 {
  display: block;
}
```

The result is that the overlay <div> is hidden unless the mouse pointer is over the image. Note that I used the :hover pseudo-class with #picture. This ensures that the overlay is displayed whenever the mouse is over the picture, rather than just when it's over the overlay.

In Lesson 9, "Using Images on Your Web Pages," you were introduced to image maps. You can also approximate image maps using positioning. For example, let's say I want to let users click the left side of the image in the previous example to move to the previous image in a set, or the right side of the image to move to the next image.

The first step is to remove the overlay from the previous example and add the links that I'm going to use:

```
<div id="picture">
  <a href="/picture2.html" id="next">Next</a>
  <a href="/picture2.html" id="previous">Previous</a>
  <img src="monet.jpg">
</div>
```

As you can see in Figure 11.6, the links appear in the normal flow above the image because I haven't positioned them yet.

First I'll apply some styles to both of the links to get them to overlay the page.

```
#picture a {
  position: absolute;
  border: 3px double #333;
  padding: 1em;
}
```

FIGURE 11.6
Inline links.

At this point, the two links will appear over the image, but they'll be stacked right on top of each other because they have been removed from the normal flow but they have not been positioned. I added a border just to make the positioning clear. The next step is to position the two links. I'm going to put the "previous" link on the upper left and the "next" link on the upper right. The results are shown in Figure 11.7.

11

```
#previous {
   left: 0;
   top: 0;
}

#next {
   right: 0;
   top: 0;
}
```

FIGURE 11.7
Links positioned in
the upper left and
right corners.

That's looking much better. As you can see, the links are now positioned correctly, in the upper corners of the image. The final step is to resize the links so that they both consume 20% of the width of the image and run the entire height of the image. Here's the updated style:

```
#picture a {
  position: absolute;
  border: 3px double #333;
  padding: 1em;
  height: 337px;
  width: 20%;
}
```

When this style is applied, the links take up the full left and right sides of the image. The links could be more attractive, but this demonstrates how you can create links that overlay images. When you resize links, the entire link remains clickable, which enables you to create large clickable regions, as I did in this example. The final image is shown in Figure 11.8.

FIGURE 11.8
An image with large links overlaid.

Fixed Positioning

11

Fixed positioning is similar to absolute positioning. Elements are positioned using the same properties, and fixed elements are removed from the normal flow. The difference is that rather than being positioned in relation to their containing block, fixed elements are positioned relative to the viewport. The obvious question is, what's the viewport?

When all of the elements on a page are laid out in the normal flow, that page may be 300 pixels wide and 100 pixels tall if it's very small, or it may be 1000 pixels wide and 8000 pixels tall if it's a long article. In the meantime, the browser window has its own size, perhaps 900 pixels wide and 700 pixels tall. The viewport is the part of the HTML page that is currently being displayed in the browser window.

When you apply the `fixed` positioning scheme to an element, the viewport is treated as the containing block, and the positioned elements remain in that position if the contents of the viewport change through scrolling or resizing the window. Here's an example. You may create a restaurant website that shows the hours, address, and phone number at the bottom of the browser window at all times. First, I add an ordinary `<div>` to the page with the ID `bottom`. Here's the code:

```
<div id="bottom">
  <strong>The Tiny Diner</strong> | 150 Water Street, Brooklyn, NY 11201
  | 718.555.1111 | 11-10 Tues - Sat
</div>
```

The next step is to apply styles to the element so that it appears at the bottom of the viewport in a fixed location. Here are the styles:

```
#bottom {
  position: fixed;
  bottom: 0;
  left: 0;
  width: 100%;
  text-align: center;
  padding: 5px;
  border-top: 3px solid blue;
  background-color: #cccccc;
}
```

First, I set the positioning of the element as `fixed`. Then, I set the `bottom` and `left` properties to 0 to position the element in the bottom-left corner of the viewport. To create a bar that runs the full length of the viewport, I set the width to 100%. Then I centered the contents of the `<div>`, added some padding, and added a border to the top and specified a background color. The results are shown in Figure 11.9.

FIGURE 11.9
A fixed bar at the bottom of a web page.

One thing you might notice in the figure is that the bar covers some of the text at the bottom of the page. Both fixed and absolute positioning remove the element from the normal flow, so the browser does not take the fixed element into account when it creates the scrollbar for the page's vertical scrolling. When you use fixed elements, you may need to strategically add whitespace to the page so that parts of the page are not permanently covered by those elements. To make sure that the bottom of the final paragraph on the page is not permanently covered by the bar I added to the bottom of the viewport, I added this style:

```
p:last-of-type {
  padding-bottom: 2em;
}
```

It adds some padding to the bottom of the last paragraph on the page, creating enough space for all of the text to be displayed. There are other ways to add whitespace as well; this is just the one I chose.

Controlling Stacking

CSS provides a way of taking control over how overlapping elements are presented. The z-index property is used to manually specify a value for the stacking order associated with a selector. By default, elements that appear in the same layer of a document are stacked in source order. In other words, an element that appears after another in the HTML source for the page will generally be stacked above it. The easiest way to think about it is to think of all of the elements on a page being numbered from first to last in the source. Larger numbers are stacked above smaller numbers.

By manually assigning z-index values for elements, however, you can put elements in specific stacking layers. If all elements appear in stacking layer 0 by default, any element in stacking layer 1 (z-index: 1) will appear above all elements in layer 0. The catch here is that z-index can be applied only to elements that are positioned. Elements in the normal flow always appear below relatively or absolutely positioned elements. The stacking layers below 0 are considered beneath the body element, so they don't show up at all.

11

TIP

If you want to have an element in the normal flow but you want to control its stacking layer, assign it the relative positioning scheme and don't specify a position. It will appear on the page normally, but you will be able to apply a z-index to it.

Let's look at another page. This one contains two paragraphs, both part of the same (default) stacking layer. As you can see in Figure 11.10, the second overlaps the first.

Input ▼

```html
<!DOCTYPE html>
<html>
<head>
  <title>Stacking Example</title>
  <style type="text/css">
#one {
  position: relative;
  width: 50%;
  padding: 15px;
  background-color: yellow;
}

#two {
  position: absolute;
  top: 15%;
  left: 15%;
  padding: 15px;
  width: 50%;
  background-color: navy;
  color: white;
}
  </style>
</head>
<body>
<p id="one">
The absence of romance in my history will, I fear, detract somewhat
from its interest; but if it be judged useful by those inquirers who
desire an exact knowledge of the past as an aid to the interpretation
of the future, which in the course of human things must resemble if
it does not reflect it, I shall be content.
</p>
<p id="two">
The absence of romance in my history will, I fear, detract somewhat
from its interest; but if it be judged useful by those inquirers who
desire an exact knowledge of the past as an aid to the interpretation
of the future, which in the course of human things must resemble if
it does not reflect it, I shall be content. In fine, I have written
my work, not as an essay which is to win the applause of the moment,
but as a possession for all time.
</p>

</body>
</html>
```

Output ▼

FIGURE 11.10
Two normally
stacked elements.

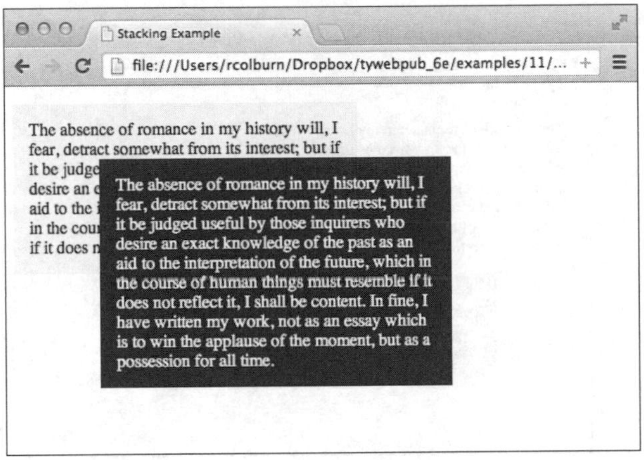

So, how do I cause the first element to overlap the second? Because I've assigned the first element the relative positioning scheme (even though I haven't specified a position), I can assign it a z-index of 1 (or higher) to move it into a stacking layer above the second paragraph. The new style sheet for the page, which appears in Figure 11.11, is as follows:

11

Input ▼

```
#one {
  position: relative;
  z-index: 1;
  width: 50%;
  padding: 15px;
  background-color: #ffc;
}

#two {
  position: absolute;
  top: 15%;
  left: 15%;
  padding: 15px;
  width: 50%;
  background-color: #060;
  color: #fff;
}
```

Output ▼

FIGURE 11.11
A page that uses
z-index to control
positioning.

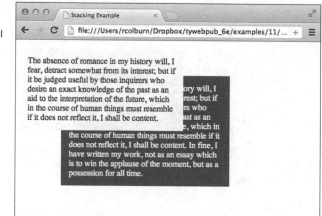

Using a combination of absolute and relative positioning, you can create complex pages with many stacked layers. Using your browser's developer tools is a great way to experiment with stacking and positioning. It's easy to open the developer tools, change the z-index values for elements, and see how the stack order changes.

Floated elements also have their own special handing. They have a higher precedence in the stacking order than elements in the normal flow, and they have a lower precedence than positioned elements. If you need to raise their precedence, you can add relative positioning and assign a z-index to them.

Creating Drop-Down Menus

Drop-down menus are one of the most common navigation techniques used on websites. They enable you to provide deep navigation without requiring a lot of screen real estate. To give a sneak preview, Figure 11.12 shows what the finished navigation menus will look like when the menu is completed. In earlier times, such elements had to be created using JavaScript, but CSS is powerful enough now that you can use it alone to build these sorts of interface elements. Indeed, this example incorporates techniques that you've already seen.

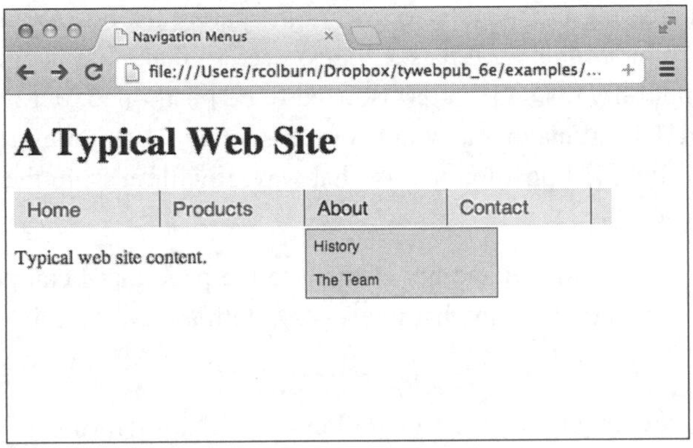

FIGURE 11.12
A navigation bar with drop-down menus.

The navigation bar starts as a regular nested HTML list. Styles will be used to convert it into the dynamic navigation bar. Here's the source code for the page:

```html
<!DOCTYPE html>
<html>
<head>
  <title>Navigation Menus</title>
  <style type="text/css">
  </style>
</head>
<body>
  <h1>A Typical Web Site</h1>
  <nav id="navigationBar">
    <ul>
      <li><a href="/home.html">Home</a></li>
      <li><a href="/products.html">Products</a>
        <ul>
          <li><a href="/products/a.html">Something Awesome</a></li>
          <li><a href="/products/b.html">Another Awesome Thing</a></li>
          <li><a href="/products/c.html">Our Best Thing</a></li>
          <li><a href="/products/d.html">A Cheap Thing</a></li>
        </ul>
      <li>
      <li><a href="/about.html">About</a>
        <ul>
          <li><a href="/history.html">History</a></li>
          <li><a href="/team.html">The Team</a></li>
        </ul>
      </li>
      <li><a href="/contact.html">Contact</a></li>
    </ul>
  </nav>
<p>Typical web site content.</p>
</body>
</html>
```

11

The first step in creating the menu is to lay out the parent list horizontally with appropriate spacing and to hide the nested lists. I'll also need to make it a positioned element. As it turns out, not only does the outer list need to be positioned, but it needs to be absolutely positioned. Unfortunately, as you know, absolutely positioning removes an element from the normal flow. If I position the list that way, it will mess up the normal flow for the rest of the page.

For this reason I'll need to add another element to the page that I can position relatively. So the real first step is to wrap the list in a `<nav>`, with an ID like this:

```
<nav id="navigationBar"> ... menu lists ... </nav>
```

You will learn more about the `<nav>` tag in Lesson 13, "Structuring a Page with HTML5."

Okay, now that's all set and I can start to style the `<nav>` and the lists nested in it. I need to take care of the following things in the style sheet to get the menus working:

- Remove the bullets from the lists
- Lay out the top-level list horizontally
- Specify sizes for all of the lists and list items to assist with positioning
- Position the submenus so that they appear in the correct place
- Hide the submenus by default
- Apply styles to customize the appearance of the menus
- Show the submenus on hover

Let's look at the styles required to make the menu work, in order of increasing specificity. First, I style the container for my `<nav>`:

```
#navigationBar {
  position: relative;
  margin: 0;
  padding: 0;
  height: 30px;
  width: 90%;
}
```

These styles position the navigation bar relatively so that I can position absolutely positioned items relative to it. I also disable the margins and padding and specify a size for the navigation bar. Next, I style the top-level list in the navigation bar:

```
#navigationBar ul {
  margin: 0;
  padding: 0;
```

```
    position: absolute;
    height: 100%;
    width: 100%;
    list-style-type: none;
    background-color: #eeeeee;
    overflow: visible;
}
```

Again, I remove the margins and padding. This time, I position the list absolutely, relative to its container. Its height and width are set to 100% so that it fills the container, and the bullets for the list are disabled. I also specify a background color and allow overflow in the list to be shown. The next step is styling the list items in the top-level list. I use the > selector to make sure that these styles only affect the list items in the top-level lists and not those in child lists.

```
#navigationBar ul > li {
    display: block;
    float: left;
    height: auto;
    /* menu header's items width */
    width: 120px;
}
```

I float the list items to the left, set them to block display, and specify a width for each list item. The next step is to style the links in the top-level list:

```
#navigationBar li > a {
    display: block;
    padding: 0 0 0 10px;
    height: 100%;
    width: 109px;
    border-right: 1px black solid;
    line-height: 30px;
    font-family: sans-serif;
    font-size: 17px;
    text-decoration: none;
    background-color: #eeeeee;
    color: #5d5636;
}
```

I apply a lot of styles to the link to get it to look just right and to get it to fit properly in the layout. Next it's time to start working on the nested lists. First, the nested list itself:

```
#navigationBar ul ul {
    margin-top: 2px;
    display: none;
    position: static;
    height: auto;
```

11

```
  width: 160px;
  border: 1px #666666 solid;
  background-color: #dddddd;
}
```

It's set to display none so that it's hidden when the page loads. The position is set to static, which is the default. I also add a border and a background color. Next, I style the list items in the submenu:

```
#navigationBar ul ul li {
  position: relative;
  float: none;
  display: block;
  height: 28px;
  width: 100%;
  border: none;
}
```

In this case, the list items are positioned relatively, float is disabled, and the list items are sized. Many of these styles override styles set for the items in the parent list. Following the pattern, I next style the links in the list:

```
#navigationBar ul ul li > a {
  height: 100%;
  width: 96%;
  padding: 0 0 0 4%;
  line-height: 28px;
  background-color: transparent;
  border: none;
  color: #000000;
  font-size: 12px;
  font-style: normal;
}
```

In this case, I set the height and width of the link, add a little padding, and set the line-height so that the link is positioned properly. I also reduce the font size a bit so that the links fit in the space allotted. Once I'm done with that, I just have to add the hover styles to make the page dynamic:

```
#navigationBar li:hover > a {
  color: #220000;
  background-color: #eeeabe;
}
#navigationBar li:hover > ul {
  display: block;
}
```

When the mouse pointer is over a list item in the navigation lists, I set the `display` property of the list that's a child of that list item to `block`. I also change the background color and color of the link so that it's highlighted. That's it for the list. The result is a dynamic menu system implemented with pure CSS.

Summary

In this lesson, I looked at the styles associated with positioning elements on the page. Using positioning, you can arrange elements in any arbitrary fashion that you like. As you saw in the final example, you can combine these properties with other styles to create complex page elements that behave like applications. You also saw that you can position elements relative to parent elements, as I did when I created the overlays for the image. Finally, you saw that fixed positioning can position elements based on the viewport. CSS positioning is what enables web developers to create websites that work like desktop applications.

Workshop

If you've made it this far, I'm sure that you still have a few questions. I've included a few that I think are interesting. Afterward, test your retention by taking the quiz, and then expand your knowledge by tackling the exercises.

11

Q&A

Q Is it possible to move absolutely positioned items around the page?

A Yes, you can move positioned elements with JavaScript. The first lesson on JavaScript is Lesson 17, "Introducing JavaScript." You can use JavaScript to modify any styles on a page. There are also libraries that enable you to apply effects when you show or hide elements, like jQuery UI, which you can find out more about at http://jqueryui.com/.

Q Where can I find more examples of using CSS for positioning?

A The Mozilla developer site provides a wide variety of examples in the Mozilla DemoStudio, at https://developer.mozilla.org/en-US/demos/. You can use it to get an idea of what can be accomplished with CSS.

Quiz

1. What is the normal flow?
2. When you position an element relatively, how does that position affect other elements on the page?
3. How do the absolute and fixed positioning schemes differ?

Quiz Answers

1. The normal flow is the default layout of the page, with elements flowing from left to right and top to bottom. Positioning is used to alter the placement of elements in the normal flow or to remove them from that flow entirely.
2. The relative positioning system does not affect other nearby elements. They are placed within the normal flow as they would be if the element were statically positioned.
3. The absolute positioning scheme positions elements relative to the closest positioned ancestor. The fixed positioning scheme positions elements relative to their viewport maintaining that position as the page scrolls.

Exercises

1. Create a page with a navigation element on the right side that follows the user as she scrolls down the page.
2. Alter the drop-down navigation menu example so that there is a second-level submenu. You should be able to follow the pattern of the submenus to create the second submenu.

LESSON 12
Designing Forms

Up to this point, you've learned almost everything you need to know to create functional, attractive, and somewhat interactive web pages. If you think about it, however, the pages you've created thus far have a one-way information flow. This lesson is about creating HTML forms to collect information from people visiting your website. Forms enable you to gather just about any kind of information for immediate processing by a server-side script or for later analysis using other applications

This lesson covers the following topics, which enable you to create any type of form possible with HTML:

- Discovering how HTML forms interact with server-side scripts to provide interactivity

- Creating simple forms to get the hang of it

- Learning all the types of form controls you can use to create radio buttons, check boxes, and more

- Using more advanced form controls to amaze your friends and co-workers

- Using other interactivity tags to make your pages more interesting

- Planning forms so that your data matches any server-side scripts you use

Understanding Form and Function

Right off the bat, you need to understand a few things about forms. First, a form is part of a web page that you create using HTML elements. Each form contains a `form` element that contains special controls, such as buttons, text fields, check boxes, Submit buttons, and menus. These controls make up the user interface for the form (that is, the pieces of the form users see on the web page). When people fill out forms, they're interacting with these elements. In addition, you can use many other HTML elements within forms to create labels, provide additional information, add structure, and so on. These elements aren't part of the form itself, but they can enhance your form's look and improve its usability.

When someone fills out an HTML form, he enters information or makes choices using the form controls. When the user submits the form, the browser collects all the data from the form and sends it to the URL specified as the form's action. It's up to the program residing at that URL to process the form input and create a response for the user.

It's important that you understand the implications of this final step. The data is what you want, after all! This is the reason you've chosen to create a form in the first place. When a user clicks the Submit button, the process ceases to be one of pure HTML and becomes reliant on applications that reside on the web server. In other words, for your form to work, you must already have a program on the server that will store or manipulate the data in some manner.

In some cases, forms aren't necessarily submitted to programs. Using JavaScript, you can take action based on form input. For example, you can open a new window when a user clicks a form button. You can also submit forms via email, which is okay for testing but isn't reliable enough for real applications.

▼ Creating a Simple Form That Accepts a Name and a Password

Okay, let's get right to it and create a simple form that illustrates the concepts just presented. It's a web page that prompts the user to enter a name and a password to continue.

Start by opening your favorite HTML editor and creating a web page template. Enter the standard HTML header information, include the `body` element, and then close the `body` and `html` elements to form a template from which to work. If you already have a template similar to this, just load it into your HTML editor:

```
<!DOCTYPE html>
<html>
<head>
<title>Page Title</title>
```

```
</head>
<body>

</body>
</html>
```

Next, add your `title` so that people will understand the purpose of the web page:

```
<title>Please Log In</title>
```

And don't forget to include a title in the `body` of the page:

```
<h1>Please Log In</h1>
```

Within the `body` of the web page, add a `form` element. I've added both the opening and the closing tags, with an empty line between them, so that I don't forget to close the `form` when I'm finished:

```
<form action="/form-processing-script" method="post">

</form>
```

Before continuing, you need to know more about the `form` element and the attributes you see within the opening tag. Obviously, `form` begins the element and indicates that you're creating an HTML form. The `action` attribute specifies the URL to the server-side script (including the filename) that will process the form when it's submitted. It's important that the script with the name you've entered is present on your web server at the location the URL specifies. In this example, I use the full URL for the script, but you can just as easily use a relative URL if it makes more sense.

12

CAUTION

Before going live with forms, contact your web hosting provider and ask whether you can use the hosting provider's scripts or add your own. You must also determine the URL that points to the directory on the server that contains the scripts. Some hosting providers rigidly control scripts for security purposes and won't allow you to create or add scripts to the server. If that's the case, and you really need to implement forms on your web pages, consider searching for a new hosting provider.

The next attribute is `method`, which can accept one of two possible values: `post` or `get`. These values define how form data is submitted to your web server. The `post` method includes the form data in the body of the form and sends it to the web server. The `get`

▼ method appends the data to the URL specified in the `action` attribute and most often is used in searches. I chose the `post` method here because I don't want to send the user's password back in plain sight as part of the URL. Now add some form controls and information to make it easy for a visitor to understand how to fill out the form. Within the `form` element, begin by adding a helpful description of the data to be entered by the user, and then add a `text` form control. This prompts the user to enter her name in a text-entry field. Don't worry about positioning just yet because you'll lay out the form controls later:

```
<form action="/form-processing-script" method="post">
  <label for="username">Username</label> <input type="text" name="username">
</form>
```

Next, add another bit of helpful text and a password control:

```
<form action="/form-processing-script" method="post">
  <label for="username">Username</label> <input type="text" name="username">

  <label for="password">Password</label> <input type="password" name="password">
</form>
```

Notice that both these form controls are created using the `input` element. The `type` attribute defines which type of control will be created. In this case, you have a text control and a password control. Each type of control has a distinct appearance, accepts a different type of user input, and is suitable for different purposes. Each control is also assigned a name that distinguishes it and its data from the other form controls.

The labels for the form fields are specified using the `<label>` tag. Each label is attached to the form field it is associated with through the `for` attribute, which should match the `name` or `id` attribute of the form tag with which it is associated. The `<label>` element doesn't provide formatting by default, but you can make it appear any way you want using CSS.

Finally, add a Submit button so that the user can send the information she entered into the form. Here's the form so far, with some `<div>` tags added to make it easier to style:

Input ▼

```
<form action="/form-processing-script" method="post">
  <div>
    <label for="username">Username</label>
    <input type="text" name="username">
  </div>
  <div>
    <label for="password">Password</label>
```
▼

```
      <input type="password" name="password">
    </div>
    <div>
      <input type="submit" class="submit" value="Log In">
    </div>
</form>
```

The Submit button is another type of `input` field. The `value` attribute is used as the label for the Submit button. If you leave it out, the default label will be displayed by the browser.

TIP

When you're naming form controls and labeling buttons, strive for clarity and meaning. If a form is frustrating or hard to figure out, visitors will leave your site for greener pastures!

Figure 12.1 contains a screenshot of the form with all the form elements in place.

Output ▼

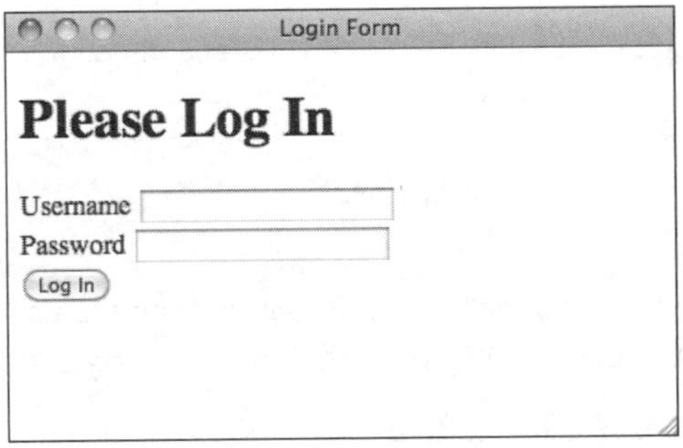

FIGURE 12.1
The form with all the input elements in place.

At this point, you've created the form and it's ready to rumble. However, if you load it into your web browser, you'll see that it doesn't look all that appealing. I can vastly improve the appearance using Cascading Style *Sheets* (CSS). Here's the code for the full page, including the style sheet:

```
<!DOCTYPE html>
<html>
  <head>
    <title>Please Log In</title>
    <style>
      div {
        margin-bottom: 5px;
```

12

```
          }
        label {
          display: block;
          float: left;
          width: 150px;
          text-align: right;
          font-weight: bold;
          margin-right: 10px;
        }
        input.submit {
          margin-left: 160px;
        }
    </style>
  </head>
  <body>
    <h1>Please Log In</h1>
    <form action="/form-processing-script" method="post">
      <div>
        <label for="username">Username</label>
        <input type="text" name="username">
      </div>
      <div>
        <label for="password">Password</label>
        <input type="password" name="password">
      </div>
      <div>
        <input type="submit" class="submit" value="Log In">
      </div>
    </form>
  </body>
</html>
```

At one time, it was rare to see forms that were laid out without the use of tables, but tables are no longer necessary thanks to CSS. Let's look at the style sheet for the form.

First, I added 5 pixels of margin to the bottom of the `<div>` elements to separate the form elements a bit. Then, I used CSS on the labels to align the form fields vertically and right-align the labels. You can only apply widths to block-level elements, so I set the display property on the labels to `block`. Then I used `float: left` and a width of 150 pixels to get the form fields to move to the right of the labels. Setting the `text-align` property to `right` for the labels moves them to the right side of the 150-pixel box I put them in. Then I just added 10 pixel margin to create some space between the labels and the form fields, and I bolded the label text. To get the Submit button, which has no label, to line up with the other form fields, I added a 160-pixel left margin. That's 150 pixels for the label and 10 pixels for the margin I added to the labels. That took a little work, but I think the final page shown in Figure 12.2 looks good.

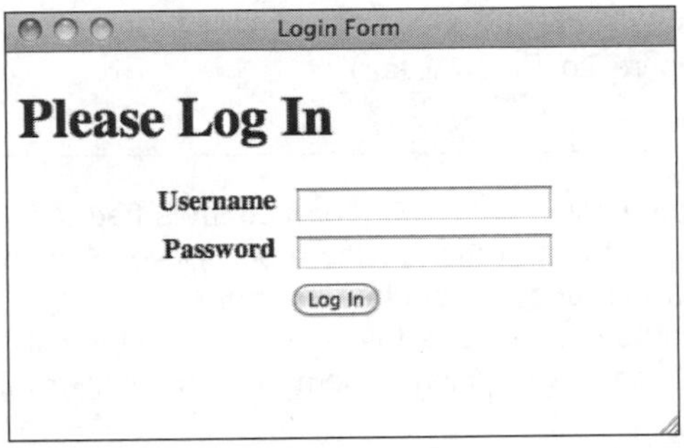

FIGURE 12.2
A simple form.

Please Log In

Username [   ]

Password [   ]

(Log In)

To complete the exercise, let's test the form to see whether it produces the data we expect. Because you don't have the script "form-processing-script" available on your hard drive, you should modify your `<form>` tag to send the data to the page with a get request:

```
<form method="get">
```

Then when you submit your form, here's what the data that's sent to the server looks like:

```
username=somename&password=somepassword
```

This data will appear at the end of the URL in your browser window as in Figure 12.3.

FIGURE 12.3
The URL field after submitting a form

x/documents/TYWebPublishing/12code01.html?username=test&password=password ☆

CAUTION

Most forms won't work if they are not on a web server. And if the URL in the `action` attribute does not exist, the form won't work when you submit it.

It's pretty measly, but you can see that the names assigned to each field are tied to the values entered in those fields. You can then use a program to use this data to process the user's request.

Using the `<form>` Tag

To accept input from a user, you must wrap all of your input fields inside a `<form>` tag. The purpose of the `<form>` tag is to indicate where and how the user's input should be sent. First, let's look at how the `<form>` tag affects page layout. Forms are block-level

▼ elements. That means when you start a form, a new line is inserted (unless you apply the `display: inline` CSS property to the `form` tag).

> **NOTE**
>
> In older versions of HTML, form controls had to be placed inside a `<form>` tag and then inside a block-level element to be valid. But HTML5 doesn't require either of these things. Instead, you should use the `<form>` tag when you need to collect a group of form controls and submit them all to the server for processing.

Take a look at the following code fragment:

Input ▼

```
<p>Please enter your username <form><input> and password
<input></form> to log in.</p>
```

You might think that your entire form would appear on a single line based on the preceding markup. As shown in Figure 12.4, the opening and closing `<form>` tags act like opening and closing paragraph tags.

Output ▼

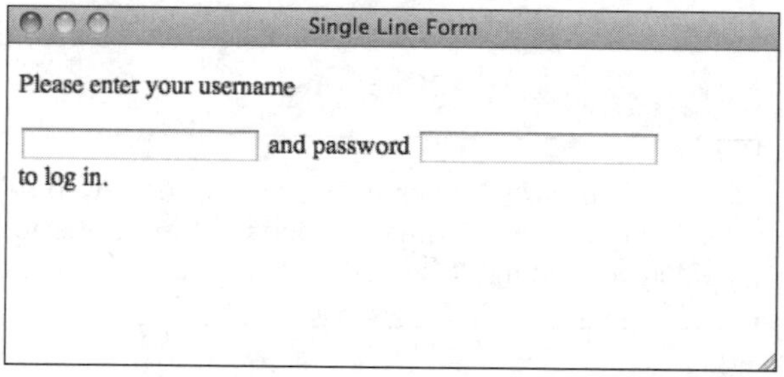

FIGURE 12.4
A line break inserted by an opening `<form>` tag.

The two most commonly used attributes of the `<form>` tag are `action` and `method`. Both of these attributes are optional. The following example shows how the `<form>` tag is typically used:

```
<form action="someaction" method="get or post">
content, form controls, and other HTML elements
```
▼ `</form>`

`action` specifies the URL to which the form is submitted. Again, remember that for the form to be submitted successfully, the script must be in the exact location you specify and must work properly.

If you leave out the `action` attribute, the form is submitted to the current URL. In other words, if the form appears on the page http://www.example.com/form.html and you leave off the `action` attribute, the form will be submitted to that URL by default. This probably doesn't seem very useful, but it is if your form is generated by a program instead of residing in an HTML file. In that case, the form is submitted back to that program for processing. One advantage of doing so is that if you move the program on the server, you don't have to edit the HTML to point the form at the new location.

Although most forms send their data to scripts, you also can make the action link to another web page or a `mailto` link. The latter is formed as follows:

```
<form action="mailto:somebody@isp.com" method="post">
```

This attaches the form data set to an email, which then is sent to the email address listed in the `action` attribute. But be aware that there are many things that can go wrong with using a `mailto` link in your forms. It's better to find a program or CGI script to link to in the `action` attribute.

TIP

> To test your forms, I recommend using the `get` method and leaving out the `action` attribute of the form tag as shown earlier in the lesson. When you submit the form, the values you entered will appear in the URL for the page so that you can inspect them and make sure that the results are what you expected.

12

The `method` attribute supports two values: `get` and `post`. The method indicates how the form data should be packaged in the request that's sent back to the server. The `get` method appends the form data to the URL in the request. The form data is separated from the URL in the request by a question mark and is referred to as the *query string*. If I have a text input field named `searchstring` and enter `Orangutans` in the field, the resulting URL would look like the following:

http://www.example.com/search?searchstring=Orangutans

The `method` attribute is not required; if you leave it out, the `get` method will be used. The other method is `post`. Instead of appending the form data to the URL and sending the combined URL-data string to the server, `post` sends the form data to the location specified by the `action` attribute in the body of the request. This is not readily visible to the user, and most forms work best with this method.

DO	**DON'T**
DO use the POST method when data on the server will be changed in any way.	**DON'T** use the GET method if you do not want the form parameters to be visible in a URL.
DO use the GET method if the form just requests data (like search forms, for example).	**DON'T** use the GET method if the form is used to delete information.
DO use the GET method if you want to bookmark the results of the form submission.	

The general rule when it comes to choosing between post and get is that if the form will change any data on the server, you should use post. If the form is used to retrieve information, using get is fine. For example, suppose that you're writing a message board program. The registration form for new users and the form used to publish messages should use the post method. If you have a form that enables the user to show all the posts entered on a certain date, it could use the get method.

HTML5 and modern browsers now offer a validation feature before the form is submitted. The browsers use a combination of rules written in the control attributes and the attribute types themselves to determine whether the content is what you're asking for. You'll learn about this in more detail later in this lesson. But because of this feature, the form tag has an attribute novalidate that lets you turn off validation on your forms. The main reason you will use this attribute is to test the JavaScript and server-side validation mechanisms you have in place. This is a Boolean attribute, so you don't need to include any values. Simply add it to your form tag:

```
<form novalidate>
```

Another new attribute of the `<form>` tag is the autocomplete attribute. It can have the value of on or off. on is the default, and it tells the browser to attempt to predict the value when a user is typing in a form control. By turning the autocomplete attribute off you tell the browser to avoid suggesting values for form fields. You can turn autocompletion on or off for your entire form by adding it to your `<form>` tag:

```
<form autocomplete="off">
```

Two other less-often used attributes of the `<form>` tag are enctype and accept-charset. enctype defines how form data is encoded when it's sent to the server, and accept-charset defines the character encodings to be used for the form submission. The default for enctype is application/x-www-form-urlencoded, and the default for accept-charset is the same as the page's character set. The only time you will ever need to use these attributes is when your form includes a file upload field (discussed a bit later) or you expect to receive data in a different language or character set than the page. If you're going to request a file upload, you need to specify that the `enctype` is `multipart/form-data`. Otherwise, it's fine to leave them out.

That about does it for the `<form>` tag, but you've really only just begun. The `<form>` tag alone is just a container for the input fields that are used to gather data from users. It indicates where the data should go and how it should be packaged. To actually gather information, you're going to need items called form controls.

Using the `<label>` Tag

Whenever you enter text that describes a form field, you should use the `<label>` tag and use the `for` attribute to tie it to the control it labels. To create a label, begin with the opening `label` tag and then enter the `for` attribute. The value for this attribute, when present, must match the `id` or `name` attribute for the control it labels. Next, enter text that will serve as the label and then close the element with the end `label` tag, as in the following:

Input ▼

```
<label for="control4">Who is your favorite NFL Quarterback?</label>
<input type="text" name="favqb" id="control4">
```

Figure 12.5 shows this text control with a label assigned to it.

Output ▼

FIGURE 12.5
You can assign labels to any form control.

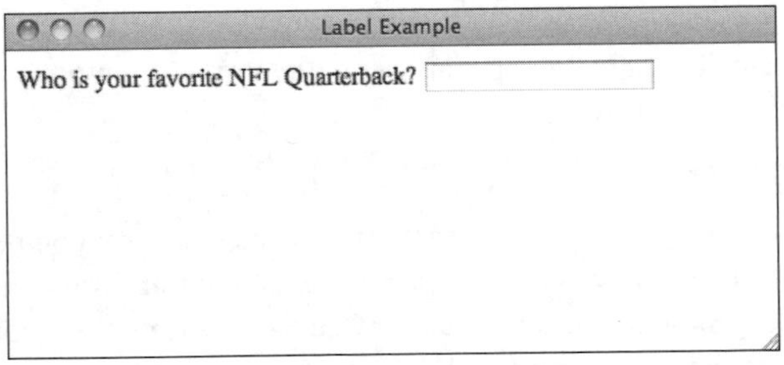

Label Example

Who is your favorite NFL Quarterback? [   ]

12

If you include your form control within the `label` element, as shown in the following code, you can omit the `for` attribute:

```
<label>User name <input type="text" name="username"></label>
```

The `<label>` tag doesn't cause visible changes to the page, but you can style it using CSS, as you saw in the sample login form earlier. One common styling approach people use is to apply a special style to the labels of required fields. For example, you may declare a style rule like this:

```
label.required { font-weight: bold; }
```

You can then set the `class` for the labels for all the required fields in your form to "required," and the labels for those fields will appear in boldface.

CAUTION

> You should not use purely visual effects (like boldface or color changes) to indicate if a field is required. These will not be accessible to users with screen readers. It's best to mention it in the text so that screen readers can read aloud that the field is required.

Creating Form Controls with the `<input>` Tag

Now it's time to learn how to create the data entry fields form. The `<input>` tag enables you to create many different types of form controls.

Form controls are special HTML tags used in a form that enable you to gather information from visitors to your web page. The information is packaged into a request sent to the URL in the form's `action` attribute.

The `input` element consists of an opening tag with attributes, no other content, and no closing tag:

```
<input attributes />
```

The key point here is using the right attributes to create the form control you need. The most important of these is `type`, which specifies what kind of form control to display. For all controls, except Submit and Reset buttons, the `name` attribute is recommended. It associates a name with the data entered in that field when the data is sent to the server. Most designers make the `name` attribute and the `id` attribute the same value to reduce confusion. The rest of this section describes the different types of controls you can create using the `input` element.

Creating Text Controls

Text controls enable you to gather information from a user in small quantities. This control type creates a single-line text input field in which users can type information, such as their name or a search term. This is the default input type and is the fallback type if a browser does not recognize the `type` you chose.

To create a text input field, create an `input` element and choose `text` as the value for the `type` attribute. Make sure to give your control an `id` so that the server script will be able to process the value:

Input ▼

```
<label for="petname">Enter your pet's name</label>
<input type="text" id="petname">
```

Figure 12.6 shows this text control, which tells the user what to type in.

Output ▼

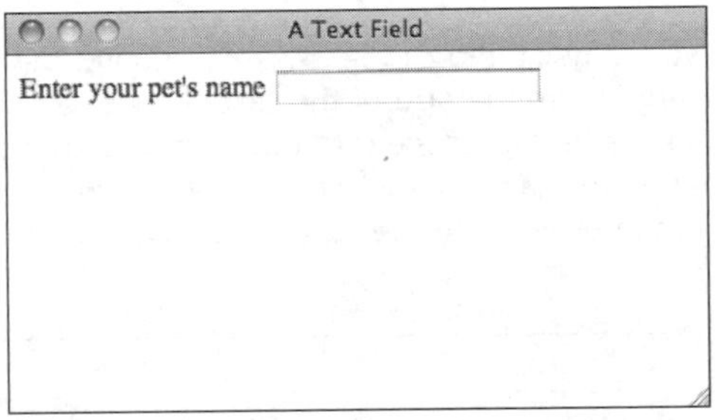

FIGURE 12.6
A text entry field.

You can modify the appearance of text controls using the `size` attribute. Entering a number sets the width of the text control in characters:

```
<input type="text" id="petname" size="15">
```

The size attribute will be overridden by any CSS widths set on the element. It is an approximate length and does not affect the number of characters the user can enter. To limit the number of characters a user can enter, add the `maxlength` attribute to the text control. This doesn't affect the appearance of the field; it just prevents the user from entering more characters than specified by this attribute. If users attempt to enter more text, their web browsers will stop accepting input for that particular control:

```
<input type="text" id="petname" size="15" maxlength="15">
```

12

You can also specify the minimum number of characters the user must enter before the form will submit with the `minlength` attribute. However, as of this writing this is only supported in Chrome (and Android) and Opera web browsers.

To display text in the text control before the user enters any information, use the `value` attribute. If the user is updating data that already exists, you can specify the current or default value using `value`, or you can prompt the user with a value:

```
<input type="text" id="petname" size="15" maxlength="15" value="Enter Pet Name">
```

In this case, `Enter Pet Name` appears in the field when the form is rendered in the web browser. It remains there until the user modifies it. It will also be submitted to the form just like anything the user writes. If you want to make a suggestion as to what the user should write, but you don't want that value submitted with the other form data, you should use the `placeholder` attribute:

```
<input type="text" id="petname" size="15" maxlength="15" placeholder="Fido">
```

This is particularly important on fields that are required. If there is a value set, the fields will not validate as empty and will not trigger the automatic browser validation.

CAUTION

> When you're using the `placeholder` attribute, using a value that's larger than the size of the text control can confuse the user because the text will appear to be cut off. Try to use only enough information to make your point. Ensure that any `placeholder` text is less than or equal to the number of characters you specified in `size`.

HTML5 adds a number of new attributes on form controls to help browsers validate the data before it is submitted to the form. The most important one is the `required` attribute. This indicates that a form field must be filled out for the form to be submitted. It is a Boolean attribute, so you just need to include the word *required* for the field to be marked required:

```
<input id="name" required>
```

The `pattern` attribute provides a regular expression against which the control's value should be checked. It uses the JavaScript regex patterns. You should include the pattern description somewhere on the page or in the input control (such as in the `title` attribute) so that your customers know what the rules are. If you wanted someone to submit a part number that has one digit followed by three uppercase letters, you would write

```
<label> Part number:
  <input pattern="[0-9][A-Z]{3}" name="part"
  title="A part number is a digit followed by three uppercase letters.">
</label>
```

Adding Options to Text Fields with `datalist`

One of the reasons that users don't like to fill out forms on the Web is because they can be very difficult to fill out. But HTML5 offers a new tag `<datalist>` that is intended to help with that. With the `datalist` tag you set up a list of options that users might want to use when filling out a text field. This is especially useful for text fields in which you'd like to get specific information, but you also want the ability to receive new values that no one has submitted before. In the past, web designers would do this with a drop-down menu or select list (I'll show you these later in this lesson) and then include an "Other" option with a text field for the user to fill out.

With a data list, you can provide a set of answers that most people fill out, and as the user types, the form guesses at what they want to write and provides suggestions as they type. To do this, first you need a data list with a bunch of options:

Input ▼

```
<datalist id="game">
  <option value="rock">
  <option value="paper">
  <option value="scissors">
  <option value="unicorn">
  <option value="sledgehammer">
</datalist>
```

Then you need to associate that list with the appropriate form control using the `list` attribute:

```
<label>
  Your Move:
  <input id="move" list="game">
</label>
```

Figure 12.7 shows how Chrome displays a data list.

Output ▼

FIGURE 12.7
A text field with a data list attached.

12

While the `datalist` tag has reasonable support in most browsers (except Safari and iOS at the time of writing), there is a way to use a select list inside your data list to get the best of both worlds:

```
<label>
  Your Move:
  <input id="move" list="game">
</label>
<datalist id="game">
<label>or select from a list:
  <select name="gameoption">
    <option value="">
    <option>rock
    <option>paper
    <option>scissors
    <option>unicorn
    <option>sledgehammer
  </select>
</label>
```

Browsers that support the `datalist` element will show the drop-down menu in the field. Browsers that don't will show the drop-down menu as a separate form control. You will learn more about creating drop-down menus later in this lesson.

Using the New HTML5 Controls

HTML5 adds more than just the `datalist` element to form controls. There are also several new form types you can use to both validate the data you collect and make it easier for your customers to fill out the forms correctly.

There are two types for which browsers will validate the contents automatically for you: `email` and `url`. This will help keep your data cleaner, but it also makes the forms easier for your customers to fill out. When a customer on an Android or iOS device (and other compatible mobile devices) gets to an `email` or `url` form control, the keyboard will change to make it easier to fill in an email address or a web page URL. For instance, with the email type, the @ sign will be visible on the keyboard without having to go into a second layer. To set up these controls, change the type to `email` or `url`:

```
<label>Email:
  <input type="email" id="address">
</label>
<label>URL:
  <input type="url" id="website">
</label>
```

On any input type you can request multiple values with the `multiple` attribute:

```
<input type="url" id="website" multiple>
```

There are several types for collecting different kinds of numbers: `tel` for collecting telephone numbers, `number` for collecting specific numbers, and `range` for collecting a number when the exact value is not important.

Telephone numbers are difficult to validate because they vary depending on your location and how specific you need to be. For instance, if you were asking for a U.S. phone number to be used internationally, you would need to include a +1 at the beginning, followed by 10 digits. However, if you were looking for a U.S. phone number from a preselected area code, all you would need would be seven digits. If you have a specific format you need your phone numbers in, you should use the `pattern` attribute discussed earlier along with some explanation or placeholder text showing how the phone number should be entered. The benefit of using the `tel` type for collecting phone numbers is that those numbers can then be passed to mobile devices as phone numbers to either call or send SMS text messages to. To collect a U.S. phone number with area code:

```
<label>Telephone:
  <input type="tel" id="phone" placeholder="xxx-xxx-xxxx" pattern="[0-9]{3}-[0-9]
{3}-[0-9]{4}">
</label>
```

With the `number` type, you can specify the minimum value, the maximum value, and even how the number picker should step through the values. Most browsers display the `number` type with a drop-down menu with the possible values. To request a whole number between 1 and 10:

```
<label>Pick a number between 1 and 10
  <input type="number" id="num" min="1" max="10" step="1">
</label>
```

If you want your readers to choose values with decimal points, add those values to the `min`, `max`, `step`, or `placeholder`:

```
<label>Pick a number between 0 and 1
  <input type="number" id="num" min="0" max="1" step="0.1" placeholder="0.5">
</label>
```

The `range` type is a little more confusing. It allows you to request a number when you don't care what the actual value is. This is perfect for customer surveys in which you want to know how people feel on a sliding scale. Rather than forcing them to choose a specific number—for instance: "rate this on a scale of 1 to 5"—you can provide a range control with the top and bottom values beside it:

12

Input ▼

```
<label>How much do you like our product?<br>
  Not at all <input type="range" id="likes" min="0" max="5" value="4.3"> More
than anything
</label>
```

As you can see in Figure 12.8, the range slider doesn't give specific values, even though they are included in the `input` element.

Output ▼

FIGURE 12.8
A range input type.

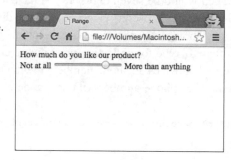

HTML5 provides several date and time types you can use to collect more specific dates from your customers.

`date`	Collects the month, day, and year you need
`datetime`	Collects the month, day, and year as well as the hours, minutes, and seconds
`datetime-local`	Collects the local date and time including time zone information
`month`	Collects the month and year
`week`	Collects the week number and year
`time`	Collects the time in hours, minutes, and seconds

Input ▼

```
<label>When can you return the book?<br>
 <input type="date" id="returndate">
</label>
```

Some browsers display a date picker automatically, as you see in Figure 12.9.

Output ▼

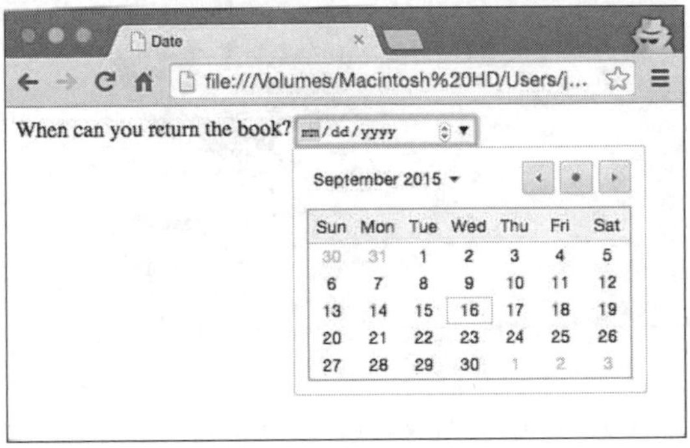

FIGURE 12.9
A date input type.

The last two types allow you to specify color values and search terms. Browsers that support the `color` type will display a color picker, and browsers that support the `search` type change the way the form control displays—adding rounded corners and sometimes a search icon inside the control. You add them the same way you add other input types:

12

Input ▼

```
<label>What is your favorite color?
  <input type="color" id="favoritecolor">
</label>

<label>Search:
    <input type="search" id="s">
</label>
```

Figure 12.10 demonstrates how Chrome displays the color picker and search control.

Output ▼

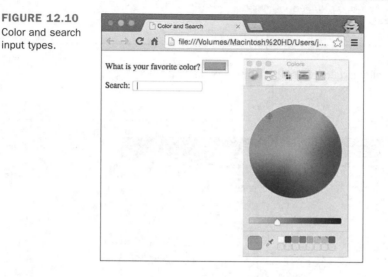

The best thing about using these new HTML5 input controls is that you don't need any fallback options to use them. You don't need JavaScript to set up special controls— although you can if you want to—because if the browser doesn't support the input type you're using it will display a text field. Because a text field is what you would have had to use to collect that form data anyway, you lose nothing. You should still validate the data that comes through your forms, even if the browser does support the input type. And that fixes bad data problems.

Creating Password Controls

The `password` and `text` field types are identical in every way except that the data entered in a password field is masked so that someone looking over the shoulder of the person entering information can't see the value that was typed into the field.

TIP

You don't have to limit your use of the `password` control to just passwords. You can use it for any sensitive material that you feel needs to be hidden when the user enters it into the form. But remember that because the text cannot be seen, it can be very easy to enter it incorrectly. And this makes password fields difficult to use.

To create a password control, create an `input` element with the `type` set to `password`. To limit the size of the password control and the maximum number of characters a user can enter, you can use the `size` and `maxlength` attributes just as you would in a `text` control. Here's an example:

Input ▼

```
<label for="userpassword">Enter your password</label> <input type="password"
id="userpassword"
  size="8" maxlength="8">
```

Figure 12.11 shows a password control.

Output ▼

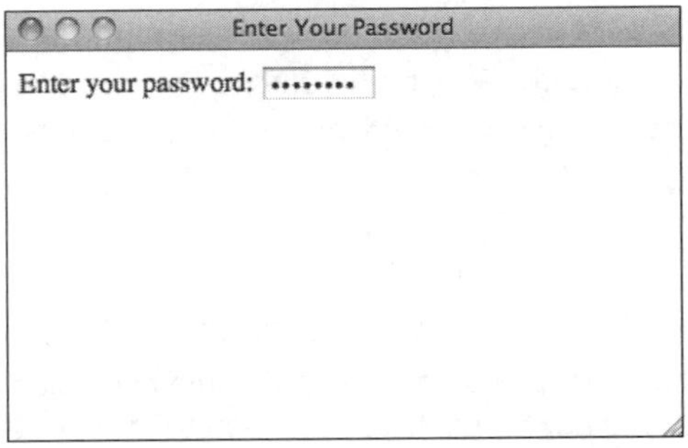

FIGURE 12.11
A password form field.

CAUTION

When data entered in a `password` field is sent to the server, it is not encrypted in any way. Therefore, this is not a secure means of transmitting sensitive information. Although the users can't read what they are typing, the `password` control provides no other security measures.

Creating Submit Buttons

Submit buttons are used to indicate that the user is finished filling out the form. Setting the `type` attribute of the form to `submit` places a Submit button on the page with the default label determined by the browser, usually `Submit Query`. To change the button text, use the `value` attribute and enter your own label, as follows:

```
<input type="submit" value="Send Form Data">
```

12

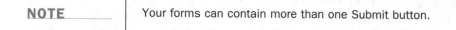

NOTE   Your forms can contain more than one Submit button.

If you include a `name` attribute for a Submit button, the `value` that you assign to the field is sent to the server if the user clicks on that Submit button. This enables you to take different actions based on which Submit button the user clicks, if you have more than one. For example, you could create two Submit buttons, both with the `name` attribute set to "action". The first might have a value of "edit" and the second a value of "delete". In your script, you could test the value associated with that field to determine what the user wanted to do when he submitted the form.

Creating Reset Buttons

Reset buttons set all the form controls to their default values. These are the values included in the `value` attributes of each field in the form (or in the case of selectable fields, the values that are preselected). As with the Submit button, you can change the label of a Reset button to one of your own choosing by using the `value` attribute, like this:

```
<input type="reset" value="Clear Form">
```

CAUTION   Reset buttons can be a source of some confusion for users. Unless you have a really good reason to include them on your forms, you should probably just avoid using them. If your form is large and the user clicks the Reset button when he means to click the Submit button, he isn't going to be very pleased with having to go back and reenter all of his data.

Creating Check Box Controls

Check boxes are fields that can be set to two states: on and off (see Figure 12.12). To create a check box, set the `input` tag's type attribute to `checkbox`. The `name` attribute is also required, as shown in the following example:

Input ▼

```
<label>Check to receive SPAM email <input type="checkbox" id="spam"></label>
```

Output ▼

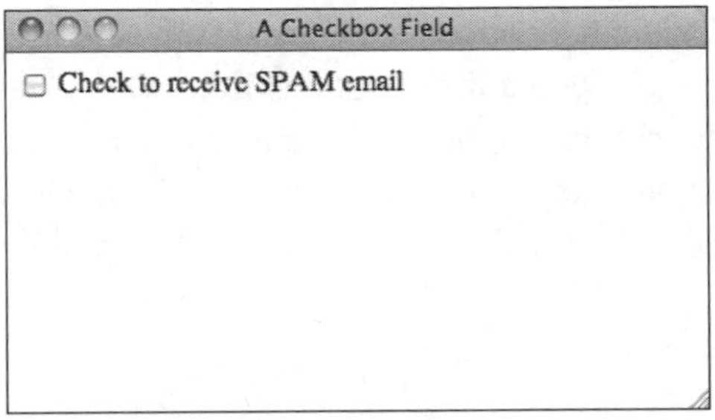

FIGURE 12.12
A check box field.

To display the check box as checked, include the `checked` attribute, as follows:

```
<input type="checkbox" id="year" checked>
```

You can group check boxes and assign them the same control name using the `name` attribute. This allows multiple values associated with the same name to be chosen:

```
<p>Check all symptoms that you are experiencing:</p>
<label><input type="checkbox" name="symptoms" value="nausea"> Nausea</label>
<label><input type="checkbox" name="symptoms" value="lightheadedness">
Light-headedness</label>
<label><input type="checkbox" name="symptoms" value="fever"> Fever</label>
<label><input type="checkbox" name="symptoms" value="headache"> Headache</label>
```

When this form is submitted to a script for processing, each check box that's checked returns a value associated with the name of the check box. If a check box isn't checked, neither the field name nor the value will be returned to the server—it's as if the field didn't exist at all.

You may have noticed that when I applied labels to these check box elements, I put the `input` tags inside the `label` tags. There's a specific reason for doing so. When you associate a label with a check box (or with a radio button, as you'll see in the next section), the browser enables you to check the box by clicking the label as well as by clicking the button. That can make things a bit easier on your user.

In the examples thus far, I have tied labels to fields by putting the field id in the `for` attribute of the label, but most designers don't identify individual check box fields, and the browser would not be able to figure out which check box the label applies to if you pointed to the checkbox name. Instead, I put the `input` tag inside the `label` tag.

12

Creating Radio Buttons

Radio buttons, which generally appear in groups, are designed so that when one button in the group is selected, the other buttons in the group are automatically unselected. They enable you to provide users with a list of options from which only one option can be selected. To create a radio button, set the `type` attribute of an `<input>` tag to `radio`. To create a radio button group, set the `name` attributes of all the fields in the group to the same value, as shown in Figure 12.13. To create a radio button group with three options, the following code is used:

Input ▼

```
<p>Select a color:</p>
<label style="display: block;"><input type="radio" name="color" value="red">
Red</label>
<label style="display: block;"><input type="radio" name="color" value="blue">
Blue</label>
<label style="display: block;"><input type="radio" name="color" value="green">
Green</label>
```

Output ▼

FIGURE 12.13
A group of radio buttons.

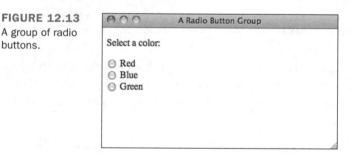

I've used the same `<label>` technique here that I did in the check box example. Placing the radio buttons inside the labels makes the labels clickable as well as the radio buttons themselves. I've changed the `display` property for the labels to `block` so that each radio button appears on a different line. Ordinarily I'd apply that style using a style sheet; I used the `style` attributes to include the styles within the example.

As with check boxes, if you want a radio button to be selected by default when the form is displayed, use the `checked` attribute. One point of confusion is that even though browsers prevent users from having more than one member of a radio button group selected at once, they don't prevent you from setting more than one member of a group as checked by default. You should avoid doing so yourself.

Using Images as Submit Buttons

Using `image` as the `type` of `input` control enables you to use an image as a Submit button:

Input ▼

```
<input type="image" src="submit.gif" id="submitformbtn">
```

Figure 12.14 shows a custom button created with an image.

Output ▼

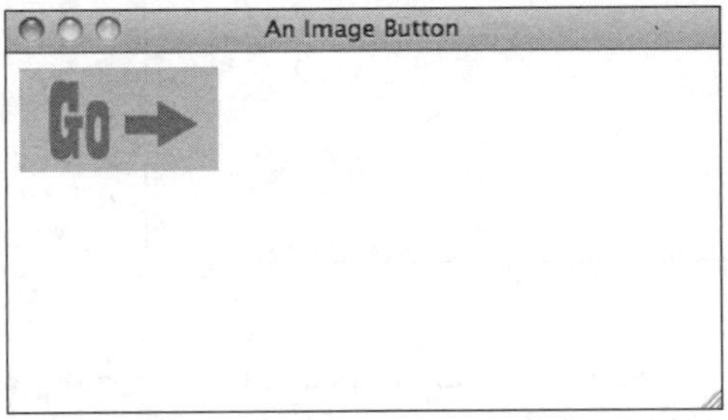

FIGURE 12.14
The image input type.

When the user clicks an image field, the x and y coordinates of the point where the user clicked are submitted to the server. The data is submitted as `name.x = x coord` and `name.y = y coord`, where `name` is the name assigned to the control. Using the preceding code, the result might look like the following:

```
submitoformbtn.x=150&submitformbtn.y=200
```

You can omit the name if you choose. If you do so, the coordinates returned would just be `x =` and `y =`. Form controls with the type `image` support all the attributes of the `<img>` tag. You can also use the same CSS properties you would use with `<img>` tags to modify the appearance and spacing of the button. To refresh your memory on the attributes supported by the `<img>` tag, go back to Lesson 9, "Using Images on Your Web Pages."

Creating Generic Buttons

In addition to creating Submit, Reset, and Image buttons, you can create buttons that generate events within the browser that can be tied to client-side scripts. To create such a

12

button, set the `type` attribute to `button`. Figure 12.15 shows a button that calls a function when it is pressed. Use the following code to create a button:

Input ▼

```
<input type="button" id="verify" value="verify" onclick="verifydata()">
```

Output ▼

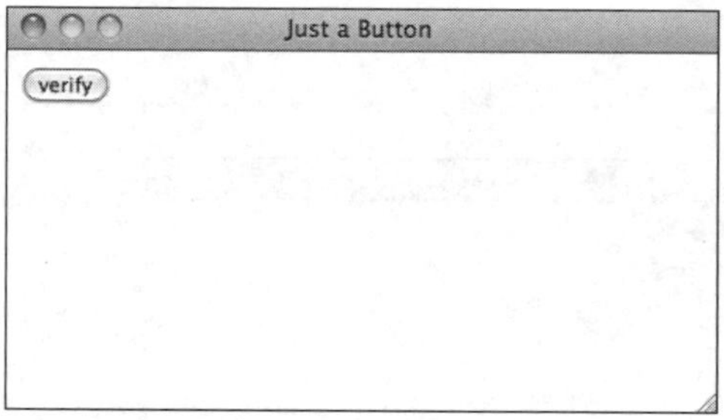

FIGURE 12.15
A button element
on a web page.

This example creates a button that runs a function called `verifydata` when it's clicked. You provide the label that appears on the button with the `value` attribute of `Verify Data`.

Unlike Submit buttons, regular buttons don't submit the form when they're clicked. I explain the `onclick` attribute when you get to Lesson 17, "Introducing JavaScript."

Hidden Form Fields

Hidden form fields are used when you want to embed data in a page that shouldn't be seen or modified by the user. The name and value pair associated with a hidden form field will be submitted along with the rest of the contents of the form when the form is submitted. To create such a field, set the field's type to `hidden` and be sure to include both the `name` and the `value` attributes in your `<input>` tag. Here's an example:

```
<input type="hidden" id="uid" value="1402">
```

Hidden form fields are generally used when data identifying the user needs to be included in a form. For example, suppose you've created a form that allows a user to edit the name and address associated with her bank account. Because the user can change her name and address, the data she submits can't be used to look up her account after she submits the form, plus there might be multiple accounts associated with one name and address. You can include the account number as a hidden field on the form so that the program on the server knows which account to update when the form is submitted.

It's important to understand that when it comes to hidden form fields, *hidden* means "won't clutter up the page" rather than "won't be discoverable by the user." Anyone can use the View Source feature in the browser to look at the values in hidden form fields, and if you use the GET method, those values will appear in the URL when the form is submitted, too. Don't think of hidden fields as a security feature but rather as a convenient way to embed extra data in the form that you know the script that processes the form input will need to use.

The File Upload Control

The file control enables a user to upload a file when he submits the form. As you can see in the following code, the `type` for the input element is set to `file`:

Input ▼

```
<label>Please select a file for upload <input type="file" name="fileupload">
</label>
```

Figure 12.16 shows a file upload control.

Output ▼

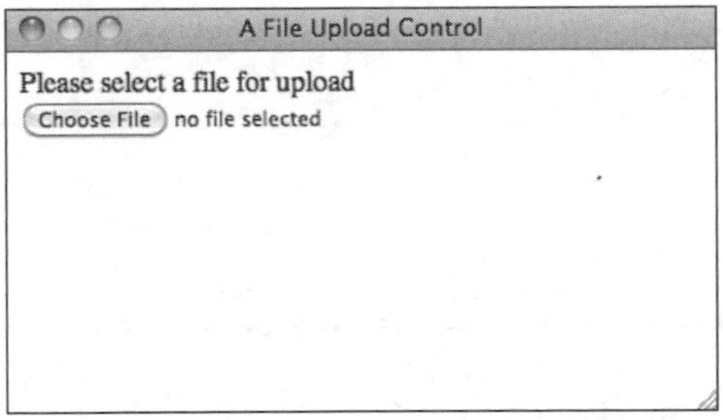

FIGURE 12.16
The file upload control.

If you want to use a file upload field on your form, you have to do a lot of behind-the-scenes work to get everything working. For one thing, the program specified in the `action` attribute of your form must be able to accept the file being uploaded. Second, you have to use the `post` method for the form. Third, you must set the `enctype` attribute of the `<form>` tag to `multipart/form-data`. Ordinarily, the default behavior is fine, but you must change the `enctype` in this particular case.

12

Let's look at a simple form that supports file uploads:

```
<form action="/upload" enctype="multipart/form-data" method="post">
  <input type="file" id="new_file">
  <input type="submit">
</form>
```

After you've created a form for uploading a file, you need a program that can process the file submission. Creating such a program is beyond the scope of this book, but all popular web programming environments support file uploads.

Using Other Form Controls

In addition to form controls you can create using the `input` element, there are three that are elements in and of themselves.

Using the `button` Element

A button you create using the `button` element is similar to the buttons you create with the `input` element, except that content included between the opening and closing button tags appears on the button.

You can create three different types of buttons: Submit, Reset, and Custom. The `<button>` tag is used to create buttons. As with other form fields, you can use the `name` attribute to specify the name of the parameter sent to the server, and the `value` attribute to indicate which value is sent to the server when the button is clicked. Unlike buttons created with the `<input>` tag, the button's label is specified by the content within the `<button>` tag, as shown in this code:

Input ▼

```
<button type="submit"><b><i>Submit button</i></b></button>
<button type="custom"><img src="recycle.gif"></button>
```

The button element is shown in a browser in Figure 12.17.

Output ▼

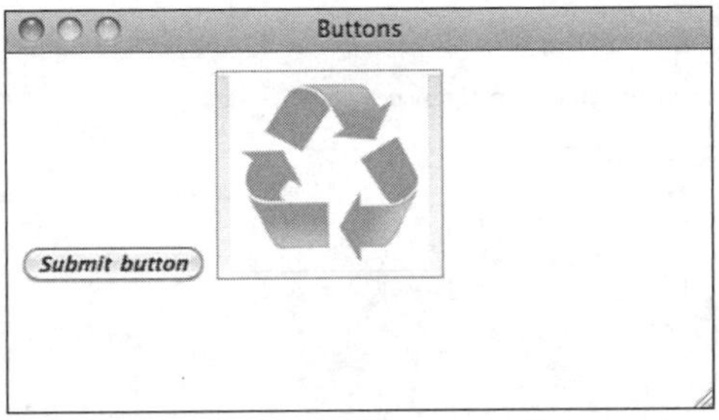

FIGURE 12.17
The `button` element provides a more flexible way to create form buttons.

Creating Large Text-Entry Fields with `textarea`

The `textarea` element creates a large text entry field where people can enter as much information as they like. To create a `textarea`, use the `<textarea>` tag. To set the size of the field, use the `rows` and `cols` attributes. These attributes specify the height and width of the text area in characters. A text area with `cols` set to 5 and `rows` set to 40 creates a field that's 5 lines of text high and 40 characters wide. If you leave out the `rows` and `cols` attributes, the browser default will be used. This can vary, so you should make sure to include those attributes to maintain the form's appearance across browsers. The closing `textarea` tag is required, and any text you place inside the `textarea` tag is displayed inside the field as the default value:

Input ▼

```
<label for="question4" style="display: block;">Please comment on our customer
service.</label>
<textarea name="question4" rows="10" cols="60">Enter your answer here
</textarea>
```

12

Figure 12.18 shows a `textarea` element in action.

Output ▼

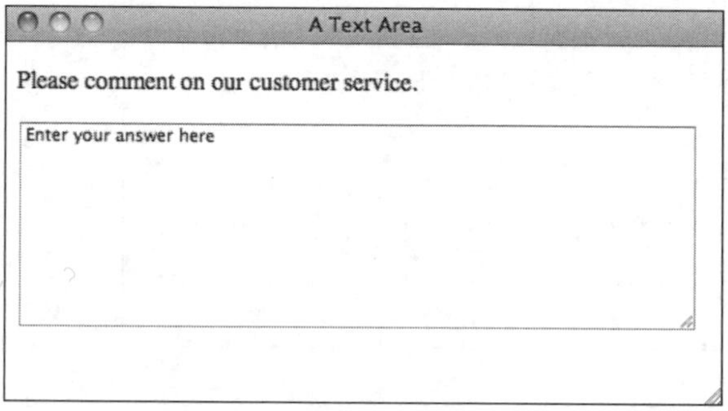

FIGURE 12.18
Use `textarea` to create large text-entry areas.

TIP

> You can also change the size of a `textarea` with the `height` and `width` CSS properties. This will override any `cols` or `rows` attributes you have set. You can alter the font in the text area using the CSS font properties, too.

Creating Menus with `select` and `option`

The `select` element creates a menu that can be configured to enable users to select one or more options from a pull-down menu or a scrollable menu that shows several options at once. The `<select>` tag defines how the menu will be displayed and the name of the parameter associated with the field. The `<option>` tag is used to add selections to the menu. The default appearance of select lists is to display a pull-down list that enables the user to select one of the options. Here's an example of how one is created:

Input ▼

```
<label for="location">Please pick a travel destination</label>
<select id="location">
  <option>Indiana</option>
  <option>Fuji</option>
  <option>Timbuktu</option>
  <option>Alaska</option>
</select>
```

As you can see in the code, the field name is assigned using the `id` attribute of the `<select>` tag. The field created using that code appears in Figure 12.19.

Output ▼

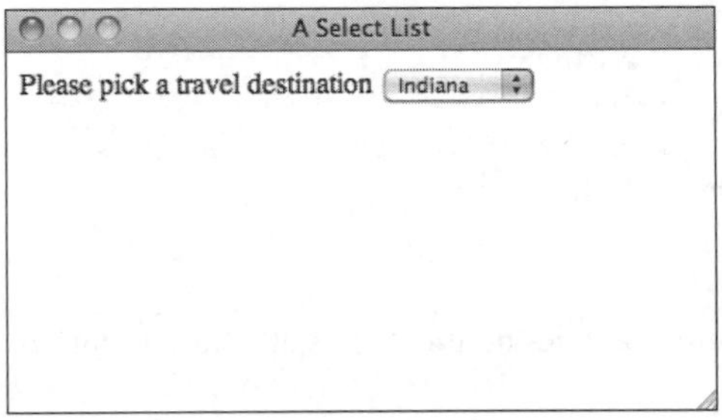

FIGURE 12.19
You can use `select` form controls to create pull-down menus.

To create a scrollable list of items, just include the `size` attribute in the opening `select` tag, like this:

Input ▼

```
<select id="location" size="3">
```

Figure 12.20 shows the same `select` element as Figure 12.19, except that the `size` attribute is set to 3. Setting the size to 3 indicates that the browser should display three options simultaneously.

Output ▼

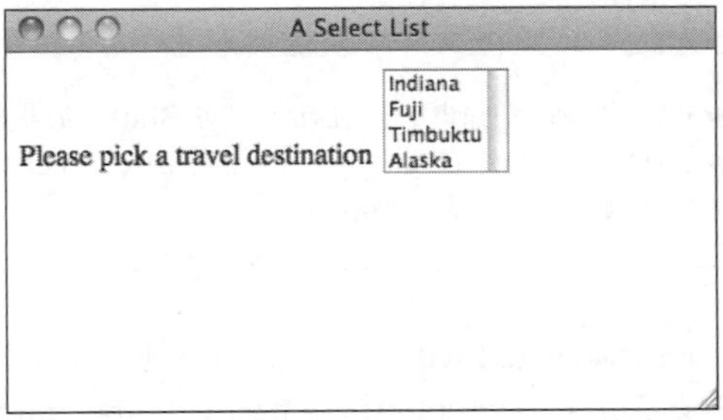

FIGURE 12.20
You also can create scrollable lists using the `select` element.

To see the fourth item, the user would have to use the scrollbar built in to the select list. By default, the value inside the `<option>` tag specifies both what is displayed in the form and what's sent back to the server. To send a value other than the display value to the server, use the `value` attribute. The following code, for example, causes `bw499` to be submitted to the server as the value associated with the `courses` field instead of `Basket Weaving 499`:

```
<select id="courses" >
  <option value="p101">Programming 101
  <option value="e312">Ecomomics 312
  <option value="pe221">Physical Education 221
  <option value="bw499">Basket Weaving 499
</select>
```

To select an option by default, include the `selected` attribute in an `option` element, as follows:

```
<select id="courses">
  <option value="p101">Programming 101</option>
  <option value="e312">Ecomomics 312</option>
  <option value="pe221" selected>Physical Education 221</option>
  <option value="bw499">Basket Weaving 499</option>
</select>
```

> **NOTE**
>
> The closing `</option>` tag is not required. You can use it or leave it off, your choice.

Thus far, you've created menus from which a user can select only one choice. To enable users to select more than one option, use the `multiple` attribute:

```
<select id="courses" multiple>
```

> **NOTE**
>
> A user can choose multiple options by Shift-clicking to select several in a row, or Ctrl-clicking (Windows) or Cmd-clicking (OS X) to select several different items.

There are some usability issues associated with select lists. When you think about it, select lists that enable users to choose one option are basically the equivalent of radio button groups, and select lists that allow multiple selections are the same as check box groups. It's up to you to decide which tag to use in a given circumstance. If you need to present the user with a lot of options, select lists are generally the proper choice. A select list with a list of states is a lot more concise and usable than a group of 50 radio buttons. By the same token, if there are four options, radio buttons probably make more sense. The same rules basically hold with check box groups versus multiple select lists.

However, sometimes a text box with some JavaScript validation is even better. Most people can type their two-letter state abbreviation a lot faster than they can find it in a select list. Drop-down menus are difficult to use and hide options that people don't realize they have. And don't forget people on small devices like cell phones: A tiny check box could be just as difficult to tap as it is to scroll through a huge select list.

The other usability issue with select lists is specific to multiple select lists. The bottom line is that they're hard to use. Most users don't know how to select more than one item, and if the list is long enough, as they move through the list they'll have problems keeping track of the items they already selected when they scroll through to select new ones. Sometimes there's no way around using a multiple select list, but you should be careful about it.

Exercise 12.2: Using Several Types of Form Controls ▼

Form controls often come in bunches. Although there are plenty of forms out there that consist of a text input field and a Submit button (like search forms), a lot of the time forms consist of many fields. For example, many websites require that you register to see restricted content, download demo programs, or participate in an online community. In this example, we'll look at a perhaps slightly atypical registration form for a website.

The purpose of this exercise is to show you how to create forms that incorporate a number of different types of form controls. In this case, the form will include a text field, a radio button group, a select list, a check box group, a file upload field, and a text area. The form, rendered in a browser, appears in Figure 12.21.

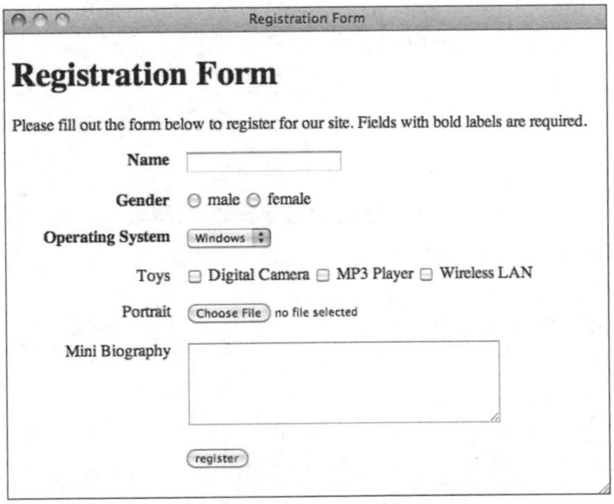

FIGURE 12.21
A registration form for a website.

12

▼ Let's look at the components used to build the form. The styles for the form are included in the page header. Here's the style sheet:

```
<style>
    form div {
        margin-bottom: 1em;
    }

    div.submit input {
        margin-left: 165px;
    }

    label.field {
        display: block;
        float: left;
        margin-right: 15px;
        width: 150px;
        text-align: right;
    }

    label.required {
        font-weight: bold;
    }
</style>
```

Looking at the style sheet, you should get some idea of how the form will be laid out. Each field will be in its own `<div>`, and I've added a margin to the bottom of each of them. Just as I did in the login form example earlier, I've added a left margin for the Submit button so that it lines up with the other fields. Most of the styling has to do with the labels.

In this form, I am using labels in two ways—first to create a left column of labels for the form, and second to add clickable labels to the radio buttons and check boxes. To distinguish between them, I'm using a class called `field`, which I apply to the field-level labels. I've also got a class called `required` that will be used with labels on required fields.

Now that you've seen the styles, let's look at the body of the page. After some introductory text, we open the form like this:

```
<form action="/register" method="post"
  enctype="multipart/form-data">
```

Because this form contains a file upload field, we have to use the `post` method and the ▼
`multipart/form-data enctype` in the `<form>` tag. The `action` attribute points to a CGI
script that lives on my server. Next, we start adding form inputs. Here's the `name` input:

```
<div>
  <label class="required field" for="name">Name</label>
  <input id="name">
</div>
```

All the inputs will follow this basic pattern. The input and its label are nested within
a `<div>`. In this case, the label has the classes `field` and `required`. The only attribute
included in the input tag is the field name because the default values for the rest of the
attributes are fine. Next is the gender field, which uses two radio buttons:

```
<div>
  <label class="required field">Gender</label>
  <label><input type="radio" name="gender" value="male"> male</label>
  <label><input type="radio" name="gender" value="female"> female</label>
</div>
```

As you can see, the radio button group includes two controls (both with the same name,
establishing the group). Because we didn't include line breaks between the two fields,
they appear side by side in the form. Here's an instance in which I used the `<label>` tag
two different ways. In the first case, I used it to label the field as a whole, and then I used
individual labels for each button. The individual labels allow you to select the radio buttons by clicking their labels. As you can see, I used the approach of putting the `<input>`
tags inside the `<label>` tags to associate them.

The next field is a select list that enables the user to indicate which operating system he
runs on his computer:

```
<div>
  <label class="required field">Operating System</label>
  <select id="os">
    <option value="windows">Windows</option>
    <option value="macos">Mac OS</option>
    <option value="linux">Linux</option>
    <option value="other">Other ...</option>
  </select>
</div>
```

This select list is a single-line, single-select field with four options. Instead of using
the display values as the values that will be sent back to the server, we opt to set them ▼

12

specifically using the value attribute of the `<option>` tag. The next form field is a check box group:

```
<div>
  <label class="field">Toys</label>
  <label><input type="checkbox" name="toy" value="digicam"> Digital Camera
</label>
  <label><input type="checkbox" name="toy" value="phone"> Smartphone</label>
  <label><input type="checkbox" name="toy" value="tablet"> Tablet</label>
</div>
```

As you can see, we use labels for each of the individual check boxes here, too. The next field is a file upload field:

```
<div>
  <label class="field" for="portrait">Portrait</label>
  <input type="file" id="portrait">
</div>
```

The last input field on the form is a text area intended for the user's bio.

```
<div>
  <label class="field" for="bio">Mini Biography</label>
  <textarea id="bio" rows="6" cols="40"></textarea>
</div>
```

After the text area, there's just the Submit button for the form. After that, it's all closing tags for the `<form>` tag, the `<body>` tag, and the `<html>` tag. The full source code for the page follows, along with a screenshot of the form as shown earlier in Figure 12.21.

Input ▼

```
<!doctype html>
<html>
  <head>
    <title>Registration Form</title>
<style>
  form div {
    margin-bottom: 1em;
  }

  div.submit input {
    margin-left: 165px;
  }

  label.field {
    display: block;
    float: left;
    margin-right: 15px;
    width: 150px;
```

```
    text-align: right;
  }

  label.required {
    font-weight: bold;
  }
</style>
  </head>
  <body>
    <h1>Registration Form</h1>
    <form action="/register" method="post"
      enctype="multipart/form-data">
        <div>
          <label class="required field" for="name">Name</label>
          <input id="name">
        </div>
        <div>
          <label class="required field">Gender</label>
          <label><input type="radio" name="gender" value="male"> male</label>
          <label><input type="radio" name="gender" value="female"> female</label>
        </div>
        <div>
          <label class="required field">Operating System</label>
          <select id="os">
            <option value="windows">Windows</option>
            <option value="macos">Mac OS</option>
            <option value="linux">Linux</option>
            <option value="other">Other ...</option>
          </select>
        </div>
        <div>
          <label class="field">Toys</label>
          <label><input type="checkbox" name="toy" value="digicam"> Digital
Camera</label>
          <label><input type="checkbox" name="toy" value="phone"> Smartphone
</label>
          <label><input type="checkbox" name="toy" value="tablet"> Tablet</label>
        </div>
        <div>
          <label class="field" for="portrait">Portrait</label>
          <input type="file" id="portrait">
        </div>
        <div>
          <label class="field" for="bio">Mini Biography</label>
          <textarea id="bio" rows="6" cols="40"></textarea>
        </div>
        <div class="submit">
          <input type="submit" value="register">
        </div>
    </form>
  </body>
</html>
```

12

Grouping Controls with `fieldset` and `legend`

The `fieldset` element organizes form controls into groupings that appear in the web browser. The `legend` element displays a caption for the `fieldset`. To create a `fieldset` element, start with the opening `fieldset` tag, followed by the `legend` element.

Next, enter your form controls and finish things off with the closing `fieldset` tag:

Input ▼

```
<fieldset>
  <legend>Oatmeal Varieties</legend>
  <label><input type="radio" name="applecinnamon"> Apple Cinnamon</label>
  <label><input type="radio" name="nuttycrunch"> Nutty Crunch</label>
  <label><input type="radio" name="brownsugar"> Brown Sugar</label>
</fieldset>
```

Figure 12.22 shows the result.

Output ▼

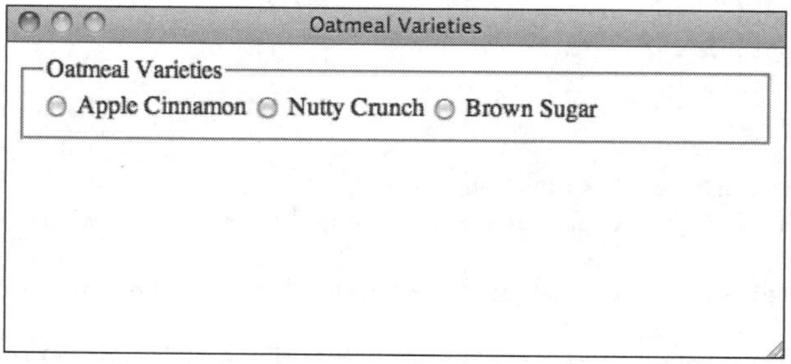

FIGURE 12.22
The `fieldset` and `legend` elements enable you to organize your forms.

The presentation of the `fieldset` in Figure 12.22 is the default, but you can use CSS to style `fieldset` elements in any way that you like. A `fieldset` is a standard block-level element, so you can turn off the borders using the style `border: none` and use them as you would `<div>` tags to group inputs in your forms.

One thing to watch out for with the `<legend>` tag is that it's a little less flexible than the `<label>` tag in terms of how you're allowed to style it. It's also not handled consistently between browsers. If you want to apply a caption to a set of form fields, use `<legend>` but be aware that complex styles may have surprising results. Figure 12.23 shows the markup from Figure 12.22 with some the following styles applied:

Input ▼

```
<style>
  fieldset {
    border: none;
    background-color: #aaa;
    width: 400px;
  }
    legend {
    text-align: right;
  }
</style>
```

Output ▼

FIGURE 12.23
The `fieldset` and `legend` elements enable you to organize your forms.

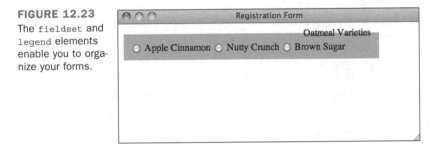

As you can see, I've changed the background color of the field set and assigned a specific width. I've also aligned the legend to the right. Because of the default browser positioning of the legend, the background color splits the legend text. This is an example of how browsers treat legends uniquely. To set a background for the field set that includes the full legend, I'd have to wrap the field set in another block-level element (like a `div`) and apply the background color to that.

Changing the Default Form Navigation

In most browsers, you can use the Tab key to step through the form fields and links on a page. When filling out long forms, it's often much easier to use the Tab key to move from one field to the next than to use the mouse to change fields. If you have a mix of form fields and links on your page, setting things up so that using Tab skips past the links and moves directly from one form field to the next can improve the usability of your applications greatly. To set the tab order for your page, use the `tabindex` attribute. You

12

should number your form fields sequentially to set the order that the browser will use when the user tabs through them. Here's an example:

```
<p>
  <label>Enter your <a href="#">name</a>
    <input type="text" name="username" tabindex="1">
  </label>
</p>
<p>
  <label>Enter your <a href="#">age</a>
    <input type="text" name="age" tabindex="2">
  </label>
</p>
<p>
  <input type="submit" tabindex="3">
</p>
```

When you tab through this page, the browser will skip past the links and move directly to the form fields.

Using Access Keys

Access keys also make your forms easier to navigate. They assign a character to an element that moves the focus to that element when the user presses a key. To add an access key to a check box, use the following code:

```
<p>What are your interests?</p>
<label>Sports <input type="checkbox" name="sports" accesskey="S"></label>
<label>Music <input type="checkbox" name="music" accesskey="M"></label>
<label>Television <input type="checkbox" name="tv" accesskey="T"></label>
```

Most browsers require you to hold down a modifier key and the key specified using accesskey to select the field. On Windows, both Firefox and Internet Explorer require you to use the Alt key along with the access key to select a field. Access keys are mostly useful for forms that will be used frequently by the same users. A user who is going to use a form only once won't bother to learn the access keys, but if you've written a form for data entry, the people who use it hundreds of times a day might really appreciate the shortcuts.

Creating `disabled` and `readonly` Controls

Sometimes you might want to display a form control without enabling your visitors to use the control or enter new information. To disable a control, add the `disabled` attribute to the form control:

```
<label for="question42">What is the meaning of life?</label>
<textarea id="question42" disabled>
```

```
Enter your answer here.
</textarea>
```

When displayed in a web browser, the control will be dimmed (a light shade of gray) to indicate that it's unavailable.

To create a read-only control, use the `readonly` attribute:

Input ▼

```
<label for="month">This month</label>
<input type="text" id="month" value="September" readonly>
```

The read-only control is not distinguished in any way from a normal form control. However, when visitors attempt to enter new information (or, in the case of buttons or check boxes, select them), they'll find that they cannot change the value. Figure 12.24 shows both a disabled control and a read-only control. You'll generally find `disabled` to be more useful because it's less confusing to your users.

Output ▼

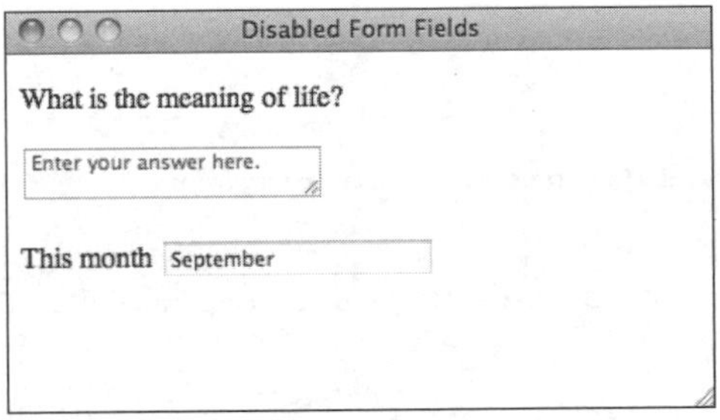

FIGURE 12.24
Disabled controls
are dimmed.
Read-only controls
appear normally—
they just can't be
changed.

12

Form Security

It's important to remember that regardless of what you do with your form controls, what gets sent back to the server when the form is submitted is really up to your user. There's nothing to stop her from copying the source to your form, creating a similar page on her own, and submitting that to your server. If the form uses the `get` method, the user can just edit the URL once the form has been submitted.

The point here is that there is no form security. In Lesson 19, "Using JavaScript in Your Pages," you'll learn how to validate your forms with JavaScript. Even in that case, you can't guarantee that users will supply the input that you intend. What this means is that you must always validate the data entered by your users on the server before you use it.

Displaying Updates with `progress` and `meter`

HTML5 adds two new tags to help you display and measure changes on your website: `progress` and `meter`. With these elements, you can indicate changes in time on your website. This is useful for web applications as well as web forms.

The `progress` tag is used to view the completion progress of a task. It is usually displayed as a progress bar. It can define either indeterminate progress or a specific amount of progress including a number from zero to a maximum with a fraction of that amount that has been completed. At its most basic, a progress bar is just the `progress` tag with a value set:

```
<p>Progress task 1:
    <progress id="prog1" value="0">0%</progress>
    </p>
```

While the `value` attribute is not required, it's a good idea to set it explicitly as some browsers default to 100% progress and some default to 0%. You should also set the `max` attribute so that the browser has a measure and include the value of the progress inside the `progress` tag so that browsers and screen readers that don't support the tag can still get the content. Figure 12.25 shows three progress bars at 0%, 45%, and 98%, written:

Input ▼

```
<p>Progress task 1:
  <progress id="prog1" value="0" max="100">0%</progress>
</p>
<p>Progress task 2:
  <progress id="prog2" value="45" max="100">45%</progress>
</p>
<p>Progress task 3:
  <progress id="prog3" value="98" max="100">98%</progress>
</p>
```

Output ▼

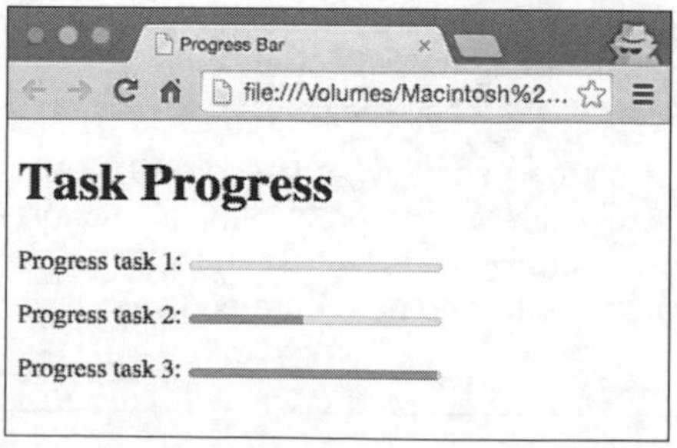

FIGURE 12.25
Three progress bars.

Different browsers style the progress bar in different ways. And even if you like the thin, rounded, blue bars that most browsers use, it might clash with your design. So, it is possible to adjust how the progress bar looks using pseudo-classes. As of this writing, there isn't a consensus as to how to style them, so you have to do a couple of extra steps to make sure that your progress bar looks as you expect it to.

In Safari and Chrome, the `-webkit-progress-bar` pseudo-class changes the `progress` tag, and the `-webkit-progress-value` changes the value—in other words, the bar inside that tracks the progress. Firefox does it slightly differently. To style the `progress` tag, you select that tag as you normally would. And to style the value, you style the `-moz-progress-bar` pseudo-class. Before you can do any of that, though, you need to remove the default styles by changing the `appearance`:

Input ▼

```
progress {
  -webkit-appearance: none;
  -moz-appearance: none;
  appearance: none;
}
```

Then you can adjust how the progress bar looks using the pseudo-classes:

```
/* Chrome and Safari */
progress::-webkit-progress-bar {
  height: 10px;
  background: #dfdfdf;
  box-shadow: 0 2px 3px rgba(0,0,0,0.2) inset;
  border-radius: 5px;
}
progress {
  height: 10px;
  background: #dfdfdf;
  box-shadow: 0 2px 3px rgba(0,0,0,0.2) inset;
  border-radius: 5px;
}
/* Mozilla Firefox */
progress::-webkit-progress-value {
  background-color: #026105;
  border-radius: 5px;
}
progress::-moz-progress-bar {
  background-color: #026105;
  border-radius: 5px;
}
```

12

Figure 12.26 shows how this would look in Chrome. But be sure to test in Safari and Firefox as well.

Output ▼

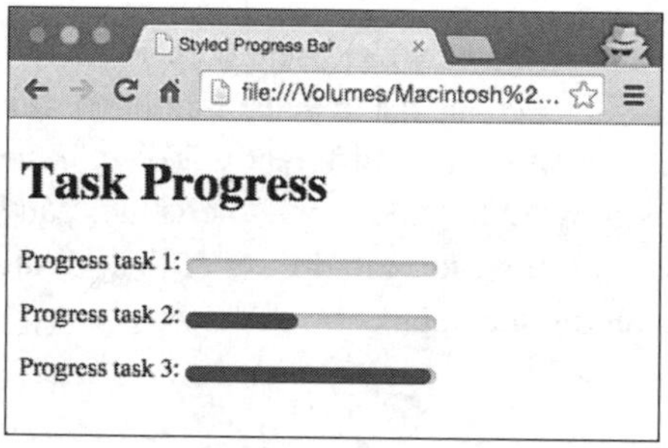

FIGURE 12.26
Styling the prog-
ress bars.

Here is the full listing for the page shown in Figure 12.26:

Input ▼

```
<!doctype html>
<html>
  <head>
    <title>Styled Progress Bar</title>
    <style>
progress {
  -webkit-appearance: none;
  -moz-appearance: none;
  appearance: none;
}
/* Chrome and Safari */
progress::-webkit-progress-bar {
  height: 10px;
  background: #dfdfdf;
  box-shadow: 0 2px 3px rgba(0,0,0,0.2) inset;
  border-radius: 5px;
}
progress {
  height: 10px;
  background: #dfdfdf;
  box-shadow: 0 2px 3px rgba(0,0,0,0.2) inset;
  border-radius: 5px;
}
/* Mozilla Firefox */
progress::-webkit-progress-value {
```

```
      background-color: #026105;
      border-radius: 5px;
}
progress::-moz-progress-bar {
      background-color: #026105;
      border-radius: 5px;
}
    </style>
  </head>
  <body>
    <h1>Task Progress</h1>
    <p>Progress task 1:
      <progress id="prog1" value="0">0%</progress>
    </p>
    <p>Progress task 2:
      <progress id="prog2" value="45" max="100">45%</progress>
    </p>
    <p>Progress task 3:
      <progress id="prog3" value="98" max="100">98%</progress>
    </p>
  </body>
</html>
```

CAUTION   It's not good code, but for the moment, you cannot combine the Firefox and Chrome styles into one style call. They don't work if they are combined.

`progress` is a useful tag for providing information to customers, but remember that it does have a semantic element to it—it is a "progress" indicator, not just a gauge. In other words, you should use this tag to track things that have a time component to them. If you need to show information that does not have a time component attached, such as a disk space monitor, use the `meter` element instead.

The `meter` element represents a measurement with a known range (for example, disk usage, search relevance, or the fraction of voters that voted "yes" on a particular initiative). You should not use `meter` to represent a value that does not have a known maximum value (for instance, height or weight).

12

Like `progress`, you can set the value of the measurement with the `value` attribute. You can also set the maximum value with the `max` attribute. But you can set several other values as well:

`min`	Defines the minimum or lower boundary of the range. Unlike the `progress` tag, this can be a number other than zero, including negative numbers.
`low`	Defines the part of the meter that is in the low range. This is not the minimum, but rather a point where the value is considered low.
`high`	Like the low value, this defines the part of the meter that is in the high range. This is not the maximum, but rather a point where the value is considered high.
`optimum`	This gives the position on the meter that is considered the best. If this is higher than the high point, this indicates that the higher the value the better. If it is lower than the low point, this indicates that the lower values are better. And if it's in between this indicates that neither high nor low values are good.

NOTE

> If you don't specify a minimum or maximum, the range is assumed to be between 0 and 1. The value, high, low, and optimum numbers must be within that range as well.

In Figure 12.27, you can see how browsers change the display of meter depending upon where the value is in relation to the low, high, and optimum values:

Input ▼

```
<p>
  Jetta:
  <meter min="0" max="14.2" high="13.5" low="3" optimum="14" value="2.5">2.5
gallons</meter>
  is getting low, we should get gas!
</p>
<p>
  Tundra:
  <meter min="0" max="22" high="20" low="5" optimum="21" value="14">14 gallons
</meter>
  is okay, we don't need gas yet.
</p>
<p>
  Vespa:
  <meter min="0" max="5" high="4.5" low="1" optimum="4.6" value="4.7">4.7
gallons</meter>
  is practically full, you just filled up!
</p>
```

Output ▼

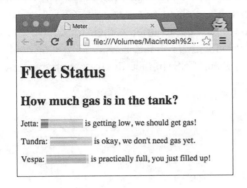

Just like the progress bar, you should also include a textual representation of your meter gauge for those browsers that don't support it.

And just like progress, to style your meters, you need to use pseudo-classes and browser prefixed properties. But rather than just the meter and the value, you need to style how it should look when the value is the best it can be, a middle value, and the worst it can be. Table 12.1 describes those values.

TABLE 12.1 Pseudo-Classes to Style the Meter Element

	Safari/Chrome	**Firefox**
Meter bar	`-webkit-meter-bar`	`-moz-meter-bar`
Best value	`-webkit-meter-bar-optimum-value`	`-moz-meter-optimum`
Middle value	`-webkit-meter-suboptimum-value`	`-moz-meter-suboptimum`
Worst value	`-webkit-meter-even-less-good-value`	`-moz-meter-sub-sub-optimum`

And, yes, the pseudo-class really is `-webkit-meter-even-less-good`. Don't blame me; I didn't name it. Style these just like you did the progress bars or any other element.

Applying Cascading Style Sheet Properties to Form Elements

In this lesson, I've already shown you some approaches you can take to managing the layout of your forms with CSS. Now I explain how to alter the appearance of form input fields themselves using style properties. As you can see from the screenshots so far, regular form controls might not blend in too well with your pages. The default look and feel of form controls can be altered in just about any way using CSS. For example, in many browsers, by default, text input fields use Courier as their font, have white backgrounds, and have beveled borders. As you know, `border`, `font`, and `background-color` are all properties that you can modify using CSS. In fact, the following example uses all those properties:

Input ▼

```
<!DOCTYPE html>
<html>
  <head>
    <title>Style Sheet Example</title>
    <style>
    input.styled
    {
    border: 2px solid #000;
    background-color: #aaa;
    font: bold 18px Verdana;
    padding: 4px;
    }
    </style>
  </head>
  <body>
    <form>
      <p><label>Default</label> <input value="value"></p>
      <p><label>Styled</label> <input value="value" class="styled"></p>
    </form>
  </body>
</html>
```

The page contains two text input fields: one with the default look and feel, and another that's modified using CSS. The page containing the form appears in Figure 12.28.

Output ▼

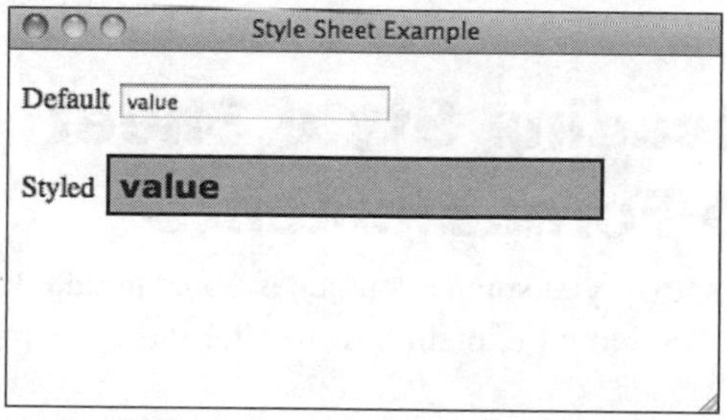

FIGURE 12.28
A regular text input field and a styled text input field.

As you can see, the field that we applied styles to is radically different from the one that uses the default decoration. You can do anything to regular form fields that you can do to other elements. In fact, you can make form fields look just like the rest of your page, with no borders and the same fonts as your page text if you like. Of course, that will make your forms extremely confusing to use, so you probably don't want to do it, but you could.

It's also fairly common to modify the buttons on your pages. Normally, Submit buttons on forms are gray with beveled edges, or they have the look and feel provided by the user's operating system. By applying styles to your buttons, you can better integrate them into your designs. This is especially useful if you need to make your buttons smaller than they are by default. I provide more examples of style usage in forms in Exercise 12.3.

Bear in mind that some browsers support CSS more fully than others. So some users won't see the styles that you've applied. The nice thing about CSS, though, is that they'll still see the form fields with the browser's default appearance.

Exercise 12.3: Applying Styles to a Form ▼

Let's take another look at the form from Exercise 12.2. The form can easily be further spruced up by tweaking its appearance using CSS. The main objectives are to make the appearance of the controls more consistent and to make it clear to users which form fields are required and which are not. In the original version of the form, the labels for the required fields were bold. We keep with that convention here and also change the border appearance of the fields to indicate which fields are required and which aren't.

Let's look at the style sheet. This style sheet is similar to the one in Exercise 11.2, but I have made some changes. First, here are three styles that I copied directly from the previous exercise:

12

```
form div {
  margin-bottom: 1em;
}
div.submit input {
  margin-left: 165px;
}
label.field {
  display: block;
  float: left;
  margin-right: 15px;
  width: 150px;
  text-align: right;
}
```

▼

These styles set up the basic form layout that I'm using in both exercises. Next, I tweak the appearance of my input fields:

```
input[type="text"], select, textarea {
    width: 300px;
    font: 18px Verdana;
    border: solid 2px #666;
    background-color: #ada;
}
```

The rule above applies to three different selectors: `select`, `textarea`, and `input[type="text"]`. The third selector is a bit different from the ones you've seen thus far. It is what's known as an attribute selector and matches only `input` tags with the value of `text` for the `type` attribute. This sort of selector can be used for any attribute. In this case, I'm using it to avoid applying this rule to Submit buttons, radio buttons, and check boxes. One catch is that the attribute has to exist, so I had to add `type="text"` to my `<input>` tag. The selector won't match if you leave out the attribute and go with the default value.

Next, I add more styles that are related to the required fields. In the previous exercise, I applied the required class to the labels, but I've moved it out to the `<div>`s this time around so that I can apply it to my labels and to my form fields. The labels are still bolded, but now I use the nested rule seen below. Also note that I apply the style only to `label.required` rather than to `label`. That's so that the other labels (used for radio buttons and check boxes) aren't bolded:

```
div.required label.field {
    font-weight: bold;
}
div.required input, div.required select {
    background-color: #6a6;
    border: solid 2px #000;
    font-weight: bold;
}
```

Finally, I have made some enhancements that make it clearer which fields are required. In the original form the labels for required fields were displayed in boldface. In this example, that remains the case. However, I moved the `required` class to the enclosing div so that I can also use it in selectors that match the form fields themselves. I also styled required input fields and select fields with a dark green background color, bold type, and a different color border than optional fields have. After the style sheet is set up, all we have to do is make sure that the `class` attributes of our tags are correct. The full source code for the page, including the form updated with classes, follows:

Input ▼

```
<!DOCTYPE html>
<html>
```

```
    <head>
      <title>Registration Form</title>
      <style>
form div {
  margin-bottom: 1em;
}
div.submit input {
  margin-left: 165px;
}
label.field {
  display: block;
  float: left;
  margin-right: 15px;
  width: 150px;
  text-align: right;
}
input[type="text"], select, textarea {
  width: 300px;
  font: 18px Verdana;
  border: solid 2px #666;
  background-color: #ada;
}
div.required label.field {
  font-weight: bold;
}
div.required input, div.required select {
  background-color: #6a6;
  border: solid 2px #000;
  font-weight: bold;
}
      </style>
    </head>
    <body>
      <h1>Registration Form</h1>
      <form action="/register" method="post"
        enctype="multipart/form-data">
          <div class="required">
            <label class="field" for="name">Name</label>
            <input id="name" type="text">
          </div>
          <div class="required">
            <label class="field">Gender</label>
            <label><input type="radio" name="gender" value="male"> male</label>
            <label><input type="radio" name="gender" value="female"> female</label>
          </div>
          <div class="required">
            <label class="field">Operating System</label>
            <select id="os">
              <option value="windows">Windows</option>
              <option value="macos">Mac OS</option>
              <option value="linux">Linux</option>
              <option value="other">Other ...</option>
            </select>
```

12

▼
```
      </div>
      <div>
        <label class="field">Toys</label>
        <label><input type="checkbox" name="toy" value="digicam"> Digital
Camera</label>
        <label><input type="checkbox" name="toy" value="phone"> Smartphone
</label>
        <label><input type="checkbox" name="toy" value="tablet"> Tablet</label>
      </div>
      <div>
        <label class="field" for="portrait">Portrait</label>
        <input type="file" id="portrait">
      </div>
      <div>
        <label class="field" for="bio">Mini Biography</label>
        <textarea id="bio" rows="6" cols="40"></textarea>
      </div>
      <div class="submit">
        <input type="submit" value="register">
      </div>
    </form>
  </body>
</html>
```

Figure 12.29 shows the page containing this form.

Output ▼

FIGURE 12.29
A form with styled
input fields.

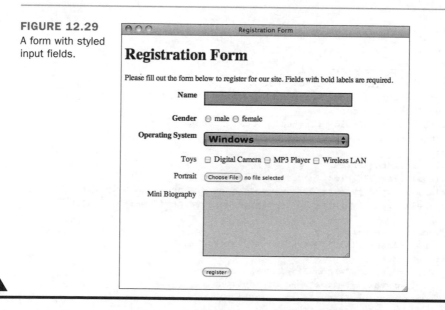

Planning Your Forms

Before you start creating complex forms for your web pages, you should do some planning that will save you time and trouble in the long run.

First, decide what information you need to collect. That might sound obvious, but you need to think about this before you start worrying about the mechanics of creating the form.

Next, review this information and match each item with a type of form control. Ask yourself which type of control is most suited to the type of questions you're asking. If you need a yes or no answer, radio buttons or check boxes work great, but the `textarea` element is overkill. Try to make life easier for the users by making the type of control fit the question. This way, analyzing the information using a script, if necessary, will be much easier.

You also need to coordinate with the person writing the CGI script to match variables in the script with the names you're assigning to each control. There isn't much point in naming every control before collaborating with the script author—after all, you'll need all the names to match. You also can create lookup tables that contain expansive descriptions and allowable values of each form control.

Finally, you might want to consider validating form input through scripting. Using JavaScript, you can embed small programs in your web pages. One common use for JavaScript is writing programs that verify a user's input is correct before she submits a form. I discuss JavaScript in more detail in Lesson 17.

Summary

As you can see, the wonderful world of forms is full of different types of form controls for your visitors. This truly is a way to make your web pages interactive.

Be cautious, however. Web surfers who are constantly bombarded with forms are likely to get tired of all that typing and move on to another site. You need to give them a reason for playing!

Table 12.2 summarizes the HTML tags used today. Remember these points and you can't go wrong:

- Use the `form` element to create your forms.
- Always assign an `action` to a form.
- Create form controls with the `input` element or the other form control elements.
- Test your forms extensively.

TABLE 12.2 HTML Tags Used in This Lesson

Tag	Use
`<form>`	Creates an HTML form. You can have multiple forms within a document, but you cannot nest the forms.
`action`	An attribute of `<form>` that indicates the server-side script (with a URL path) that processes the form data.
`enctype`	An attribute of the `<form>` tag that specifies how form data is encoded before being sent to the server.
`method`	An attribute of `<form>` that defines how the form data is sent to the server. Possible values are `get` and `post`.
`<input>`	A `<form>` element that creates controls for user input.
`<button>`	Creates a button that can have HTML content.
`<textarea>`	A text-entry field with multiple lines.
`<select>`	A menu or scrolling list of items. Individual items are indicated by the `<option>` tag.
`<option>`	Individual items within a `<select>` element.
`<progress>`	Progress bar to measure the progress of a task.
`<meter>`	Gauge to show a scalar measurement within a known range.
`<label>`	Creates a label associated with a form control.
`<fieldset>`	Organizes form controls into groups.
`<legend>`	Displays a caption for a `<fieldset>` element.
`type`	An attribute of `<input>` that indicates the type of form control. Possible values are shown in the following list:

`text`	Creates a single-line text entry field.
`color`	Creates a color entry field.
`date`	Creates a date picker.
`datetime`	Creates a date and time picker.
`datetime-local`	Creates a local date and time picker.
`email`	Creates an email entry field.
`month`	Creates a month picker.
`number`	Creates a number picker.
`range`	Creates a range slider.
`search`	Creates a search entry field.

Tag	Use
tel	Creates a telephone entry field.
url	Creates a URL entry field.
week	Creates a week picker.
password	Creates a single-line text entry field that masks user input.
submit	Creates a Submit button that sends the form data to a server-side script.
reset	Creates a Reset button that resets all form controls to their initial values.
checkbox	Creates a check box.
radio	Creates a radio button.
image	Creates a button from an image.
button	Creates a pushbutton. The three types are Submit, Reset, and Push, with no default.
hidden	Creates a hidden form control that cannot be seen by the user.
file	Creates a file upload control that enables users to select a file with the form data to upload to the server.

12

Workshop

If you've made it this far, I'm sure that you still have a few questions. I've included a few that I think are interesting. Afterward, test your retention by taking the quiz, and then expand your knowledge by tackling the exercises.

Q&A

Q Are there security issues associated with including forms on my website?

A Yes and no. The forms themselves are not a security risk, but the scripts that process the form input can expose your site to security problems. Using scripts that you can download and use on your own site can be particularly risky because malicious people will already know how to exploit any of their bugs. If you are going to use publicly available scripts, make sure they are approved by your hosting provider and that you are using the latest release.

Q **I want to create a form and test it, but I don't have the script ready. Is there any way I can make sure that the form is sending the right information with a working script?**

A I run into this situation all the time! Fortunately, getting around it is very easy.

Within the opening `<form>` tag, modify the `action` attribute and make it a `mailto` link to your email address, as in the following:

```
<form action="mailto:youremailaddress@isp.com" method="post">
```

Now you can complete your test form and submit it without having a script ready. When you submit your form, it will be emailed to you as an attachment. Just open the attachment in a text editor, and presto! Your form data is present.

Quiz

1. How many forms can you have on a web page?
2. How do you create form controls such as radio buttons and check boxes?
3. Are passwords sent using a `password` control secure?
4. Explain the benefit of using hidden form controls.
5. What other technology do forms rely on?

Quiz Answers

1. You can have any number of forms on a web page.
2. These form controls are created with the `input` element. Radio buttons have the `type` attribute set to `radio`, and check boxes are created using the type `checkbox`.
3. No! Passwords sent using a `password` control are not secure.
4. Hidden form controls are intended more for you than for the person filling out the form. By using unique `value` attributes, you can distinguish between different forms that may be sent to the same script or sent at different times.
5. For you to process the data submitted via forms, they must be paired with a server-side script through the `action` attribute. You can also use JavaScript to process the form data.

Exercises

1. Ask your hosting provider for scripts that you can use to process your forms. If you can use them, ask how the data is processed and which names you should use in your form controls. If you need to use forms and your hosting provider won't allow you to use its scripts, start looking elsewhere for a place to host your website.

2. Visit some sites that might use forms, such as http://www.fedex.com. Look at which form controls they use and how they arrange them, and peek at the source to see the HTML code.

12

LESSON 13

Structuring a Page with HTML5

Once you've designed a few websites, you begin to notice a pattern. Most web pages have a similar structure, with a header, footer, navigation, and sections. The authors of the HTML5 specification added support for additional structural tags to make it easier for authors to create web pages with a tag structure that matches the meaning behind those tags. Most of the new tags in HTML5 are new structural elements.

This lesson will cover the following topics:

- A review of how page layout approaches have evolved over the history of HTML
- How to lay out a page using HTML5 tags
- An overview of the new structural tags in HTML5
- How the browser creates an outline of a web page
- How to use HTML5 scripts that don't yet provide HTML5 support

A Short History of HTML Page Layout

On the early Web, most pages tended to be a single column of text that ran down the page from top to bottom, mainly because that was the only option available. Early browsers didn't even support tables, so you could create paragraphs, lists, and other basic elements that were laid out left to right and top to bottom.

The first attempts to adjust the layout of pages were done with transparent images. A GIF image was created that was 1 pixel by 1 pixel and transparent using GIF transparency. This image was then given a width and height and placed beside text or other images to push them over on the screen. It was a crude form of layout, but with a lot of effort it got the job done.

Once tables were added to HTML, they immediately became the best option for creating page layouts with multiple columns, borders around elements, and other approaches that moved beyond the normal page flow. This quickly led to unwieldy pages that contained large numbers of nested tables and often rendered very slowly. This was also the point at which semantic use of HTML elements was at its lowest ebb. Designers tended to ignore whatever semantic meaning had been intended for elements and instead used them only for whatever physical effect they had on the page. For example, designers would frequently wrap entire articles in `<blockquote>` tags to add wider margins.

Gradually, after CSS was introduced in 1996, styles began to replace HTML tags. As browser support for CSS improved and more people upgraded to newer browsers, web developers switched from using HTML tags to CSS. First, style rules gradually replaced tags that were used for character styles. For example, the `<font>` tag was one of the most-used HTML tags for a long time, particularly because some browsers did not inherit the `<font>` specification from their parent elements, so you had to include a `<font>` tag in every cell of a table. The `<font>` tag has since been completely replaced by CSS.

As more of the design and layout of pages switched from HTML to CSS, usage of tags with semantic meaning was replaced by use of the generic container tags `<div>` and `<span>`.

In the days before you could use CSS to control the layout of your pages, it was common for pages to be laid out entirely within a large table. In fact, pages often consisted of multiple nested tables that were laid out to create designs.

There were a number of problems with this approach, starting with the fact that tables have a specific semantic meaning—they are meant to present tabular data—and using them for everything removed that meaning. Some browsers also ran into performance problems trying to render pages with all of those nested tables. Finally, all of those table-related tags were really confusing and made pages difficult to maintain.

When support for style sheets was widespread enough to be relied upon, table-based layout gradually gave way to layouts based on elements positioned using CSS, and this is still the current state of the art. Pages are usually structured using nested `<div>` elements that are assigned `id` or `class` values that represent the structure of the page.

The authors of the HTML5 specification noticed that many of the names people were assigning to their `<div>` elements were the same on just about every website and decided to add elements to describe page structure that have semantic meaning.

Of course, elements like `<body>`, `<p>`, `<blockquote>`, and headings already exist. HTML5 adds elements that represent page headers and footers, navigation sections, and parts of typical documents, like articles, sections, and asides. As browser support for these new elements expands, they will gradually come to replace the nested `<div>` structures that make up just about every current web page.

Laying Out a Page in HTML5

Before digging into the new elements provided by HTML5, I want to talk about the structure of a typical web page. Here's the source code for a sample web page:

```
<!DOCTYPE html>
<html>
  <head>
    <meta charset="utf-8">
    <title>A Typical Website</title>
  </head>
  <body>
    <div id="header">
      <h1>A Typical Website </h1>
      <div class="nav" id="topmenu">
        <ul>
          <li><a href="/">Home</a></li>
          <li><a href="/products.html">Products</a></li>
          <li><a href="/about.html">About</a></li>
          <li><a href="/contact.html">Contact</a></li>
        </ul>
      </div>
    </div>

    <div id="article">
      <h2>A Headline</h2>
      <p>The text of an article.</p>
        <div class="aside">
          <p>This is an aside.</p>
        </div>
      <p>More article text.</p>
    </div>
```

13

```
<div id="footer">
  Copyright 2015-2016
</div>
</body>
</html>
```

As you can see, the page is constructed using `<div>` tags that represent typical sections included in a web page. I chose the classes and IDs for this page to correspond exactly to the equivalent tags in HTML5. Using the new elements, here's how the same page would be constructed:

```
<!DOCTYPE html>
<html>
  <head>
    <meta charset="utf-8">
    <title>A Typical Website </title>
  </head>
  <body>
    <header>
      <h1>A Typical Website </h1>
      <nav id="topmenu">
        <ul>
          <li><a href="/">Home</a></li>
          <li><a href="/products.html">Products</a></li>
          <li><a href="/about.html">About</a></li>
          <li><a href="/contact.html">Contact</a></li>
        </ul>
      </nav>
    </header>

    <article>
      <h2>A Headline</h2>
      <p>The text of an article.</p>
        <aside>
          <p>This is an aside.</p>
        </aside>
      <p>More article text.</p>
    </article>

    <footer>
      Copyright 2015-2016
    </footer>
  </body>
</html>
```

As you can see, this page has no `<div>` tags. Instead, I've used the new top-level elements in HTML5 to represent the structure of the page. One of the key design goals of HTML5 was to make HTML better represent the structure of web pages the way developers are actually building them.

HTML5 Structural Tags

Now that you've seen a full page built using HTML5, let's look at the individual structural tags and which semantics they represent. The new tags don't provide an advantage in terms of styling your pages; you can provide the structure you need for styling using `<div>` tags, IDs, and classes. The advantage of the new tags is that they provide a standard vocabulary for describing the structure of a page. This vocabulary makes it easier to build software that extracts information from structured pages so that it can be presented in alternate ways. The key, though, is for developers who are using these tags to use them in the manner consistent with that vocabulary.

Sections

It's helpful to think of the structure of a web page as an outline. The top-level structural element of a page is the `<html>` element. The next level is represented by the `<head>` and `<body>` elements. In HTML4, the only element available for dividing the page into further sections is the `<div>` element. HTML5 provides a number of other others, starting with the `<section>` element.

As you might expect, the `<section>` element is used to define a generic section of the document. The other structural tags in HTML5 are used to define document sections with more specific semantic meaning. A `<section>` tag is expected to include a heading tag for that section. You'll learn in more detail how headings and document sections interact a little further on.

Here's an example of a section:

```
<section>
    <h1>Board Members</h1>
    <p>The board members for 2014 to 2016 term are as follows.</p>
    <ul>
        <li>Lisa Smith, Chairman</li>
        <li>Joe Brown, President</li>
        <li>Sheila Robinson, Vice President</li>
        <li>Wanda Nichols, Treasurer</li>
        <li>Ronald Jones, Secretary</li>
    </ul>
</section>
```

13

While styles can be applied to the `<section>` element, it does not alter the appearance of a page on its own. You can also nest `<section>` elements on the page to create subsections. That said, you should use more specific elements when possible to avoid the `<section>` tag becoming the new `<div>` tag.

Header

The `<header>` element, seen in the example HTML5 page that I showed earlier, is a container for elements that generally appear at the top of the page and are carried across an entire site. HTML5 distinguishes between sectioning elements, like `<section>`, that are considered part of the document outline, and elements that are removed from the outline, usually because they are boilerplate that appears on many pages. The `<header>` element is excluded from the outline.

The header should contain general content like logos and navigational elements. For example, Figure 13.1 contains the part of the *New York Times* home page that should be enclosed within a `<header>` element.

FIGURE 13.1
The header of the *New York Times* website.

You can also add `<header>` elements to other sectioning elements or even nest one `<header>` within another. So, the `<body>` element can have a header, and each `<section>` can have its own `<header>`.

All of the HTML5 structural tags, including `<header>`, have no visible effect on the page.

Footer

The `<footer>` element is just like the `<header>` element, except that it's a footer. It speaks well of the design of HTML5 that it's challenging to define the structural tags without using the name of the tag in the definition. The `<footer>` contains the footer material for the nearest sectioning ancestor. What does that mean? If a `<footer>` element is nested inside a `<section>` element, it is considered to be the footer of that section, not the footer for the page itself.

Like the `<header>` element, the `<footer>` element is not considered part of the page outline. You can probably imagine the sorts of things you might put in a `<footer>` element, and if you can't, most web pages have footers. They usually contain copyright information, contact information for the creator of the page, and often some navigational elements. The footer for a section of a page may contain information about the author of the content in that section. Figure 13.2 contains a typical page footer.

FIGURE 13.2
The footer of a
page on the *New
York Times* web-
site.

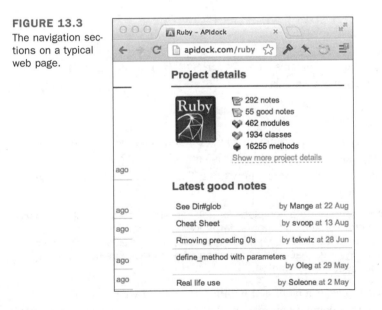

Navigation

HTML5 also provides a `<nav>` element, a sectioning element that is intended to contain
groups of navigational links on the page. When should it be used? The specification
says that "the element is primarily intended for sections that consist of major navigation
blocks." So, it's a judgment call for the creator of the page. You can use the `<nav>`
element on all your navigation lists or only on the primary navigation for the page—
whatever makes more sense.

Figure 13.3 shows a typical web page with navigation sections.

FIGURE 13.3
The navigation sec-
tions on a typical
web page.

The figure shows the types of elements that would best be enclosed in `<nav>` elements.
You can also assign `<nav>` elements to specific sections. For example, the article tools
in Figure 13.4 are a typical example of a navigation element associated with a particular
section.

13

FIGURE 13.4
Section-specific
navigation.

Here's how the `<nav>` element is used in the earlier HTML5 example:

```
<header>
  <img src="logo.png">
  <nav id="topmenu">
    <ul>
      <li><a href="/">Home</a></li>
      <li><a href="/products.html">Products</a></li>
      <li><a href="/about.html">About</a></li>
      <li><a href="/contact.html">Contact</a></li>
    </ul>
  </nav>
</header>
```

A page can contain many `<nav>` elements, and it's perfectly fine to add `id` or `class` attributes to distinguish them from one another.

Articles

The `<article>` element is another sectioning element, but unlike `<header>` and `<footer>`, it is included in the document outline. It is equivalent to the `<section>` element, with special semantic meaning. Here's how the HTML5 specification defines an article:

> "The article element represents a complete, or self-contained, composition in a document, page, application, or site and that is, in principle, independently distributable or reusable, e.g. in syndication. This could be a forum post, a magazine or newspaper article, a blog entry, a user-submitted comment, an interactive widget or gadget, or any other independent item of content."

One thing to note is that articles can be nested within sections and vice versa. For example, a section of the page may contain multiple articles, or an article can contain multiple sections.

Just like ordinary sections, articles can also contain their own header, footer, or navigation. They can also contain their set of headers.

Here's an example of an `<article>` element in a page:

```
<article>
  <h2>A Headline</h2>
  <p>The text of an article.</p>
    <aside>
      <p>This is an aside.</p>
    </aside>
  <p>More article text.</p>
</article>
```

Asides

Asides are represented by the `aside` element. When used inside an `article`, they are meant to represent content that is related to the surrounding article but not part of it. For example, an `aside` may contain a list of links for further reading, or a glossary list of terms used in the article, or a sidebar. You can also place advertisements within an `aside` element. The `aside` tag can also be used outside an article to contain content on the page that is not directly relevant to the main content on the page. However, be sure that you're not using an `aside` tag when you should be using `header`, `footer`, or `nav`.

The `aside` tag can be used for any content that belongs in a section but isn't considered part of the main page flow. That means you can also use it for things like advertisements that you want to display but wouldn't want to treat as part of the page's content.

Here's an example of an `aside` for an `article`:

```
<article>
  <h2>A Headline</h2>
  <p>The text of an article.</p>
    <aside>
      <p>This is an aside.</p>
    </aside>
  <p>More article text.</p>
</article>
```

13

The Page Outline

In discussing the various sectioning tags in HTML5, I talked about the page outline quite a bit. You already know that HTML is structured in a hierarchical fashion—tags are nested and make up a tree-like structure. That's one outline, but it's not the one I'm talking about. The browser also creates a semantic outline of the page that represents the structure of the document in terms of the content.

Prior to HTML5, sections in a document were defined using the `div` tag, and the relative precedence of the content was specified using heading tags. Anytime a new heading tag was encountered, it was treated as the beginning of a new section, with the precedence of that section in the document structure indicated by the level of the heading. Here's an example:

```
<h1>Top Level Heading</h1>
<p>Some content.</p>
<h2>Second Level Heading</h2>
<p>More content.</p>
<h3>Third Level Heading</h3>
<p>Even more content.</p>
<h2>Second Level Heading</h2>
<p>Content.</p>
```

In this case, the outline would read like this:

1. Top Level Heading

   1.1 Second Level Heading

       1.1.1 Third Level Heading

   1.2 Second Level Heading

The typical page has a number of divs, headings, and other structural elements, but given that `div` has no special semantic meaning, it is impossible to infer an accurate outline from the structure of a typical page. Instead, the headings were used to define the outline of the page.

The sectioning elements in HTML5 rectify this situation, enabling Web publishers to control the page outline precisely. With HTML5, the first heading inside a sectioning element defines the heading for that section rather than starting a new section. The subsequent headings in a section are considered to start a new section. This is referred to as implicit sectioning. If you want to force explicit sectioning, you must place every header with a corresponding sectioning element.

Why does this matter? Obviously, Web browsers like Chrome and Firefox don't present an outline of a web page; they present a rendered web page. That's not the case, however, for Web browsers that use assistive technology for visitors with vision impairment. Well thought-out page structure makes it much easier for such browsers to present the most important information on the page to users and skip over the parts that are not critical.

The most important difference between HTML5 and previous versions is that HTML5 offers more structural elements than HTML 4 did. The second difference is that HTML5 excludes some structural elements in the document outline, so they are ignored by assistive technology like screen readers.

Elements with Their Own Outlines

Some elements are semantically understood to represent external content. The sectioning elements nested in these kinds of elements are ignored when the document outline is produced. These elements are `blockquote`, `details`, `fieldset`, `figure`, and `td`.

Using HTML5 Structural Elements

As a creator of web pages, HTML5 structural elements provide a much cleaner and more semantically useful alternative to plain old `div` tags for creating web pages. And these days all modern browsers support them.

Polyfill Scripts

If you have users who are using extremely old browsers like Internet Explorer 7 or 8, you can still use HTML5 elements, but you might need fallback options. There are scripts, referred to as polyfills, that provide functionality found in browsers that do not support that functionality natively.

Modernizr is one such script. It's a JavaScript library that can be used to automatically alter web pages and style sheets when they are loaded in Internet Explorer so that they are displayed properly in the browser.

There are three lessons all about JavaScript starting with Lesson 17, "Introducing JavaScript." JavaScript is a programming language that browsers understand how to interpret and execute. You can load JavaScript libraries on your web pages in basically the same way you load external style sheets. You can also embed JavaScript in your pages using the `script` tag.

You need to download Modernizr to use it. You can get it from the website at http://modernizr.com/download/. For performance reasons, you can create a custom build that includes the features that you need, but it's easiest to start by downloading the whole thing.

Explaining how Modernizr works is beyond the scope of this lesson, but if you need to support older browsers with specific HTML5 features, you can use Modernizr to ensure that users of older browsers see an equivalent experience when they use your page.

13

Summary

HTML5 provides a new set of tags that enable you to structure pages using tags that provide sematic meaning about the page, rather than just `<div>` tags. Not only do these tags describe the structure of a page, but they also enable you to clearly differentiate between sections of a page that should be treated as page content, and parts that are boilerplate used across multiple pages like headers, footers, and navigational elements. The structural elements are combined into a page outline that represents the overall structure of the page and leaves out the sections that are not part of the page content. In Table 13.1, there's a list of the new elements introduced in this lesson. As you'll see, the descriptions of most of them include the names of the elements themselves. That was the intention behind the design of HTML5.

TABLE 13.1 New Tags Discussed in Lesson 13

Tag	Description
`<header>`	Represents the header of an HTML document. Excluded from the page outline.
`<footer>`	Represents the footer of an HTML document. Excluded from the page outline.
`<nav>`	A section containing navigation elements. Included in the page outline.
`<section>`	Represents a section of a page. Included in the page outline.
`<article>`	An article. Included in the page outline.
`<aside>`	An aside, sidebar, or other supplemental content. Not included in the page outline.

Workshop

The workshop contains a Q&A section, quiz questions, and activities to help reinforce what you've learned in this lesson. If you get stuck, the answers to the quiz can be found after the questions.

Q&A

Q You talk a lot about sematic markup. What are the tangible advantages?

A For regular desktop browsers, web pages look the same whether they are written in semantically correct markup or not. That said, proper semantic markup makes web pages much easier for users with disabilities who use screen readers to browse the Web. It also makes it easy to process the content of web pages with software and extract meaning from them. Finally, as a developer, it's easier to understand how a web page is constructed when it uses semantically accurate tags.

Q How do you decide when to start using HTML5 structural tags?

A If you're creating web pages for an audience that uses known browsers, you can use whichever tags those browsers support. For example, at my job, all of the employees use Google Chrome, so we can use HTML5 tags whenever we're working on internal applications. However, on our public website, we continue to need to support browsers that do not yet provide HTML5 support. Furthermore, we have a large web application that was written before HTML5 existed, so we would have to change all of our pages to use the new tags. These days the majority of websites are written in HTML5, and if you haven't upgraded your site yet, you should be considering it.

Quiz

1. In HTML4, which elements are used to construct the page outline?
2. How does the behavior of a heading tag change when it's placed within a `<section>` tag?
3. How does the `<nav>` element change the appearance of a page?
4. Does the `<div>` tag define a new section on a page?

Quiz Answers

1. In HTML4, the page outline is defined based on the headers used on the page.
2. Placing headings in a `<section>` tag doesn't change the heading behavior at all. It just gives the section a title for the outline.
3. This was a trick question. None of the new HTML5 structural elements affect the layout of the page.
4. The `<div>` tag does not define a new page section.

Exercise

Take a look at one of your favorite websites and think about how you would organize the page using HTML5 structural elements.

13

LESSON 14

Integrating Multimedia: Video and Sound

Video and sound are a core part of the modern Web. You can watch television online at sites like Hulu, watch movies on demand through Netflix and Amazon.com, and watch videos uploaded by anyone at sites like Vimeo and YouTube. Sites that sell downloadable music provide audio previews of the music they sell. Pandora and Last.fm enable their users to create their own radio stations starting with the name of a single song.

Understanding how to incorporate video, audio, and Flash into your own web pages is an important part of building modern websites. In this lesson you'll learn how to:

- Embed videos hosted at Vimeo and YouTube in your pages
- Convert video files to common web formats
- Use the HTML5 `<video>` and `<audio>` tags
- Embed Flash movies in web pages using the `<object>` tag
- Use Flash audio and video players

Embedding Video the Simple Way

There's a lot to be learned about embedding video: tags for embedding video in web pages, new audio and video elements in HTML5, and browser incompatibilities. First, however, it's worth discussing the way the vast majority of videos are embedded in web pages these days. People upload their video to a website that specializes in video hosting or use videos that other people have uploaded and then copy and paste the code those sites provide for embedding the videos in their own sites.

The two most popular video hosting sites, YouTube and Vimeo, provide the code to embed the videos they host on the web pages for each video. You can see the form that allows you to generate the embed code for YouTube in Figure 14.1.

FIGURE 14.1
The embed form on YouTube.

If you want to add a video hosted on YouTube, you just click the Share button and then choose Embed, and the form shown in the figure is displayed. If you want to customize it, click on the Show More button and choose your customization options. Then copy the HTML code from the box into your own page. The result is shown in Figure 14.2.

YouTube (and other sites) automatically generates the markup that you can paste into your own web pages to embed their videos. There's nothing magic about it; I'll describe the tags they use when I discuss embedding video later.

FIGURE 14.2
A YouTube video embedded in a web page.

Advantages and Disadvantages of Hosting Videos on External Sites

You can upload your own videos to YouTube and embed them in your pages, too. Other sites, like Vimeo (https://vimeo.com/), also offer free hosting for video. There are a number of advantages to hosting your videos on an external site rather than on your own web server. For one thing, video files tend to be rather large, and hosting them on YouTube or Vimeo means that you don't have to figure out a place to put them. You also get to take advantage of their video player, which supports multiple quality levels and full-screen playback. It's used by millions of people and is widely tested. There are also applications for mobile platforms like Apple iOS and Google Android, so videos can be viewed on them, whereas they cannot be with other Flash players. As you'll see, another advantage is that it's very easy to get started with YouTube or Vimeo. You just upload your video file, go to the new page for the video, and then copy the embed code and paste it on your own site to get things working.

Another advantage of hosting your video on an external video site is that you can take advantage of YouTube's and Vimeo's audience in addition to the audience at your own website. When you upload a video to YouTube and make it public, it shows up in search results and on the lists of related videos when people watch other videos on the site. So in the end, using YouTube or Vimeo for video hosting can lead more people to your website than hosting videos on your own.

14

The disadvantages of using external video hosting sites are that you cede some control over your video and how it is presented. The YouTube player works well, but it's obvious to your users that it's the YouTube player—the same is true of the Vimeo player. Plus there are restrictions to what you can post to these sites, such as longer videos. There are also automated systems to check for copyright violations, but there can be false-positives that may flag your videos and have them automatically removed. Although it's important to not post copyrighted videos (or the music in the videos), it can be a hassle to prove that you have the rights to something if YouTube or Vimeo decide to remove your content. You may want to host the video yourself if you don't want your customers to be distracted by YouTube, you need to host extremely large videos, or you want to use your own player.

Uploading Videos to YouTube

YouTube provides a number of ways to upload video to the site. You can take video with your webcam and upload it directly, or even send video taken on a smartphone to YouTube. In this case, I'm going to upload an existing video file using the web interface. To start the process, go to https://www.youtube.com/upload and drag a video you want to upload onto the upload box, as in Figure 14.3.

FIGURE 14.3
The YouTube file upload page.

NOTE

YouTube supports a wide variety of video formats, including those used by most camcorders. Supported formats include MP4, MOV, AVI, MWV, and FLV.

After you've selected a file, you'll immediately be taken to the video processing page. The page shows a progress indicator that lets you know how long your video is going to take to upload and enables you to enter information about the video you've uploaded. Using the form, you can enter a title, description, category, and tags for your video, all of which are important if you want YouTube users to be able to find your video.

As you can see from the screenshot, you can also choose a privacy setting for your video. You can choose public, which allows people to find your video through YouTube, or private, meaning that you can specify exactly who's allowed to see it. The third option is unlisted. This option makes the video publicly available, but only to people who know the URL. It's useful if you want to embed the video on your own website, but you don't want people to find it by browsing YouTube. The scheduled option lets you set a time when you want the video to be made public on the YouTube servers.

YouTube provides the URL and embed code for your video before it's even finished uploading, so you can link to it immediately.

Customizing the Video Player

After you've uploaded your video, you can embed it in your own web pages. Embedding videos of your own is just like embedding other videos found on YouTube; you can just click the Embed button and copy the code for your own page. However, you can do some things to customize the embedded player. You can see all the embedding options in Figure 14.4.

FIGURE 14.4
Customization options for embedded YouTube videos.

14

As you tweak the embed settings, the page automatically updates the embed code with your new settings. There are four check boxes you can select. The first allows you to disable the list of related videos that YouTube normally displays when a video finishes playing. You may want to disable these if you want your visitors to stick around on your site after watching your video instead of wandering off to look at other videos on YouTube. Enabling Show player controls adds visible controls to the YouTube player (and adjusts the height and width to accommodate the controls without shrinking the video). This is useful if your customers have trouble getting videos started with the controls hidden by default. Show Video Title and Player Actions leaves the title of the video at the top of the screen along with the watch later and share buttons. Privacy-enhanced mode prevents YouTube from storing identifying information about the user if he didn't click the player.

After you've chosen all of your customization options, you can copy the embed code and use it in your page.

Other Services

YouTube is the most popular video hosting service, but there are many others, too. Vimeo (https://vimeo.com/) is a popular video hosting service that's a lot like YouTube. YouTube offers unlimited uploads but limits the length of video uploads to 15 minutes. Vimeo offers a professional (paid) account that enables subscribers to upload videos of any length.

FIGURE 14.5
Vimeo's video player.

The process of uploading video files to Vimeo is nearly identical to the process for YouTube. You just choose your file and information, like the name and description. Both sites will convert video from nearly any common format to the format used by their player.

Here's a list of some other popular video hosting services:

- **Dailymotion**—http://www.dailymotion.com/
- **Flickr**—https://www.flickr.com/
- **SmugMug**—https://www.smugmug.com/
- **Viddler**—http://www.viddler.com/
- **VideoPress**—http://videopress.com/

Which video hosting site you choose is a matter of taste. Each site has its own video player and its own community, and you should choose whichever suits you best. Be sure to check out the restrictions on video length and video resolution when choosing. For example, the maximum length of videos on Flickr is 90 seconds, and only users with Pro accounts are allowed to view them in high definition (HD). There's also no rule that says that you can't upload your videos to more than one site. You may want to upload your videos to Vimeo for the purpose of embedding them on your own site and upload them to YouTube to make them available to YouTube's audience.

Hosting Your Own Video

For any number of reasons, you might want to host video yourself instead of relying on a third-party service such as Vimeo or YouTube to host it for you. For one thing, you can use your own player rather than using the one they provide. You also may not want to include branding or advertising from a third party on your own site, and you might not want to distract your users with a link to YouTube. As is the case with most third-party services on the Web, hosting your own video gives you more control over the end result but requires more work and expertise on your part.

At one time, a wide variety of methods were used to embed video in web pages, each with its own browser plug-in and file format. These days, just two common methods are in use. The first is to use a Flash movie to play back the video, and the second is to use the HTML5 `<video>` tag to play the video using the browser itself. I'll explain how to use both approaches and how to combine the two to support as many browsers and platforms as possible.

14

Before diving into the tags used to publish video on the Web, it's important to first explain how to create video files that can be played in a browser. Understanding how to create video files for the Web is the first step in getting video from your camcorder or mobile phone onto web pages.

Video and Container Formats

Before discussing how to embed video within a web page, it's important to discuss video formats. All video files are compressed using what's known as a codec, short for coder/decoder. After a video has been encoded, it must be saved within a container file, and just as there are a number of codecs, there are a number of container file formats, too. To play a video, an application must understand how to deal with its container file and be able to decode whatever codec was used to compress the video. For example, H.264 is one of the most popular video codecs and is supported by a number of container formats, including FLV (Flash Video) and MP4.

It's not uncommon to run into situations in which a video player can open the container file used to package the video but does not support the codec used to encode the video. Likewise, if a video player doesn't recognize the container file used to package the video, it won't be able to play it back, regardless of the codec used. Whereas many, many video codes and container formats exist, only a few are relevant in terms of video on the Web. The extension for a video file indicates its container format, not the codec of the video in it. For example, the extension for Apple's QuickTime container format is .mov, regardless of which codec is used to encode the video.

H.264 is a commercial format that is supported natively by Microsoft Internet Explorer 9, Apple Safari, and Google Chrome. It's also supported by Flash. The problem with H.264 is that it is patented, and there are license fees associated with the patents. Companies that implement the codec must pay for a license, as must companies that use the codec to deliver H.264 video to users. Mozilla held out for a long time and did not support H.264 in Firefox because of the patent licenses required, but as of around version 20 it began supporting it. H.264 is the most popular format for delivering video content over the Web by far. It's also used for satellite and cable television and to encode the video on Blu-Ray discs.

Most commonly, H.264 video is associated with MP4 (.mp4) containers, or occasionally Flash Video (.flv) containers. MP4 files are supported by the Flash player and by all the browsers that support H.264 video, making it the most widely supported container for distributing video on the Web.

Theora is an open, freely licensed video codec released by the Xiph.org Foundation. Mozilla Firefox and Google Chrome offer Theora support, but Apple and Microsoft have no plans to support it. It's usually associated with the Ogg container format, and the files are usually referred to as Ogg Theora files. Ogg files that contain video usually have the extension `.ogv`. There's also an associated audio codec, Vorbis. Ogg Theora audio files have the extension `.oga`.

In 2010, Google released a new container format called WebM. WebM files use the VP8 codec for video and the Vorbis codec for audio. VP8 was originally created by a company called On2, which was acquired by Google, who then released the codec to the public without licensing requirements. WebM is supported by Google Chrome and will also be supported by Mozilla Firefox, Microsoft Internet Explorer, and Adobe Flash.

Currently, if you want to encode your video only once, you can use H.264/MP4 and play it natively in browsers that support it using the `<video>` tag. All modern browsers support this format. Internet Explorer 8 is the only browser that cannot, so if you need to support Internet Explorer 8, you can play the same video file using a Flash video player.

Converting Video to H.264

One of the nicest features of video hosting services is that they free you from worrying about codecs and container formats because they do the conversion for you. It's up to you to create a video file with the desired resolution, but the hosting service takes it from there. If you're hosting video yourself, you'll need to convert your video to MP4 and perhaps Flash, too.

A number of tools are available for dealing with video, but when it comes to converting video from other formats to H.264, there's only one you need to worry about: HandBrake. HandBrake is a free, open source application that enables you to convert video stored in pretty much any format to H.264. There are versions for Windows, OS X, and Linux that all work basically the same. You can download HandBrake at http://handbrake.fr/.

If you just want to convert your video to H.264, you can open it in HandBrake and click Start. However, you'll probably want to tweak some of the settings to optimize your video for use on the Web. Check out the interface for HandBrake in Figure 14.6. I'll walk you through the options you'll want to set to optimize your video for the Web.

14

FIGURE 14.6
The interface for
HandBrake.

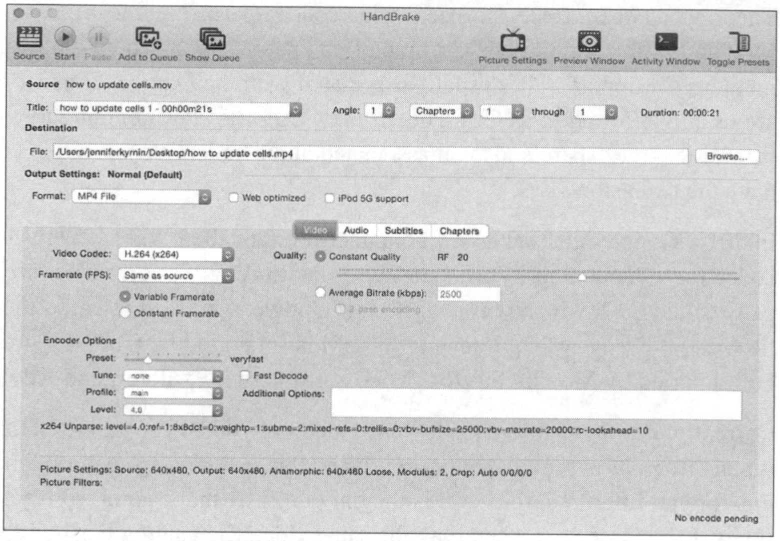

First, choose a filename for your video using the Destination field. You'll also want to stick with the default output format: MP4. The four tabs at the bottom enable you to optimize the video output for your purpose. First, though, check the Web Optimized button for your video. It enables your video to start playing immediately as it's being downloaded and makes it easier for players to skip around in the video. The only cost is slightly longer encoding time. If you think your customers will be using the older iPod fifth-generation models to play your video, you should select the iPod 5G Support.

Under the video options, the default codec is H.264. Keep that. Under Framerate, the default is to stick with the framerate in the video you're converting, but you can choose another option. The higher the framerate, the larger the resulting file. If you change the framerate, you can enable two-pass encoding, which causes encoding to take longer (by adding the additional pass) but results in higher-quality video for a given file size.

Finally, you'll tweak the Quality settings. Video encoding is all about tradeoffs. The higher the picture quality, the larger the resulting file. Larger files take up more space on the server and take longer to download. On the other hand, they look better. You can change three variables that affect the overall size of the file: the height and width of the video (a 320×240 video will be much smaller than a 640×480 video), the framerate, and the quality. If your video will be played in a small box embedded on a web page, you can afford to lower these settings to create smaller videos. If your video will be played on a 42-inch television, you'll probably want to raise the quality settings. Bear in mind that your web pages will be viewed by people using many different size screens, so don't go too small or too large.

There are three ways to specify the quality for your video, and understanding them requires that you know about bit rate. The bit rate of a video is the amount of data used by one second of video. The bigger the number, the more space the video will use. The default method of specifying quality is "constant quality." What this means is that the entire video will be compressed by the same factor. H.264 is like the JPEG image format in that some data is lost when the video is compressed. The Constant Quality setting applies the same compression factor to the whole video. When you set a video to Constant Quality, the video uses whatever bit rate is required to provide that quality, so the bit rate will vary throughout depending on how well the video can be compressed at the specified quality level.

The Average Bit Rate option varies the quality of the video to satisfy the bit rate that you specify. Both it and the target file size option are more predictable—the video will be the size you expect when you get to the end.

Instead of manipulating the settings on your own, you can use one of the presets that HandBrake provides. To view the presets, click the Toggle Presets button on the upper right. The list of settings in Figure 14.7 will appear. (I've fully expanded the list.) These presets are already optimized for certain uses. The one that works best for web video is the iPhone & iPod Touch preset. The simplest approach, if you're starting out, is to select it and then click the Web Optimized check box.

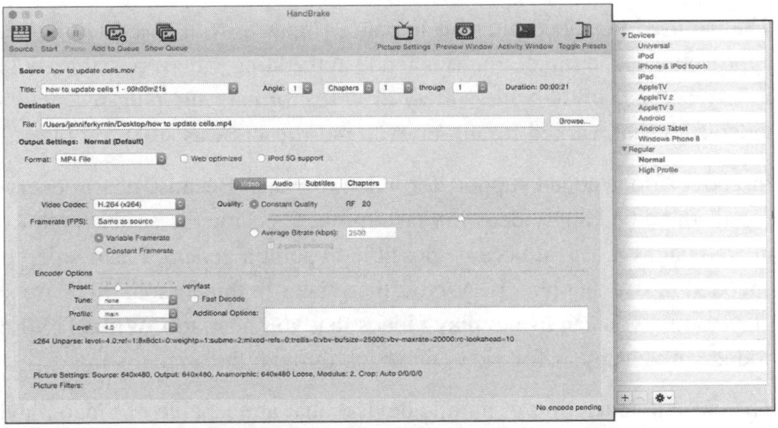

FIGURE 14.7
The list of HandBrake presets.

You'll also want to click the Picture Settings button in the toolbar to specify the height and width of your video. 320×240 is a pretty standard size for smaller videos. 640×480 is also a common setting. For HD video, set the size to at least 1280×720. From Picture

14

Settings, you can also crop your video or adjust the filter settings. The HandBrake documentation has more on the filter settings.

One option you have is to create multiple copies of your file and display them using media queries. This allows you to create responsive versions of your videos. You'll learn more about how to do this in Lesson 16, "Using Responsive Web Design."

After you've specified the settings, just click the Start button to encode your video as H.264. When the encoding is complete, preview the video, preferably in the player you'll be using on the Web, to make sure that the quality is sufficient. If it's not, encode the video again using different settings. Likewise, if the video file is larger than you'd like, you may want to encode the video again with the compression turned up. Afterward, watch the video and make sure that it still looks okay.

Embedding Video Using `<video>`

The methods used to embed video in web pages have changed a great deal over the years. In the early days of the Web, to present video, the best approach was just to link to video files so that users could download them and play them in an application other than their browser. When browsers added support for plug-ins through the `<embed>` tag, it became possible to embed videos directly within web pages. The catch was that to play the video, the user was required to have the proper plug-in installed.

The tag used to embed plug-ins in pages changed from `<embed>` to `<object>`, but the approach was the same. Plug-ins made embedding videos possible, but they didn't make it easy because of the wide variety of video formats and plug-ins available. Publishing video files that worked for all, or even most, users was still a problem.

In 2002, Adobe added support for video to Flash. Because nearly everyone had Flash installed, embedding videos in Flash movies became the easiest path to embedding video in web pages. Later, it became possible to point a generic Flash video player at a properly encoded movie and play it. As you'll see later in this lesson, there are some Flash video players that you can use to play videos that you host, too. With HTML5, browsers have added native support for video playback through the `<video>` tag.

The current generation of mobile devices that are capable of video playback (like the iPhone and phones based on Google's Android operating system) support the HTML5 `<video>` tag and do not support Flash. So, the best approach for providing video to the widest number of users is to use both the `<video>` tag and a Flash player. After introducing the `<video>` tag, I'll explain how to use it with a Flash movie in such a way that users only see one video player—the appropriate one for their environment.

The `<video>` Tag

The `<video>` tag is new in HTML5. It embeds a video within a web page and uses the browser's native video playback capabilities to do it, as opposed to Flash or some other plug-in. Here's a simple version of the `<video>` tag:

```
<video src="myvideo.mp4">
```

If the browser is capable of playing the video at the URL specified in the `src` attribute, it will do so. Or, it would, if there were some way of telling the browser to play the video. In this case, the video will have no controls and won't start playing automatically. To take care of that, I need to use some of the attributes of the `<video>` tag, which are listed in Table 14.1.

TABLE 14.1   `<video>` Attributes

Attribute	Description
`src`	The URL for the video to be played.
`height`	The height of the element.
`width`	The width of the element.
`controls`	Boolean attribute that indicates that the browser should supply its own controls for the video. The default is to leave out the controls.
`autoplay`	Boolean attribute that indicates that the video should play immediately when the page loads.
`loop`	Boolean attribute. If present, the video will loop when it reaches the end, replaying until the user manually stops the video from playing.
`preload`	Boolean attribute. If present, the browser will begin downloading the video as soon as the page loads to get it ready to play. Ignored if `autoplay` is present.
`poster`	Image to show prior to starting playback.
`muted`	Boolean attribute. If present, the video will have no sound.

Because the video above doesn't have the `controls` or `autoplay` attributes, there's no way to get it to play. Figure 14.8 shows the video, embedded using the following tag, with `controls` included:

```
<video src="myvideo.mp4" controls>
```

14

FIGURE 14.8
A video embedded
using the `<video>`
tag, with `controls`.

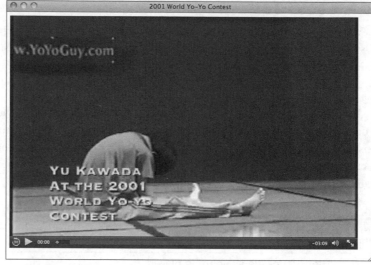

When embedding a video, make sure that you give users some way to control the video playback. Be conservative with `autoplay` and `loop`, too. Many users don't want a video to start playing immediately when they get to a page. If you include the `loop` attribute and you don't include controls, the user will have to leave the page to stop the video.

By default, the `<video>` element will be the same size as the video in the video file. You can change the size of the element on the page using the `height` and `width` attributes, however, the browser will preserve the aspect ratio of the video file and leave blank space where needed. For example, my movie was created using a 3:2 aspect ratio. If I create a `<video>` element with a 9:5 aspect ratio, the movie will appear centered within the element, as shown in Figure 14.9:

```
<video style="background: black;" src="http://www.yo-yo.org/mp4/yu.mp4" controls
width="675" height="375">
```

I set the background color of the `<video>` element to black to make it clear where the browser puts the extra space when the movie's aspect ratio does not match the aspect ratio of the element.

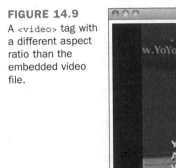

FIGURE 14.9
A `<video>` tag with a different aspect ratio than the embedded video file.

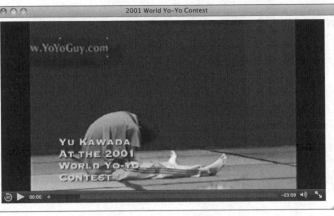

Finally, if you're fairly certain that most people who come to your page will want to view the video, but you want to let them play the video themselves, you may want to include the `preload` attribute, which tells the browser to go ahead and download the video when the page loads but to wait for the user to play the video. Usually this means users will not have to wait as long to see the video after they try to play it, but the disadvantage is that you'll use bandwidth sending the video to everyone, whether or not they actually play the movie.

Using the `<source>` Element

There is one major drawback to using the `<video>` tag. Not all browsers support the same video containers or codecs. As you've seen, this problem requires you to encode your videos in multiple formats if you want to reach most browsers, but the good news is that the `<video>` element provides a means of dealing with this issue so that your users won't notice.

To embed a single video file, you can use the `src` attribute of the video tag. To provide videos in multiple formats, use the `<source>` element nested within your `<video>` tag. Here's an example, the results of which are shown in Figure 14.10:

```
<video width="320" height="240" preload controls>
  <source src="movie.mp4"
    type='video/mp4; codecs="avc1.42E01E, mp4a.40.2"'>
  <source src="movie.ogv"
    type='video/ogg; codecs="theora, vorbis"'>
</video>
```

14

FIGURE 14.10
A video embedded using the `<video>` tag with `<source>` tags, with controls.

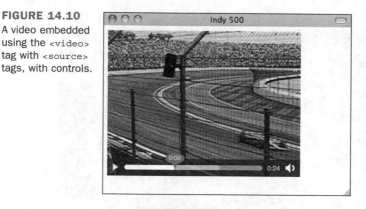

As you can see, in this case I've left the `src` attribute out of my `<video>` tag. Instead, I've nested two `<source>` elements within the tag. The `src` attribute of `<source>` contains the URL of a video file, and the `type` attribute provides information to the browser about the format of that file. The browser examines the types of each of the movie files and chooses one that is compatible.

The syntax of the `type` attribute can be a little bit confusing because of the punctuation. Here's the value:

```
video/ogg; codecs="theora, vorbis"
```

The first part is the MIME type of the video container. The second part lists the codes that were used to encode the audio and video portions of the file. So in this case, the container type is `video/ogg`, the video codec is `theora`, and the audio codec is `vorbis`. If the browser supports both the file type and the codecs, it will use that video file. The values for the `type` attribute are as follows:

- **MP4/H.264**—`video/mp4; codecs="avc1.42E01E, mp4a.40.2"`
- **Ogg Theora**—`video/ogg; codecs="theora, vorbis"`
- **WebM**—`video/webm; codecs="vp8, vorbis"`

Embedding Flash Using the `<object>` Tag

The `<object>` tag is used to embed media of all kinds in web pages. Although it is most often used to embed Flash movies, it can also be used for audio files, video files, images, and other media types that require special players. Unlike all the other HTML tags you've learned about so far, the `<object>` tag works very differently from browser to browser. The problem is that browsers use different methods to determine which plug-in should be used to display the media linked to through the `<object>` tag.

First, the version of the `<object>` tag that works with older versions of Internet Explorer:

```
<object classid="clsid:D27CDB6E-AE6D-11cf-96B8-444553540000" width="780"
height="420">
  <param name="movie" value="movie.swf" />
</object>
```

The `height` and `width` attributes are necessary to define how much space the `<object>` will take up. The `classid` attribute identifies the ActiveX control that will be used to display the content in the browser. That long, random-looking collection of letters and numbers is the address of the ActiveX control in the Windows Registry. Your best bet is to find an example of Flash embedding and copy it from there.

TIP

When you're specifying the height and width for a Flash movie, be sure to take the size of the player into account, too. Some players include a border, and nearly all of them provide controls for the video playback. You need to account for these parts of the window to make sure your video is shown at the resolution you anticipated.

The `<param>` element is used with `<object>` to provide additional information about the content being embedded to the plug-in referenced by the `<object>` tag. The `<param>` element has two attributes: `name` and `value`. This `<param>` element provides the Flash player with the URL of the movie to be played.

The preceding markup will work in Internet Explorer 8, embedding the Flash movie named `movie.swf`. Here's the markup for the `<object>` tag for other browsers:

```
<object type="application/x-shockwave-flash" data="myContent.swf" width="780"
height="420">
</object>
```

For non-Internet Explorer browsers, you specify the plug-in to use with the `type` attribute, and the URL of the movie to play with the `data` attribute. As you can see, the `height` and `width` attributes are included here, too. The `type` attribute is used to provide an Internet media type (or content type). The browser knows which content types map to which plug-ins, so it can figure out whether you have the proper plug-in installed. If you do, it can load it and render the content at the URL specified by the `data` attribute. In the sidebar, I explain exactly what Internet media types are.

14

Internet Content Types

Internet media types, also referred to as content types or MIME types, are used to describe the format of a file or resource. They're a more robust version of a file extension. For example, a PNG image usually has the extension `.png`. The MIME type for PNG files is `image/png`. Microsoft Word documents have the extension `.doc` (or more recently, `.docx`) and the MIME type `application/msword`. These types were originally used to identify the types of email attachments—MIME is short for Multipurpose Internet Mail Extensions—but these days, they're used in other cases where information about file types needs to be exchanged.

In the case of the `<object>` tag, you specify an Internet media type so that the browser can determine the best way to render the content referenced by that tag. The Internet media type for Flash is `application/x-shockwave-flash`; if that type is specified, the browser knows to use the Flash plug-in.

There's one other important use for these types when it comes to video and sound files. When a web server sends a resource to the Web, it includes a `content` type. The browser looks at the `content` type to determine what to do with the resource. For example, if the content type is `text/html`, it treats it as a web page.

When a web server sends files to users, it figures out the Internet media type using the file extension. So if a user requests `index.html`, the web server knows that an extension of `.html` indicates that the files should have the content type `text/html`. Later in this lesson, I discuss how to make sure that your web server sends the right content types for video and audio files that you use.

With most tags, you could just combine all the attributes and wind up with an `<object>` that works with all the popular browsers. With `<object>`, it doesn't work that way. However, there's a way around this problem. Here's a version that will work:

```
<object classid="clsid:D27CDB6E-AE6D-11cf-96B8-444553540000" width="780"
height="420">
  <param name="movie" value="movie.swf" />
  <object type="application/x-shockwave-flash" data="myContent.swf" width="780"
height="420">
  </object>
</object>
```

In this example, one of the `<object>` tags is nested inside the other. This works because browsers ignore tags they don't understand, so browsers that aren't Internet Explorer ignore the outer `<object>` tag. Internet Explorer ignores tags nested inside an `<object>` tag, except for the `<param>` tag, so it ignores the inner `<object>`. That's the simplest approach to using the `<object>` tag in a way that works with all browsers. But you're even better off just using the `<object>` tag as a fallback for older browsers (like Internet Explorer 8) that don't understand the `<video>` tag.

A number of other attributes are supported by the `<object>` tag, too (see Table 14.2).

TABLE 14.2 `<object>` Attributes

Attribute	Description
`data`	The URL for the data that will be presented in the `<object>` element. Flash uses a `<param>` to specify this instead.
`form`	Enables the element to be associated with a specific form.
`height`	The height of the element.
`name`	A name for the element.
`type`	The MIME type of the content to be displayed in the object.
`usemap`	The URL of a client-side image map to be applied to the object.
`width`	The width of the element.

In HTML5, you may find yourself using the `<video>` tag rather than the `<object>` tag for video files, but the `<object>` tag will still be used for other Flash movies and for other multimedia content, such as Microsoft Silverlight.

Alternative Content for the `<object>` Tag

What happens when a user hasn't installed the plug-in that the `<object>` tag requires? The browser will either display an error message or just display nothing at all. However, you can provide alternate content that will be displayed if the browser cannot find the correct plug-in. All you have to do is include the alternate content inside the `<object>` tag. If the `<object>` tag works, it will be ignored. If it doesn't, it will be displayed. Here are the nested `<object>` tags with some alternative content included. You can see alternative content displayed in a browser that does not have Flash installed in Figure 14.11. Here's the code:

```
<object classid="clsid:D27CDB6E-AE6D-11cf-96B8-444553540000" width="780"
height="420">
   <param name="movie" value="movie.swf" />
   <object type="application/x-shockwave-flash" data="myContent.swf" width="780"
height="420">
     <p>You need the Flash player to view this page.
     <a href="http://get.adobe.com/flashplayer/">Get Flash.</a></p>
   </object>
</object>
```

14

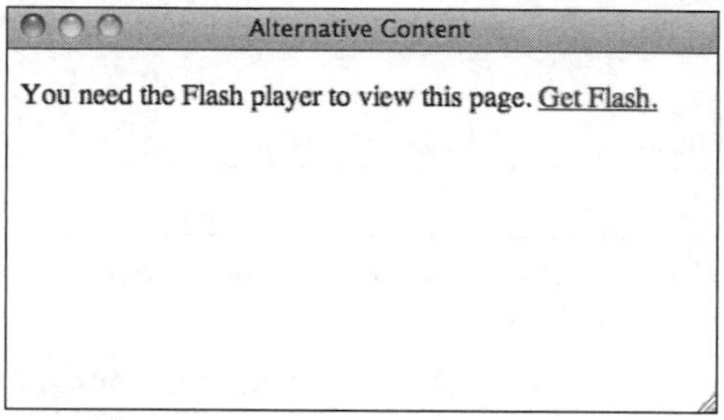

FIGURE 14.11
Alternative content displayed in a browser that doesn't support Flash.

TIP

It's often a good idea to make your alternate content the same size as the `<object>` tag to preserve the layout of your page. You can style your alternate content with CSS or use an image of the same size as a placeholder for the `<object>`.

Remember that it's better to include an alternative that is equivalent to what they get with the `object` element rather than simply suggesting they download Flash or some other program to get your content. It's a rare customer who will decide to download and install a new program because a website said it wouldn't work without it. Here's a better alternative:

```
<p>This page works best with <a href="http://get.adobe.com/flashplayer/">Flash
</a>,
but if you can't use Flash, you can download this movie as a
<a href="movie.mov">MOV</a> file and watch it on your local machine instead.</p>
```

Telling people they are using the wrong browser, software, or whatever is not acceptable, and it just annoys people.

The `<embed>` Tag

The `<embed>` element has been added to HTML5, mainly as a recognition of the fact that it has been in wide use since Netscape created it when they added plug-in support to their browser. Browsers continue to support it, mainly because many pages out there still use it.

First, let's look at the required attributes of the `<embed>` element:

```
<embed src="a01607av.avi" height="120" width="160"
  type="application/x-shockwave-flash">
```

The `src` attribute contains the location of the multimedia file you want to embed in the web page. The `type` attribute contains the content type. (It's the same as the type attribute of the `<object>` tag.) The `height` and `width` attributes specify the dimensions of the embedded file in pixels.

Table 14.3 summarizes the `<embed>` attributes that are part of HTML5.

TABLE 14.3   `<embed>` Attributes

Attribute	Description
height	The height of the element.
src	The URL of the multimedia file.
type	The MIME type of the multimedia file indicated by the `src` attribute.
width	The width of the element.

There are also some other attributes that only Internet Explorer supports. If you need to support older versions of Internet Explorer, consider using the nonconforming attributes in Table 14.4 to improve embedded videos for that browser.

TABLE 14.4   `<embed>` Attributes of Internet Explorer

Attribute	Description
allowfullscreen	Specifies whether the embedded element can occupy the full screen. Values are `true` and `false`.
allowscriptaccess	Determines whether the embedded object can communicate with external scripts or link to external pages. Values are `always`, `samedomain`, and `never`.
flashvars	Used to pass configuration parameters to the Flash player. Only used if the embedded object is Flash.
plug-inspage	The URL of the page where you can download the plug-in used to view this object.

The bottom line on `<embed>` is that you shouldn't use it. I've included it here because you'll probably see it on other sites, but there are better ways to embed media into a web page.

14

Embedding Flash Movies Using SWFObject

SWFObject is a combination of markup and JavaScript that provides a way to embed Flash movies in web pages using standards-compliant markup that still supports all the browsers that are currently in use. JavaScript is a programming language that runs within the context of a web page, I explain how it works in more detail in Lesson 17, "Introducing JavaScript." You don't need to know how to program in JavaScript to use SWFObject; you just need to copy and paste some code and fill in a few blanks. To download SWFObject and read the documentation, go to https://code.google.com/archive/p/swfobject/.

Aside from providing a reliable way to present Flash movies using standards-compliant markup, SWFObject also works around a problem that can't be dealt with using markup alone. When the version of the Flash player a user has installed is too old to play a movie, the movie will not be presented, and any alternative content you provided will not be displayed. The browser hands off the movie to the Flash player assuming it will work and doesn't handle things gracefully if it does not. SWFObject uses JavaScript to catch these errors and show the correct alternative content when they occur.

SWFObject provides two approaches to embedding content; one uses markup augmented by a bit of JavaScript (called the static publishing method), and the other uses pure JavaScript (called the dynamic publishing method). Using markup provides better performance and offers some level of functionality if JavaScript is disabled or the content is republished in an environment where the JavaScript is not included. The dynamic version is a bit more flexible in that it enables you to configure the embedded player on the fly.

Using SWFObject with markup requires three steps: adding the `<object>` tags, including the `swfobject.js` file in the page, and registering the player with the SWFObject library.

First you should add the JavaScript to the `<head>` of your document:

```
<script src="swfobject.js"></script>
```

This loads the external JavaScript to the page. You'll need to make sure that the `src` attribute points to the correct location for your copy of `swfobject.js`. You'll learn more about JavaScript and external JavaScript files in Lesson 17.

Then you should embed your Flash player. Here's the code:

```
<object id="myId" classid="clsid:D27CDB6E-AE6D-11cf-96B8-444553540000"
width="780" height="420">
  <param name="movie" value="mymovie.swf" />
  <!--[if !IE]>-->
  <object type="application/x-shockwave-flash" data="mymovie.swf" width="780"
height="420">
```

```
<!--<![endif]-->
  <p>Alternative content</p>
<!--[if !IE]>-->
</object>
<!--<![endif]-->
</object>
```

The next three lines are some JavaScript code that's embedded within the page:

```
<script>
  swfobject.registerObject("myId", "9.0.115", "mymovie.swf");
</script>
```

The italicized text represents placeholders for the values that you need to plug in to register SWFObject. As you can see, SWFObject requires the ID of the `<object>` tag (`myId`), the version of Flash that your movie requires (`9.0.115`), and the URL of the movie to be played (`mymovie.swf`).

The other option is to use dynamic publishing. First put the JavaScript in the `<head>` of your document as before:

```
<script src="swfobject.js"></script>
```

Then embed your SWF file and include alternative content:

```
<script>
  swfobject.embedSWF("myContent.swf", "myContent", "300", "120", "9.0.115");
</script>
<div id="myContent">
  <p>Alternative content</p>
</div>
```

As you can see, the main difference is that the `<object>` tags are gone entirely. Instead, I've got a `<div>` tag that serves as the container for the Flash movie. The alternate content that will be displayed if the Flash player is not present or does not satisfy the version requirement is placed within the `<div>`. The JavaScript call to dynamically publish Flash movies is a bit different from the one used in the static publishing method:

```
swfobject.embedSWF(movie URL, ID of the target div, width, height, required Flash
version);
```

Many Flash movies enable configuration through a parameter named `FlashVars`. You can specify them using the `<param>` tag:

```
<param name="FlashVars" value="controls=on">
```

14

The configuration variables that are available depend entirely on the Flash movie that you're using. You can also configure the movie through the dynamic publishing approach, but it requires a bit more knowledge of JavaScript. For more information, check out the online documentation for SWFObject after the JavaScript lessons.

In the next section, I talk about some specific Flash video players, both of which can be embedded in a page using SWFObject.

Flash Video Players

You've learned how to embed video in pages with the `<video>` tag and how to embed Flash content in pages. Next I introduce some Flash players that can play the same videos you created for use with the `<video>` tag. These players are useful because they enable anyone who has Flash to view your videos. A number of such video players are available. In this section, I discuss two of them: JW Player and Flowplayer.

JW Player

JW Player is a popular Flash video (and audio) player. It is licensed under a Creative Commons noncommercial license, so it's free to use so long as it's not for a commercial purpose. It also requires you to attribute the work to its creator when you use it; in other words, you have to link back to the JW Player website when you embed the player. There's also a commercial version available that you can use for any purpose without the link to the JW Player website. If your website includes advertising, you must use the commercial version of JW Player.

To download JW Player, go to https://github.com/jwplayer/jwplayer.

After you've downloaded the player, you'll need your video file as well as the Flash player itself: `player.swf`. JW Player includes a sample file that uses the `<object>` and `<embed>` tags, but you should use a standards-complaint approach. You can use SWFObject to embed JW Player, as shown in Figure 14.12 using the following code:

```
<script src="swfobject.js"></script>
<script>
  swfobject.registerObject("myId", "9", "expressInstall.swf");
</script>
<div>
  <object id="myId" classid="clsid:D27CDB6E-AE6D-11cf-96B8-444553540000"
width="400" height="315">
    <param name="movie" value="player.swf" />
    <param name="flashvars" value="file=video.mp4" />
    <!--[if !IE]>-->
      <object type="application/x-shockwave-flash" data="player.swf"
        width="400" height="315">
```

```
        <param name="flashvars" value="file=video.mp4" />
    <!--<![endif]-->
    <div>
        <!-- Alternative content -->
        <p><a href="http://www.adobe.com/go/getflashplayer">Download Flash</a></p>
    </div>
    <!--[if !IE]>-->
        </object>
    <!--<![endif]-->
    </object>
</div>
```

FIGURE 14.12
A video played
using JW Player.

The code starts with the `<script>` tags used to include the SWFObject script and register
the player. If you look at the line that registers the player, you'll see that I'm registering the `<object>` tag with the ID `myId` and that I'm specifying that version 9 of Flash
is required because that's the first version of Flash that supported MP4 and H.264.
Finally, there's a reference to `expressInstall.swf`, a Flash movie that's included with
SWFObject that enables users to upgrade their Flash player in place if it's out-of-date.

Both the `<object>` tag for Internet Explorer and the nested `<object>` tag for other browsers refer to the JW Player Flash file, `player.swf`. They also both use the `flashvars`
param to point to the video file, `video.mp4`. I've included some alternate content that
points the user to the Flash download site if they don't have Flash installed.

JW Player is highly customizable. There's a detailed list of the configuration parameters
in the documentation at the JW Player website. All the configuration options are specified

14

in the `flashvars` parameter. Figure 14.13 shows an example that moves the control bar to the top of the player:

```
<param name="flashvars" value="file=video.flv&amp;controlbar=top">
```

FIGURE 14.13
JW Player with the control bar moved to the top.

There are two configuration parameters in that `<param>` tag: `file` and `controlbar`. Each is separated from its value by an equals sign, and the two parameters are separated by an encoded ampersand (`&amp;`). The `flashvars` is formatted in the same way as a URL query string, the same format used for encoding form parameters when they're sent to the server. For more information about how to format query strings, take a look at the Wikipedia article at http://en.wikipedia.org/wiki/Query_string.

Using Flowplayer

Flowplayer is another popular Flash-based video player. The base version is free and open source and can be used on commercial sites. The only catches are that the base version displays the Flowplayer logo at the end of the video and you can only have a maximum of 4 minutes per video. If you want to get rid of the branding or display your own logo, you can purchase a commercial version of Flowplayer. The price is based on the number of domains on which you want to use the player. You can download it at http://flowplayer.org/.

Flowplayer is used similarly to dynamic publishing with SWFObject. To embed a video in a page using Flowplayer, you must include the custom JavaScript file supplied with Flowplayer, using a `<script>` tag:

```
<script src="path/to/the/flowplayer-3.2.2.min.js"></script>
```

Then you have to add a container to the page in which the video will appear:

```
<a href="myvideo.mp4"
  style="display: block; width: 425px; height: 300px;"
  id="player">Download video</a>
```

And finally, you need to install the player in the target element:

```
<script>
flowplayer("player", "path/to/the/flowplayer-3.2.2.swf");
</script>
```

Instead of using the `<object>` tag or using a `<div>` as the container for the player, Flowplayer recommends using the `<a>` tag. The player will play the video referenced in the `href` attribute of the `<a>` tag. Here's the full example page, which is shown in Figure 14.14:

```
<!DOCTYPE html>
<html>
<head>
  <script src="flowplayer-3.2.2.min.js"></script>
</head>
<body>
  <a href="http://e1h13.simplecdn.net/flowplayer/flowplayer.flv"
    style="display:block; width:520px; height:330px"
                    id="player"></a>
  <script>
    flowplayer("player", "flowplayer-3.2.2.swf");
  </script>
</body>
</html>
```

FIGURE 14.14
A video played
using Flowplayer.

There are a number of customization options for Flowplayer. The easiest way to change them is to use Flowplayer's Setup application, available at https://flowplayer.org/designer/. You can also configure Flowplayer yourself, using JavaScript. There's a full list of configuration options on the Flowplayer website at http://flowplayer.org/documentation/configuration/.

Using the `<object>` Tag with the `<video>` Tag

The `<object>` tag can be used as an alternative for presenting video for browsers like Internet Explorer 8 that don't support the `<video>` tag. All that you need to do is include a proper `<object>` tag inside your `<video>` tag. The way HTML support works in browsers ensures that this works. Browsers ignore tags that they don't recognize, so Internet Explorer will ignore your `<video>` tag. Browsers that do support the `<video>` tag will ignore any `<object>` tags that are nested within them, recognizing that they are included as an alternative means of presenting the video.

So when you use them together, you wind up with markup that looks like this:

```
<video width="320" height="240" controls>
  <source src="path/to/movie.mp4"
    type='video/mp4; codecs="avc1.42E01E, mp4a.40.2"'>
  <source src="path/to/movie.ogv"
    type='video/ogg; codecs="theora, vorbis"'>
    <object classid="clsid:D27CDB6E-AE6D-11cf-96B8-444553540000"
      width="320" height="240">
      <param name="movie" value="/movie.mp4">
    </object>
</video>
```

The `<video>` tag with its `<source>` elements will present video in browsers that support it, and for those that don't, the `<object>` element is included to present the video using Flash.

You can even further nest tags, including the `<object>` tags used by both Internet Explorer and other browsers as children of the `<video>` tag:

```
<video width="320" height="240" controls>
  <source src="path/to/movie.mp4"
    type='video/mp4; codecs="avc1.42E01E, mp4a.40.2"'>
  <source src="path/to/movie.ogv"
    type='video/ogg; codecs="theora, vorbis"'>
    <object classid="clsid:D27CDB6E-AE6D-11cf-96B8-444553540000"
      width="320" height="240">
      <param name="movie" value="/movie.mp4">
      <object type="application/x-shockwave-flash" data="myContent.swf"
width="780" height="420">
        <p>You need the Flash player to view this page.
```

```
        <a href="http://get.adobe.com/flashplayer/>Get Flash.</a></p>
      </object>
    </object>
</video>
```

In this case, browsers that support the native `<video>` tag will use it. Then Internet Explorer will use the nested `<object>` tag. Finally, other browsers will use the inner `<object>` tag.

Embedding Audio in Your Pages

The nice thing about embedding audio is that it's similar to embedding video. HTML5 provides an `<audio>` tag that works almost identically to the `<video>` tag. The `<embed>` tag can also be used with audio, but you should use the `<audio>` and `<object>` tags instead.

Four main file formats and codecs are used for audio on the Web: MP3, Ogg Vorbis, AAC, and WAV. MP3 is supported natively by Internet Explorer 9+, Firefox, Opera, iOS, Android, Safari, and Chrome and can be played using Flash-based players. The WAV format is supported by all browsers except Internet Explorer. Ogg Vorbis, the open format, is supported by Firefox, Opera, Android, and Chrome. AAC is the format used by iTunes when you rip CDs. It is supported natively by all browsers but Firefox and also by Flash. Firefox only supports it in an MP4 container.

Your best bet for reaching the largest audience is to use the `<audio>` tag with MP3 files for browsers that support it, including mobile browsers that support HTML5 but not Flash, and then use a Flash-based player to play the MP3 files for those users whose browsers do not support HTML5 or don't support the MP3 format.

The `<audio>` Tag

The `<audio>` tag is similar to the `<video>` tag. It attempts to use the native capabilities of the browser to play an audio file. Its attributes are the same as the `<video>` tag, except that the `height` and `width` attributes are not used. Here's an example of the `<audio>` tag:

```
<audio src="song.mp3" controls>
```

If the browser is capable of playing the video at the URL specified in the `src` attribute, it will present the audio, which you can use to control playback. The audio player appears in Figure 14.15.

14

FIGURE 14.15
An embedded
audio player.

Table 14.5 lists the attributes of the `<audio>` tag.

TABLE 14.5 `<audio>` Attributes

Attribute	Description
src	The URL for the audio to be played.
controls	Boolean attribute that indicates that the browser should supply its own controls for the file. The default is to leave out the controls.
autoplay	Boolean attribute that indicates that the audio should play immediately when the page loads.
loop	Boolean attribute. If present, the audio will loop when it reaches the end, replaying until the user manually stops the file from playing.
mediagroup	Groups media elements with an implicit media controller.
muted	Boolean attribute. If present, the audio file will be silent.
preload	Boolean attribute. If present, the browser will begin downloading the video as soon as the page loads to get it ready to play. Ignored if `autoplay` is present.

To provide background music for the page, you can add the `autoplay` and `loop` attributes to the tag. Chances are, if you use `autoplay`, or even worse, `autoplay` and `loop` without also providing controls for the audio, your users will leave in a hurry.

Flash Audio Players

Embedding Flash audio players is the same as embedding Flash video players in a page. You can use the `<object>` tag, nested `<object>` tags, or SWFObject to embed your Flash movie. You can also nest `<object>` tags within `<audio>` tags to maximize browser support.

Both JW Player and Flowplayer can play audio as well as video files. To do so, supply the path to an MP3 file rather than to a video file. A number of Flash players are just for audio.

One popular Flash audio player is called WordPress Audio Player. You'll want to download the standalone version from http://wpaudioplayer.com/. It is also available as a plug-in for the WordPress blogging tool; be sure not to download that version.

After you've downloaded it, copy the `audio-player.js` and `player.swf` files to your website. Then set up the audio player, as shown in this example page, which appears in Figure 14.16:

```
<!DOCTYPE html>
<html>
  <head>
    <title>Audio Player</title>
    <script src="audio-player.js"></script>
    <script>
      AudioPlayer.setup("player.swf", {
        width: 325
      });
    </script>
  </head>
  <body>
    <p id="myaudio"><a href="song.mp3">Download MP3 file</a></p>
    <script>
      AudioPlayer.embed("myaudio", {soundFile: "song.mp3"} );
    </script>
  </body>
</html>
```

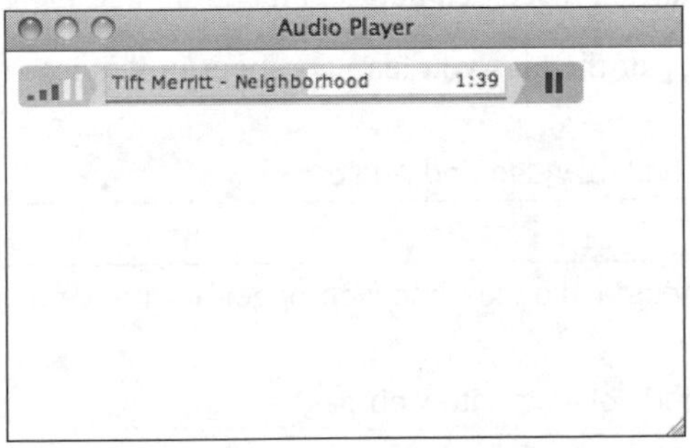

FIGURE 14.16
An embedded
audio player.

14

Audio Player uses JavaScript to embed the player in a target element using a technique similar to the SWFObject dynamic publishing technique. In the header of the page, I included the JavaScript file provided with Audio Player and then set up the player in the next `<script>` tag. Copy that code and replace the size with the size that works for you. (The player in my example is set to be 325 pixels wide.)

Then in the body of the page, I included a `<p>` tag that will contain the player. My alternate content goes inside the `<p>` tag. It's replaced when the JavaScript that follows adds the player to the page. In this case, I added a link that points to the MP3 file that the player is going to play. Finally, I embedded the player using JavaScript. For it to work, I specified the ID of the element that will contain the player and specified the location of the audio file. In this case, it's `song.mp3`, found in the same directory as the page.

Summary

In this lesson, you learned about the wide world of tags, codecs, and file formats associated with publishing audio and video on the Web. First, you learned how to upload your video files to YouTube and publish them on your site. You also learned about some alternative sites, such as Vimeo, that provide video hosting. Then you learned about the file formats associated with video on the Web and how to convert videos to those formats. You learned a lot about the limitations of the various browsers in terms of the tags and formats they support, and you discovered how to work around those limitations to deliver your video and audio content to as many users as possible.

Next, I discussed the option of hosting your own videos. You learned how to embed video in web pages using the `<video>` tag and the `<object>` tag and how to combine them to support the largest number of browsers. You also learned about SWFObject, a tool that makes it easier to embed Flash movies in your pages in a standards-compliant way. The lesson also covered two Flash movies that can used to embed video or audio files in your web pages. Finally, I discussed audio embedding and the `<audio>` tag.

Table 14.6 shows a summary of the tags you learned about in this lesson.

TABLE 14.6   Tags for Embedding Video and Audio

Tag	Use
`<audio>`	Embeds audio files into web pages for native playback by the browser.
`<embed>`	Embeds objects into web pages.
`<object>...<object>`	Embeds objects into web pages.

Tag	Use
`<param>...</param>`	Specifies parameters to be passed to the embedded object. Used in the `object` element.
`<source>`	Points to a source audio or video file to be played by an `<audio>` or `<video>` tag.
`<video>`	Embeds an audio file into a web page for native playback.

Workshop

The following workshop includes questions you might ask about embedding video and audio in your web pages, questions to test your knowledge, and three exercises.

Q&A

Q What's the quickest way to get started adding video to my site?

A The quickest way is to use a site like YouTube or Vimeo that makes it easy to upload your video files and then embed them using the code provided. For most publishers, using sites such as these is all that's needed to provide video to users. Going the extra mile to host your own video is probably not worth it for the vast majority of applications, especially when you can subscribe to a site such as Vimeo for a nominal fee and publish videos hosted there without linking back to them.

Q Should I be worried about web browser compatibility and standards compliance when it comes to audio and video?

A Unfortunately, yes. When it comes to video and audio, it's easy to wind up writing markup that isn't standards compliant or to leave out part of your audience by using markup that won't work with their browser. Fortunately, as long as you use the techniques listed in this lesson, you can embed video or audio in your pages in a standards-compliant way that supports all the browsers that are currently in use.

Q What is the difference between H.264 and Ogg Theora?

A H.264 and Ogg Theora are both video codecs. They are slightly different in terms of performance, but the main difference is in how they are licensed. Ogg Theora is an open technology that can be implemented by anyone without restraint. To use the `<video>` tag and reach the widest number of users, you should make your videos available in both formats.

14

Quiz

1. How do you accommodate users whose browsers do not support the `<video>` tag and do not have Flash installed?

2. Why is SWFObject a more robust approach to embedding Flash than just using the `<object>` tag?

3. Why are two `<object>` tags required to embed Flash movies in pages that work in most browsers?

4. Which video format is supported by all web browsers that support the `<video>` tag?

Quiz Answers

1. The key to accommodating users who cannot view your video because of the browser they're using or because they don't have the proper plug-in installed is to use alternate content. Content placed inside the `<video>` tag or `<object>` tag will be ignored by browsers that understand those tags, and displayed by those that don't. You can include a link to the proper plug-in, a new browser, or even a direct link to the video itself so that the user can download it and play it with an application on his computer.

2. The two main advantages of SWFObject are that it enables you to create valid markup that still supports a wide variety of browsers, and that it gracefully handles cases in which the user is missing the Flash plug-in or the version of the Flash plug-in she has installed is out of date.

3. Two `<object>` tags are required because one set of attributes works with Internet Explorer and another set of attributes works with other browsers, like Firefox and Safari.

4. This is a trick question. No one container format or codec is supported by all browsers and browser versions. To reach your entire audience, you must encode your video in multiple formats and use Flash for browsers without native support for the `video` tag.

Exercises

1. Upload a video to YouTube or Vimeo, and then create a web page with that video embedded in it.

2. Use one of the two video players listed in this chapter, JW Player or Flowplayer, to embed a video in a web page. Look into the configuration options and try changing the appearance of the player.

3. Try rewriting the YouTube embed code for a video on the site in a standards-compliant fashion. There's no reason why you must use YouTube's non-standards-compliant code to embed their movies in your pages.

LESSON 15

Advanced CSS: Page Layout in CSS

One of the major draws of modern CSS is the freedom to replace clunky HTML with structured HTML markup, styled by CSS rules. In Lesson 8, "Using CSS to Style a Site," you learned how to place individual portions of your web page in specific locations using absolute positioning or floating content. You can use the same types of style rules to build the visual structure of the page.

In this lesson, you'll learn about the following:

- The different strategies for laying out a page in CSS
- Why it's a bad idea to use `<table>` for page layout
- The steps to replacing a table-based layout with a CSS-based structure
- How to write HTML code for CSS-based layouts
- How to use positioned content to lay out a page
- How to use floating columns to lay out a page
- Which questions you need to ask yourself before starting on a style sheet
- How to organize your style sheets to make them easier to use and edit

Laying Out the Page

This lesson brings together many of the techniques you've learned in previous lessons for using Cascading Style Sheets (CSS) properties to lay out an entire page or even an entire website.

The examples in this lesson use a redesigned version of the website for the Dunbar Project in Tucson, Arizona. The site as it appeared before the makeover is shown in Figure 15.1. It is mostly a dark purple color, and although it's not bad, it could be improved through the use of CSS, as you'll see.

FIGURE 15.1
The Dunbar Project's original website.

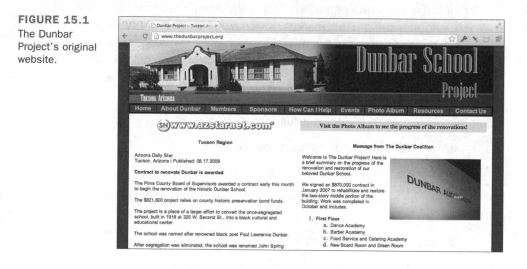

The Problems with Layout Tables

Figure 15.2 shows the source view for the original version of the Dunbar Project website, which was not designed with CSS. Instead, multiple nested `<table>` tags provide the page layout, and `<font>` is used extensively.

Tables for layout are problematic for a number of reasons. HTML purists argue against tables on principle: The `<table>` tag is meant to identify data in rows and columns of information and is not intended for page layout. Accessibility mavens will tell you that screen readers employed by visually impaired users struggle with table layout.

Table-based layouts are often more difficult to maintain than CSS-based layouts, requiring extensive rewriting of HTML tags to make simple changes. Later this lesson, you'll see how a few CSS rules can easily move entire sections around without touching the HTML document at all.

FIGURE 15.2
Table-based layout can be very convoluted.

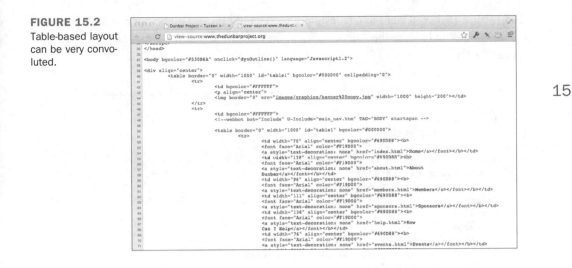

CSS-based layouts make it easier to maintain your HTML pages without cluttering them up with `<tr>` and `<td>` tags and make for simpler transitions to new layouts by just swapping in a new style sheet. Your web pages laid out with CSS will be smaller (and thus load more quickly) than table-based pages. You can write web pages with the main content first in the HTML source and the navigation and footer information after, making your page friendlier to screen readers and search engines.

NOTE

While it's very important, as you've just learned, to not use tables for layout, HTML5 has declared that it is still a valid use of the tag. The important thing is to make it clear to browsers and user agents that the table is used for layout. The best way to do this is to include the `role=presentation` attribute on the table tag. This attribute tells the browser explicitly that the table is intended for layout.

Writing HTML with Structure

The first step to laying out a page is to start with well-written HTML that is divided into sections for styling. This is done with HTML5 structural elements you learned in Lesson 13, "Structuring a Page with HTML5," that correspond to the different sections of the page. If you have an area of the page that doesn't fit with those elements, you can use the `<div>` tags to provide additional layout structure.

In Listing 15.1, you can see a redesign of the Dunbar Project home page, which uses simple markup to store the site navigation, the content, the side navigation links, and the page footer.

LISTING 15.1   Using HTML5 Sectioning Tags to Create Sections for Positioning

```
<!doctype html>
<!-- dunbar-15.1.html -->
<html>
  <head>
    <meta charset="utf-8">
    <title>The Dunbar Project</title>
  </head>
  <body>
    <header>
      <h1>The Dunbar Project</h1>
      <h2>In the Shadow of Downtown Tucson</h2>
      <nav id="sitenav">
        <ol><li><a href="index.html">Home</a></li>
            <li><a href="about/">About the Dunbar Project</a></li>
            <li><a href="gallery/">Photo Galleries</a></li>
            <li><a href="donate/">Donate</a></li>
            <li><a href="contact/">Contact</a></li></ol>
      </nav> <!-- sitenav -->
    </header> <!-- header -->
    <div id="main">
      <article id="content">
        <h3>Welcome to The Dunbar Project Website</h3>
        <img src="DunbarTop.jpg" alt="[Dunbar School]">
        <p>Dunbar School was completed in January 1918, for the
           purpose of educating Tucson's African-American students.
           The school was named after <a href="poet.html">Paul
           Laurence Dunbar</a>, a renowned African-American poet.
           African-American children in first through ninth grades
           attended Dunbar until 1951, when de jure segregation was
           eliminated from the school systems of Arizona.  When
           segregation in Arizona was eliminated, Dunbar School
           became the non-segregated John Spring Junior High School,
           and continued as such until 1978 when the school was
           closed permanently.</p>
        <!-- ... more content omitted ... -->
      </article> <!-- content -->
      <aside id="sidebar">
        <h3>Dunbar Project</h3>
        <ol><li><a href="plan/">The Dunbar Site Plan</a></li>
            <li><a href="auditorium/">Dunbar Auditorium</a></li>
            <li><a href="history/">School History</a></li>
            <li><a href="proposal/">Project Proposal</a></li>
            <li><a href="donors/">Dunbar Donors</a></li>
```

```
            <li><a href="poet.html">About Paul Laurence Dunbar,
                Poet</a></li>
            <li><a href="links/">Related Links</a></li></ol>
        <h3>Coalition Partners</h3>
        <ol><li>The Tucson Urban League</li>
            <li>The Dunbar Alumni Association</li>
            <li>The Dunbar/Spring Neighborhood Association</li>
            <li>The Juneteenth Festival Committee</li></ol>
        <h3>Individual Members</h3>
        <ol> <!-- ... list of donors omitted ... --> </ol>
      </aside> <!-- sidebar -->
      <footer>
        <p id="note501c3">The Dunbar Project is a 501c(3)
           organization, and your contributions are tax
           deductible.</p>
        <p id="copyright">Copyright &copy; 2006 by the Dunbar
           Project. Questions?
           <a href="mailto:webmaster@thedunbarproject.com"
           >Mail the Webmaster.</a></p>
      </footer> <!-- footer -->
    </div> <!-- main -->
  </body>
</html>
```

The structure of this page is defined by the HTML5 tags with `id` attributes. The general skeleton (with content omitted) consists of the following:

```
<header>
  <nav id="sitenav"></nav>
</header>
<div id="main">
  <article id="content"></article>
  <aside id="sidebar"></aside>
  <footer></footer>
</div>
```

Comments are used with the closing tags as reminders about which section is being closed; it makes the page easier to edit later.

The page is constructed of two sections: a header and a main body. Each of these has one or more subsections. This structure provides what's needed to redesign and lay out the page.

Why this particular structure? There are actually many ways you could structure such the page, inserting tags appropriately. This skeleton is simply the method chosen for this example, to get the specific styles used later on. During the web development process, you might go back to your HTML and add or remove tags while styling to give more flexibility when creating page layouts.

Remember to use the HTML5 sectioning elements for parts of the page that have that particular meaning (section, article, aside, header, footer, and nav). If you just need to add an HTML tag to hook your CSS styles to, that is when you should use the `<div>` tag, which has no semantic meaning.

Figure 15.3 shows the new HTML page without styles applied.

FIGURE 15.3
An unstyled page, ready for layout.

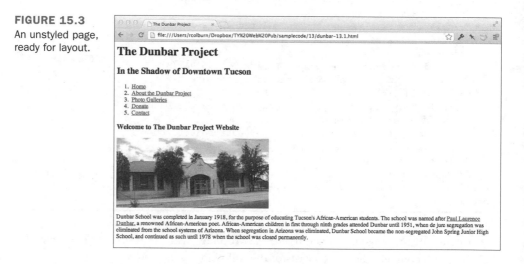

Writing a Layout Style Sheet

With an HTML page ready for styling, the next step is to write the style sheet. There are several questions to consider regarding how to lay out the page.

The first is a technical question: Will you use absolute positioning for layout, or will you use floated columns? You can get the same general layout effects from both techniques. Absolute positioning is a little bit easier to grasp, at first, so this example uses absolute positioning. Later this lesson, however, you'll learn how to lay out the same HTML page with the `float` property.

You need to figure out how many columns you want. There's a slight increase in complexity when you have more columns, but the specific techniques remain the same whether you're using two columns, three columns, or more. In this redesign, two columns are used to avoid making the example overly complex.

Finally, you need to determine whether you are using a fixed layout or a liquid layout. A fixed layout is one that defines a specific width for an entire page; for example, it may be always 700 pixels across, and excess space in the browser simply becomes wider margins. A liquid layout is one that grows larger (or smaller) based on the user's screen resolution and browser window size. There is a greater variety of devices used to access the Web these days, and there's also the challenge of presenting your site well on all of those devices. You'll learn about some techniques to help with that in Lesson 21, "Designing for the Mobile Web," and how to change your layout depending on the device viewing it in Lesson 16, "Using Responsive Web Design."

There are advantages and disadvantages to both fixed and liquid layouts. A fixed layout may be easier to create and easier to read on larger monitors; a liquid layout is more adaptable but could result in overly long lines, which are harder to read. In this example, the Dunbar Project site will use a liquid design with margin size based on em units.

Listing 15.2 is a style sheet that starts to set up the layout choices.

LISTING 15.2 A Style Sheet for Page Layout

```
body         { margin: 0; padding: 0;
               background-color: silver; }
header       { background-color: black; color: white; }
#sitenav ol  { padding: 0; margin: 0;
               display: inline; }
#sitenav li  { display: inline; padding-left: 1em;
               margin-left: 1em;
               border-left: 1px solid black; }
#sitenav li:first-child
             { padding-left: 0; border-left: none;
               margin-left: 0; }
#sitenav li a { color: white; }
#main        { padding: 0 12em 2em 2em;
               position: relative;
               background-color: gray; }
#content     { background-color: white; }
#sidebar     { position: absolute; width: 10em;
               right: 1em; top: 1em; }
#sidebar h3  { color: white;
               background-color: black; }
#sidebar ol  { margin: 0 0 1em 0;
               background-color: white;
               border: 2px solid black; }
footer       { background-color: white; }
```

This style sheet is deliberately plain and simple, with colors of black, gray, silver, and white to make it easier for you to identify the various sections of the page.

So what's happening here?

- The first rule sets the margin and padding of the `<body>` to `0`. This is an important first rule for layout because browsers typically add one or the other (or both) to any web page.

- The `#sitenav` rules in Listing 15.2 are used to turn the ordered list of links into a horizontal navigation bar.

- The `#main` section is set to `position: relative` to become the containing block around the `#content`, `#sidebar`, and `footer` sections.

- The `#main` section is also given a large padding on the right, `12em`. This is where the `#sidebar` will be located.

- Absolute positioning is used to move the `#sidebar` into the margin, out of its place in the normal flow of content. It is positioned 1 em to the left of the right edge of its containing block (`#main`) by `right: 1em`, and 1 em down from the top edge of the containing block by `top: 1em`.

Figure 15.4 shows the results of linking this style sheet to the HTML file from Listing 15.1.

FIGURE 15.4
Positioning properties define the rough outline of the page.

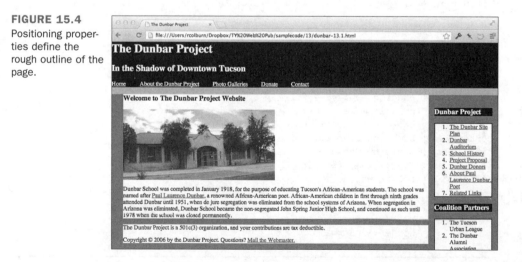

It's still quite rough, but you can see the different sections moved into place. You should note the silver bars above and below the header. Where did they come from, and why?

The silver bars are the result of the background color set on the `<body>` showing through. They are formed because of the default margin properties set on the `<h1>` and `<h3>`

headings used on the page. Remember that margins are outside of the border of an element's box, and the `background-color` property on a box colors only the interior content, not the margin. This applies even when you have a `<header>` wrapped around a heading, such as `<h1>`. The margin extends beyond the edge of the `<header>`'s background-color.

To fix this, we explicitly set the heading margins to zero on the heading tags. Listing 15.3 is a style sheet that not only does that, but also assigns colors, fonts, and other styles on the site. The teal, purple, white, and yellow colors were chosen to reflect the original design of the website, and the actual colors used at the Dunbar school auditorium.

LISTING 15.3 A Style Sheet for Colors and Fonts

```
body       { font-family: Optima, sans-serif; }
a:link     { color: #055; }
a:visited  { color: #404; }

header     { text-align: center;
             color: white; background-color: #055; }
header h1, header h2
           { margin: 0; }
header h1  { color: #FFFF00; font-size: 250%; }
header h2  { font-weight: normal; font-style: italic; }

#sitenav    { color: white; background-color: #404; }
#sitenav ol { font-size: 90%; text-align: center; }
#sitenav li { margin-left: 1em;
             border-left: 1px solid #DD0; }
#sitenav li a:link, #sitenav li a:visited
           { color: white; text-decoration: none; }
#sitenav li a:hover
           { color: #DDDD00; }

#main      { background-color: #055; }

#content    { background-color: white; padding: 1em 5em; }
#content h3 { margin-top: 0; }
#content p  { font-size: 90%; line-height: 1.4; }

#sidebar h3 { font-size: 100%; color: white; margin: 0;
             font-weight: normal; padding: 0.125em 0.25em;
             background-color: #404; }
#sidebar ol { background-color: white; border: 2px solid #404;
             border-top: 0; margin: 0 0 1em 0;
             padding: 0.125em 0.25em; }
#sidebar li { font-size: 85%;
             display: block; padding: 0.125em 0; }
```

15

```
#sidebar li a:link, #sidebar li a:visited
          { text-decoration: none; color: #055; }
#sidebar li a:hover { color: #404; }

footer      { background-color: #404; color: white;
              padding: 0.5em 5em; }
footer p    { margin: 0em; font-size: 85%; }
footer p a:link, footer p a:visited
          { color: #DDDD00; }
```

Figure 15.5 shows the HTML file from Listing 15.1 with both the layout style sheet from Listing 15.2 and the colors and fonts style sheet from Listing 15.3.

FIGURE 15.5
Fonts and colors help define the website's look.

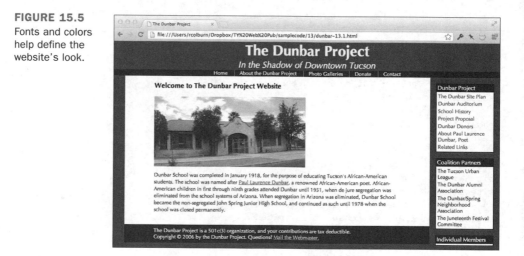

As you can see, the styled page in Figure 15.5 looks quite different from the unstyled version in Figure 15.3.

Reordering Sections with Positioning Styles

The page in Figure 15.5 looks okay, but let's say that you got this far into the web design process and you suddenly decide that you want to have the site navigation bar located above the headline, rather than below it.

You could go in and change your HTML source around. This would work, but it would introduce a problem. The order of the HTML in Listing 15.1 is sensible—the name of the site is given first, and then the navigation menu. This is how users of non-CSS browsers such as Lynx will read your page, and also how search engines and screen readers will understand it. Moving the title of the page after the list of links doesn't make much sense.

Instead, you can use CSS positioning properties to reformat the page without touching the HTML file. Listing 15.4 is a style sheet to do exactly that.

15

LISTING 15.4   Moving One Section Before Another

```
/* dunbar-move-15.4.css */

header    { padding: 1.25em 0 0.25em 0;
            position: relative;
            background-color: #404; }
#sitenav  { position: absolute;
            top: 0; right: 0;
            border-bottom: 1px solid #DDDD00;
            width: 100%;
            background-color: #055; }
```

What's happening here?

- The `header` section encloses the `#sitenav` in the HTML source, so by setting it to `position: relative`, it now becomes the containing block for the site navigation links.

- Padding is added to the top of the `#header` section. This is where subsequent rules will place the site navigation menu; the padding reserves the space for it.

- Absolute positioning properties align the top-right corner of the `#sitenav` section with the top-right corner of its containing block, the `#header`.

- Giving a `width` of `100%` to the `#sitenav` ensures it will reach across the full width of its containing block, which is, in this case, as wide as the browser display window.

- Finally, colors are swapped on the `#header` and the `#sitenav` to make them fit in better with the overall design in their new locations, and a yellow border is added to the bottom of the navigation links.

Figure 15.6 shows the effects of these changes.

FIGURE 15.6
The navigation menu is now above the page headline.

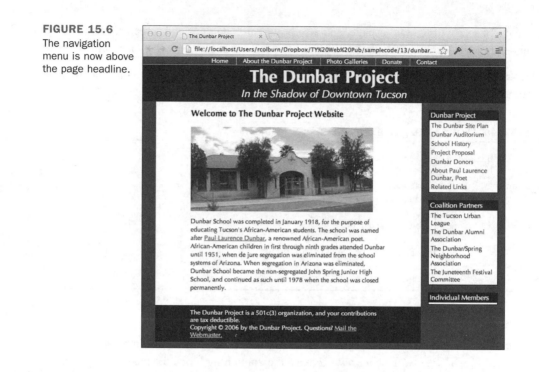

Exercise 15.1: Redesign the Layout of a Page

You just learned how to move the site navigation menu around. What if you want to make further changes to the page? Try these steps to get familiar with how easy it is to change the layout with CSS:

1. Download a copy of the source code for editing. The file `dunbar.html` contains the complete HTML page, and `dunbar-full.css` has all the style rules listed in this chapter combined into a single style sheet.

2. Move the sidebar to the left side of the page instead of the right. To do this, you need to make space for it in the left gutter by changing the padding rule on the `#main` section to

   `#main { padding: 0 2em 2em 12em; }`

3. Then change the positioning offset properties on the `#sidebar`. You don't even have to change the rule for the `top` property; just replace the property name `right` with `left`.

4. Reload the page. You should now see the menu bar on the left side of the screen.

5. Next, move the `footer` section. Even though it is semantically the footer, there's nothing magical about that name that means it needs to be at the bottom of the page. Place it on the right side, where the sidebar used to be located. First clear some space:

```
#main { padding: 0 12em 2em 12em; }
```

6. Then reposition the footer with these rules:

```
footer { position: absolute;
         top: 1em; right: 1em;
         width: 10em;
         padding: 0; }
footer p { padding: 0.5em; }
```

7. Reload the page. The `footer` is now no longer a footer, but a third column on the right side of the page.

The Floated Columns Layout Technique

You can also lay out a web page by using the `float` property rather than positioning properties. This method is a little bit more complex but is favored by some designers who prefer the versatility. In addition, floated columns deal better with side columns that are shorter than the main text in some cases.

Listing 15.5 is a style sheet demonstrating how you can float entire columns on a page with CSS. This is a replacement for the `dunbar-layout-15.2.css` style sheet in Listing 15.2. The new style sheet places the menu bar on the left instead of the right, just for variety's sake; there's nothing inherently left-biased about floated columns (or right-biased about positioning).

LISTING 15.5 Float-Based Layouts in CSS

```
/* dunbar-float-15.5.css */

body        { margin: 0; padding: 0; }
#sitenav ol { padding: 0; margin: 0;
              display: inline; }
#sitenav li { display: inline; padding-left: 1em;
              margin-left: 1em; border-left: 1px
              solid black; }
#sitenav li:first-child
            { padding-left: 0; border-left: none;
              margin-left: 0; }

/* This is what positions the sidebar: */
#main       { padding: 0 2em 2em 12em; }
#content    { float: left; }
#sidebar    { float: left; width: 10em;
              position: relative;
```

```
        right: 11em; top: 1em;
        margin-left: -100%; }
#sidebar ol { margin: 0 0 1em 0; }
```

What does this style sheet do?

- The first section just duplicates the site navigation bar code from Listing 15.2 so that the entire style sheet can be replaced by this one.

- Starting at the second comment, the code for positioning the columns appears. The first rule sets the `#main` section to have a wide gutter on the left, which is where we will be placing the sidebar.

- Both the `#content` and `#sidebar` sections are set to float. This means that they line up on the left side of the `#main` section, just inside the padding.

- A width is given to the `#sidebar` of `10em`. The size was chosen because that allows 1 em of space around it, after it is placed inside the 12 em gutter set by the `padding` rule on `#main`.

- A negative margin is set on the left side of the `#sidebar`, which actually makes it overlay the `#content` section. Relative positioning is then used, via the `right` and `top` rules, to push the sidebar into the correct place in the gutter.

Figure 15.7 shows this style sheet applied to the HTML file in Listing 15.1, along with the colors and fonts style sheet in Listing 15.3 and the style sheet from Listing 15.4, which relocated the site navigation menu.

FIGURE 15.7
The sidebar is positioned as floating content.

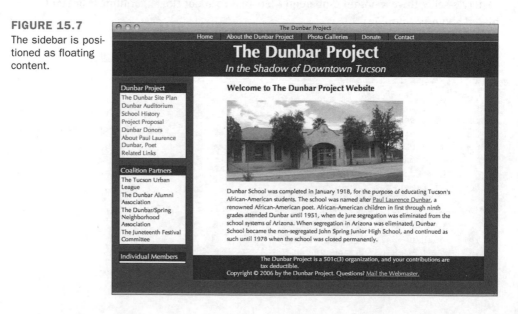

The Role of CSS in Web Design

As a web developer, skilled in HTML, CSS, and possibly other web languages and technologies, you have a web development process. Even if you haven't planned it out formally, you've got a method that works for you, whether it's as simple as sitting down and designing whatever strikes your fancy or as complex as working on a team with multiple developers, each with their own responsibilities.

Adding CSS to your repertoire has made you an even better web developer than before; your skill set has expanded, and the types of designs you can create are nearly limitless. The next step is to integrate your CSS skills into your web development process. I'm not going to tell you exactly how you'll do that—people have their own methods—but I'll help you think about how you can go about using CSS in your web designs.

In a few cases, you might be able to develop your style sheets completely separately from your HTML pages. More commonly, you'll use an iterative process, in which you make changes to the style sheet, then changes to the HTML page, and then go back to the style sheet for a few more tweaks until you're satisfied with the results. The adaptive nature of style sheets makes it easy to create these kinds of changes, and you may find yourself continuing to perfect your styles even after you post your content on the Web.

NOTE

You might not be starting with a blank slate and an uncreated website when you begin using CSS. Redesigns are common in web development, and you may want to take advantage of a new site design to convert to a CSS-based presentation. It can sometimes be harder, but it's certainly possible to keep the same look and feel of your site when converting it to use CSS. If you're using a content management system (CMS) that automatically generates your website from a database, converting to style sheets may be a snap. CSS is very compatible, on a conceptual level, with the idea of templates as used by content management systems.

As mentioned at the start of this lesson, CSS design involves balancing a number of factors to arrive at the best compromise for your site and its users. Questions will arise as you work with CSS on any site, and you'll need to answer them before you go on. Here are several of these key questions to help you plan your site:

- **Which browsers will you support?** By "support," I mean investing the effort to work around the quirks of certain older browsers. There are a number of workarounds for these temperamental browsers, plus ways to exclude certain browsers from viewing styles. But if you are designing just for CSS-enabled browsers, such as recent Chrome, Firefox, Safari, or Opera versions, those workarounds become less important. Even the latest versions of Internet Explorer have good support for HTML5 and CSS3.

- **Are you using positioning CSS for layout?** It's relatively easy to use CSS for formatting text, controlling fonts, and setting colors. Using it for layout is trickier, especially with inconsistent browser support among some of the older versions.

- **Will you use embedded or linked style sheets?** Here, I'll give you advice: Use linked style sheets whenever you can. Some of the examples in this book may use embedded style sheets, but that's mainly because it's easier to give you one listing than two.

The preceding list isn't exhaustive; you'll encounter more choices to make when designing and using CSS, but you should have learned enough by now to answer them.

Style Sheet Organization

The way you organize your style sheet can affect how easy it is for you to use and maintain your CSS, even if the effects are not evident in the presentation. This becomes even more critical if you're in a situation whereby someone else may have to use your styles in the future. You may work with an organization in which multiple people will be working on the same site, or perhaps when you move on to another job your successor will inherit your style sheets.

To make a great style sheet, be organized and clear in what you're doing, and above all, use comments. Web developers often overlook comments in CSS, but if you have to come back later and try to figure out why you did something, they're invaluable. Comments can also be used to group related styles into sections.

A comment in CSS is written /*, then the text of your comment, and then */ to close it. You can enclose entire blocks of CSS inside a comment if you want to prevent it from being used.

Reasonable names for `class` and `id` attributes can make your style sheet easier to read; choose names for these important selectors that reflect the functions of the elements. If you can, avoid selectors based solely on appearance characteristics, such as the `boldtext` or `redbox` classes. Instead, try something descriptive of why you've chosen those styles, such as `definition` or `sidebar`. That way, if you change your page styles later, you won't have to rewrite your HTML. There are few things as confusing as a rule, like the following:

```
.redbox { color: blue; background-color: white; }
```

In what way is that box red? Well, it probably was red in some prior incarnation of the style rules, but not now.

When you list your rules in your style sheet, do them in a sensible order. Generally speaking, it's best to start with the body rules first and then proceed down from there, but because the cascade order matters only in case of conflict, it's not strictly necessary to mirror the page hierarchy. What's more important is that you are able to locate the rules that apply to a given selector and to discern which styles should be applied.

An example of bad style sheet organization is shown in Listing 15.6. This is part of the style sheet from a high-quality website but with the rules in a scrambled order. How hard is it for you to figure out what is going on here?

LISTING 15.6 A Randomly Organized Style Sheet

```
#sidebar0 .section, #sidebar1 .section { font-size: smaller;
border: 0px solid lime; text-transform: lowercase;
margin-bottom: 1em; }
gnav a:link, #nav a:visited, #footer a:link, #footer
a:visited { text-decoration: none; color: #CCCCCC; }
#nav .section, #nav .shead, #nav .sitem, #nav h1 { display:
inline; }
#sidebar1 { position: absolute; right: 2em; top: 3em;
width: 9em; } a:link { color: #DD8800; text-decoration: none; }
#main { } a:hover { color: lime; }
#nav .shead, #nav .sitem { padding-left: 1em; padding-right:
1em; }
#nav { position: fixed; top: 0px; left: 0px; padding-top:
3px; padding-bottom: 3px; background-color: #333333; color:
white; width: 100%; text-align: center; text-transform:
lowercase; }
#nav .section { font-size: 90%; } #layout { padding: 1em; }
body { background-color: white; color: #333333; font-family:
Verdana, sans-serif; margin: 0; padding: 0; }
#nav h1 { font-size: 1em; background-color: #333333; color:
white; } a:visited { color: #CC8866; text-decoration: none; }
#nav { border-bottom: 1px solid lime; } #main { margin-left:
11.5em; margin-right: 11.5em; border: 0px solid lime;
margin-bottom: 1.5em; margin-top: 1.5em; }
#nav a:hover, #footer a:hover { color: lime; }
#sidebar0 { position: absolute; left: 2em; top: 3em;
width: 9em; text-align: right; }
```

If that was hard to follow, don't feel bad; the difficulty was intentional. CSS rules are easily obfuscated if you're not careful. Most style sheets grow organically as piecemeal additions are made; discipline is necessary to keep the style sheet readable.

The style sheet in Listing 15.7 is really the same style sheet as in Listing 15.6. Both are valid style sheets, and both produce the same results when applied to the web page, but the second one is easier to understand. Comments make clearer what each section of the style sheet does, indentation and whitespace are used effectively, and the order is much easier to follow.

LISTING 15.7   A Better-Organized Style Sheet

```
/* default styles for the page */
body       { background-color: white;
             color: #333333;
             font-family: Verdana, sans-serif;
             margin: 0;
             padding: 0; }

a:link    { color: #DD8800; text-decoration: none; }
a:visited { color: #CC8866; text-decoration: none; }
a:hover   { color: lime; }

/* layout superstructure */
#layout  { padding: 1em; }

/* top navigation bar */
#nav      { position: fixed;
            top: 0px;          left: 0px;
            color: white;      width: 100%;
            padding-top: 3px;  padding-bottom: 3px;
            background-color: #333333;
            text-align: center;
            text-transform: lowercase; }
            border-bottom: 1px solid lime; }
#nav .section, #nav .shead, #nav .sitem, #nav h1
          { display: inline; }
#nav .section
          { font-size: 90%; }
#nav .shead, #nav .sitem
          { padding-left: 1em; padding-right: 1em; }
#nav h1   { font-size: 1em;
            background-color: #333333; color: white; }
#nav a:hover, #footer a:hover
          { color: lime; }
#nav a:link, #nav a:visited,
#footer a:link, #footer a:visited
          { text-decoration: none; color: #CCCCCC; }

/* main content section */
#main     { margin-left: 11.5em;   margin-right: 11.5em;
            margin-bottom: 1.5em;  margin-top: 1.5em;
            border: 0px solid lime; }
```

```
/* two sidebars, absolutely positioned */
#sidebar1 { position: absolute;
            right: 2em; top: 3em; width: 9em; }
#sidebar0 { position: absolute;
            left: 2em; top: 3em; width: 9em;
            text-align: right; }
#sidebar0 .section, #sidebar1 .section
          { font-size: smaller;
            border: 0px solid lime;
            text-transform: lowercase;
            margin-bottom: 1em; }
```

15

Site-Wide Style Sheets

The style sheet given in Listing 15.7 was created to be used on the entire site, not just on one page. Linking to an external style sheet is an easy way for you to apply style sheets over your entire set. You just use the `<link>` tag on every page, with the `href` attribute set to the location of your site-wide style sheet.

A site-wide style sheet can be used to enforce a consistent appearance on the website, even if you have multiple web developers working on different parts of the same site. Additional styles can be added in embedded style sheets or in additional linked CSS files that are created for each department or business unit. For example, each department at a school may use the school's global style sheet for design elements common to the entire site, and individual departmental style sheets for that department's unique color, layout, and font choices.

Summary

Tables have long been used in web design to lay out a web page. However, this use of `<table>` markup introduces a plethora of complications, from accessibility concerns to complexity problems. Using CSS for layout can clean up your HTML code and produce flexible designs that can be updated easily to new styles.

Laying out a page with CSS starts with adding sections to the HTML, using HTML5 sectioning elements. These are then arranged in vertical columns, through the use of either positioning rules or the `float` property. With CSS layouts, it's not difficult to reorder and reshape the page simply by changing the style sheet.

Workshop

The workshop contains a Q&A section, quiz questions, and activities to help reinforce what you've learned in this lesson. If you get stuck, the answers to the quiz can be found after the questions.

Q&A

Q Is it ever okay to use tables for layout?

A CSS layouts generally are more efficient and versatile than `<table>`-based code, but if you are careful to test your layout tables in a browser such as Lynx to make sure that the site is usable without tables and you always use the `role=presentation` attribute, you can probably get away with it. Tables aren't awful for laying out a page, and CSS can be tricky when you're dealing with grid-based designs. In general, though, you're better off using CSS whenever you can.

Q Which are better measurements for layouts, pixels or percentages?

A Some web designers, especially those from a print background or who have picky clients to please, swear by pixels. With some patience, you can get close to pixel-perfect designs in CSS. Other designers like percentage measurements, which scale with the size of the text window. There's no clear-cut advantage to any approach, however; all have their pros and cons. You can experiment with a variety of measurement types, and don't be afraid to mix and match them sensibly on your site—for example, designating column widths in percentages but also setting pixel-based `min-width` and `max-width` values.

Q Are there problems with using ems for layout?

A Only if you're not careful. The biggest problems result from setting margins, padding, or positioning properties based on em values and then changing the font size of those values. For example, you might overlook the effects of the `font-size` rule buried in these declarations:

```
#sidebar { right: 1em; top: 1em;
           text-align: right; color: white;
           font-family: Verdana, sans-serif;
           font-size: 50%; }
```

This won't actually be located 1 em in each direction from the corner of its containing block; it will be 0.5 em from the right and 0.5 em from the top. If you are going to change the font size within a section that uses ems for dimensions or placement, set the `font-size` rules on the contents of the box, as done in this chapter's style sheets with `#sidebar h3 { ... }` and `#sidebar ol { ... }` rules. You could also add an extra `<div>` inside the sidebar and set the `font-size` rule on that `<div>`.

Quiz

1. Which property tells the text to start flowing normally again, after a floated column?
2. How do you designate the containing block for an absolutely positioned element?
3. What kind of rules would you write to change an ordered list of navigation links into a horizontal navigation bar?

15

Quiz Answers

1. The `clear` property can be used after floated columns—for example, if you want a footer to reach across the entire browser window below the floated columns.
2. You set the containing block by changing the `position` property, usually to a value of `relative` (with no offset properties designated).
3. Listing 15.7 has an example of a style sheet with rules to do that, using the `display` property.

Exercises

1. What kind of layouts can you create with CSS? Choose your favorite sites—either your own or some you enjoy using—and duplicate their layout styles with CSS. Existing sites make good models for doing your own practice, but keep in mind that unless you get permission, you shouldn't just steal someone else's code. Start with the visual appearance as you see it on the screen, and draw out boxes on paper as guidelines showing you where various columns are located. Use that as your model to write the HTML and CSS for building a similar layout.
2. Try both of the techniques described in this lesson—using absolutely positioned content and using floating columns. Start with one version and convert it over to the other. Find a style of page that looks right to you and the CSS code that you think is easiest to understand, apply, and modify consistently.

LESSON 16
Using Responsive Web Design

Responsive web design, or RWD, is a way of thinking about web pages that assumes that every person, every browser, every device that views the page is different, and yet they should all get access to the same content. This is a step away from how web pages were built in the past, when web designers often expected their users to use the same browser, operating system, and sometimes even monitor to view the page.

In this lesson, you will take the HTML and CSS you've studied in earlier lessons and learn how to use that to make your sites change depending on what type of device or browser is viewing it. You will learn the following:

- How theories of web design like Mobile First work with RWD

- How to plan a responsive website

- How to build media queries

- Tips for making elements like images, videos, and tables responsive

- Best practices for designing a responsive site

What Is Responsive Web Design?

RWD is an approach to web design that attempts to adapt a site's design to look as good as possible on whatever device is displaying it. The ultimate goal of a responsive site is that it has one codebase of HTML, CSS, and JavaScript that can then be displayed on any device that wants to view it. This means that the same HTML document could be viewed on a small cell phone and then a large 5K monitor, and while it might not look identical, it would be functional in both places.

History of Responsive Web Design

In the 1990s, when web pages were first starting to be built, programmers built them rather than designers. Those builders cared a lot less about how the pages looked and more about whether they displayed at all. This may be dating myself, but I remember when images first got added to web pages. Everyone in my office gathered around the desk of a co-worker who had just found this wonderful browser, NCSA Mosaic, that could display images. Up until that point, we'd been using Lynx, which was a text-only web browser. Along with images came color, and along with those features came designers and their desire to change how a site looks.

Then CSS came around giving designers more and more control over the pages. At first there was a lot of difference in how a page looked when it came to different browsers. And the smartphone was still a few years off. So it was more convenient to write a web page that looked great in the browser that you preferred (or your boss preferred) and just tell others to go download that one. More progressive designers would attempt to write hacks to make their pages look the same on different browsers. But that was difficult too, as there were a lot of browsers.

But once mobile devices grew in popularity, that became more and more difficult. Netscape Navigator might be available for Windows and Macintosh, but it wouldn't run on cell phones. And while cell phones quickly gave rise to smartphones and tablets, by that time there were so many different devices and browsers that it was impossible to design for every possible combination, and you couldn't tell people what browser to get because it probably wouldn't run on their phone anyway.

The other thing that was different with smartphone and tablet devices was that they were not as big as the desktop computers that most designers worked on. A page that would look great on a browser maximized on a 5K screen would be completely unusable on a small phone screen. Ethan Marcotte coined the term *responsive web design* as a way to design pages and sites that responded to the device viewing it and changed to meet the needs of that device.

Why RWD Is Important

RWD is important because the number of browsers and devices capable of viewing web pages is only growing. And every time a new device joins the market it adds new features to support and often changes the way it supports existing features. A designer of a cooking website might have his pages shown in a 5K monitor at one house and a touchpad screen on a refrigerator at another. And the smart designer wants the pages to work well in both places.

RWD Is More Than Just Changing the Number of Columns

16

It's very common to see people dismiss RWD as a form of layout adjustment. And often the most striking changes to a design come from how the pages are presented on a desktop screen versus a mobile screen. But good RWD does more than that. Good RWD includes the following:

- Adjusting the content to put the important things first for each device
- Recognizing what the critical content is for a page, and making sure that everyone who visits can see and access it
- Providing alternatives for elements that don't work on smaller screens
- Keeping bandwidth costs in mind when designing a page
- Using technology that is appropriate and providing fallback options for critical features

Mobile Devices Should Come First

As I mentioned previously, it used to be very common for web designers to use the most modern, up-to-date browsers on huge monitors. Their web pages would look amazing at 5120 pixels wide on the latest nightly of Chromium, but anyone viewing on a smaller screen or with an older browser was out of luck. But what these designers forgot is that they are not their customers. When I bought my first 4K monitor, my mother was still browsing the Web on a 12-inch screen. Her monitor was about the same size or a little smaller than my tablet! And before you dismiss my mother as a Luddite, as of January 2015 over 50% of visitors to W3Schools had a resolution of 1366×768 or lower (see http://www.w3schools.com/browsers/browsers_display.asp).

But resolution is only part of the picture. More and more people are moving to tablet and mobile phones. In fact, in 2015 Google began penalizing sites that were not mobile friendly. That means that in order to get decent placement in one of the largest search engines in the world, your site needs to work on mobile devices.

Mobile First

Instead of focusing on the desktop and how your website looks on your personal browser, you should start by building a website that looks amazing on a mobile device. When you design first for mobile devices, you have to focus on what the content is for the site. Phones are small and don't have a lot of room for extraneous bells and whistles. Instead, you need to develop a laser focus determining what content the customers really need and what is only nice to have. Mobile first websites make sure that everyone can see the critical content.

I'll go into more details about what makes a site mobile friendly in Lesson 21, "Designing for the Mobile Web," but there are a few things you should remember:

- **Limit your designs to one column.** Feature phones can only effectively view one column, and even smartphones work better if the layout is simple.

- **Limit the navigation choices.** This doesn't mean you limit your mobile site—the best sites let their customers get to any of the content. But the navigation should be simple. What are the three or four most important (to mobile customers, at least) pages? Those are the ones that should be in your navigation.

- **Limit the file size.** Mobile phones can download quickly, but even on the most advanced mobile networks, a page that takes too long to download is a page no one will visit. But more importantly, many mobile users have data limits that can result in large charges if they go over. No one wants to visit a site if they think it will cost them a lot of money.

- **Limit URL lengths while making links longer.** Typing in a long URL on a phone is difficult, and so is tapping on a tiny link. People don't do things that are difficult.

- **Limit your use of frames, Flash, and tables.** Frames are not valid in HTML5 (except, of course, inline frames), and they don't work well on smaller screens. Flash isn't supported on most mobile operating systems. And tables are hard to read on most small screens; some mobile phones won't display them at all.

- **Do not limit your testing.** The one thing you should not limit is your testing. Test on actual devices, if you can, not just emulators. And test on as many devices as you can.

Affecting the Viewport

The first thing you should do to your web pages to help them look better on mobile devices is to set viewport settings. The viewport is the rectangular shape that web browsers display in. On mobile phones and tablets the viewport is typically the full screen of the device. On a desktop the viewport is the width and height of the browser window.

It's important to understand the viewport because mobile devices display web content differently depending upon how the viewport is configured. But as a web designer you can affect how you want mobile browsers to render your pages. As you can see in Figure 16.1, if you don't configure the viewport, your page can look very different, even for a very simple page.

16

FIGURE 16.1
The same page on an iPhone 6 displayed with (right) and without (left) the viewport configured.

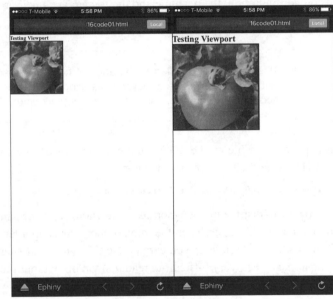

Here is the HTML for the page without the viewport configured:

```
<!doctype html>
<html>
<head>
<meta charset="UTF-8">
<title>Testing Viewport</title>
<style>
html, body, * { margin: 0; }
body { width: 600px; }
```

```
</style>
</head>
<body>
<h1>Testing Viewport</h1>
<img src="16pic01.png">
</body>
</html>
```

There is just a style sheet to remove the margins and set the width of the page to 600px. Then I've got a headline and a picture. If you were to preview this page in your web browser, both the headline and the image would be fairly big. The image is 320 pixels wide. The iPhone has an approximate width of 375 pixels, but it is a Retina display, so it displays at double that resolution, or around 750 pixels wide. When you view the page without viewport configuration, the headline and the tomato are small and don't fill the screen.

NOTE

This is a very simplified explanation of how Retina screens work. But explaining Retina is beyond the scope of this book. For more accurate information, check out the Apple website.

To make this page more usable on the iPhone and other mobile devices, you just need to add one line of HTML to the head of your document:

```
<meta name="viewport" content="width=device-width">
```

This tells the browser to display the viewport as if the width were the same as the actual device width, or around 375 pixels. Then the tomato photo takes up a larger chunk of the window and the headline is legible. If you extrapolate this out to full sites, you can see where a site might have been very difficult to read and tap on without the viewport meta tag.

Previously in this lesson, I mentioned that Google penalizes sites that aren't mobile friendly. But just adding this one line can get your site back into the search engine giant's good graces.

Here's the full HTML:

Input ▼

```
<!doctype html>
<html>
<head>
<meta charset="UTF-8">
```

```
<meta name="viewport" content="width=device-width">
<title>Testing Viewport</title>
<style>
html, body, * { margin: 0; }
body { width: 600px; }
</style>
</head>
<body>
<h1>Testing Viewport</h1>
<img src="16pic01.png">
</body>
</html>
```

16

Planning a Responsive Website

Planning how you're going to make your website responsive is an important first step before you jump right in and start writing HTML and CSS. By planning what you need to do you can avoid problems later.

Check Your Analytics

First you should check your website analytics. If your site is brand new, this will be difficult or impossible, but if it's been live for even a few weeks you can get a sense of what types of people are currently visiting your website.

Don't assume that your site must be responsive. Sometimes just adding the viewport tag listed previously is enough to support your mobile customers. But you won't know how many mobile customers you have until you look at your stats. You'll learn more about site analytics in Lesson 23, "How to Publish Your Site."

Try the Site with Your Own Phone

If you have a low number of mobile viewers to your site, you might think that you don't need to make your site responsive. But if your site doesn't work well on a mobile device, then mobile customers won't stick around and won't come back. So the second step you should do when planning is find a smartphone or other mobile device and go visit your website. How does it look? Is it easy to use? Can you tap on the links and the navigation? If you can, talk to some of your customers and get their thoughts on how your site works on their mobile devices.

Decide What Content Is Critical

Once you know how important mobile users are to your site and how your site looks on mobile devices, think about the content your site has. Is there content that is going to be more useful for mobile customers than for desktop customers? For example, a restaurant website will want to show mobile customers their address right away, as someone browsing on his phone is probably looking for a place to eat lunch.

But remember that mobile customers are the same people whether they are on their phone or their laptop. If you have your menu on your website for computer browsers, it should be available for mobile browsers as well. You don't want to limit your customers; you just want to make what they typically want to do as easy as possible.

Writing Media Queries

Media queries are what most people think of when they think of RWD. A CSS media query is a logical expression that is either true or false. If the expression evaluates as true, the browser should use that CSS, and if it evaluates as false, it should not. They are called media queries because they originally checked the media type of the device viewing the page. Media types were introduced in CSS2, and they were used to check whether a device was a screen or if it was print, among other things. CSS3 introduced media queries, and they got more sophisticated allowing designers to check things like device width, aspect ratio, resolution and even if a screen was a Retina display or not.

Media Types

There are 10 media types you can test for with CSS media queries:

- `all`—All media
- `braille`—Braille and tactile feedback devices
- `embossed`—Paged Braille printers
- `handheld`—Small-screen, low-bandwidth handheld devices
- `print`—Paged media and documents in print preview mode
- `projection`—Projected presentations
- `screen`—Color computer screens
- `speech`—Speech synthesizers
- `tty`—Teletypes and media with a fixed-pitch character grid
- `tv`—Television

You can set the media type with the `media` attribute on the `<style>` tag:

```
<style media="print">
```

You can also add it to the `<link>` tag when you link an external style sheet:

```
<link href="styles.css" media="screen">
```

You can add media query expressions to existing style sheets with the `@media` attribute:

```
@media all { ... }
```

Media Features

Media features are what make media queries interesting. There are 13 media features you can test for:

- `aspect-ratio`—A ratio of the width of the device to the height.
- `color`—The number of bits per color component.
- `color-index`—The number of colors in the device's color input title.
- `device-aspect-ratio`—The ratio of the device width to the device height.
- `device-height`—The height of the rendering surface.
- `device-width`—The width of the rendering surface.
- `grid`—If the device is a grid (such as TTY devices or phones with only one font) or bitmap.
- `height`—The height of the display area.
- `monochrome`—The number of bits per pixel in monochrome devices. If the device isn't monochrome, the value will be 0.
- `orientation`—Whether the device is in portrait or landscape mode.
- `resolution`—The pixel density of the device; in print, this would be the dots per inch or dpi of the printer.
- `scan`—The scanning process of TV output devices; for example, progressive scanning.
- `width`—The width of the display area.

Along with these features, there are two prefixes you can add to them: `min-` and `max-`. For example, to set a style sheet for all devices with at least a width of 320 pixels:

```
@media (min-width: 320px) { ... }
```

And to style devices that are narrower than 1024 pixels:

```
@media (max-width: 1024px) { ... }
```

16

You can combine them with the keyword and. For example, to add styles to any browser that is wider than 320 pixels and narrower than 1024 pixels:

```
@media (min-width: 320px and max-width: 1024px) { ... }
```

Breakpoints

A CSS breakpoint is a media query to separate the style sheet into two parts: the part outside the query and the part inside. Breakpoints are typically based on the browser's width, but they don't have to be. You can set them to any media feature or combination you would like. The thing to remember is that for every breakpoint there will be one additional design. In other words, one breakpoint equals two designs, two breakpoints equals three designs, and so on.

Here is the HTML and CSS to make a page with two breakpoints. As you can see, there are two media queries, so there will be three possible designs:

Input ▼

```
<!doctype html>
<html>
<head>
<meta charset="UTF-8">
<title>Two Breakpoints</title>
<style>
body {
  color: blue;
  font-family: "Handwriting - Dakota", "Lucida Calligraphy Italic", Papyrus;
}
@media all and (min-width:480px) and (max-width:800px){
  body { color: red; }
}
@media screen and (min-width:801px){
  body { color: green; }
}
</style>
</head>

<body>
<p>Lorem ipsum dolor sit amet, consectetur adipiscing elit. Etiam id purus nec
eros semper luctus. Proin nisl lectus, ullamcorper ultrices leo in, tristique
rutrum risus. Morbi congue diam tempor lorem semper, congue tempor turpis
pretium. Nunc eget dui ut lorem auctor ornare. Vivamus lectus purus, vehicula eu
velit eu, iaculis ultrices dui. Aliquam consectetur risus non ligula blandit, et
gravida lectus bibendum. Etiam laoreet luctus nibh. Nulla sit amet lorem quis
arcu accumsan mollis.</p>

</body>
</html>
```

Figure 16.2 shows how the colors change depending upon how wide the screen is.

Output ▼

FIGURE 16.2
The same page previewed in Dreamweaver at 320×480 and 768×1024.

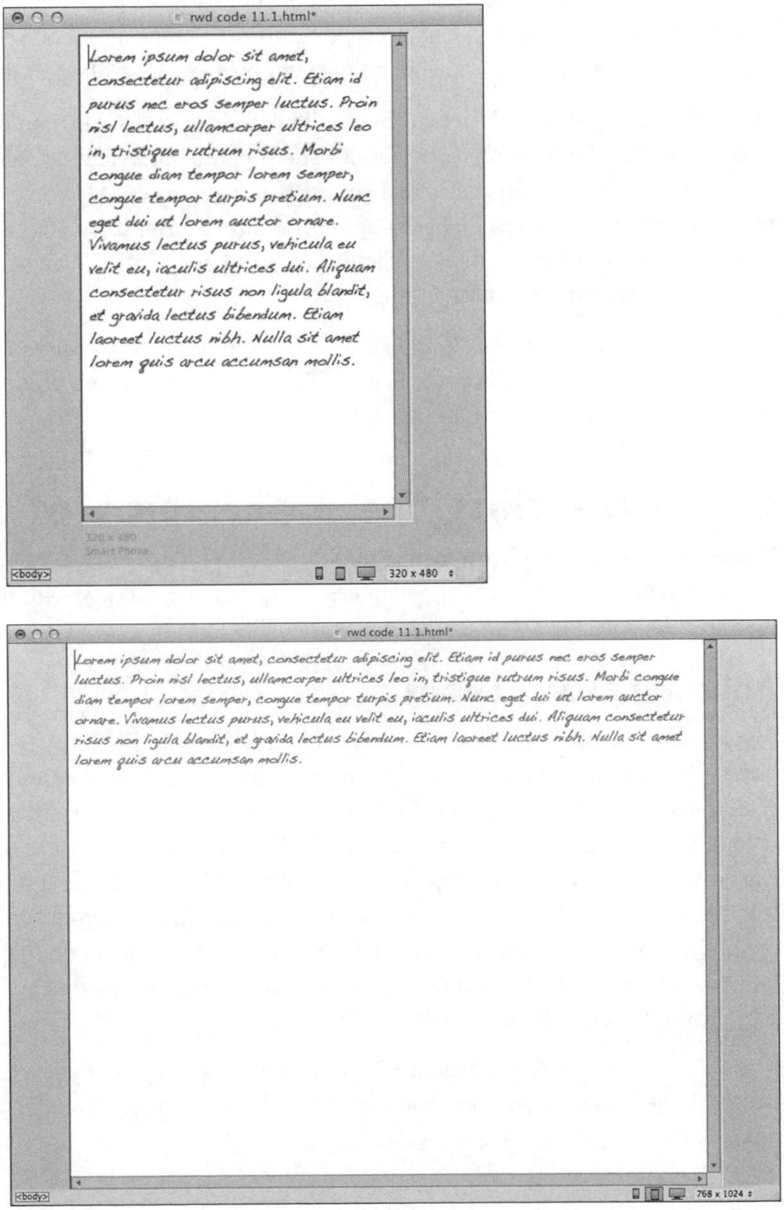

16

Building a Style Sheet with Media Queries

As mentioned previously, you should start by designing for mobile devices first. And the easiest way to do that is to start writing your style sheet for mobile devices without media queries. This will be the basic design for your site, so you should stick to one column and add all the colors, typography, and iconography you want everyone to see. Because this is not inside a query, it will be applied to every browser regardless of the specifications.

Once you have your site designed for mobile devices, you should start adding your media queries to affect larger screen devices. Most designers immediately want to know what widths they should set for their breakpoints. Is it better to use 800px to target smartphones, or should you aim higher to design for tablets? But this is the wrong question. Instead of asking what widths you should set to target specific devices, you should ask at what widths your design starts falling apart.

For instance, with a single column design, there comes a point where it gets too wide for the text to be readable. How wide is that? That is the point where you might set a breakpoint and divide your page into two columns.

Understanding the Mechanics of RWD

When you start working with media queries and RWD, there are a lot of things you can adjust. Whatever you can change with CSS, you can also modify with media queries and CSS inside them.

Adjusting the Layout

The layout is the most common adjustment you'll see with RWD. A typical two-breakpoint design might have one column for small screens, two columns for medium-sized screens, and three columns for large screens. There are many ways to do web layout. But the three most common types are fixed width layout, fluid or liquid layout, elastic layout, and hybrid layouts that use aspects of fixed and liquid or elastic layouts. It is possible to create a responsive design using any of these layout types. So choose the method you prefer. Lesson 11, "Using CSS to Position Elements on the Page" covered how to do basic positioning, and then you learned more advanced page layout in Lesson 15, "Advanced CSS: Page Layout in CSS."

I've found that it's best to create a wireframe or mockup of how you want the site to look two or three device sizes. Then you can use CSS media queries to adjust your layout to match those.

One fun way to create columns of your page is to use the new CSS3 columns properties. There are 13 new properties in CSS3 to help you create columns:

- `column-width`—Defines the width of each column
- `column-count`—Defines the number of columns
- `columns`—A shorthand property to define the column width and count
- `column-gap`—Defines the length of the gap between columns
- `column-rule-color`—Defines the color of the line between columns
- `column-rule-style`—Defines the style (like solid, dashed, or dotted) of the line between the columns
- `column-rule-width`—Defines the width of the line between columns
- `column-rule`—A shorthand property to define the width, style, and color of the line between columns
- `break-before`, `break-after`, and `break-inside`—All define the page or column break behavior before, after or inside the box
- `column-span`—Defines how many columns the element should span across
- `column-fill`—Defines how to fill the columns either balanced between the columns (balance) or filled sequentially (auto)

In the previous lesson, we modified the Dunbar Project website to have multiple columns. But what if I want small devices to have one column and then larger devices have the content show in newspaper style columns? That is easy if you start with the HTML I showed you back in Lesson 15:

Input ▼

```
<!doctype html>
<html>
  <head>
    <meta charset="utf-8">
    <title>The Dunbar Project</title>
    <meta name="viewport" content="width=device-width">
  </head>
  <body>
    <header>
      <h1>The Dunbar Project</h1>
      <h2>In the Shadow of Downtown Tucson</h2>
      <nav id="sitenav">
        <ol><li><a href="index.html">Home</a></li>
            <li><a href="about/">About the Dunbar Project</a></li>
            <li><a href="gallery/">Photo Galleries</a></li>
```

16

```
            <li><a href="donate/">Donate</a></li>
            <li><a href="contact/">Contact</a></li></ol>
      </nav> <!-- sitenav -->
    </header> <!-- header -->
    <div id="main">
      <article id="content">
        <h3>Welcome to The Dunbar Project Website</h3>
        <p>Dunbar School was completed in January 1918, for the
           purpose of educating Tucson's African-American students.
           The school was named after <a href="poet.html">Paul
           Laurence Dunbar</a>, a renowned African-American poet.
           African-American children in first through ninth grades
           attended Dunbar until 1951, when de jure segregation was
           eliminated from the school systems of Arizona.  When
           segregation in Arizona was eliminated, Dunbar School
           became the non-segregated John Spring Junior High School,
           and continued as such until 1978 when the school was
           closed permanently.</p>
        <!-- ... more content omitted ... -->
      </article> <!-- content -->
      <aside id="sidebar">
        <h3>Dunbar Project</h3>
        <ol><li><a href="plan/">The Dunbar Site Plan</a></li>
            <li><a href="auditorium/">Dunbar Auditorium</a></li>
            <li><a href="history/">School History</a></li>
            <li><a href="proposal/">Project Proposal</a></li>
            <li><a href="donors/">Dunbar Donors</a></li>
            <li><a href="poet.html">About Paul Laurence Dunbar,
                   Poet</a></li>
            <li><a href="links/">Related Links</a></li></ol>
        <h3>Coalition Partners</h3>
        <ol><li>The Tucson Urban League</li>
            <li>The Dunbar Alumni Association</li>
            <li>The Dunbar/Spring Neighborhood Association</li>
            <li>The Juneteenth Festival Committee</li></ol>
        <h3>Individual Members</h3>
        <ol> <!-- ... list of donors omitted ... --> </ol>
      </aside> <!-- sidebar -->
    </div> <!-- main -->
    <footer>
      <p id="note501c3">The Dunbar Project is a 501c(3)
         organization, and your contributions are tax
         deductible.</p>
      <p id="copyright">Copyright &copy; 2006 by the Dunbar
         Project. Questions?
         <a href="mailto:webmaster@thedunbarproject.com"
         >Mail the Webmaster.</a></p>
    </footer> <!-- footer -->
  </body>
</html>
```

I removed the image so that we could focus on just the layout for the site. Figure 16.3 shows how this would look on a small-screen device.

Output ▼

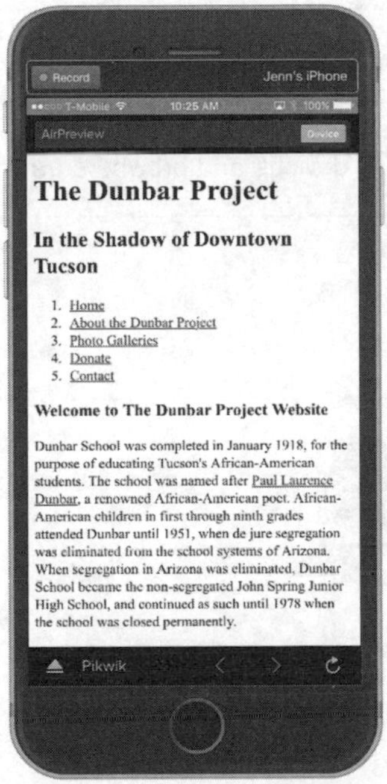

FIGURE 16.3
An iPhone showing
a single-column
layout.

16

I then will add a style sheet to the document to create the styles for larger-screen devices.

Input ▼

```
<style>
  #main {
    -moz-column-count: 2;
    -webkit-column-count: 2;
    column-count: 2;
  }
  aside {
    -webkit-column-break-before: always;
    break-before: always;
  }
</style>
```

This style sheet makes the section with the id of `main` have a column count of two. And then I set it so there is always a column break before `aside` tags. As you can see, I used browser prefixes (`-moz-column-count`, `-webkit-column-count`, and `-webkit-column-break-before`) to help browsers provide the styling I want.

CAUTION

Even if there are browser prefixes, there is no guarantee that the browsers will work with the styles. In my example, Firefox version 40 does not implement the `break-before` property. Always make sure to test in as many devices and browsers as you can.

Figure 16.4 shows how these styles affect the page.

Output ▼

FIGURE 16.4
An iPhone showing the layout with two columns.

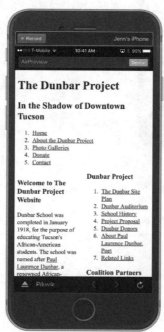

As you can see, there are now two columns, but they are very narrow and hard to read. So this is a candidate for a breakpoint. We know that having no styles looks fine on the iPhone as far as the layout goes, so our breakpoint needs to be around 400 pixels:

Input ▼

```
@media ( min-width: 400px ) {
  #main {
    -moz-column-count: 2;
    -webkit-column-count: 2;
    column-count: 2;
  }
  aside {
    -webkit-column-break-before: always;
    break-before: always;
  }
}
```

16

Figure 16.5 shows how this style sheet looks on a desktop browser.

Output ▼

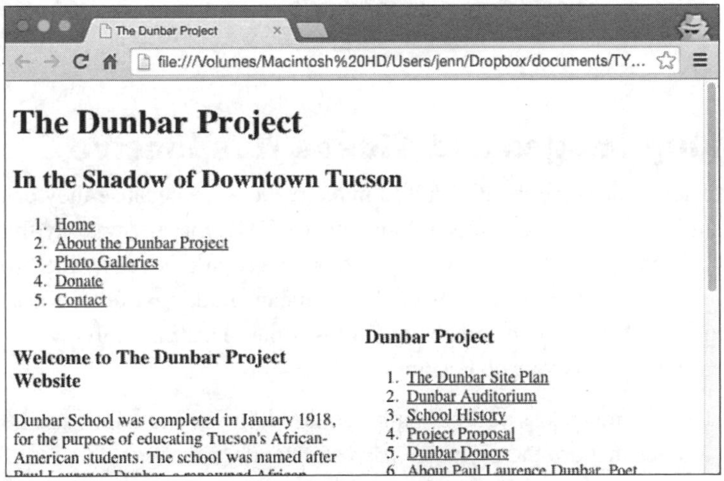

FIGURE 16.5
The layout in Chrome has two columns.

And Figure 16.6 shows how it appears on an iPhone.

Output ▼

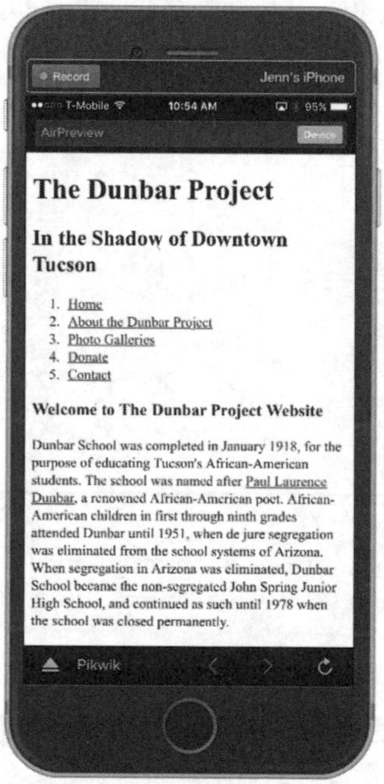

FIGURE 16.6
The layout on the iPhone has one column again.

Making Images and Videos Responsive

Images and videos can be difficult to make responsive because they can end up being huge and thus slow to download. Plus, most HTML instructions say that you should always define the height and width of your images and never let the browser resize them for you. Thus, making a responsive design means making a few choices; no matter what you choose, there will be someone who loses out. There are three ways you can deal with images in a responsive web design:

- Use the images as you normally would, defining the width and height and creating images that are the right size for your standard design.
- Set the image width to something flexible, and save the image in a large file size so that it can flex to fit large and small screens.
- Change the images that display depending upon the device that is viewing it.

With the first method, the losers are typically small screen devices because web designers usually build their pages to look good on desktop machines. So, the images are either too big to fit in the window or too big to download quickly. Either way, the website is the ultimate loser because Google frowns on images not optimized for mobile devices, and mobile users simply leave the site.

The second method is appealing because it ensures that the image will fit on both mobile and desktop machines. But if the images are too big, they take too long to download on smartphones, and if they are too small, they look awful if they are resized above their absolute limit.

The third method attempts to solve both the download size and the dimension problems. By serving different images to different devices, you can ensure that customers on mobile devices get small images that download quickly, while customers on large screen 5K monitors get gorgeous gigantic images. The problem is you need to have a web server that can run the programs required to test for devices, and you need a tool like WURFL that can be used to test against.

NOTE   WURFL stands for Wireless Universal Resource File. It is a community-based effort to do mobile device detection. You can learn more about WURFL at http://wurfl.sourceforge.net/.

Most responsive websites use the second method, but if you have to have really large images, you can use the third.

Making the images flexible is a great method for most RWD websites because it's almost as easy as doing nothing at all. But your images will flex to fit the width of the browser or the width of the container. All you need to do in your style sheet is set the `width` to 100%, the `height` to auto, and the `max-width` to the absolute width of your images. For example, you might have a large picture of a dog that is 1920×1142 pixels in dimensions. If you put that straight into your web page, it would be way too wide for nearly any mobile browser. But if you view it in a window that is wider than 2000 pixels, the image will start to distort and look bad. You don't want it to resize to larger than 1920, so that's what you set the maximum width to be. Here is the HTML I used:

Input ▼

```
<!doctype html>
<html>
  <head>
    <meta charset="UTF-8">
    <meta name="viewport" content="width=device-width">
```

```
    <title>Flexible Width Images</title>
    <style>
img {
  width: 100%;
  height: auto;
  max-width: 1920px;
}
    </style>
  </head>

  <body>
    <article>
      <h1>Flexible Width Images</h1>
      <figure>
        <img src="swiss-shepherd-dog-354536_1920.jpg" alt="Swiss Shepherd Dog">
        <figcaption> Image courtesy Pixabay</figcaption>
      </figure>
    </article>
  </body>
</html>
```

And as you can see in Figure 16.7, it fills up the screen on an iPhone in landscape mode.

Output ▼

FIGURE 16.7
The image fills up the screen on an iPhone.

In many ways, making videos responsive is even easier than images. This is because the HTML5 `video` tag allows you to embed multiple source files. Absent any other information, the browser will use the source file that is best for it. But media queries let you provide even more information. Here is the HTML for adding a video:

```
<video controls>
  <source src="video.mp4">
</video>
```

The `video.mp4` file was shot at 1920×1080, and although it will look fine on some devices, it might be too big or too small for others. So, you can add in another video recorded at 720×480 for smaller screens. To display the small version on small screens, you use a media query right on the `source` tag:

```
<source src="video-small.mp4" media="(max-width:480px)">
```

Any browser that is wider than 480 pixels will automatically load and play the larger file instead of the smaller one.

Building Responsive Tables

16

Data tables are a sensitive subject for responsive web designers because they are often very big and can thus be difficult to handle on smaller screens. It can be tempting to add `display: none;` to tables and only display them on larger screen sizes (by setting the display back to table: `display: table;` inside the media queries), but that isn't an option if the table is required content.

Designers typically handle tables in RWD in three ways:

- Resize the cells.
- Rearrange the table.
- Remove or hide the content.

Resizing the cells is the easiest way to handle tables because it's the way that tables rearrange themselves by default. First you should make the main table tag 100% in width:

```
<table style="width:100%;" border="1">
```

This will help the table flex to fit various size devices. But what about tables with wide columns, like this HTML?

Input ▼

```
<!doctype html>
<html>
  <head>
    <meta charset="UTF-8">
    <meta name="viewport" content="width=device-width">
    <title>Responsive Tables</title>
    <style>

    </style>
  </head>

  <body>
    <article>
```

```
        <h1>Responsive Tables</h1>
<table style="width:100%;" border="1">
  <thead>
    <tr>
      <th>Name</th>
      <th>URL</th>
      <th>RWD?</th>
      <th>Windows</th>
      <th>Macintosh</th>
    </tr>
  </thead>
  <tbody>
    <tr>
      <td>Adobe Dreamweaver</td>
      <td>http://www.adobe.com/products/dreamweaver.html</td>
      <td>yes</td>
      <td>yes</td>
      <td>yes</td>
    </tr>
    <tr>
      <td>Macaw</td>
      <td>http://macaw.co/</td>
      <td>yes</td>
      <td>yes</td>
      <td>yes</td>
    </tr>
    <tr>
      <td>Coffee Cup Responsive Layout Maker Pro</td>
      <td>http://www.coffeecup.com/responsive-layout-maker-pro/</td>
      <td>yes</td>
      <td>yes</td>
      <td>yes</td>
    </tr>
    <tr>
      <td>Microsoft Notepad</td>
      <td>http://www.notepad.org/</td>
      <td>no</td>
      <td>yes</td>
      <td>no</td>
    </tr>
    <tr>
      <td>Tummult Hype</td>
      <td>http://tumult.com/hype/</td>
      <td>no</td>
      <td>no</td>
      <td>yes</td>
    </tr>
  </tbody>
</table>
    </article>
  </body>
</html>
```

If you view that on a smartphone, it would be too large for the screen and require horizontal scrolling. But by resizing the text inside the table, you can help it fit better. Here is the CSS I added:

```
/* styles for all devices */
table {   border-collapse: collapse;    font-size: 14px; }
/* zebra stripe the table */
table tr:nth-child(2n+1) { background-color: #dfdfdf; }
/* styles for devices larger than 650px wide */
@media screen and ( min-width:651px ) {
  table { font-size: 16px; }
}
```

Figure 16.8 shows that there is no horizontal scrollbar on an iPhone.

Output ▼

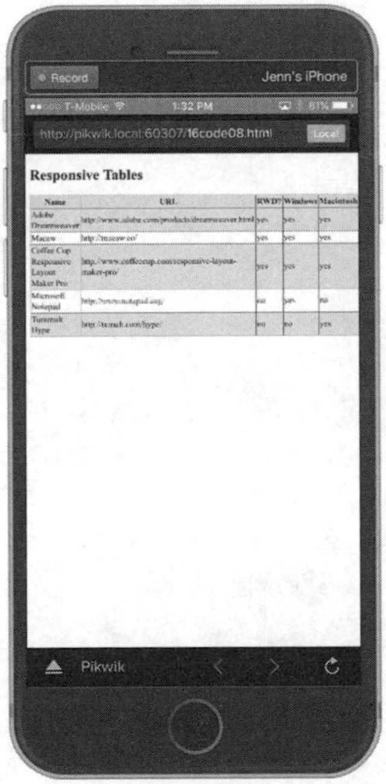

FIGURE 16.8
No horizontal
scrolling to see the
table on an iPhone.

16

While there is no horizontal scrolling, the table is very difficult to read on the iPhone without zooming. So instead of making the font size smaller, you could rearrange the table when it's displaying on a small screen. If you replace the CSS in the table with this:

Input ▼

```
/* styles for all devices */
table { border-collapse: collapse; }

/* styles for small devices */
@media (max-width:720px){
  table { border: none; }
  /* display the whole table as a block */
  table, thead, tbody, th, td, tr { display: block; }
  /* Hide the headers */
  thead tr { position: absolute; top: -9999px; left: -9999px; }
  tr { border: 1px solid #ccc; margin-bottom: 1em; }
  tr:nth-of-type(odd) { background: #eee; }
  td {
    /* Behave  like a "row" */
    border: none;
    border-bottom: 1px solid #eee;
    position: relative;
    padding-left: 20%;
  }
  td:before {
    /* Now like a table header */
    position: absolute;
    /* Top/left values mimic padding */
    top: 1px;
    left: 2px;
    width: 45%;
    padding-right: 10px;
    white-space: nowrap;
  }
  /* Label the data */
  td:nth-of-type(1):before { content: "Name "; }
  td:nth-of-type(2):before { content: "URL "; }
  td:nth-of-type(3):before { content: "RWD? " ; }
  td:nth-of-type(4):before { content: "Win "; }
  td:nth-of-type(5):before { content: "Mac "; }
}

/* styles for larger devices */
@media (min-width:721px) {
  tr:nth-child(2n+1) { background-color: #80C5F5; }
  table thead tr:nth-child(n) { background-color: #3d447e; color: #dfdfdf; }
}
```

That will make your table look better on the iPhone, as you can see in Figure 16.9.

Output ▼

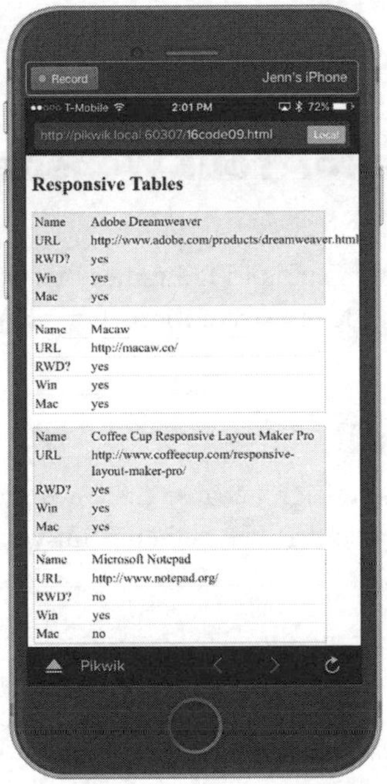

FIGURE 16.9
The format of the table changes on the iPhone.

As you can see, the first URL still scrolls off the screen, but it is much easier to read than the initial version. But if this were a problem, you could remove that column either with JavaScript or by using the `display: none;` property. But this is a bad solution because it removes content from mobile customers. It's better to work with your tables, changing either the size or the arrangement so that they best fit on the screen of mobile devices.

Responsive Web Design Best Practices

Methods of doing responsive web design are changing all the time, so it's always a good idea to read what other web developers are coming up with. But there are a few things you can do to make your site work out the best.

Give Everyone the Best Experience

Make sure that your site is as accessible and inclusive as you can make it. It's very easy, as a web designer, to get hung up on the way that you're used to viewing the Web, but there are lots of other ways. Here are some ways you can improve the experience of your site for everyone:

- Think mobile first.
- Write semantic HTML.
- Use HTML5 and CSS3.

Use the Best Breakpoints for Your Website, Not for Devices

Focus your breakpoints on where your design starts to fail rather than worrying about specific devices or widths. It's also a good idea to strive for as few breakpoints as your design can handle and not be broken.

Be Flexible But Think Small

Web design is a lot more flexible than print design because there's no way to really control how your pages will look on every device that views them. But you want to make sure of the following:

- Your layouts should fit the screen they are on.
- Images should fit the screen, too.
- Video needs to be small so that it downloads quickly.
- Compress everything that you can.
- Don't use more than two or three external resources (like web fonts).

If you keep these best practices in mind, you will create a really great, responsive website.

Summary

Responsive web design covers a lot of areas of web design, from designing for mobile devices through images and optimization and even into how your pages display on various devices.

When you're building a responsive website, first you need to plan your site so that you know what it's going to need and what the customers want. Then you can create a layout and add multiple columns to larger screen devices. Responsive images and videos flex with the width of the container but are never larger than their source file. And the best responsive designs try to stay small so that they load quickly no matter who is viewing them.

Workshop

Put on your thinking cap again because it's time for another review. These questions, quizzes, and exercises will remind you about the items that you should (or should not) include on your pages.

Q&A

Q Are there other areas I should focus on when doing RWD?

A Just about any aspect of your site can be made responsive. You can change the fonts and typography depending on the device viewing your page. You can adjust what fields show up in a form. The two places I would focus on next if you want to go further with RWD are typography and navigation. Both of these can impact your site significantly, and RWD can make them even more impressive.

Q Are there websites that focus just on mobile devices and ignore the desktop?

A Like Mobile First, there is also a Mobile Only movement. These people believe that mobile is the future and that web designers should focus on building their sites first and only for mobile (and desktop users can view it without much issue). There is a huge benefit to this type of thinking; your site will be much more likely to take advantage of some of the features like GeoLocation that are only truly useful on mobile devices.

Quiz

1. Why is RWD important?
2. What does the `column-rule` property do?
3. Why should you use responsive images?
4. What attribute can you use to make videos responsive?

Quiz Answers

1. Responsive web design, or RWD, helps designers focus on making their sites accessible and available to every device or person who visits. This is important for the site owner because he gets more pageviews. And it's important for the web community as a whole because it helps make the Web easier to use for everyone.

2. The `column-rule` property is a CSS3 property that defines the width, color, and style of lines between columns.

3. You should use responsive images so that your images flex with your designs and don't look too large on small screens or too small on large screens.

4. You can use the `media` attribute on the `source` tag to define video (and audio) source files specific to a certain media query.

Exercises

1. Come up with a mockup for two designs for your website: one for small screens that is one column wide and one for larger screens that is two or three columns wide.

2. Once you are satisfied with your mockup, build it with CSS media queries.

LESSON 17
Introducing JavaScript

JavaScript is a programming language that's used to turn web pages into applications. JavaScript is used to manipulate the contents of a web page and to allow users to interact with web pages without reloading the page.

This is the first of three lessons in a row on JavaScript. In this lesson, I explain how JavaScript works and how to use it in your pages. In the next lesson, "Using jQuery," I discuss jQuery, a library that makes it much simpler to work with JavaScript, and then in the following lesson, "JavaScript Examples," I'll walk you through some real world examples. In this lesson, you learn about the basics of JavaScript by exploring the following topics:

- What JavaScript is
- Why you would want to use JavaScript
- The `<script>` tag
- An overview of the JavaScript language
- The browser as a programming environment
- Using JavaScript to handle browser events

Why Would You Want to Use JavaScript?

JavaScript changes the browser from an application for displaying documents to a platform for writing applications. It's useful because it enables the developer to manipulate the contents of a web page after it has loaded, making it possible to provide users with instant feedback when they make a change in a form, loading resources on demand for performance reasons, or building full-blown user interfaces that resemble desktop applications.

JavaScript is useful because it's deeply integrated with the browser. This integration allows programmers to manipulate various aspects of the browser behavior, as well as objects included on the page. JavaScript uses what's referred to as an *event-driven model* of execution. When you embed JavaScript code in a web page, it isn't run until the event it's associated with is triggered.

The types of events that can call JavaScript include loading the page, leaving the page, interacting with a form element in some way, clicking a link, or even just scrolling up or down. Plenty of other events are available, too. Often these events are utilized in what most users would consider to be annoying ways. For example, many sites open an additional window containing an advertisement when you navigate to one of their pages. This is accomplished using JavaScript and the page load event. Other sites open additional windows when you leave them; this is also accomplished using JavaScript triggered by the page unload event. Less annoying applications include validating forms before they are submitted or displaying extra information on a page when a user clicks a link without requiring a complete page refresh.

> **NOTE**
>
> This introduction will by necessity be briskly paced. There are many books written about JavaScript alone. The goal of these lessons is to introduce you to JavaScript, enable you to get started accomplishing tasks, and hopefully kindle your interest to dig into the language more deeply.

JavaScript enables you to manipulate web pages without sending a request back to the server or to send a request to the server to retrieve information without leaving the page that the user is on. Using these capabilities, you can change the contents of a page, change the style of elements on a page, validate user input before a user submits a form, and modify the behavior of the browser—all by using scripts embedded within your web pages. Let's look at some of the advantages of using JavaScript to enhance your web pages.

Ease of Use

JavaScript is a real programming language and is regularly used to build large, complex applications, including some you've probably seen, like Google Maps. At the same time, compared to many other programming languages, it's very easy to get started with JavaScript. You can add useful behavior to a web page with just a little bit of JavaScript added to the `onclick` attribute of a link or to a `script` tag at the top of an HTML document. And as you'll learn in Lesson 18, jQuery makes it easy to add functionality to a page using just a few lines of code. The point is, don't be intimidated by JavaScript. You can start accomplishing things almost immediately.

Improving Performance

One of the main advantages of JavaScript is that it can provide user feedback instantly. Instead of requiring users to submit a form to see if their input was valid, you can let them know in real time. Not only can this improve user experience, but it can also make life easier for your server by preventing unnecessary form processing on the server. You can also use JavaScript to load resources when they're needed rather than when the page first loads. For example, you can load images that are not displayed immediately after the page loads to display the site more quickly. You can also use JavaScript to alter only the parts of the page that need to change when users interact with it. For example, you can process a search form using JavaScript and display the results on the same page so that a page reload isn't required.

Integration with the Browser

JavaScript enables you to manipulate objects on the page, such as links, images, and styles. You can also use JavaScript to control the browser itself by changing the size of the browser window, moving the browser window around the screen, and activating or deactivating elements of the interface. Technologies like Flash can provide an interactive interface, but they are not integrated into the browser in the same way that JavaScript is.

The `<script>` Tag

The `<script>` tag is used to include a JavaScript script in a web page, in much the same way that the `<style>` tag is used to add a style sheet to a page. The contents of the `<script>` tag are expected to be JavaScript source code. There are a couple of other ways to use JavaScript in your pages, too, but the `<script>` tag is a good place to start.

For the best results across all browsers, you should include the `type` attribute in the script tag, which specifies the type of content that the tag contains. For JavaScript, use `text/javascript`. HTML5 uses `text/javascript` as the default value for the `type` attribute, so if that is the type your script uses, you can leave it off.

The Structure of a JavaScript Script

When you include any JavaScript code in an HTML document (apart from using the `<script>` tag), you should also follow a few other conventions:

- HTML standards prior to HTML5 required that the `<script>` tag be placed between the `<head>` and `</head>` tags at the start of your document, not inside the `<body>` tag. However, for performance reasons, it's almost always a better idea to put your `<script>` tags at the bottom of the page. I'll discuss the reasons why later on.

- Unlike HTML, which uses the `<!-- comment tag -->`, comments inside JavaScript code use the `//` symbol at the start of a line. Any line of JavaScript code that starts with these characters will be treated as a comment and ignored.

Taking these three points into consideration, here's how the `<script>` tag is normally used:

```
<html>
<head>
<title>Test script</title>
</head>
<body>
  Your Web content goes here
<script>
// Your JavaScript code goes here
</script>
</body>
</html>
```

You can place your `<script>` tag in either the head or the body of your document. But because JavaScript forces the browser to load it as a single thread, it's best to place it at the bottom of your pages, right before the closing `</body>` tag. This ensures that your pages load as quickly as possible.

The `src` Attribute

Besides the `language` attribute, the `<script>` tag can also include an `src` attribute, which allows a JavaScript script stored in a separate file to be included as part of the current web page. This feature enables you to share JavaScript code across an entire website, just as you can share a single style sheet among many pages.

When used this way, the `<script>` tag takes the following form:

```
<script src="http://www.example.com/script.js">
```

The `src` attribute will accept any valid URL, on the same server or on another. Naming your JavaScript files with the extension `.js` is customary.

JavaScript and the Chrome Development Tools

You've already seen how useful the Chrome Development Tools are when it comes to inspecting the source code of a page and diagnosing CSS issues on a web page. Developer tools like these were originally introduced to help people who were writing JavaScript. There are two incredibly useful features for JavaScript developers in the Developer Tools. The first is the JavaScript Debugger, which I'll discuss a bit later on. The second is the JavaScript Console, which provides a place to enter JavaScript code, execute it, and view the results interactively.

As I walk you through the JavaScript language, you can use the Console of the Chrome Development Tools (or the JavaScript Console in whichever browser you prefer) to run the examples. JavaScript errors that occur as you interact with the page are also printed in the Console, so when you're adding JavaScript to your own pages, you'll use it to investigate the bugs that inevitably crop up as you write your own JavaScript. You can see what the Console looks like in Figure 17.1.

17

FIGURE 17.1
The Chrome Developer Tools JavaScript Console.

To view the Console, you open the Developer Tools and click on the Console tab. The > prompt is where you enter your JavaScript code to be evaluated. The Console is what's known as a REPL, which is short for Read-eval-print Loop. That's because it reads the code you enter, evaluates it, and then prints the results. It's a place you can experiment more easily than editing the JavaScript on a page, loading it in a browser, and then viewing the results.

To see how it works, open the Console and type `"1 + 1"` at the prompt. On the next line, you'll see the number 2, the results of that mathematical expression. That expression happens to be valid JavaScript, and the Console automatically evaluates it and prints the results for you. Now try this:

```
alert(1 + 1);
```

You can see what the results look like in Figure 17.2.

FIGURE 17.2
Expressions evaluated using the Console.

When you enter that line, an alert dialog will pop up containing the number 2. As you can see, you can affect the browser environment using the Console. The word *undefined* is printed in the Console. `alert`, which I'll discuss further later, opens the dialog box. It is also an expression, just like `1 + 1`, and the results of evaluating that expression are printed in the Console window. In this case, the expression's result is `undefined`, which is why that's printed. That's what any expression that does not return a useful value returns in JavaScript. If you're not already a programmer, you may be wondering what an expression is at all. I'll get into that a bit later as well.

The JavaScript Language

When JavaScript is included in a page, the browser executes that JavaScript as soon as it is read. Here's a simple page that includes a script; the output is included in Figure 17.3:

Input ▼

```
<!DOCTYPE html>
<html>
<head>
    <title>A Simple JavaScript Example</title>
</head>
<body>

<p>Printed before JavaScript is run.</p>

<p>
<script>
    document.write("Printed by JavaScript.");
```

```
</script>
</p>

<p>Printed after JavaScript is run.</p>

</body>
</html>
```

Output ▼

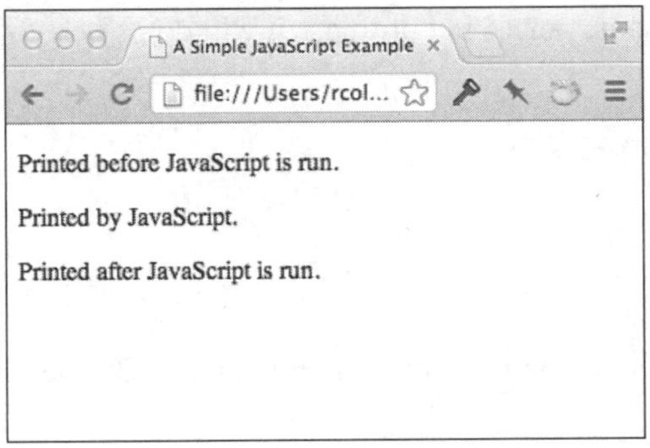

FIGURE 17.3
The results of a
simple script.

Printed before JavaScript is run.

Printed by JavaScript.

Printed after JavaScript is run.

17

The page includes a single line of JavaScript, which writes the "Printed by JavaScript" on the page. The text is printed between the other two paragraphs on the page, demonstrating that the browser executed the JavaScript as soon as it got to it.

Before I start talking about what this code does, let me talk for just a moment about its structure. JavaScript programs are made up of individual statements, which are terminated by a semicolon. This program consists of a single statement or line of code.

As you can see, this line adds text to the page. Let me break down what this does, exactly. First, you might notice that `document.write()` and `window.alert()`, which I use earlier, look similar. Both `window` and `document` are things. `write` and `alert` are messages that you can send to those things. In both cases, you need content for those messages. In the latter example, the content of the `write` message is "Printed by JavaScript."

In programming, the term used for things is *objects*, and the term used for the messages is *methods*. The content of the message is said to be passed to the method and is referred to as the method's *argument*. So in programmer jargon, I'd say that I called the `write` method of the `document` object with the argument "Printed by JavaScript." The `document` and `window` objects are provided by the browser—the environment in which JavaScript runs. You can also declare objects of your own; they'll be discussed further along.

The document object is a representation of the current page that is accessible by JavaScript. Whenever you manipulate the page using JavaScript, you do so by calling methods of the document object.

The bit of text that I passed to the document.write() method in the previous example is called a string in the vocabulary of programming. The document.write() method expects a string argument, which it then adds to the source of the document. Some programming languages are strict about data types, so if a method expects you to give it a string as an argument and you give it a number instead, an error will occur. JavaScript isn't like that. If you pass a string to the document.write() method, it will print it out unchanged. If you pass it some other kind of thing, it will do its best to convert it to a string and print it out.

So, for example, you can give it a number:

```
<script>
        document.write(500);
</script>
```

It will convert the number to a string and print it on the page. Or you can even pass it an object, like this:

```
<script>
        document.write(document);
</script>
```

The results are in Figure 17.4.

Output ▼

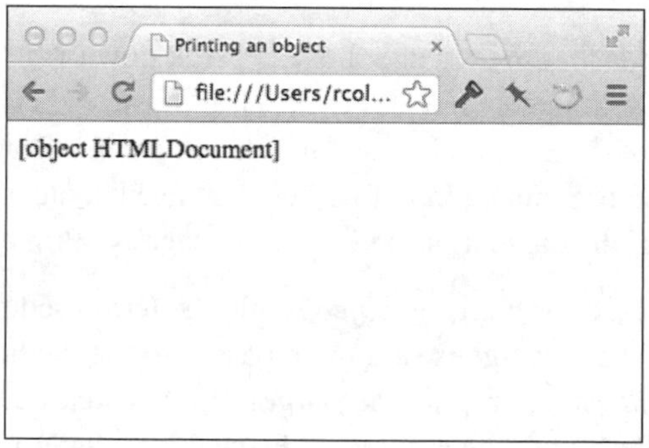

FIGURE 17.4
Attempting to write an object to the page.

[object HTMLDocument]

That's the string representation of the `document` object. Many programming languages would print an error if you tried to use an object like `document` with a method that accepts a string. Not JavaScript. It makes do with what you give it.

Operators and Expressions

In my introduction to the JavaScript Console in the Chrome Web Developer Tools, I talked a bit about expressions. An *expression* is a snippet of code that can be evaluated to return a result. You may recognize the term expression from math, and indeed, many expressions are mathematical expressions. Here's a simple mathematical expression that you can enter in the Console:

```
10 * 50
```

In this case, JavaScript will multiply 10 by 50. That's an expression. There are also string expressions. For example, you can use the + operator to join strings together, like this:

```
"The bird a nest," + " the spider a web," + " man friendship."
```

17

Expressions are built using operators. You've already seen a couple: * for multiplication and + for combining strings or adding numbers. Table 17.1 lists more operators provided by JavaScript, along with examples. (For a full list of all the supported operators, refer to the online JavaScript documentation.)

TABLE 17.1 JavaScript Operators and Expressions

Operator	Example	Description
+	5 + 5	Adds the two numeric values; the result is 10.
+	"Java" + "Script"	Combines the two string values; the result is JavaScript.
-	10 - 5	Subtracts the second value from the first; the result is 5.
*	5 * 5	Multiplies the two values; the result is 25.
/	25 / 5	Divides the value on the left by the value on the right; the result is 5.
%	26 % 5	Obtains the modulus of 26 when it's divided by 5. (Note: A *modulus* is a function that returns the remainder.) The result is 1.

There are many other operators, too. All the examples here used literal values in the expressions, but there are other options as well. You can use values returned by methods in expressions if you choose, as in the following example:

```
Math.sqrt(25) - Math.sqrt(16)
```

This example uses the `Math` object, another object built in to JavaScript. It provides a number of methods that perform a variety of mathematical operations so that you don't have to write the code to perform them yourself. `Math.sqrt()` is a method that returns the square root of a number. In this case, I subtracted the square root of 16 from the square root of 25. You can enter any of these expressions in the Console and see the results.

Variables

Thus far, I've been manipulating values and printing them directly to the page. The next fundamental building block of writing scripts is temporary storage of those values so that they can be reused. Like all programming languages, JavaScript supports the use of variables. A *variable* is a user-defined container that can hold a number, text, or an object. Creating variables and retrieving their values is simple in the Console, as shown in Figure 17.5.

Input ▼

```
var message = "Message"
 message
```

Output ▼

FIGURE 17.5
A variable declaration in the console.

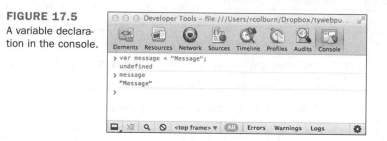

In that example, I created a variable called `message` and then printed its value by entering it as an expression in the Console. You can also assign the results of an expression to a variable:

```
var sum = 5 + 5;
```

And you can use variables in your expressions:

```
var firstName = "George";
var lastName = "Washington";
var name = firstName + " " + lastName;
```

Let's break down a variable declaration into pieces. Here's a declaration:

```
var message = "My message";
```

The line begins with `var`, which indicates that this is a variable declaration. The name of this variable is `message`. There are a number of rules that apply to naming variables, which I will list shortly. The assignment operator (=) is used to assign a value to the variable when it's declared. The value returned by the expression on the right side of the operator is assigned to the newly declared variable.

Variable names must conform to the following rules:

- Variable names can include only letters, numbers, and the underscore (_) or dollar sign ($) character.
- Variable names cannot start with a number.
- You cannot use reserved words as a variable name. Reserved words are words that have a specific meaning for the JavaScript interpreter. For example, naming a variable `var` won't work. Table 17.2 contains a full list of JavaScript reserved words.
- As a matter of style, JavaScript variables begin with a lowercase letter. If a variable name contains multiple words, usually an underscore is used to join the two words, or the first letter of the second word is uppercase. So you would write `my_variable` or `myVariable`.

17

TABLE 17.2 JavaScript Reserved Words

abstract	final	return
arguments	finally	short
boolean	float	static
break	for	super
byte	function	switch
case	goto	synchronized
catch	if	this
char	implements	throw
class	import	throws
const	in	transient
continue	instanceof	true
debugger	int	try
default	interface	typeof
delete	let	var

do	long	void
double	native	volatile
else	new	while
enum	null	with
eval	package	yield
export	private	
extends	protected	
false	public	

Not all the reserved words in Table 17.2 are currently used in JavaScript; some have been placed off limits because they might be added to the language in the future.

Here are a couple of additional notes on variable assignment. You don't have to assign a value to a variable when you declare it. You can declare the variable without an assignment so that it can be used later. For example:

```
var myVariable;
```

If you entered `myVariable` in the console as an expression, it would be evaluated to undefined because nothing has been assigned to it. However, if you enter the name of an as yet undeclared variable (like `myNewVariable`), you'll see an error message.

You can also assign new values to variables after they've been declared, as follows:

```
myVariable = "My value";
```

Control Structures

To get your scripts to actually do something, you'll need control structures, which come in two main varieties. There are conditional statements, which are used to make decisions, and loops, which enable you to repeat the same statements more than once.

The `if` Statement

The main conditional statement you'll use is the `if` statement. The statements inside an `if` statement are executed only if the condition in the `if` statement is true. If you were writing code in English rather than JavaScript, an `if` statement would read like this: "If the background of this element is blue, turn it red." There's also an `else` clause associated with `if`. The statements in the `else` clause are executed if the `if` statement's condition is false. An `if` statement with an `else` clause reads like this: "If the value of this variable is blue, change it to red; otherwise, change it to blue."

Let's look at a simple example, which will work in the Console:

```
var color = "red";
if (color == "blue") {
    color = "red";
} else {
    color = "blue";
}
color;
```

In this example, I've created a variable named `color` and use that in my `if` statement. Later, I'll explain how to retrieve information from the page, style sheets, and form elements in your JavaScript code and make changes to them. For now, it's easier to explain the conditional statements with hard-coded values. The statement begins with the `if` keyword, followed by the condition enclosed within parentheses. The statements to be executed if the condition is true are placed within curly braces. In this case, I've also included an `else` clause. The statement associated with it is also enclosed in curly braces. Finally, let's look at the condition. It is true if the variable `color` is equal to the value `"blue"`. In this case, the condition is false, so the `else` clause will be executed.

The `==` operator tests for equality and is but one of several conditional operators available in JavaScript. Table 17.3 contains all the conditional operators.

TABLE 17.3   JavaScript Comparison Operators

Operator	Operator Description	Notes
==	Equal to	a == b tests to see whether a equals b.
!=	Not equal to	a != b tests to see whether a does not equal b.
<	Less than	a < b tests to see whether a is less than b.
<=	Less than or equal to	-a <= b tests to see whether a is less than or equal to b.
>=	Greater than or equal to	-a >= b tests to see whether a is greater than or equal to b.
>	Greater than	a > b tests to see whether a is greater than b.

You can also enter conditional expressions in the Console to see their results. As you'll see, they all return either `true` or `false`. For example, `1 == 2` will evaluate as `false`, and `5 > 3` will evaluate as `true`. If you're curious about the result of a conditional expression, you can always test it there.

17

484 LESSON 17: Introducing JavaScript

You can also use the ! operator, which reads as "not," to negate any Boolean expression. For example, if you enter !true in the Console, the result of the expression will be false. If you want to negate an expression that uses a conditional operator, you'll need to use parentheses. For example, try this expression in the Console:

```
!(1 == 2)
```

The result will be true.

Loops

You'll occasionally want a group of statements to be executed more than once. JavaScript supports two kinds of loops. The first, the for loop, is ideal for situations in which you want to execute a group of statements a specific number of times. The second, the while loop, is useful when you want a set of statements to be executed until a condition is satisfied.

for Loops   Here's a for loop:

```
for (var count = 1; count <= 10; count++) {
    console.log("Iteration number " + count);
}
```

The loop starts with the for keyword, followed by all the information needed to specify how many times the loop body will be executed. (Trips through a loop are referred to as *iterations*.) Three expressions are used to define a for loop. First, a variable is declared to keep track of the loop iterations. The second is a Boolean expression (evaluates to true or false) that terminates the loop when it is false. The third is an expression that increments the loop counter so that the loop condition will eventually be satisfied. In the preceding example, I declared the variable count with an initial value of 1. I specified that the loop will execute until the value of count is no longer less than or equal to 10. Then I used an operator you haven't seen, ++, to increment the value of count by one each time through the loop.

The body of the loop uses console.log to print out a message in the console every time the loop executes. The console object refers to the Console in the web developer tools, and the log method prints whatever is passed as an argument to the console directly. It's useful for debugging, especially when you add it to your scripts within pages to get a sense of the state of your scripts while they're running.

CAUTION   As you can see, the for statement is self-contained. The count variable is declared, tested, and incremented within that statement. You shouldn't modify the value of count within the body of your loop unless you're absolutely sure of what you're doing.

while Loops   The basic structure of a `while` loop looks like this:

```javascript
var color = 'blue';
while (color == 'blue') {
    console.log("Color is still blue.");
    if (Math.random() > 0.5) {
        color = 'not blue';
    }
}
```

TIP

One thing you may notice when you're entering code in the Console is that multiline statements will return an error if you enter part of the statement and press Return. To enter multiline statements yourself, you can either paste them into the Console instead of typing them, or you can press Shift-Return at the end of the lines to indicate that they are part of a multiline block. When you press the Return key at the end, all the lines will be evaluated together.

17

The `while` loop uses only a condition. The programmer is responsible for creating the condition that will eventually cause the loop to terminate somewhere inside the body of the loop. It might help you to think of a `while` loop as an `if` statement that's executed repeatedly until a condition is satisfied. As long as the `while` expression is true, the statements inside the braces following the `while` loop continue to run forever—or at least until you close your web browser.

In the preceding example, I declare a variable, `color`, and set its value to `"blue"`. The `while` loop will execute until it is no longer true that `color` is set to `"blue"`. Inside the loop, I print a message indicating that the color is still blue, and then I use an `if` statement that may set the `color` variable to a different value. The condition in the `if` statement uses `Math.random()`, another method of the `Math` object that returns a value between `0` and `1`. In this case, if it's greater than 0.5, I switch the value so that the loop terminates.

If you prefer, you can write `while` loops with the condition at the end, which ensures that they always run once. These are called `do ... while` loops and look like this:

```javascript
var color = "blue";
do {
  // some stuff
}
while (color != "blue");
```

Even though the test in the loop will not pass, it will still run once because the condition is checked after the first time the body of the loop runs.

CAUTION

When you're using `while` loops, avoid creating infinite loops. This means that you must manipulate one of the values in the looping condition within the body of your loop. If you do manage to create an endless loop, about the only option you have is to shut down the web browser. If you're going to iterate a specific number of times using a counter, it's usually best to just use a `for` loop.

Functions

Functions are a means of grouping code together so that it can be called whenever you like. To create a function, you declare it. The following code includes a function declaration:

```
function writeParagraph(myString) {
    document.write("<p>" + myString + "</p>");
}
```

A function declaration consists of the `function` keyword, a function name, a list of parameters the function accepts (in parentheses), and the body of the function (enclosed in curly braces). This function is named `writeParagraph`, and it accepts a single parameter, `myString`. Function parameters are variables that are accessible within the body of the function. As you can see, this function prints out the value passed in as an argument inside a `<p>` tag. After I've declared this function, I can then use the following code later in the page:

```
writeParagraph("This is my paragraph.");
```

It will produce the output:

```
<p>This is my paragraph.</p>
```

NOTE

When it comes to the values passed to functions, you'll see them referred to as *parameters* or as *arguments*. Technically, the variables listed in the function declaration are parameters, and the values passed to the function when it is called are arguments.

Functions can be written to accept multiple arguments. Let's look at another function:

```
function writeTag(tag, contents) {
    document.write("<" + tag + ">" + contents + "</" + tag + ">");
}
```

This function accepts two arguments: a tag name and the contents of that tag. There's one special statement that's specific to functions: the return statement. It is used to specify the return value of the function. You can use the value returned by a function in a conditional statement, assign it to a variable, or pass it to another function. Here's a function with a return value:

```
function addThese(value1, value2) {
    return value1 + value2;
}
```

Here are a couple of examples of how you might use that function:

```
if (addThese(1, 2) > 10) {
    document.write("Sum is greater than 10.");
}
var sum = addThese(1, 2);
```

One other thing to note is that the values passed to function as arguments are copies of those values unless the arguments are objects.

Here's one more example, and the results are shown in Figure 17.6:

Input ▼

```
<script language="JavaScript">
function modifyValue(myValue) {
    document.write(myValue + "<br>");
    myValue = "new value";
    document.write(myValue + "<br>");
}

var value = "old value";
modifyValue(value);
document.write(value + "<br>");
</script>
```

17

Output ▼

Functions are called using the function name, followed by parentheses. If you are passing arguments to a function, they are included in the parentheses in a comma-separated list. Even if you're not using arguments, the parentheses are still required. This is true whether you're calling a function you wrote yourself or a function that's built in to JavaScript.

Data Types

I've mentioned JavaScript's type system, but I haven't talked much about JavaScript data types. JavaScript supports the following types of values:

- Strings, like `"Teach Yourself Web Publishing"`.
- Boolean values (true or false).
- Numbers, integer or decimal.
- `null`, which is used to represent an unknown or missing value.
- `undefined`, the value associated with variables that have been declared but have not yet had a value assigned to them. Also the return value of methods that don't return anything.

This is the full set of primitive data types that JavaScript supports. JavaScript attempts to convert data to whatever type it needs in a given context. So if you take a Boolean value and use it in a context where a string is expected, JavaScript will convert it to a string. In some cases, this automatic conversion process can lead to odd results. For example, if you try to use a value that's not a number in a context where a number is expected, JavaScript will return a special value, NaN, which is short for "not a number":

```
Math.sqrt("a string"); // The value of squareRoot is NaN
```

Boolean values represent a state of either true or false. You've already seen some examples that involve Boolean values. For example, `if` statements and `while` loops require conditional expressions that return a Boolean value. Any JavaScript value or expression can ultimately be converted to a Boolean. The values that are treated as false are the number zero, empty strings, `null`, `undefined`, and `NaN`. Everything else is true.

To explicitly convert data from one type to another, you can type casting functions. They are `Number()`, `Boolean()`, and `String()`. Type casts to Boolean are the most interesting because they allow you to see the Boolean value of an expression. For example, to confirm that NaN is false, you could type the following in the Console:

```
Boolean(Math.sqrt("a"))
```

Arrays

Arrays are lists of things. They can be lists of values, lists of objects, or even lists of lists. There are a couple of ways to declare arrays. The first is to create your own `Array` object, like this:

```
var list = new Array(10);
```

That declares an array with 10 slots. Arrays are numbered (or indexed) starting at 0, so an array with ten elements has indexes from 0 to 9. You can refer to a specific item in an array by placing the index inside square brackets after the array name. So, to assign the first element in the array, you use the following syntax:

```
list[0] = "Element 1";
```

If you want to add elements to your array when you declare it, you can use what's called an array literal, like this:

```
var list = ["red", "green", "blue"];
```

To find out how many elements are in an array, you can use a property of the array called `length`. Here's an example:

```
listLength = list.length
```

Objects

You've already been introduced to a few objects—most recently, the `Array` object. JavaScript features a number of built-in objects, and the browser supplies even more (as discussed in the next section). The first thing you need to know about objects is that they have properties. You just saw one property: the `length` property of the `Array` object.

17

Object properties are accessed through what's known as dot notation. You can also access properties as though they are array indexes. For example, if you have an object named `car` with a property named `color`, you can access that property in two ways:

```
car.color = "blue";
car["color"] = "red";
```

You can also add your own properties to an object. To add a new property to the `car` object, I just have to declare it:

```
car.numberOfDoors = 4;
```

There are a number of ways to create objects, but you should stick to the best one. To create an object, you can use an object literal, which is similar to the array literal I just described:

```
var car = { color: "blue", numberOfDoors: 4, interior: "leather" };
```

That defines an object that has three properties. As long as the properties of the object follow the rules for variable names, there's no need to put them in quotation marks. The values require quotation marks if their data type dictates that they do. You can name properties whatever you like, though, as long as you use quotation marks.

In addition to properties, objects can have methods. Methods are just functions associated with the object in question. This may seem a bit odd, but methods are properties of an object that contain a function (as opposed to a string or a number). Here's an example:

```
car.description = function() {
        return color + ' car ' + ' with '
            + numberOfDoors + ' and a ' + interior + ' interior';
}
```

As you can see, this is a bit different from the function declarations you've seen before. When you declare a method, instead of specifying the function name in the `function` statement, you assign an anonymous function to a property on your object. You can specify parameters for your methods just as you specify them for functions.

After you've added a method to an object, you can call it in the same way the methods of built-in objects are called. Here's how it works:

```
document.write(car.description());
```

NOTE —————— | The core JavaScript language contains lot of built-in objects—too many to cover here. For more information about these objects, look at the JavaScript documentation provided by Mozilla or Microsoft.

The JavaScript Environment

I've taken you on a very brief tour of the JavaScript language, but beyond the basic language syntax, which involves declarations, control structures, data types, and even core objects that are part of the JavaScript language, there's also the browser environment. When your scripts run, they have access to the contents of the current page, to other pages that are open, and even to the browser itself. I've mentioned the document object, which provides access to the contents of the current page.

Now let's look at a specific object. The top-level object in the browser environment is called window. The window object's children provide information about the various elements of a web page. Here are some of the most commonly used children of window:

location Contains information about the location of the current web document, including the URL and components of the URL, such as the protocol, domain name, path, and port.

history Holds a list of all the sites that a web browser has visited during the current session and gives you access to built-in functions that enable you to send the user forward or back within the history.

document Contains the complete details of the current web page. All the tags and content on the page are included in a hierarchy under document. Not only can you examine the contents of the page by way of the document object, but you can also manipulate the page's contents, too.

You can find a complete list of the available objects in the Mozilla JavaScript documentation at https://developer.mozilla.org/en-US/docs/Web/JavaScript.

Because the entire browser environment is accessible through this hierarchical set of objects, you can access anything as long as you know where it lives in the hierarchy. For example, all the links on the current page are stored in the property document.links, which contains an array. Each of the elements in the array has its own properties as well, so to get the location to which the first link in the document points, you use document.links[0].href.

Events

All the examples you've seen so far are executed as soon as the page loads. JavaScript is about making your pages more interactive, which means writing scripts that function based on user input and user activity. To add this interactivity, you need to bind your

JavaScript code to events. The JavaScript environment monitors user activity and provides the opportunity for you to specify that code will be executed when certain events occur.

There are three ways to bind JavaScript code to an event handler. The first is to use an HTML attribute. For example, if you want to display an alert when a user clicks a link, you could bind the event like this:

```
<a href="/whatever.html" onclick="alert('Be careful')">Link</a>
```

The disadvantage of this approach is that it makes your JavaScript hard to maintain. You wind up with JavaScript scattered throughout your documents, and it makes it difficult to reuse the same JavaScript code on many pages. You should not use this approach for any but the simplest things.

The second is to bind the event to the appropriate property of the element. If you have a reference to a link called `myLink` in JavaScript, you can add a click event like this:

```
myLink.onclick = function(event) { alert('Be careful'); };
```

This approach enables you to separate your JavaScript from your HTML, but it allows you to bind only one function to the click event of the link. This can come back to bite you in the future or cause problems if you include other JavaScript code on your page that might also need to bind an event to the click event of that link.

Finally, you can use the `addEventListener()` method to attach an event handler to an event on an element. Here's an example:

```
myButton.addEventListener('click', function(){ alert('Be careful!'); }, false);
```

You can use `addEventListener()` to attach any number of event handlers to the same event on the same element. It's the preferred method for event binding currently. If you need to support older browsers like Internet Explorer 8, there are a number of JavaScript libraries that will handle the binding of event handlers to events in a safe, cross-platform way. In the next lesson, you will learn how to use one of the most popular libraries, `jQuery`.

Table 17.4 provides a list of the event handlers that JavaScript provides.

TABLE 17.4 JavaScript Event Handlers

Event Handler	When It's Called
onblur	Whenever a visitor leaves a specified form field
onchange	Whenever a visitor changes the contents of a specified form field
onclick	Whenever a visitor clicks a specified element

Event Handler	When It's Called
onfocus	Whenever a visitor enters a specified form field
onload	Whenever a page and all of its images have finished loading
onmouseover	Whenever a visitor places the mouse cursor over a specified object
onselect	Whenever a visitor selects the contents of a specified field
onsubmit	Whenever a visitor submits a specified form
onunload	Whenever the current web page is changed

First, let me explain how to bind an event using HTML attributes. All the event handlers listed in Table 17.4 can be used as attributes for tags that respond to them. For example, the onload handler is associated with the body tag. As you know, JavaScript code is executed as soon as it is encountered. Suppose you want to write a script that modifies all the links on a page. If that script is executed before all the links have been loaded, it will miss some of the links. Fortunately, there's a solution to this problem. The onload event does not occur until the entire page has loaded, so you can put the code that modifies the links into a function and then bind it to the page's onload event. Here's a page that uses onload:

17

```
<!DOCTYPE html>
<html>
<head>
    <title>Modifying Links with JavaScript</title>
</head>
<body onload="linkModifier()">
    <ul>
        <li><a href="http://google.com/">Google</a></li>
        <li><a href="http://www.nytimes.com/">New York Times</a></li>
    </ul>
    <script type="text/javascript">
        function linkModifier() {
            for (var i = 0; i < document.links.length; i++) {
                document.links[i].href = "http://example.com";
            }
        }
    </script>
</body>
</html>
```

This page contains a script tag, and that script tag contains a single function declaration. The function, linkModifier(), changes the href attribute of all the links on the page to http://example.com/. To access the links, it uses document.links, which is a reference to an array of all the links in the document. It iterates over each of those links, changing their `href` properties from the values specified in the HTML to the new URL. The main point of this example, though, is the `onload` attribute in the `body` tag, which contains the call to `linkModifier()`. It's important to associate that call with the `onload` event so that all the links on the page have been processed before the function is called. If I'd put the function call inside the `<script>` tag, the function call might have occurred before the page was loaded.

Most often, when using attributes to bind events, function calls are used, but the value of the attributes can be any JavaScript code, even multiple statements, separated by semicolons. Here's an example that uses the `onclick` attribute on a link:

```
<a href="http://google.com/" onclick="alert(this.href); return false;">Google</a>
```

In this example, the value of the `onclick` attribute contains two statements. The first uses the built-in `alert()` function to display the value in the `href` attribute of the link. The second prevents the link from taking the user to a new page. So clicking the link will display the alert message in Figure 17.7 and do nothing after the user acknowledges the alert.

FIGURE 17.7
A JavaScript alert message.

Whether you're writing code in your event binding attribute or writing a function that will be used as an event handler, returning false will prevent the default browser action for that event. In this case, it prevents the browser from following the link. If the `onsubmit` action for a form returns `false`, the form will not be submitted.

The Meaning of `this`

You might be a bit puzzled by the use of `this` as a variable name in an event handler. Here, `this` is shorthand for the current object. When you're using an event handler in a tag, `this` refers to the object represented by that tag. In the previous example, it refers to the link that the user clicked on. The advantage of using `this` is that it places the event in a useful context. I could use the same attribute value with any link and the code would still work as expected. It's particularly useful when you're using functions as event handlers and you want to make them easy to reuse.

At one time, using event-handler attributes to bind functions to events was the most common approach, but these days, it's more common to bind events to elements in other ways. It's considered poor style to include JavaScript throughout your web pages, and using the event-handler attributes can override event bindings that are applied from JavaScript rather than in the HTML. In Lesson 18, I explain how to bind events to elements without changing your markup.

> **Learning More About JavaScript**
>
> The list of statements, functions, and options included in this lesson represents only part of the potential offered by JavaScript.
>
> For this reason, I cannot overemphasize the importance of the online documentation provided by Mozilla. All the latest JavaScript enhancements and features will be documented first at https://developer.mozilla.org/en-US/docs/Web/JavaScript.

17

Summary

JavaScript enables HTML publishers to include simple programs or scripts within a web page without having to deal with the many difficulties associated with programming in high-level languages such as Java or C++.

In this lesson, you learned about the `<script>` tag and how it's used to embed JavaScript scripts into an HTML document. In addition, you explored the basic structure of the JavaScript language and how to use JavaScript in the browser environment.

With this basic knowledge behind you, in the next lesson, you'll explore some real-world examples of JavaScript and learn more about the concepts involved in JavaScript programming.

Workshop

The following workshop includes questions, a quiz, and exercises related to JavaScript.

Q&A

Q Don't I need a development environment to work with JavaScript?

A Nope. As with HTML, all you need is a text editor and a browser that supports JavaScript. You might be confusing JavaScript with Java, a more comprehensive programming language that needs at least a compiler for its programs to run. However, tools like the Chrome Developer Tools, FireBug for Firefox, and Safari's Web Inspector can make your life easier. Consult the documentation on those tools to learn more about their JavaScript features.

Q What is AJAX?

A One topic we haven't covered yet is AJAX. AJAX is a term used to describe scripts that communicate with the server without requiring a web page to be fully reloaded. For example, you can use it to fetch information and display it on the page or to submit a form for processing, all without changing the full page in the browser.

Q When I use JavaScript, do I need to accommodate users whose browsers may not support JavaScript or who have disabled it?

A Some estimates indicate that over 95% of web users have JavaScript enabled. However, unless you have a really good reason not to, you should make accommodations for users without JavaScript. You need not offer users who don't have JavaScript an identical experience to those who have it, but they should be able to access your site. For example, if you run an online store, do you really want to shut out users because of their browser configuration?

Q In Java and C++, I previously defined variables with statements such as `int`, `char`, and `string`. Why can't I do this in JavaScript?

A As I mentioned previously, JavaScript is a loosely typed language. This means that all variables can take any form and can even be changed on-the-fly. As a result, the context in which the variable is used determines its type.

Quiz

1. What HTML tag is used to embed JavaScript scripts in a page?
2. What are *events*? What can JavaScript do with them?
3. Is an expression that evaluates to the value `0` true or false? How about the string `"false"` inside quotation marks?
4. How do you make sure that a variable you create in a function is only visible locally in that function?
5. How are functions different from methods?

Quiz Answers

1. To accommodate the inclusion of JavaScript programs in a normal HTML document, Netscape introduced the `<script>` tag. By placing a `<script>` tag in a document, you tell the web browser to treat any lines of text inside the tag as script rather than as content for the web page.

2. Events are special actions triggered by things happening in the system (windows opening, pages being loaded, forms being submitted) or by reader input (text being entered, links being followed, check boxes being selected). Using JavaScript, you can perform different operations in response to these events.

3. The number `0` is false, and the string `"false"` is true. The only false values are `0`, `null`, an empty string, `undefined`, `NaN` (not a number), and the Boolean value `false` itself.

4. The `var` statement is used to define a local variable inside a function.

5. Methods are associated with a specific object, and functions are standalone routines that operate outside the bounds of an object.

Exercises

1. If you haven't done so already, take a few minutes to explore the documentation for JavaScript at https://developer.mozilla.org/en-US/docs/Web/JavaScript. See whether you can find out what enhancements were included in the latest version of JavaScript that weren't included in earlier versions.

2. Find a simple JavaScript script somewhere on the Web—either in use in a web page or in an archive of scripts. Look at the source code and see whether you can decode its logic and how it works.

17

LESSON 18
Using jQuery

JavaScript is a programming language that makes it possible to manipulate the contents of web pages after they have loaded. jQuery and other JavaScript libraries make it much easier to take advantage of JavaScript. jQuery enables JavaScript programmers to code without worrying about differences among browsers. It also provides a number of other features that make it easy to build powerful JavaScript features without writing very much code. In this lesson, you'll learn about the following:

- What JavaScript libraries are and why you might want to use one

- How to use the jQuery library in your pages

- How to select elements on a page with jQuery

- How to bind events using jQuery

- How to manipulate styles on a page

- How to change the content of a page

- How to fetch content from an external source using AJAX

What Are JavaScript Libraries?

In this book, I've talked about browsers and incompatibilities between them. The popular browsers differ in their support for HTML and CSS and in their support for JavaScript. Unlike CSS and HTML, though, JavaScript can actually be used to solve the problem of incompatibilities in JavaScript implementations. You can write code that detects which browser is being used or even the specific capabilities of the browser and then add logic to make sure the program works correctly for whatever environment that it's in.

For example, some browsers allow you to retrieve elements from the document by class name using the `getElementsByClassName()` method, and others do not. If your script depends on that method, it will break in some browsers. You can work around the problem by checking to see whether the method exists before you use it, and if it doesn't, using another technique that works in the browsers that don't support it.

JavaScript libraries were created by people who had to do this sort of thing too many times and decided to package up all of these kinds of workarounds to create a simpler interface to common functionality that hides all the incompatibilities of the various browsers. In doing so, the authors also added many other features to make life more convenient for JavaScript developers. The most popular JavaScript libraries make it easier to bind code to events, select elements on the page to act on in your programs, and even make calls to the server from JavaScript to dynamically change elements on the page, using a technique referred to as AJAX.

You might have noticed that I am referring to JavaScript libraries as a group. That's because there are a number of libraries that provide roughly the same set of features. They were all independently developed and work differently from one another, and each has its own set of advantages and disadvantages. If you're starting from scratch, choosing between them is a matter of taste.

Getting Started with jQuery

Entire books are published about each of the popular JavaScript libraries, so it would be foolish to try to cover them all in this lesson. Instead, I'm going to focus on introducing jQuery. I've chosen it mainly because it's the easiest library to get started with, especially if you already know CSS. Even if you don't wind up using jQuery, you'll still get an idea of how JavaScript libraries work by reading this section. You'll just have to follow up by digging into the documentation to learn how to apply the same concepts with the library that you use instead.

jQuery is a regular JavaScript file that you can include in your page using the `<script>` tag. To get started, download your own copy at http://jquery.com/. After you've downloaded jQuery, you can start using it in your pages. The easiest way to include it in a page, especially for local testing, is to rename the downloaded file to `jquery.js` and put it in the same directory as the HTML page:

```
<script type="text/javascript" src="jquery.js"></script>
```

NOTE The file you download will have a different name than `jquery.js` because it will include the jQuery version number. You'll have to rename it as `jquery.js` or use the full filename in your `<script>` tag. You can download jQuery in production or development configurations. The production configuration is "minified"— compressed so that it downloads as quickly as possible. Unfortunately, the minified file is unreadable by humans; so if you think you may need to look at the jQuery source, download the development version. Just be sure to replace it with the minified version when you make your site live.

Your First jQuery Script

18

jQuery is built around the idea of selecting objects on the page and then performing actions on them. In some ways, it's very similar to CSS. You use a selector to define an element or set of elements, and then you write some code that is applied to those elements. Here's an example of a page that includes a simple jQuery script:

```
<!DOCTYPE html>
<html>
<head>
  <title>jQuery Example</title>
</head>
<body>
  <a href="1.html">A link</a>
  <script src="jquery.js"></script>
  <script>
    $(document).ready(function() {
      $("a").click(function(event) {
        alert("You clicked on a link to " + this.href );
      });
    });
  </script>
</body>
</html>
```

The first `<script>` tag loads the external jQuery script. The second contains the script I wrote. This script causes an alert to be displayed whenever a user clicks a link. I'll break it down line by line.

The first line is important because you'll see it or a variation of it in nearly every jQuery script:

```
$(document).ready(function() {
```

First, `$` is the name of a function declared by jQuery, and `document` is an argument to that function. The `$` function selects the set of elements matched by the selector provided as an argument. In this case, I've passed `document` as the argument, and it matches the `document` object—the root object of the page's document object model. Usually, the selector is a CSS selector, but the `document` object is an alternative that you can use, as well.

To the right, you'll see a call to the `ready` method, which is applied to the elements that the selector matches. In this case, it's the `document` object. jQuery provides convenient methods for binding events to objects or elements, and in this case, it will be used to bind an anonymous function to the document's `ready` event. The "ready" event is provided by jQuery.

The `window` object supports the `onload` event, which is what's normally used to execute JavaScript when the page is displayed. The `window.onload` event doesn't "fire" (call any methods that are bound to it) until the page has fully loaded. This can be a problem for pages that contain large images, for example. The JavaScript code won't run until the images load, and that could lead to strange behavior for users.

jQuery's `document.ready` event, however, fires when the page has been fully constructed. This can cause the JavaScript to run a bit earlier in the process, while images are being downloaded. With jQuery it's customary to perform all the work you want to occur when the page loads within an anonymous function bound to the `document.ready` event. It's so common, in fact, that a shortcut is provided to make doing so even easier. The line above can be rewritten as follows:

```
$(function() {
```

jQuery knows that you intend to bind the function to the `document.ready` event. Here's the code that's bound to the event:

```
$("a").click(function(event) {
  alert("You clicked on a link to " + this.href );
});
```

This code binds a function that prints an alert message containing the URL of the link that the user clicked on to every link on the page. In this case, I use `"a"` as the selector

I pass to jQuery, and it works exactly as it does with CSS. The `click()` method binds a function to the `onclick` event for all the elements matched by the selector it's called on, in this case, all the `<a>` tags on the page.

Selecting Elements from the Document

In the previous example, I used a jQuery selector to bind an event handler to all the links on a page. The important thing to know about jQuery is that jQuery selectors are a superset of CSS selectors; pretty much any selector you can use with CSS can also be used with jQuery. This is a fantastic shortcut, but it's worth discussing what happens behind the scenes a bit as well.

When a web page is loaded in the browser, the browser creates a programmatic representation of the page structure called the Document Object Model. This representation of the page is what's shown in the Elements tab of the Developer Tools. You'll notice that implied tags (like `tbody` for tables) are included and that broken HTML is repaired in this representation.

In JavaScript, the built-in `document` object is the entry point for manipulating the DOM. It provides methods like `getElementById`, `getElementByName`, and `getElementByTagName` to enable you to query the DOM directly from JavaScript. There are also methods that enable developers to add and remove elements from the DOM and to modify them. However, using these methods is much more cumbersome than using jQuery. For example, here's some JavaScript code that accomplishes the same thing as the jQuery code above accessing the DOM directly:

```
<script>
  window.addEventListener('load', function() {
    var links = document.getElementsByTagName("a");

    for (var i = 0; i < links.length; i++) {
      links[i].addEventListener('click', function() {
        alert("You clicked on a link to " + this.href );
      });
    }
  });
</script>
```

As you can see, that's an awful lot more code than I wrote for the jQuery example. The other problem is that this code does not take browser incompatibilities into account. It works in most browsers, but not all of them. Most of the incompatibilities between browsers are in their DOM implementations. So if you write code to manipulate the DOM from scratch, you have to account for these differences. That would entail writing even more code.

18

jQuery translates the selectors that developers use into the calls it needs to make on the `document` object to retrieve the proper list of elements. Thus, you can use a selector like `a` to find all the links on a page or `a.archives` to find all the links with the class `archives`, and jQuery will access the DOM in whatever way works with the user's browser and return the list of elements they selected.

Binding Events

Most JavaScript development involves binding event handlers to events. Whether it's making sure that JavaScript code that initializes things loads at the right time, or adding interactivity by associating code with actions the user takes on the page, you're dealing with event binding.

jQuery properly binds events so that multiple handlers can be bound to the same event, across all browsers. If you bind your events using jQuery, you never have to worry about overriding events bound in another script. Also, as you saw in the previous example, jQuery makes it easy to bind handlers to multiple elements at once. For example, the following code would disable all the links on the page:

```
$("a").click(function(event) { event.preventDefault(); }
```

jQuery enables you to refer to the object representing the event itself in your handler. To do so, add the `event` parameter to the anonymous function representing the event handler. You can name the parameter whatever you like, in this case. I named it `event`. I then call the `preventDefault` method on the event. That method, provided by jQuery, indicates that the default action associated with the event should not be performed. The default action of a link is to change the browser's location to the URL in the link, but this event handler prevents that from happening.

Here's a more useful example. Let's say that I want links to external sites to open in a new window, and all the links to external sites use a fully qualified URLwhereas local links do not. I could use the following event handler:

```
$(function () {
  $("a").click(function (event) {
    if (null != this.href && this.href.length > 4
      && this.href.substring(0, 4) == "http") {
      event.preventDefault();
      window.open(this.href);
    }
  });
});
```

The `if` statement tests whether the `href` attribute of the link starts with "http." The other tests in the `if` statement are checks that prevent the `substring` method from raising an error if the URL is not present or is too short. If the URL does start with "http," I open a new window for that URL and prevent the default action. If it doesn't, the default action is allowed to continue. Instead of adding special classes to external links on the page or using the `onclick` attribute for each of them to open new windows, I just used jQuery's selector functionality and a bit of programming to take care of it for me.

> **CAUTION**
>
> If you can't get the previous script to work correctly, make sure that the `if` statement is all on one line: `if (null != this.href && this.href.length > 4 && this.href.substring(0, 4) == "http") {`. Some browsers don't like whitespace in the middle of `if` statements.

jQuery provides methods for binding most events to jQuery objects. For more a full list of events jQuery supports, see http://api.jquery.com/bind/.

Modifying Styles on the Page

Another powerful feature of jQuery is that it enables you to modify styles on the page on-the-fly. jQuery enables you to modify the page styles indirectly through convenience methods that hide and show elements, for example, and enables you to change styles directly.

Hiding and Showing Elements

For example, you can hide and show elements easily based on activity by the user. Here's a sample page that swaps out two elements whenever they are clicked:

```
<!DOCTYPE html>
<html>
<head>
  <title>Anchors</title>
</head>
<body>

  <div id="open" style="padding: 1em; border: 3px solid black;
    font-size: 300%;">We are open</div>

  <div id="closed" style="padding: 1em; border: 3px solid black;
    font-size: 300%;">We are closed</div>
```

18

```
<script src="jquery.js"></script>
<script type="text/javascript" charset="utf-8">
$(function () {
  $("#closed").hide();
  $("#open, #closed").click(function (event) {
    $("#open, #closed").toggle();
  });
});
</script>
</body>
</html>
```

The page contains two `<div>`s, one containing the text "We are closed" and one containing the text "We are open." In the event handler for the document's ready state, I hide the `<div>` with the ID `closed`:

```
$("#closed").hide();
```

That method sets the `display` style of the elements matched by the selector to `none` so that when the page finishes loading, that `<div>` will not be visible, as shown in Figure 18.1.

FIGURE 18.1
The initial state of the page. "We are closed" is hidden.

Then I bind an event handler to the `onclick` event of those `<div>`s containing the following code:

```
$("#open, #closed").toggle();
```

As you can see, this selector matches both the IDs `open` and `closed` and calls the `toggle()` method on each of them. That method, provided by jQuery, displays hidden items and hides items that are being displayed. So, clicking the `<div>` will cause the other `<div>` to appear and hide the one you clicked. After you click the `<div>` and the two elements have been toggled, the page appears, as shown in Figure 18.2.

FIGURE 18.2
The state of the page after the element has been clicked.

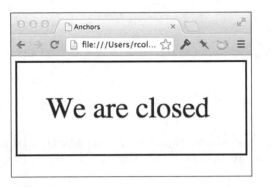

Retrieving and Changing Style Sheet Properties

You can also modify styles on the page directly. If I change the event handler in the previous example to contain the following code, the text will be underlined when the user clicks the `<div>`, as shown in Figure 18.3:

```
$(this).css("text-decoration", "underline");
```

FIGURE 18.3
The text is underlined after the user clicks on the `<div>`.

18

jQuery enables you to manipulate any styles on the page in this fashion. You can also retrieve the values of CSS properties using the `css()` method; just don't leave out the argument. If I instead change the body of the event handler to the following, the browser will display the current font size used in the `<div>` that the user clicked:

```
alert("The font size is " + $(this).css("font-size"));
```

A browser window with the alert displayed appears in Figure 18.4.

FIGURE 18.4
An alert box displaying the value of a CSS property.

JavaScript Alert

The font size is 48px

OK

Using these techniques, you can build pages with expanding and collapsing lists, add borders to links when users mouse over them, or allow users to change the color scheme of the page on-the-fly.

Modifying Content on the Page

Not only can you modify the styles on the page using jQuery, but you can also modify the content of the page itself. It provides methods that enable you to remove content from the page, add new content, and modify existing elements.

Manipulating Classes

jQuery provides a number of methods for manipulating the classes associated with elements. If your page already has a style sheet, you might want to add or remove classes from elements on-the-fly to change their appearance. In the following example page, shown in Figure 18.5, the class `highlighted` is added to paragraphs when the mouse is moved over them, and it's removed when the mouse moves out:

```
<!DOCTYPE html>
<html>
<head>
  <title>Altering Classes on the Fly</title>
  <style>
    p { padding: .5em;}
    p.highlighted { background: #666666; }
  </style>
</head>
<body>

  <p>This is the first paragraph on the page.</p>
  <p>This is the second paragraph on the page.</p>

  <script src="jquery.js"></script>
  <script type="text/javascript">
    $(function () {
      $("p").mouseenter(function () {
        $(this).addClass("highlighted");
      });

      $("p").mouseleave(function () {
```

```
            $(this).removeClass("highlighted");
        });
    })
  </script>
</body>
</html>
```

FIGURE 18.5
No paragraphs are
highlighted initially.

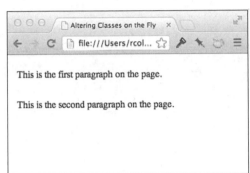

On this page, I have two paragraphs that have no classes assigned to them by default.
I also have a style sheet that applies a gray background to any paragraph with the class
highlighted. Most important, I have the following two event handlers:

```
$("p").mouseenter(function () {
  $(this).addClass("highlighted");
});
$("p").mouseleave(function () {
  $(this).removeClass("highlighted");
});
```

In this example, I use the jQuery mouseenter and mouseleave events to fire events whenever the user moves his mouse over or away from a paragraph. As you can see in Figure
18.6, when the user's mouse is over the paragraph, the class highlighted is applied to it.
When the mouse moves away, the class is removed.

FIGURE 18.6
Paragraphs are
highlighted when
the mouse is over
them.

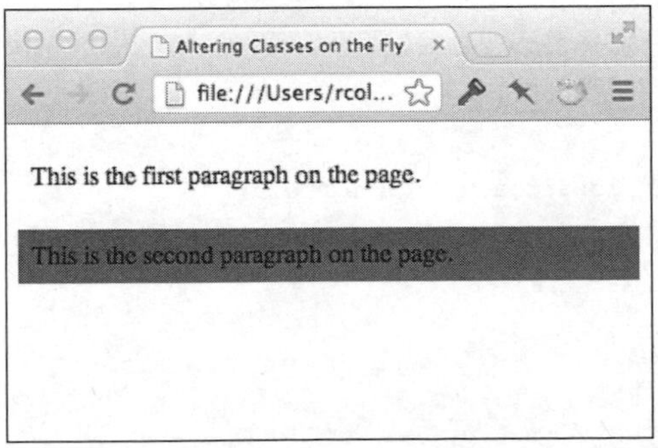

You can use jQuery's `toggleClass()` method to reverse the state of a particular class on an element. In the following example, the elements in the list are highlighted the first time the user clicks them, and the highlighting is removed the next time the user clicks them. All that's required is to toggle the `highlighted` class with each click:

```html
<!DOCTYPE html>
<html>
<head>
  <title>Altering Classes on the Fly</title>
  <style>
    li.highlighted { background: yellow; }
  </style>
</head>
<body>
  <ul>
    <li>One</li>
    <li>Two</li>
    <li>Three</li>
    <li>Four</li>
  </ul>

  <script src="jquery.js"></script>
  <script type="text/javascript" charset="utf-8">
    $(function () {
      $("li").click(function () {
        $(this).toggleClass("highlighted");
      });
    });
  </script>
</body>
</html>
```

Finally, jQuery can check for the presence of a class using the `hasClass()` method. If I change the body of the event handler in the previous example to the following function, the first time the user clicks a list item, the `highlighted` class will be applied. The second time, an alert (shown in Figure 18.7) will be displayed indicating that the item is already highlighted:

```javascript
$("li").click(function () {
  if (!$(this).hasClass("highlighted")) {
    $(this).addClass("highlighted");
  }
  else {
    alert("This list item is already highlighted.");
  }
});
```

FIGURE 18.7
An alert is displayed when users click a paragraph the second time.

In this example, I use the `hasClass()` method to determine whether the class is already present. If it isn't, I add it. If it is, I display the alert.

Manipulating Form Values

You can also use jQuery to modify the contents of form fields. The `val()` method can be used to both retrieve the value of form fields and modify them. In many cases, websites put an example of the input that should be entered into a form field in the field until the user enters data. In the following example, the form starts with sample data in the field, but it's removed automatically when the user focuses on the field. If the user doesn't enter data, the sample data is restored. Figure 18.8 shows the initial state of the page.

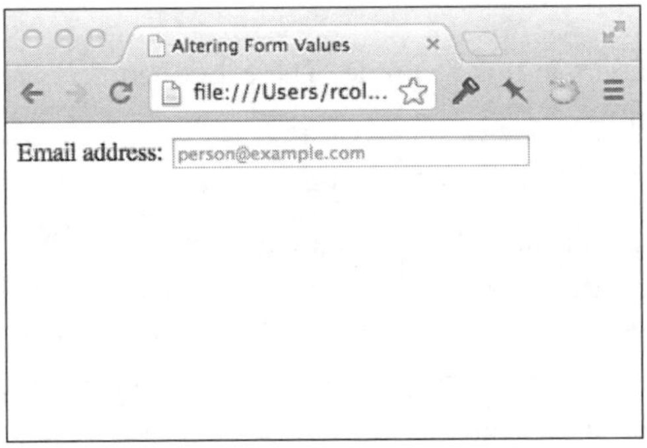

FIGURE 18.8
When the page loads, the sample content appears in the form field.

18

```
<!DOCTYPE html>
<html>
<head>
  <title>Altering Form Values</title>
  <style>
    input[name="email"] { color: #999; }
  </style>
</head>
<body>
  <form>
```

```
   <label>Email address: <input name="email" value="person@example.com"
size="40" /></label>
  </form>

  <script src="jquery.js"></script>
  <script type="text/javascript" charset="utf-8">
  $(function () {
    $("input[name='email']").focus(function () {
      if ($(this).val() == "person@example.com") {
        $(this).val("");
        $(this).css("color", "black");
      }
    });

    $("input[name='email']").blur(function () {
      if ($(this).val() == "") {
        $(this).val("person@example.com");
        $(this).css("color", "#999");
      }
    });
  });
  </script>
</body>
</html>
```

Again, I use two event handlers in this example. The event handlers are new, as is the selector. Here's one of them:

```
$("input[name='email']").focus(function () {
```

In this case, I'm using a selector that's based on an attribute value. It matches an input field in which the `name` attribute is set to `email`, and it binds to the `focus` event. This event fires when the user places the cursor in that field. The event handler for the focus event does two things: sets the value of the field to an empty string, and changes the color from gray to black, but only if the value is `person@example.com`. If it's something else, it's a value the user entered and should be left alone. Figure 18.9 shows what the form looks like when the user initially clicks in the field.

The other event handler is bound to the blur event, which fires when the cursor leaves the field. If the field has no value, it changes the color back to gray and puts the example input back into the field.

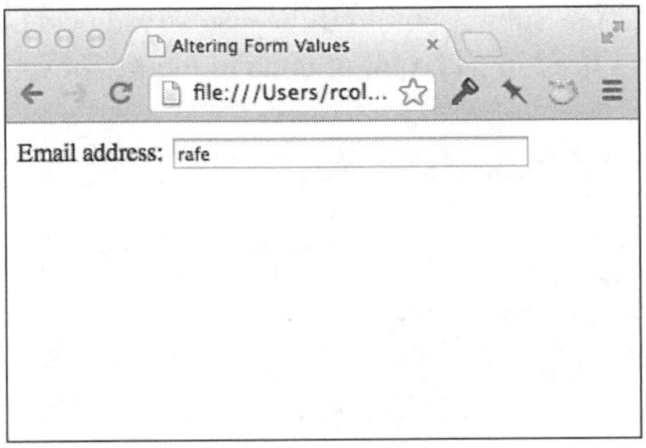

FIGURE 18.9
The contents of
the email field are
removed when the
user clicks in it.

Email address: rafe

Manipulating Attributes Directly

You can also use jQuery to manipulate the attributes of elements directly. For example, disabling a form field entirely requires you to modify the `disabled` attribute of that field.

I've added a Submit button to the form from the previous example and set it to `disabled`. Here's the new form:

```
<form>
  <label>Email address: <input name="email" value="person@example.com" size="40">
  <input id="emailFormSubmit" type="submit" disabled>
</form>
```

18

Figure 18.10 shows the form with the sample content and the disabled Submit button.

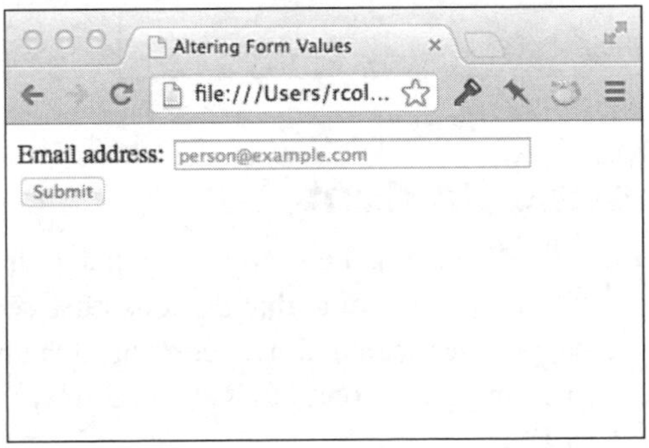

FIGURE 18.10
This form contains
sample content,
and the Submit
button is disabled.

Email address: person@example.com
Submit

I only want to let users click the Submit button if they've already entered an email address. To add that check, I need to add a bit of code to the `blur` event for the email field, as shown:

```
$("input[name='email']").blur(function () {
  if ($(this).val() == "") {
    $(this).val("person@example.com");
    $(this).css("color", "#999");
    $("#emailFormSubmit").attr("disabled", "disabled");
  }
  else {
    $("#emailFormSubmit").removeAttr("disabled");
  }
});
```

If the user leaves the field having set a value, the `disabled` attribute is removed from the Submit button, as shown in Figure 18.11. If the user leaves the field without having entered anything, the `disabled` attribute is added, just in case it was previously removed.

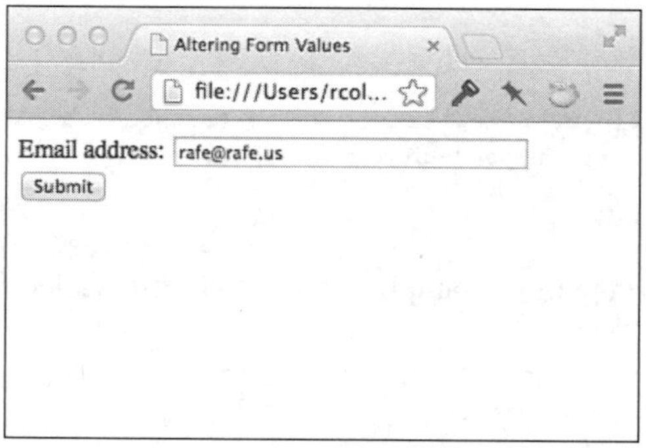

FIGURE 18.11
The Submit button is no longer disabled after an email address is entered.

Adding and Removing Content

jQuery provides a number of methods that can be used to manipulate the content on the page directly. Here's a more complex example that demonstrates several ways of manipulating the content on a page—users can add new content to the page, remove content from the page, and even wipe out all the content inside an element in one click. The initial page appears in Figure 18.12.

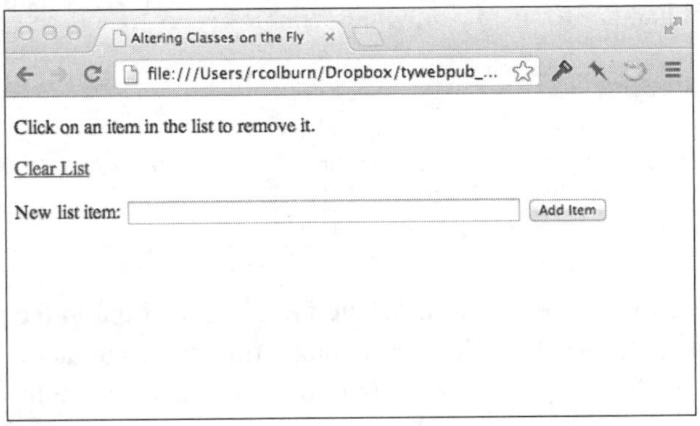

FIGURE 18.12
A page that allows
you to add and
remove content on
the fly.

I'll start with the markup for the page. First, I need a list. In this example, the user will be able to add elements to the list and remove elements from the list. All I need is an empty list with an ID:

```
<ul id="editable">
</ul>
```

Next, I have a form that enables users to add a new item to the end of the list. It has a text input field and a Submit button:

```
<form id="addElement">
  <label>New list item: <input name="liContent" size="60" /></label>
  <input type="submit" value="Add Item" />
</form>
```

Finally, I've added a link that removes all the elements the user has added to the list:

```
<p><a id="clearList" href="#">Clear List</a></p>
```

The action is on the JavaScript side. Let's look at each of the event handlers for the page one at a time. First, here's the event handler for the Clear List link:

```
$("#clearList").click(function (event) {
    event.preventDefault();
    $("#editable").empty();
});
```

This event handler prevents the default action of the link (which would normally return the user to the top of the page) and calls the `empty()` method on the list, identified by selecting its ID. The `empty()` method removes the contents of an element.

Next is the event handler for the form, which enables users to add new items to the list:

```
$("#addElement").submit(function (event) {
  event.preventDefault();
  $("#editable").append("<li>"
    + $("#addElement input[name='liContent']").val() + "</li>");
  $("#addElement input[name='liContent']").val("");
});
```

I bind this handler to the `submit` event for the form, just as I did in the previous example. First, it prevents the form submission from completing its default action—submitting the form to the server. Then I append the content to the list. I select the list using its ID, and then I call the `append()` method, which adds the content in the argument just inside the closing tag for the elements that match the selector. In this case, I put the value in the text field, which I obtain using the `val()` method that you've already seen, inside an opening and closing `<li>` tag, and pass that to the `append()` method. I also remove the content from the text field because it has been appended to the list. Figure 18.13 shows the list once a few elements have been added.

FIGURE 18.13
A page with items added by a user.

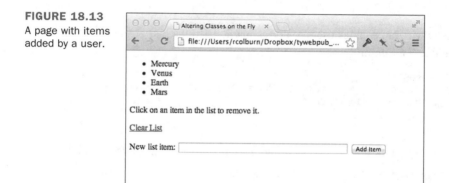

Finally, I allow users to remove items from the list by clicking them. There's one trick here. As you've seen, to do so I'll need to use the `click` handler for the `<li>` elements in the list. In this case, there's a catch. When the page loads and the `document.ready` event for the page initially fires, there are no elements in the list to bind events to. Fortunately, jQuery provides a way to set up an event handler so that it's automatically bound to newly created elements on the page. Here's the code:

```
$(document).on('click', "#editable li", function () {
  $(this).remove();
});
```

As you can see, the event binding is slightly different here. Instead of using the `click()` method, I've used the `on()` method with `document` as the selector. This indicates that I want to monitor changes to the page and perform the event binding that follows any time an element matching the selector (the second argument) is added. The first argument is the name of the event to bind—it's the name of the event to be bound, placed in quotation marks. The second argument is the selector to match. The third is the event handler as it would normally be written. The `on()` method is one of the most powerful features of jQuery because it enables you to automatically treat dynamically generated content the same way you'd treat content that's on the page at the time that it loads.

Here's the full source for the page:

```html
<!DOCTYPE html>
<html>
<head>
  <title>Altering Form Values</title>
</head>
<body>
  <ul id="editable">
  </ul>
  <form id="addElement">
    <label>New list item: <input name="liContent" size="60" /></label>
    <input type="submit" value="Add Item" />
  </form>
  <p><a id="clearList" href="#">Clear List</a></p>

  <script src="jquery.js"></script>
  <script type="text/javascript" charset="utf-8">
  $(function () {
    $("#clearList").click(function (event) {
      event.preventDefault();
      $("#editable").empty();
    });
    $("#addElement").submit(function (event) {
      event.preventDefault();
      $("#editable").append("<li>"
        + $("#addElement input[name='liContent']").val() + "</li>");
      $("#addElement input[name='liContent']").val("");
    });
    $(document).on('click', "#editable li", function () {
      $(this).remove();
    });
  });
  </script>
</body>
</html>
```

18

There are other methods for adding content in different locations in relation to a selected element. For example, if I change the `append()` call to `prepend()`, new items will be added to the top of the list rather than the bottom. You can also use the `before()` method to add content before another element, and the `after()` element to add it after. The difference is that when you use those methods, the content is placed outside the tags matched by the selector, rather than inside those tags.

Special Effects

It can be a little jarring when elements just appear or disappear instantly. Most JavaScript libraries, including jQuery, provide a library of effects that enable you to animate transitions on the page when items appear, disappear, or move. jQuery has a few basic effects built in to the core library. Supplemental effects are also available as part of jQuery UI, which you can obtain at http://jqueryui.com/.

The four effects that are part of jQuery are fade in, fade out, slide up, and slide down. I'm going to build on the previous example to show you how they can be used to soften the transitions when you add items to the page or remove items from it. Adding the effects to the page just requires a few small tweaks to the event handlers that I already created.

The first effect I added applies the fade-out effect when users click a list item to remove it. To cause an element to fade out, you call the `fadeOut()` method on the results of a selector that matches that element. Here's the code:

```
$(document).on('click', "#editable li", function () {
  $(this).fadeOut('slow', function() { $(this).remove() });
});
```

When you call `fadeOut()`, it sets the `display` property for the element to `none`—essentially, it's a fancy replacement for `hide()`. Figure 18.14 shows a list item that's in the process of fading out.

In this case, I want to actually remove the element from the page entirely. To do so, I need a callback, which is included as the second argument to `fadeOut()`. The callback is run whenever the animation is complete, and in this case, it removes the element from the page. The first argument is used to specify the speed of the animation. Setting it to `slow` means that it will take 600 milliseconds to complete. By default, the animation takes 400 milliseconds. You can also set it to `fast` (200 milliseconds), or you can enter a number of milliseconds yourself.

FIGURE 18.14
The jQuery fade-out effect in progress.

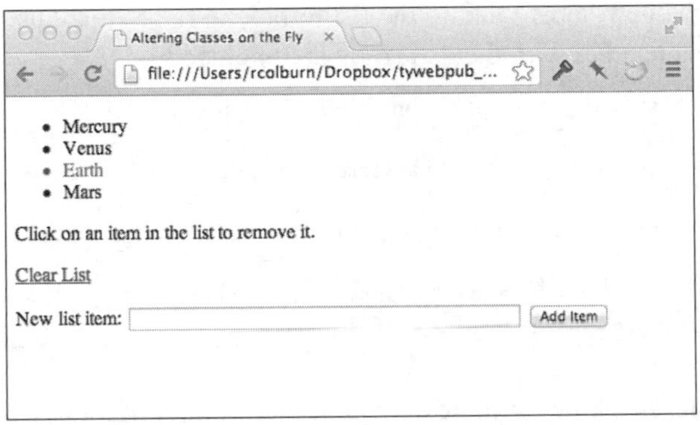

I've also updated the event handler for the Clear List link. In this case, I use the slide-up effect, shown in Figure 18.15, when the list is cleared. Here's the updated event handler:

```
$("#clearList").click(function (event) {
    event.preventDefault();
    $("#editable").slideUp('slow', function () {
      $("#editable").empty()
      $("#editable").show();
    });
});
```

18

FIGURE 18.15
The jQuery slide-up effect.

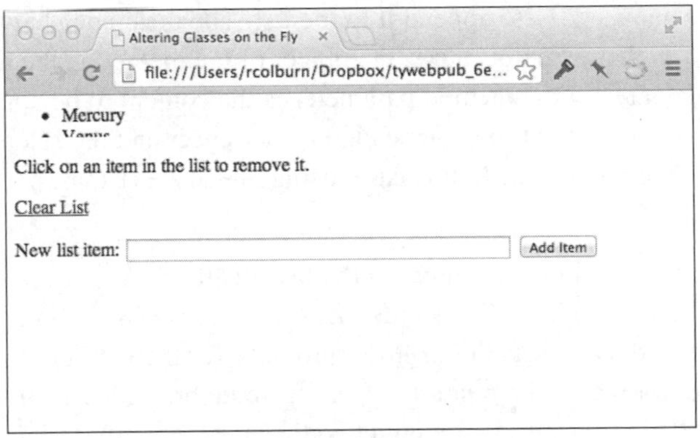

The changes here are similar to those for the previous event handler. After the animation is complete and the list is hidden, I call the `empty()` method to remove the contents of the list and then call `show()` on the now hidden list so that when the user adds new elements to it, the list will be visible.

Finally, I want the new items I add to the list to fade in rather than just appearing. Here's the updated event handler with the `fadeIn()` call included:

```
$("#addElement").submit(function (event) {
    event.preventDefault();
    var content = "<li>" + $("#addElement input[name='liContent']").val() +
"</li>";
    $(content).hide().appendTo("#editable").fadeIn('slow').css("display",
"list-item");
    $("#addElement input[name='liContent']").val("").focus();
});
```

This event handler is a little bit more complex. First, I initialize a new variable with the content to add to the page, just to make the code a little more readable. Then I go through all the steps required to fade the new content in. At this point, I should explain one of the other nifty features of jQuery—method chaining. Nearly all jQuery methods return the object of the method. So if I use `hide()` to hide something, the method returns whatever it was that I hid. This makes it convenient to call multiple methods on the same object in succession.

In this case, I call `hide()`, `appendTo()`, `fadeIn()`, and `css()` on the jQuery object representing the new content that I created. First, I pass the content variable to `$()`, which allows me to call jQuery's methods on the content. Then I call `hide()` on it so that it doesn't appear instantly when I append it to the list.

After that, I use `appendTo()` to append it to the list. The difference between `append()` and `appendTo()` is that with `append()`, the object of the method is the selector that represents the container, and the method parameter is the content to be appended, whereas with `appendTo()`, the content to be appended is the object and the selector for the container is the method parameter. In this case, using `appendTo()` makes it easier to chain all of these method calls.

After I've appended the hidden content to the list, I call `fadeIn('slow')` to make it gradually appear. Then, finally, I call `css("display", "list-item")` on the new content. When `fadeIn()` is done, it sets the `display` property for the list item to `block`, which causes the bullet for the list item not to appear in some browsers. Setting the `display` property to `list-item` ensures that a bullet is displayed.

AJAX and jQuery

One of the primary reasons programmers started adopting JavaScript libraries was that they made it much easier to use AJAX techniques on their websites and applications. What's AJAX? It's a description for functionality that uses a JavaScript feature called

`XmlHttpRequest` to make requests to the server in the background and use the results within the page.

The Web is based around the concept of pages. When you click a link or submit a form, usually you leave the page that you're on and go to a new page with a different URL (or refresh the current page). AJAX is about retrieving content from the server and then placing it on the page using JavaScript.

The previous example demonstrated how to use JavaScript to process data entered in a form and add it to a page instantly. Using AJAX, you can use the same techniques to retrieve data from the server and add it to the page. It's possible to write the code necessary to do this sort of thing from scratch, but jQuery makes it a whole lot easier.

Usually, AJAX is associated with server-side applications. For example, you can create a search engine and then use AJAX to retrieve search results and present them without ever leaving the current page. Unfortunately, there's not enough space in this book to teach you how to create a search engine. jQuery also provides the ability to retrieve information from a different static page using AJAX and present it in the current page. I'm going to present an example that takes advantage of that feature to show you how AJAX can be used.

Using AJAX to Load External Data

I've created a simple page, shown in Figure 18.16, that allows users to look up information about South American countries. When a user clicks one of the links, the information about that country is retrieved from the server and displayed inline on the page.

NOTE

Because of the way AJAX works, this example will only work if it's deployed on a web server. If you load the files directly in your browser, the JavaScript code that retrieves the information won't work. This is because browsers have a security feature that prevents JavaScript on one server from loading content from another server.

The sample consists of two files. The first is the page shown in Figure 18.16, which loads the data from the second page.

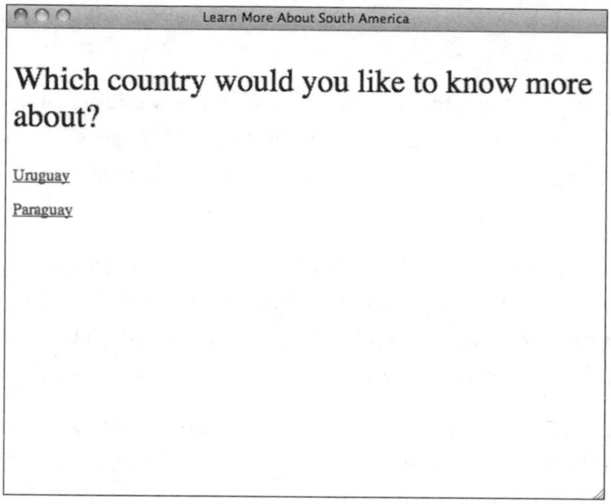

FIGURE 18.16
A page that loads
data from an exter-
nal source using
AJAX.

FIGURE 18.16
A page that loads data from an external source using AJAX.

The second is the page containing the information about the countries. Here's the source for the second page, `countries.html`, which contains information about the countries:

```html
<!DOCTYPE html>
<html>
<head>
    <title>South American Countries</title>
</head>
<body>
<div id="uruguay">
  <h2>Uruguay</h2>

  <p>Uruguay, officially the Oriental Republic of Uruguay, is a country located
in the southeastern part of South America. It is home to some 3.5 million people,
of whom 1.4 million live in the capital Montevideo and its metropolitan area. An
estimated 88% of the population are of European descent.</p>
  <p>Uruguay's only land border is with Rio Grande do Sul, Brazil, to the north.
To the west lies the Uruguay River, to the southwest lies the estuary of Rio de
la Plata, with Argentina only a short commute across the banks of either of these
bodies of water, while to the southeast lies the southern part of the Atlantic
Ocean. Uruguay, with an area of approximately 176 thousand km2, is the second
smallest nation of South America in area after Suriname.</p>
</div>

<div id="paraguay">
  <h2>Paraguay</h2>
  <p>Paraguay, officially the Republic of Paraguay, is a landlocked country in
South America. It is bordered by Argentina to the south and southwest, Brazil to
the east and northeast, and Bolivia to the northwest. Paraguay lies on both banks
of the Paraguay River, which runs through the center of the country from north to
south. Because of its central location in South America, is sometimes referred to
```

```
as Corazon de America, or the Heart of America.</p>
  <p>As of 2009 the population was estimated at 6.3 million. The capital and
largest city is Asuncion. The official languages are Spanish and Guarani, both
being widely spoken in the country. Most of the population are mestizos.</p>
</div>
</body>
</html>
```

For a real application, instead of this simple page, you'd have a more robust service that could return lots of information about every country in South America on demand. This sample page illustrates the concept without requiring knowledge of server-side programming.

Now that the raw information is in place to be used on the page, I'll explain how the page works. When a link is clicked, the information is retrieved from `countries.html` and displayed on the initial page, as shown in Figure 18.17.

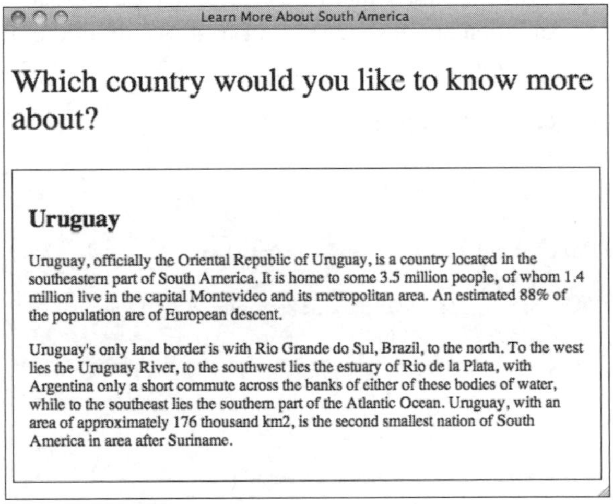

FIGURE 18.17
The information about Uruguay was loaded from an external source.

First, let's look at the two links:

```
<p class="countryOption"><a href="countries.html #uruguay">Uruguay</a></p>
<p class="countryOption"><a href="countries.html #paraguay">Paraguay</a></p>
```

They almost look like regular links. The one difference is that I've included a space between the filename and the anchor in the URL. That's because it's not really an anchor; it's the ID of a `<div>` on the `countries.html` page.

Here's the event handler for the click event for the links:

```
$("p.countryOption a").click(function (event) {
  event.preventDefault();
  $("p.countryOption").fadeOut();
  $("#country").load($(this).attr('href'));
  $("#country").fadeIn();
});
```

You should be used to most of this by now. The first line prevents the link from actually taking you to the link referenced in the `href` attribute. The second line fades out the links, because they'll be replaced by the country data.

The third line actually performs the AJAX request. It instructs jQuery to load whatever is in the `href` of the link the user clicked on into the element with the ID "country." In this case, the links refer to jQuery selectors of sorts. Remember the URLs in the links? They consist of two parts, the first being the file to load, and the second being a jQuery selector, in this case, the ID of the country that I'll be displaying information about. jQuery loads the entire page, and then applies the selector to it to extract the information I care about.

Here's the full source code for the page:

```
<!DOCTYPE html>
<html>
  <head>
    <title>Learn More About South America</title>
      <style>
        #country { border: 1px solid black; padding: 15px; }
        p.question { font-size: 200%; }
      </style>
  </head>
<body>
<p class="question">
  Which country would you like to know more about?
</p>

<div id="country">Foo</div>

<p class="countryOption"><a href="countries.html #uruguay">Uruguay</a></p>
<p class="countryOption"><a href="countries.html #paraguay">Paraguay</a></p>

  <script src="jquery.js"></script>
  <script type="text/javascript" charset="utf-8">
    $(function () {
      $("#country").hide();

      $("p.countryOption a").click(function (event) {
        event.preventDefault();
        $("p.countryOption").fadeOut();
```

```
      $("#country").load($(this).attr('href'));
      $("#country").fadeIn();
    });
  });
</script>
</body>
</html>
```

To read about other AJAX-related methods offered by jQuery, take a look at the jQuery API documentation. Most of the other jQuery methods are more suitable to application development, but they essentially work in a similar fashion to the `load()` method that you saw here.

Summary

In this lesson, I explored some of the powerful features common to most JavaScript libraries using jQuery. You learned which JavaScript libraries are available and why you might want to use them. You also learned how to include jQuery in a web page and take advantage of its functionality through the `document.ready()` event. I explained how event binding works with jQuery and how to dynamically modify the styles on a page as well as the content of a page itself. Finally, I explained what AJAX is and how jQuery and other JavaScript libraries enable you to make requests to external data sources from within a web page.

18

Workshop

As always, we wrap up the lesson with a few questions, quizzes, and exercises. Here are some questions and exercises that should refresh what you've learned about jQuery.

Q&A

Q Won't adding jQuery cause my pages to load more slowly?

A Yes, adding any JavaScript library will add to your overall page size. However, the browser will cache the external JavaScript file, so users should only have to download it once, when they get to the first page of your site. When they go to subsequent pages, the JavaScript library will already be in the cache.

Another option to help speed up your pages that use jQuery is to use a content delivery network or CDN. These are repositories of many different JavaScript libraries that you can link to in your web pages to take advantage of the global cache. Chances are your customers have already visited a page that uses a CDN for jQuery so it's already in their cache and you can take advantage of that. The CDN I use for jQuery is at https://code.jquery.com/. Simply link to the version of jQuery you want to use on your site the way you would any other script file. For example, to link to the 2.1.4 version you would write: `<script src="https://code.jquery.com/jquery-2.1.4.min.js"></script>`.

Q What about users who don't have JavaScript enabled?

A It's generally agreed that less than 3% of users have JavaScript disabled these days. However, that is still a lot of people, so you'll want to make sure that essential functionality still works for users who don't have JavaScript access. That's one of the big advantages of the unobtrusive JavaScript approach that jQuery reinforces. The markup should work fine without the JavaScript, which enhances the experience but is not essential to making the pages work.

Quiz

1. What is the purpose of jQuery's `document.ready()` handler?
2. How do I select an item with the ID `navigationLink` in jQuery?
3. What does the variable `this` refer to in an event-handling function?

Quiz Answers

1. The `document.ready()` event, provided by jQuery, fires when the HTML document is fully constructed and before resources like images are loaded. It's generally a safe point at which you can begin initializing JavaScript for a page.
2. jQuery uses CSS-style selectors. So to select an item with the ID `navigationLink`, you'd use `$("#navigationLink")`.
3. In an event handler, `this` refers to the object that the event was fired from. So if it's a click event on a link, `this` refers to the link that was clicked.

Exercises

1. Download jQuery and use the `<script>` tag to load it in a web page.
2. Use jQuery to disable all the links on a web page.
3. Use jQuery to cause a border to appear around all the links on a web page when the user mouses over them. Make sure to remove the borders when the user moves the pointer away from the link.
4. Try to add a link to a web page that uses AJAX to retrieve the local temperature from a weather site for your city. You'll need to find the URL for a page with your city's weather on it and then create the correct selector to extract only the information you want from that page. After you find the weather page, view the source on it to figure out how to extract the information using a jQuery selector.

LESSON 19
Using JavaScript in Your Pages

Now that you have some understanding of what JavaScript is all about, you're ready to look at some practical applications of JavaScript.

In this lesson, you'll learn how to complete the following tasks:

- Validate the contents of a form
- Create a list that expands and collapses
- Add new content to a web page

Validating Forms with JavaScript

Remember the sample form that you created back in Lesson 12, "Designing Forms"? It's shown again in Figure 19.1. It's a typical registration form for a website, with several required fields.

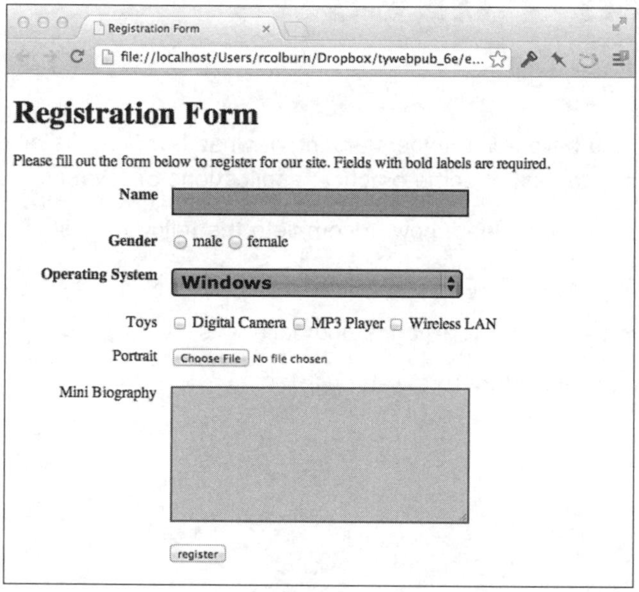

FIGURE 19.1
The registration form.

What happens when this form is submitted? In the real world, a script on the server side validates the data that the visitor entered, stores it in a database, and then thanks the visitor for her time.

But what happens if a visitor doesn't fill out the form correctly—for example, she doesn't enter her name or choose a value for gender? The script can check all that information and return an error. The good thing about server-side validation is that it's reliable. The web developer can be completely certain that the user's input has been validated before the script tries to store it in the database. However, validating the form input in the browser before it's submitted has some advantages as well. The validation can be designed to occur when it makes the most sense for the form in question, as opposed to waiting for the user to click the Submit button. Furthermore, saving round trips to the server conserves resources and offers better performance for users.

Exercise 19.1: Form Validation ▼

Now take a look at how the registration form is validated with JavaScript. Whenever you click the Submit button on a form, two events are triggered: the `onclick` event for the button and the `onsubmit` button for the form. For form validation, `onsubmit` is the better choice because some forms can be submitted without clicking the Submit button. When the `onsubmit` event is fired, the validation function is called.

First open the HTML for your form. It looks like this:

```html
<!DOCTYPE html>
<html>
<head>
<title>Registration Form</title>
<style type="text/css" media="screen">
    form div {
        margin-bottom: 1em;
    }

    div.submit input {
        margin-left: 165px;
    }

    label.field {
        display: block;
        float: left;
        margin-right: 15px;
        width: 150px;
        text-align: right;
    }

    input[type="text"], select, textarea {
      width: 300px;
      font: 18px Verdana;
      border: solid 2px #666;
      background-color: #ada;
    }

    div.required label.field {
        font-weight: bold;
    }

    div.required input, div.required select {
        background-color: #6a6;
        border: solid 2px #000;
        font-weight: bold;
    }
</style>
</head>
<body>
```

19

▼

▼
```
<h1>Registration Form</h1>

<p>Please fill out the form below to register for our site. Fields
with bold labels are required.</p>

<form action="/register" method="post" enctype="multipart/form-data"
id="registrationForm">

  <div class="required">
    <label class="field" for="name">Name</label>
    <input name="name" type="text" />
  </div>

  <div class="required">
    <label class="field">Gender</label>
    <label><input type="radio" name="gender" value="male" /> male</label>
    <label><input type="radio" name="gender" value="female" /> female</label>
  </div>

  <div class="required">
    <label class="field">Operating System</label>
    <select name="os">
      <option value="windows">Windows</option>
      <option value="macos">Mac OS</option>
      <option value="linux">Linux</option>
      <option value="other">Other ...</option>
    </select>
  </div>

  <div>
    <label class="field">Toys</label>
    <label><input type="checkbox" name="toy" value="digicam" /> Digital Camera
</label>
    <label><input type="checkbox" name="toy" value="mp3" /> MP3 Player</label>
    <label><input type="checkbox" name="toy" value="wlan" /> Wireless LAN</label>
  </div>

  <div>
    <label class="field">Portrait</label>
    <input type="file" name="portrait" />
  </div>

  <div>
    <label class="field">Mini Biography</label>
    <textarea name="bio" rows="6" cols="40"></textarea>
  </div>

  <div class="submit">
    <input type="submit" value="register" />
  </div>
```
▼
```
</form>
```

```
</body>
</html>
```

I'll be using jQuery to write the form validation code. So, I'll add the following code to the page right above the closing `</body>` tag:

```
<script src="https://code.jquery.com/jquery-2.1.4.min.js"></script>
```

This loads jQuery from a CDN so that your page will load faster.

Then load the `form.js` script. I placed mine in the `scripts` subdirectory, like this:

```
<script src="scripts/form.js"></script>
```

In this script I use jQuery's `document.ready` handler to bind an anonymous function to the submit event of the form, which has the ID `registrationForm`:

```
$(function() {
  $("#registrationForm").submit(function (event) {
    alert("Form submitted");
    event.preventDefault();
  });
});
```

The Validation Function   When you write an event-handling function for jQuery, you can specify that the function accepts an argument, which represents the event that the handler is handling. In this case, I named the argument `event` for simplicity. In the handler, I display an alert, just to demonstrate that the JavaScript is working, and I call the `event.preventDefault()` method. This is a special method provided by jQuery that indicates that the default behavior associated with the event should not occur. In the case of a form submission, it prevents the form from being submitted. When the form validation is complete, the default action will only be prevented when the form input is not valid.

Testing For Required Fields   The form has three required fields: Name, Gender, and Operating System. The validation function is responsible for checking that they each contain a value. The `name` field is a text input field. Here's the markup for the field:

```
<input name="name" type="text" />
```

Before writing the test to verify that the form field is not empty, the trick is accessing the value in the field. I've updated my event handler to look like this:

```
$("#registrationForm").submit(function (event) {
    event.preventDefault();
    console.log($(this.name).val());
});
```

19

▼ I'm still preventing the form's submission, and now I'm using the `console.log()` method to log the value of `$(this.name).val()`. The `console.log()` method is provided as a convenience so that you can print out your own messages to the Console tab in the Development Tools window. In this case, I want to print out the value of the form field. Remember that `this` is an object representing the form. The form object has properties representing each of its fields, so I can access a field with the name "name" using `this.name`. jQuery provides the `val()` method to normalize accessing the values of form fields. So, `$(this.name).val()` returns the current value of the field named "name" in the form. That line prints it on the console.

Using this information and an `if` statement, you can test the contents of `name` to see whether a name has been entered:

```
if (!$(this.name).val()) {
  event.preventDefault();
  alert("You must enter a name.");
}
```

The expression in the `if` statement evaluates the value of the form field in a Boolean context. So if the field's value is null or an empty string, the expression will be false. In that case, the function displays an error message and prevents the form from being submitted.

If the name is valid, the next step is to validate the gender radio button group. Validation of these fields differs slightly because radio button groups consist of multiple fields with the same name. So in this case, I need to alter my selector to access the value of the radio button field. Remember that only one element in a set of radio buttons can be selected. I can use the CSS selector for attribute values to locate the selected radio button. The code to validate the radio button looks like this:

```
if (!$(this).find("input[name='gender']:checked").length) {
  event.preventDefault();
  alert("You must select your gender.");
}
```

I access the `Gender` field on the form the same way I accessed the `Name` field. Then I used the jQuery `find` method to search for elements with the "checked" attribute checked using the `:checked` selector. I could also pass the context for a jQuery query as a second argument to the jQuery method, like this:

```
$("input[name='gender']:checked", this)
```

If neither radio button is selected, the length of the matched set will be zero and therefore
▼ be false in the context of the `if` statement, and the error message will be displayed.

The form indicates that the Operating System field is also required, but because it's impossible to not select an item in that list, there's no need to validate it.

You can use the JavaScript debugger built in to Chrome (or whichever browser you're using) to inspect this function further. In Chrome, open the Developer Tools and click on the Sources button. Then click the button on the upper left, just below the toolbar, to view a list of the scripts on the page. From there, select form.js from the list. You should see a view like the one in Figure 19.2.

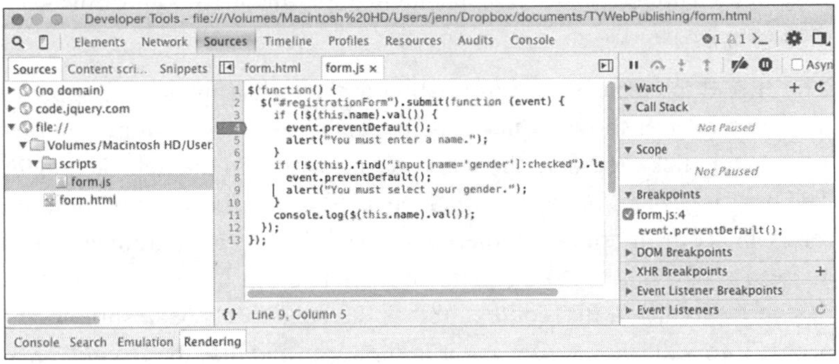

FIGURE 19.2
The Chrome Developer Tool Sources view.

In the middle pane, you can see the source code for the script. Each line of the script is numbered. If you click the line number for line 3, an arrow will appear. This sets what's called a *breakpoint*. Before the browser executes this line of the script, it will stop execution and let you inspect the inner workings of the script as it runs. This is incredibly useful when you're looking into problems in your scripts. You can see which variables are set and what their values are, and you can control execution of the script from that point on, resuming execution or proceeding one line at a time. After you've set the breakpoint on line 3, click the Submit button on the form. The Developer Tools window will be updated to look as it does in Figure 19.3.

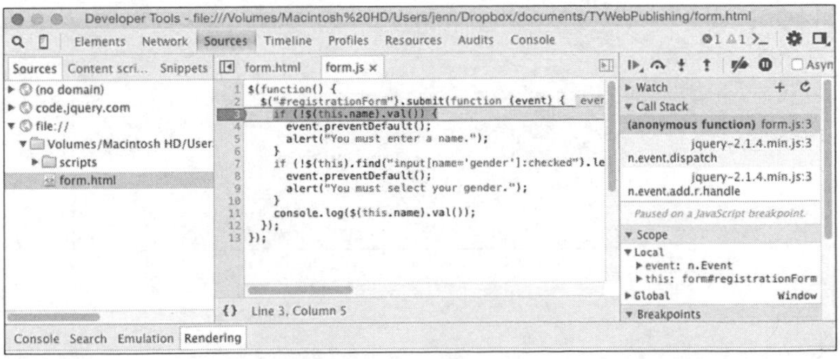

FIGURE 19.3
Running a script in the debugger.

19

▼ The blue arrow next to the line number for line 3 indicates that it is the where the debugger is stopped. The buttons above the right pane allow you to control execution from there. The buttons, from left to right, are Resume, Step Over, Step Into, Step Out, and Deactivate Breakpoints. The Deactivate button causes subsequent breakpoints to be ignored. The Resume button continues execution until the script finishes or it hits another breakpoint. Step Over moves to the next statement in the current function, and Step Into debugs whatever function is being called from the current line (if there is a function call on that line). Step Out executes the remainder of the current function and resumes debugging in the calling function. You should experiment with all of these to get a feel for how the debugger works.

You'll find three pieces of information in the right pane useful immediately. The first is the *Call Stack*. It shows which function calls led to the current statement being called. When you click Step Out, the debugger moves up to the next statement in the call stack. The next is *Scope Variables*, which enables you to inspect any variables that are currently in scope. In this case, there's `event`, which is the parameter of your event handler, and `this`, which is set to the element that the event handler is bound to. If you inspect it, you'll see that in this context, this is the `form` that's been submitted. You'll need to access it to validate the user input in the form. Finally, the *Breakpoints* section shows all of the breakpoints that have been set. Sometimes it's hard to remember which breakpoints you've set and where you set them. You can use the Breakpoints list to unset them. You should definitely experiment with the debugger. Being able to use it effectively makes it very easy to track down many kinds of bugs.

The Completed Registration Form with JavaScript Validation When the JavaScript script that you just created is integrated with the original registration form document from Lesson 12, the result is a web form that tests its contents before they're transmitted to the server for further processing. This way, no data is sent to the server until everything is correct. If a problem occurs, the browser informs the user (see Figure 19.4).

FIGURE 19.4
An alert message.

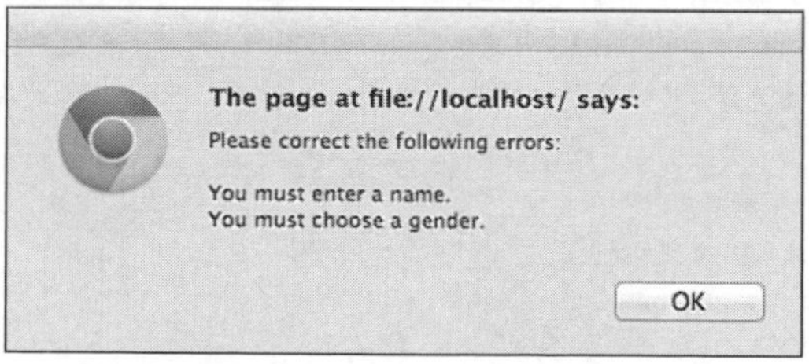

The page at file://localhost/ says:

Please correct the following errors:

You must enter a name.
You must choose a gender.

OK

▼

There was no need to change the source code for the page at all other than to add the JavaScript tags to load the jQuery library and the custom script for the page, as mentioned previously.

Then there's the custom script itself. Here are the full contents:

```
$(function() {
  $("#registrationForm").submit(function (event) {
    if (!$(this.name).val()) {
      event.preventDefault();
      alert("You must enter a name.");
    }
    if (!$(this).find("input[name='gender']:checked").length) {
      event.preventDefault();
      alert("You must select your gender.");
    }
    console.log($(this.name).val());
  });
});
```

Improving Form Validation   The form validation code in this exercise works, but it could be better. The biggest problem is that it shows an alert for each field with an error. A better approach is to show an error on the page and highlight the fields that need to be corrected before the page can be submitted. The validation code is the same; what's different is what happens when errors are found.

In this case, I'm going to print an error message above the form, and I'm going to mark each field with invalid input to indicate that it needs to be corrected. Before I get to the JavaScript, I'm going to add a few styles to the style sheet that will be used for the validation messages. Here are the new styles:

```
div.error label {
  color: red;
}

div.errors {
  border: 2px solid red;
  color: red;
  width: 50%;
  padding: 10px;
}
```

The first style is applied to labels inside div elements with the error class. The second style is applied to a div with the class errors. This should provide some insight into how the validation code will work. When a field is found to have invalid input, an error message will be saved so that it can be placed in the errors div, and the class error will be applied to the div containing that field.

▼ The conditional code in the validation JavaScript is the same. The first change I'm making is to get rid of the lines that display the alert box and replace them with the lines that add the appropriate class to the document. The updated JavaScript looks like this:

```
$(function() {
  $("#registrationForm").submit(function (event) {
    if (!$(this.name).val()) {
      $(this.name).parents("div.required").addClass("error");
      event.preventDefault();
    }

    if (!$("input[name='gender']:checked", this).length) {
      $("input[name='gender']", this).parents("div.required").addClass("error");
      event.preventDefault();
    }
  });
});
```

The trick here is to write the proper selectors to add the error class to the appropriate element. First, here's the line that adds the error class to the enclosing `div` for the Name field:

```
$(this.name).parents("div.required").addClass("error");
```

I start by selecting the Name field. Then I use jQuery's `parents()` method to apply the `div.required` selector to all the ancestors of the form field. It matches the appropriate element, and then I use the `addClass()` method to apply the `error` class to the `div`. If you try this out, you'll see that when you submit invalid data the labels for the invalid fields suddenly turn red.

Now let's look at printing a proper error message on the page. First, I declare a variable in which to collect the error messages for each field. If a field is invalid, the error message is appended to the list. Once all the fields have been validated, if there are any error messages in the list, the `div` containing the error messages is formatted and printed at the top of the form. Here's the script:

```
$(function() {
  $("#registrationForm").submit(function (event) {
    var errors = [];

    if (!$(this.name).val()) {
      errors.push("<li>You must enter a name.</li>");
      $(this.name).parents("div.required").addClass("error");
      event.preventDefault();
    }

    if (!$("input[name='gender']:checked", this).length) {
      errors.push("<li>You must select a gender.</li>");
      $("input[name='gender']", this).parents("div.required").addClass("error");
      event.preventDefault();
```
▼

```
    }

    if (errors.length > 0) {
      $(this).prepend("<div class='errors'>You must "
         + "correct the following errors:<ul>"
         + errors.join("") + "</ul></div>");
    }
  });
});
```

If you include this code in your page and test it, you'll see that when you submit an invalid form, it properly marks the labels of invalid fields, prints the error message at the top form, and prevents the form from being submitted. However, one bug should be fixed. What happens when you submit the form with invalid input a second time? As you'll see, a second set of error messages will be printed at the top of the page. To fix this bug, I just need to add the following line to the event handler:

```
$("div.errors", this).remove();
```

I added it right before the `if` statement that checks whether to print the error messages. It uses the jQuery `remove()` method to remove any elements that match the selector.

The final form with all of the error messages for invalid input displayed appears in Figure 19.5.

FIGURE 19.5
An alert message
for multiple fields.

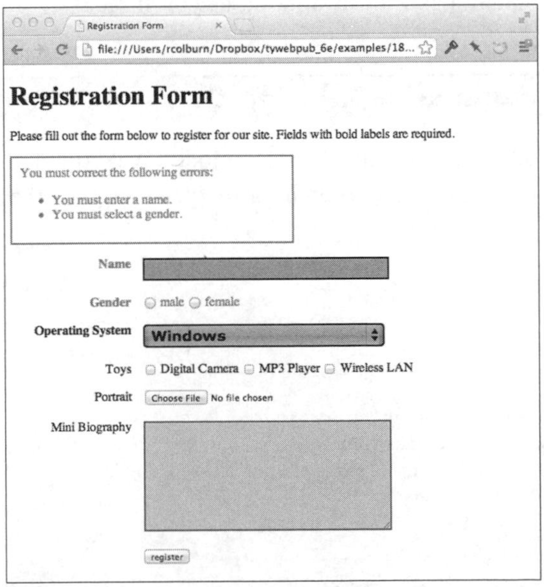

19

Hiding and Showing Content

One way to help users deal with a lot of information presented on a single page is to hide some of it when the page loads and to provide controls to let them view the information that interests them. In this example, I create a frequently asked questions page. On this page, the questions will be organized in sections. Each section will start out collapsed, and the answers to the questions will be hidden as well. Users can display the answers by clicking the corresponding questions.

In this example, I apply an approach referred to as unobtrusive JavaScript. The philosophy behind it is that the behavior added by JavaScript should be clearly separated from the presentation applied using HTML and *Cascading Style Sheets* (CSS). The page should work and be presentable without JavaScript, and JavaScript code should not be mixed with the markup on the page.

In practice, what this means is that event handlers should be specified in scripts instead of HTML attributes. Also, in this example, using JavaScript unobtrusively means that if the user has JavaScript turned off, she will see all the questions and answers by default, rather than seeing a page with the questions hidden and no means of displaying them.

In the previous lesson, you learned how to hide and show content using jQuery. In this example, I'm going to explain how to accomplish the same thing using plain JavaScript, and then provide the jQuery version as a comparison. jQuery is a convenience, but it's not necessary for building things with JavaScript, as you'll see.

▼ Exercise 19.2: Hiding and Showing Content

The exercise starts with a web page that doesn't include JavaScript and that displays the frequently asked questions. Here's the source for the page. Figure 19.6 shows the page in a browser.

Input ▼

```
<!DOCTYPE html>
<html>
<head>
    <title>Frequently Asked Questions</title>
    <style type="text/css" media="screen">
        dt { margin-bottom: .5em; font-size: 125%;}
        dd { margin-bottom: 1em;}
    </style>
</head>
<body>
<h1>Frequently Asked Questions</h1>
```

```
<dl id="faq">
    <dt>Don't I need a development environment to work with JavaScript?</dt>
    <dd>Nope. As with HTML, all you need is a text editor and a browser that sup-
ports JavaScript. You might be confusing JavaScript with Java, a more comprehen-
sive programming language that needs at least a compiler for its programs to run.
However, tools like FireBug for Firefox, the Internet Explorer Developer Toolbar,
and Safari's Web Inspector can make your life easier. Consult the documentation
on those tools to learn more about their JavaScript features.</dd>
    <dt>What is AJAX?</dt>
    <dd>One topic we haven't covered yet is AJAX. AJAX is a term used to describe
scripts that communicate with the server without requiring a Web page to be
fully reloaded. For example, you can use it to fetch information and display it
on the page, or to submit a form for processing, all without changing the full
page in the browser. I'll discuss AJAX in detail in Lesson 16, "Using JavaScript
Libraries."</dd>
    <dt>When I use JavaScript, do I need to accommodate users whose browsers may
not support JavaScript or who have disabled it?</dt>
    <dd>Some estimates indicate that over 90% of Web users have JavaScript
enabled. However, unless you have a really good reason not to, you should make
accommodations for users without JavaScript. You need not offer users who don't
have JavaScript an identical experience to those who have it, but they should be
able to access your site. For example, if you run an online store, do you really
want to shut out users because of their browser configuration? </dd>
</dl>
</body>
</html>
```

Output ▼

FIGURE 19.6
The FAQ page.

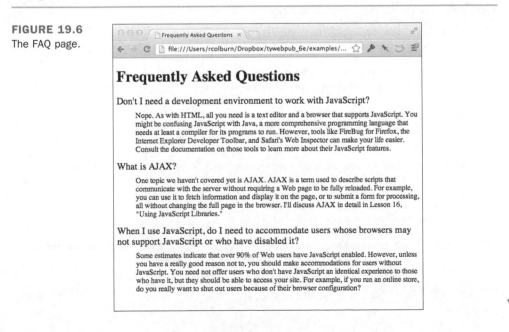

▼ The page is designed so that it works perfectly well without JavaScript; all the questions and answers are displayed so that the user can read them. This is what unobtrusive JavaScript is all about.

Adding the Script　After the page has been created and you've confirmed that it's working correctly, the next step is to add JavaScript into the mix. To include the script on the page, I just need to add the link to the external script to the header:

```
<script type="text/javascript" src="faq.js"></script>
```

That `<script>` tag loads and executes the script in the file `faq.js`. After the JavaScript has been added, the answers to the questions are hidden, as shown in Figure 19.7.

FIGURE 19.7
The FAQ page with the JavaScript included.

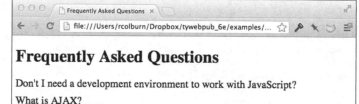

Here's the JavaScript contained in the `faq.js` file:

```
window.onload = function() {
    var faqList, answers, questionLinks, questions, currentNode, i, j;

    faqList = document.getElementById("faq");
    answers = faqList.getElementsByTagName("dd");

    for (i = 0; i < answers.length; i++) {
        answers[i].style.display = 'none';
    }

    questions = faqList.getElementsByTagName("dt");

    for (i = 0; i < questions.length; i++) {
        questions[i].onclick = function() {
            currentNode = this.nextSibling;
            while (currentNode) {
                if (currentNode.nodeType == "1" && currentNode.tagName == "DD") {
                    if (currentNode.style.display == 'none') {
```

▼

```
                currentNode.style.display = 'block';
            }
            else {
                currentNode.style.display = 'none';
            }

            break;
        }

        currentNode = currentNode.nextSibling;
    }

    return false;
    };
  }
}
```

This JavaScript code is significantly more complex than any used previously in the book. Take a look at the first line, which is repeated here:

```
window.onload = function() {
```

This is where the unobtrusiveness comes in. Instead of calling a function using the onload attribute of the <body> tag to start up the JavaScript for the page, I assign an anonymous function to the onload property of the window object. The code inside the function will run when the onload event for the window is fired by the browser. Setting up my JavaScript this way allows me to include this JavaScript on any page without modifying the markup to bind it to an event. That's handled here.

This is the method for binding functions to events programmatically. Each element has properties for the events it supports. To bind an event handler to them, you assign the function to that property. You can do so by declaring an anonymous function in the assignment statement, as I did in this example, or you can assign the function by name, like this:

```
function doStuff() {
    // Does stuff
}
window.onload = doStuff;
```

In this case, I intentionally left the parentheses out when I used the function name. That's because I'm assigning the function itself to the onload property, as opposed to assigning the value returned by doStuff() to that property.

▼

NOTE

When you declare an anonymous function in an assignment statement, you must make sure to include the semicolon after the closing brace. Normally when you declare functions, a semicolon is not needed, but because the function declaration is part of the assignment statement, that statement has to be terminated with a semicolon or you'll get a syntax error when the browser tries to interpret the JavaScript.

On the next line, I declare all the variables I use in this function. JavaScript is a bit different from many other languages in that variables cannot have "block" scope. For example, in most languages, if you declare a variable inside the body of an `if` statement, that variable will go away once the `if` statement is finished. Not so in JavaScript. A variable declared anywhere inside a function will be accessible from that point onward in the function, regardless of where it was declared. For that reason, declaring all your variables at the top of the function is one way to avoid confusing bugs.

Looking Up Elements in the Document   The preceding lesson discussed the `document` object a little bit and mentioned that it provides access to the full contents of the web page. The representation of the page that is accessible via JavaScript is referred to as the *Document Object Model*, or DOM. The entire page is represented as a tree, starting at the root element, represented by the `<html>` tag. If you leave out the `<html>` tag, the browser will add it to the DOM when it renders the page. The DOM for this page is shown in Figure 19.8.

FIGURE 19.8
The DOM for the FAQ page, shown in the Chrome Developer Tools.

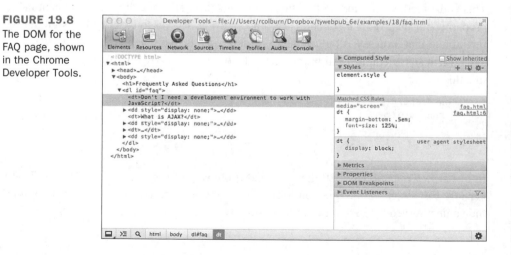

▼

There are a number of ways to dig into the DOM. The browser provides access to the parent of each element, as well as its siblings and children, so you can reach any element that way. However, navigating your way to elements in the page that way is tedious. Fortunately, there are some shortcuts available.

These shortcuts, methods that can be called on the `document` object, are listed in Table 19.1.

TABLE 19.1   Methods for Accessing the DOM

Method	Description
getElementsByTagName(name)	Retrieves a list of elements with the supplied tag name. This can also be called on a specific element, and it will return a list of the descendants of that element with the specified tag name.
getElementById(id)	Retrieves the element with the specified ID. IDs are assigned using the `id` attribute. This is one of the areas in which JavaScript intersects with CSS.
getElementByName(name)	Retrieves elements with the specified value as their `name` attribute. Usually used with forms or form fields, both of which use the `name` attribute.

To set up the expanding and collapsing properly, I must hide the answers to the questions and bind an event to the questions that expands them when users click them. First, I need to look up the elements I want to modify in the DOM.

```
faqList = document.getElementById("faq");
answers = faqList.getElementsByTagName("dd");
```

The first line gets the element with the ID `faq`. That's the ID I assigned to my definition list in the markup. Then the next line returns a list of all the `dd` elements that are children of the element now assigned to `faqList`. I could skip the step of looking up the `faq` list first, but then if this page included multiple definition lists, the behavior would be applied to all of them rather than just the `faq`. This is also a useful precaution in case this JavaScript file is included on more than one page. In the end, I have a list of `dd` elements.

Changing Styles   I grabbed the list of `dd` elements so that they can be hidden when the page loads. I could have hidden them using a style sheet or the style attribute of each of the `dd` elements, but that wouldn't be unobtrusive. If a user without JavaScript visited the page, the answers to the questions would be hidden and there wouldn't be any way to reveal the answers. It's better to hide them with JavaScript.

19

▼ There are two ways to hide elements with CSS: you can set the `display` property to `none` or the `visibility` property to `hidden`. Using the `display` property will hide the element completely and remove it from the DOM. The `visibility` property hides the content in the element but leaves the space it takes up empty. So for this case, using the `display` property makes more sense. Every element in the document has a `style` property, and that property has its own properties for each CSS property. Here's the code that hides each of the `dd` elements:

```
for (i = 0; i < answers.length; i++) {
      answers[i].style.display = 'none';
  }
```

The `for` loop iterates over each of the elements, and inside the loop, I set the `display` property to `none`. Once the page loads, the answers will be hidden.

Traversing the Document   The final step is to bind the event that toggles the display of the answers to each of the questions. This is the most complex bit of code on the page. First, let me explain how the event handler works:

```
function() {
  currentNode = this.nextSibling;
  while (currentNode) {
      if (currentNode.nodeType == "1" && currentNode.tagName == "DD") {
          if (currentNode.style.display == 'none') {
              currentNode.style.display = 'block';
          }
          else {
              currentNode.style.display = 'none';
          }
          break;
      }
      currentNode = currentNode.nextSibling;
  }

  return false;
};
```

That's the function that will be used as the `onclick` handler for each of the questions. As you may remember, in the context of an event handler, `this` is the element associated with the event. The main challenge in this function is locating the answer associated with the question the user clicked on, and displaying it.

To do so, the function will navigate through the DOM to find the next DD element in the DOM tree following the DT element that the user clicked on. First, I use the `nextSibling` property of `this`, and then I start a `while` loop that will iterate over each of the siblings of that element. The `while` condition ensures that the loop will run until `this`
▼ runs out of siblings.

The nextSibling property is a reference to the next node in the DOM tree. A node is different from an element. HTML elements are nodes, but the whitespace between tags is a node, as is the text inside a tag. So the nextSibling of a node might very well be the return character at the end of the line following the tag. There are a number of other properties associated with nodes as well that can be used to traverse the document. Some are listed in Table 19.2.

TABLE 19.2 Node Properties for Navigating the DOM

Method	Description
childNodes	An array of all the children of a node.
firstChild	The first child node of a node.
innerHTML	The markup and content inside a node. You can set this property to change the contents of a node.
lastChild	The last child of a node.
nextSibling	The next sibling of the node (at the same level of the DOM tree).
parentNode	The parent of the current node.
previousSibling	The node that precedes the current node at the same level of the tree.

All the properties in the table are null if it's not possible to traverse the DOM in that direction. For example, if a node has no child nodes, its lastChild property will be null.

Here's what happens when a user clicks one of the questions. As mentioned, a while loop will iterate over the siblings of the question. Inside the while loop, I check the nodeType and tagName of the current node.

The nodeType property contains a number that identifies what type of node is being processed. Element nodes have a node type of 1. Attributes are node type 2, and text nodes are type 3. There are 12 total node types, but those three are the main ones you'll use. In this function, I'm searching for the <dd> tag that follows the DT tag that contains the question. I have to check the node type before checking the tagName property because only elements (that have node type 1) support the tagName property. If I didn't check the node type first, other node types would cause errors.

Each sibling node that follows the original <dt> is tested, and as soon as a <dd> element is found, the script toggles the visibility of that element. It then uses the break statement to stop executing the loop. If the node is not a <dd> element, then the next sibling of currentNode is assigned to the currentNode variable, and the loop is executed again. If the <dd> element is never found, then when there are no more siblings, the currentNode variable will be set to null, and execution of the loop will stop.

19

▼ At the end, the function returns `false`:

```
questions = faqList.getElementsByTagName("dt");
for (i = 0; i < questions.length; i++) {
    questions[i].onclick = function() {
        // The actual event handling code goes here.
    }
}
}
```

First, I use `getElementsByTagName()` to get a list of all the `<dt>` tags that are children of `faqList`. Then I use a `for` loop to iterate over them and bind the function described previously to their `onclick` event.

The Same Code with jQuery

Now here's a look at code that achieves the same results using jQuery. There are some flaws in the previous code as well that this solution gets around. For example, for reasons of simplicity and cross-browser compatibility, I specified the click event handler, attaching it directly to the `onclick` property of the relevant element. I did the same thing with the `body.onload` handler. As you know, this approach can interfere with other scripts you might want to use on the page.

First I load jQuery from the CDN with this line of HTML:

```
<script src="https://code.jquery.com/jquery-2.1.4.min.js"></script>
```

Here's the new `faq.js` script:

```
$(function() {
  $("#faq dd").hide();
  $("#faq dt").click(function(event) {
      event.preventDefault();
      $(this).next("dd").toggle();
  });
});
```

▲ As you can see, the libraries enable me to accomplish a lot more than I could writing raw JavaScript with just a few lines of code.

Adding New Content to a Page

The last example demonstrated how to modify styles on a page. In this example, I explain how to modify the content on a page using JavaScript. You can create new elements in JavaScript and then attach them to the document in any location that you choose. You can also modify elements that are already on the page or remove elements if you need to do so.

Exercise 19.3: Add an Expand All/Collapse All Link to the FAQ ▼

In this example, I'll be adding a new feature to the FAQ page presented in the previous example. In that example, I illustrated how to add new features to a page using JavaScript without modifying the markup in any way. This example will continue along those lines. In fact, I won't be making any changes to the markup on the page; all the changes will take place inside the JavaScript file.

In this example, I add a link to the page that expands all the questions in the FAQ, or, if all the questions are already expanded, will collapse all the questions. The label on the link will change depending on its behavior, and the function of the link will change if the user individually collapses or expands all the questions.

Adding the Link to the Page   Because the link only functions if the user has JavaScript enabled, I am going to add it dynamically using JavaScript. I've added a new function to the JavaScript file that takes care of adding the link, which I call from the `onload` handler for the page. The function adds more than just a link to the page. It adds a link, a `<div>` containing the link, and the `onclick` handler for the link. Here's the function, which I've named `addExpandAllLink()`:

```
function addExpandAllLink() {
  var expandAllDiv, expandAllLink, faq;

  expandAllDiv = document.createElement("div");
  expandAllDiv.setAttribute("id", "expandAll");

  expandAllLink = document.createElement("a");
  expandAllLink.setAttribute("href", "#");
  expandAllLink.setAttribute("id", "expandAllLink");
  expandAllLink.appendChild(document.createTextNode("Expand All"));

  expandAllDiv.appendChild(expandAllLink);

  expandAllLink.onclick = function() {
    var faqList, answers;
    faqList = document.getElementById("faq");
    answers = faqList.getElementsByTagName("dd");

    if (this.innerHTML == "Expand All") {
      for (i = 0; i < answers.length; i++) {
          answers[i].style.display = 'block';
      }
      this.innerHTML = "Collapse All";
    }
    else {
      for (i = 0; i < answers.length; i++) {
          answers[i].style.display = 'none';
```

19

▼

▼
```
        }
        this.innerHTML = "Expand All";
      }
      return false;
    };

    faq = document.getElementById("faq");
    faq.insertBefore(expandAllDiv, faq.firstChild);
}
```

First, I declare the variables I use in the function, and then I start creating the elements. The `createElement()` method of the `document` object is used to create an element. It accepts the element name as the argument. I create the `<div>` element and then call the `setAttribute()` method to add the `id` attribute to that element. The `setAttribute()` method takes two arguments: the attribute name and the value for that attribute. Then I create the link by creating a new `<a>` element. I set the `href` attribute to `#`, because the event handler for the link's `onclick` event will return `false` anyway, and I add an `id` for the link, too. To add the link text, I call the `document.createTextNode()` method:

`expandAllLink.appendChild(document.createTextNode("Expand All"));`

I pass the results of that method call to the `appendChild()` method of `expandAllLink`, which results in the text node being placed inside the `<a>` tag. Then on the next line I append the link to the `<div>`, again using `appendChild()`. The last thing to do before appending the `<div>` to an element that's already on the page (causing it to appear) is to add the `onclick` handler to the link.

I'm again attaching the `onclick` handler using an anonymous function, as I did in the previous example. In this case, I use the same technique I did in the previous example, obtaining a reference to the `<div>` with the ID `faq` and then retrieving a list of `<dd>` elements inside it.

At that point, I inspect the contents of `this.innerHTML`. In an event handler, `this` is a reference to the element upon which the event was called, so in this case, it's the link. The `innerHTML` property contains whatever is inside that element—in this case, the link text. If the link text is "Expand All," I iterate over each of the answers and set their `display` property to `block`. Then I modify the `this.innerHTML` to read `"Collapse All"`. That changes the link text to `Collapse All`, which not only alters the display but causes the same function to hide all the answers when the user clicks on the link again. Then the function returns `false` so that the link itself is not processed.

Once the `onclick` handler is set up, I add the link to the document. I want to insert the link immediately before the list of frequently asked questions. To do so, I get a reference to its `<div>` using `getElementById()` and then use `insertBefore()` to put it in the right place:

```
faq = document.getElementById("faq");
faq.insertBefore(expandAllDiv, faq.firstChild);
```

Table 19.3 contains a list of methods that can be used to modify the document. All of them are methods of elements.

TABLE 19.3 Methods for Accessing the DOM

Method	Description
`appendChild(element)`	Adds the element to the page as a child of the method's target
`insertBefore(new, ref)`	Inserts the element `new` before the element `ref` on the list of children of the method's target
`removeAttribute(name)`	Removes the attribute with the supplied name from the method's target
`removeChild(element)`	Removes the child of the method's target passed in as an argument
`replaceChild(inserted, replaced)`	Replaces the child element of the method's target passed as the `inserted` argument with the element passed as the parameter `replaced`
`setAttribute(name, value)`	Sets an attribute on the method target with the name and value passed in as arguments

19

There's one other big change I made to the scripts for the page. I added a call to a new function in the handler for the click event for the questions on the page:

```
updateExpandAllLink();
```

That's a call to a new function I wrote, which switches the Expand All / Collapse All link if the user manually collapses or expands all the questions. When the page is opened, all the questions are collapsed, and the link expands them all. After the user has expanded them all one at a time, this function will switch the link to Collapse All. The function is called every time the user clicks on a question. It inspects the answers to determine whether they are all collapsed or all expanded, and it adjusts the link text accordingly. Here's the source for that function:

```
function updateExpandAllLink() {
  var faqList, answers, expandAllLink, switchLink;
```

```
faqList = document.getElementById("faq");
answers = faqList.getElementsByTagName("dd");
expandAllLink = document.getElementById("expandAllLink");
switchLink = true;

if (expandAllLink.innerHTML == "Expand All") {
  for (i = 0; i < answers.length; i++) {
    if (answers[i].style.display == 'none') {
      switchLink = false;
    }
  }

  if (switchLink) {
    expandAllLink.innerHTML = "Collapse All";
  }
}
else {
  for (i = 0; i < answers.length; i++) {
    if (answers[i].style.display == 'block') {
      switchLink = false;
    }
  }

  if (switchLink) {
    expandAllLink.innerHTML = "Expand All";
  }
}
}
```

This function starts with some setup. I declare the variables I will be using and retrieve the elements I need to access from the DOM. I also set the variable switchLink to true. This variable is used to track whether I need to switch the link text in the Expand All link. Once everything is set up, I use an if statement to test the state of the link. If the link text is set to Expand All, it checks each of the answers. If any of them are hidden, it leaves the link as is. If all of them are displayed, it changes the link text to Collapse All. If the link text is already Collapse All, the test is the opposite. It switches the link text to Expand All if all the questions are hidden.

Now let's look at how I could accomplish the same thing using jQuery. Inside the main ready function, I add the following code:

```
$("<a href='#' id='expandAll'>Expand All</a>").insertAfter("h1");

$("#expandAll").click(function (event) {
    event.preventDefault();

    if ($(this).html() == "Expand All") {
        $("#faq dd").show();
```

```
        $(this).html("Collapse All");
    } else {
        $("#faq dd").hide();
        $(this).html("Expand All");
    }
});
```

First, I add the new link to the page. I use the jQuery `insertAfter()` method, which adds the content specified after the selector passed to it. Had the selector matched multiple elements, the content would have been appended after each of them.

After I add the new element to the page, I add a click handler for the link. It performs the same functions as does the non-jQuery version I presented previously, but it uses jQuery methods to accomplish the same thing with less code.

Summary

This lesson demonstrated a number of common tasks associated with programming in JavaScript. It illustrated how to access the values in forms and check them for errors. It also explained how you can manipulate the styles on a page and even the contents of a page using JavaScript. The final two examples were written in a style referred to as unobtrusive JavaScript, which involves writing JavaScript in such a way that the page still works even if the user has disabled JavaScript or his browser does not offer JavaScript support. JavaScript is used to enhance the user's experience, but the functionality of the page is not dependent on JavaScript. This approach is generally favored as the preferable way to write JavaScript these days. It separates JavaScript code from the markup on the page and ensures support for the largest number of users, including users with mobile browsers that may not support JavaScript functionality.

19

Workshop

The following workshop includes questions, a quiz, and exercises related to the uses of JavaScript.

Q&A

Q Can you point me in the direction of more scripts that I can integrate with my pages?

A A number of sites provide JavaScript you can copy and paste for use on your own pages, but this approach has fallen out of favor. Given the simplicity of building functionality with jQuery and other libraries, the best bet is to find libraries that provide the building blocks you need to write your own scripts and then put the pieces together to accomplish your goals.

Q **In what cases might you want to use JavaScript without a library like JavaScript?**

A If your JavaScript is very simple, it may be worth it to leave out supporting libraries. But for most web developers, starting with a tool that accounts for differences between browsers is a great way to avoid bugs and get things done quickly and simply. It's generally better to make use of these sorts of libraries to write JavaScript from scratch. It's a good idea to know how to write JavaScript without libraries, but using them almost always makes sense.

Quiz

1. What happens whenever a user clicks a link, button, or form element on a web page?

2. In an event handler, what does `this` refer to?

3. What kinds of nodes on a page can be associated with properties like `nextChild` and `previousChild`?

4. How does form validation with JavaScript conserve server resources?

Quiz Answers

1. Whenever a user clicks a link, a button, or any form element, the browser generates an event signal that can be captured by one of the event handlers mentioned in the previous lesson.

2. In event handlers, `this` is a reference to the element on which the event was called. So in an event handler for the `onclick` event of a link, `this` would refer to the link that the user clicked on.

3. Nodes in the DOM can include HTML elements, text inside HTML elements, and even whitespace between elements.

4. JavaScript enables you to do error checking in forms on the browser side before the form is ever submitted to the server. A script must access the server before it can determine the validity of the entries on a form. (Note that even if you use JavaScript form validation, you must validate user input on the server, too, because users can bypass the JavaScript if they choose.)

Exercises

1. Change the HTML validation example to add error messages to the page above the form when validation fails.

2. Add a Preview button to the form validation example that displays the values the user entered below the form.

3. Modify the FAQ example so that users can click a link for each question to remove that question from the page entirely.

19

LESSON 20
Working with Frames and Linked Windows

In the early days of the Web, two significant limitations of web browsers were that they could only display one document in a browser window at a time and that sites couldn't open more browser windows if needed. The Web has evolved to enable developers to combine web pages in browser windows in all sorts of ways. Inline frames enable you to embed web pages within other pages in the same way you would an image, and linked windows enable you to create links that open pages in new browser windows. These tools offer a lot of power, but improper usage can make your sites far less usable. It's important to learn not only how to use them, but when to use them. You'll learn all about the following topics:

- What inline frames are and how they can affect your layout

- How to work with linked windows

- What happened to frames

What Are Frames?

HTML5 enables you to embed a second document into an existing page using what's called an *inline frame*. Inline frames are like images or video players; they can be included anywhere within a page. Over time, inline frames became more commonly used, and frames created using framesets were made obsolete. HTML5 does not include support for frames created using framesets, leaving only inline frames.

Why Were Frames Removed from HTML5?

Frames were removed from the HTML specification for several reasons. The primary reason that they were removed was because the `<frameset>` tag replaces the `<body>` tag. This can cause problems with some assistive technology as they are built to expect a body on any web page.

But there are other reasons why frames caused problems. Frames prevent customers from correctly bookmarking web pages. You visit a frame site and then click some links, but when you try to bookmark the internal pages, your bookmark records only the top-level page. Some designers tried to solve this problem with JavaScript, but that simply added to the complexity of the pages and made them even more difficult for screen readers to use.

Printing pages in frames is also difficult. Although most browsers will print the first page or screen, they struggle with getting all the content. Plus, if the frameset doesn't fit on the page, it can result in some strange use of paper.

Linking to frames from external sites can be difficult. Often you have the choice of linking to the front page or to an internal framed page that is missing navigation and other elements contained in the frameset. This means that a framed page that is referenced in search engine results could end up being displayed with no navigation or any site references. This is not a good user experience, and most designers want their site logo and navigation to appear on every page.

What About Iframes?

Iframes are different from frames because they are simply embedded into the web page, just like an image or other multimedia. Iframes add all the benefits of frames with none of the drawbacks. You can embed content from other parts of your website or completely different websites right inside your web pages.

HTML5 adds a few new features to the `<iframe>` tag to add security and flexibility to your frames. I will discuss those features later in this lesson.

Working with Linked Windows

Before you learn how to use iframes, you need to learn about the `target` attribute of the `<a>` tag. It enables you to direct a link to open a page in an inline frame or a new window. This attribute takes the following form:

`target="browsing_context"`

To drop a bit of jargon on you, the value of the `target` attribute is the name of a browsing context. Usually, when you click a hyperlink, the page to which you're linking replaces the current page in the browser window. When you use the `target` attribute, you can open links in new windows, or in existing windows other than the one that the link is in. With frames, you can use the `target` attribute to display the linked page in a different frame. There are also some keywords you can use that represent browsing contexts by function rather than name.

When you use the `target` attribute inside an `<a>` tag, the browser first checks whether a browsing context with the name that matches the value of the attribute exists. If it does, the document pointed to by the hyperlink replaces the current contents of that browsing context. On the other hand, if the named browsing context does not exist, a new browser window or tab opens with that name assigned to it. Then the document pointed to by the hyperlink is loaded into the newly created window.

Browsing Context Keywords

The `target` attribute works not only with window names but also with keywords that represent a type of context. All of these keywords are case sensitive and begin with an underscore (_) character. They enable you to target links at specific browsing context relative to the current browsing context.

Table 20.1 lists the browsing context keywords and describes their use.

TABLE 20.1 Magic `target` Names

target Name	Description
target="_blank"	Forces the document referenced by the `<a>` tag to be loaded into a new unnamed window.
target="_self"	Causes the document referenced by the `<a>` tag to be loaded into the current browsing context—the window or frame that contains the `<a>` tag. This is the default behavior of links.
target="_parent"	Specifically for use with frames. Forces the link to load into the parent of the current browsing context. If the current document has no parent, however, target="_self" will be used.

20

target Name	Description
target="_top"	Forces the link to load into the full web browser window, replacing the current page entirely. If the current document is already at the top, however, target="_self" will be used. More often than not, when you create links to other sites on the Web, you don't want them to open within a frame. Adding target="_top" to the link will prevent this from occurring.

▼ Exercise 20.1: Working with Windows

Each of the hyperlinks in the following exercise uses the target attribute to open a web page in a different browser window. The concepts you'll learn here will help you understand later how targeted hyperlinks work with frames.

In this exercise, you create four separate HTML documents that use hyperlinks, including the target attribute. You use these hyperlinks to open two new windows, called yellow_page and blue_page, as shown in Figure 20.1. The top window is the original web browser window (the red page), yellow_page is at the bottom right, and blue_page is at the bottom left.

FIGURE 20.1
Using the target attribute indicates that links should open new windows.

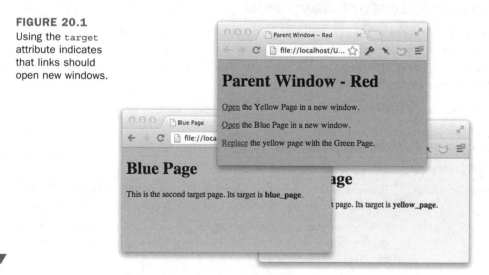

▼

First, create the document to be displayed by the main web browser window, shown in Figure 20.2, by opening your text editor of choice and entering the following lines of code:

Input ▼

```html
<!DOCTYPE html>
<html>
<head>
<title>Parent Window - Red</title>
</head>
<body style="background-color: #ff9999;">
    <h1>Parent Window - Red</h1>
    <p><a href="yellow.html" target="yellow_page">Open</a> the Yellow Page in a
new window.</p>
    <p><a href="blue.html" target="blue_page">Open</a> the Blue Page in a new
window.</p>
    <p><a href="green.html" target="yellow_page">Replace</a> the yellow page with
the Green Page.</p>
</body>
</html>
```

Output ▼

FIGURE 20.2
The parent window
(the red page).

This creates a light-red page that links to the other three pages. Save this HTML source as `parent.html`.

20

▼ Next, create a document called `yellow.html` (see Figure 20.3) by entering the following code:

Input ▼

```
<!DOCTYPE html>
<html>
<head>
<title>Yellow Page</title>
</head>
<body style="background-color: #ffff33;">
    <h1>Yellow Page</h1>
    <p>This is the first target page. Its target is <b>yellow_page</b>.</p>
</body>
</html>
```

Output ▼

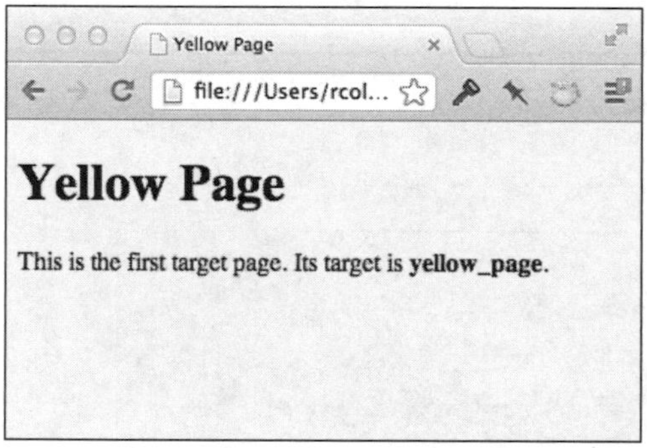

FIGURE 20.3
`yellow.html` web browser window named `yellow_page`.

After saving `yellow.html`, create another document called `blue.html` (see Figure 20.4) by entering the following code:

Input ▼

```
<!DOCTYPE html>
<html>
<head>
<title>Blue Page</title>
</head>
<body style="background-color: #99ccff;">
    <h1>Blue Page</h1>
    <p>This is the second target page. Its target is <b>blue_page</b>.</p>
</body>
</html>
```

Output ▼

FIGURE 20.4
blue.html
displayed in the
web browser
window named
blue_window.

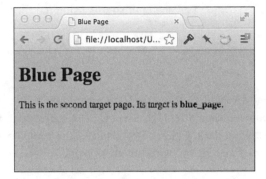

Next, create a fourth document called green.html, which looks like the following:

```
<!DOCTYPE html>
<html>
<head>
<title>Green Page</title>
</head>
<body style="background-color: #ccffcc;">
    <h1>Green Page</h1>
    <p>This is the third target page. Its target is <b>yellow_page</b>. It should
    replace the yellow page in the browser.</p>
</body>
</html>
```

To complete the exercise, load parent.html (the red page) into your web browser. Click the first hyperlink to open the yellow page in a second browser window. This happens because the first hyperlink contains the attribute target="yellow_page", as the following code from parent.html demonstrates:

```
<p><a href="yellow.html" target="yellow_page">Open</a> the Yellow Page in a new
window.</p>
```

Now return to the red page and click the second link. The blue page opens in a third browser window. Note that the new windows won't be laid out like the ones shown in Figure 20.1; modern browsers open new windows as new tabs. The following target="blue_page" statement in the parent.html page is what causes the new window to open:

```
<a href="blue.html" target="blue_page">Open</a> the Blue Page in a new window.
</p>
```

20

▼

▼ The previous two examples opened each of the web pages in a new browser window. The third link, however, uses the `target="yellow_page"` statement to open the green page in the window named `yellow_page`. You accomplish this using the following code in `parent.html`:

```
<p><a href="green.html" target="yellow_page">Replace</a> the yellow page
 with the Green Page.</p>
```

Because you already opened the `yellow_page` window when you clicked the link for the yellow page, the green page should replace the page that's already in it. To verify this, click the third hyperlink on the red page. This replaces the contents of the yellow page (with the `yellow_page` target name) with the green page (`green.html`), as shown in Figure 20.5.

FIGURE 20.5
green.html displayed in the web browser window named green_page.

▲

The `<base>` Tag

When you're using the `target` attribute with links, you'll sometimes find that all or most of the hyperlinks on a web page should point to the same browsing context. For example, you might want all the links on a page to open in a new window, so customers don't forget about your home page.

In such cases, instead of including a `target` attribute for each `<a>` tag, you can use another tag, `<base>`, to define a global target for all the links on a web page. The `<base>` tag is used as follows:

```
<base target="window_name">
```

If you include the `<base>` tag in the `<head>`...`</head>` block of a document, every `<a>` tag that doesn't have a `target` attribute will use the value of the `base` tag's `target` attribute as its default target . For example, if you had included the tag

`<base target="yellow_page">` in the HTML source for `parent.html`, the three hyperlinks could have been written as follows:

```
<!DOCTYPE html>
<html>
<head>
<title>Parent Window - Red</title>
<base target="yellow_page"> <!-- add base target="value" here -->
</head>
<body style="background-color: #ff9999">
    <h1>Parent Window - Red</h1>

    <p><a href="yellow.html">Open</a>
    <!-- no need to include a target -->
        the Yellow Page in a new window.</p>
    <p><a href="blue.html" target="blue_page">Open</a> the Blue Page in a new
window.</p>
    <p><a href="green.html">Replace</a>
    <!-- no need to include a target -->
        the yellow page with the Green Page.</p>
</body>
</html>
```

In this case, `yellow.html` and `green.html` load into the default window assigned by the `<base>` tag (yellow_page); `blue.html` overrides the default by defining its own target window of `blue_page`.

You also can override the window assigned with the `<base>` tag by using one of two special window names. If you use `target="_blank"` in a hyperlink, it opens a new browser window that doesn't have a name associated with it. Alternatively, if you use `target="_self"`, the current window is used rather than the one defined by the `<base>` tag.

NOTE

> If you don't provide a `target` using the `<base>` tag and you don't indicate a target in a link's `<a>` tag, the link will load the new document in the same window as the link.

20

Inline Frames

The main advantage of inline frames is that you can position them anywhere on a web page, just as you can other elements like images or movies. You can incorporate content from another page or even another site into a page in a seamless way through the use of inline frames. In fact, inline frames, which are specified using the `<iframe>` tag, are very commonly the means by which "widgets" offered by popular websites are incorporated into other websites. For example, sites like Twitter and Facebook offer widgets that you can incorporate into your own site that are implemented using inline frames. The embed code that YouTube provides uses an `iframe` for the movie.

Here's a brief run-through of how to create inline frames. First, you define them using the `<iframe>` tag. Like images, these frames appear within the normal flow of an HTML document (hence the `i` for inline). The `<iframe>` tag supports attributes like `src`, which contains the URL of the document to be displayed in the frame, and `height` and `width`, which control the size of the frame.

Table 20.2 lists the attributes of the `<iframe>` element.

TABLE 20.2 Key Attributes

Attribute	Description
`width`	Specifies the width, in pixels, of the floating frame that will hold the HTML document.
`height`	Specifies the height, in pixels, of the floating frame that will hold the HTML document.
`src`	Specifies the URL of the HTML document to be displayed in the frame.
`srcdoc`	Specifies HTML content to be displayed in the frame. This is new in HTML5.
`name`	Specifies the name of the frame for the purpose of linking and targeting.
`sandbox`	Enables extra restrictions for the content of an iframe. This is new in HTML5.

Because you know how to use inline images, using the `<iframe>` tag is fairly easy. The following code displays one way to use the Away from My Desk pages in conjunction with an inline frame. In this example, you begin by creating a page with a red background. The links that the user clicks appear on a single line, centered above the iframe. For clarity, I've placed each of the links on a separate line of code.

Following the links (which target the inline frame named `reason`), the code for the frame appears within a centered `<div>` element. As you can see in the following HTML, the floating frame will be centered on the page and will measure 450 pixels wide by 105 pixels high:

Input ▼

```
<!DOCTYPE html>
<html>
  <head>
    <title>I'm Away From My Desk</title>
```

```
  <style>
    body { background-color: #ffcc99; }
  </style>
</head>
<body>
  <h1>I'm away from my desk because ...</h1>
  <p style="text-align: center;">
    <a href="reason1.html" target="reason">Reason 1</a> |
    <a href="reason2.html" target="reason">Reason 2</a> |
    <a href="reason3.html" target="reason">Reason 3</a> |
    <a href="reason4.html" target="reason">Reason 4</a> |
    <a href="reason5.html" target="reason">Reason 5</a> |
    <a href="reason6.html" target="reason">Reason 6</a>
  </p>

  <div style="margin: 0 auto; width: 450px;">
    <iframe name="reason" src="reason1.html" style="width: 450px; height:
105px;"></iframe>
  </div>
</body>
</html>
```

Figure 20.6 shows the result.

Output ▼

FIGURE 20.6
An inline frame.

You then create the reasons in separate HTML documents named `reason1.html`,
`reason2.html`, `reason3.html`, and so on. These can be complete HTML documents with

everything you might expect from a web page. But I made the reasons very simple. For example, here is the HTML for `reason2.html`:

```
<!doctype html>
<html>
  <head>
    <title>Reason 2</title>
  </head>
  <body>
    <p>I knew you were coming, so I'm baking a cake</p>
  </body>
</html>
```

This page is really simple and seems like a lot of work to change the text of the iframe. But with the new attribute `srcdoc`, you can place the HTML you want to display in the frame right in the iframe tag. Instead of referencing an entire page, the browser will load the HTML you specify. Here's how to set reason 1 as the default source document:

```
<iframe name="reason" src="reason1.html"
  srcdoc="<p>My chair is trying to kill me</p>"
  style="width: 450px; height: 105px"></iframe>
```

NOTE

> You don't need a complete HTML document inside the `srcdoc` attribute. If the browser doesn't support the `srcdoc` attribute, however, it will show the HTML in the `src` attribute instead. So, don't leave that out. As of this writing, only Internet Explorer, Edge, and Opera Mini don't support the `srcdoc` attribute.

HTML5 also adds a security feature to iframes: the `sandbox` attribute. If you include this on your iframes, it will load them with extra restrictions. You can load your frames with all the restrictions by just including the attribute on your iframe tag like this:

```
<iframe src="frame.html" sandbox></iframe>
```

This will add the following security features to your framed content:

- The content will be treated as if it's coming from a foreign domain, even if it's not.
- Forms cannot be submitted from within the iframe.
- Scripts cannot be executed in the iframe.
- APIs are disabled.
- Links cannot target other browser contexts.
- Content cannot use embedded content, such as through the `<object>` or `<embed>` tags.

- Content cannot navigate to the top-level browsing context.
- Autoplay features such as video or form focus controls are blocked.

These features allow web designers to point to untrusted source material with less worry that a malicious script could be run on their web server. But the `sandbox` attribute also lets you open up the security for trusted sites with space-separated values of the `sandbox` attribute. These values are explained in Table 20.3.

TABLE 20.3 Sandbox Values

Attribute	Description
`allow-forms`	Enables form submission
`allow-pointer-lock`	Enables APIs
`allow-popups`	Enables pop-ups
`allow-same-origin`	Allows the iframe content to be treated as being from the same origin
`allow-scripts`	Enables scripts
`allow-top-navigation`	Allows the iframe content to navigate its top-level browsing context

If you use inline frames to point to pages on websites you don't control, you should always sandbox them as much as possible. This will keep both your website and your customers more secure.

Opening Linked Windows with JavaScript

Pop-up windows are used all over the Web. They are often used to display advertisements, but they can be used for all sorts of other things as well, such as creating a separate window to show help text in an application or to display a larger version of a graph that's embedded in a document. You've seen how you can use the `target` attribute to open a link in a new window, but that approach isn't very flexible. You can't control the size of the window being displayed, nor which browser window controls are displayed.

Fortunately, with JavaScript you can take more control of the process of creating new windows. You've already learned that one of the objects supported by JavaScript is `window`. It refers to the window that's executing the script. To open a new window, you

20

use the `open` method of the `window` object. Here's a JavaScript function that opens a window:

```
function popup(url) {
  mywindow = window.open(url, 'name', 'height=200,width=400');
  return false;
}
```

The function accepts the URL for the document to be displayed in the new window as an argument. It creates a new window using the `window.open` function and assigns that new window to a variable named `mywindow`. (I explain why we assign the new window to a variable in a bit.)

The three arguments to the function are the URL to be displayed in the window, the name for the window, and a list of settings for the window. In this case, I indicate that I want the window to be 400 pixels wide and 200 pixels tall. The name is important because if other links target a window with the same name, either via the `window.open()` function or the `target` attribute, they'll appear in that window.

At the end of the function, I return `false`. That's necessary so that the event handler used to call the function is stopped. To illustrate what I mean, it's necessary to explain how this function is called. Instead of using the `target` attribute in the `<a>` tag, the `onclick` handler can be used, as follows:

```
<a href="whatever.html" target="_blank" onclick="popup('whatever.html')">Pop up
</a>
```

Of course, it's preferable to use unobtrusive JavaScript and add an appropriate event handler in a `script` tag. However, this works for the purposes of an example.

Ordinarily, when a user clicks the link, the browser calls the function and then goes right back to whatever it was doing before, navigating to the document specified in the `href` attribute. Returning `false` in the `popup()` function tells the browser not to continue what it was doing, so the new window is opened by the function, and the browser doesn't follow the link. If a user who had JavaScript turned off visited the page, the link to `whatever.html` would still open in a new window because I included the target attribute, too.

In the preceding example, I specified the `height` and `width` settings for the new window. There are several more options available as well, which are listed in Table 20.4.

TABLE 20.4 Settings for Pop-Up Windows

Setting	Purpose
height	Height of the window in pixels.
width	Width of the window in pixels.
resizable	Enable window resizing.
scrollbars	Display scrollbars.
status	Display the browser status bar.
toolbar	Display the browser toolbar.
location	Display the browser's location bar.
menubar	Display the browser's menu bar (not applicable on Mac OS X).
left	Left coordinate of the new window onscreen (in pixels). By default, pop-up windows are placed slightly to the right of the spawning window.
top	Top coordinate of the new window onscreen (in pixels). By default, pop-up windows are placed slightly below the top of the spawning window.

When you specify the settings for a window, you must include them in a comma-separated list, with no spaces anywhere. For the settings that allow you to enable or disable a browser interface component, the valid values are `on` or `off`. Here's a valid list of settings:

```
status=off,toolbar=off,location=off,left=200,top=100,width=300,height=300
```

Here's an invalid list of settings:

```
status=off, toolbar=off, location=false, top=100
```

Including spaces (or carriage returns) anywhere in your list will cause problems. It's also worth noting that when you provide settings for a new window, the browser automatically assumes a default of `off` for any on/off settings that you don't include. So, you can leave out anything you want to turn off.

Here's a complete example that uses JavaScript to create a new window:

```
<!DOCTYPE html>
<html>
  <head>
    <title>Popup example</title>
  </head>
  <body>
    <h1>Popup Example</h1>
    <p>
      <a href="popup.html" onclick="popup(this.href)">Launch popup</a>
```

20

```
    </p>
    <script>
      function popup(url) {
        var mywindow = window.open(url, 'name', 'height=200,width=400');
        return false;
      }
    </script>
  </body>
</html>
```

When a user clicks the Launch pop-up link, a new 200×400 pixel window appears with the contents of `popup.html`.

The unobtrusive approach is to skip the `onclick` attribute entirely and bind the `popup()` function to the link in your JavaScript code. First, change the link on the page to look like this:

```
<a href="popup.html" id="launchpopup">Launch popup</a>
```

Then you should edit the `<script>` tag so that it looks like this:

```
<script>
  function popup(url) {
      var mywindow = window.open(url, 'name', 'height=200,width=400');
      return false;
  }
  window.onload = function () {
    var link = document.getElementById("launchpopup");
    link.onclick = function () {
        return popup(this.href);
    }
  }
</script>
```

In this case, when the page loads, I retrieve the link by its ID and then bind a new anonymous function to it that calls the original `popup()` function. Instead of hard coding the URL, I pass `this.href` to the `popup()` function so that it opens the URL in the link.

Using a library like jQuery can make things even easier. Suppose you want any link tag with the class `popup` to open a new window with the URL associated with the link. Here's the code:

```
<script>
$(document).ready(function () {
    $("a.popup").click(function (event) {
        var mywindow = window.open(this.href, 'newwindow',
'height=200,width=400');
        event.preventDefault();
```

```
    });
});
</script>
```

When the page is ready, I apply the same `onclick` handler to all the links on the page with the class `popup`. The anonymous event handler opens a new window with the URL stored in `this.href`, which returns the URL in the link that the user clicked. It then calls the `preventDefault()` method on the event. It's used instead of just returning `false` because it doesn't disrupt other event handlers that may be fired in addition to this one.

Summary

In this lesson, you learned how to link a document to a new or existing window. In addition, you learned how to create inline frames and link them by using the tags listed in Table 20.5.

TABLE 20.5 New Tags Discussed in Lesson 20

Tag	Attribute	Description
`<base target="window">`		Sets the global link window for a document.
`<iframe>`		Defines an inline frame.
	`src`	Indicates the URL of the document to be displayed in the frame.
	`srcdoc`	Provides the HTML source to be displayed in the frame.
	`name`	Indicates the name of the frame for the purpose of linking and targeting.
	`width`	Indicates the width of the frame in pixels.
	`height`	Indicates the height of the frame in pixels.
	`sandbox`	Enables extra restrictions for the content of the frame. Possible values include `allow-forms`, `allow-pointer-lock`, `allow-popups`, `allow-same-origin`, `allow-scripts`, and `allow-top-navigation`. If none are listed, all restrictions apply.

20

Workshop

As if you haven't had enough already, here's a refresher course of questions, quizzes, and exercises that will help you remember some of the most important points you learned in this lesson.

Q&A

Q Is there any reason why you should sandbox iframe content from your own server?

A The decision to sandbox content shouldn't be made based on where the content is coming from, but rather how reliable and trustworthy you find the source. If you are posting your pages to a shared domain, you might have no knowledge of the designers of another site on that domain. Sandboxing helps you maintain security.

Q What if I use the `<frame>` tag anyway?

A Most browsers still support frames, so your content will still work. However, it is considered poor form. And with iframes and CSS, there are many options that don't have the drawbacks of frames while providing the same functionality.

Quiz

1. Where does the keyword `_self` take readers if they click a link with that target?
2. If you want a link to open in a named iframe, what attribute do you need to use?
3. When a web page includes the `<frameset>` element, what element cannot be used at the beginning of the HTML document?
4. What attribute of the `<iframe>` tag provides security for the reader and the website loading the content?

Quiz Answers

1. The `_self` target is the default action for a link. The link will open in the same browser context as the link itself.
2. The `target` attribute of the `<a>` tag directs linked pages to load into the appropriate iframe.
3. When a web page includes the `<frameset>` element, it cannot include the `<body>` element at the beginning of the page. They're mutually exclusive. And this is why frames are no longer part of HTML5.
4. The `sandbox` attribute provides some security for the reader and the website by putting restrictions on what the iframe content can do.

Exercises

1. Create an iframe that links to another page on your website. Size it so that it fits in the main content area of your page.

2. For the preceding frameset, create a page that you will use for a table of contents beside the frame. Create two links in the table of contents that open in the inline frame.

20

LESSON 21
Designing for the Mobile Web

In this lesson we will move away from the desktop computer that you are used to using and look at how your customers are using web pages on mobile devices. As you learned in Lesson 16, "Using Responsive Web Design," more and more people are moving to mobile to consume Web-based content. And if your designs are stuck in the 20th century—focused on desktop computers—your customers will find some other site to visit that better meets their needs.

With everything you've learned in this book so far, you could easily set it down and start building an amazing website. Your site would be responsive to mobile customers, have beautiful CSS layouts, and be well designed using the most up-to-date HTML tags and attributes. But if you continue reading, you will learn the techniques and tricks that the best Web designers know—the ones that make a site not just good but amazing.

This lesson covers mobile Web design best practices, including the following:

- How browsing habits on mobile differ from desktop
- Standards for writing mobile web pages
- How to write for mobile and online customers
- Designing pages and layout for mobile
- Optimizing your content
- Other habits you should get into for mobile web design

People Browse Differently on Mobile Phones

The first thing you should be aware of when considering designing for mobile devices is that the way people browse the Web on mobile phones is very different from how they browse the Web on their computers. They are more likely to know exactly what they are looking for, and once they find it they will take action. Consumers use mobile to access local information, stay up-to-date, buy products, and purchase music and video. If you think about how you use your phone, that is probably true for you as well. I know that it's definitely true for me.

In a study from Google, it was found:

- Mobile users visited search engines, social networking, retail, and video sharing sites.

- Nine out of ten smartphone searches ended with them either buying something or visiting a business.

- Nearly 80% of smartphone consumers use their phones to help with shopping.

- More than 90% of all smartphone users have searched for local information.

- And after searching, most take action within one day.

This study was done in 2011, but the numbers continue to rise. What you should consider is that mobile customers are task oriented. They usually have come to your site for a specific purpose. And unlike desktop browsers, that task is often to buy something. If they can't make that task happen, they will quickly go elsewhere.

That means that your site needs to be optimized for mobile customers. You want to give them what they want as quickly and painlessly as you can so they never feel the need to go to some other site.

The only caveat to this is location. If your business runs out of a country where mobile device usage is even more prevalent than it is in the United States, then you will have even more need to create a site that works well on mobile. Ultimately, whether your site is based in the United States, Australia, Africa, or somewhere else, mobile devices are growing more and more popular, and your website will suffer if it doesn't cater to them.

Standards Compliance and the Mobile Web

You might think you don't need to worry about standards compliance. After all, most people use a modern web browser, and mobile users upgrade their phones every 1 to 2 years, right? To some extent, that is true. The standards have come together in a way they never had in the past, with browser makers working together along with web designers to develop techniques that actually work—both for the browsers and the people building the pages.

Currently, browser makers are working together to a greater extent than ever before. The current versions of Internet Explorer/Edge, Firefox, Safari, Chrome, and Opera all offer strong standards support, and the browsers for popular mobile phones are based on the same codebase as their desktop brethren. Given the strong standards support in current browsers, the biggest question most developers face is how they want to deal with older feature phones that don't display web pages very well.

And even though most mobile browsers support the same HTML and CSS as desktop browsers, they still differ in terms of capabilities. The most obvious example is the size. Even the largest tablet, phablet, or oversized phone screen is smaller than most desktop monitors. But mobile devices aren't more limited than desktop or tablet computers. Their capabilities are different. For example, most desktop computers don't offer geolocation, and even if they do, it's not particularly useful, as you don't see people lugging 30-inch screens around with them. The ability to "click to call" is starting to get implemented on some computers with the use of Skype and other Internet calling services. But in general that is a phone-only feature.

Progressive Enhancement

Progressive enhancement is a popular approach to creating web pages. It describes an approach that enables web designers to use the latest and greatest technology available without leaving people using browsers with different capabilities behind. The idea is that you start with simple but completely functional web pages and then layer on enhancements that add to the experience. This should also help you stop considering mobile devices as somehow inferior to computers. After all, if you're building a web scavenger hunt game, the person with the desktop computer will be at more of a disadvantage than the one with the smartphone in her pocket.

21

You'll want to start with valid, standards-compliant HTML when you're creating web pages. This means HTML5. Your initial pages should consist only of HTML markup with no JavaScript or CSS, and they should look fine and work properly. All of your navigation should be present and should work properly, but it won't be pretty (no CSS, remember?). Your main page content should be visible. In other words, you should start out with a fully functional, very plain website. This ensures that your site will work for even the most rudimentary browsers and for assistive technology like screen readers. Taking this approach also ensures that your markup reflects the content of your site rather than how you want to present it.

Once that is complete, you can start layering on the more advanced functionality. First, implement the visual design for your website using CSS. As you learned in Lesson 16, you should focus on mobile-first designs and use media queries to affect how the pages are displayed to different size devices. Later on in this lesson I'll go into the specifics for designing things like layout, where to place navigation, and dealing with images and text.

Given the robust support for CSS in the current browsers, there should be no need to use HTML to define the appearance of your website. You might find you need to add container elements to your page that provide the necessary structure for your styles. For example, if your page layout is split into columns for larger screens, it will be necessary to add `<div>` tags for the contents of each column. Fortunately, such tags do not create visual differences unless they are styled, so your page's appearance will not be altered for users who don't have CSS support.

Finally, add dynamic technology like JavaScript or Flash. Back in Lesson 19, "Using JavaScript in Your Pages," I discussed unobtrusive JavaScript. That approach complements progressive enhancement. When you add JavaScript to the page, make sure the page provides some minimum level of functionality without the JavaScript, and then use JavaScript to enhance that baseline functionality. For example, if your page includes collapsed elements that can be expanded with JavaScript, make sure to start out with them expanded on the page, and then collapse them when the page loads using JavaScript. That way, content will not be permanently hidden from users who don't have JavaScript.

This is what progressive enhancement is all about. It ensures that everyone with a browser of any kind will be able to view your site, while the site still provides an enhanced experience for those who can benefit from it.

Validating Your Pages

One way to be sure that your pages will have a good base for mobile devices is to make sure that the HTML (and CSS and JavaScript) is written well, or *valid*. This removes one place where your pages might get into trouble—if you know the HTML is valid, then you can look elsewhere to figure out why something isn't working.

It's all well and good to attempt to write valid pages, but how do you know whether you've succeeded? It's easy enough to determine whether your pages look okay in your browser, but verifying that they're valid is another matter. Fortunately, the W3C, which is responsible for managing the HTML recommendations, also provides a service to validate your pages. It's a web application that enables you to upload an HTML file or to validate a specific URL to any W3C recommendation. The URL is http://validator.w3.org/.

Figure 21.1 is a screenshot of the validator in action. I've sent it off to validate https://www.pearson.com/.

FIGURE 21.1
The W3C Validator validating Pearson.com.

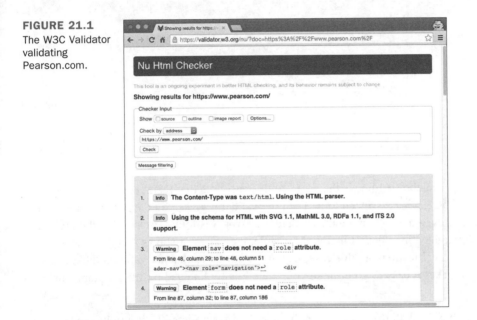

When I validate the page, I can see that there are ten messages from the validator: two info messages, four warnings, and four errors. The first two messages tell me about how the validator is working. I learn that it used the HTML parser because it detected the page was in HTML. Then I learned that it was using the schema for HTML with support for a few other languages like MathML and SVG. The warnings are messages that indicate lines in your code that you should be aware of. They are not saying that your code is wrong or that you should rewrite it, but rather that you might be using an unnecessary attribute or something similar.

The messages you want to pay attention to are the errors. Figure 21.2 shows the sixth message, an error, on the Pearson site validation.

21

FIGURE 21.2
The W3C Validator
validating
Pearson.com.

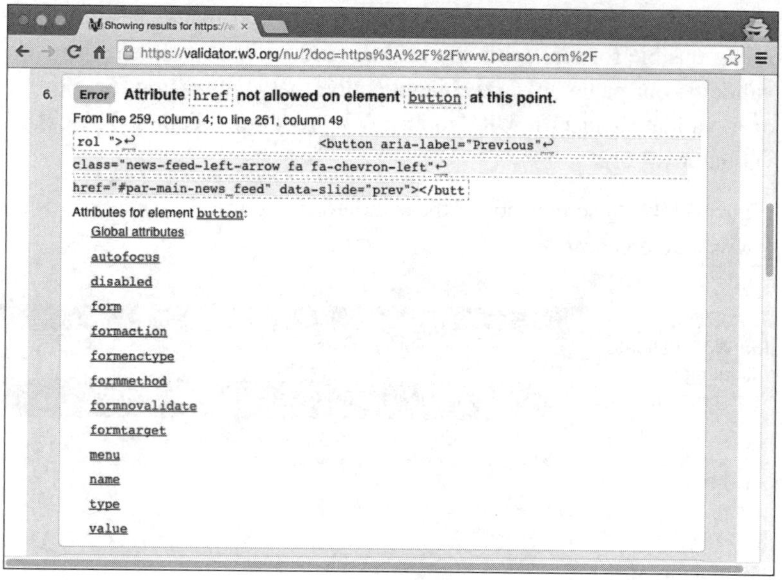

As you can see, the first line is the error. In this case, it's that the `button` tag has an illegal attribute, `href`, assigned to it. Then the validator gives you the line number in the HTML and even the column number where the error was found. Below that the problem tag is highlighted in yellow. Finally, if possible, the validator shows you the relevant part of the specification—in this case, listing the attributes that are valid on the `button` tag. This makes it easy to go through your page line by line and fix the problems that are found.

After you've fixed all the errors, the only messages your site will get will be the two informational messages, as you can see in Figure 21.3.

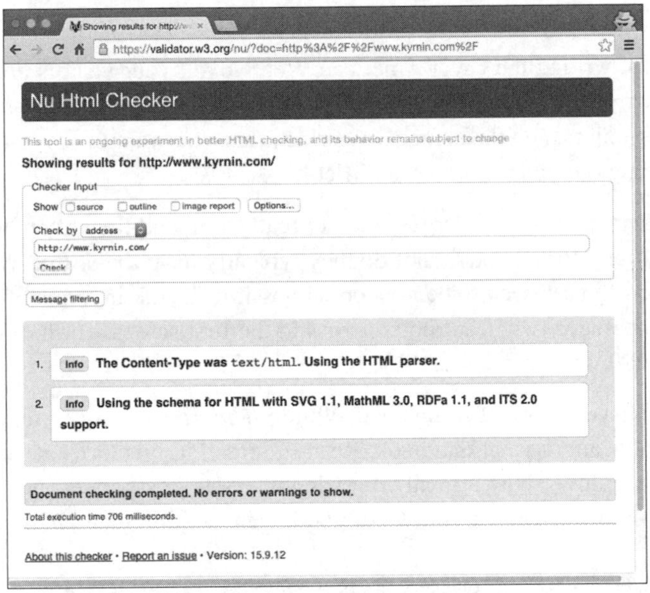

FIGURE 21.3
The W3 Validator acknowledges a job well done.

Writing for the Mobile Web

Writing on the mobile Web is no different from writing in the real world. Although it's not committed to hard copy, it's still published and is still a reflection of you and your work. In fact, because your writing is online and your visitors have many other options when it comes to finding something to read, you'll have to follow the rules of good writing that much more closely.

Because of the vast quantities of information available on the Web, your visitors aren't going to have much patience if your web page is poorly organized or full of spelling errors. They're likely to give up after the first couple of sentences and move on to someone else's page. After all, there are several million pages out there. No one has time to waste on bad pages.

I don't mean that you have to go out and become a professional writer to create a good web page, but I give you a few hints for making your web page easier to read and understand as well as some tips for optimizing your writing for mobile devices.

21

Write Clearly and Be Brief

Unless you're writing the Great American Web Novel, your visitors aren't going to linger lovingly over your words. You should write as clearly and concisely as you possibly can, present your points, and then stop. Obscuring what you want to say with extra words just makes figuring out your point more difficult.

Mobile readers don't have a large screen to read from, and they often don't have a lot of time to read long form content, nor do they typically have the desire. Web pages written for mobile customers need to be as short as possible. Think in terms of screen chunks. Try to get the majority of your point across in the first screen worth of text—this could be the first 200 words or fewer.

If you don't have a copy of Strunk and White's *The Elements of Style*, put down this book right now and go buy that book. Read it, reread it, memorize it, inhale it, sleep with it under your pillow, show it to all your friends, quote it at parties, and make it your life. You'll find no better guide to the art of good, clear writing than *The Elements of Style*.

Organize Your Pages for Quick Scanning

Even if you write the clearest, briefest, most scintillating prose ever seen on the Web, chances are good that your visitors won't start at the top of your web page and carefully read every word down to the bottom.

In this context, *scanning* is the first quick look your visitors give to each page to get the general gist of the content. Depending on what your users want out of your pages, they may scan the parts that jump out at them (headings, links, other emphasized words), perhaps read a few contextual paragraphs, and then move on. By writing and organizing your pages for easy "scannability," you can help your visitors get the information they need as quickly as possible.

To improve the scannability of your web pages, follow these guidelines:

- **Don't bury important information in text**—If you have a point to make, make it close to the top of the page or at the beginning of a paragraph. Forcing readers to sift through a lot of information before they get to what's important means that many of them won't see the important stuff at all.

- **Use headings to summarize topics**—Note that this book has headings and sub-headings. You can flip through quickly and find the parts that interest you. The same concept applies to web pages.

- **Use lists**—Lists are wonderful for summarizing related items. Every time you find yourself saying something like "each widget has four elements" or "use the following steps to do this," the content after that phrase should be in an ordered or unordered list.

- **Don't forget link menus**—As a type of list, the link menu has all the same advantages of lists for scannability, and it doubles as an excellent navigation tool.

- **Write short, clear paragraphs**—Long paragraphs are harder to read and make gleaning the information more difficult. The further into the paragraph you put your point, the less likely it is that anybody will read it.

The most important thing to remember when writing for mobile is the first guideline. Put the most important information first. Mobile readers won't sift through, and they aren't very likely to even scroll to scan the whole page. If they don't find what they are looking for on the first screen full of text, they will hit the back button and be gone.

Make Each Page Stand on Its Own

As you write, keep in mind that your visitors could jump to any of your web pages from anywhere. For example, you can structure a page so that section four distinctly follows section three and has no other links to it. Then someone you don't even know might create a link to the page starting at section four. From then on, visitors could find themselves at section four without even knowing that section three exists.

Be careful to write each page so that it stands on its own. The following guidelines will help:

- **Use descriptive titles**—The title should provide not only the direct subject of this page, but also its relationship to the rest of the pages on the site.

- **Provide a navigational link**—If a page depends on the one before it, provide a navigational link back to that page (and a link up to the top level, preferably).

- **Avoid initial sentences such as the following**—"You can get around these problems by...," "After you're done with that, do this...," and "The advantages to this method are...." The information referred to by *these*, *that*, and *this* are off on some other page. If these sentences are the first words your visitors see, they're going to be confused.

As I've said previously, you should also focus on keeping the first screen full of content the most relevant. In other words, to optimize your content for mobile, you should focus on making each section of each page standalone. And the first part of any page is the most important.

Be Careful with Emphasis

Use emphasis sparingly in your text. Paragraphs with a whole lot of words in **boldface** or *italics* or ALL CAPS are hard to read, whether you use them several times in a paragraph or to emphasize long strings of text.

21

Link text also is a form of emphasis. Use short phrases for link text, but as you'll see later in this lesson, avoid making links too short—two to three words is best. By removing some of the boldface and using less text for your links, you can considerably reduce the amount of clutter on your pages.

Be especially careful of emphasis that moves or changes, such as marquees, blinking text, or animation. Unless the animation is the primary focus of the page, use movement and sound sparingly.

Don't Use Browser-Specific Terminology

Avoid references in your text to specific features of specific browsers. For example, don't use the following wording:

- **"Click here"**—Users of smartphones and tablets tap on links. A more generic phrase is "Follow this link."

- **"To save this page, pull down the File menu and select Save"**—Most mobile devices don't work that way, and some don't even allow you to save files to the device. Even desktop browsers have different menus and different ways of accomplishing the same actions. If at all possible, do not refer to specifics of browser operation in your web pages.

- **"Use the Back button to return to the previous page"**—Each browser has a different set of buttons and different methods for going back. If you want your visitors to be able to go back to a previous page or to any specific page, link those pages.

It's also not a good idea to assume you know what mobile device they are using. Many Android users get offended if a website assumes they are on an iPhone and vice versa. Many smartphones have such large resolutions they appear to be tablets, and many tablets masquerade as laptop computers. By avoiding any reference to specific technology in your writing, you avoid the mistakes that would come with that.

Spell Check and Proofread Your Pages

Spell checking and proofreading may seem like obvious suggestions, but they bear mentioning given the number of pages I've seen on the Web that obviously haven't had either.

The process of designing a set of web pages and making them available on the Web is like publishing a book, producing a magazine, or releasing a product. Publishing web pages is considerably easier than publishing books, magazines, or other products, of course, but just because the task is easy doesn't mean your product should be sloppy.

Thousands of people may be reading and exploring the content you provide. Spelling errors and bad grammar reflect badly on you, on your work, and on the content you're describing. It may be irritating enough that your visitors won't bother to delve any deeper than your home page, even if the subject you're writing about is fascinating. If you don't believe me, just do a quick Internet search on annoying grammar mistakes to see how many people complain about grammar errors online.

Proofread and spell check each of your web pages. Remember that the spelling and grammar checking tools available aren't perfect. It's common to see homophones—words that sound the same but are spelled differently—used on web pages incorrectly. If possible, have someone else read your writing. Often other people can pick up errors that you, the writer, can't see. Even a simple edit can greatly improve many pages and make them easier to read and navigate.

Design and Page Layout

Probably the best rule of web design to follow at all times is this: *Keep the design of each page as simple as possible*. Reduce the number of elements (images, headings, and paragraphs), and make sure that visitors' eyes are drawn to the most important parts of the page first.

Remember that mobile devices come in all different shapes and sizes with different levels of quality and different resolutions. Some devices support zooming in and out on content, and some don't. Many feature phones can access the Web but cannot scroll horizontally. By keeping your design simple, more devices will be able to view your pages.

Keep this cardinal rule in mind as you read the next sections, which offer some other suggestions for basic design and layout of web pages.

Use Headings as Headings

Headings tend to be rendered in larger or bolder fonts in graphical browsers. Therefore, using a heading tag to provide some sort of warning, note, or emphasis in regular text can be tempting, but this is just another form of emphasis.

Headings stand out from the text and signal the start of new topics, so they should be used only as headings. Some mobile devices and many assistive devices use the headlines as a page outline. If you really want to emphasize a particular section of text, consider using CSS to change the background color, add a border, or add a shadow. Remember that you can use CSS to change the color, background color, font size, font face, and border for a block of text.

21

Group Related Information Visually

Grouping related information within a page is a task for both writing and design. As I suggested in the "Writing for the Mobile Web" section, grouping related information under headings improves the scannability of that information. Visually separating each section from the others helps to make it distinct and emphasizes the relatedness of the information.

If a web page contains several sections, find a way to separate those sections visually—for example, with a heading, a border, or tables.

Use a Consistent Layout

When you're reading a book, each page or section usually has the same layout. The page numbers are placed where you expect them, and the first word on each page starts in the same place.

The same sort of consistent layout works equally well on web pages. Having a single look and feel for each page on your website is comforting to your visitors. After two or three pages, they'll know what the elements of each page are and where to find them. If you create a consistent design, your visitors can find the information they need and navigate through your pages without having to stop at every page and try to find where certain elements are located.

Consistent layout can include the following:

- **Consistent page elements**—If you use second-level headings (`<h2>`) on one page to indicate major topics, use second-level headings for major topics on all your pages. If you have a heading and a rule line at the top of your page, use that same layout on all your pages.

- **Consistent forms of navigation**—Put your navigation menus in the same place on every page (usually the top or the bottom of the page, or even both), and use the same number of them. If you're going to use navigation icons, make sure that you use the same icons in the same order for every page.

- **The use of external style sheets**—You should create a master style sheet that defines background properties, text and link colors, font selections and sizes, margins, and more. The appearance of your pages maintains consistency throughout your site.

But remember that consistency doesn't mean identical. If you have a pull-out navigation for mobile devices, that doesn't mean that larger screens must also have a pull-out navigation. But the navigation that small screens see should have access to the same information that the larger screen navigation has.

Using Links

Without links, web pages would be really dull, and finding anything interesting on the Web would be close to impossible. In many ways, the quality of your links can be as important as the writing and design of your actual pages. Here's some friendly advice on creating and using links for mobile design.

Mobile Users Tap; They Don't Click

This is an important distinction when you're working on your links, for more than just the words you use, as I mentioned previously. Tapping a screen is a different action than clicking and can have different results. For example, it's difficult to "click and drag" on a smartphone. And "tap and drag," if it does anything, often does something different. You also can't "right-click" a smartphone.

But more important, tapping requires that people use their fingers or a stylus to touch your web page. If the items they touch are too difficult, this can result in a lot of frustration. Some of the most frustrating things a Web designer can do with his links include the following:

- Put too many links too close together. The closer links are to one another, the more likely it is that the customer will tap on the wrong item.

- Linking just one word. When the links are small, they are also hard to tap, and single-word links, although they might look more interesting on the page, are difficult for mobile users to tap.

- Links that move. As I've said before, mobile users are coming to your site to take some form of action. When they see the link they want, they tap it immediately. If the link moves for any reason—such as if the page continues to load content above it—they may end up tapping on something they didn't expect.

Test your web pages in a mobile device, not just an emulator. This will give you a better idea of how tappable your links are.

Use Link Menus with Descriptive Text

As I've noted throughout this book, using link menus is a great way of organizing your content and the links on a page. If you organize your links into lists or other menu-like structures, your visitors can scan their options for the page quickly and easily.

21

Just organizing your links into menus might not be enough, however. Make sure that your descriptions aren't too short. For example, using menus of filenames or other marginally descriptive links in menus can be tempting, but if your readers don't know what they are going to get, they aren't going to tap on the link. A better plan is to provide some extra text describing where the link goes.

Use Links in Text

The best way to provide links in text is to first write the text as if it isn't going to have links at all—for example, as if you were writing it for hard copy. Then you can highlight the appropriate words that will link to other pages. Make sure that you don't interrupt the flow of the page when you include a link. Once the text is linked, it will stand on its own in most designs. That way, the links provide additional or tangential information that your visitors can choose to follow or ignore at their own whim. Don't be shy about what you link; longer links are much easier to tap than shorter ones.

Probably the easiest way to figure out whether you're creating links within text properly is to print out the formatted web page from your browser. In hard copy, without hypertext, does the paragraph still make sense? If the page reads funny on paper, it'll read funny online, too.

Avoid the "Here" Syndrome

A common mistake that many web authors make when creating links in body text is using the "here" syndrome. This is the tendency to create links with a single highlighted word (here) and to describe the links somewhere else in the text. Look at the following examples, with underlining to indicate link text:

Information about ostrich socialization is contained here.
Follow this link for a tutorial on the internal combustion engine.

Because links are highlighted on the web page, the links visually pop out more than the surrounding text (or *draw the eye*, in graphic design lingo). Your visitors will see the link before reading the text.

So the first thing they see in those two lines are "here" and "link." Because "here" says nothing about what the link is used for, your poor visitors have to search the text before and after the link itself to find out what's supposed to be "here." In paragraphs that have many occurrences of *here* or other nondescriptive links, matching up the links with what they're supposed to link to becomes difficult. This forces your visitors to work harder to figure out what you mean.

Plus, these links are just one word long. As mentioned several times, short links are difficult to tap. Here is an example of how you could rewrite those lines to make the links more mobile friendly and easier to understand:

Get more information about ostrich socialization.
This is a great tutorial on the internal combustion engine.

Both of these links are longer, which makes them easier to tap. They are also more descriptive, which gives the user a better understanding of where they are going to go.

To Link or Not to Link

Just as with graphics, every time you create a link, consider why you're linking two pages or sections. Is the link useful? Does it give your visitors more information or bring them closer to their goal? Is the link relevant in some way to the current content?

Each link should serve a purpose. Just because you mention the word *coffee* on a page about some other topic, you don't have to link that word to the coffee home page. Creating such a link may seem cute, but if a link has no relevance to the current content, it just confuses your visitors.

The following list describes some of the categories of useful links in web pages. If your links don't fall into one of these categories, consider the reasons why you're including them in your page:

- Explicit navigation links indicate the specific paths that visitors can take through your web pages: forward, back, up, and home. These links are often indicated by navigation icons, as shown in Figure 21.4.

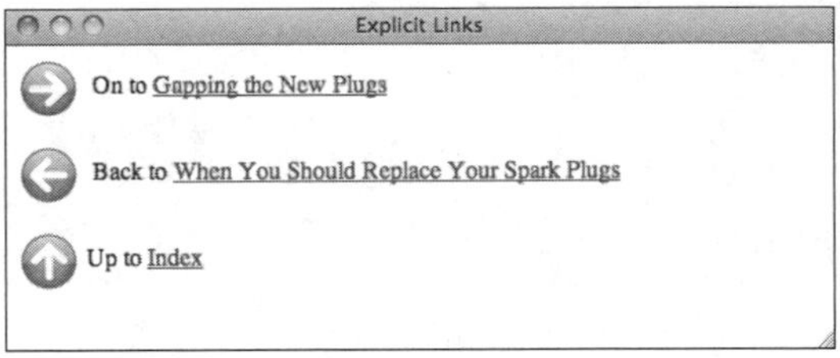

FIGURE 21.4
Explicit navigation links.

- Implicit navigation links (see Figure 21.5) are different from explicit navigation links because the link text implies, but does not directly indicate, navigation between pages. Link menus are the best example of this type of link. The highlighting of the link text makes it apparent that you'll get more information on this topic by selecting the link, but the text itself doesn't necessarily say so. Note the major difference between explicit and implicit navigation links: If you print a page containing both, you won't be able to pick out the implicit links.

  Implicit navigation links also can include tables of contents or other overviews made up entirely of links.

21

FIGURE 21.5
Implicit navigation
links.

> ⊙ ○ ○   Implicit Navigation
>
> # Welcome to Foozle Industries, Inc.
>
> *Keeping the world warm.*
>
> ──────────────────────────────
>
> What's New at Foozle?
> Company Overview
> Our Products
> Product Support
> Job Opportunities at Foozle

■ Definitions of words or concepts make excellent links, particularly if you're creating large networks of pages that include glossaries. By linking the first instance of a word to its definition, you can explain the meaning of that word to visitors who don't know what it means without distracting those who do. Figure 21.6 shows an example of this type of link.

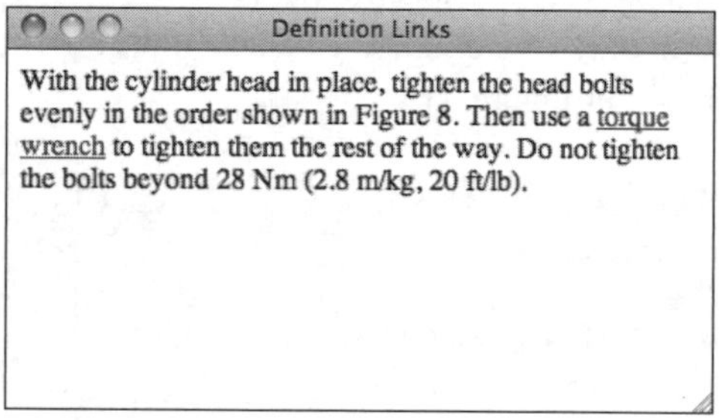

FIGURE 21.6
Definition links.

> ⊙ ○ ○   Definition Links
>
> With the cylinder head in place, tighten the head bolts
> evenly in the order shown in Figure 8. Then use a torque
> wrench to tighten them the rest of the way. Do not tighten
> the bolts beyond 28 Nm (2.8 m/kg, 20 ft/lb).

■ Finally, links to tangents and related information are valuable when the text content will distract from the main purpose of the page. Think of tangent links as footnotes or endnotes in printed text (see Figure 21.7). They can refer to citations to other works or to additional information that's interesting but isn't necessarily directly relevant to the point you're trying to make.

FIGURE 21.7
Footnote links.

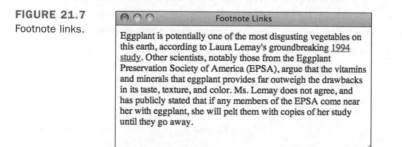

> ⊙ ○ ○   Footnote Links
>
> Eggplant is potentially one of the most disgusting vegetables on
> this earth, according to Laura Lemay's groundbreaking 1994
> study. Other scientists, notably those from the Eggplant
> Preservation Society of America (EPSA), argue that the vitamins
> and minerals that eggplant provides far outweigh the drawbacks
> in its taste, texture, and color. Ms. Lemay does not agree, and
> has publicly stated that if any members of the EPSA come near
> her with eggplant, she will pelt them with copies of her study
> until they go away.

Be careful that you don't get carried away with definitions and tangent links. You might create so many tangents that your visitors spend too much time following links elsewhere to get the point of your original text. Resist the urge to link every time you possibly can, and link only to tangents that are relevant to your own text. Also, avoid duplicating the same tangent—for example, linking every instance of the letters *WWW* on your page to the WWW Consortium's home page. If you're linking twice or more to the same location on one page, consider removing most of the extra links. Your visitors can select one of the other links if they're interested in the information.

Using Images and Multimedia

In Lesson 9, "Using Images on Your Web Pages," you learned all about creating and using images in web pages. And in Lesson 14, "Integrating Multimedia: Video and Sound," you learned all about how to add video and audio files into your web pages. This section summarizes many of those hints and gives suggestions for optimizing them for mobile users.

Don't Overuse Images

Be careful about including a large number of images on your web page. Besides the fact that each image adds to the amount of time it takes to load the page, having too many images on the same page makes it look cluttered and distracts from the point you're trying to get across. This is especially true for mobile customers. Sometimes, though, people think that the more images they include on a page, the better it is. Remember the hints I gave you in Lesson 9. Consider how important each image really is before you put it on the page. If an image doesn't directly contribute to the content, consider leaving it out. Often one feature image per page is enough to get the point across.

Keep Images Small

Keep in mind that each image you use is a separate network connection and takes time to load over a network. This means that each image adds to the total time it takes to view the page, and data minutes deducted from your mobile customers' download limits. Try to reduce the number of images on the page, and keep them small both in file size and in actual dimensions. In particular, keep the following hints in mind:

- For larger images, consider using thumbnails on your main page and then linking to the images rather than putting them inline.

- Save your image in both the PNG and GIF formats to see which creates a smaller file for the type of image you're using. You might also want to increase the level of compression for your JPEG images or reduce the number of colors in the palette of

21

the GIF images to see whether you can save a significant amount of space without adversely affecting image quality.

- You can reduce the physical size of your images by cropping them (using a smaller portion of the overall image) or scaling (shrinking) them. When you scale an image, you might lose some of the detail.

CAUTION

> Remember that reducing the size of your images using the `height` and `width` CSS properties or the `height` and `width` attributes of the `<img>` tag only makes them take up less space on the page; it doesn't affect the size of the image file or the download speed.

Watch Out for Assumptions About Your Visitors' Hardware

Many web designers create problems for their visitors by making a couple of careless assumptions about their hardware. When you're developing web pages, be kind and remember that not everyone has the same screen and browser dimensions as you do.

Just because that huge image you created is narrow enough to fit in your browser doesn't mean that it'll fit in someone else's. An image that's too wide is annoying because the visitors need to resize their windows or scroll sideways.

Most developers limit the overall width of their pages to 750 pixels or 950 pixels, and for the sake of readability, limit the width of containers used to display text to 500 or 600 pixels. Pages meant to be displayed on mobile devices need to be even smaller.

Don't Make Your Videos Annoying

The same rules about file sizes and download times apply to videos and other multimedia just as much as images. While you might want to film your videos in HD or 4K or some huge resolution, most of your mobile customers will just find it annoying if you expect them to download a gigantic file on their data plan.

But there are other so-called features that web designers often add to their videos that are particularly annoying to mobile users. Setting a video to play automatically when the page loads annoys just about everyone who comes to the page. This is especially true if the sound is turned on. That means that that wonderful sound file you added as "background music" to your web page does more than set the mood—it drives people away.

But multimedia can also annoy mobile users when you try to speed things up for them by preloading the files. This is a very tempting technique because many Web designers believe that if the video doesn't start within a few seconds the customer will disappear. That might be true for nonmobile customers, but it's not true for mobile. For one thing, most mobile customers know that they will have to wait at least a short time to watch videos on their devices. But also, when you start downloading a video that they haven't requested, you are, in effect, stealing their bandwidth. You are forcing them to use data minutes for a file they might not even want.

One popular technique on the Web right now is a video background. And while you can do that with CSS, you risk driving away your customers if your page is too distracting. But more important, this is also downloading a video file that your mobile customers then have to pay for without requesting it. There's nothing stopping you from creating a video background, but they can annoy your customers, and annoying your customers turns them into ex-customers.

Avoid Flash

Depending upon who you ask, Flash is either the best thing to ever happen to the Web or the worst. Regardless of which side of the fence you fall on, you should be aware that mobile and Flash simply don't mix.

Apple has never supported Flash on its iOS devices, and Google stopped doing much with it for its Android devices after a year or two. The final nail in the coffin came when Adobe, the makers of Flash, announced in 2011 that it was no longer adapting Flash Player for mobile devices.

The majority of mobile devices can't use Flash, so you should not use Flash either.

Making the Most of CSS and JavaScript

Web design these days is about minimal markup, styled using CSS. Sticking with the following rules of thumb will make sure that your sites load quickly and efficiently on mobile devices as well as computers.

Put Your CSS and JavaScript in External Files

Nearly all browsers maintain a cache of recently loaded content. The more content on your site that can be cached, the more quickly pages on your site after the first one will load. You should put your styles in external style sheets and your JavaScript in linked scripts whenever you can. Linked files will be cached when users first visit your site and then will be retrieved from the cache on subsequent page views.

There are also advantages to this approach in terms of saving you time. If the styles for each page on your site live in `<style>` tags on those pages, you have to update every

21

page when you decide to make a change. It's much easier to make those changes in an external style sheet.

You can even include styles for specific pages in a single external style sheet if you use the class and id attributes cleverly. The `<body>` tag for a page can have a class or id, just like any other element. So if you want the pages in the news section of your site to have one background color and the pages in the "about us" section to have another, you could use this `<body>` tag for "about us":

```
<body class="aboutus">
```

For news, you'd use this one:

```
<body class="news">
```

And then in your style sheet, you'd include the following styles:

```
body.aboutus { background-color: black; }
body.news { background-color: grey; }
```

The same rule applies to JavaScript, too. If you'd use unobtrusive JavaScript, discussed in Lesson 19, you can often put all the JavaScript for a site in a single file.

Location Matters

HTML5 requires links to external style sheets and the `<style>` tag to reside within the `<head>` element. You should be sure to follow this rule, because placing style sheets elsewhere in your document can cause your pages to take longer to display. By the same token, whenever possible, it's best to put `<script>` tags at the bottom of your document, just before the closing `</body>` tag. JavaScript loads in a single thread, which means when browsers are downloading an external script file, they don't try to download other page elements. This can slow down overall page loading time. Putting the scripts last on the page enables JavaScript to download everything else on the page in parallel before it gets to the scripts. It can make your pages load a bit more quickly.

Shrink Your CSS and JavaScript

Once you're done writing your CSS and JavaScript, it's a good idea to compress them so that they download more quickly. Yahoo! has created a tool called the YUI Compressor that shrinks JavaScript and CSS to the smallest size possible. The resulting files aren't really readable by humans, but browsers understand them just fine. You'll work on your files in the human-readable form, but shrink them before putting them on the server. Shrinking these files can save on download time. This shrinking is sometimes referred to as *minifying*. You can download the YUI Compressor from http://yui.github.io/yuicompressor/.

If you use third-party libraries like jQuery, be sure to deploy the minified versions. Your JavaScript files and style sheets might not be very big, but these libraries can be quite large. For example, the regular version of jQuery 1.4.2 is 160k, and the minified version is 70.5k. Most JavaScript libraries can be downloaded in either the regular or the minified form.

Google hosts versions of the popular AJAX libraries (like jQuery, Dojo, and YUI) so that you don't have to host them on your own server. This provides a number of advantages. The first is that you don't have to keep your own copy around. The second is that Google's infrastructure speeds up the delivery of these files. And third, if one of your users has already visited a site that is using the Google-hosted version of the file you're using, it's probably already cached so that the browser won't have to download it at all. You can find out how to use Google's copies of the files at https://developers.google.com/speed/libraries/.

Take Advantage of Mobile Features

Mobile devices are not inferior Web browsers; they are different web browsers. And as such, they have features that are not available on computer web browsers. When you write for the mobile Web, you should take advantage of these features as much as you can.

Geolocation

Geolocation lets users share their location with websites they trust. This is a feature of mobile devices that, while available on nonmobile devices, doesn't make a lot of sense there. HTML5 includes a geolocation *application programming interface* (API) to let web designers detect where a user is when he accesses the website. You can then use that information to provide more help to your customers.

As mentioned previously in this lesson, most mobile users use their smartphones to look up local information. This often means that they want to know where a local business is or find out whether there are special deals near where they currently are.

You can use geolocation on your website to do the following:

- Set up check-in links for your customers to connect to social media sites.
- Send notifications to customers when they are near your store.
- Provide maps to and from your business.

21

But while most desktop computers don't move around a lot, you shouldn't discount them when building your web applications. Getting their location could be helpful, even if they never move. For example, in the near future a Web-enabled refrigerator might be able to connect to your site, place an order for more milk, and send you its location using geolocation.

Make Phone Calls

While the first mobile devices were really PDAs or palmtops (my dad and I both had HP 200LX palmtop computers back in the 1980s), most people think of cell phones as the first mobile devices. And phones are how most people get to the mobile Web. Of course, a feature of phones is that they can make phone calls. And, as a mobile web designer, you can add phone numbers to your website and make them work. This is called *click to call*.

You write a link like you would any other link, but instead of linking to a URL or web page address, you link to a phone number:

```
<a href="tel:4255025366">
```

On mobile phones, when customers tap the link, they are asked if they want to make a call, as in Figure 21.8.

FIGURE 21.8
Click to call.

Of course, desktop browsers are catching up with this feature as well. Apple will open Facetime (voice) when presented with a click to call link. And other computers can link to Skype and other Internet phone services. So maybe nonmobile will be catching up soon.

SMS

One advantage that mobile devices have over computers is that mobile phones can also send SMS or text messages, but most nonmobile devices cannot.

NOTE

Apple has connected all its machines, but if you don't have an iPhone on the same network as your Mac, you can't send SMS text messages using it.

But as a mobile web designer, you can give your mobile customers a link to send you a text message. It works the same way as the phone links:

```
<a href="sms:4255025366">
```

When a user clicks on the link, she is taken to her messaging app with the phone number as the recipient.

Other Good Habits and Hints for Mobile Web Design

In this section, I've gathered several other miscellaneous hints and advice about building mobile websites.

Link Back to Home

Consider linking back to the top level or home page on every page of your site. This link will give visitors a quick escape from the depths of your site. Using a home link is much easier than trying to navigate backward through a hierarchy or repeatedly clicking the back button. This is especially important because visitors to most sites are directed there by search engines. If a search engine leads users to an internal page on your site, you'll want to give them a way to find their way to the top. The easiest way to do this is to link your logo to the home page. People tend to tap on images anyway, so if your logo image takes them to your home page, you haven't lost them.

21

Don't Split Topics Across Pages

Each web page works best if it covers a single topic in its entirety. Don't split topics across pages; even if you link between them, the transition can be confusing. It will be even more confusing if someone jumps in on the second or third page and wonders what's going on.

Plus, it's really common to see long documents or search results pages or the like with links that are single-digit numbers. These are *way too short* to tap on a mobile device. If you must have this type of pagination on a site, make the links large with CSS padding and then set the entire link to `display:block;` or `display:inline-block;`. This will tell the browser to make the entire box, including padding, tappable on smaller screens.

If you think that one topic is becoming too large for a single page, consider reorganizing the page so that you can break up the topic into subtopics. This tip works especially well in hierarchical organizations. It enables you to determine the exact level of detail that each level of the hierarchy should go and exactly how big and complete each page should be. You can then make the links out of the subtopic titles as long as they are at least two words long.

Sign Your Pages

Each page should contain some sort of information at the bottom to act as the signature. I mentioned this tip briefly in Lesson 7, "Formatting Text with HTML and CSS," as part of the description of the `<address>` tag. That particular tag was intended for just this purpose.

Consider putting the following useful information in the `<address>` tag on each page:

- Contact information for the person who created this web page or who is responsible for it. This information should include the person's name and an email address, at the least.

- The status of the page. Is it complete? Is it a work in progress? Is it intentionally left blank?

- The date this page was most recently revised. This information is particularly important for pages that change often or are time sensitive. Include a date on each page so that people know how old it is.

- Copyright or trademark information, if it applies.

Another nice touch is to link a Mailto URL to the text containing the email address of the site owner, as in the following:

```
<address>
Laura Lemay <a href="mailto:lemay@lne.com">lemay@lne.com</a>
</address>
```

This way, the visitors can simply select the link and send mail to the person responsible for the page without having to retype the address into their mail programs.

CAUTION

> One downside of putting your email address on your web page is that there are programs that search websites for email addresses and add them to lists that are sold to spammers. You'll want to consider that risk before posting your email address on a public web page.

Finally, if you don't want to clutter each page with a lot of personal contact information or boilerplate copyright info, a simple solution is to create a separate page for the extra information and then link the signature to that page. Here's an example:

```
<address>
<a href="copyright.html">Copyright</a> and
<a href="contact.html">contact</a> information is available.
</address>
```

One Final Secret to Mobile Web Design

For the end of this lesson I will let you in on a little secret about mobile web design: *It is not all that different from nonmobile web design.* You can apply all of these techniques to your web pages even if you never have a mobile customer. Your desktop customers will also benefit. The great thing about focusing on mobile web design is that you are making your pages easier for everyone to use, not just mobile customers. And that is a good thing for everyone.

Summary

The main Do's and Don'ts for mobile web page design are as follows:

21

- Do use HTML standards like HTML5 and CSS3 when designing for the mobile Web.
- Do provide fallback options for any feature that might not be supported.

- Do test your pages in multiple devices.
- Do write your pages clearly and concisely.
- Do organize the text of your page so that your visitors can scan for important information.
- Do put the most important information first.
- Do validate your HTML and CSS, and check your JavaScript for errors.
- Do spell check and proofread your pages.
- Do group related information both semantically (through the organization of the content) and visually (by using headings or separating sections CSS features).
- Do use a consistent layout across all your pages.
- Do use descriptive links.
- Do have good reasons for using links.
- Do make your links large and tappable.
- Do keep your layout simple.
- Do provide alternatives to images for text-only browsers.
- Do use features like geolocation and click to talk that are only available on mobile devices.
- Do try to keep your images and multimedia small so that they load faster over the network.
- Do use external CSS and JavaScript files whenever possible.
- Do provide a link back to your home page.
- Do match topics with pages.
- Do provide a signature block or link to contact information at the bottom of each page.
- Do write context-independent pages.
- Don't link to irrelevant material.
- Don't overuse emphasis (such as boldface, italic, all caps, link text, blink, or marquees).
- Don't use terminology that's specific to any one browser or device ("click here," "use the Back button," and so on).
- Don't use heading tags to provide emphasis.
- Don't fall victim to the "here" syndrome with your links.
- Don't autoplay or preload videos or audio files.

- Don't link repeatedly to the same site on the same page.
- Don't clutter the page with a large number of pretty but unnecessary images.
- Don't split individual topics across pages.

Workshop

Put on your thinking cap again because it's time for another review. These questions, quizzes, and exercises will remind you about the items that you should (or should not) include on your pages.

Q&A

Q **I've been creating pages, and they work when I test them in the browser. Is it really important to validate them?**

A It's impossible to test your web pages in all of the browsers on all the mobile devices people are using, and making sure that they validate provides a baseline level of assurance that your pages are built correctly and that they'll work in situations that you haven't personally tested them with.

Q **I'm converting existing documents into web pages. These documents are text heavy and are intended to be read from start to finish instead of being scanned quickly. I can't restructure or redesign the content to better follow the guidelines you've suggested—that's not my job. What can I do?**

A All is not lost. You can still improve the overall presentation of these documents by providing reasonable indexes to the content (summaries, tables of contents pages, subject indexes, and so on) and including standard navigation links. In other words, you can create an easily navigable framework around the documents themselves. This can go a long way toward improving content that's otherwise difficult to read online. But if it really isn't your job to restructure the content for the mobile Web, you should provide feedback to the content creators. They need to know that the format they are providing you won't work well for mobile Web customers. You can even suggest they get this book so they better understand what they should be doing.

21

Q   **I have a standard signature block that contains my name and email address, revision information for the page, and a couple of lines of copyright information that my company's lawyers insisted on. It's a little imposing, particularly on small pages. Sometimes the signature is bigger than the page itself! How do I integrate it into my site so that it isn't so obtrusive?**

A   If your company's lawyers agree, consider putting all your contact and copyright information on a separate page and then linking to it on every page rather than duplicating it every time. This way, your pages won't be overwhelmed by the legal stuff. Also, if the signature changes, you won't have to change it on every page. Failing that, you can always just reduce the font size for that block and perhaps change the font color to something with less contrast to the background of the page. This indicates to users that they're looking at fine print.

Quiz

1. What are some ways you can organize your pages so that visitors can scan them more easily?

2. True or false: Headings are useful when you want information to stand out because they make the text large and bold.

3. True or false: Mobile web design applies only to mobile devices.

4. True or false: You can reduce the download time of an image by using the `width` and `height` style properties on the `<img>` tag to scale down the image.

5. Why does it improve performance to put your CSS in a linked style sheet rather than including it on the page?

Quiz Answers

1. You can use headings to summarize topics, lists to organize and display information, and link menus for navigation, and you can separate long paragraphs with important information into shorter paragraphs.

2. False. You should use headings as headings and nothing else. You can emphasize text in other ways or use a graphic to draw attention to an important point.

3. False. Mobile web design improves your web pages for everyone who views them, not just mobile customers.

4. False. When you use the `width` and `height` style properties to make a large image appear smaller on your page, it may reduce the dimensions of the file on the screen, but it won't decrease the download time. The visitor still downloads the same image, but the browser just fits it into a smaller space.

5. Putting your CSS in an external file enables the browser to cache the file so that it doesn't have to download the same information as the user moves from one page on the site to another.

Exercises

1. Go visit several of your favorite sites using a mobile device, preferably a small smartphone. How do they look? Do they break any of the rules you learned in this lesson? What do they do right?

2. How would you improve the sites that you visited in exercise 1 for mobile devices?

LESSON 22
Designing for User Experience

In previous lessons, you learned about what you should and shouldn't do when you plan your website and design your pages. You learned how to design for mobile first and some best practices around designing for mobile users. But there is more to the web design universe than just mobile users, and the best designers try to be as inclusive as possible.

You should already know that the real world consists of many different users with many different computer systems who use many different browsers. Some of the things we haven't yet addressed, however, are the many different preferences and experience levels that the visitors to your site will have. By anticipating these real-world needs, you can better judge how you should design your pages. I also explain how you can make sure that your websites are usable for people who are disabled and must use accessibility technologies to browse the Web.

In this lesson, you'll learn some ways that you can anticipate these needs, as well as the following:

- Things to consider when you're trying to determine the preferences of your audience

- Various ways of helping users find their way around your site

- HTML code that displays the same web page in each of the XHTML 1.0 specifications (Transitional, Frameset, and Strict)

- What accessibility is, and how to design accessible sites

- Using an accessibility validator

Considering User Experience Level

The people viewing your website have varying levels of experience. Although most people visiting your site will be interested in the Web, some of them might have barely used a web browser, while others might have been browsing the Web for 20 years. When you design your site, consider that the people who visit it might have varying levels of experience and browsing requirements.

Will the topics that you discuss on your site be of interest to people with different levels of experience? If so, you might want to build in some features that help them find their way around more easily. The key, of course, is to make your navigation as intuitive as possible. By keeping your navigation scheme consistent from page to page throughout the site, you'll do a favor for users of all experience levels. There are a number of features you can add to your site that will improve its usability for everyone.

Add a Search Engine

Many users go straight to the search engine when they want to find something on a site. No matter how much time and effort you put into building a clear, obvious navigation scheme, someone looking for information about Frisbees is going to look for a box on your page where she can type in the word *Frisbee* and get back a list of the pages where you talk about them.

Unfortunately, locating a good search engine package and setting it up can be an awful lot of work, and difficult to maintain. On the other hand, there are some alternatives. Some search engines enable you to search a specific site for information. You can add a link to them from your site. Some search engines even allow you to set things up so that you can add their search engine to your site, such as Google:

http://www.google.com/cse/

By signing up, you can add a search box to your site that enables your users to search only pages on your own site for information. For a list of other ways to add search functionality to your site, see the following page in the Open Directory Project:

http://www.dmoz.org/Computers/Software/Internet/Servers/Search/

Use Concise, Sensible URLs

One common mistake made by web designers is not considering how users share URLs. If your site is interesting at all, people are going to email the URL to their friends, paste it into instant messaging conversations, and talk about it around the water cooler. Making your URLs short and easy to remember makes them that much easier for people to share. There's a reason why people have paid huge sums for domain names like business.com and computers.com in the past. They're easy to remember, and you don't have to spell them out when you tell them to people.

You might not have control over your domain name, but you can exercise control over the rest of your URLs. Say that you have a section of your site called "Products and Services." All the pages in that section are stored in their own directory. You could call it any one of the following:

```
/ps
/prdsvcs
/products
/products_services
/products_and_services
```

There are plenty of other options, too (you could call it /massapequa if you wanted to), but the preceding list seems like a reasonable group of options. Of the list, a few stand out to me as being poor choices. /products_service and /products_and_services just seem too verbose. If the pages under those directories have long names at all, you're suddenly in very long URL territory, which isn't conducive to sharing. However, /prdsvcs may be short, but it's also difficult to remember and almost certainly has to be spelled out if you tell it to anyone. It's probably no good. That leaves two remaining choices: /ps and /products. The first, /ps, is nice and short and probably easy to remember. Using it would be fine. However, there's one other principle of URLs that I want to talk about: guessability.

Chances are that most of the people who visit your website have been using the Web for awhile. There's some chance that they might just assume that they know where to go on your site based on experience. If they want to read about your products, they may guess—based on their experience with other sites they've visited—that your products will be listed at http://www.your-url.com/products. Any time you can put your content where your users will assume it to be, you're doing them a favor. Using standard directory names such as /about, /contact, and /products can make things ever so slightly easier for your users at no cost to you.

TIP

Several URL shortening services are available that you can use to help your readers when your URLs get too long. My favorite is https://bitly.com/.

22

My final bit of advice on URLs is to make sure that they reflect the structure of your site. One time, I worked on a site that consisted of hundreds of files, all in a single directory. The site itself had structure, but the files were not organized based on that structure. Whether the user was on the home page or five levels deep within the site, the URL was still just a filename tagged onto the hostname of the server. Not only did this make the site hard to work on, but it also kept some useful information away from users.

Suppose you have a site about cars, and you want users to get the latest information about the Honda Fit. What's more useful to your users?

http://www.example.com/fit.html

or

http://www.example.com/cars/honda/2016/fit.html

The second URL provides a lot more information to the user than the first one does. As an added bonus, you can set up your site so that the user can take `fit.html` off the end and get a list of all Honda models for 2016. He can also remove `2016/fit.html` to display all the Honda model years your site covers or take `honda/2016/fit.html` off the end and get a list of all car makes discussed on the site. This URL would be very useful to someone with a lot of experience on the Web.

While veteran web users are accustomed to dealing with URLs, newcomers might not be as comfortable with a long, complicated URL. One way to solve this is to set up redirects on your web server to make shorter URLs point to their longer, more fleshed-out destinations. In other words, you could make http://www.example.com/fit.html point to http://www.example.com/cars/honda/2016/fit.html. Most web hosting services offer redirection help. Contact their support if you don't know how to do it on your website.

Navigation Provides Context

The key purpose of navigation is obviously to enable your users to get from one place to another within your site. However, its secondary purpose is to let your users know where they are within the site. This is something that "breadcrumb" navigation provides to users—a sense of location. Take a look at the screenshot from the DMOZ directory in Figure 22.1.

Just below the search box, you can see a list of links that start at the top of the directory and lead down to the page that I'm actually on. The first thing it does is give me the ability to go back to any level of the directory between the home page (called "Top") and the Cats page that I'm actually on. The second thing it does is let me know that I'm six levels into the directory; the page I'm on is part of the Shopping category of the directory and all the subcategories between that category and the page that I'm on. That's a lot of utility packed into a small feature.

FIGURE 22.1
A page from the DMOZ directory.

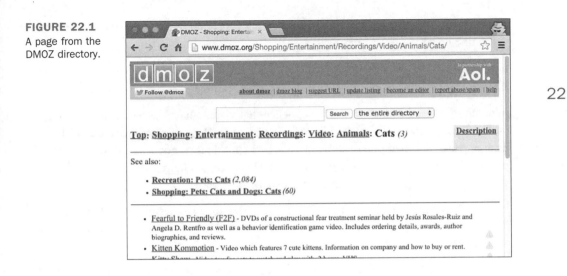

Not all sites have as large and complex a structure as DMOZ, but you can still provide context for your users through your navigation scheme. By altering your navigational elements based on the page that the user is on, you can indicate to them not only where she can go but also where she is. This is also particularly helpful to users who arrive at your site not via the home page, but from an external link. Enabling users to immediately deduce where they are in the larger scheme of things makes it more likely that they'll take in more of your site.

Are Your Users Tourists or Regulars?

When you're designing a site, one of the things you need to remember is that your users are generally either tourists or regulars. If many of your users are tourists, which means that they don't use your site very often or will probably only ever use it one time, you should design your site so that the first-timer can easily figure out what he should be doing and where he needs to go.

However, if your site is normally used by the same existing group of users who come back once a day or once a week, your emphasis should be on providing shortcuts and conveniences that enable them to use your site as efficiently as possible. It's okay if it takes a bit of work to learn about the conveniences because it's worth your users' time.

Clearly, the secret is to strike a balance for two reasons: You want to continue to grow your user base, and that means constantly getting new users. And, you want to make sure that your existing customers get what they need as quickly and easily as possible. The holy grail is a site that's obvious and clear to new users but also provides the features that repeat users crave. However, understanding what sort of audience you have can help you determine how to assign your resources.

Determining User Preferences

In addition to the various levels of experience that visitors have, everyone has his own preferences for how he wants to view your web pages. How do you please users? The truth is, you can't. But you *can* give it your best shot. Part of good web design is anticipating what visitors want to see on your site. This becomes more difficult if the topics you discuss on your site are of interest to a wider audience.

Everyone sees the Web differently. Sometimes this is due to user interests, but other times it's because of special needs. Therein lies the key to anticipating what your customers need on your web pages.

A topic such as "Timing the Sparkplugs on Your 300cc Motorcycle Engine" is of interest to a more select audience. It will attract only those who are interested in motorcycles—more specifically, those who want to repair their own motorcycles. It should be relatively easy to anticipate the types of things these visitors would like to see on your site. Step-by-step instructions can guide them through each process, while images or multimedia can display techniques that are difficult to describe using text alone.

"The Seven Wonders of the Ancient World," however, will attract students of all ages as well as their teachers. Archaeologists, historians, and others with an interest in ancient history also might visit the site. Now you have a wider audience, a wider age range, and a wider range of educational levels. It won't be quite as easy to build a site that will please them all.

In cases such as this, it might help to narrow your focus a bit. One way is to design your site for a specific user group, such as the following:

- **Elementary school students and their teachers**—This site requires a basic navigation system that's easy to follow. Content should be simple and easy to read. Bright, colorful images and animations can help keep the attention of young visitors.

- **High school students and their teachers**—You can use a slightly more advanced navigation system. Multimedia and the latest in web technology will keep these students coming back for more.

- **College students and their professors**—A higher level of content is necessary, whereas multimedia may be less important. Properly citing the sources for your information will be important.

- **Professional researchers and historians**—This type of site probably requires pages that are heavier in text content than multimedia.

> **NOTE**   Not all websites are focused on education. For instance, a site dedicated to college student parties might need to be all videos and pictures and no citations of any kind.

It's not always possible to define user groups for your website, so you'll need to start with your *own* preferences. Survey other sites that include similar content. As you browse through them, ask yourself what you hope to see there. Is the information displayed well? Is there enough help on the site? Does the site have too much or too little multimedia? If you can get a friend or two to do the survey along with you, it helps you get additional feedback before you start your own site. Take notes and incorporate those ideas into your own web pages.

After you design some initial pages, ask your friends, family members, and associates to browse through your site and pick it apart. Even better is if you can find a few people in your target market to check out your beta site. Keep in mind that when you ask others for constructive criticism, you might hear some things that you don't want to hear. However, this process is important because you'll often get many new ideas on how to improve your site even more.

What Is Accessibility?

Accessibility is basically the effort to make websites as usable as possible for people with disabilities. This involves the creation of software and hardware that enables people with various disabilities to use computers and the Web. It also means addressing accessibility concerns in the design of HTML as a markup language and efforts on the part of web designers to incorporate accessibility into their websites. When a person with impaired vision uses a screen reader to visit a website, there are things the site's author can do to make that experience as rich and fulfilling as possible given the user's disability.

The good news is, because you already design with a Mobile First mindset, making your inclusive site accessible will be a breeze.

Common Myths Regarding Accessibility

Historically, there has been some resistance among web designers toward building websites in an accessible manner. This resistance has arisen not due to a want to discriminate against people who might benefit from accessible design, but rather from a fear that accessibility will limit designers' options in how they create their sites. There's also the fact that accessibility seems like it will add additional work, and most people have too much to do already.

For a long time, many people thought that *accessible* was a code word for *all text*. It was believed that adding accessibility meant putting all of your content in a single column running straight down the page and avoiding the bells and whistles that many people believe are necessary for an attractive website. The fact is that this couldn't be further from the truth. Although some common techniques can interfere with accessibility, that doesn't mean that you must remove any images, sounds, or multimedia from your website. Nor does it dictate that your layout be simplified.

The demand that accessibility places on designers is that they write clean, standards-compliant markup, take advantage of HTML features that improve accessibility, and use tags as they are intended to be used in the specification rather than based on how they make your pages look in the browser. If you've been following along with the lessons in this book, you're already doing these things.

The other common misapprehension with regard to accessibility is that it will require a lot of extra work on your part. The fact is that it does require some extra work—creating your pages so that they take advantage of accessibility features in HTML is more work than leaving them out. However, in many cases, coding for accessibility will help all of your users, not just those using alternative browsers.

Section 508

Section 508 is a government regulation specifying that U.S. federal government agencies must provide access for all users, including those with disabilities, to electronic and information technology resources. It requires that federal agencies consider the needs of disabled users when they spend money on computer equipment or other computer resources. What this boils down to is that federal websites must be designed in an accessible fashion.

Not only did Section 508 change the rules of the game for many web designers (anyone involved with federal websites), but it raised the profile of accessibility in general. Thanks in part to the fact that people didn't really understand the implications of Section 508 at first, people started thinking a lot about accessibility and what it meant for the Web.

NOTE	For more information on Section 508, see http://www.section508.gov/.

Alternative Browsers

Just as there are a number of disabilities that can make it more challenging for people to use the Web, there are a number of browsers and assistive technologies that are designed to level the playing field to a certain degree. I discuss some common types of assistive technologies here so that when you design your web pages you can consider how they'll be used by people with disabilities.

22

Disabled users access the Web in a variety of ways, depending on their degree and type of disability. For example, some users just need to use extra large fonts on their computer, whereas others require a completely different interface from the standard used by most people.

Let's look at some of the kinds of browsers specifically designed for disabled users. For users who read Braille, a number of browsers provide Braille output. Screen readers are also common. Instead of displaying the page on the screen (or in addition to displaying it), screen readers attempt to organize the contents of a page in a linear fashion and use a voice synthesizer to speak the page's contents. Some browsers also accept audio input—users who are uncomfortable using a mouse and keyboard can use speech recognition to navigate the Web.

Another common type of assistive technology (AT) is a screen magnifier. Screen magnifiers enlarge the section of the screen where the user is working to make it easier for users with vision problems to use the computer. More and more touch screen devices make it trivial to pinch to zoom in on a web page and make the text and images larger. Most standard web browsers support zooming with a keyboard shortcut like Ctrl-+ to zoom in and Ctrl-- to zoom out (use the Cmd key on a Mac).

One type of AT that almost everyone has experienced is closed-captioning for the hearing impaired. You see this at loud restaurants and airports when it's impossible to hear the overhead TVs. And although most web pages rely on text and images, which don't impact the hearing impaired, if you use video or audio your site will become inaccessible to them unless you include captioning.

Writing Accessible HTML

When it comes to writing accessible HTML, there are two steps to follow. The first step is to use the same tags you normally use as they were intended. The second step is to take advantage of HTML features specifically designed to improve accessibility. I've already mentioned a number of times that tags should be used based on their semantic meaning rather than how they're rendered in browsers. For example, if you want to print some bold text in a standard size font, `<h4>` will work, except that it not only boldfaces the text, it also indicates that it's a level 4 heading. In screen readers or other alternative browsers, that might cause confusion for your users. So if all you need is the text to be bold, use the CSS `font-weight` property.

Tables

Accessibility issues are particularly difficult when it comes to tables. I've already mentioned that it's not a good idea to use tables for page layout when you're designing for accessibility. Alternative browsers must generally indicate to users that a table has been encountered and then unwind the tables so that the information can be presented to the user in a linear fashion. To make things easier on these users, you should use tables for tabular data where you can. If you can't avoid using tables to lay out your page, make sure to indicate it's a presentation table with the `role="presentation"` attribute and be aware of how the table will be presented to users.

When you're presenting real tabular data, it's worthwhile to use all the supplemental tags for tables that are all too often ignored. When you're inserting row and column headings, use the `<th>` tag. If the default alignment or text presentation is not to your liking, use CSS to modify it. Some browsers will indicate to users that the table headings are distinct from the table data. Furthermore, if you label your table, using the `<caption>` tag is a better choice than just inserting a paragraph of text before or after the table. Some browsers indicate that the text is a table caption.

Here's an example of a table that's designed for accessibility:

```
<p>This is the famous Boston Consulting Group Product
Portfolio Matrix. It's a two by two matrix with labels.</p>
<table border="1" cellpadding="12">
  <caption>Boston Consulting Group Product Portfolio Matrix</caption>
  <tr>
    <td colspan="2" rowspan="2"><br></td>
    <th colspan="2">Market Share</th>
  </tr>
  <tr>
    <th>High</th>
    <th>Low</th>
  </tr>
  <tr>
    <th rowspan="2">Market Growth</th>
    <th>High</th>
    <td align="center">Star</td>
    <td align="center">Problem Child</td>
  </tr>
  <tr>
    <th>Low</th>
    <td align="center">Cash Cow</td>
    <td align="center">Dog</td>
  </tr>
</table>
```

Links

As mentioned in Lesson 21, "Designing for the Mobile Web," avoiding the "here" syndrome is imperative for mobile design, but it's also important when it comes to accessibility. Having all the links on your page described as "click here" or "here" isn't very helpful to disabled users (or any others). Just thinking carefully about the text you place inside a link to make it descriptive of the link destination is a good start.

To make your links even more usable, you can use the `title` attribute. The `title` attribute is used to associate some descriptive text with a link. It is used not only by alternative browsers, but many standard browsers will display a tool tip with the link title when the user holds her mouse pointer over it. Here are some examples:

```
<a href="http://www.dmoz.org/" title="The volunteer maintained directory.">DMOZ</a>
<a href="document.pdf" title="1.5 meg PDF document">Special Report</a>
```

Navigational links are a special case because they usually come in sizable groups. Many pages have a nice navigation bar right across the top that's useful to regular users who are able to skim the page and go directly to the content they want. Users who use screen readers with their browsers and other assistive technologies aren't so lucky. You can imagine what it would be like to visit a site that has 10 navigational links across the top of the page if you relied on every page being read to you. Every time you move from one page to the next, the navigation links would have to be read over again.

There are a few ways around this that vary in elegance. If you're using CSS to position elements on your page, it can make sense to place the navigational elements after your main content in your HTML file but use CSS to position them wherever you like. When a user with a screen reader visits the site, he'll get the content before getting the navigation. You can then include a link that skips to the navigation at the top of the page and hide it using CSS. Users with screen readers can jump to the navigation if they need to but won't be required to listen to it on every page.

TIP

It's worth remembering that many disabled users rely on keyboards to access the Web. You can make things easier on them by using the `accesskey` and `tabindex` attributes of the `<a>` tag to enable them to step through the links on your page in a logical order. This proves particularly useful if you also include forms on your page. For example, if you have a form that has links interspersed in the form, setting up the `tabindex` order so that the user can tab through the form completely before he runs into any links can save him a lot of aggravation. This is the sort of convenience that all of your users will appreciate, too.

Images and Multimedia

Images are a sticky point when it comes to accessibility. Users with impaired vision might not be able to appreciate your images or videos. Users with bad hearing might not enjoy your audio files and find videos without captioning annoying. However, clever design and usage of the tools provided by HTML can, to a certain degree, minimize the problems multimedia cause.

Images are known for having probably the best-known accessibility feature of any HTML element. The `alt` attribute has been around as long as the `<img>` tag and provides text that can stand in for an image if the user has a text-only browser or the image wasn't downloaded for some reason. Back when everybody used slow dialup connections to the Internet, it was easy to become intimately familiar with `alt` text because it displayed while the images on a page downloaded. Later, some browsers started showing `alt` text as a tool tip when the user let her mouse pointer hover over an image.

Despite the fact that `alt` text is useful, easy to add, and required by the HTML5 specification, many pages on the Internet still lack meaningful alternative text for most (if not all) of their images. Taking a few extra minutes to enter `alt` text for your images is a must for anyone who uses HTML that includes images. Also bear in mind that while using `alt=""` is perfectly valid, it is a bad idea. If you have images that don't need alternative text, put them as background images in your CSS. Text-based browsers will, in the absence of `alt` text, generally display something like [IMAGE] on the page. If the image is a design feature rather than actual content, this can make the page more difficult to comprehend when the screen reader simply says "image" in the middle of a paragraph.

There's one final area to discuss when it comes to images: the marriage of images and links in the form of image maps. As you might imagine, image maps can be an accessibility issue. But you can use the `alt` attribute on your `<area>` tags in the same way as you would use it on your `<img>` tags to provide alternate text for each link area:

```
<area shape="rect" coords="50,50,100,100" alt="square box" href="box.html">
```

Many browsers also provide tool tips for alternate text on image maps for non-AT browsers, which makes it more useful for all your users.

With video and audio, it's even easier to provide fallback options for users who can't view or hear them. The first thing you do is include HTML inside the `<video>` or `<audio>` tags that provides fallback information. This might be a text description of the video, links to alternative text or other versions of the video, or even a full written transcript of the audio file.

HTML5 provides another tag to help make audio and video more accessible: `<track>`. Although this tag doesn't have widespread support—as of this writing only Internet

Explorer 10 and Safari/iOS browsers support it—it's still a good idea to start at least thinking about it. The `track` tag lets you provide multiple audio tracks to make your media more accessible. You place it in your HTML inside the `video` or `audio` tags and give it a label that is human readable explaining what the track is for. The last attribute you need is the `kind` attribute that indicates what type of track it is. To caption a video with English text you might write the following:

```
<track kind="captions" src="brave.en.hoh.vtt"
srclang="en" label="English for the Hard of Hearing">
```

You can use several kinds of tracks with HTML5. Table 22.1 explains them.

TABLE 22.1 Keywords for the `kind` Attribute of the `track` Tag

Keyword	Description
subtitles	Transcription of the dialog. Typically overlaid on video.
captions	Transcription of dialog, sound effects, relevant musical cues, and other audio information. Typically overlaid on video.
descriptions	Text descriptions of the video portion of a media element. Typically synthesized as audio.
chapters	Chapter titles used as navigating within the media file. Typically displayed as an interactive list.
metadata	Tracks intended for use from script. Not typically shown to the end user.

Designing for Accessibility

Just as important as taking advantage of the HTML features provided specifically for accessibility is taking care to design your pages in a manner that's as accommodating as possible for users who are in need of assistance. Most of these techniques are relevant to all users, not just those using alternative browsers or assistive technologies.

Using Color

A common pitfall designers fall into is using color to confer meaning to users. For example, they print an error on the page and change the font color to red to indicate that something went wrong. Unfortunately, visually impaired users won't be able to distinguish your error message from the rest of the text on the page without reading it. Needless to say, putting two elements on the page that are the same except for color (such as using colors to indicate the status of something) is not accessible. The best alternative is to label them with text. For example, you might display an error message this way:

```
<p class="error">ERROR: You must enter your full name.</p>
```

Remember, too, that color impacts not just people who cannot see, but also people who are color blind. If you have content on your page that relies on a difference between two colors, your page will not be accessible. It will have the problem of using color I just mentioned, but it may also run the risk of looking like two identical colors to a color blind person.

You can also cause difficulty reading your page if the colors don't contrast enough, especially your text and background colors. There is a reason that most word processors use black text on white or pale backgrounds: The high contrast makes them easy to read, and that makes it accessible to everyone.

Fonts

When you specify fonts on your pages, you can cause accessibility problems if you're not careful. In some cases, font specification doesn't matter at all because the user accesses your site with a screen reader or alternative browser that completely ignores your font settings. However, users who simply see poorly can have an unpleasant experience if you set your fonts to an absolute size—particularly if you choose a small size. If a user has set his browser's default font to be larger than normal, and your pages are hard coded to use 9-point text, that user will probably dump your site altogether.

In many cases, it makes sense to leave the default font specification alone for most of the text on your site. That way, users can set their fonts as they choose, and you won't interfere with their personal preferences. If you do modify the fonts on the page, make sure that the fonts scale with the user's settings so that the user can see the text at a comfortable size.

CAUTION

Be sure to test your pages with a variety of text size settings when you do browser testing. Many users increase the size of fonts in the browser to make them easier to read, and you should make sure that if users have done so, your pages still work for them. And, as mentioned previously, zooming on mobile devices is just a pinch away.

Take Advantage of All HTML Tags

It's easy to fall into the trap of using `<i>` or `<b>` rather than more specific tags when you need to add emphasis to something. For example, suppose you're citing a passage from a book. When you enter the book title, you could indicate to your users that it's a proper title by putting it inside the `<i>` tag, or you could use the `<cite>` tag. There are plenty of other underutilized tags, as well, all of which provide some semantic meaning in addition to the text formatting they're associated with.

Even in cases in which you really just want to emphasize text, it's preferable to use `<em>` and `<strong>` over `<i>` and `<b>`. These tags provide a lot more meaning than the basic text formatting tags that are often used. Not all alternative browsers will take advantage of any or all of these tags, but conveying as much meaning as possible through your choice of tags won't hurt accessibility for sure, and will help some now and could help more in the future. There's no downside to taking this approach, either.

Frames

Frames are, to put it bluntly, not accessible. That is why they were removed from HTML5. This doesn't exactly apply to inline frames, but they are still difficult for most AT to use. This is especially true if you put an entirely different site inside your iframe. In this case, the site you're framing needs to be accessible as well, and that's not a guarantee. My recommendation is to avoid even inline frames unless you absolutely must use them, and provide alternative content—like links to the framed content—when you do.

Forms

Forms present another thorny accessibility issue. Nearly all web applications are based on forms, and failure to make them accessible can cost you users. For example, large online stores have a serious financial interest in focusing on form accessibility. How many sales would Amazon or eBay lose if their sites weren't accessible? Some work on making sure the forms that enable you to purchase items are accessible can really pay off.

One key thing to remember is that disabled users often navigate using only the keyboard. As I mentioned when talking about links, assigning sensible `tabindex` values to your form fields can really increase both the usability and the accessibility of your forms. The other advanced form tags, such as `fieldset`, `optgroup`, and `label`, can be beneficial in terms of usability, too.

22

Validating Your Sites for Accessibility

There's no reason to rely on luck when it comes to determining whether your site measures up when it comes to accessibility. Just as you can use the W3C validator to verify that your HTML files are standards compliant, you can use a number of validators to check your site for accessibility problems. Cynthia Says is one such validator, and you can find it at http://cynthiasays.com/. It can validate a site against the Section 508 guidelines mentioned earlier or against the Web Content Accessibility Guidelines developed by the W3C.

Its operation is nearly identical to that of the HTML validator provided by the W3C. If you submit your page to the validator, it generates a report that indicates which areas of your page need improvement, and it provides general tips that can be applied to any page. Figure 22.2 shows a Cynthia Says report for InformIT.

FIGURE 22.2
An accessibility report generated by Cynthia Says.

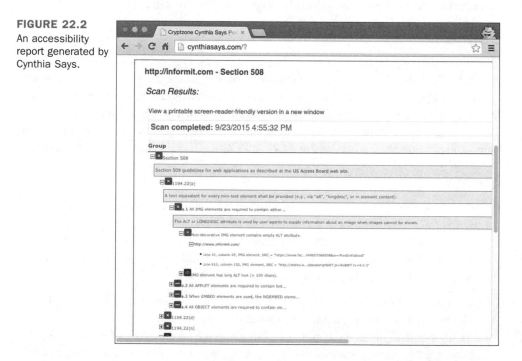

If you don't want to do a full-scale validation, you can use the WCAG (Web Content Accessibility Guidelines) conformance levels to evaluate your site yourself. You can read more about the conformance levels at the W3C: http://www.w3.org/TR/WCAG20/.

22

Further Reading

This lesson is really the tip of the iceberg when it comes to handling accessibility on websites. If you're going to make a commitment to creating an accessible site, you'll probably want to research the issue further. Your first stop should be online accessibility resources. The W3C provides a huge body of information on accessibility as part of their Web Accessibility Initiative. The home page is http://www.w3.org/WAI/.

If you maintain a personal site, you might also find Mark Pilgrim's online book, *Dive into Accessibility* (http://diveintoaccessibility.info/), to be a useful resource.

There have also been several books written on web accessibility. Joe Clark's *Building Accessible Websites* is very well regarded. You can find out more about the book at the book's website: http://joeclark.org/book/.

Summary

I hope you now realize that the needs of your visitors should affect the approach you use in your website design. The key is to anticipate those needs and try to address them as broadly as possible. Not every site has to be filled with multimedia that implements the latest and greatest web technologies. On the other hand, certain topics almost demand higher levels of page design. Listen to the needs of your visitors when you design your pages, and you'll keep them coming back.

Even though accessibility issues ostensibly affect only a small percentage of web users, they should not be ignored. Many accessibility-related improvements actually improve the web experience for most users. Leaving out disabled users by not accounting for them in your designs is inconsiderate and can often be a poor business decision. Adding accessibility features to an existing site can be challenging, but when you build new sites from scratch, making them accessible can often be done with little additional effort. If I've convinced you of the importance of accessibility in this lesson, you'll probably want to dig into the resources listed previously for more information.

Workshop

As if you haven't had enough already, here's a refresher course. As always, there are questions, quizzes, and exercises that will help you remember some of the most important points in this lesson.

Q&A

Q Feedback from visitors to my site varies a lot. Some want my pages to use less multimedia, whereas others want more. Is there an easy way to satisfy both of them?

A You've already learned that you can provide links to external multimedia files. This is the best approach for visitors who want less multimedia because they won't see it unless they click the link. Often the objections to multimedia have less to do with the videos being on the site than with how you implement them. For example, most people find autoplaying videos and sound files to be annoying but don't mind if there's just a box with a triangle in the middle of it. As you learned in Lesson 21, setting up autoplay is bad for mobile usability, and it affects accessibility and user experience for nonmobile customers.

Q I use a lot of external files on my website, and they can be downloaded from several different pages. Wouldn't it be more efficient to include a link to the correct readers or viewers on the pages where the external files appear?

A Although it's much easier for the visitor to download an external file and the appropriate reader or helper application from the same page, it might be more difficult for you to maintain your pages when the URLs for the helper applications change. A good compromise is to include a Download page on your website with links to all the helper applications that the visitor will need. After the visitor downloads the external file, she can then navigate to your Download page to get the helper application she needs to view that file.

Q If I don't make my site accessible, what percentage of my audience will I lose?

A Even if you weren't wondering about this yourself, there's a good chance your boss probably wants to know. Unfortunately, there's no hard-and-fast number. I've seen it reported that 10% of the population has disabilities, but not all of those disabilities affect one's ability to access the Web. And you have to remember that a lot of things you do to make your site accessible will help your nondisabled customers as well. Older customers generally need larger font sizes and zooming, many people are color blind, and lots of companies don't allow sound cards on their company computers. By making your site accessible to blind and deaf people, you help those others as well.

Q Can I run into legal trouble if I don't bother with making my site accessible?

A If you're in the United States, the answer to this question is no, unless you're working on a site for the federal government and are bound by Section 508. This may be different in other countries, especially in Europe. Contact a legal advisor if you are concerned.

Quiz

1. How do real-world user needs vary?
2. What are some important things to include on your site to help those who are new to computers or the Internet?
3. True or false: It's better to have a lot of frames in a frameset because you can keep more information in the browser window at the same time.
4. True or false: To make a site truly accessible, no images can be used for navigation or links.
5. What should you do with images that are part of the design and don't have alternative text?
6. How should navigation be placed on a page to make it most accessible?
7. Name attributes of tags aimed specifically at accessibility.

Quiz Answers

1. Different users will have different levels of experience. Browser preferences will vary. Some want to see a lot of multimedia, whereas others prefer none at all. Some prefer images and multimedia that are interactive, whereas others prefer simpler pictures that demonstrate a process or technique on how to do something. Other preferences are more specific to the interests of the visitors.
2. Include pages on your site that help visitors find the information they're looking for. Also include pages that help them find their way around the site.
3. False. This was a trick question. Frames are no longer part of HTML, and you shouldn't use them. The only exception is the `iframe` tag, and you should avoid using it because it's still not as accessible as plain HTML.
4. False; however, you must use the images in an accessible manner, specifically by including alternative text.
5. Images that are part of the design should be loaded using CSS to avoid them appearing as content to screen readers.
6. Navigation should be placed after the main content on a page to make it accessible with users who must navigate the page in a linear fashion.
7. Some attributes designed to improve accessibility are the `title` attribute of the `<a>` tag and the `alt` attribute of the `<img>` and `<area>` tags.

Exercises

1. Design a simple navigation system for a website and describe it in a manner that makes sense to you. Then ask others to review it and verify that your explanations are clear to them.

2. Make a list of the topics that you want to discuss on your website. Go through the list a second time and see whether you can anticipate the types of people who will be interested in those topics. Finally, review the list a third time and list the special needs that you should consider for each user group.

3. Visit Cynthia Says, the accessibility validator, and see how your site rates against the accessibility guidelines.

4. Make sure that all the `<img>` tags on your site have `alt` attributes. It's a good first step toward accessibility.

LESSON 23
How to Publish Your Site

Just uploading your site to a web server somewhere doesn't mean that you'll attract many visitors. In fact, with millions of sites online already, you'll need to promote your site if you want to build an audience.

So, how do you entice people to come to your site? This lesson shows you some of the ways, including the following:

- Learning what a web server does and why you need one

- Finding web hosting

- Deploying your website

- Determining your URL

- Testing and troubleshooting your web pages

- Advertising your site

- Submitting your site to search engines

- Using business cards, letterheads, and brochures

- Promoting your site on social networks

- Using analytics to find out who's viewing your pages

What Does a Web Server Do?

To publish web pages, you need a web server. The server listens for requests from web browsers and returns the resources specified in the URL in those requests. Web servers and web browsers communicate using the *Hypertext Transfer Protocol* (HTTP), a protocol created specifically for the request and transfer of hypertext documents over the Web. Because of this use, web servers often are called *HTTP servers*.

Other Things Web Servers Do

Although the web server's primary purpose is to answer requests from browsers, it's responsible for several other tasks. You'll learn about some of them in the following sections.

File and Media Type Determination

In Lesson 14, "Integrating Multimedia: Video and Sound," you learned about content types and how browsers and servers use file extensions to determine file types. Servers are responsible for telling the browsers what kinds of content the files contain. Web servers are configured so that they know which media types to assign to files that are requested so that the browser can tell audio files from HTML pages from style sheets.

File Management

The web server also is responsible for rudimentary file management—mostly in determining how to translate URLs into the locations of files on the server. If a browser requests a file that doesn't exist, the web server returns the HTTP error code 404 and sends an error page to the browser. You can configure the web server to redirect from one URL to another, automatically pointing the browser to a new location if resources move or if you want to retire them. Servers can also be set up to return a particular file if a URL refers to a directory on a server without specifying a filename.

Finally, servers keep log files for information on how many times each URL on the site has been accessed, including the address of the computer that accessed it, the date and, optionally, which browser they used, and the URL of the page that referred them to your page. Web servers also keep a log of any errors that occur when browsers submit requests so that you can track them down and fix them.

Server-Side Scripts and Forms Processing

In addition to serving up static documents such as HTML files and images, most web servers offer the option of running scripts or programs that generate documents on-the-fly. These scripts can be used to create catalogs and shopping carts, discussion boards, clients to read email, or content management systems to publish documents dynamically.

In fact, any website that you find that does more than just publish plain old documents is running some kind of script or program on the server. A number of popular scripting platforms are available for writing web applications. Which one is available for your use depends in part on which web server you're using. PHP is the most popular choice. It's easy to get started with and runs on most servers. Other popular choices include Microsoft .NET, which runs on Windows, or Java Server Pages (JSP), which can run on most servers. Newer choices include Go, R, Ruby on Rails, and Django, all of which can be used to build web applications.

Server-Side File Processing

Some servers can process files before they send them along to the browsers. On a simple level, there are server-side includes, which can insert a date or a chunk of boilerplate text into each page, or run a program. Also, you can use server-side processing in much more sophisticated ways to modify files on-the-fly for different browsers or to execute small bits of code embedded in your pages.

Authentication and Security

Password protection is provided out of the box by most web servers. Using authentication, you can create users and assign passwords to them, and you can restrict access to certain files and directories. You can also restrict access to files or to an entire site based on site names or IP addresses. For example, you can prevent anyone outside your company from viewing files that are intended for employees. It's common for people to build custom authentication systems using server-side scripts, too.

For security, some servers also provide a mechanism for encrypted connections and transactions using the *Secure Sockets Layer* (SSL) protocol. SSL allows the browser to authenticate the server, proving that the server is who it says it is, and an encrypted connection between the browser and the server so that sensitive information between the two cannot be understood if it is intercepted. SSL is becoming more and more important to search engines as well; they use them to assign authority to websites that are secured and identified.

How to Find Web Hosting

Before you can put your site on the Web, you must find a web server. How easy this is depends on how you get your access to the Internet.

Using a Web Server Provided by Your School or Work

If you get your Internet connection through school or work, that organization might allow you to publish web pages on its own web server. Given that these organizations usually

23

have fast connections to the Internet and people to administer the site for you, this situation is ideal.

You'll have to ask your system administrator, computer consultant, webmaster, or network provider whether a web server is available and, if so, what the procedures are for putting up your pages. You'll learn more about what to ask later in this lesson.

Using a Commercial Web Host

You may pay for your Internet access through an *Internet service provider* (ISP), or a commercial online service. Many of these services allow you to publish your web pages, although it may cost you extra. Restrictions might apply as to the kinds of pages you can publish or whether you can run server-side scripts. You can probably find out more about the web hosting options offered by your Internet service provider on the support section of their website.

Many companies specialize in web hosting. These services, most commonly known as *web hosts*, usually provide a way for you to transfer your files to their server (usually a web-based tool, but sometimes FTP or Secure FTP too). They also usually supply the disk space and the actual web server software that provides access to your files. In addition, they have professional systems administrators onsite to make sure the servers are running well at all times.

Generally, you're charged a flat monthly rate, with added charges if you use too much disk space or network bandwidth. Many web hosts provide support for server-side scripts written in PHP and often install some commonly used scripts so that you don't even have to set them up for yourself. Most also enable you to set up your site with your own domain name, and some even provide a facility for registering domain names. These features can make using commercial web hosting providers an especially attractive option. Some popular commercial web hosts include BlueHost (http://www.bluehost.com/), DreamHost (https://www.dreamhost.com/), and MediaTemple (https://mediatemple.net/).

> **CAUTION**
>
> Make sure that when you register your domains, they are registered in your name rather than in the name of the hosting provider or domain registrar who registers them on your behalf. You want to make sure that you own the domain names you register.

To get your own domain name, you need to register it with an authorized registrar. The initial cost to register and acquire your domain name can be as low as $2 per year. Thereafter, an annual fee keeps your domain name active. After you have your own domain name, you can set it up at your hosting provider so that you can use it in your

URLs and receive email at that domain. Your site will have an address such as http://www.example.com/.

Many ISPs and web hosts can assist you in registering your domain name. You can register your domain directly with an authorized registrar such as Network Solutions (http://www.networksolutions.com/), Register.com, dotster.com, or Google Domains (https://domains.google.com/about/). Most of these services also offer *domain parking*, a service that allows you to host your domain with them temporarily until you choose a hosting provider or set up your own server. The prices vary, so shop around before registering your domain.

23

Commercial Web Builders

A new area that is becoming more popular in the web hosting space is web builders. These are companies that offer hosting, building, and management software all in one package. The advantage of these tools is that they offer sophisticated sites and site templates without requiring the work involved in building and maintaining it yourself.

These tools are especially popular with small business owners who want to maintain their own website but don't want to learn a lot about web design or building web pages. If you've gotten this far in the book, you already know more about building web pages than you need to use these services. But they are a quick, and sometimes free, way to get a website up quickly. Some of the best of these include Weebly (http://www.weebly.com/), Squarespace (http://squarespace.com/), and Webs (http://www.webs.com/).

Setting Up Your Own Server

If you're really courageous and want the ultimate in web publishing, running your own website is the way to go. You can publish as much as you want and include any kind of content you want. You'll also be able to use forms, scripts, streaming multimedia, and other options that aren't available to people who don't have their own servers. Other web hosts might not let you use these kinds of features. However, running a server definitely isn't for everyone.

You have two options here. The first is to set up an actual computer of your own and use it as a server. However, the cost and maintenance time can be daunting, and you need a level of technical expertise that the average user might not possess. Furthermore, you need some way to connect it to the Internet. Many Internet service providers won't let you run servers over your connection, and putting your server in a colocation facility or getting a full-time Internet connection for your server can be costly. However, this might be the right answer if you are setting up a website for internal use at your company or organization.

The second option is to lease a virtual server. Applications exist that enable companies to treat a single computer as multiple virtual computers. They then lease those virtual computers to people to use for whatever they like. So for a modest price, you can lease a virtual server over which you have full control. From your perspective, it is your computer. Companies such as Linode (http://linode.com) and RackSpace (http://www.rackspace.com/cloud) offer virtual servers, as does Amazon.com through its EC2 service (https://aws.amazon.com/ec2/).

Free Hosting

If you can't afford to pay a web hosting provider to host your website, some free alternatives exist. For the most part, free sites do not offer the opportunity to create your own pages by hand and deploy them. Instead, there are services that host particular kinds of content, such as weblogs (https://www.blogger.com/home), journals (http://www.livejournal.com/), and photos (https://www.flickr.com/). The tradeoff is that the pages on these sites have advertisements included on them and that your bandwidth usage is generally sharply limited. There are often other rules regarding the amount of space you can use, too. Free hosting can be a good option for hobbyists, but if you're serious about your site, you'll probably want to host it with a commercial service.

Organizing Your HTML Files for Publishing

After you have access to a web server, you can publish the website you've labored so hard to create. Before you actually move it into place on your server, however, it's important to organize your files. Also, you should have a good idea of what goes where to avoid lost files and broken links.

Questions to Ask Your Webmaster

The *webmaster* is the person who runs your web server. This person also might be your system administrator, help desk administrator, or network administrator. Before you can publish your site, you should get several facts from the webmaster about how the server is set up. The following list of questions will help you later in this book when you're ready to figure out what you can and cannot do with your server:

- **Where on the server will I put my files?** In most cases, someone will create a directory on the server where your files will reside. Know where that directory is and how to gain access to it. On many hosting providers, this is the only directory you will have access to.

- **What's the URL of my top-level directory?** This URL will usually be different from the actual path to your files.

- **What is the operating system of my web server?** Most web servers run on Linux or UNIX using Apache as the web server software, but there are Windows and Macintosh web servers. The operating system (and web server software) will affect what types of scripts and files you can use on the site.

- **What's the name of the system's default index file?** This file is loaded by default when a URL ends with a directory name. Usually it's `index.html` or `index.htm`, but it may be `default.htm` or something else.

- **Can I run PHP, ASP, or other types of scripts?** Depending on your server, the answer to this question may be a decisive "no," or you might be limited to certain programs and capabilities.

- **Do you support special plug-ins or file types?** If your site will include multimedia files (Flash, MP3, MP4, or others), your webmaster might need to configure the server to accommodate those file types. Make sure that the server properly handles special types of files before you create them.

- **Are there limitations on what or how much I can put up?** Some servers restrict pages to specific content (for example, only work-related pages or no adult content) or restrict the amount of storage you can use. Make sure that you understand these restrictions before you publish your content.

- **Is there a limit to the amount of bandwidth that my site can consume?** This is somewhat related to the previous question. Most web hosts only allow you to transfer a certain amount of data over their network over a given period of time before they either cut you off or start charging you more money. You should ask what your bandwidth allotment is and make sure that you have enough to cover the traffic you anticipate. (The bandwidth allotment from most web hosts is more than enough for all but the most popular sites, and more and more hosts offer unlimited bandwidth.)

- **Do you provide any canned scripts that I can use for my web pages?** If you aren't keen on writing your own scripts to add advanced features to your pages, ask your service provider whether it provides scripts that might be of assistance. For example, many web hosts provide a script for creating an email contact form. Others might provide access to form-processing scripts, too. More and more hosting companies are offering package managers to add external programs like WordPress and Drupal as well.

23

Keeping Your Files Organized with Directories

Probably the easiest way to organize your site is to include all the files in a single directory. If you have many extra files—images, for example—you can put them in a subdirectory under that main directory. Your goal is to contain all your files in a single place rather than scatter them around. You can then set all the links in those files to be relative to that directory. This makes it easier to move the directory around to different servers without breaking the links.

Having a Default Index File and Correct Filenames

Web servers usually have a default index file that's loaded when a URL ends with a directory name rather than a filename. One of the questions you should ask your webmaster is, "What's the name of this default file?" For most web servers, this file is called `index.html`. Your home page, or top-level index, for each site should have this name so that the server knows which page to send as the default page. Each subdirectory should also have a default file if it contains HTML files. If you use this default filename, the URL to that page will be shorter because you don't have to include the actual filename. For example, your URL might be http://www.example.com/pages/ rather than http://www.examplecom/pages/index.html.

CAUTION

> If you don't put an index file in a directory, many web servers will enable people to browse the contents of the directory. If you don't want people to snoop around in your files, you should include an index file or use the web server's access controls to disable directory browsing. Ask your webmaster for help.

Also, each file should have an appropriate extension indicating its type so that the server can map it to the appropriate file type. If you've been reading this book in sequential order, all your files should have this special extension already and you shouldn't have any problems. Table 23.1 lists the common file extensions that you should be using for your files and multimedia.

TABLE 23.1   Common File Types and Extensions

Format	Extension
HTML	`.html`, `.htm`
ASCII Text	`.txt`
GIF	`.gif`

Format	Extension
JPEG	`.jpg`, `.jpeg`
PNG	`.png`
Scalable Vector Graphics	`.svg`
Shockwave Flash	`.swf`
WAV Audio	`.wav`
MPEG Audio	`.mp3`
MPEG Video	`.mp4`
QuickTime Video	`.mov`
Portable Document Format	`.pdf`

If you're using multimedia files on your site that aren't part of this list, you might need to configure your server to handle that file type. You'll learn more about this issue later in this lesson.

Publishing Your Files

Got everything organized? Then all that's left is to move everything to the server. After your files have been uploaded to a directory that the server exposes on the Web, you're officially published on the Web. That's all there is to putting your pages online.

Where's the appropriate spot on the server, however? You should ask your webmaster for this information. Also, you should find out how to access that directory on the server, whether it's just copying files, using FTP to put them on the server, or using some other method.

Moving Files Between Systems

If you're using a web server that has been set up by someone else, usually you'll have to upload your web files from your system to theirs using FTP, SCP (secure copy), or some other method. Although the HTML markup within your files is completely cross-platform, moving the actual files from one type of system to another sometimes has its drawbacks. In particular, be careful to do the following:

- **Watch out for filename restrictions**—Make sure that your filenames don't have spaces or other funny characters in them. Keep your filenames as short as possible, use only letters, dashes (-), underscores (_), and numbers, and you'll be fine. You can use periods (.) in your filenames, but that can confuse readers who type them in, so I recommend avoiding them.

- **Watch out for uppercase or lowercase sensitivity**—Filenames on computers running Microsoft Windows are not case sensitive. On UNIX and Mac OS X systems, they are. If you develop your pages on a computer running Windows and publish them on a server that has case-sensitive filenames, make sure that you have entered the URLs in your links properly. If you're linking to a file named `About.html`, on your computer running Windows, `about.html` would work, but on a UNIX server it would not. It's best to get in the habit of using all lowercase letters for file and directory names on your web pages.

- **Be aware of carriage returns and line feeds**—Different systems use different methods for ending a line. The Macintosh uses carriage returns, UNIX and Linux use line feeds, and DOS and Windows use both. When you move files from one system to another, most of the time the end-of-line characters will be converted appropriately, but sometimes they won't. The characters that aren't converted can cause your file to come out double spaced or all on a single line when it's moved to another system.

  Most of the time, this failure to convert doesn't matter because browsers ignore spurious returns or line feeds in your HTML files. The existence or absence of either one isn't terribly important. However, it might be an issue in sections of text that you've marked up with `<pre>`; you might find that your well-formatted text that worked so well on one platform doesn't come out that way after it's been moved.

  If you do have end-of-line problems, you have two options. Many text editors enable you to save ASCII files in a format for another platform. If you know the platform to which you're moving, you can prepare your files for that platform before moving them. If you don't know, save your file to a UNIX or Linux format.

Uploading Your Files

In the preceding list of tips about moving files, I mentioned FTP. FTP, short for *File Transfer Protocol*, is one of the ways to move files from your local computer to the server where they will be published, or to download them so that you can work on them, for that matter. Some other protocols that can be used to transfer files include SFTP (*Secure FTP*) and SCP (*Secure Copy*). They all work a bit differently; the most important difference is that SCP and SFTP are encrypted, whereas FTP is not.

TIP

If your server provides multiple methods for uploading files, you should choose SCP or SFTP rather than FTP. With FTP, your password for the server will be transmitted unencrypted over the Internet. That's a security risk. It's preferable to use the encrypted uploading options. And many hosting providers are switching to only secure transfer methods.

A number of clients support FTP, SCP, and SFTP through the same interface. As long as you have the name of the server, your username, your password, and the name of the directory where you want to put your files, you can use any of these clients to upload your web content.

One option that's often available is publishing files through your HTML editing tool. Many popular HTML and text editors have built-in support for FTP, SCP, and SFTP. You should definitely check your tool of choice to see whether it enables you to transfer files using FTP from directly within the application. Some popular tools that provide FTP support include Adobe Dreamweaver, Panic Coda, and HTML-Kit. Text editors such as UltraEdit, Textmate, and jEdit support saving files to a server via FTP, too. If your HTML editor doesn't support FTP, or if you're transferring images, multimedia files, or even bunches of HTML files simultaneously, you'll probably want a dedicated FTP client. A list of some popular choices follows:

23

- **CuteFTP (Windows, OS X)**—http://www.cuteftp.com/
- **FTP Explorer (Windows)**—http://www.ftpx.com/
- **FileZilla (Windows, OS X, Linux)**—https://filezilla-project.org/
- **Cyberduck (Windows, OS X)**—https://cyberduck.io/
- **Transmit (OS X)**—https://www.panic.com/transmit/
- **Fetch (OS X)**—http://fetchsoftworks.com/

All the tools listed support FTP, SFTP, and SCP, and some support other transfer options like WebDAV and Dropbox. How the FTP client is used varies depending on which client you choose, but there are some commonalities among all of them that you can count on (more or less). You'll start out by configuring a site consisting of the hostname of the server where you'll publish the files, your username and password, and perhaps some other settings that you can leave alone if you're just getting started.

CAUTION

If you're sharing a computer with other people, you probably won't want to store the password for your account on the server in the FTP client. Make sure that the site is configured so that you have to enter your password every time you connect to the remote site.

After you've set up your FTP client to connect to your server, you can connect to the site. Depending on your FTP client, you should be able to simply drag files onto the window that shows the list of files on your site to upload them or drag them from the listing on the server to your local computer to download them.

Troubleshooting

What happens if you upload all your files to the server and try to display your home page in your browser and something goes wrong? Here's the first place to look.

I Can't Access the Server

If your browser can't even get to your server, this probably isn't a problem you can fix. Make sure that you have entered the right server name and that it's a complete hostname (usually ending in .com, .edu, .net, or some other common suffix). Make sure that you haven't mistyped your URL and that you're using the right protocol. If your webmaster told you that your URL included a port number, make sure that you're including that port number in the URL after the hostname.

Also make sure that your network connection is working. Can you get to other URLs? Can you get to the top-level home page for the site itself?

If none of these ideas solve the problem, perhaps your server is down or not responding. Call your webmaster to find out whether she can help.

I Can't Access Files

What if all your files are showing up as Not Found or Forbidden? First, check your URL. If you're using a URL with a directory name at the end, try using an actual filename at the end—like index.html. Double-check the path to your files; remember that the path in the URL might be different from the path on the actual disk. Also, keep case sensitivity in mind. If your file is MyFile.html, make sure that you're not trying myfile.html or Myfile.html.

If the URL appears to be correct, check the file permissions. On UNIX systems, all your directories should be world-executable, and all your files should be world-readable. You can ensure that all the permissions are correct by using the following commands:

```
chmod w+r filename
chmod 755 directoryname
```

> **TIP**
>
> Most FTP clients will allow you to modify file and directory permissions remotely.

I Can't Access Images

You can get to your HTML files just fine, but all your images are coming up as icons or broken icons. First, make sure that the references to your images are correct. If you've used relative pathnames, you shouldn't have this problem. If you've used full pathnames or file URLs, the references to your images may have been broken when you moved the files to the server. (I warned you.)

In some browsers, you get a pop-up menu when you select an image with the right mouse button. (Hold down the Option key while you click on a Macintosh mouse.) Choose the View This Image menu item to try to load the image directly. This will give you the URL of the image where the browser thinks it's supposed to be (which might not be where *you* think it's supposed to be). You can often track down strange relative pathname problems this way.

23

Inspecting the image with the Google Chrome developer tools is another way to find the problem. Open web developer tools on the page, and scroll down to the broken image. You will then see the URL the site is using and even change it temporarily to see if you can fix the problem.

If you're using Internet Explorer for Windows, you can also select the Properties option from the menu that appears when you right-click an image to see its address. You can check the address that appears in the Properties dialog box to see whether it points to the appropriate location.

If all the references look good and the images work just fine on your local system, the only other place a problem could have occurred is in transferring the files from one system to another. Try reuploading the image. And if that doesn't work, delete the image from your web hosting service first, waiting a few minutes, and then reuploading. By waiting a few minutes, you give the web server a chance to update the cache and possibly fix the problem. If none of these things work, you'll need to talk to your webmaster or web hosting support.

My Links Don't Work

If your HTML and image files are working just fine but your links don't work, you most likely used pathnames for those links that applied only to your local system. For example, you might have used absolute pathnames or file URLs to refer to the files to which you're linking. As mentioned for images, if you used relative pathnames and avoided file URLs, you shouldn't have a problem. The most common mistake new designers make is in using file system paths in their links. If you see a link that starts out `file://` or has `D:///` (or any other drive name), those links aren't going to work when your page is on the web host. These will work fine while they are on your local computer, which is how they creep into the process. Go back and switch them to relative paths and reupload the page.

My Files Are Being Displayed Incorrectly

Suppose you have an HTML file or a file in some multimedia format that's displayed correctly or links just fine on your local system. After you upload the file to the server and try to view it, the browser gives you gobbledygook. For example, it displays the HTML code itself instead of the HTML file, or it displays an image or multimedia file as text.

This problem can happen in two cases. The first is that you're not using the right file extensions for your files. Make sure that you're using one of the correct file extensions with the correct uppercase and lowercase.

The second case is that your server is not properly configured to handle your files. If all your HTML files have extensions of .htm, for example, your server might not understand that .htm is an HTML file. (Most modern servers do, but some older ones don't.) Or you might be using a newer form of media that your server doesn't understand. In either case, your server might be using some default content type for your files (usually text/plain), which your browser probably can't handle. This can happen with server-side scripts, too. If you put up .php files on a server that doesn't support PHP, the server will often send the scripts to the browser as plain text.

To fix this problem, you'll have to configure your server to handle the file extensions for the correct media. If you're working with someone else's server, you'll have to contact your webmaster and have him set up the server correctly. Your webmaster will need two types of information: the file extensions you're using and the content type you want him to return. If you don't know the content type you want, refer to the Wikipedia article on MIME at https://en.wikipedia.org/wiki/MIME.

Promoting Your Web Pages

To get people to visit your website, you need to promote it. The more visible your site, the more pageviews it will attract.

A *pageview* is a visit to your website. Be aware that although your site may get, say, 50 pageviews in a day, that doesn't necessarily mean that it was visited by 50 different people. It's just a record of the number of times a copy of your web page has been downloaded.

You can promote your site in many ways. You can make sure that it's in search engine indexes, promote your site via social media, put the URL on your business cards, and so much more. The following sections describe each approach.

Getting Links from Other Sites

It doesn't take much surfing to figure out that the Web is huge. It seems like there's a site on every topic, and when it comes to popular topics, there may be hundreds or thousands of sites. After you've done the hard work of creating an interesting site, the next step is to get other people to link to it.

The direct approach is popular but often yields the wrong results. It can be tempting to simply find other sites like your own and send a personal email to the people who run them, introducing yourself and telling them that you have a site similar to theirs that they may be interested in. If they are interested, it's possible that they'll provide a link to your site. More often than not, though, they won't see your email, or if they do see it, they will think you're a spammer and go out of their way to avoid your website.

23

It's much better to get links from sites that you've already shown your value to. In other words, you have already visited their site numerous times and participated, giving back to their community. Once the website owner recognizes you, she will be much more ame-nable to linking to your site. And the way you get her to know you is by participating on her site. You can participate by answering or asking questions in comments, providing feedback (when requested), joining forums, and making yourself known. Most website comment forms have a field for URL, which you can use to put your URL on their pages. It won't get you search engine results, but it still will be seen by the site owner and might be clicked on by other participants on the site.

When you're sure that the site owner will recognize you, then sending a direct email mes-sage asking for a link is a good idea. But remember that the biggest sites often get hun-dreds or thousands of link requests a day. So even if they know you, don't be surprised if they ignore your request.

Content Marketing Through Guest Posting

The thing about asking for links is you are asking the website owner to give you some-thing while he gains little or nothing. In fact, if search engines decide that your site is a spam site or link farm, they could ultimately hurt their own authority by linking to you. A better way to get links to your site on other sites is to start doing guest posting.

Guest posting occurs when you write an article on your topic of interest, but instead of posting it on your own website, you post it on another website—for free. You see guest posts on sites all over the Internet on topics ranging from auto repair to zoology. If there is a topic, there is probably a website related to it, and most sites are willing to post guest posts if you ask them to.

If you are going to use guest posting to help promote your website, you need to remember a few things:

- Make sure that they will post your name and URL along with the guest post in either a byline or a biography section.

- Write the best article you can write. Save your best article ideas for your guest posts, as those are the ones you want to use as advertising for your website.

- Find out what their policy is on shared posting. Some sites don't want posts that are duplicated, even if you only posted it to your own site first. Other sites have laxer policies.

- Make sure that you retain your rights regarding the work. Just because an article is posted on the Web doesn't mean that copyright doesn't apply.

To start guest posting, you need to come up with a list of sites that you want to post to. Be sure to list the most popular sites in your topic area as well as some that are less popular. Don't assume either that you are too unknown to write for the "big boys" or that you won't get enough traffic from the smaller sites. Large sites, especially content-driven sites, are often looking for new sources of content. And smaller sites can provide you with a wider audience, especially when you're just getting started.

DO	DON'T
DO use guest posts as a way to get your name and site URL out to the world.	**DON'T** get discouraged if a site turns down your guest post idea.
DO follow all writing guidelines you receive.	**DON'T** spam websites asking to be a guest author.

Promoting Your Site Through Social Media

First, what is social media? Most people define social media as websites that enable their users to socialize with one another. Sites such as Twitter and Facebook are popular examples. Weblogs like Tumblr and WordPress.com can be considered social media, too. There are also link sharing sites like Digg and Reddit, where users can submit links, vote for them, or comment on them. Links that get more votes are featured more prominently on the site. Social media is about people connecting to one another, and promoting a site through social media is as simple as talking about your site on those sites. The tricky part is doing so in a way that makes you a valuable participant in the conversation rather than a tedious self-promoter.

Many people talk about "viral" marketing. The concept is simple: Instead of purchasing an advertisement that may be displayed for hundreds or thousands of people, you tell just a few interested people about your site (or essay, or product, or movie, or whatever it is that you've created), and then they in turn share it with people they think will be interested, and so on, until it has reached a large audience. The advantage, assuming that it works, is that it's inexpensive, and your message has been delivered by people who the audience is actually willing to listen to—people they already know. The difficulty is in creating something that is interesting to large audiences in the first place and in telling the right people about it so that they are interested in sharing in what you've created. Taking advantage of social media is one way to accomplish the second part of the task.

Regardless of the outlet, the two steps are to establish a presence and to be interesting. Twitter (https://twitter.com) is one of the most popular social media sites these days. After you've signed up for an account, you can follow other people on Twitter, and people who find you interesting will follow you. A lot of people on the Web give advice on how to attract large numbers of followers, and a lot of people on Twitter follow thousands of people in hopes that people will follow them in return.

Focusing on follower counts is the wrong approach. Remember, the goal with social media is to establish an audience of people who actually care about what you're doing. Let's say you've created a new website for knitting enthusiasts, and in hopes of promoting the site, you've created a Twitter account to go along with it.

NOTE

Creating a Twitter account is easy and free. To create a Twitter account, you need only supply an account name, a full name, an email address, and a password of your choosing. The account name and full name can be anything you like. After you've followed those steps, you're all set.

For starters, you should create posts on Twitter with links back to your site whenever you publish something new. You should also follow people who say interesting things, preferably on the subject of knitting. If they say something you find particularly interesting, you should retweet it; this means you repeat it, mentioning their Twitter handle, to your followers. You should respond to people when you have something interesting to say, too. If you do so, eventually they may follow you in return. If things go well, eventually you'll have a great outlet for promoting your site, and even if they go poorly, you'll be participating in a community of people who like to talk about the subject of your site—knitting. That's social media in a nutshell.

Creating a Facebook Page for Your Site

There's an additional way to promote your site on the popular social networking site Facebook. You can create a page that represents your site to the Facebook community. To do so, you need a Facebook account. After you've signed up, go to https://www.facebook.com/pages/create/. You will be asked what type of page you want to create, as shown in Figure 23.1.

FIGURE 23.1
The Facebook Create a Page start page.

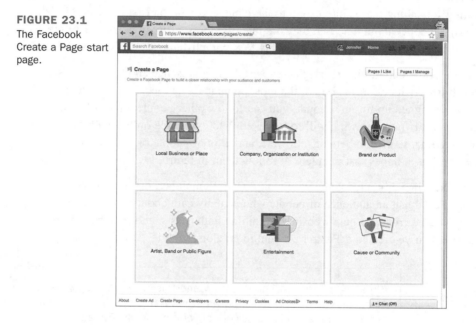

I chose Brand or Product and then Website to create a new page for this book. Then I was given a chance to add a description of the page, include a profile picture, give it a Facebook URL, and even specify the audience I wanted to target. The Facebook Page setup screen is shown in Figure 23.2.

After the page has been created, I can customize it in a variety of ways, controlling who's allowed to post on it and what kinds of content they're allowed to post. The Facebook page gives Facebook users who are interested in this book a place to congregate to discuss it, share links related to the book, and meet one another.

FIGURE 23.2
The Facebook Page
setup screen.

Site Indexes and Search Engines

Nearly all web users know how to find things using search engines, and you'll want to make sure that they can find your site. Search engines work by creating an index of all the sites they can find. You need to be sure to add your site to the index when you publish it so that search engines will start including it in search results. As long as people link to your site, search engines will find it eventually whether you tell them about it or not, but asking them to index your site will ensure that it's added immediately. Here's a list of the top four search engines:

Google	https://www.google.com/
Bing	http://www.bing.com/
Yahoo	https://www.yahoo.com/
Ask	http://www.ask.com/

Lesson 25, "Search Engines and SEO," goes into more detail about how and why to submit your sites to some of the popular search engines. There's a set of interlocking relationships among search engine providers that can make it difficult to keep track of who is providing search functionality for whom. The search engines listed previously maintain their own indexes. After your site is included in their index, it will be available via all the search engines that use their index, too. The art of so-called *search engine optimization*, or SEO, is also covered in detail in Lesson 25.

NOTE For more information about search engines, I strongly recommend you read Search Engine Watch at http://www.searchenginewatch.com/.

Business Cards, Letterhead, Brochures, and Advertisements

Although the Internet is a wonderful place to promote your new website, many people fail to consider some other great advertising methods.

Most businesses spend a considerable amount of money each year producing business cards, letterhead, and other promotional material. These days it's rare to see any of these materials without web and email information on them. By printing your email address and home page URL on all your correspondence and promotional material, you can reach an entirely new group of potential visitors.

Even your email signature is a good place to promote your site. Just put in a link and the title and maybe a short description so that everyone you correspond with can see what you're publishing on the Web.

When you're promoting your website, the bottom line is lateral thinking. You need to use every tool at your disposal if you want to have a successful and active site.

Finding Out Who's Viewing Your Web Pages

Now you've got your site up on the Web and ready to be viewed, you've advertised and publicized it to the world, and people are flocking to it in droves. Or are they? How can you tell? You can find out in a number of ways, including using log files and access counters.

Log Files

One way to figure out how often your pages are being seen, and by whom, is to get access to your server's log files. How long these log files are kept depends on how your server is configured. The logs can take up a lot of disk space, so some hosting providers remove old logs pretty frequently. If you run your own server, you can keep them as long as you like, or at least until you run out of room. Many commercial web providers allow you to view your own web logs or get statistics about how many visitors are accessing your pages and from where. Ask your webmaster for help.

If you do get access to these raw log files, you'll most likely see a whole lot of lines that look something like the following. (I've broken this one up into two lines so that it fits on the page.)

```
vide-gate.coventry.ac.uk - - [17/Feb/2015:12:36:51 -0700]
  "GET /index.html HTTP/1.0" 200 8916
```

What does this information mean? The first part of the line is the site that accessed the file. (In this case, it was a site from the United Kingdom.) The two dashes are used for authentication. (If you have login names and passwords set up, the username of the person who logged in and the group that person belonged to will appear here.) The date and time the page was accessed appear inside the brackets. The next part is the actual file-name that was accessed; here it's the `index.html` at the top level of the server. The GET part is the actual HTTP command the browser used; you usually see GET here. Finally, the last two numbers are the HTTP status code and the number of bytes transferred. The status code can be one of many things: 200 means the file was found and transferred correctly; 404 means the file was not found. (Yes, it's the status code you get when pages aren't found in your browser.) Finally, the number of bytes transferred usually will be the same number of bytes in your actual file; if it's a smaller number, the visitor interrupted the load in the middle.

Most web hosts provide log processing software that will take the logs generated by the server when users visit your site and turn them into reports, often with graphs and other visual aids, that you can use to easily see how many users are visiting your site as well as how those servers are finding your site, whether it's through search engines or links on other web pages. You'll want to check out the support site for your web host to determine how to set things up so that your logs are processed and find out the URL of the reports that are generated.

Google Analytics

There are other ways to keep track of who's visiting your site and what pages they're viewing. Processing log files is one way to get an idea of who's visiting your site. Another option is to use Google Analytics, a tool provided for free by Google that keeps track of all the visitors to your site and generates reports about your visitors.

The nice thing about Google Analytics is that you don't have to deal with log files. Google Analytics works by providing you with a code that uniquely identifies your site. On each of the pages that you want to track, you include a reference to a JavaScript file that Google provides and pass in the code for your site. Whenever users visit the pages with a link to the tracking script, Google records information about their visit. Google then uses this information to create the reports for you.

<table>
<tr><td>CAUTION</td><td>This benefit can also be a drawback as Google Analytics will *only* track pages that have the code on them. If you forget to add the code to a page, it won't show up in your reports.</td></tr>
</table>

One particularly nice thing about Google Analytics is that you can usually add it to your site even if the site is on a server you don't control. So if you create a weblog (blog) on a site like Tumblr, you can edit the theme of the site and paste in the Google Analytics code.

Installing Google Analytics

To get started with installation, you'll need to go to the Google Analytics website, http://www.google.com/analytics/, and sign up for an Analytics account. If you don't already have a Google account, you'll need to sign up for one, too.

After you've signed up for your account, you'll need to create a profile for your website. Click the Add New Property link to create the profile, and you'll see the form in Figure 23.3.

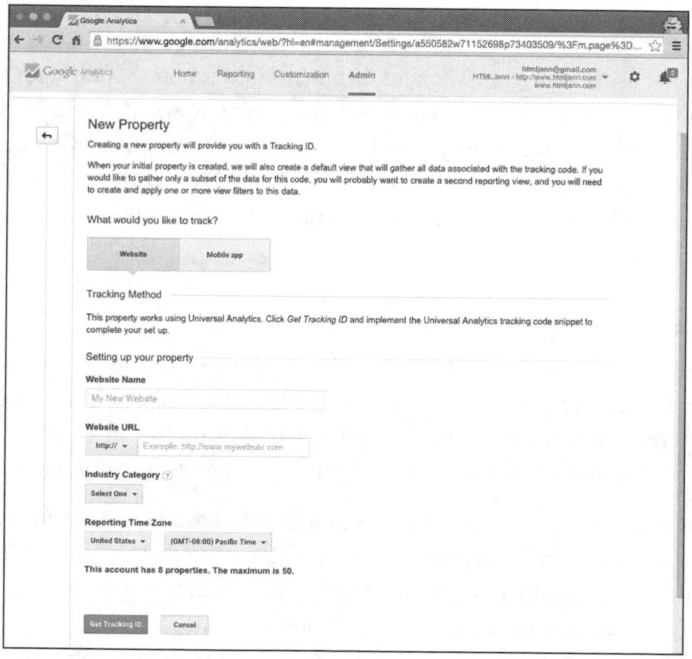

FIGURE 23.3
Setting up a new Google Analytics profile.

To add a profile, you just enter the name and URL of your website in the form provided and choose the industry category and time zone for your site. After you've saved your new profile, Google provides the code to paste into your own web page so that customer visits can be tracked. The code itself is a snippet of JavaScript that loads the Google tracking code. To install the Google tracking code on your site, copy the code that Google provides into your own pages. Google recommends that you paste the tag just before the closing `</body>` tag on your pages. To start out, edit the HTML for your site's home page and paste in the Google Analytics code. Upload the page to your server if necessary, and then visit that page in your browser.

After the page has been loaded with the Google Analytics tracking code in place, Google Analytics will indicate that it has started tracking visits to your site. At that point, add the Google tracking code to your other pages and upload them, too.

Using the Google Analytics Reports

After Google Analytics has been installed, it will start creating reports for your site anywhere from 1 to 24 hours later. To view the main report for your site, just click the Reporting tab. The Dashboard shows some basic statistics about use of your site—how many visits you've gotten each day for the past month, a map showing where most of your visitors come from, and which pages on your site are the most popular. You can see an example of the Dashboard in Figure 23.4.

FIGURE 23.4
The Google Analytics Dashboard.

Other numbers on the page provide insight into how users are interacting with your site. Bounce Rate shows the percentage of users who leave after visiting your landing page instead of sticking around to visit more pages on your site. The average pages per visit and average time on site provide a further idea of the degree to which users are drilling down on your site. In some cases, low numbers here may be fine. If your page is a set of links to other sites, a high bounce rate and low time on the site may indicate that users are finding what they're looking for and following the links. Your interpretation of the statistics should be based on your goals.

Each of the reports on the Dashboard links to a report with more detailed information. For example, if you click the report link for Traffic Sources, you'll see a more detailed breakdown of where your traffic originated, including which search terms people used to find your site.

One report shows which browsers and operating systems your visitors are using, so you can figure out which features your audiences will be able to take advantage of. Other reports show how many of your users visited for the first time and how many were repeat visitors. There are reports that show which sites link to yours. Keeping a close eye on your Analytics reports will enable you to figure out which parts of your site are working and which aren't, whether you use Google Analytics or some other analytics package.

Summary

In this lesson, you published your site on the Web through the use of a web server, either one installed by you or that of a network provider. You learned what a web server does and how to get one, how to organize your files and install them on the server, and how to find your URL and use it to test your pages. You also learned the many ways that you can advertise and promote your site and how to use log files and Google Analytics to keep track of the number of visitors. At last, you're on the Web and people are coming to visit!

Workshop

As always, we wrap up the lesson with a few questions, quizzes, and exercises. Here are some pointers and refreshers on how to promote your website.

Q&A

Q **I've published my pages at an ISP I really like. The URL is something like http://www.thebestisp.com/users/mypages/. Instead of this URL, I'd like to have my own hostname, something like http://www.mypages.com/. How can I do this?**

A You have two choices. The easiest way is to ask your ISP whether you're allowed to have your own domain name. Many ISPs have a method for setting up your domain so that you can still use their services and work with them—it's only your URL that changes. Note that having your own hostname might cost more money, but it's the way to go if you really must have that URL. Many web hosting services have plans starting as low as $5 a month for this type of service, and it currently costs as little as $16 to register your domain for two years.

The other option is to set up your own server with your own domain name. This option could be significantly more expensive than working with an ISP, and it requires at least some background in basic network administration.

Q **There are so many search engines! Do I have to add my URL to all of them?**

A No, mainly because eventually they will find your site whether you add it to them or not. Adding your URL to a search engine may get it into the results more quickly, so if you already know about a search engine and can submit your site, do so. Otherwise, don't worry about it.

23

Quiz

1. What's the basic function of a web server?
2. What are default index files, and what's the advantage of using them in all directories?
3. What are some things that you should check immediately after you upload your web pages?
4. Name some of the ways that you can promote your website.
5. What's a pageview?

Quiz Answers

1. A web server is a program that sits on a machine connected to the Internet (or an intranet). It determines which resource is associated with a URL and delivers that resource to the user. Some people also refer to the machine that runs the server software as a web server.

2. The default index file is loaded when a URL ends with a directory name rather than a filename. Typical examples of default index files are `index.html`, `index.htm`, and `default.htm`. If you use default filenames, you can use a URL such as http://www.mysite.com/ rather than http://www.mysite.com/index.html to get to the home page in the directory.

3. Make sure that your browser can reach your web pages on the server, that you can access the files on your website, and that your links and images work as expected. After you've determined that everything appears the way you think it should, have your friends and family test your pages in other browsers.

4. Some ways you can promote your site include using major web directories and search engines, asking for links, writing guest posts, and adding site links to business cards and other promotional materials.

5. A pageview is a view of a file from your website.

Exercises

1. Start shopping around and consider where you want to host your website. Find a couple of web hosting firms that look like good options and do some research online to see what their existing customers have to say about them.

2. Upload and test a practice page to learn the process, even if it's just a blank page that you'll add content to later. You might work out a few kinks this way before you actually upload all your hard work on the Web.

3. Visit some of the search engines listed in this lesson to obtain a list of the sites where you want to promote your web page. Review each of the choices to see whether there are special requirements for listing your page.

4. Sign up for a Google Analytics account and install it on your site. Explore the reports to see what kind of information it provides about your site.

LESSON 24
Taking Advantage of the Server

At this point, you've learned how to publish websites using *Hypertext Markup Language* (HTML). This lesson takes things a step further and explains how to build dynamic websites using scripts on the server. Most websites utilize some kind of server-side processing. Search engines take the user's request and search an index of web pages on the server. Online stores use server-side processing to look up items in the inventory, keep track of the user's shopping cart, and handle the checkout process. Newspaper websites keep articles in a database and use server-side processing to generate the article pages. This lesson introduces server-side programming using the PHP language. PHP is the most common scripting platform provided by web hosts, can be easily installed on your own computer, and is completely free. It's also easy to get started with. Even if you wind up developing your applications using some other scripting language, you can apply the principles you'll learn in this lesson to those languages.

In this lesson, you'll learn the following:

- How PHP works

- How to set up a PHP development environment

- The basics of the PHP language

- How to process form input

- Using PHP includes

How PHP Works

PHP enables programmers to include PHP code in their HTML documents, which is processed on the server before the HTML is sent to the browser. Normally, when a user submits a request to the server for a web page, the server reads the HTML file and sends its contents back in response. If the request is for a PHP file and the server supports PHP, the server looks for PHP code in the document, executes it, and includes the output of that code in the page in place of the PHP code. Here's a simple example:

```
<!DOCTYPE html>
<html>
<head><title>A PHP Page</title></head>
<body>
<?php echo "Hello world!"; ?>
</body>
</html>
```

If this page is requested from a web server that supports PHP, the HTML sent to the browser will look like this:

```
<!DOCTYPE html>
<html>
<head><title>A PHP Page</title></head>
<body>
Hello world!
</body>
</html>
```

When the user requests the page, the web server determines that it is a PHP page rather than a regular HTML page. If a web server supports PHP, it usually treats any files with the extension .php as PHP pages. Assuming this page is called something like hello.php, when the web server receives the request, it scans the page looking for PHP code and then runs any code it finds. PHP code is distinguished from the rest of a page by PHP tags, which look like this:

```
<?php // your code here ?>
```

Whenever the server finds those tags, it treats whatever is within them as PHP code. That's not so different from the way things work with JavaScript, where anything inside <script> tags is treated as JavaScript code.

In the example, the PHP code contains a call to the echo function. This function prints out the value of whatever is passed to it. In this case, I passed the text "Hello world!" to the function, so that text is included in the page. The concept of functions should also be familiar to you from Lesson 19, "Using JavaScript in Your Pages." Just like JavaScript, PHP lets you define your own functions or use functions built in to the language. echo is a built-in function.

Statements in PHP, as in JavaScript, are terminated with a semicolon. (You can see the semicolon at the end of the statement in the example.) There's no reason why you can't include multiple statements within one PHP tag, like this:

```php
<?php
  echo "Hello ";
  echo "world!";
?>
```

PHP also provides a shortcut if all you want to do is print the value of something to a page. Instead of using the full PHP tag, you can use the expression tag, which just echoes a value to the page. Instead of using

```php
<?php echo "Hello world!"; ?>
```

You can use this:

```php
<?= "Hello world!" ?>
```

24

Replacing `php` with `=` enables you to leave out the call to the `echo` function and the semicolon. This style of tag is referred to as a *short tag*. Not all PHP installations have short tags enabled, so be sure to test these on your server before you release your PHP pages.

Getting PHP to Run on Your Computer

Before you can start writing your own PHP scripts, you need to set up a PHP environment. The easiest approach is probably to sign up for a web hosting account that provides PHP support. Even if you do so, though, there are some advantages to getting PHP to work on your own computer. You can edit files with your favorite editor and then test them right on your own computer rather than uploading them to see how they work. You'll also be able to work on them even if you're not online. Finally, you can keep from putting files on a server that your users will be able to see without your having tested them first.

To process PHP pages, you need the PHP interpreter and a web server that works with the PHP interpreter. The good news is that PHP and the most popular web server, Apache, are both free, open source software. The bad news is that getting PHP up and running can be a bit of a technical challenge.

Fortunately, if you're a Windows or Mac user, someone else has done this hard work for you. A tool called XAMPP, available for both Windows and OS X, bundles up versions of Apache, PHP, and MySQL (a database useful for storing data associated with web applications) that are already set up to work together. (The last P is for Perl, another scripting language.) You can download it from https://www.apachefriends.org/index.html.

If you're a Mac user, you also have the option of using MAMP, another free package that combines Apache, PHP, and MySQL. You can download it from https://www.mamp.info/en/.

> **TIP**
>
> If you like to tinker with your Mac, you have the option of using the version of Apache and PHP that are included with OS X. But this can be challenging. Using a prebuilt system is quicker.

After you've installed XAMPP (or MAMP), you just have to start the application to get a web server up and running that you can use to develop your pages. To test your PHP pages, you can put them in the `htdocs` directory inside the XAMPP install directory. For example, if you want to test the `hello.php` page I talked about earlier, you could put it in the `htdocs` directory. To view it, just go to http://localhost/hello.php.

If that doesn't work, make sure that XAMPP has started the Apache server. If you're using MAMP, the steps are basically the same. Just put your pages in the `htdocs` folder, as with XAMPP.

The PHP Language

When you think about the English language, you think about it in terms of parts of speech. Nouns name things, verbs explain what things do, adjectives describe things, and so on. Programming languages are similar. A programming language is made up of various "parts of speech," too. In this section, I explain the parts of speech that make up the PHP language—comments, variables, conditional statements, and functions.

It might be helpful to think back to Lesson 19 as you read this lesson. PHP and JavaScript share a common ancestry, and many of the basic language features are similar between the two. If things such as the comment format, curly braces, and control statements look similar from one to the other, it's because they are.

Comments

Like HTML and JavaScript, PHP supports comments. PHP provides two comment styles: one for single-line comments, and another for multiple comments. (If you're familiar with comments in the C or Java programming language, you'll notice that PHP's are the same.) First, I'll cover single-line comments. To start a single-line comment, use `//` or `#`. Everything that follows either on a line is treated as a comment. Here are some examples:

```
// My function starts here.
$old_color = 'purple';
```

```
$color = 'red'; // Set the color for text on the page
# $color = 'blue';
$color = $old_color; # Sets the color to the old color.
// $color = 'red';
```

The text that precedes // is processed by PHP, so the second line assigns the $color variable. On the third line, I've turned off the assignment by commenting it out. PHP also supports multiple-line comments, which begin with /* and end with */. If you want to comment out several lines of code, you can do so like this:

```
/*
$color = 'red';
$count = 55; // Set the number of items on a page.
// $count = $count + 1;
*/
```

PHP ignores all the lines inside the comments. Note that you can put the // style comment inside the multiline comment with no ill effects. You cannot, however, nest multiline comments. This is illegal:

```
/*
$color = 'red';
$count = 55; // Set the number of items on a page.
/* $count = $count + 1; */
*/
```

NOTE	The generally accepted style for PHP code is to use // for single-line comments rather than #.

Variables

Variables provide a way for the programmers to assign a name to a piece of data. In PHP, these names are preceded by a dollar sign ($). Therefore, you might store a color in a variable called $color or a date in a variable named $last_published_at. Here's how you assign values to those variables:

```
$color = "red";
$last_published_at = time();
```

The first line assigns the value "red" to $color; the second returns the value returned by the built-in PHP function time() to $last_published_at. That function returns a timestamp represented as the number of seconds since what's called the "UNIX epoch," or the beginning of UNIX time.

One thing you should notice here is that you don't have to indicate what kind of item you'll be storing in a variable when you declare it. You can put a string in it, as I did when I assigned `"red"` to `$color`. You can put a number in it, as I did with `$last_published_at`. I know that the number is a timestamp, but as far as PHP is concerned, it's just a number. What if I want a date that's formatted to be displayed rather than stored in seconds so that it can be used in calculations? I can use the PHP `date()` function. Here's an example:

```
$last_published_at = date("F j, Y, g:i a");
```

This code formats the current date so that it looks something like "June 10, 2010, 8:47 pm." As you can see, I can change what kind of information is stored in a variable without doing anything special. It just works. The only catch is that you have to keep track of what sort of thing you've stored in a variable when you use it. For more information about how PHP deals with variable types, see http://www.php.net/manual/en/language.types.type-juggling.php.

TIP

> If you get a warning about not setting a time zone when you enter the previous `date()` line, you should add a line setting your time zone above it in the script: `date_default_timezone_set('America/Los_Angeles')`. Change the "America/Los Angeles" to your time zone. You can find a list of supported time zones at http://php.net/manual/en/timezones.php.

Despite the fact that variables don't have to be declared as being associated with a particular type, PHP does support various data types, including string, integer, and float (for numbers with decimal points). Not all variable types work in all contexts. One data type that requires additional explanation is the array data type.

Arrays

All the variables you've seen so far in this lesson have been used to store single values. Arrays are data structures that can store multiple values. You can think of them as lists of values, and those values can be strings, numbers, or even other arrays. To declare an array, use the built-in `array` function:

```
$colors = array('red', 'green', 'blue');
```

This declaration creates an array with three elements in it. Each element in an array is numbered, and that number is referred to as the *index*. For historical reasons, array indexes start at 0, so for the preceding array, the index of `red` is 0, the index of `green` is

1, and the index of `blue` is 2. You can reference an element of an array using its index, like this:

```
$color = $colors[1];
```

By the same token, you can assign values to specific elements of an array, too, like this:

```
$colors[2] = 'purple';
```

You can also use this method to grow an array, as follows:

```
$colors[3] = 'orange';
```

What happens if you skip a few elements when you assign an item to an array, as in the following line?

```
$colors[8] = 'white';
```

In this case, not only will element 8 be created, but elements 4 through 7 will be created, too. If you want to add an element onto the end of an array, you just leave out the index when you make the assignment, like this:

```
$colors[] = 'yellow';
```

In addition to arrays with numeric indexes, PHP supports associative arrays, which have indexes supplied by the programmer. These are sometimes referred to as *dictionaries* or as *hashes*. Here's an example that shows how they are declared:

```
$state_capitals = array(
  'Texas' => 'Austin',
  'Louisiana' => 'Baton Rouge',
  'North Carolina' => 'Raleigh',
  'South Dakota' => 'Pierre'
);
```

When you reference an associative array, you do so using the keys you supplied, as follows:

```
$capital_of_texas = $state_capitals['Texas'];
```

To add a new element to an associative array, you just supply the new key and value, like this:

```
$state_capitals['Pennsylvania'] = 'Harrisburg';
```

If you need to remove an element from an array, just use the built-in `unset()` function, like this:

```
unset($colors[1]);
```

24

The element with the index specified will be removed, and the array will decrease in size by one element. The indexes of the elements with larger indexes than the one that was removed will be reduced by one. You can also use `unset()` to remove elements from associative arrays, like this:

```
unset($state_capitals['Texas']);
```

Array indexes can be specified using variables. You just put the variable reference inside the square brackets, like this:

```
$i = 1;
$var = $my_array[$i];
```

This also works with associative arrays:

```
$str = 'dog';
$my_pet = $pets[$str];
```

As you'll see a bit further on, the ability to specify array indexes using variables is a staple of some kinds of loops in PHP.

As you've seen, nothing distinguishes between a variable that's an array and a variable that holds a string or a number. PHP has a built-in function named `is_array()` that returns `true` if its argument is an array and `false` if the argument is anything else. Here's an example:

```
is_array(array(1, 2, 3));  // returns true
is_array('tree'); // returns false
```

NOTE   When PHP returns a `true` value, it returns the number 1. PHP doesn't return a value when it returns `false`.

To determine whether a particular index is used in an array, you can use PHP's `array_key_exists()` function. This function is often used to do a bit of checking before referring to a particular index, for example:

```
if (array_key_exists("Michigan", $state_capitals) ) {
    echo $state_capitals["Michigan"];
}
```

As mentioned previously, it's perfectly acceptable to use arrays as the values in an array. Therefore, the following is a valid array declaration:

```
$stuff = ('colors' => array('red', 'green', 'blue'),
          'numbers' => array('one', 'two', 'three'));
```

In this case, I have an associative array that has two elements. The values for each of the elements are arrays themselves. I can access this data structure by stacking the references to the array indexes, like this:

```
$colors = $stuff['colors']; // Returns the list of colors.
$color = $stuff['colors'][1]; // Returns 'green'
$number = $stuff['numbers'][0]; // Returns 'one'
```

Strings

The most common data type you'll work with in PHP is the string type. A string is just a series of characters. An entire web page is a string, as is a single letter. To define a string, just place the characters in the string within quotation marks. Here are some examples of strings:

```
"one"
"1"
"I like publishing Web pages."
"This string
spans multiple lines."
```

Take a look at the last string in the list. The opening quotation mark is on the first line, and the closing quotation mark is on the second line. In PHP, this is completely valid. In some programming languages, strings that span multiple lines are illegal—not so in PHP, where strings can span as many lines as you like, so long as you don't accidentally close the quotation marks.

There's more to strings than just defining them. You can use the . operator to join strings, like this:

```
$html_paragraph = "<p>" . $paragraph . "</p>";
```

The $html_paragraph variable will contain the contents of $paragraph surrounded by the opening and closing paragraph tag. The . operator is generally referred to as the *string concatenation operator*.

Up to this point, you might have noticed that sometimes I've enclosed strings in double quotation marks, and that other times I've used single quotation marks. They both work for defining strings, but there's a difference between the two. When you use double quotation marks, PHP scans the contents of the string for variable substitutions and for special characters. When you use single quotation marks, PHP just uses whatever is in the string without checking to see whether it needs to process the contents.

Special characters are introduced with a backslash, and they are a substitute for characters that might otherwise be hard to include in a string. For example, \n is the substitute for a newline, and \r is the substitute for a carriage return. If you want to include a newline in a string and keep it all on one line, just write it like this:

```
$multiline_string = "Line one\nLine two";
```

Here's what I mean by variable substitutions. In a double-quoted string, I can include a reference to a variable inside the string, and PHP will replace it with the contents of the variable when the string is printed, assigned to another variable, or otherwise used. In other words, I could have written the preceding string-joining example as follows:

```
$html_paragraph = "<p>$paragraph</p>";
```

PHP will find the reference to $paragraph within the string and substitute its contents. On the other hand, the literal value "$paragraph" would be included in the string if I wrote that line like this:

```
$html_paragraph = '<p>$paragraph</p>';
```

You need to do a bit of extra work to include array values in a string. For example, this won't work:

```
$html_paragraph = "<p>$paragraph['intro']</p>";
```

You can include the array value using string concatenation:

```
$html_paragraph = "<p>" . $paragraph['intro'] . "</p>";
```

You can also use array references within strings if you enclose them within curly braces, like this:

```
$html_paragraph = "<p>{$paragraph['intro']}</p>";
```

One final note on defining strings is escaping. As you know, quotation marks are commonly used in HTML as well as in PHP, especially when it comes to defining attributes in tags. There are two ways to use quotation marks within strings in PHP. The first is to use the opposite quotation marks to define the string that you're using within another string. Here's an example:

```
$tag = '<p class="important">';
```

I can use the double quotes within the string because I defined it using single quotes. This particular definition won't work, though, if I want to specify the class using a variable. If that's the case, I have two other options:

```
$tag = "<p class=\"$class\">";
$tag = '<p class="' . $class . '">';
```

In the first option, I use the backslash character to "escape" the double quotes that occur within the string. The backslash indicates that the character that follows is part of the string and does not terminate it. The other option is to use single quotes and employ the string concatenation operator to include the value of `$class` in the string.

Conditional Statements

Conditional statements and loops are the bones of any programming language. PHP is no different. The basic conditional statement in PHP is the `if` statement. Here's how it works:

```php
if ($var == 0) {
  echo "Variable set to 0.";
}
```

The code inside the brackets will be executed if the expression in the `if` statement is true. In this case, if `$var` is set to anything other than 0, the code inside the brackets will not be executed. PHP also supports `else` blocks, which are executed if the expression in the `if` statement is false. They look like this:

```php
if ($var == 0) {
  echo "Variable set to 0.";
} else {
  echo "Variable set to something other than 0.";
}
```

24

When you add an `else` block to a conditional statement, it means that the statement will always do something. If the expression is true, it will run the code in the `if` portion of the statement. If the expression is not true, it will run the code in the `else` portion. Finally, there's `elseif`:

```php
if ($var == 0) {
  echo "Variable set to 0.";
} elseif ($var == 1) {
  echo "Variable set to 1.";
} elseif ($var == 2) {
  echo "Variable set to 2.";
} else {
  echo "Variable set to something other than 0, 1, or 2.";
}
```

As you can see, `elseif` allows you to add more conditions to an `if` statement. In this case, I added two `elseif` conditions. There's no limit on `elseif` conditions—you can use as many as you need. Ultimately, `elseif` and `else` are both conveniences that enable you to write less code to handle conditional tasks.

PHP Conditional Operators

It's hard to write conditional statements if you don't know how to write a Boolean expression. First of all, Boolean means that an expression (which you can think of as a statement of fact) is either true or false. Here are some examples:

```
1 == 2 // false
'cat' == 'dog' // false
5.5 == 5.5 // true
5 > 0 // true
5 >= 5 // true
5 < 10 // true
```

PHP also supports logical operators, such as "not" (which is represented by an exclamation point), "and" (&&), and "or" (||). You can use them to create expressions that are made up of multiple individual expressions, like these:

```
1 == 1 && 2 == 4 // false
'blue' == 'green' || 'blue' == 'red' // false
!(1 == 2) // true, because the ! implies "not"
!(1 == 1 || 1 == 2) // false, because ! negates the expression inside the ()
```

Furthermore, individual values also evaluate to true or false on their own. Any variable set to anything other than 0 or an empty string ("" or '') will evaluate as true, including an array with no elements in it. So if $var is set to 1, the following condition will evaluate as true:

```
if ($var) {
  echo "True.";
}
```

If you want to test whether an array is empty, use the built-in function empty(). So if $var is an empty array, empty($var) will return true. Here's an example:

```
if (empty($var)) {
  echo "The array is empty.";
}
```

You can find a full list of PHP operators at http://www.php.net/manual/en/language.operators.php.

Loops

PHP supports several types of loops, some of which are more commonly used than others. As you know from the JavaScript lesson, loops execute code repeatedly until a condition of some kind is satisfied. PHP supports several types of loops: `do...while`, `while`, `for`, and `foreach`. I discuss them in reverse order.

foreach Loops

The `foreach` loop was created for one purpose—to enable you to process all the elements in an array quickly and easily. The body of the loop is executed once for each item in an array, which is made available to the body of the loop as a variable specified in the loop statement. Here's how it works:

```
$colors = array('red', 'green', 'blue');
foreach ($colors as $color) {
  echo $color . "\n";
}
```

This loop prints each of the elements in the `$colors` array with a linefeed after each color.

24

> **NOTE**
>
> Don't forget that web pages display the line feed as a single space. If you want them to appear on a new line, you must include a `br` tag (for example, `echo $color . "<br>\n";`).

The important part of the example is the `foreach` statement. It specifies that the array to iterate over is `$colors` and that each element should be copied to the variable `$color` so that it can be accessed in the body of the loop.

The `foreach` loop can also process both the keys and the values in an associative array if you use slightly different syntax. Here's an example:

```
$synonyms = array('large' => 'big',
                  'loud' => 'noisy',
                  'fast' => 'rapid');

foreach ($synonyms as $key => $value) {
    echo "$key is a synonym for $value.\n";
}
```

As you can see, the `foreach` loop reuses the same syntax that creates associative arrays.

`for` **Loops**

Use `for` loops when you want to run a loop a specific number of times. The loop statement has three parts: a variable assignment for the loop's counter, an expression (containing the index variable) that specifies when the loop should stop running, and an expression that increments the loop counter. Here's a typical `for` loop:

```
for ($i = 1; $i <= 10; $i++)
{
  echo "Loop executed $i times.\n";
}
```

`$i` is the counter (or index variable) for the loop. The loop is executed until `$i` is larger than 10 (meaning that it will run 10 times). The last expression, `$i++`, adds one to `$i` every time the loop executes. The `for` loop can be used instead of `foreach` to process an array. You just have to reference the array in the loop statement, like this:

```
$colors = array('red', 'green', 'blue');
for ($i = 0; $i < count($colors); $i++) {
  echo "Currently processing " . $colors[$i] . ".\n";
}
```

There are a couple of differences between this loop and the previous one. In this case, I start the index variable at 0 and use `<` rather than `<=` as the termination condition for the loop. That's because `count()` returns the size of the `$colors` array, which is 3, and loop indexes start with 0 rather than 1. If I start at 0 and terminate the loop when `$i` is equal to the size of the `$colors` array, it runs three times, with `$i` being assigned the values 0, 1, and 2, corresponding to the indexes of the array being processed.

`while` **and** `do...while` **Loops**

Both `for` and `foreach` are generally used when you want a loop to iterate a specific number of times. The `while` and `do...while` loops, on the other hand, are designed to be run an arbitrary number of times. Both loop statements use a single condition to determine whether the loop should continue running. Here's an example with `while`:

```
$number = 1;
while ($number != 5) {
  $number = rand(1, 10);
  echo "Your number is $number.\n";
}
```

This loop runs until `$number` is equal to 5. Every time the loop runs, `$number` is assigned a random value between 1 and 10. When the random number generator returns a 5, the `while` loop will stop running. A `do...while` loop is basically the same, except the condition appears at the bottom of the loop. Here's what it looks like:

```
$number = 1;
do {
  echo "Your number is $number.\n";
  $number = rand(1, 10);
} while ($number != 5);
```

Generally speaking, the only time it makes sense to use `do ... while` is when you want to be sure the body of the loop will execute at least once.

Controlling Loop Execution

Sometimes you want to alter the execution of a loop. Sometimes you need to stop running the loop immediately, and other times you might want to just skip ahead to the next iteration of the loop. Fortunately, PHP offers statements that do both. The `break` statement is used to immediately stop executing a loop and move on to the code that follows it. The `continue` statement stops the current iteration of the loop and goes straight to the loop condition.

Here's an example of how `break` is used:

```
$colors = array('red', 'green', 'blue');
$looking_for = 'red';
foreach ($colors as $color) {
  if ($color = $looking_for) {
    echo "Found $color.\n";
    break;
  }
}
```

In this example, I'm searching for a particular color. When the `foreach` loop gets to the array element that matches the color I'm looking for, I print the color out and use the `break` statement to stop the loop. When I've found the element I'm looking for, there's no reason to continue.

I could accomplish the same thing a different way using `continue`, like this:

```
$colors = array('red', 'green', 'blue');
$looking_for = 'red';
foreach ($colors as $color) {
  if ($color != $looking_for) {
    continue;
  }

  echo "Found $color.\n";
}
```

24

In this case, if the color is not the one I'm looking for, the `continue` statement stops executing the body of the loop and goes back to the loop condition. If the color is the one I'm looking for, the `continue` statement is not executed and the `echo` function goes ahead and prints the color name I'm looking for.

The loops I'm using as examples don't have a whole lot of work to do. Adding in the `break` and `continue` statements doesn't make my programs much more efficient. Suppose, however, that each iteration of my loop searches a very large file or fetches some data from a remote server. If I can save some of that work using `break` and `continue`, it could make my script much faster.

Built-In Functions

PHP supports literally hundreds of built-in functions. You've already seen a few, such as `echo()` and `count()`. There are many, many more. PHP has functions for formatting strings, searching strings, connecting to many types of databases, reading and writing files, dealing with dates and times, and just about everything in between.

You learned that most of the functionality in the JavaScript language is built using the methods of a few standard objects such as `window` and `document`. PHP is different—rather than its built-in functions being organized via association with objects, they are all just part of the language's vocabulary.

If you ever get the feeling that there might be a built-in function to take care of some task, check the PHP manual to see whether such a function already exists. Chances are it does. Definitely check whether your function will manipulate strings or arrays. PHP has a huge library of array- and string-manipulation functions that take care of most common tasks.

User-Defined Functions

PHP enables you to create user-defined functions that, like JavaScript functions, enable you to package up code you want to reuse. Here's how a function is declared:

```
function myFunction($arg = 0) {
  // Do stuff
}
```

The `function` keyword indicates that you're creating a user-defined function. The name of the function follows. In this case, it's `myFunction`. The rules for function names and variable names are the same—numbers, letters, and underscores are valid. The list of arguments that the function accepts follows the function name, in parentheses.

The preceding function has one argument, $arg. In this example, I've set a default value for the argument. The variable $arg would be set to 0 if the function were called like this:

```
myFunction();
```

However, $arg would be set to 55 if the function were called like this:

```
myFunction(55);
```

Functions can just as easily accept multiple arguments:

```
function myOtherFunction($arg1, $arg2, $arg3)
{
  // Do stuff
}
```

As you can see, myOtherFunction accepts three arguments, one of which is an array. Valid calls to this function include the following:

```
myOtherFunction('one', 'two', array('three'));
myOtherFunction('one', 'two');
myOtherFunction(0, 0, @stuff);
myOtherFunction(1, 'blue');
```

24

One thing you can't do is leave out arguments in the middle of a list. So if you have a function that accepts three arguments, there's no way to set just the first and third arguments and leave out the second, or set the second and third and leave out the first. If you pass one argument in, it will be assigned to the function's first argument. If you pass in two arguments, they will be assigned to the first and second arguments to the function.

Returning Values

Optionally, your function can return a value, or more specifically, a *variable*. Here's a simple example of a function:

```
function add($a = 0, $b = 0) {
  return $a + $b;
}
```

The return keyword is used to indicate that the value of a variable should be returned to the caller of a function. You could call the previous function like this:

```
$sum = add(2, 3); // $sum set to 5
```

A function can just as easily return an array. Here's an example:

```
function makeArray($a, $b) {
  return array($a, $b);
```

```
}

$new_array = makeArray('one', 'two');
```

Your function can also return the result of another function, whether it's built in or one you wrote yourself. Here are a couple of examples:

```
function add($a = 0, $b = 0) {
  return $a + $b;
}

function alsoAdd($a = 0, $b = 0) {
  return add($a, $b);
}
```

Processing Forms

You learned how to create forms back in Lesson 12, "Designing Forms," and although I explained how to design a form, I didn't give you a whole lot of information about what to do with form data once it's submitted. Now I explain how PHP makes data that has been submitted available to your PHP scripts.

When a user submits a form, PHP automatically decodes the variables and copies the values into some built-in variables. Built-in variables are like built-in functions—you can always count on their being defined when you run a script. The three associated with form data are $_GET, $_POST, and $_REQUEST. These variables are all associative arrays, and the names assigned to the form fields on your form are the keys to the arrays.

$_GET contains all the parameters submitted using the GET method (in other words, in the query string portion of the URL). The $_POST method contains all the parameters submitted via POST in the response body. $_REQUEST contains all the form parameters regardless of how they were submitted. Unless you have a specific reason to differentiate between GET and POST, you can use $_REQUEST. Let's look at a simple example of a form:

```
<form action="post.php" method="post">
  Enter your name: <input type="text" id="yourname" /><br />
  <input type="submit" />
</form>
```

When the user submits the form, the value of the yourname field will be available in $_POST and $_REQUEST. You could return it to the user like this:

```
<p>Hello <?= $_REQUEST['yourname'] ?>. Thanks for visiting.</p>
```

Preventing Cross-Site Scripting

You have to be careful when you display data entered by a user on a web page because malicious users can include HTML tags and JavaScript in their input in an attempt to trick other users who might view that information into doing something they might not want to do, such as entering their password to your site and submitting it to another site. This is known as a *cross-site scripting attack*.

To prevent malicious users from doing that sort of thing, PHP includes the `htmlspecialchars()` function, which automatically encodes any special characters in a string so that they are displayed on a page rather than letting the browser treat them as markup. Or, if you prefer, you can use `htmlentities()`, which encodes all the characters that are encoded by `htmlspecialchars()` plus any other characters that can be represented as entities. In the preceding example, you really want to write the script that displays the user's name like this:

```
<p>Hello <?= htmlspecialchars($_POST['yourname']) ?>.
Thanks for visiting.</p>
```

That prevents the person who submitted the data from launching a successful cross-site scripting attack.

If you prefer, you can also use the `strip_tags()` function, which just removes all the HTML tags from a string.

Finally, if your form is submitted using the POST method, you should refer to the parameters using `$_POST` rather than `$_REQUEST`, which also helps to avoid certain types of attacks by ignoring information appended to the URL via the query string.

24

Once you have access to the data the user submitted, you can do whatever you like with it. You can validate it (even if you have JavaScript validation, you should still validate user input on the server as well), store it in a database for later use, or send it to someone via email.

Handling Parameters with Multiple Values

Most form fields are easy to deal with; they're simple name and value pairs. If you have a text field or radio button group, for example, you can access the value submitted using `$_REQUEST`, like this:

```
$radio_value = $_REQUEST['radiofield'];
$text_value = $_REQUEST['textfield'];
```

However, some types of fields submit multiple name and value pairs—specifically check boxes and multiple select lists. If you have a group of five check boxes on a form, that field can actually submit up to five separate parameters, all of which have the same name and different values. PHP handles this by converting the user input into an array rather than a regular variable. Unfortunately, you have to give PHP a hint to let it know that a field should be handled this way. (PHP has no idea what your form looks like; all it knows about is the data that has been submitted.)

If you include [] at the end of the name of a form field, PHP knows that it should expect multiple values for that field and converts the parameters into an array. This occurs even if only one value is submitted for that field. Here's an example:

```
<form action="postmultiplevalues.php" method="post">
  <input type="checkbox" name="colors[]" value="red" /> Red<br />
  <input type="checkbox" name="colors[]" value="green" /> Green<br />
  <input type="checkbox" name="colors[]" value="blue" /> Blue
</form>
```

When the form is submitted, you can access the values as you would for any other parameter, except that the value in the $_REQUEST array for this parameter will be an array rather than a single value. You can access it like this:

```
$colors = $_REQUEST['colors'];
foreach ($colors as $color) {
  echo "$color<br />\n";
}
```

If the user selects only one check box, the value will be placed in an array that has only one element.

▼ Exercise 24.1: Validating a Form

One of the most common tasks when it comes to server-side processing is form validation. When users submit data via a form, it should be validated on the server, even if your page includes JavaScript validation, because you can't guarantee that JavaScript validation was actually applied to the form data.

I use a simplified version of the user registration form from Lesson 12 in this exercise. Figure 24.1 is a screenshot of the form I'll be using. Here's the HTML source:

Input ▼

```
<!DOCTYPE html>
<html>
  <head>
    <title>Registration Form</title>
  </head>
  <body>
    <h1>Registration Form</h1>
```

```
<p>Please fill out the form below to register for our site. Fields
with bold labels are required.</p>

<form method="post">
  <p><label for="name"><b>Name:</b></label><br>
  <input id="name"></p>

  <p><label for="age"><b>Age:</label></b><br>
  <input id="age"></p>

  <p><b>Toys:</b><br>
  <label><input type="checkbox" name="toys[]" value="Digital Camera">
         Digital Camera</label><br>
  <label><input type="checkbox" name="toys[]" value="MP3 Player"> MP3
Player</label><br>
  <label><input type="checkbox" name="toys[]" value="Tablet">Tablet</label></
p>

  <p><input type="submit" value="register" /></p>
</form>
</body>
</html>
```

24

Output ▼

FIGURE 24.1
A simple user registration form.

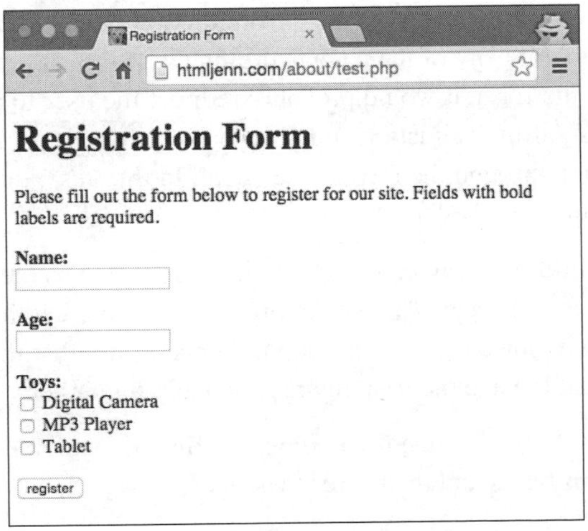

As you can see, the form has three fields: one for the user's name, one for the user's age, and one that enables the user to select some toys he owns. All three of the fields are required. The form submits to itself, using the POST method. I've specified the action for ▼

▼ the form using a built-in PHP variable that returns the URL for the page currently being displayed. That way I can make sure the form is submitted to itself without including the URL for the page in my HTML. Here's the basic structure of the page:

```php
<?php
// Form processing code
?><!doctype html>
<html>
    <head>
        <title>Page Structure</title>
        <style>
            /* Page styles go here. */
        </style>

    </head>
    <body>
        <h1>Sample Page</h1>
        <!-- Print form errors here -->
        <form method="post" action="<?php echo htmlspecialchars($_SERVER["PHP_
SELF"]);?>">
            <!-- Present form fields here -->
        </form>
    </body>
</html>
```

This structure is pretty common for pages that present a form and process that form, too. The PHP processor runs the scripts on the page from top to bottom, so all the form processing will take place before any of the page is presented. If this page were going to do more than just validate the form, it would probably redirect the user to a page thanking him or her for registering if the validation code found no errors. It would also probably save the values submitted through the form somewhere. In this case, though, I'm just explaining form validation.

As you can see, the form-processing code lives on the same page as the form itself, so the form will be submitted to this page. The validation code will live within the script section at the top of the page. My objective for this page is to make sure that the user enters all the required data and that the age the user enters is actually a number.

The first thing I need to do is initialize my PHP and define my variables. I need to set variables for all my form fields and their error messages, as well as the array of toys:

```php
// define variables
$nameErr = $ageErr = $toysErr = $errors =  "";
$name = $age =  "";
$toys = array();
```

Then I wrote the PHP to validate my fields:

```php
if ($_SERVER['REQUEST_METHOD'] == 'POST') {
  if ( empty( $_POST['name'] ) ) {
      $nameErr = 'You must enter your name.';
      $errors = 1;
  } else {
    $name = $_POST['name'];
  }

  $agecheck = (isset($_POST['age']) ? $_POST['age'] : null);
  if ( !is_numeric( $agecheck ) ) {
    $ageErr = "You must enter a valid age.";
      $errors = 1;
  } else {
    $age = $_POST['age'];
  }

  if ( empty( $_POST['toys'] ) ) {
      $toysErr = 'You must choose at least one toy.';
      $errors = 1;
  } else {
    $toys = $_POST['toys'];
  }
}
```

This function validates each of the fields on the form and then places all the errors in
separate error messages named $nameErr, $ageErr, and $toysErr, respectively. When an
error is detected, the error variable is updated with a string. Later on, I display the error
messages and use the field names to mark the fields that have errors.

On the first line, I check to see whether a form has been submitted via POST. Then I start
checking each field one at a time. PHP has a built-in function called empty() that checks
to see whether a variable is empty. In this case, I use it to check $_POST['name'], which
was set automatically when the form was submitted. If that variable is empty, meaning
that the user did not submit her name, I add an entry to $nameErr. If that value is not
empty, I assign the submitted information to the $name variable.

For the age field, I want to make sure that it is not empty and that it's a number. The line
$agecheck = (isset($_POST['age']) ? $_POST['age'] : null); assigns a variable
$agecheck to the submitted value if it is there and to null if it isn't. This uses a short-
hand format for the if/then/else conditional statement. It is written in the following
format:

```
if ? then : else ;
```

First the conditional statement, followed by a question mark, then the value if it's true
followed by a colon, and finally the value if it's false.

▼ I use the `is_numerical()` function to check if the `$agecheck` variable (which was assigned the age submitted or 'null') is a number. If it isn't I set the `$ageErr` error variable, and if it is, I set the `$age` variable to the submitted value.

Finally, I check to make sure that the user has selected a toy. As you saw, this field is actually a check box group, meaning that the contents of the field are submitted as an array (assuming I've named the field properly). Again, I use `empty()` here. It works with regular variables and arrays, and it returns `true` if an array contains no elements. If there are no elements in the array, no toys were submitted, and the error message is added to the `$toysErr` variable.

That is the end of my PHP script. The benefit of doing it this way is that if there are no submitted values, the form is displayed like normal. But if any parameters are submitted via POST, the fields are validated as I just described.

Presenting the Form

Aside from validating form submissions, one of the other important functions of server-side processing is to prepopulate forms with data when they are presented. Many web applications are referred to as *CRUD applications*, where CRUD stands for create/update/delete. It describes the fact that the applications are used to mostly manage records in some kind of database. If a user submits a form with invalid data, when you present the form for the user to correct, you want to include all the data that the user entered so that he doesn't have to type it all in again. By the same token, if you're writing an application that enables a user to update his user profile for a website, you will want to include the information in his current profile in the update form. This section explains how to accomplish these sorts of tasks.

Separating Presentation and Logic

The point here is that it's common to mix PHP and HTML in this way. You create your loop using PHP, but you define the HTML in the page rather than in `echo()` calls inside your PHP code. This is generally considered the best practice for PHP. You should write as much HTML as possible outside your PHP scripts, using PHP only where it's necessary to add bits of logic to the page. Then you can keep the bulk of your PHP code at the top or bottom of your page or in included files to separate the presentation of your data and the business logic implemented in code. That makes your code easier to work on in the future. As an example, rather than sprinkling the validation code throughout my page, I put it in one function so that a programmer can work on it without worrying about the page layout. By the same token, I could have built the unordered list inside the validation function and just returned that, but then my HTML would be mixed in with my PHP. Cleanly separating them is generally the best approach.

▼

If there are errors, I want to load the form and show the errors inline. This is the easiest way to show customers exactly what mistakes they made. Before I do that, let me show you one more thing I've added to the page. I included a style sheet that defines one rule: .error. The error messages for any fields with errors will be assigned to this class so that they can be highlighted when the form is presented. Here's the style sheet:

```
<style>
.error { color: red; }
</style>
```

Okay, now that everything is set up, let's look at how the name field is presented. Here's the code:

```
<p>
<label for="name"><b> labels </b></label>
<br>
<input id="name" value="<?php echo htmlspecialchars($name);?>">
<span class="error"><?php echo $nameErr;?></span>
</p>
```

This code is different from the old code I used to present the name field in the original listing in this example. I included the value as an escaped version of what might have been submitted in the $name variable with `<?php echo htmlspecialchars($name);?>`. I also included a span with the $nameErr error message inside it. If there is no error, then that tag will display nothing. This message will be red, indicating to the user that she needs to fix that field.

The age field is identical to the name field in every way except its variable names, so I skip that and turn instead to the toys field. Here's the code:

```
<p>
<label><b>Toys:</b></label>
<br>
<?php
  $options = array('Digital Camera','MP3 Player','Tablet');
  foreach ($options as $option) {
    echo '<label><input type="checkbox" name="toys[]" ';
    echo 'value="' . $option . '"';
    if ( is_array($toys) && in_array($option, $toys ) ) {
      echo " checked";
    }
    echo ">" . $option . "</label><br>" ;
  }
?>
<span class="error"><?php echo $toysErr; ?></span>
</p>
```

24

▼ As you can see, the code for marking the label for the field as an error is the same for this field as it was for `name`. The more interesting section of the code here is the loop that creates the check boxes.

The values and labels in the `<input>` tags are in an array I called `$options`. I then walked through that array with the `foreach` function, calling each entry `$option`. Inside the loop, I print out the `<input>` tags, using `toys[]` as the parameter name to let PHP know that this field can have multiple values and should be treated as an array. I include the value of the tag as `$option`, and I use it again to print out the label for the check box after the tag. The last bit here is the `if` statement found within the `<input>` tag. Remember that if you want a check box to be prechecked when a form is presented, you have to include the `checked` attribute. I use the `in_array()` function to check whether the option currently being processed is in `$toys`. If it is, I then print out the `checked` attribute using `echo()`. This ensures that all the items the user checked before submitting the form are still checked if validation fails.

A browser displaying a form that contains some errors appears in Figure 24.2. Here's the full source listing for the page:

Input ▼

```php
<?php
// define variables
$nameErr = $ageErr = $toysErr =  "";
$name = $age =  "";
$toys = array();

if ($_SERVER['REQUEST_METHOD'] == 'POST') {
  if ( empty( $_POST['name'] ) ) {
    $nameErr = 'You must enter your name.';
  } else {
    $name = $_POST['name'];
  }

  $agecheck = (isset($_POST['age']) ? $_POST['age'] : null);
  if ( !is_numeric( $agecheck ) ) {
    $ageErr = "You must enter a valid age.";
  } else {
    $age = $_POST['age'];
  }

  if ( empty( $_POST['toys'] ) ) {
    $toysErr = 'You must choose at least one toy.';
  } else {
    $toys = $_POST['toys'];
  }
▼ }
```

```php
?><!DOCTYPE html>
<html>
  <head>
    <title>Registration Form</title>
    <style>
      .error { color: red; }
    </style>
  </head>
  <body>
    <h1>Registration Form</h1>

    <p>Please fill out the form below to register for our site. Fields
    with bold labels are required.</p>

    <form method="post" action="<?php echo htmlspecialchars($_SERVER["PHP_
SELF"]);?>">
    <p>
    <label for="name"><b>Name:</b></label>
    <br>
    <input id="name" value="<?php echo htmlspecialchars($name);?>">
    <span class="error"><?php echo $nameErr;?></span>
    </p>


      <p>
      <label for="age"><b>Age:</label></b><br>
      <input id="age" value="<?php echo htmlspecialchars($age);?>">
      <span class="error"><?php echo $ageErr;?></span>
      </p>

<p>
<label><b>Toys:</b></label>
<br>
<?php
  $options = array('Digital Camera','MP3 Player','Tablet');
  foreach ($options as $option) {
    echo '<label><input type="checkbox" name="toys[]" ';
    echo 'value="' . $option . '"';
    if ( is_array($toys) && in_array($option, $toys ) ) {
      echo " checked";
    }
    echo ">" . $option . "</label><br>" ;
  }
?>
<span class="error"><?php echo $toysErr; ?></span>
</p>

        <p><input type="submit" value="register" /></p>
      </form>
    </body>
</html>
```

24

▼ Output ▼

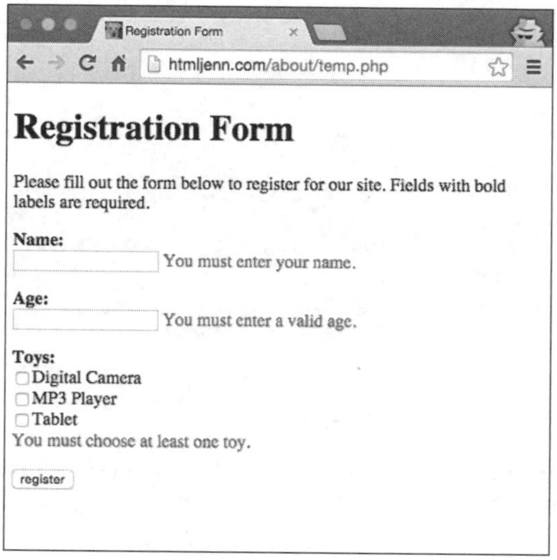

FIGURE 24.2
A form with some
errors that were
caught during vali-
dation.

Using PHP Includes

PHP and all other server-side scripting languages provide the ability to include snippets of code or markup in pages. With PHP, the ability to include files is built in to the language. Because the include statements are part of the language, you don't need to include parentheses around the name of the file to be included. You can conditionally include files, specify which file to include dynamically, or even nest include function calls within included pages. Here's a simple example of an `include` call:

```
include "header.php";
```

On encountering that function call, PHP will try to read in and process a file named `header.php` in the same directory as the current page. If it can't find this file, it will try to find the file in each of the directories in its *include path*, too. The include path is a list of directories (generally specified by the server administrator) where PHP searches for files to include, and it's generally set for the entire server in a configuration file.

Four `include`-related functions are built in to PHP: `require`, `require_once`, `include`, and `include_once`. All these functions include an external file in the page being processed. The difference between `include` and `require` is how PHP reacts when the file being included isn't available. If `include` or `include_once` is used, the PHP page prints a warning and continues on. If `require` or `require_once` is used, an unavailable include file is treated as a fatal error and page processing stops.

If you use `require_once` or `include_once` to include a file that was already included on the page, the function call will be ignored. If you use `require` or `include`, the file will be included no matter what.

PHP includes are like HTML links in that you can use relative or absolute paths in your includes. The difference is that absolute PHP paths start at the root of the file system rather than the web server's document root. So if you want to include a file using an absolute path on a computer running Windows, you write the `include` like this:

```
require_once 'c:\stuff\myfile.php';
```

That's almost never a good idea. You should always use relative paths where possible. In other words, if the included file is in the directory above the one where the including file is located, you should use a path like this:

```
require_once "../myinclude.php";
```

If the file being included is not stored with your other web documents, try to have that directory added to your server's include path rather than using absolute paths to access it.

24

CAUTION	Never pass data entered by a user to an include function; it's a big security risk. For example, this would be inappropriate and very dangerous: `require_once $_POST['file_to_include'];`

PHP includes can be useful even if you don't plan on doing any programming in PHP. You can turn parts of your website that you use frequently into files to be included, saving you from having to edit the same content in multiple places when you're working on your site. Using PHP includes this way can provide the same advantages that putting your CSS and JavaScript into external files does. For example, you might create a file called `header.php` that looks like this:

```
<!DOCTYPE html>
<html>
<head>
    <title><?= $title ?></title>
    <script src="site.js"></script>
    <link rel="stylesheet" href="site.css">
</head>
<body>
```

This file includes all the tags for the start of my page, including links to external JavaScript and CSS files. There's a PHP short tag in the title that prints out the value of the `$title` variable. That enables you to use the header file for all of your pages and to specify individual titles for each of them. To include this file, you use the following code:

```php
<?php
$title = "Welcome!";
include "header.php";
?>
```

Choosing Which Include Function to Use

Given these four very similar functions, how do you choose which makes the most sense to use? The most important factor in making that decision is the content of the file to be included. Generally, there are two types of include files: snippets of markup that will be presented on your page, and PHP code libraries that provide code you are using on multiple pages throughout a site.

If the file you are including is a library, you just about always want to use `require_once`. If you're using code from the library on a page, chances are the page will not work if the library file is not available, meaning that you should use `require` rather than `include`. If the file contains library code, you're not going to want to include it more than once. Let's look at an example. You've written a library called `temperature_converter.php`. The contents of the file are shown here:

```php
<?php
function celsiusToFahrenheit($temp = 0) {
    return round(($temp * 9/5) + 32);
}
?>
```

This file contains one function, `celsiusToFahrenheit()`, which converts a Celsius temperature to Fahrenheit and then rounds the result so that the function returns an integer. Now let's look at a page that includes this file:

```php
<?php
require_once "temperature_converter.php";
?>
<html>
  <head>
    <title>Current Temperature</title>
  </head>
  <body>
    <p>Current temperature in Fahrenheit: <?= celsiusToFahrenheit(25) ?></p>
  </body>
</html>
```

As you can see, in this case the page won't have meaning if the function in the library page is not available, so using `require` makes sense. On this page, it wouldn't matter whether I used `require` or `require_once` because there are no other includes. Suppose that the page included another file—one that prints the current temperatures around the world. If that page also had a `require()` call for `temperature_converter.php`, the same code would be included twice. An error would cause the page to fail, because each function name can only be declared once. Using `require_once` ensures that your library code is available and that it is not accidentally included in your page multiple times.

However, if you're including content that will be displayed within your page, `include` or `require` makes more sense. You don't have to worry about conflicts, and if you're including something to be displayed on the page, chances are you want it to appear, even if you've already included the same thing.

Expanding Your Knowledge of PHP

24

PHP is a full-featured scripting language for creating web applications and even writing command-line scripts. What you've seen in this lesson is just a brief introduction to the language. There are more statements, lots more built-in functions, and plenty of other things about the application for which there isn't space to discuss in this lesson. Fortunately, an online version of the PHP manual is available that will fill in most of the blanks for you. You can find it at http://www.php.net/docs.php.

Also, shelves of books about PHP are available to you. Some that you might want to look into are *Sams Teach Yourself PHP, MySQL, and Apache All in One* by Julie Meloni, and *PHP and MySQL Web Development* by Luke Welling and Laura Thomson.

There's more to PHP than just the core language, too. Lots of libraries have been written by users to take care of common programming tasks that you might run into. There's an online repository for these libraries called PEAR, which stands for PHP Extension and Application Repository. You can find it at http://pear.php.net/.

When you're writing your applications, make sure to check the PHP manual to ensure there's not already a built-in function to take care of whatever you're doing. If there isn't, check PEAR.

As I said before, I left out huge swaths of PHP functionality in this lesson for the sake of space. Here are some areas that you'll want to look into before developing your own PHP applications.

Database Connectivity

I mentioned CRUD applications already. A CRUD application is generally just a front end for a relational database, which in turn is an application optimized for storing data within tables. Databases can be used to store content for websites, billing information for an online store, payroll for a company, or anything else that can be expressed as a table. It seems like there's a relational database providing the storage for just about every popular website.

Because databases play such a huge role in developing web applications, PHP provides a lot of database-related functionality. Most relational databases are applications that can be accessed over a network, a lot like a web server. PHP is capable of connecting to every popular relational database. To communicate with relational databases, you have to use a language called SQL (the Structured Query Language). That's another book unto itself.

Regular Expressions

Regular expressions comprise a small language designed to provide programmers with a flexible way to match patterns in strings. For example, the regular expression `^a.*z$` matches a string that starts with *a*, ends with *z*, and has some number of characters in between. You can use regular expressions to do much more fine-grained form validation than I did in Exercise 24.1. They're also used to extract information from files, search and replace within strings, parse email addresses, or anything else that requires you to solve a problem with pattern matching. Regular expressions are incredibly flexible, but the syntax can be a bit complex.

PHP actually supports two different varieties of regular expression syntax: Perl style and POSIX style. You can read about both of them in the PHP manual.

Sending Mail

PHP provides functions for sending email. For example, you could write a PHP script that automatically notifies an administrator by email when a user registers for a website or sends users a password reminder if they request one when they forget their password. PHP also provides functions that enable your applications to retrieve mail as well as send it, making it possible to write web-based email clients and other such applications.

Object-Oriented PHP

PHP provides features for object-oriented development if you prefer that style of programming. For more information on object-oriented PHP, refer to the manual.

Cookies and Sessions

Cookies are a browser feature that lets websites set values that are stored by your browser and returned to the server any time you request a page. For example, when users log in to your site, you can set a cookie on their computers to keep track of who they are so that you don't have to force them to log in any time they want to see a password-protected page. You can also use cookies to keep track of when visitors return to your site after their initial visit. PHP provides full support for cookies. It also provides a facility called *sessions*. Sessions enable you to store data between requests to the server. For example, you could read a user's profile into her session when that user logs in to the site, and then reference it on every page without going back and loading it all over again. Generally, cookies are used with sessions so that the server can keep track of which session is associated with a particular user.

File Uploads

Back in Lesson 12 you learned about file upload fields for forms. PHP can deal with file uploads, enabling the programmer to access and manipulate them. With PHP, file uploads are stored to a temporary location on the server, and it's up to the programmer to decide whether to store them permanently and, if so, where to put them.

24

Other Application Platforms

PHP is just one of many programming languages that people use to write web applications. It is the language used to create popular web applications like Drupal, WordPress, and Expression Engine. It's also the tool used by major web companies like Facebook and Yahoo! However, other options are available. If you're just diving into web programming yourself, PHP is probably a good choice, but you might find yourself working on applications written in another language. Here's a brief overview of the languages you may encounter.

Microsoft ASP.NET

Microsoft provides the ASP.NET environment for writing web applications that run on Windows servers. ASP.NET is similar to PHP in that it supports embedding server-side code in HTML pages. It supports Visual Basic and C# as programming languages, and it runs on Microsoft's Internet Information Server, which is included with Windows Server. You can read more about ASP.NET and download free tools for developing and running ASP.NET applications at http://www.asp.net/.

Java EE

Java is a programming language originally created by Sun that runs on many operating systems, including Windows, OS X, and Linux. EE stands for "Enterprise Edition," an umbrella under which the server-side Java technologies live. Java is widely used by large companies to build internal and external applications.

There are two ways to write web applications in Java—servlets, which are programs that run on the server and can produce web content as output; and Java Server Pages, which allow you to embed Java code in HTML pages so that it can be executed on the server. You can read more about Java EE at http://www.oracle.com/technetwork/java/index.html.

Ruby on Rails

Ruby on Rails is a newer application platform that is gaining popularity because it enables developers to get a lot done with just a few lines of code. It uses the Ruby programming language and is designed with the philosophy that applications can be written quite efficiently if developers adhere to the conventions that the creators of the Ruby on Rails framework built in to it. You can read more about Ruby on Rails at http://rubyonrails.org/.

Summary

This lesson provided a whirlwind tour of the PHP language, and it explained how server-side scripts are written in general. Although the syntax of other languages will differ from PHP, the basic principles for dealing with user input, processing forms, and embedding scripts in your pages will be quite similar. I also listed some other application platforms you might encounter. They are all similar to PHP in function, even though the syntax of the languages they use differs from PHP to varying degrees.

In the next lesson, you'll learn how to take advantage of applications that other people have written rather than writing them yourself. Just as PHP has lots of built-in functions to take care of common tasks, so too are there many popular applications that you can download and install rather than writing them from scratch yourself.

Workshop

The following workshop includes questions you might ask about server-side development, quizzes to test your knowledge, and three quick exercises.

Q&A

Q At work, all of our applications are written using Active Server Pages. Why didn't you write about that?

A There are a number of popular platforms for writing web applications. PHP has the advantage of running on a number of operating systems, including Windows, Mac OS X, and Linux. Furthermore, support for PHP is offered by many web hosting providers. Finally, as you'll learn in the next lesson, there are many applications already written in PHP that you can take advantage of. Knowledge of PHP can be helpful in working with them.

Q Do I need a special application to edit PHP files?

A Just as with HTML, PHP files are normal text documents. Some text editors have specialized features that make working with PHP easier, just as there are for HTML. If you're just starting out, using Notepad or any other regular text editor will work fine, but you'll probably want to find a more powerful tool for writing PHP if you find yourself programming in PHP a lot.

24

Q How do I deploy PHP files to a server?

A There are no special requirements for deploying PHP files. You can just transfer them to the server as you would regular HTML files. As long as the server is configured to handle PHP, you should be fine. The one thing you do need to be careful to do is to make sure your directory structure is the same on the server and on your local computer. If you are using includes and directory paths change, your includes will break.

Q Are PHP scripts browser dependent in any way?

A All the processing in PHP scripts takes place on the server. They can be used to produce HTML or JavaScript that won't work with your browser, but there's nothing in PHP that will prevent it from working with a browser.

Quiz

1. What is the difference between double and single quotes in PHP?
2. How do the `include_once` and `require_once` functions differ?
3. Which functions can be used to help avoid cross-site scripting attacks?
4. How do you declare an associative array in PHP?

Quiz Answers

1. In PHP, strings in double quotes are parsed for variable references and special characters before they are presented. Strings in single quotes are presented as is.

2. The `include_once` function does not return a fatal error if the file being included is not found. With `require_once`, if the file is not found, a fatal error occurs and the rest of the page is not processed.

3. You can use `htmlspecialchars()` to escape the characters used to generate HTML tags for a page. You can use `strip_tags()` to remove HTML tags from a string. Either approach should prevent users from using malicious input to attempt a cross-site scripting attack.

4. Associative arrays are declared as follows:
```
$array = ('key' => 'value, 'key2' => 'value2');
```

Exercises

1. Get PHP up and running on your own computer.

2. Write a script that enables a user to show the current date and time on a web page.

3. Go to the PHP manual online and find a built-in function that wasn't introduced in this lesson. Use it in a script of your own.

LESSON 25
Search Engines and SEO

Just uploading your site to a web server somewhere doesn't mean that you'll attract many visitors. In fact, with millions of sites online already, you'll need to promote your site if you want to build an audience. And the way that most people promote their site is through search engines. There is no one proven way to ensure that your site shows up in the number one slot in a search engine, but you can do some things to make sure your site isn't penalized and may rank a little better. This is called search engine optimization, or SEO.

So, how do you do SEO? This lesson shows you some of the ways, including the following:

- What SEO is and whether your site really needs it
- How search engines find your site
- What makes a site "search engine friendly"
- What keywords are and how you can use them
- How accessibility, user experience, and your content affect SEO
- SEO myths
- How to submit your site to search engines
- Free tools you can use to improve SEO
- Using analytics to verify that your SEO is helping

What Is SEO?

SEO, or search engine optimization, is a marketing technique that focuses on getting traffic from organic (nonpaid) search results in sites like Bing, Google, and Yahoo!. You can do many things to help search engines better index your site and give them hints about how your site should be referenced and linked to. Some people consider SEO an art form, as there are no clear and fast rules. But there are some guidelines you can follow to help improve your search rankings.

The first thing you should bear in mind is that *there are no guarantees*. Every search engine has a different algorithm for ranking sites, finding new links, and removing pages from their index. And some change those algorithms constantly. I have run sites that consistently ranked (and some still rank) in the top five on Google, often in the number one slot. But those positions change daily. The best I hope for when working on SEO is that my sites are clear and easy to use for my existing customers. If my sites work well for people, they will work well for search engines.

Why You Need SEO

The fact is that if your site survives on pageviews then you need to think about SEO. The vast majority of web traffic comes from the major search engines: Google, Bing, and Yahoo!. If your site doesn't show up in those search engines, chances are no one will find it.

But it's more than just people finding your site; it's the quality of the people finding your site. If your pages are well optimized for search, they will bring people who are looking for what your site is offering. Someone who is looking to buy a tractor is not going to want to end up on my site, html5in24hours.com, but if they want information about HTML and web design, they would be happy to end up there. And the best search engines strive to direct people to what they are looking for rather than just link them at random.

What About Social Media?

One thing that is very popular right now is social media—sites like Facebook, Twitter, and Instagram. These sites are an important part of a complete website marketing strategy, but they don't drive a lot of traffic. In fact, most companies that use Facebook find the most success in building their brand rather than driving pageviews to their website.

This is because the goal of sites like Facebook and Twitter is different from search engines. Facebook and Twitter want people to stay on Facebook and Twitter. They make money as long as the ads they are displaying get seen by people. They don't make money if someone leaves to go to your website.

Search engines, in general, make their money either by other services they offer or by the ads they show within the search results themselves. The entire purpose of a search engine is to aggregate information and provide the links to it so that customers can access it.

You Can Do Your Own SEO

The beauty of SEO is that it's not difficult to do. It can get very complex, requiring server access and even possibly programming skills, but the basics are easy to understand and apply to every website. And the beauty of well-done SEO is that it improves your site for your customers—the *people* visiting your pages—not just the search engines.

Why Don't Search Engines Find Sites Without SEO?

You should be aware that search engines do find sites without SEO. The Google spiders are constantly out crawling the Web looking for new pages and adding them to their index. Depending on where your site is linked from, it can be found by a spider in as little as a few hours to a couple of days.

CAUTION

> You shouldn't rely on "security through obscurity" as a way of protecting your web pages. Just because you have not publicized your site doesn't mean it won't be found. Search robots can fill out forms, read referral codes, and follow links. And when they come across new pages, they add them to their index, sometimes even when you've asked them explicitly not to.

25

Search engines are just computer programs—complex ones, but just programs. The major search engines are constantly updating their algorithms to improve how their search results work, how their robots crawl the Web, and how their users respond to the results they get.

But search results are only as good as the content they have to index. If your web pages are confusing or hard to read for your customers, it's likely that they will be confusing and hard to read for search engine robots. And when the robots are confused, your site gets buried in the results rather than ranking where you'd like it to rank.

How Search Engines Work

Search engines work using a program, called a *robot*, to crawl through the Web reading pages and adding them to their indexes. These programs are sometimes called *crawlers* or *spiders*. Once these spiders have found a new page, they read the HTML (and CSS and JavaScript) and store the contents in huge databases. This information is then recalled later when a customer submits a *search query* to the search engine. Search engine companies use complex, and secret, algorithms to determine which pages will be shown for which search queries and in what order, or rank. There are often hundreds, possibly thousands, of variables that go into the ranking algorithms, and each engine is different. But some of them include

- Trust of the domain and domain quality
- Links to the site from trusted domains and sites
- Relevant content
- Length and readability of the content
- Engagement—how long people stay on the site after they've clicked from search
- Social metrics like tweets from Twitter or mentions on Facebook

These are not all the possible things your pages could be measured on when being ranked by search engines. You'll learn in more detail about how you can affect your search engine rankings later in this lesson.

Google

Google is currently the most popular search engine. Its search results are ranked based on a secret algorithm known only to Google developers. Google is constantly updating its search algorithm to improve its results for its users.

This search algorithm does a remarkably good job of pushing the most relevant sites to the top of the search results. It also rewards people who publish useful, popular sites rather than those who've figured out how to manipulate the algorithms that other search engines use. Many sites that aren't dedicated to providing search functionality use Google's index, so getting into the Google index provides wide exposure.

Google recommends that you focus on making your pages primarily for your users, *not* for search engines. Your site should have a clear hierarchy, and every page should be reachable from a static text link somewhere on your site. Sites that rank well in Google tend to be information-rich and have accessibility features like alternative text on images and descriptive `title` attributes on links. Google also recommends that your URLs include keywords relevant to the page that are human-readable.

Microsoft Bing

Bing is Microsoft's web search offering. Like Google, Microsoft maintains its own index of the Web. Bing was launched in May 2009, and as of February 2015, it is the second largest search engine in the United States.

Like Google, Bing has begun adding "instant answers" into its search results to make things easier for its customers. If you look up things like sports scores or definitions, those results will show up right at the top of the search, not forcing readers to go to another site.

Bing Webmaster Guidelines recommend that your URLs be clean and keyword-rich. You should not bury your content inside rich media like Flash or JavaScript. Your content should be fresh and updated regularly. Bing also suggests that you should not put text you want indexed into images. For example, your company name should appear in text on your page, not just in a logo.

Yahoo!

Yahoo! has been around since 1994. In fact, it was the first search engine I ever used, only I accessed it at akebono.stanford.edu. Yahoo! provides both a human-edited directory of the Web, which I discussed earlier, and web search. Yahoo!'s search engine currently uses the Bing index for its search results. It is the third most popular search engine in the United States.

25

Don't Forget International Searches

If you are in the United States it's easy to forget that there are other search engines out there, but the fact is that the Web is international, and search engines are, too. While the three most popular search engines in the United States are currently Google, Bing, and Yahoo!, there is another search engine—Baidu (http://www.baidu.com)—that is second only to Google worldwide. If you haven't heard of it, that's probably because you don't read Chinese.

Although Google still continues to dominate search worldwide, it doesn't reign everywhere. In Russia, Yandex (http://www.yandex.ru) is more popular, Baidu is most popular in China, South Koreans use Naver (http://www.naver.com), and Japan and Taiwan prefer Yahoo! Japan (http://www.yahoo.co.jp) and Yahoo! Taiwan (https://tw.yahoo.com/), respectively.

If your site has any aspirations to serving a worldwide audience, be aware of the search engines in other countries. There are many more than listed here, especially region-specific sites. Use your favorite search engine to find out more about the country or region you want to target.

SEO Techniques

You can do some specific things with your HTML to make your web pages easier to read and index for search engines. Your pages need to be well structured and indexable—in other words, they must be friendly to search engines.

Is Your Site "Friendly?"

Many people refer to a product as being "user friendly" as a way of saying that it's easy to use and people like using it. The same could be true of a website that is "search engine friendly." Search engines don't read websites the way humans do, so it's important to structure your content in a way that the search engines can read it. For instance

- Your most important content should be in HTML text. Search engines find it harder, if not impossible, to read text in images, Flash, Java applets, videos, and so on. This content is often ignored completely by search engines. **If it's important, write it out in text.**

- Provide alternative text. If you must use things that are not readable by search engines (like Flash, images, etc.), provide a text alternative. Use the HTML attributes and features like the `alt` attribute on images or include alternate text inside the `video` and `audio` tags. **Everything should have a text alternative somewhere on the page.**

- Make your navigation crawlable. Include a text link to every page on your site somewhere on the site. Note, I don't mean you should include a text link to every page *on* every page. The spiders can crawl from one page to the next and find all the pages, as long as the text link exists somewhere. **Link all your pages.**

- Include transcripts to audio and video. As you learned in Lesson 22, "Designing for User Experience," including transcripts helps make your multimedia more accessible, and it helps search spiders too. **Make your pages accessible.**

- Use correct HTML, CSS, and JavaScript. Most spiders can navigate even the most error-filled HTML, but they work better and more efficiently on pages that use standards compliant code. **Validate your pages.**

If these suggestions sound a lot like the accessibility you learned about in earlier lessons, you'd be right. Search engine spiders are like a fairly limited AT (assistive technology) device. If you try to make your site as accessible as possible, you will not only help search engines better index your site, but you'll also make them more accessible to your human customers.

Using Keywords and Keyword Research

Keywords are the basis of search. Customers go to a search engine and type in a word or two and then see what results come up. As search engine spiders crawl through pages, they keep track of key words and phrases that are used often and then use that frequency to rank pages. This is why a page about sequoias will not rank well in a search for "english sheepdog"—the keywords are too dissimilar.

CAUTION — Watch out for companies that promise "#1 ranking on Google" or similar claims. Often they will fulfill this promise by showing that a page ranks number one for a highly unlikely keyword phrase. It does you no good to rank at number one for the search "english sheepdog sequoia beat down" if no one else is searching for that.

When you are working on optimizing your web pages for search keywords, it can be tempting to focus on the number of times your keyword phrase is mentioned on the page. You will see many SEO experts (including old sites of mine) that recommend finding keyword phrases, using them in specific places (like titles, URLs, headlines, and image alternate text), and even tracking the *density* of your keywords (number of times the keyword phrase is used compared to the rest of the words on the page). But the fact is that all this is overkill. Here are my recommendations for using keyword phrases on your web pages:

1. Decide what your page is about, but don't worry too much about what keyword phrase you're targeting. Just write the content.
2. Make sure the title and main headline reflect the content of the page.
3. Keep the most relevant content at the top.
4. Write the page well, with correct spelling and grammar. Use bullets to make things easier to read.
5. Post the page to your website, and make sure it has a text link to it somewhere on the site.

25

You might notice that no where in those instructions did I have you look up popular keywords or place the phrases in specific locations on the page. The fact is that Google and other search engines are starting to penalize sites that are over optimized. And although they are unlikely to drop your ranking because you used a keyword phrase too many times on one page, they will lower rankings of pages that customers don't like. And most people don't like pages that are obviously keyword focused.

Keywords used to be thought of as the most important part of SEO. There were hundreds of sites dedicated to figuring out the "best" keywords and teaching you how to optimize your pages for specific keywords and keyword phrases. While it's true that keywords are at the heart of the search process, they are no longer the primary thing you should focus on. Instead, focus on creating great content, as you'll learn in the next section.

Creating Content for Customers Is the Best SEO

The first and best thing you can do to improve your site's rankings in search engines is to create and continually update content. Google and other search engines want to have the best content possible to show to their customers, so your pages should contain relevant, useful information about whatever they are covering. The sites that consistently rank well in search engines all have some things in common:

- They are easy to use. This means that both people and search robots won't have any problem finding their way around the sites or any difficulty understanding what the site is about.

- They are concise, yet actionable. In other words, you should make your pages as long as they need to be to cover the topic at hand, *but no longer*. A wordy page that blathers on at length about nothing is not going to be as useful as a short, 500-word explanation of the topic. But don't let that word-count number be your metric. If you need 5,000 words to cover the topic, use all of them. Just make sure that they all count for something.

- They use modern web design practices. This means they use HTML5 and CSS3. They are standards compliant and accessible. They are everything you've learned to create by reading this book.

- They provide high-quality content. This should be self-explanatory, but it includes having few or no typos, correct spelling and grammar, and above all being factually accurate.

When you're thinking about SEO, think on a page level rather than on a site level. For the most part, it's nearly impossible for a site these days to optimize its home page for any keywords other than its company name. Instead of worrying that your dog groomer home page isn't ranking well for the phrase "dog grooming," you should start building content (if you haven't already) around topics related to dog grooming. Write an article about your favorite breeds to groom—even one page per breed, if you have enough interesting things to say. Write reviews of dog shampoos and the best leashes. Post editorials on why dogs are better than cats. Then when people come to read your how-to on removing skunk smell from dog paws, they will stay to learn that you offer full-service grooming as well.

Myths and Facts About SEO

There are a lot of myths and misunderstandings surrounding SEO. Some of these things used to be true but are no longer, and others were never true. The following are some of the most persistent myths about SEO and some facts that people don't believe, but really are true:

- **Myth: You must submit your site to search engines.** Back in the 1990s, search engines were just getting started, and many of them didn't have effective spiders that could wander the Web at will. So, web page owners had to submit their sites to the search engine indexes for inclusion. Since 2001, however, submitting your site to search engines has become completely unnecessary. You can still submit your sites if you want, but it won't help you rank higher.

- **Myth: You must use meta tags.** Back in the early days of the Web, meta tags were considered the only way to get search engine ranking. You were expected to post meta keywords and a meta description tag on every page that you wrote, and search engines would then use that information to both index your site and describe it in their results. These days, the keywords tag is universally ignored as the spam technique it became, and the description is typically ignored in favor of the visible content on the page. Focus on writing a descriptive title, headline, and body copy and leave the meta tags for things like your character set.

- **Myth: Keyword density gets you higher rankings.** This has been disproved over and over, yet many SEO experts continue to recommend that you increase the number of times a keyword phrase is mentioned on your page. I think the reason it's still so popular is that it's easy to check. But you'll get much better rankings from one link to your site from another high-quality site on the same topic.

- **Myth: Paid search affects your rankings in organic search.** Many people believe that the search engines deliberately penalize sites that don't advertise with them or pay them in some other fashion. But in fact, Google, Bing, and Yahoo! all have walls around the arms of their companies that work with search and advertising for exactly this reason.

- **Fact: Cloaking can get your site removed from the search engine results.** Cloaking is a technique in which one type of content is shown to human visitors and another type of content is shown to the search engines. The simplest form of cloaking is hiding text in the HTML that your site visitors can't see, such as in comments. More complex forms use programs to detect the search engine spider and deliberately show it different content from what a non-spider would see. It is possible to cloak website content for a positive reason, such as to improve user

25

experience, but if you are considering doing it to affect search rankings, you could affect your rankings—by being booted out of the results altogether.

- **Fact: Schemes to get links will only get you banned.** Most people know that the best way to get higher rankings is to get more and higher-quality links back to your site. While it can be difficult to manipulate a high-quality site to link to you, many unscrupulous SEO managers have resorted to link farms, paid links, and directory links to get the absolute number of links to a page increased. Google in particular takes a dim view of this type of link manipulation and will devalue sites that do it.

- **Fact: Duplicate content hurts your site.** One of the ways people would try to increase their search rankings was to increase the amount of content on their site. And to do this, they would simply copy the content from one page into another page and another and another. Search engines don't like duplicate content because it fills up their index with repetitive information. And while it can be argued that they don't penalize sites that have duplicate content, they take time away from indexing that site that could be used on nonduplicate content. Ultimately, whether you believe Google (or Bing, or Yahoo!) penalizes sites with duplicate content or not, the result is the same—fewer of your pages make it into the index to rank well. If you have duplicate content on your site, get rid of it either by deleting the duplicates or using redirects or the `robots.txt` file discussed later in this lesson.

- **Fact: Search engines are not obligated to include your site.** If you suspect that your site has been removed from one of the major search indexes, you should find out why directly from them. Google offers Webmaster Tools (https://www.google.com/webmaster), and Bing does too (http://www.bing.com/toolbox/webmaster/). These tools will give you hints and messages explaining what problems they might have encountered when indexing your site and give you suggestions for fixing them.

Tools for Tracking and Managing SEO

When you're doing SEO, there are a lot of tools out there to help you. Some were created by the search engines themselves.

Using Sitemaps

Sitemaps are a great way to list all the files on your site in one place for the search engines to find it. They help search engines find and identify any content that they might not have found on their own. There are three ways most sites provide a sitemap: XML, RSS, and plain text.

An XML sitemap is the best method. It is widely accepted by all major search engines, and it is extremely easy for them to parse. You can create an XML sitemap yourself with any text editor, but it's better to use a sitemap generator.

RSS sitemaps are easy to maintain because they are often built automatically by site tools like blogs. RSS sitemaps are often updated automatically, but they can be large and harder to manage because they provide more information than the plain XML format does.

Text sitemaps are the easiest to maintain. They are typically built as one URL per line with up to 50,000 lines. But these text files provide no information outside of the URLs themselves.

If you want to learn more about sitemaps, visit Sitemaps.org, or you can build your own sitemap at XML-Sitemaps.com.

The `robots.txt` File

The `robots.txt` file is a file of that exact name stored in the root of your web server. It provides instructions to spiders and other web page crawlers about what pages of your site they should and should not visit. When you use a `robots.txt` file, you can indicate to search engines where your sitemap is, directories and pages you do not want them to visit, and even how often they should return to your site to find new content.

A sample `robots.txt` file looks like this:

```
User-agent: *
Disallow: /includes/
Disallow: /misc/

User-agent: googlebot
Disallow: /nosearch/
```

The first section says that all robots should not visit the `/includes/` and `/misc/` directories. The second section suggests that just the Googlebot should not visit the `/nosearch/` directory.

CAUTION   Not all web robots read or follow the `robots.txt` file. Some are not well written and don't check the file, and others have nefarious purposes and will deliberately seek out directories you've marked private. If the directories you've disallowed are critical, use some other form of protection like HTAccess to prevent robots from crawling them.

25

You can use a meta tag to request that specific pages not be indexed or follow any of the links on them:

```
<meta name="robots" content="noindex, nofollow">
```

You can also use the `rel="nofollow"` attribute on your links. This tells search engines not to follow this specific link from your pages. Some search engines will still follow the links, but they will not afford them the same amount of authority your site might lend to a link that doesn't have that attribute.

Understanding Canonical Links

Creating duplicate content is not only a bad thing when it comes to search engines, it's also very easy to do accidentally (or on purpose, but without malice). For example, every directory on your server probably has a default page called something like `default.html`. That means that someone can visit both http://www.example.com/ and http://www.example.com/default.html and get the same content. This can happen if you have a secure server (https://) that serves the same content as the nonsecure server (http://) or a subdomain like www that serves the same content as the site URL without the www subdomain (http://www.example.com/ and http://example.com/).

One of the ways that search engines deal with duplicate content is by allowing you to define which page is the authoritative or "canonical" version of the page with the canonical link in the head of the document:

```
<link rel="canonical" href="http://www.example.com/">
```

The benefit of using this tag is that you can place it on a page and then not worry about whether your server is creating duplicates like the subdomain or the default page. The canonical URL is defined.

Redirecting Duplicate Content

Another tool you can use for dealing with duplicate content is to redirect the duplicate content to the canonical page. If you use a 301 redirect, you are telling the web server that not only has this page moved, but it has moved permanently. You can do a redirect in many ways; check with your hosting provider for the best way to redirect on your site. Some hosting providers even provide tools to make creating redirects easy.

The most common way to create a redirect is with the HTAccess tool. This is only available on Apache sites. To create an HTAccess redirect, open the file `.htaccess` (note the period at the beginning of the filename) in the root directory of your web server and type the following:

```
Options +FollowSymLInks
RewriteEngine on
```

```
RewriteRule http://www.example.com/dupe.html http://www.example.com/canonical-
file.html [r=301,L]
```

You can also do it with PHP:

```
<?php
  Header("HTTP/1.1 301 Moved Permanently");
  Header("Location: http://www.example.com/canonical.html");
?>
```

Place that at the top of the duplicate page, and it will redirect to the new one.

Checking How Your Site Looks to Search Engines

One way to make sure that your SEO efforts are working is to try to see your site as a
search spider might see it. There are several tools you can use to see your site as a search
engine does. The first place you should look is the Google cache. View the text-only version to see what your site looks like to Google. Figure 25.1 shows what the InformIT site
looks like to Google.

FIGURE 25.1
The Google Web
cache of InformIT.

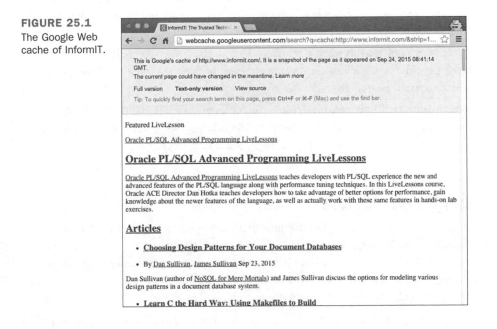

25

Other tools you can use to view your site include SEO-browser.com and the MozBar
(https://moz.com/tools/seo-toolbar/). These tools can give you a better idea of why your

site might not be ranking the way you want it to because you can see clearly what the search engines are seeing.

Tracking Your SEO Efforts

The final thing you should do when working on SEO is make sure that you track your progress. Analytics programs, as mentioned in other lessons, can help you not only see what pages are doing well but also where you need to improve your efforts.

Some things you should pay attention to include the following:

- **Search engine referrals**—These are the search engines that are sending you traffic. This can be particularly useful if you get more content from a search engine other than Google. This may mean that Google has a problem with your site (check Google Webmaster Tools) or that you have content that appeals to a different demographic than typical.

- **Keywords**—Most analytics software will tell you what keywords are generating traffic to your site. This will help you to both focus your SEO efforts and understand where you're not ranking well. Watching how these referrals trend on your site can give you a good sense of whether you've lost ranking or something else has happened.

- **What pages get search engine traffic**—This is good to know as it tells you which pages have the best ranking and which pages either are not linked well or are unknown to the search engines.

- **Where your traffic is coming from**—Search engines might be the lion's share of your referrals, or they might be almost nothing. If you are getting lots of referrals from a site you don't recognize, you might want to check it out.

Paying for Links

All the popular search engines have programs that allow you to pay for links on their search results pages. In other words, you can pay to have a link to your site displayed when users enter search terms that you choose. Most sites charge on a per-click basis—you pay every time a user clicks on the link, up to a maximum that you set. After you've used up your budget, your advertisement doesn't appear any more.

Most search engines display paid links separately from the regular search results, but this approach still provides a way to get your site in front of users who may be interested immediately. You just have to be willing to pay.

Remember that, as mentioned previously, this is not a way to get higher rankings. The top search engine companies keep their paid search links divisions separate from their organic search links.

Summary

In this lesson, you learned what SEO is and why it's important to your website. You learned about how SEO differs from social networking and got tips for doing your own SEO. One of the key factors in doing SEO is to apply the rules that you've learned in the earlier lessons in this book: write standards-based HTML, make your pages accessible, put mobile design first, and make content the most important part of your web pages. You learned that there is no fool-proof way to make your site appear in the number one slot on Google or any other search engine, but there are several techniques you can employ to improve your site for both your customers and search engines.

Workshop

As always, we wrap up the lesson with a few questions, quizzes, and exercises. Here are some pointers and refreshers on how to promote your website.

Q&A

Q You mentioned analytics were important to SEO, but do I have to use Google Analytics to be ranked well on the Google search engine?

A No, you are not required to use Google Analytics to rank well in Google search. Just like their advertising division, this is a separate division of the company. Google Analytics is a good analytics option that shows you a lot of information about your site including SEO. But there are other options. Yahoo! offers a free analytics tool called Yahoo! Web Analytics, and one of my favorite tools is Piwik, which is open source and runs on your own server.

Q There are so many search engines! Do I have to add my URL to all of them?

A No, in fact, most search engines will ignore your submission if you are able to find a submission form. They feel that the links they find through natural organic search are more valuable because they better reflect how real customers might find your site. So it's better to focus on writing great content and getting others to link to you than worrying about whether you've submitted a page to every search engine.

25

Quiz

1. What's the basic function of SEO?

2. What are five ways to make sure your site is search engine friendly?

3. What is the only thing you need to do for good SEO?

4. What is the `rel=canonical` link for?

Quiz Answers

1. SEO's purpose is to help web designers make their sites more visible and rank higher in search engines. The best SEO is done by focusing on content rather than gimmicks.

2. There are five rules of thumb for creating search engine friendly pages: If it's important, write it out in text. Everything should have a text alternative somewhere on the page. Link all your pages. Make your pages accessible. Validate your pages.

3. The only thing you need to do for good SEO is create great content.

4. The `rel=canonical` link tells the search engine the URL of the canonical version of the current page. This ensures that any duplicate content will not be indexed as a separate page in search engine indexes.

Exercises

1. Check out your site in the Google cache and see how it looks to search engines. Make some decisions about how you can improve your site in search engine results based on what you see.

2. Sign up for a Google Analytics account and install it on your site. Explore the reports to see what kind of information it provides about your site. Check out what search engines send traffic to your site and what pages get the most search engine traffic for what keywords.

Index

Symbols

A

B

G

O

S

U

V

W

X

Y

Z

REGISTER YOUR PRODUCT at informit.com/register

Access Additional Benefits and SAVE 35% on Your Next Purchase

- Download available product updates.

- Access bonus material when applicable.

- Receive exclusive offers on new editions and related products.
  (Just check the box to hear from us when setting up your account.)

- Get a coupon for 35% for your next purchase, valid for 30 days. Your code will
  be available in your InformIT cart. (You will also find it in the Manage Codes
  section of your account page.)

Registration benefits vary by product. Benefits will be listed on your account page
under Registered Products.

InformIT.com—The Trusted Technology Learning Source

InformIT is the online home of information technology brands at Pearson, the world's foremost
education company. At InformIT.com you can

- Shop our books, eBooks, software, and video training.
- Take advantage of our special offers and promotions (informit.com/promotions).
- Sign up for special offers and content newsletters (informit.com/newsletters).
- Read free articles and blogs by information technology experts.
- Access thousands of free chapters and video lessons.

Connect with InformIT—Visit informit.com/community

Learn about InformIT community events and programs.

informIT.com
the trusted technology learning source

Addison-Wesley • Cisco Press • IBM Press • Microsoft Press • Pearson IT Certification • Prentice Hall • Que • Sams • VMware Press